ADMINISTERING THE EMPIRE, 1801–1968

Frontispiece. The General Registry of the Colonial Office [1942]:
Miss Heritage, a member of the registry staff, consults a register of correspondence now in CO 378.
(With thanks to Pictorial Press)

ADMINISTERING THE EMPIRE, 1801–1968

A GUIDE TO THE RECORDS OF THE COLONIAL OFFICE IN THE NATIONAL ARCHIVES OF THE UK

Mandy Banton

LONDON
INSTITUTE OF HISTORICAL RESEARCH
THE NATIONAL ARCHIVES OF THE UK

Published by

UNIVERSITY OF LONDON
SCHOOL OF ADVANCED STUDY
INSTITUTE OF HISTORICAL RESEARCH
Senate House, London WC1E 7HU

in conjunction with

THE NATIONAL ARCHIVES OF THE UK
London

First edition published 2008
Revised edition published 2011
Second edition published 2015

ISBN 978 1 909646 12 4

Cover illustrations:

Cover: Map of the world on Mercator's projection showing the British empire, 1926 (with submarine cable routes shown in red), *The Dominions Office and Colonial Office List for 1926*, by Sir W H Mercer, A J Harding, and G E J Gent (Waterloo & Sons Limited, London, Dunstable & Watford, 1926)

Back: The General Registry of the Colonial Office [1942]: Miss Heritage, a member of the registry staff, consults a register of correspondence now in CO 378 (With thanks to Pictorial Press)

Contents

List of figures and tables

Figures

Tables

Foreword to first edition

The handbook on colonial records at The National Archives prepared by Mandy Banton serves at least three important and useful purposes. First and foremost it is a new and extensively revised guide that takes fully into account records that have become accessible in recent decades, together with corrected and expanded lists of earlier eras. It covers the Colonial Office's relations with other government departments, including the Admiralty, the Cabinet Office, the Foreign Office, the Prime Minister's Office, the Treasury and the War Office. In view of the complexity of the classification systems at The National Archives, researchers may wish to visit the Colonial Office handbook as their first port of call in clarifying other destinations, whether academic or genealogical.

A second function of the guide is historical perspective and comprehensive coverage of complicated and extensive lists of documents. Those using the handbook will be able to trace records on the evolution of the War and Colonial Office of the early 19th century and the creation of the geographical departments. The Colonial Office came into its own in 1854, and a half century later the creation of the Dominions Division in 1907 marked another major development. In 1925 the Dominions Office became a separate department, though relations remained close. The most recent era in the Colonial Office's history, as summarised in the handbook, is the period of decolonisation leading to the closing down of the Colonial Office in 1966 by its merger with the Commonwealth Relations Office, eventually becoming what we know today as the Foreign and Commonwealth Office.

The third useful aspect of the handbook is its range and depth of historical detail. It is a historical work in its own right. It comments usefully on the 'informal' as well as the formal British empire and reveals the extent to which the Colonial Office was involved in the affairs of China, Argentina and Egypt, even listing, in Foreign Office records, the papers of Lord Cromer. It defines as well as guides. Readers will find helpful the distinctions in the nomenclature of British dependencies, the legal as well as the conventional meanings of such categories as colony, protectorate and mandate, and the nuances of meaning from decade to decade.

As one who has used the documents at the Public Record Office, now The National Archives, since 1960, and thus approaching my 50th year of archival experience, I can testify to the utility of the new handbook. It contains useful guidance on the registration of original correspondence, file numbers, arrangements of files, secret registers, confidential prints and other more mysterious matters such as the purpose and methods of minuting. The handbook also discusses rather arcane sets of records such as the private office papers, as well as more well-known series of secret correspondence such as the indispensable CO 537 files. Seasoned historians and genealogists as well as those using The National Archives for the first time will find the handbook an indispensable guide and source of invaluable historical detail.

Wm. Roger Louis
17 November 2007

Preface to first edition

This guide is intended as an introduction to the records of British government departments responsible for the administration of colonial affairs, and now held in The National Archives of the United Kingdom, and covers the period from about 1801 to 1968. It is not intended to replace Anne Thurston's revised edition of the earlier handbook written by R. B. Pugh (although sadly the former is now out of print), nor to repeat the detailed information about the internal organisation and staffing of the Colonial Office and Dominions Office/Commonwealth Relations Office provided there. Instead it has been planned as a user-friendly guide concentrating on the organisation of the records, the information they are likely to provide and how to use the contemporary finding aids. It provides a brief outline of the expansion of the British empire during the period, and says a little about the organisation of colonial governments. It includes references to the roles of other government departments in colonial affairs, and to some of their records.

Many people have added to my knowledge of these records, particularly the colleagues, too numerous to name individually, with whom I have worked over the years. I am also grateful to the editors of the British Documents on the End of Empire project, particularly Stephen Ashton, Roger Louis, the late Martin Lynn, and Philip Murphy, with whom I have had many useful discussions. Many more of my acknowledgements must be to people whose names I do not know – the researchers who have honed my knowledge over the years by asking difficult questions about the records, and who continue to find new and complex queries. My greatest debt is perhaps to R. B. Pugh. A copy of his handbook, *The Records of the Colonial and Dominions Offices*, was put into my hand by a member of staff of the Public Record Office on my first visit there as a research student. Some years later I learned a great deal more from discussions with Anne Thurston while she was revising and updating Pugh's guide. And Pugh's chapter on 'The Colonial Office' in the *Cambridge History of the British Empire* is a model of the now old-fashioned administrative history without which the archivist can hardly survive.

I am particularly grateful to Aidan Lawes for commissioning this guide and for his encouragement and practical assistance.

Preface to second edition

When the first edition of this guide was published, in 2008, it was 40 years since the Colonial Office had been merged with other departments to form the Foreign and Commonwealth Office. It seemed reasonable to assume that under the thirty-year rule most of its records would have already been transferred to The National Archives, and that sufficient information about those comparatively few collections still to be transferred would be known to TNA staff and could be incorporated. Hopefully the guide could be the last word on the subject. But there have been subsequent developments. First, a number of collections from the former Colonial Office Library – incorporated into the Foreign and Commonwealth Office Library – were, in 2008, in process of transfer or under discussion; second, in 2011 the FCO admitted that it was holding a collection of records removed from 37 colonial governments at independence which were to be transferred to TNA; and third, in 2013, it became clear that the FCO had for many years failed to assess for transfer all of the records of its predecessors in accordance with UK public records legislation, and that a residue of Colonial Office records was included in the vast collection of 'out of time' material stored in its high security facility at Hanslope Park, north of London. There is still little that can be said about this last category, but researchers should be aware that it may include material of importance for their work, and of the possibility of using FOI procedures to request access. An inventory is available.[1] In the case of material transferred from FCO library, or still to be transferred, information has been added to this guide as appropriate; and the so-called 'migrated archives' are discussed in an expanded Chapter 3, and listed in appendix 1 under the names of the former dependencies concerned.

In addition, I have continued to learn more about the documents in the course of my own research, and in the light of queries from others, at least some of which seems worth recording.

I am grateful to those of my former colleagues at TNA who have been generous in updating me on developments, and have commented on new drafts, especially Stephen Cable who contributed much of the content of the new chapter on photographs.

Mandy Banton, Institute of Commonwealth Studies, London, 25 January 2015

[1] https://www.gov.uk/government/publications/foreign-offices-archive-inventory (accessed 6 Jan. 2015). See also chapter 8.

Glossary

A number of terms are used within this guide, within the records or by The National Archives which may be unfamiliar. Some of these are explained here:

At once	instruction concluding a series of Colonial Office minutes, being an instruction for action to be taken as agreed (occasionally – 'so proceed').
Blue book	term used in the Colonial Office for locally printed statistics.
Calendar	summary or précis of the contents of a series of documents, normally presented in chronological order.
Class	see Series.
Clerk	term used until the early 20th century for any government official.
Confidential print	copies or extracts of documents printed by a government department for circulation internally or to other departments, especially the Cabinet.
Cut	material between two points in a thumb index.
Despatch	formal written communication to or from a governor or other official administering a colonial dependency.
Disturbance	term commonly used by British government departments for a riot, demonstration or major civil unrest (and therefore a useful term to use in catalogue searches).
Docket	endorsement upon a despatch or a letter noting its origin, date, content and method of disposal; index slip forming a means of reference to a registered file.
Dummy sheet	a note inserted in place of a paper, map or other item that has been extracted from a document giving brief details and the new reference.
For consideration (or 'For conson.')	for discussion and approval.
Gazette	official government newspaper.
Governor	head of a colonial government.
Item	a single document in whatever format, e.g. file, bound volume, flat sheet. See also Piece.

Letter	semi-official communication from a colonial official or correspondence between government departments.
Letter code	alphabetical reference code used by The National Archives to denote the creating government department or other record-creating body (also departmental code). Often takes the form of an acronym, for example CO for Colonial Office, but more recently letter codes have been allocated which have no direct significance, for example FD for the Medical Research Council.
Lithographed form	a printed pro forma letter, a variety of which were used by the Colonial Office for routine matters. Usually abbreviated to LF (plural, LFF).
Minute	comment, recommendation or direction attached to an official communication; internal memorandum or instruction. Not in this sense a formal record of a decision taken.
Officer administering the government (o.a.g.)	any head of a colonial government, but almost always used to mean the governor's deputy rather than the governor himself.
Original correspondence	term used in the Colonial Office to describe incoming correspondence with related minutes and drafts of outgoing correspondence.
Paper	a despatch or letter covered by a minute sheet.
Parliamentary under-secretary of state	deputy to the secretary of state; equivalent to a minister.
Permanent under-secretary of state	the senior civil servant in a government department.
Piece	an orderable file, volume, paper, map, etc. within a record series.
Registered file	a file created within a system having a unique numeric or alpha-numeric reference code.
Secretary of state	head of a government department (a politician).
Series	a collection of records created for a particular function or activity and of similar physical form and allocated a numerical reference by The National Archives. Formerly called a class.
So proceed	see 'At once'.
Transmits	sends or forwards.
Wanting	term used in the catalogue meaning that the document was missing at the time of transfer to The National Archives.

1. The British empire

The map reproduced on the front and back cover of this volume shows the extent of the British empire in 1926. Many more would be required to reflect the detail of its expansion and decline throughout its history. Original manuscript and published maps do, of course, survive, both in The National Archives (see chapter 10) and elsewhere, but the most comprehensive and accessible cartographic information is almost certainly that provided in the *Atlas of British Overseas Expansion*[1] which includes nearly 140 maps and covers the period from the late 15th to the late 20th centuries. Maps of the empire as a whole, and of individual territories, are also included in the annual *Colonial Office List*,[2] which is referred to throughout this guide and described in some detail in appendix 4.

'The British empire' has meant different things at different periods, not only in its geographical extent but also in its varied definitions. Does the term refer only to a formal and internationally recognised network of colonies, protectorates, dominions and mandated territories, or does it include much wider spheres of influence and authority? Much has been written on these matters in recent years, and the bibliography provided lists some of these studies. It is not necessary, however, to dwell on these questions here; this guide is concerned with the records of those departments of the British government which were responsible for the administration of empire in its formal sense. The wider picture is not completely ignored, and is discussed briefly below. An attempt is also made to point users to appropriate sources within The National Archives, but the subject must necessarily take a minor place.

In terms of period, the core of the information provided in this guide is concentrated on the years from 1801 to 1966. This is a reflection of administrative reality rather than a marking of significant dates in the history of the empire; the War and Colonial Department was established in 1801, and its direct successor, the Colonial Office, was abolished in 1966. As will be seen, however, the arrangement of the records virtually ignores the fairly arbitrary date at the beginning of this period, and is distinctly fluid at the end. Care has been taken to ensure that researchers working across either date line will not find an abrupt cut-off in the information provided.

Dates at which Britain acquired its individual dependencies, and usually the processes of such acquisitions, are given in appendix 1, but it may be useful to provide here a broad overview of the geographical extent of empire, and its development in our period. A more logical start date

[1] *Atlas of British Overseas Expansion*, ed. A. N. Porter (London, 1991; 1994).

[2] For 1862–1966 only; maps were not included after the 1940 edition but a separate map supplement was published in 1948.

for this guide should perhaps be 1783, when Britain formally recognised the loss of most of its possessions in North America – the thirteen colonies which formed the nucleus of the United States of America. But some important redrawing of empire had also been seen at the close of the Seven Years' War[3] 20 years earlier. Although most territories conquered during that war were returned to their pre-war owners, Britain acquired Quebec and Cape Breton from France, together with its claims to the territory east of the Mississippi River, and Florida from Spain. Bengal, the richest of the East India Company's client states, became a directly ruled province, and, in the Caribbean, Britain took Dominica, Grenada, St Vincent and the Grenadines, and Tobago. In West Africa Britain gained settlements on the Senegal River. This war also explains the presence among the Colonial Office records of a small collection of papers relating to the British expedition against the Spanish province of Havana in 1762.[4]

Independence of the thirteen American colonies was formally recognised by the Treaty of Paris of 1783, and associated agreements with France and Spain further adjusted imperial relationships. Montserrat, Dominica, Grenada, St Christopher (St Kitts) and St Vincent, which had been captured by France, were restored to Britain, as were the Bahamas, which had been captured by Spain. St Lucia and Tobago were restored to France. But no period of stability ensued; the long years of the French Revolutionary and Napoleonic wars again re-shaped the European empires and the British became heavily involved in conquest overseas. They took from their enemies places of strategic importance – the Cape of Good Hope, Mauritius and Ceylon – and kept them at the peace. In addition Trinidad was taken from the Spanish, and Guiana from the Dutch. Gibraltar, which had been British since 1704, remained British throughout this turbulent period, having withstood a combined French and Spanish force during the Great Siege of 1779–83. Britain also acquired an additional Mediterranean possession of key strategic value: Malta, which had been given to the Knights of St John of Jerusalem in 1530, was captured by the French in 1798, but was surrendered to Britain in 1801 and formally ceded in 1814. Minorca, in the Balearic Islands, had been British for much of the 18th century, but was restored to Spain by the Treaty of Amiens of 1802.

The first great period of exploration might have been over, but following the end of the Seven Years' War a number of expeditions left England and France to explore the Pacific. Captain James Cook described the east coast of Australia as suitable for European settlement, and in 1788 a start was made by the British with the establishment of a penal colony at Botany Bay. A by-product of the loss of the American colonies was their unavailability for convict deportation and settlement. West Africa had already been rejected as a suitable convict destination,[5] but in 1787 a settlement at Sierra Leone – the Province of Freedom – was established for London's 'Black Poor', who were later joined by Black loyalists from the American War of Independence who had been initially settled in Nova Scotia (see figure 55), Jamaican Maroons, and Bussa rebels from Barbados. A company was incorporated to manage the settlement in 1791, and continued to administer it until 1808 when Sierra Leone became a British colony.

[3] Also known as the French and Indian War; the peace treaties concluded in 1763 were the Treaty of Paris and the Treaty of Hubertusburg.

[4] CO 117, Secretary of State: Havana, Original Correspondence, 1762–3.

[5] See W. Oldham, *Britain's Convicts to the Colonies* (Library of Australian History, Sydney, 1990).

By the end of the 18th century Britain was the largest exporter of slaves from West Africa, with a network of trading posts on the coast controlled by the African companies,[6] but by 1807, the year of British Parliamentary abolition of the trade, there were only two British dependencies in Africa: Sierra Leone and the Cape of Good Hope. This picture changed gradually during the 19th and early 20th centuries, partly as a result of the 'scramble' for Africa of the late 1800s. Fernando Po was used as a Royal Navy base for action against the slave trade from 1827 to 1834, but was subsequently returned to Spain. Gambia and the British settlements in the Gold Coast were placed under Sierra Leone in 1821 following the abolition of the African Company. Gambia became a separate colony in 1843, but the Gold Coast not until 1874 after the last Danish and Dutch settlements there had been ceded to Britain. Lagos, which had been a British colony since 1862, then became part of Gold Coast Colony until 1886 when it again became a separate colony and the Lagos Protectorate was created from bordering territories. From 1849 British consuls, responsible to the Foreign Office,[7] had been appointed to the eastern part of what is now the Nigerian coast. The Oil Rivers Protectorate was established over that part of the coast in 1885; in 1893 it was extended and named the Niger Coast Protectorate. In 1900 the protectorate was united with territories administered by the Royal Niger Company to form the Protectorate of Southern Nigeria, which itself merged with Northern Nigeria – also a protectorate since 1900 – in 1914.

In East Africa British involvement had been based at Zanzibar, where the first British consul was posted in 1841. In 1832 the Arab ruler of Oman in the Persian Gulf had transferred his capital to Zanzibar, which soon became the principal urban centre of East Africa and commanded the coast.[8] German claims to the island were finally settled in 1890 when Britain ceded the North Sea island of Heligoland, and Zanzibar became a British protected state. In 1888 the Imperial British East Africa Company was incorporated to administer mainland territory, known as the East Africa Protectorate, allocated to Britain by an agreement with Germany. The protectorate, later Kenya, was administered through the Foreign Office from 1895, and transferred to the control of the Colonial Office in 1905. Uganda, which had been previously claimed by Germany, was also assigned to the Imperial British East Africa Company in 1890. Somaliland became a British protectorate in 1884 when Egypt withdrew its claims; until 1905 it was administered by the resident at Aden as a dependency of the government of India.

In the meantime British influence in Southern and Central Africa had been steadily extended from its base at the Cape. Natal was annexed to the Cape in 1844, and Basutoland in 1871. Bechuanaland became a British protectorate in 1885, Zululand in 1887, Nyasaland in 1889 and Amatongaland in 1895. In 1889 the British South Africa Company was granted a charter to develop and administer the Rhodesias.

[6] Usually known simply as the 'African companies' and so referred to here, the full name changed over time as follows: Company of Royal Adventurers of England Trading with Africa, 1663–72; Royal African Company of England, 1672–1750; Company of Merchants Trading to Africa, 1750–1821. Records of the companies are at TNA in the Treasury record series T 70. See also figures 53 and 54.

[7] And, therefore, with records in Foreign Office series: primarily FO 2 and FO 84 (see chapter 12).

[8] Correspondence from British consuls at Zanzibar is to be found in the Foreign Office Muscat series FO 54, as well as the Zanzibar and East Africa series FO 107 and other more general series.

British settlement in Australia also spread gradually during the first half of the 19th century, although much of the eastern part of Australia was initially administered from New South Wales. Tasmania was separated in 1825, Victoria in 1851 and Queensland in 1859. New Zealand, settled from 1814, was also under the jurisdiction of New South Wales until 1841. In 1867 the British North America Act united the provinces of Ontario, Quebec, New Brunswick and Nova Scotia as the Dominion of Canada. Other provinces were added later as noted in appendix 1.

In the Pacific the early European explorers 'were followed first by missionaries and then by traders, whalers, deserters, escaped convicts and others on the make or on the run from settlements in Australia and New Zealand'.[9] When the Western Pacific High Commission was set up in 1877, three years after Fiji was ceded to Britain, it was largely to control labour recruitment in the region; its jurisdiction was gradually extended. The interests of other European powers in the region led to one particularly novel form of colonial administration – the Anglo-French condominium established over New Hebrides in 1906.[10] Similarly Canton (or Kanton) and Enderbury islands, now part of Kiribati, were under joint UK/US administration from 1939 to 1968.

British territorial advances in South and South East Asia were largely determined by the needs of India. India itself is scarcely mentioned in this volume simply because records of the East India Company and the India Office, successively responsible for the British administration of India, are held separately in the Asia, Pacific and Africa Collections of the British Library.[11] The same is true of neighbouring territories such as Burma. Ceylon was annexed to the presidency of Madras when it was first seized from the Dutch in 1796, but it became a separate colony in 1802. Penang, in what is now Malaysia, was ceded to the East India Company in 1786 for use as a trading post, and Province Wellesley was acquired by the company in 1800. Malacca was ceded to Britain by the Dutch in 1824, and Singapore recognised as British in the same year. In 1876 these territories, known as the Straits Settlements, were transferred from the control of the India Office to that of the Colonial Office. The Cocos or Keeling Islands, formerly administered by Ceylon, joined them in 1886, Christmas Island in 1900 and Labuan in 1907. British supremacy was subsequently achieved elsewhere in the Malayan archipelago, in what were known as the Federated and the Unfederated Malay States, through a system of residents and 'advisers' to the indigenous rulers. Demands for increased freedom to trade with China led to the ceding of Hong Kong to Britain in 1842. The Kowloon peninsula was added in 1860, and in 1898 the New Territories and Wei-Hai-Wei were leased to Britain, the latter as a naval harbour.

A number of dependencies fall outside the geographical arrangement adopted above. After periods of British, French and Spanish settlement in the 1760s and 1770s, the Falkland Islands and their dependencies became British in 1833. St Helena, formerly governed by the East India Company,

[9] Porter, p. 142.

[10] For a brief and light-hearted account of some of the absurdities of this dual administration, see A. Stuart, 'French & English: a colonial game or a colonial war?', in *Administering Empire: the British Colonial Service in Retrospect*, ed. J. Smith (London, 1999), pp. 295–303.

[11] India Office Records (http://www.bl.uk/reshelp/findhelpregion/asia/india/indiaofficerecords/indiaofficescope/indiaofficehistoryscope.html [accessed 28 Nov. 2014]). See appendix 1 for records in TNA for the period of independence.

became a colony in 1834. In the Indian Ocean Seychelles was annexed to Britain in 1814 after a period of conquest and re-conquest by Britain and France. It was administered through Mauritius until 1897. In the Mediterranean, in addition to Gibraltar, Malta and Minorca, which have already been mentioned, the Ionian Islands were made a British protectorate in 1814. They had been held by Venice for over four centuries before being captured by France in 1797 and by Russia in 1800, and subsequently made a Russo-Turkish protectorate before being returned to France in 1807. Cyprus, formerly part of the Ottoman empire, was handed over to Britain for administrative purposes in 1878 and annexed to Britain on the outbreak of war with Turkey in 1914.

The First World War had other long-term effects on the composition of the British empire. Following the war, territories formerly in the possession of Germany and the Ottoman empire were allocated to the victors under mandates of the League of Nations. Britain thus acquired responsibilities for parts of Togoland and Cameroon in West Africa, for that part of the former German East Africa subsequently known as Tanganyika, and for Transjordan (Jordan), Palestine and Iraq. South West Africa (Namibia) was allocated to the Union of South Africa, and in the Pacific Nauru and the former German protectorate of New Guinea became the responsibility of Australia. With these acquisitions the British empire reached its widest bounds.[12]

'Informal' empire

As noted above, beyond the limits of its recognised dependencies British interests and influence spread over many independent countries. Some foreign governments were compelled to make great concessions to British power while in other countries trade was financed and dominated by British capital; in Argentina, China and Siam (Thailand), for example, British influence was enforced through commercial agreements. British expatriate communities formed privileged elites in cities such as Cairo, Shanghai[13] and Buenos Aires. The balance of power in such situations varied; sometimes the relationship was almost an imperial/colonial one, while in other cases it was much looser. But it did not equate to formal rule, and the Colonial Office was never the responsible department within the British government even for a country such as Egypt which had many of the attributes of a British colony, and which is used here as one of just two examples. In the case of Egypt and all other countries forming part of the 'informal' empire the records of the Foreign Office should be consulted first (see 'Foreign Office', pp. 163–4).

Only for the brief period from 1914 to 1922 was Egypt a British protectorate (albeit one unilaterally declared), but for nearly three-quarters of a century after Britain's invasion to put down Arabi Pasha's nationalist 'revolt' in 1882 it was part of Britain's informal empire of indirect control and

[12] The exclusion of the mandated territories from the maps showing the empire as a whole printed in successive editions of the *Colonial Office List* suggests that they were not formally part of the empire. They were, however, treated as such.

[13] In addition to the more usual Foreign Office collections, some legal records of the British settlement at Shanghai can be found in the series FO 656, Supreme Court, Shanghai, China: General Correspondence; FO 917, Supreme Court, Shanghai, China: Probate Records; and FO 1092, Shanghai Courts, China: Judges' and Magistrates' Notebooks.

influence. Even before 1882 Britain played a significant role; it had controlled Egypt's finances jointly with France following the bankruptcy of the khedive in 1875. Britain declared its intention to recognise Egypt's independence in 1922, but reserved certain matters to its discretion: 'the security of the communications of the British Empire in Egypt; the defence of Egypt against all foreign aggression or interference, direct or indirect; the protection of foreign interests in Egypt and the protection of minorities; and the Sudan.'[14] Under the terms of a further agreement, concluded in 1936 for a 20-year period, British control was relaxed but not eliminated; it continued to a certain extent in the areas of defence, imperial communications and Sudan. In 1952 a coup led by Gamal Abdul Nasser and other army officers forced the abdication of King Farouk, and four years later Nasser nationalised the Suez Canal, precipitating the Suez crisis and war. Throughout this long period relations with Egypt remained the responsibility of the Foreign Office and records will be found in a range of 'FO' record series. For obvious reasons the records of the Cabinet, the Prime Minister's Office and the defence departments are also important. The papers of Evelyn Baring, later Lord Cromer, who was officially British agent and consul-general but virtually the ruler of Egypt from 1883 to 1907, are held at TNA (in the series FO 633). So too are the papers of one of his successors in the role, Lord Kitchener (PRO 30/57). Records of the mission to Egypt of Lord Milner, who commenced negotiations leading to the 1922 declaration, are in FO 848.

The second example of a foreign country falling within Britain's sphere of influence is Iran (Persia), where the historic connection was based on commerce, India, Anglo-Russian competition in Central Asia and oil. In 1907, after decades of rivalry, Britain and Russia agreed spheres of influence in Iran. The British and Indian governments subsequently built up strong economic control in the south of the country by supporting road and rail concessions and subsidising shipping services in an attempt to prevent any penetration of the region by Russia and the strategic disaster of a Russian foothold in the Persian Gulf. In 1908 a British syndicate struck oil, and a major new economic stake in the area rapidly developed and continued until Prime Minister Musaddiq nationalised the Anglo-Iranian Oil Company (previously known as Anglo-Persian) in 1951. It is significant that after the Foreign Office it is the Treasury records that contain the bulk of material relating to the oil company, followed by those of the Ministry of Fuel and Power.

Into a rather different category falls the British administration between 1941 and 1952 of the former Italian dependencies in Africa: Cyrenaica, Tripolitania, Eritrea and Somalia. These territories were then the responsibility of the War Office until 1949 and subsequently of the Foreign Office. Records are in WO 230 and FO 1015.

Despite what has been said above it should not be thought that the Colonial Office had no interest in territories within Britain's 'informal empire'; a search of the catalogue of its records for material relating to Egypt, Iran, Thailand or China, etc. will show otherwise.

[14] Quoted in P. Mansfield, *The British in Egypt* (London, 1971), p. 242.

'Miscellaneous islands'

The Colonial Office found itself to be technically responsible for some very tiny lands – all without any system of government and most without inhabitants – which it felt obliged to include in its yearbooks. With one or two exceptions none of the 'islands and rocks' listed below has a discrete series of Colonial Office documents allocated to it and so is not included in appendix 1, but researchers may find material among others of its records – perhaps those associated with a neighbouring territory – or those of other government departments. An enquiry to TNA about the first mentioned below, the Ashmore Group, revealed documents among the records of the Admiralty and the Dominions Office (although the query related to a period before the establishment of the latter department), and suggested that a search of Foreign Office records relating to the United States and The Netherlands might be worthwhile given the objections of those countries to British annexation of the islands, as well as of Colonial Office records relating to Western Australia.

The following is taken directly from the *Colonial Office List* of 1901 and describes the situation at that date.

> A number of islands and rocks through the world are British territory, or under British protection, but are not included in any Colony or separate Protectorate. Many of these have no permanent inhabitants, but are, or have been, leased by the Lords Commissioners of the Treasury for guano collection, or for cocoanut [*sic*] planting. The rents are paid into the Exchequer. Among such may be mentioned the Ashmore Group (Indian Ocean), Bird Island and Cato Island (in the Norfolk Island Group), Sombrero (West Indies, with a Board of Trade Lighthouse costing £520 annually), Raine Island, Bell Cay and Bramble Cay (near British New Guinea), Sydney Island, Phoenix Group, leased to the Pacific Islands Company Limited (4° 25′ S. lat., 171° 13′ W. long.), the Caroline and Flint Islands (Pacific Ocean, leased to the same Company, 9° 56′ S. lat, 150° 6′ W. long., and 11° 26′ S. lat. and 151° 48′ W. long.), Malden Island (4° 1′ S. lat., 155° 57′ W. long), leased to Messrs. Grice, Sumner, and Co., Pilgrim Island, Ducie Island, Bauman, Roggewein, and Teinhoven Islands, Coral Island and Dudosa, Starbuck Island, Little Scrub Island, Palmerston Island, Vostoc, Willis's Islets (all in the Pacific Ocean), and there are many others.
>
> Humphrey (Manahiki), and Rierson (Rakahanga) Islands, lying to the north of the Cook Islands, about 160° W. long. and 10° S. lat., were annexed in 1889. Christmas, Fanning, and Penrhyn Islands were annexed in March, 1888, in view of the possibility of their being utilised in connection with the projected telegraph cable from Vancouver to Australasia. Christmas Island (1° 57′ N. lat., 157° 27′ W. long.) is an atoll 90 miles in circumference, barren, with only brackish water. A trading firm collects mother of pearl shells. Fanning Island (3° 51′ N. lat., 159° 22′ W. long.) is a small atoll 9 miles by 4, covered with cocoanut trees, copra and guano being exported. Penrhyn Island (9° S. lat., 158° 3′ W. long.) is an atoll 30 miles in circumference, partly covered with cocoanut trees and having a population of 300. Mother of pearl is exported. Suwarrow Island (13° 13′ S. lat., 163° 9′ W. long.) was annexed for a similar reason, 22nd April, 1888; a protectorate was established over Jarvis Island, the Phoenix group, comprising Phoenix, Birnie, Hull, Gardner and Sydney Islands, Washington or New York Island and Palmyra Island and Johnson Island. [A footnote then reads: 'Afterwards withdrawn, and acknowledged to belong to Hawaii, on condition that the right to

land a cable is conceded if desired'.] It is now proposed that Palmerston, Penrhyn, Suwarrow, and one or two other small islands should be annexed to New Zealand.

The Great and Little Basses and Minicoy are small islets in the Indian Ocean, with lighthouses maintained by the Board of Trade out of shipping dues levied on vessels passing, and collected at Ceylon, Mauritius, Straits, and Indian ports.

The Kuriyan-Muriyan Islands, five in number, off the south-east coast of Arabia, were ceded by the Imam of Muskat for the purpose of landing the Red Sea telegraph cable. On one of them, Hallaniyah, is the signalling station maintained by the Telegraph Company. The whole group is leased for the purpose of guano collection.

Amboyna Cay and Sprattley Island (lat. 8° 38′ N., 111° 54′ E. long.; lat. 7° 52′ N., 112° 55′ E. long.), two uninhabited sandbanks in the middle of the China Sea, lying about 240 miles N.W. of Borneo and 100 miles N. of Labuan, were annexed in 1877, and leased for guano collection. They are annually visited by Chinese junks for the purpose of collecting turtle.

Decolonisation

Despite the growing credibility of the independence movement in India, Britain's confidence in the enduring nature of her colonial empire remained largely intact until the end of the Second World War. Then pressure from wartime allies and rapidly developing nationalist feeling within the colonies created a demand for a reassessment of policy. In 1941 Roosevelt and Churchill had expressed their respect for 'the rights of all peoples to choose the form of government under which they live'.[15] Although they had in mind those European countries occupied by Germany, implications for the colonies were obvious.[16]

In 1943 Oliver Stanley, secretary of state for the colonies, announced in the House of Commons that the British government was 'pledged to guide Colonial people along the road to self-government within the framework of the British Empire'.[17] Five years later one of his successors, Arthur Creech Jones, declared that the basic aim of British policy was to guide the colonies to responsible self-government in conditions which would ensure a fair standard of living, and freedom from oppression, for all their peoples – a formulation derived from high-level policy discussion in the context of India, Burma and Ceylon, all of which achieved independence in 1947–8. No formal time-scale was set out, however, and the British government showed itself prepared to resist forcibly any development which it considered undesirable, such as the so-called 'Mau Mau rebellion' in Kenya and communist insurgency in Malaya. Indeed, by the late 1940s

[15] The 'Atlantic Charter' was published for Parliament as Cmd. 6321. A copy is in the Cabinet Office file CAB 166/304.

[16] See the Prime Minister's Office files PREM 4/43A/3, application of Atlantic Charter to coloured races, Sept. to Dec. 1941, an extract from which is at figure 52; and PREM 4/45/6, application of Atlantic Charter to India, Aug. to Dec. 1941.

[17] Hansard, *Parliamentary Debates*, 5th ser., *Commons*, 391 (13 July 1943), col. 48; TNA reference ZHC 2/899.

Britain's American allies considered communism to be a much greater danger than residual colonialism. In 1956 the policy of steady development intended to lead gradually to autonomy was dealt a blow by the politically disastrous attack on Egypt launched by Britain and France. Although the Gold Coast achieved independence, as Ghana, the following year as part of the planned and gradual process, by 1960 Harold Macmillan, in his famous 'winds of change' speech to the Cape Parliament, signalled an altogether more rapid dissolution of empire.[18]

Most former colonies became members of the Commonwealth of Nations;[19] responsibility for British relations with Commonwealth countries went first to the Commonwealth Relations Office (the renamed Dominions Office), then to the Commonwealth Office, and subsequently to the Foreign and Commonwealth Office. The Commonwealth Relations Office retained a role in the organisation of meetings of Commonwealth prime ministers and officials – the forerunners of the Commonwealth Heads of Government Meetings (CHOGM) – and for related matters until 1965 when the Commonwealth Secretariat was set up with headquarters in London.[20] The secretariat maintains its own records.[21]

With the return of Hong Kong to China in 1997 many British commentators claimed that the sun had finally set on the British empire. But there is a substantial residue. The first edition of this guide stated that Britain's remaining dependencies (now known as UK Overseas Territories) number 15: Anguilla; Ascension; Bermuda; British Antarctic Territory; British Indian Ocean Territory; British Virgin Islands; Cayman Islands; Falkland Islands; Gibraltar; Montserrat; Pitcairn, Henderson, Ducie and Oeno Islands; St Helena; South Georgia and Sandwich Islands; Tristan da Cunha (which is a dependency of St Helena); and the Turks and Caicos Islands. However, a new constitution dated 1 September 2009 created a single dependency of Saint Helena, Ascension and Tristan da Cunha giving the three islands equal status within the territory. Details of the current administration of overseas territories, and related matters such as the application of international treaties to the dependencies, can be found through the Foreign and Commonwealth Office website, https://www.gov.uk/government/organisations/foreign-commonwealth-office/.

Many of the most significant documents in TNA relating to decolonisation have been reproduced in the volumes of the British Documents on the End of Empire project, the main purpose of which was to publish papers from British official archives on the ending of colonial and associated rule and on the context in which this took place. The project consists of general volumes describing the policies of successive British governments, a series of territorial studies and two supporting volumes providing guides to the records (see bibliography for details).

[18] Copies of the speech are at TNA in the Colonial Office Social Services Department file CO 859/1477, race relations: speech by Prime Minister, Rt. Hon. Harold Macmillan, in Cape Town, 3 Feb. 1960; and the Commonwealth Relations Office file DO 35/10570, which includes a souvenir brochure of the event.

[19] Formerly known as the British Commonwealth of Nations, the word 'British' was dropped in April 1949 to reflect the changing nature of the association.

[20] For records of these meetings, held both at TNA and at the Secretariat, see *Imperial and Commonwealth Conferences* (London, List and Index Society, 280, 2000).

[20] For details, see http://thecommonwealth.org/library-and-archives/ [accessed 8 Oct. 2014].

2. Colonial government structure and relations with London

Colonies, dominions, protectorates and mandated territories

'Colony' tends to be used as a blanket term for all dependencies within the British empire, and, indeed, is so used within this guide. Technically, however, there were at least four different types of dependency: colonies, dominions, protectorates and mandated territories. Distinctions were often blurred and, as shown below, not always clear even to officials within the Colonial Office, but it may be useful to attempt some definitions here. First, however, it should be stressed that British dependent territories were separate units and not extensions of the United Kingdom.

Colonies

As T. O. Lloyd has written, 'it was a very large empire but at times it does seem to have been even more confusing than was absolutely necessary. Perhaps there really was a rule at the Colonial Office that no colony should have a constitution exactly like that of any other colony; if so, it was enforced with an entirely untypical uniformity'.[1] Individual researchers may need a detailed understanding of the precise constitutional arrangements existing within 'their' colonial dependency during 'their' period. Because of the huge variety of such governmental and administrative arrangements it is possible here only to give generalisations, and generalisations which are not necessarily applicable to earlier and later periods.

By 1878 the Colonial Office was classifying colonies into three categories:

1. Crown Colonies, in which the Crown has the entire control of legislation, while the administration is carried on by public officers under the control of the Home Government.
2. Colonies possessing Representative Institutions but not Responsible Government, in which the Crown has no more than a veto on legislation, but the Home Government retains the control of public officers.
3. Colonies possessing Representative Institutions and Responsible Government, in which the Crown has only a veto on legislation, and the Home Government has no control over any public officer except the Governor.[2]

[1] T. O. Lloyd, *The British Empire 1558–1995* (Oxford, 1996), p. ix.
[2] *Colonial Office List* (1878), p. 273.

The succeeding paragraphs in the *Colonial Office List* for that year, which provide more detail and claim to place individual dependencies into their appropriate categories, are, however, unclear and are hedged about with expressions such as 'generally' and 'for the most part', and with exceptions to every rule. The *List* should, however, be considered a good starting point for details of the constitutional position of individual territories in the 1862–1966 period if no more detailed secondary source is available. More information is given about this publication at appendix 4. Details of constitutional change may also be found in the original correspondence series and government gazettes for individual territories (see chapter 6), and in the series CO 380, Colonial Office and Predecessors: General Draft Letters Patent, Commissions, Royal Instructions, Warrants, etc., 1764–1925.

The introduction to the comparable classification of colonies in the 1901 *List* commences with the statement that

> The British Colonial Empire comprises forty-three distinct and independent governments [excluding the Transvaal and Orange River Colonies, the government of which has not yet been organised]. But in addition to these organised communities, there are a number of scattered dependencies under the dominion or protection of the Queen which do not possess regularly formed administrations, and vast territories controlled by British Companies.

Although three categories of dependency are retained, the term 'administration' is used in preference to 'colony', perhaps reflecting uncertainties about terminology. More significantly, the third category listed in the 1878 definition – 'Colonies possessing Representative Institutions and Responsible Government' – is specifically excluded, with the territories of Canada, Newfoundland, Cape Colony, Natal, the Australian Commonwealth, the six Australian States and New Zealand being listed separately. The three constitutional distinctions of the remainder are now described as:

1. No Legislative Council. Legislative power delegated to the officer administering the Government.
2. Legislative Council nominated by the Crown.
3. Legislative Council partly elected.[3]

Almost at the end of our period Sir Charles Jeffries, a deputy under-secretary of state, wrote: 'A Colony, in modern constitutional definition, is a territory which, by settlement, conquest, cession or annexation has become a part of Her Majesty's dominions and over which Her Majesty, as Queen of the United Kingdom, exercises absolute sovereignty.'[4]

Dominions

Although the term is not used in the introductory section to the 1901 *List* quoted above, from the early 20th century 'dominion' was increasingly used for dependencies possessing responsible government. The gradual movement to responsible government in colonies of settlement outside

[3] *Colonial Office List* (1901), p. xxiii.

[4] Sir Charles Jeffries, *The Colonial Office* (London, 1956), p. 29.

the Caribbean eventually resulted in a system of administration of government not by officials appointed by the governor, but by ministers responsible to an assembly which eventually became the parliament. Such a colony was for all practical purposes internally self-governing.

Demands of the dominions for exceptional treatment by the British government led to the creation of the Colonial Office Dominions Division in 1907, and, subsequently, to the establishment of a separate Dominions Office (see pp. 42–3 and 48–9). In 1917 dominions prime ministers called for a readjustment of constitutional relations, greater involvement in imperial affairs and an adequate voice in foreign policy. The Balfour Declaration of 1926 defined the constitutional relationship between Great Britain and the dominions as 'autonomous communities within the British Empire, equal in status, in no way subordinate one to another', although it was not until 1931 that the Statute of Westminster clarified the legal position of the dominions parliaments. These changes not only removed any theoretical British authority over internal affairs but also gave the dominions some recognition in international affairs. After 1945 the term 'dominion' was less used and the territories were treated as independent states, although there was no formal declaration of independence. They subsequently came to be referred to as the 'Old' Commonwealth – in distinction to the 'New' Commonwealth of those former dependencies which joined the association of the Commonwealth of Nations from the 1940s onwards on achieving independence. More recently nations without a prior constitutional connection to the UK have joined the Commonwealth, for example Mozambique in 1995, and Rwanda in 2009. Others have expressed an interest in joining.

Protectorates

The terms 'protectorate' and 'protected state' seem to be peculiarly difficult to define, which perhaps accounts for their omission from the indexes of a number of recent studies of the British empire. Bernard Porter, however, describes the establishment of protectorates as a means of avoiding colonial annexation and minimising Britain's responsibilities:

> In a "protectorate" the metropolitan country had some responsibilities, but not many. The word implied that some indigenous authority did the actual ruling, but with the privilege of being allowed to call on the metropolitan country's help and protection if they were needed. Protectorates were generally legitimised by treaties between both parties to this effect. In practice the "protection" afforded by Britain took a number of guises, and in some cases it was a legal fiction covering what was in effect a piece of political puppetry.[5]

Perhaps surprisingly, officials in the Colonial Office also found it difficult to define these terms. A simple enquiry to them in 1930 created considerable work for J. J. Paskin, who subsequently reported:

> *A British Protectorate* is not part of His Majesty's dominions. The native inhabitants are not, by reason of birth there, British subjects, but are under His Majesty's protection, and are generally known as British Protected Persons.

[5] B. Porter, *The Lion's Share: a Short History of British Imperialism 1850–1995* (3rd edn., Harlow, 1996), p. 114.

No authoritative definition of the term "Protectorate" has ever been enacted by the Imperial Parliament, but the following general descriptions (which must not be taken to be legal definitions) may be regarded as representing the classification adopted by the Colonial Office:-

A. Territories, in and over which His Majesty possesses no powers of sovereignty but in which he has jurisdiction (and exercises it under the Foreign Jurisdiction Act, 1890) over all persons, subject (in respect of the nationals of Foreign Powers) to Treaty obligations (if any).

   (a) Territories (such as Nyasaland and Northern Rhodesia) not under a recognised Sovereign Ruler, and the administration of which is, in practice, hardly distinguishable from that of a Colony.

   (b) Territories in which there are one or more local Rulers recognised as possessing a certain measure of sovereignty over certain areas within their limits but not over the whole of the territory, e.g. Uganda, which includes the Native Kingdoms of Buganda, Toro, Ankole and Bunyoro.

   (c) Zanzibar, in which His Majesty possesses and exercises jurisdiction, and in which (while there is also a local Ruler, recognised as possessing sovereign rights over the whole of the territory) the administration (subject to the rights of the Sultan over his own subjects,) is essentially British.

B. States in which there is a recognised Sovereign Ruler, but which, being under His Majesty's protection, have no political relations with Foreign Powers except through or by permission of His Majesty's Government. These States are usually referred to as "Protected States". They may be roughly classified as follows:-

   (a) States in which His Majesty does not possess jurisdiction (e.g. the various Malay States and Sarawak). In certain of these States, although *de jure*, His Majesty may have no control over the internal affairs of the State, such control is *de facto* exercised through the medium of British Residents or Advisers.

   (b) States in which His Majesty, although possessing jurisdiction, does not exercise it under the Foreign Jurisdiction Act 1890 (e.g. North Borneo).

   (c) Tonga, in which (like Zanzibar) His Majesty possesses and exercises jurisdiction and in which there is also a local ruler, recognised as possessing sovereign rights over the whole of the Territory. The administration of Tonga is however vested mainly in the King and his government.[6]

Britain's relationship with the protectorates and protected states was usually administered initially through the consular service, and correspondence from the consuls and related material can be found in the Foreign Office collections (see chapter 12). The transfer of responsibilities to the Colonial Office in the late 19th and early 20th centuries is detailed for each territory in appendix 1. To complicate matters further, some territories consisted of both a colony and a protectorate. In 1886, for example, Lagos, which for 12 years had been part of the Gold Coast Colony, became a separate colony. In the same year Lagos Protectorate was created from bordering territories.

[6] CO 323/1105/6, file 71376, 1930, 'colony' and 'protectorate': meaning of terms.

Twenty years later both colony and protectorate amalgamated with the Protectorate of Southern Nigeria to form the Colony and Protectorate of Southern Nigeria. Similarly, when the East Africa Protectorate was renamed Kenya in 1920, the coastal strip originally leased from the sultan of Zanzibar became the Protectorate of Kenya, and the remaining territory became Kenya Colony. The *Colonial Office List* (see appendix 4) provides details of the geographical limits of colony and protectorate in such cases.

Mandated territories

As noted above, the mandated territories were former dependencies of Germany and the Ottoman empire entrusted to Britain by the League of Nations following the First World War. Terms of the mandates required Britain to administer the territories in the interests of their inhabitants, and with a view to their eventual independence. In effect Transjordan (Jordan) and Iraq were treated as protectorates, and Palestine and the ex-German territories in Africa – parts of Togoland, Cameroon and German East Africa (Tanganyika) – were treated as colonies.[7] Although the British government was responsible to the Permanent Mandates Commission of the League for the good government of the mandated territories, in practice such territories were simply absorbed into the empire and treated in the same way as colonial possessions. British policy in, for example, the mandated territory of Tanganyika was rarely distinguishable from policy in the neighbouring colony of Kenya. After 1945 the remaining mandated territories became United Nations trust territories.[8]

Given the complexities touched upon above, it will, I hope, be clear that no universal form of local colonial government can be described here; it simply never existed. Colonies were not extensions of the United Kingdom, but separate entities. What follows is a very general outline of the types of structure used.

The colonial government

The governor

Whatever the variation in the constitutional arrangements for the dependencies, we can be confident that a named individual would have held the position of head of each colonial government. His[9] title varied: governor, governor-general, governor-in-chief, governor and commander-in-chief, and captain-general have all been used. In a mandated territory he may have been called a 'high commissioner', although his role was essentially the same. In the case of protectorates, possessing their own indigenous rulers, the title 'high commissioner' was also

[7] Other parts of the former German territories in Africa were allocated to France and to Belgium. Namibia was allocated to the Union of South Africa; Nauru and German New Guinea were allocated to Australia.

[8] The mandate over Iraq had come to an end in 1932.

[9] The masculine term is used with some reluctance; however, it reflects the true situation until 1968 when Dr Hilda Louisa Gibbs Bynoe was appointed governor of Grenada. She served in that capacity until Grenada's independence in 1974. I am grateful to Tony Kirk-Greene for suggestions which led me to this information.

sometimes used, although less authoritative forms such as 'adviser', 'resident' or 'agent' were often preferred. Throughout this guide the simple term 'governor' is used.

Governors were appointed by the Crown for a temporary period; by at least 1828 generally not more than six years.[10] The governor was (and of course in some cases still is) head of state; the representative of the British monarch.[11] Technically he was also responsible to the reigning monarch, although in practice reporting to the secretary of state. He exercised virtually all the constitutional functions of the Crown within his territory, and was described by Lugard as combining the functions of king and prime minister.[12] Furthermore he was, in the term so commonly used, 'the man on the spot'. As Jeffries has noted, it may seem that governors were subject to the direction of the secretary of state, but this is true only up to a point:

> The Secretary of State does not function in a vacuum. He must have information before him in order that he may decide upon any action. And he necessarily relies mainly upon the Governor to lay before him all the necessary information and considerations which affect … the decision which has to be taken. Further, the Secretary of State is answerable to his Ministerial colleagues, and the Government as a whole is answerable to Parliament, for his actions. To overrule the considered and maintained advice of a Governor is a thing which no Secretary of State would do lightly …[13]

Some governors headed a federation of small dependencies, in which cases a lieutenant-governor, administrator or president of the council would be appointed to administer each constituent territory. Such appointees reported, at least in theory, to the federal governor rather than directly to London.

If a governor was temporarily absent from his seat of government – whether touring a distant part of his dependency, on an official or private visit away from that dependency, or on leave in the UK or elsewhere – a nominated deputy assumed his responsibilities, and will be generally described in the records as the 'officer administering the government' or 'o.a.g'. The same is true of periods between the transfer, retirement or death of a governor and the arrival in the dependency of his successor.

The legislature

Occasionally there was no legislature. For example, Sir Frederick Lugard (later Lord Lugard), as high commissioner of Northern Nigeria from 1900, was himself empowered to enact legislation by 'proclamation' and similar arrangements existed elsewhere at various times. More usually a governor would be supported by a formal advisory structure – a privy council or executive council – comprised initially of senior officials but gradually expanding to include 'unofficial' (or 'non-official') members. In almost all territories there would also be an assembly or legislative council responsible for discussing financial matters and legislation.[14] Arrangements were diverse,

[10] See circular despatches of 1 and 31 May 1828, CO 854/1, f. 274.

[11] Independent states within the Commonwealth which have not adopted a republican form of government, such as for example Canada and Jamaica, retain the post of governor-general.

[12] Sir F. D. Lugard [later Lord Lugard], *The Dual Mandate in British Tropical Africa* (Edinburgh and London, 1926), p. 95.

[13] Jeffries, p. 36.

[14] For a study of one such council, see M. Wight, *The Gold Coast Legislative Council* (London, 1947).

but details for each dependency, charting constitutional development over the years and listing council members, are given in the annual *Colonial Office List* for the period from 1862 to 1966. Three examples are given here.

In Jamaica, following major constitutional reform in 1866 after the so-called Morant Bay Rebellion of the previous year, there was a Privy Council comprised of senior officials appointed by, or with the approval of, the British monarch. The governor was required to consult the Privy Council on important matters. He was not obliged to accept its advice, but was likely to ignore it only in exceptional circumstances. In addition there was a Legislative Council, under the presidency of the governor, consisting of the official members of the Privy Council and an equal number of unofficial members. Although the unofficial members were technically representatives of local interests, they were appointed rather than elected. Very similar arrangements existed elsewhere, although the two councils were more commonly called the executive council and the legislative council. In Mauritius they were known as the Executive Council and the Council of Government.

Malta, from 1849, had only one council, the Council of Government. By 1878 the council consisted of 18 members, 10 official and eight elected. The elected councillors were returned by an electorate of about 2,700 selected through a property qualification from a total population of almost 150,000.[15]

In New Zealand a 'Central Legislation' was established in 1852 consisting of the governor, a Legislative Council and a House of Representatives. In addition the governor was assisted by an Executive Council. By 1878 there were 43 appointed members of the Legislative Council. The House of Representatives comprised 88 elected members, including four Maori members returned by the Maori electorate. The *Colonial Office List* for 1878 describes the franchise as 'practically amount[ing] to household suffrage' but does not say if that was true for the Maori population which at the time was estimated to amount to just over one-tenth of the whole.

Many legislative councils included both appointed and elected unofficial members, with the proportion of elected councillors gradually increasing. Although unofficial members were appointed or elected as representatives of the local population, in the absence of any truly democratic process it was often only a tiny proportion of that population that was directly represented. In East and Central Africa before the Second World War only the white settler community was represented in the main organs of government; the member representing African interests was always a European – and often a missionary.[16]

Records of the proceedings of the legislative bodies are held at TNA among the Colonial Office, Dominions Office and Commonwealth Relations Office records in the series known as 'sessional papers'; they are included in the territorial listing in appendix 1, and described at pp. 122–3.

[15] The property qualification required a minimum income of £8 from immovable property, or payment of a rent of £4 per annum.

[16] 'The composition of the Legislative and Executive Councils', in Lord Hailey, *An African Survey* (1938), pp. 163–73.

The executive

Under the head of state – the governor – there existed varied arrangements for the day-to-day administration of a dependency. Invariably civil establishments differed considerably in size and detail, but in the modern period they can be equated with the government departments of any independent state. Typically a chief secretary or colonial secretary might act as head of the civil service with overall responsibility for a range of departments: treasury, customs and audit departments, public works, medical and sanitary departments, police and prisons, etc., etc. As geography dictated there might be a harbour department or a forestry department. New departments would be added as circumstances developed. It might be recognised, for example, that education could not be left entirely to the missionaries, and that an education department was required, or that the addition of a labour department would serve to control recruiting and ensure the welfare of workers. Older colonies often had a structure of local government which will be familiar to historians of England – based for example on parish vestries – while in modern Africa district commissioners and district officers filled both administrative and magisterial roles in the various localities.

Records of colonial government departments are not part of the Colonial Office records at TNA, but must be sought in the national archives of the independent territories (for exceptions to this rule see chapter 3). TNA does hold collections of the annual reports of such departments, although these are not fully comprehensive. They are to be found in the 'sessional papers' series for each territory (see pp. 122–3) and are usually described in the catalogue as 'departmental reports' or 'administration reports'; the catalogue does not list the individual reports contained in each volume but there is usually an internal contents list.

Varied arrangements were in place for the appointment of individuals to the myriad posts in colonial government departments. Many senior appointments were made from London, although an individual recommended, or temporarily appointed, by the governor was often confirmed in post. For specialist posts it might be necessary for the Colonial Office to seek suggestions from other UK government departments or from specialist institutions or professional bodies. In the case of more junior staff the situation varied enormously from place to place. In some colonies they were usually local appointees; elsewhere there might be far fewer opportunities for local people.

Colonial civil servants below the rank of governor were employed by their colonial government, not directly by the British government or by the Colonial Office in London, although a colonial civil service gradually developed with responsibilities for central recruitment, training, placement and what we would now call career development.[17]

[17] For a comprehensive history of the overseas civil services, see A. Kirk-Greene, *Britain's Imperial Administrators, 1858–1966* (Basingstoke, 2000). A research project and a series of witness seminars organised by the Overseas Service Pensioners' Association have provided a record and assessment of the varied work of HM Overseas Civil Service in the period before and immediately after independence. For lists of associated publications see http://www.ospa.org.uk.

From about 1820 through to the 1940s very brief career details of individuals employed by the colonial governments can be found in the annual blue books of statistics in the Colonial Office 'miscellanea' series (see pp. 127–30 for details and appendix 1 for series references for each dependency). More detailed information concerning senior officials can be found in the *Colonial Office List* (1862–1966). In both cases it is exclusively career information rather than personal or family detail, although entries in the *List* will almost certainly refer to any previous military service and may mention universities (and sometimes schools) attended. For further details and a discussion of the utility of other Colonial Office records for research into the careers of colonial officials see appendix 8.

Judicial establishment

Each dependency had its own judiciary, court system and legal officers. Again, individual arrangements vary considerably, but there was generally a chief justice, attorney-general, solicitor-general, Crown advocate and a network of courts and judges and/or magistrates as required. The records of these departments, courts and individuals do not form part of the Colonial Office archives at TNA, and must be sought in the former dependencies. The legal officer whose work tends to be most prominent among Colonial Office records is the attorney-general, whose reports on new or amended legislation can be found among the original correspondence series under cover of governors' despatches. Reports from the stipendiary or 'special' magistrates appointed during the transitional period of 'apprenticeship' following the emancipation of slaves, and from the appeal courts which replaced them, can sometimes also be found.[18] Overall, however, records of judicial proceedings are found very rarely in either the correspondence or the 'miscellanea' series. Occasional references, and even transcripts, generally relate to cases involving matters of precedent, commutation of death sentences, or where there is a legal query which cannot be resolved locally. In 1920, for example, the synopsis of a Jamaican court case was forwarded to London because of the 'difficulty of proving that the prisoner has been "leading persistently a dishonest or criminal life"' and the potential effect of such a difficulty on the application of the Habitual Criminals Law of 1917.[19] Figures 10 and 11 relate to a piracy trial at Grand Turk.

In the early 19th century commissions of inquiry were appointed to investigate legal and judicial systems in newly acquired dependencies. Details of the records of the commissioners of eastern inquiry relating to the Cape, Ceylon and Mauritius are noted in appendix 1. The work of the commissioners of legal enquiry in the West Indies was extended to the older colonies in the region; the majority of its records are in the West Indies series CO 318, with some further references in records relating to the individual dependencies. Commissions also investigated the judicial establishments of New South Wales and Tasmania in the 1820s. Reports of all these commissions were published for Parliament (see pp. 101 and 104).

[18] Where these are included in the 'miscellanea' series of records they are listed in appendix 1. In other cases they can be found in the correspondence series.

[19] CO 137/738 fos. 179–89.

The Judicial Committee of the Privy Council is the court of final appeal for the remaining UK overseas territories, and for those Commonwealth countries that have retained the appeal to Her Majesty in Council or, in the case of republics, to the Judicial Committee. Records of the committee held at TNA (in PCAP series) do not, however, appear to include any references to colonial cases. Records are with the Judicial Committee; details of recent judgments can be found on the council's website.[20] Correspondence about individual cases can sometimes be found among Colonial Office and Dominions Office/Commonwealth Relations Office correspondence.[21]

Civil proceedings relating to colonial matters may have been heard in English courts. Writing specifically of land and property in the Caribbean, Guy Grannum has noted that

> The equity side of the courts of Chancery and Exchequer dealt with a large and varied range of disputes such as inheritance, lands, debts, bankruptcy and marriage settlement. Papers such as accounts, deeds, journals and correspondence were provided as evidence ... Those that were not returned to the owner have survived as Chancery Masters Exhibits (C 103–C 114 and J 90) and Exchequer Exhibits (E 140, E 192, E 214 and E 219).[22]

Defence

Defence of the colonies was primarily an imperial rather than a colonial responsibility. Units of the British Army were based in various parts of the empire at various times and in various circumstances. In 1901, for example, the headquarters of British forces in West Africa was at Freetown in Sierra Leone. It consisted of six companies of the West India Regiment, the West African Regiment, detachments of the Royal Engineers and the Royal Artillery and locally raised companies of artillery and engineers.[23] There was also an establishment for victualling and coaling ships of the Royal Navy. In other territories there might be a locally raised militia in addition to, or instead of, a regular army presence.

Records of the local militias, if they survive, will be held locally. Operational and other records of British forces (including in many cases service records) will be found among the records of the War Office, Admiralty and Air Ministry held at TNA. Some records of men of the West India regiments, first raised in 1795, are included in the general series of War Office musters, pension registers, description books, casualty returns and soldiers' documents (see also under West Indies in appendix 1). Records of locally raised units which fought in the South African (Boer) War are also among the War Office collection. The Colonial Office was responsible for the administration of the King's African Rifles and the West Africa Frontier Force, records of which are listed in appendix

[20] http://www.jcpc.uk/decided-cases/ [accessed 8 Oct. 2014].

[21] For example, CO 96/759/41, Privy Council appeal: I. T. A. Wallace Johnson vs. the King (1939–40); CO 295/608/4, Grant to Uriah Butler for special leave to appeal to the Privy Council ..., following his conviction and sentence of two years' imprisonment for sedition (1938).

[22] G. Grannum, *Tracing your Caribbean Ancestors* (London, 2012), p. 60. For further information about these records, see H. Horwitz, *Chancery Equity Records and Proceedings, 1600–1800* (Public Record Office, Handbook No. 27, 1998); and H. Horwitz, *Exchequer Equity Records and Proceedings, 1649–1841* (Public Record Office, Handbook No. 32, 2001).

[23] *Colonial Office List* (1901), p. 256. Sierra Leone also maintained an armed police force 'especially organised for frontier work' and at that time numbering 623.

1. Their administration was brought together in a Colonial Office Military Branch in 1927. The archival collections of the Rhodesian Army Association, formerly held by the British Empire and Commonwealth Museum at Bristol, have yet to find a permanent home. Neither the collections nor the electronic catalogue compiled as part of a project at the University of the West of England (UWE) are currently available to researchers.[24] The museum also held records of the Palestine Police.[25]

TNA holds records relating to the Royal Irish Constabulary, including service records, and to the South African Constabulary (see appendix 1 for further details).

Ecclesiastical establishment

As will be seen from the *Colonial Office List*, ecclesiastical establishments varied considerably. For Mauritius in 1878, for example, the only individuals listed are a civil chaplain and two Roman Catholic priests. For Trinidad in the same year the *List* includes an Anglican bishop and a total of 18 rectors, curates, catechists and chaplains. In addition there was a Roman Catholic archbishop and 26 curés, assistant curés and chaplains. By 1901 clergy of the Presbyterian, Wesleyan and Baptist churches are also listed for Trinidad. Although Colonial Office records include a quite considerable amount of correspondence[26] with or relating to the churches and individual incumbents, records of the churches themselves should be sought locally or through their appropriate headquarters. The same is true of records of the British and foreign missionary societies which operated in the British dependencies.[27]

Lambeth Palace Library holds the correspondence and papers of the bishops of London, including extensive documentation of the Church of England in colonial America and the West Indies.[28]

The relationship between the Colonial Office and the colonies

In 1936 a Colonial Office official complained, with some exasperation, that a former parliamentary under-secretary had held the fixed idea that 'colonies are governed from here'.[29] This is still a common misconception. But although the secretary of state for the colonies was ultimately

[24] The UWE project, 'Wars of Liberation, Wars of Decolonisation: The Rhodesian Army Archive Project', was managed first by Professor Diana Jeater, and subsequently by Dr Kent Fedorowich.

[25] Following closure of the British Empire and Commonwealth Museum in late 2012, the Palestine Police Force records were removed for safe keeping by the Department for International Development (DfID), which had deposited the records with the Museum some years earlier. At time of writing an assessment of the collection is underway. Once this is completed options for its future will be considered by DfID and TNA. Another separate collection of Palestine Police records is held at St Antony's College, Oxford.

[26] As well as scattered communications there are small discrete collections of correspondence with the bishops of Barbados and of Jamaica for the period 1824 to the early 1840s, when the religious instruction of enslaved and newly emancipated inhabitants was considered a priority (in CO 28 and CO 137 respectively).

[27] For a guide to sources, see *Missionary Encounters: Sources and Issues*, ed. R. A. Bickers and R. Seaton (Richmond, 1996); the Mundus Gateway is a web-based guide to more than 400 collections of overseas missionary materials held in the UK (http://mundus.ac.uk [accessed 8 Oct. 2014]).

[28] Lambeth Palace Library (http://www.lambethpalacelibrary.org/content/collections/ [accessed 8 Oct. 2014]).

[29] CO 866/29 file 1166, J. E. W. Flood minute, 3 Oct. 1936.

responsible to the British government, and thence to the UK Parliament, for the peace, order and good government of the colonies, day-to-day responsibility for administration was effectively devolved to the governors and the colonial governments. There were occasions when London made demands on the colonial authorities – which might be accepted or vigorously resisted – but in most respects British colonies were governed internally rather than by the imperial centre. As Jeffries has put it, 'The Governor … is not a "stooge" of Her Majesty's Government', although admittedly 'he could hardly hope or wish to retain his office if he were in fundamental disagreement with the policies or principles of Her Majesty's Ministers'.[30] A comparison is sometimes made with the French system in which colonies were governed much more directly. It is, perhaps, helpful to see the relationship between the Colonial Office and the colonies as analogous to the modern relationship between UK central government and the local authorities.

Henry Hall, in his study of the 19th-century Colonial Office, has stressed that the distance between the centre and the periphery required a 'policy of trust'.[31] He quotes one secretary of state, Earl Grey, informing a Parliamentary committee in the late 1840s that to 'attempt to conduct the details of the administration from this country is absolutely impracticable'. Twenty years later Sir Charles Adderley, parliamentary under-secretary, endorsed this view: 'in distant Crown Colonies the Home Government can only *supervise* – they cannot *judge* except on the Governor's local information. Their original act is sending a good governor, and their check is dismissing him.'[32] Hall has also stated, however, that 'those who think that the Office knew no more than the Governor chose to tell it are mistaken, for abundant information from other sources arrived by every mail'.[33]

The 'arm's length' approach was a factor in creating the widely differing policies and practices which developed in the dependencies; as noted in chapter 5 (pp. 43–7) it was not until the late 1920s that there was any real attempt within the Colonial Office to co-ordinate policy in individual subject areas. It also informs the current distribution of archival sources. The National Archives of the United Kingdom holds the records of the Colonial Office in London. It does not (with the exception of collections described in chapter 3) hold the locally created records of the colonial governments.

Details of the respective roles of the individual colonial governments and the Colonial Office in legislative development are outlined in chapter 6 (pp. 118–21), and a little more about the relationship is said in the section on 'original correspondence'. The role of other UK government departments is discussed briefly in chapter 12.

[30] Jeffries, p. 36.
[31] H. L. Hall, *The Colonial Office: a History* (London, 1937), p. 113.
[32] Hall, p. 113.
[33] Hall, p. 5.

3. Records of colonial governments

Many new users of records relating to the colonies deposited in TNA appear to believe that all records created by the colonial governments have been transferred, or copied, to London. This is not the case. TNA does hold certain, often printed, material supplied by the colonial governments, for example the series of statutes, sessional papers, gazettes and blue books of statistics described below, but it does not hold the local records of the governors' and colonial secretaries' offices, the local government departments, the courts and magistrates, the parish vestries, the district commissioners and district officers, and the myriad temporary bodies which might exist from time to time. Such records must be sought in the national archives of the independent territories.

Inevitably there are exceptions to this rule. The first edition of this guide described the few series of locally created records then held among the Colonial Office collections in TNA – information repeated in this chapter and included in the geographical listings in appendix 1. During 2012–13, however, an additional collection of records created by the governments of former dependent territories was transferred to TNA, and deposited not in a Colonial Office record series, but in a new Foreign and Commonwealth Office series, FCO 141. The background to this transfer is described briefly below.

Locally created records in Colonial Office series[1]

British Guiana: records of the Dutch West India Company relating to the administration of Essequibo, Demerara and Berbice between 1686 and 1792 (CO 116/18 to 136). They include Dutch Association papers; ordinances and instructions; grants and surveys of land; church accounts; registers of legal instruments; records of the court of policy and criminal justice; statistics of soldiers, slaves, buildings, etc.; and taxation returns.

Ceylon: 50 volumes of records of the government of Ceylon, 1800–5, including ledgers and journals of the Military Auditor General's Office, proceedings of the Military Board at Colombo and of the Committee of Superintendence of Charitable Institutions in Ceylon, and diaries and proceedings of the Military, Public and Secret Departments (CO 55/11–60).

[1] This list is believed to be comprehensive for Colonial Office content, but other locally created records may be found elsewhere in TNA, for example records of the Irish Revenue Board and Irish Board of Customs in CUST 1, and of the mixed commission courts established to try cases of illegal slave trading held in a variety of collections. For the latter, see the TNA research guide 'British transatlantic slave trade' (http://www.nationalarchives.gov.uk/records/research-guides/slave-trade-slavery.htm [accessed 6 January 2015]).

Ionian Islands: the islands were occupied by Britain in 1809/10 and made a British protectorate in 1814. Local records of the islands were sent to the UK when the protectorate was surrendered to Greece in 1864. This considerable collection is not catalogued in any detail; a proportion is in Italian (CO 136/300–1433).

Ireland: records of the Chief Secretary's Office in Dublin Castle, which was the central office of the Irish administration serving both the lord lieutenant and the chief secretary (CO 904, 1795–1926, 232 boxes and files).

Heligoland: one volume only of papers from the office of the chief secretary to the government (CO 122/1, 1844–89).

Malta: records of the officers at arms, 1826–70, left in the charge of the chief secretary to the government of Malta and forwarded to the Colonial Office in 1872 (CO 745/3). Eight files of the governor's office, 1958–69, relating to the Bailey Dockyard case (CO 1062). The series CO 1053 has been raised for records of the governor and commander-in-chief's office, but at the time of writing no papers have been transferred.

New South Wales: the records of the superintendent of convicts in New South Wales were transferred to the government of New South Wales in 1973. Microfilm copies are retained in TNA (CO 207/9–11, 1788–1868).

North Borneo: the territory was governed by the British North Borneo Company from 1882 to 1942. The company transferred its surviving records to the Public Record Office following the winding up of its affairs in 1952 (CO 874, 1,114 files and volumes).

Palestine: a small collection of records of the Palestine custodian of enemy property, 1939–1952 (CO 1044, 6 files and volumes).

Sierra Leone: records of the Colony of Sierra Leone including three volumes of governors' despatches to the under-secretaries of state (CO 269/9–11, 1826–35), 17 volumes of council minutes (CO 270/1–18, 1792–1827), three volumes of council letter books (CO 268/12–14, 1834–66), and one volume of letters to the court of directors (CO 268/5, 1794–8).

Tangier: the territory was ceded to England by Portugal in 1661 as part of the dowry of Catherine of Braganza, the wife of Charles II. Records held in TNA include court books of the municipal assemblies under English rule and local notarial documents (CO 279/34–49, 1664–86).

Wei-Hai-Wei: the territory was leased to Britain by China in 1898 for use as a naval harbour. Administration was first undertaken by the senior naval officer and in 1899 it was transferred to a military and civil commissioner appointed by the War Office. In 1901 the War Office handed over control to the Colonial Office, and a civil commissioner was appointed in 1902. The civil commissioner's files were stored in the British Embassy at Peking (Beijing) from 1930 until 1961 when they were sent to the Colonial Office; they are now in CO 873.

In addition TNA holds small discrete collections for territories held temporarily in wartime: Corsica, Curaçao, Guadeloupe, Havana, Martinique, St Croix, St Eustatius, St Thomas, Santo Domingo, and Suriname (details in appendix 1). In contrast, records of the five years of British administration of Reunion (1810–15) are held in the Archives départementales de la Réunion.

TNA also holds microform copies of the records of the Hudson's Bay Company (BH 1, 1667–1991, 3640 films). See under Hudson's Bay in appendix 1 for details of custody of the originals.

FCO 141, Foreign and Commonwealth Office and predecessors: Records of Former Colonial Administrations: Migrated Archives

In June 2009 five elderly Kenyans brought a claim against the British government alleging that they had suffered mistreatment and torture at the hands of British colonial and military personnel during the Mau Mau Emergency (1952–60). As a result of the case, and the unrelenting efforts of lawyers and expert witnesses, the Foreign and Commonwealth Office was forced in April 2011 to reveal the existence of some 1,500 government files removed from Kenya at independence. The FCO subsequently announced that it held files from 37 former dependencies, a collection first estimated at 8,800 items but in fact amounting to about 20,000. A report commissioned by the Foreign Secretary to examine 'what went wrong and what lessons should we draw?' emphasised bureaucratic incompetence and loss of corporate memory rather than any deliberate intention to conceal the existence of the archives.[2] The report also recommended that an audit be made of all 'out of time' documentation held by the FCO, that is material not assessed for transfer to TNA in accordance with the timescales prescribed by UK public records legislation. It is clear that this includes Colonial Office documentation. See chapter 8 for further information.

Inevitably a considerable amount of media and scholarly attention has been given to the story of the 'discovery' and release of the 'migrated archives'.[3] Professor Stephen Howe has noted, 'Potentially, almost every part of the narrative of decolonisation … will have to be rewritten'.[4] However, as some of these records date back to the 19th century they may well throw new light on events from much earlier periods.

FCO 141 consists of documents from the former dependencies as follows:

[2] https://www.gov.uk/government/publications/cary-report-on-release-of-the-colonial-administration-files [accessed 7 Jan. 2015].

[3] See, for example, articles by Anderson, Bennett and Elkins in *Journal of Imperial and Commonwealth History*, 39 (2011), and by Banton in *Journal of Imperial and Commonwealth History*, 40 (2012).

[4] Stephen Howe, 'Flakking the Mau Mau catchers', in *Journal of Imperial and Commonwealth History*, 39 (2011).

Aden, 1949–67, 47 items
Anguilla, 1967–72, 274 items
Bahamas, 1962–73, 40 items
Botswana (listed in catalogue as Bechuanaland), 1921–66, 304 items
British Indian Ocean Territory and Seychelles, 1930–76, 275 items
Brunei, 1847–1965, 927 items
Cameroon, 1922–62, 148 items
Cyprus, 1879–1960, 2859 items
Fiji (see also Western Pacific), 1931–70, 29 items
Gambia, 1932–65, 93 items
Ghana (listed in catalogue as Gold Coast), 1932–64, 274 items
Jamaica, 1927–63, 352 items
Kenya, 1906–82, 2,726 items (including 915 items from the Kenya Land Transfer Programme, 1955–82)
Kiribati and Tuvalu (listed in catalogue as Gilbert and Ellice Islands), 1943–78, 40 items
Lesotho (listed in catalogue as Basutoland), 1909–66, 771 items
Malawi (listed in catalogue as Nyasaland), 1946–64, 162 items
Malaysia (listed in catalogue as Malaya), 1884–1963, 821 items
Malta, 1852–1971, 4,359 items
Mauritius, 1942–68, 265 items
Nigeria, 1895–1962, 451 items
Palestine, 1926–50, 53 items
Seychelles (see under British Indian Ocean Territory)
Sierra Leone, 1943–61, 64 items
Singapore, 1847–1963, 2934 items
Solomon Islands, 1936–78, 325 items
Sri Lanka (listed in catalogue as Ceylon), 1835–1948, 694 items
Swaziland, 1888–1968, 339 items
Tanzania (listed separately in catalogue as Tanganyika – 1920–64, 332 items – and Zanzibar, 1888–1964, 327 items)
Trinidad, 1874–1972, 37 items
Turks and Caicos, 1945–73, 26 items
Tuvalu (see under Kiribati and Tuvalu above)
Uganda, 1900–63, 459 items
Vanuatu (listed in catalogue as New Hebrides), 1936–82, 280 items
West Indies (records of the West Indian Development and Welfare Organisation and the West Indian Federation), 1940–63, 262 items
Western Pacific High Commission, 1884–1978, 59 items
Zambia (listed in catalogue as Northern Rhodesia), 1924–64, 583 items
Zimbabwe (listed in catalogue as Southern Rhodesia), 1959–68, 15 items

This information has been added to appendix 1 as appropriate. The series is reasonably well catalogued although no attempt has been made to record the original provenance of individual files although this is sometimes readily identifiable. It should be noted that information about one country is sometimes included in the subseries for another. For example the sub-series for Singapore includes files on the Federated Malay States.

The series FCO 141 also includes over 60 Colonial Office and Foreign and Commonwealth Office files relating to the migrated archives, their removal from the dependencies, and their custody in the UK.

The FCO has previously held other collections of locally created records on a temporary basis. For example, records from Antigua transferred to the UK pending the establishment of a viable local archive, and returned in 1990, and records of the Western Pacific High Commission now at the University of Auckland (see p. 307).

4. Administration of British colonial affairs before 1801: the organisation in London

The Privy Council and the Board of Trade

In the early days of the British colonial empire several committees of the Privy Council (the advisory body which had developed from the King's Council) and special commissions were appointed to deal with questions concerning particular trades and colonies. Trade and 'plantations',[1] as Britain's earliest colonies were known, were intimately inter-related. The first such body to deal with all the colonies, and the first to have an executive rather than a purely advisory function, was the Committee for Foreign Plantations, which existed from 1634 to at least 1641. It was replaced by a Parliamentary commission, and later by the Council of State working through a variety of standing and ad hoc committees which included merchants as well as officials. In 1660 two separate councils, for trade and for foreign plantations, were established, but this system did not last, and the Privy Council experimented with a variety of other arrangements until 1675 when the Committee of Lords of Trade and Plantations was established. This committee was reconstituted in 1688, and replaced by William III in 1696 by 'the Lords Commissioners for promoting the Trade of our Kingdom, and for inspecting and improving our Plantations in America and elsewhere' – known usually as the Board of Trade. The new body was not, unlike its predecessors, a subsidiary of the Privy Council, but a separate entity. It remained in existence until 1782, when it was temporarily abolished, and during that period colonial affairs were the responsibility of the secretaries of state and the Board of Trade in partnership. The interest of the Privy Council in colonial affairs did not disappear, however, and, as a far more powerful body than the board, it continued on occasion to make decisions on which it might consult the latter but not defer to it. Parliament also showed a fluctuating interest in colonial affairs, and at times a great deal of the work of the board was undertaken in response to orders from the House of Commons. For the continuing involvement of the Privy Council and the re-established Board of Trade in colonial affairs see chapter 12.

[1] 'Plantation' in the sense of a British settlement 'planted' in a faraway land, rather than a horticultural enterprise. The term was first widely applied to settlements on expropriated lands in early seventeenth-century Ulster, but came to be extended to colonies in north America. The 17th-century philosopher Thomas Hobbes defined plantations as 'numbers of men sent out from the commonwealth, under a conductor or governor, to inhabit a foreign country, either formerly void of inhabitants, or made void by war' (Thomas Hobbes, *Leviathan* (1839), II. xxiv. 239).

The secretaries of state

By the mid 16th century two secretaries of state shared the routine work of foreign and domestic affairs, and played a large part in the presentation of information to the Privy Council. After 1660 the secretaries began to be called formally the secretary of state for the Northern Department and the secretary of state for the Southern Department. The Northern Department dealt with the mainly Protestant countries, while the Southern Department dealt with the Catholic countries, and also had oversight of the colonies, Ireland and the Channel Islands. This arrangement was not formal or rigid, however, and on occasion the northern secretary involved himself in colonial affairs. In the 17th century the secretaries of state were, in fact, little concerned with the colonies, except in so far as they were always (from 1675) 'Lords of Trade' and were also the sovereign's channel of communication with the board and the colonial governors.

During the 18th century the secretaries came, generally as a result of wartime conditions, to take a larger part in colonial affairs. In 1768 a third post of secretary of state was created, to whom the colonial functions of the southern secretary were transferred; the department working to him was known either as the American Department or the Colonial Department or Office. At the same time the constitution of the Board of Trade was amended and the third secretary became its president. With the loss of the American colonies both the third secretaryship and the Board of Trade were abolished in 1782.[2] The board was re-established two years later but did not resume a fundamental role in colonial affairs, although it continued to exercise a considerable influence on the review of colonial legislation and in some other matters. Instead, responsibility for the colonies was placed with the secretary of state for home affairs. Although a third secretary was again appointed in 1794, his primary responsibility was to manage the war with France, and colonial affairs remained with the Home Office. In 1801, however, colonial affairs were transferred to the third secretary, and the War and Colonial Department was established.

India and associated territories were administered separately, and the main body of records of the East India Company (1600–1858), the Board of Control or Board of Commissioners for the Affairs of India (1784–1858) and the India Office (1858–1947) is held at the British Library (http://www.bl.uk).

Records of the secretaries of state and the Board of Trade

Records of the War and Colonial Department and of the Colonial Office are described in chapter 6, and much of what is said there relates also to this earlier period. There are, however, certain features of the arrangement of the earlier records of the secretaries of state and the Board of Trade, especially the official correspondence between colonial governors and London, which merit a mention here. Most importantly, the correspondence no longer follows its original arrangement.

[2] By the Civil List and Secret Service Money Act, 22 Geo. III, c. 82.

The respective responsibilities for the colonies of the secretaries of state and the Board of Trade have been defined as a division between political and military matters on the one hand, and trade and economic development on the other, but this is a simplification which was not always clear at the time, as the official correspondence of colonial governors often shows. One editor of the *Calendar of State Papers, Colonial* complained that the 'existence of the Board of Trade … often leads to an excessive duplication of information. Some over-zealous Governors wrote Despatches to the Secretary and the Board which, though not copies, contain substantially the same material'.[3] The records of the two bodies were consequently rearranged by the Public Record Office. Before 1860, the first editor of the *Calendar* arranged the colonial papers dating to 1688 in a single chronological sequence to simplify calendaring, and in 1907 the decision was made that the bulk of the remaining State Paper Office and Board of Trade colonial records should be merged into an arrangement by colony. They are now held in record series under the 'CO' departmental code, the majority of which continue into the post-1801 period. This re-arrangement was considered at the time to be 'more convenient'[4]; it is, of course, contrary to modern archival practice.

Published finding aids

Original finding aids prepared by the responsible government departments are described below. For any search of the records in the period to 1739, however, the *Calendar of State Papers, Colonial Series, 1574–1739* is the primary finding aid.[5] The *Calendar* provides transcripts, abstracts or brief summaries of documents relating to the American and West Indian colonies held in The National Archives. It includes material on French, Dutch and Spanish possessions, and, in view of the importance of the Atlantic slave trade, some relating to the west coast of Africa. It covers the period from 1574 to 1739, and was originally intended to continue to the years of the American Revolution. A parallel, but much smaller, series covers records relating to the East Indies.[6] Publication of the *Calendar* contributed to a programme designed to increase the

[3] *Calendar of State Papers, Colonial Series, America and West Indies*, 42: *1735–1736* (London, HMSO, 1953), introduction, p. vi.

[4] *Calendar of State Papers, Colonial Series, 1574–1660*, ed. W. N. Sainsbury (HMSO, London, 1860), introduction, p. ix.

[5] Published by HMSO in over 40 volumes between 1860 and 1994; a CD-ROM edition under the title *Calendar of State Papers, Colonial: North America and the West Indies, 1574–1739* was published by Routledge in association with the Public Record Office in 2000. For the period from 1740 a useful introduction is provided by C. M. Andrews, *Guide to the Materials for American History, to 1783, in the Public Record Office* (2 vols., Carnegie Institution of Washington, Washington, DC, 1912). ProQuest published images of the series CO 1, America and West Indies, Colonial Papers (General Series), linked to the *Calender of State Papers, Colonial*, in the autumn of 2007; for further details see http://www.proquest.com [accessed 28 Nov. 2014]. The Institute of Historical Research published the *Calendar of State Papers, Colonial Series* in 2008, as free content in its digital library, British History Online (http://www.british-history.ac.uk [accessed 28 Nov. 2014]).

[6] *Calendar of Colonial Papers, Colonial Series, East Indies, China and Japan 1513–1624*; *East Indies, China and Persia, 1625–1629*; and *East Indies and Persia, 1630–1634* (5 vols., London, HMSO, 1862–92). The calendar includes the TNA series CO 77 and a range of material from the State Papers, Domestic and State Papers, Foreign collections, together with documents from the East India Company records held at the British Library and some published sources.

accessibility of the archives by making available a variety of lists, catalogues, transcripts and calendars. Calendars were intended to provide a précis full enough, for most purposes, to replace the original documents. The published material was presented in chronological order (hence 'calendar'): the originals as well were often rearranged in date order by the editors.

In addition to the records of the secretaries of state and the Board of Trade and its predecessors, the *Calendar*, particularly in its earlier volumes, includes documents from many other record series. This results primarily from the lack of a clearly separate administration of colonial affairs before the late 17th century, but also from the presence of some colonial content in papers belonging to another sphere of government. For example, it is appropriate to cite correspondence between the English ambassador and authorities of the United Provinces, held in a series of State Papers Foreign, where it concerns the settlement of Walloons and French in Virginia. Similarly there is much in the State Papers Domestic series which concerns the colonies, and which is included. References provided are often to the entries in the published calendars for those series, as well as to the original documents. The domestic series also contain accounts of the pre-colonisation explorations of men such as Sir Martin Frobisher and Sir Francis Drake, which are not included in the calendar of colonial papers. Some private papers are included in the colonial *Calendar*, for example the papers of the earls of Shaftesbury concerning the early settlement of Carolina, which were presented to the Public Record Office by the seventh earl in 1871. There are also occasional references to published sources.

Some other material which is central to the English administration of colonial affairs is omitted from the *Calendar*. The colonial records of the Privy Council were separately calendared,[7] and the journals of the Board of Trade dating from 1704 onwards have been printed[8] (although earlier entries will be found in the *Calendar of State Papers, Colonial*). Despite the best efforts of the successive keepers of the state papers, some secretaries of state removed papers when they left office and researchers should be aware of the existence of much relevant material in collections of private papers held both in The National Archives and in other record offices and libraries.[9] The records of the trustees of Georgia from 1732 were omitted from the *Calendar* until the 1737 volume, on the grounds that they were private, not public, records.[10]

As noted above, it was originally planned to continue the calendaring of the correspondence, but this labour intensive project was finally abandoned in the 1990s. In the meantime, however, a separate series of calendars covering the American revolutionary period was published.[11]

[7] *Acts of the Privy Council of England, Colonial Series, 1613–1783* (London, HMSO, 1908–12). For more details of the role and records of the Privy Council, see p. 161.

[8] *Journal of the Commissioners for Trade and Plantations, 1704–1782* (London, HMSO, 1920–38).

[9] See appendix 9 for details of means of reference.

[10] See Allen D. Candler *et al.*, eds., *The Colonial Records of the State of Georgia*, 28 vols. (vols. 1–26 reprinted, New York, 1970), (vols. 27–32 reprinted, Athens, Ga., 1977–89).

[11] *Documents of the American Revolution, 1770–1783*, ed. K. G. Davies (21 vols., Shannon, 1972–81).

Original finding aids

Registers and indexes of correspondence consist of various finding aids maintained in the Board of Trade and the War and Colonial Department; they are held together at TNA in the record series CO 326. Their description as 'general registers' has led some to assume that they relate to the correspondence of the General Department in the series CO 323, but they are 'general' in the sense of covering all incoming correspondence. The registers cover the period 1623–1782 (although the catalogue suggests that there may be some gaps for some colonies) and then from 1810 to 1817, although apparently not complete for 1817 itself. There is then another gap until 1822 when a registrar was first appointed in the War and Colonial Department. Given the existence of the published *Calendar* for the years to 1739 the registers for that period would appear to be redundant, but they may be of continuing interest to some researchers, and one example is given here.

CO 326/3 is described in the catalogue as a subject index to trade papers. On folio 169 there is a reference to a 1700 paper about 'pestilential fevers' in Barbados with three references given in three separate columns (see figure 1). The first column is headed 'Journal' and gives the reference E 41; the second is headed 'Entries', with the reference B 51; and the third is headed 'Bundle' and gives the reference D 4. The three entries can be explained as follows:

1. The correspondence was read at a meeting of the Board of Trade as recorded in the Board of Trade journal held in the series CO 391. Reference to the catalogue shows that the journal designated 'E' is at CO 391/13 (see figure 2). As noted above, from 1704 onwards the Board of Trade journals have been separately printed.
2. 'Entries' refers to the 'entry books' for Barbados in the series CO 29. Again reference to the catalogue shows that volume 'B' is at CO 29/7 (see figure 3). In this case only a copy of the incoming correspondence is included, although the entry books might usually be expected to provide a copy of the response or 'out-letter'.
3. The original correspondence is filed as item 4 in bundle D of the Barbados correspondence in CO 28. Reference to the catalogue shows that bundle D is included in the volume CO 28/4 (see figure 4).

This is clearly an elaborate system and one which is inevitably reliant on the care of the clerks maintaining it. Also on folio 169 of this 'subject index' is a reference to 'the Scots settlement at Darien [Panama] and the Spaniards resentment thereon'. This gives the correspondence ('bundle') reference as D 11, but D 11 in CO 28/4 concerns the appointment of members of council. The correspondence about the Scottish settlement is actually at D 12.

After 1739 when the *Calendar* finishes, the registers in CO 326 are usually the only means of identifying relevant material. The format continues much as in the example given above, although it has been noted that not all of the three columns have always been completed. Researchers using the catalogue to identify correspondence in the geographical record series such as CO 28

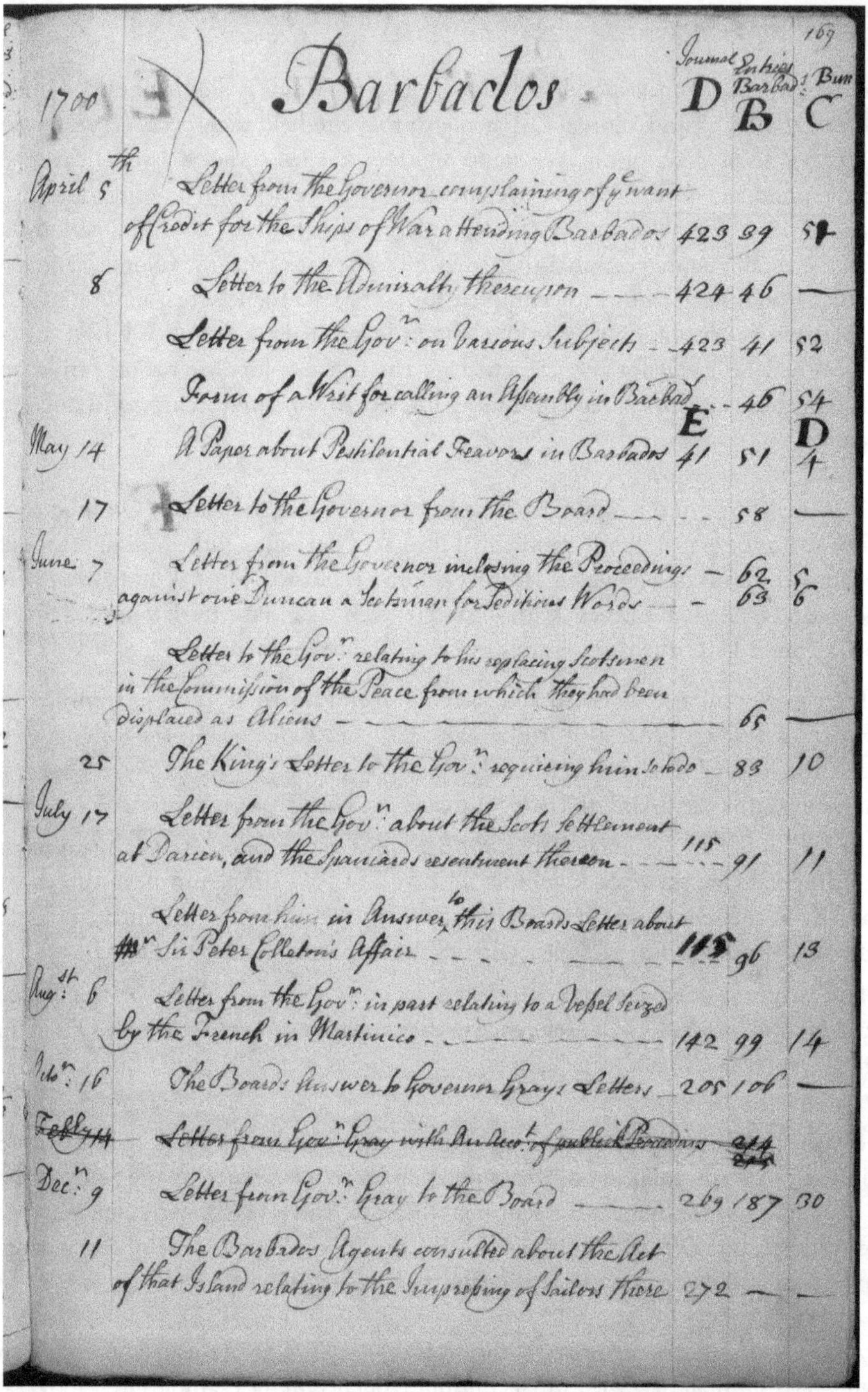

1700	Barbados	Journal D	Entries Barbad.s B	Bun C
April 5th	Letter from the Governor complaining of ye want of Credit for the Ships of War attending Barbados	423	39	54
8	Letter to the Admiralty thereupon	424	46	—
	Letter from the Gov.r on Various Subjects	423	41	52
	Form of a Writ for calling an Assembly in Barbad.		46	54
		E		D
May 14	A Paper about Pestilential Feavors in Barbados	41	51	4
17	Letter to the Governor from the Board		58	—
June 7	Letter from the Governor inclosing the Proceedings against one Duncan a Scotsmen for Seditious Words		62 63	6
	Letter to the Gov.r relating to his replacing Scotsmen in the Commission of the Peace from which they had been displaced as Aliens		65	—
25	The King's Letter to the Gov.r requiring him so to do		83	10
July 17	Letter from the Gov.r about the Scots Settlement at Darien, and the Spaniards resentment thereon	115	91	11
	Letter from him in Answer to this Boards Letter about Sir Peter Colleton's Affair	115	96	13
Aug.st 6	Letter from the Gov.r in part relating to a Vessel seized by the French in Martinico	142	99	14
Octo.r 16	The Boards Answer to Governor Grays Letters	205	106	—
~~Feb.y 14~~	~~Letter from Gov.r Gray with an Acc.t of publick Records~~	~~214~~		
Dec.r 9	Letter from Gov.r Gray to the Board	269	187	30
11	The Barbados Agents consulted about the Act of that Island relating to the Impressing of Sailors there	272	—	—

Figure 1. CO 326/3, subject index to Trade papers, 1696–1714, fo. 169. Entry of 14 May 1700 for 'a Paper about Pestilential Feavors in Barbados' giving references to Board of Trade journal, entry book, and original correspondence (bundle).

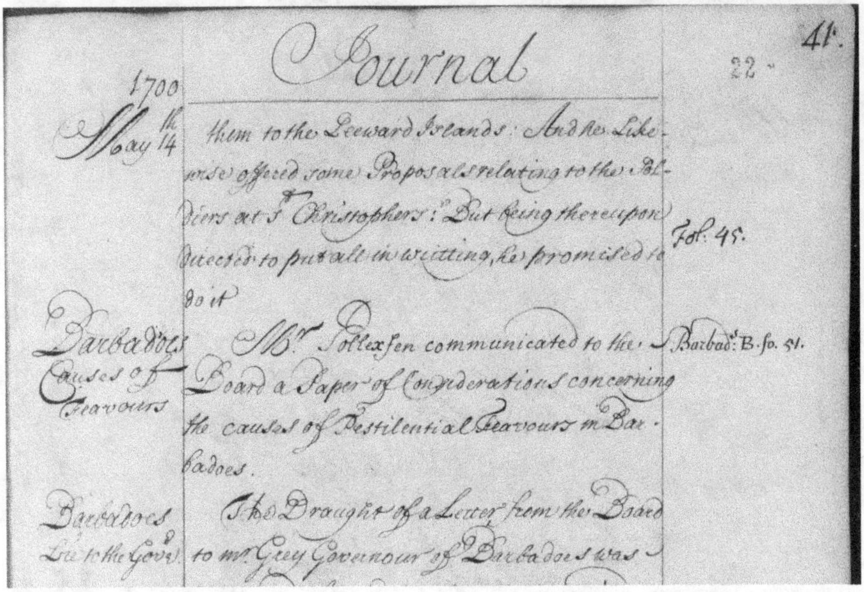

Journal — 41. — 22

1700 May 14th

them to the Leeward Islands: And he Likewise offered some Proposals relating to the Soldiers at St Christophers: But being thereupon directed to put all in writting, he promised to doe it — Fol. 45.

Barbadoes. Causes of Feavours — Mr Pollexfen communicated to the Board a Paper of Considerations concerning the causes of Pestilential Feavours in Barbadoes. — Barbad: B. fo. 51.

Barbadoes. Lre to the Govr — The Draught of a Letter from the Board to Mr Grey Governour of Barbadoes was

Figure 2. CO 391/13, Board of Trade journal, volume E, 1700–1, p. 41 (fo. 22). Entry reporting the receipt of 'a Paper of Considerations concerning the causes of Pestilential Feavours in Barbadoes'.

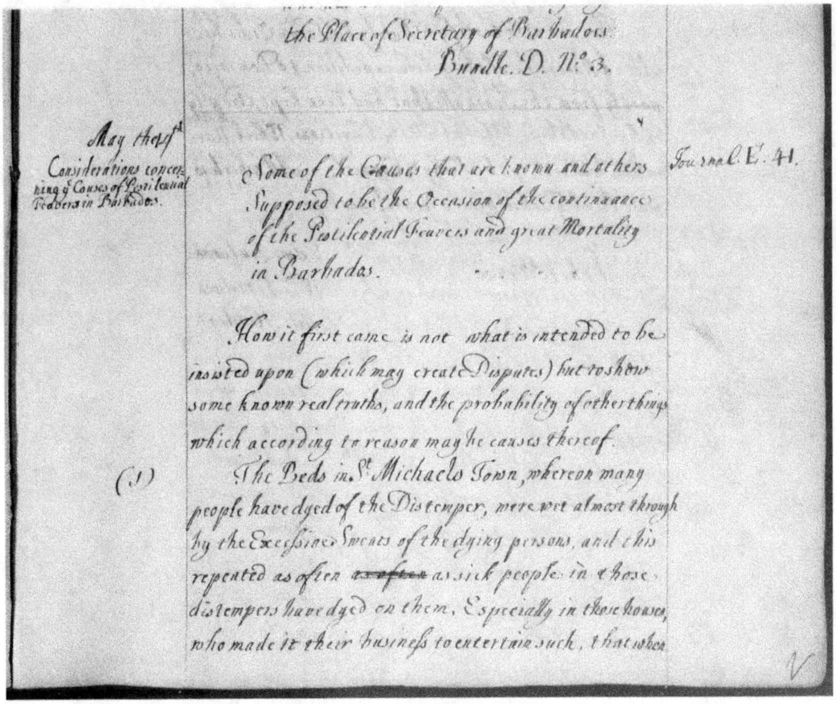

the Place of Secretary of Barbados.
Bundle. D. No 3.

May the 14th. Considerations concerning ye Causes of Pestilential Feavers in Barbados. — Journal E. 41.

Some of the Causes that are known and others Supposed to be the Occasion of the continuance of the Pestilential Feavers and great Mortality in Barbados.

How it first came is not what is intended to be insisted upon (which may create Disputes) but to show some known real truths, and the probability of other things which according to reason may be causes thereof.

(1) The Beds in St Michaels Town, whereon many people have dyed of the Distemper, were wet almost through by the Excessive Sweats of the dying persons, and this repeated as often ~~as often~~ as sick people in those distempers have dyed on them, Especially in those houses, who made it their business to entertain such, that when

Figure 3. CO 29/7, Barbados entry book, volume B, 1699–1792, p. 51.
Copy of a paper concerning the causes of 'Pestilential Feavers and great Mortality in Barbados'.

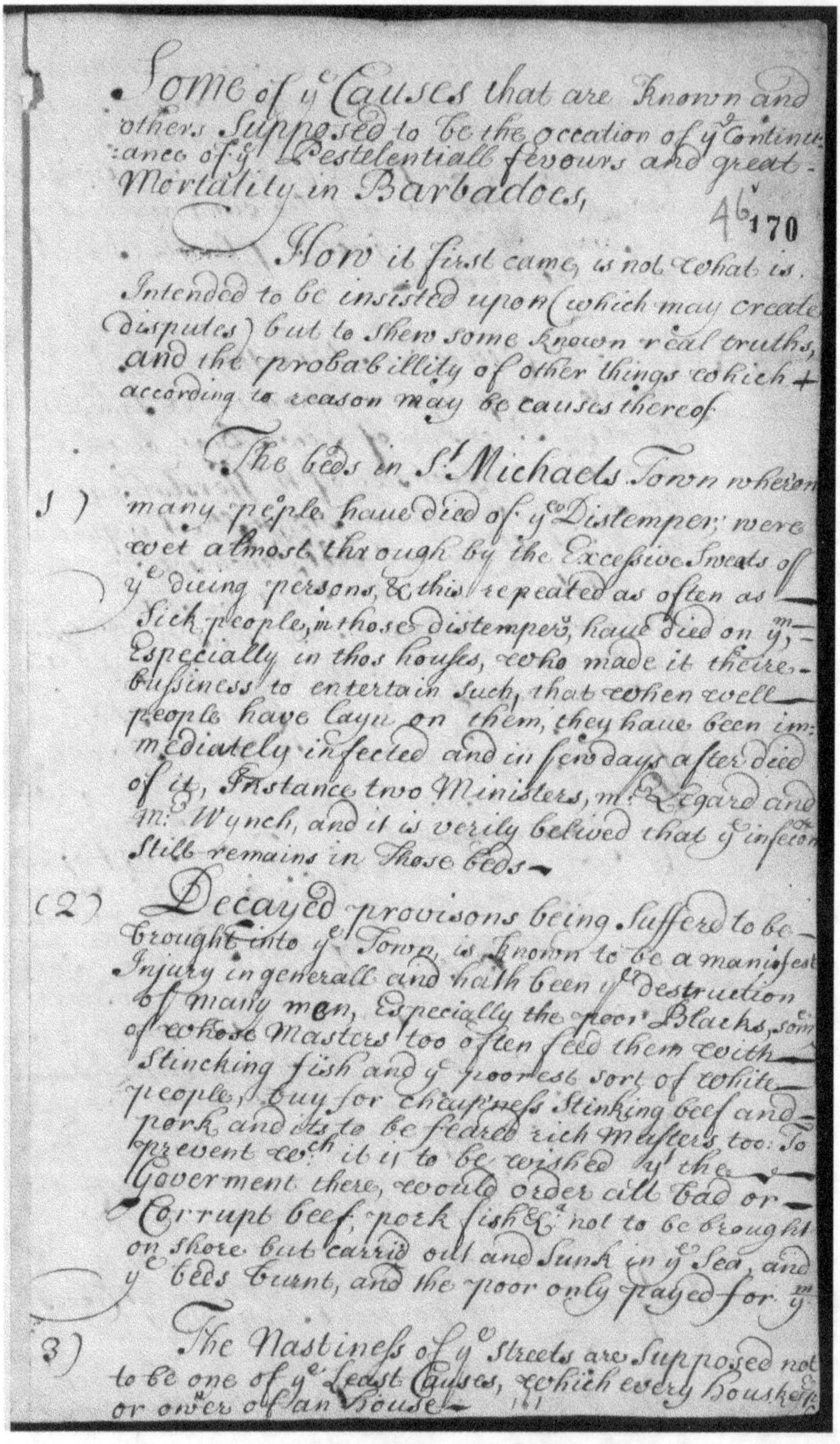

Some of ye Causes that are known and others Supposed to be the occation of ye Continu:ance of ye Pestelentiall fevours and great Mortality in Barbadoes,

46 170

How it first came, is not what is Intended to be insisted upon (which may create disputes) but to shew some known real truths, and the probabillity of other things which according to reason may be causes thereof

1) The beds in St Michaels Town whereon many people have died of ye Distemper; were wet almost through by the Excessive Sweats of ye dieing persons, & this repeated as often as Sick people, in those distempers, have died on ym, Especially in thos houses, who made it theire bussiness to entertain such, that when well people have layn on them, they have been im:mediately infected and in few days after died of it, Instance two Ministers, mr Legard and mr Wynch, and it is verily belived that ye infection Still remains in those beds

(2) Decayed provisons being suffered to be brought into ye Town, is known to be a manifest Injury in generall and hath been ye destruction of many men, Especially the poor Blacks, some of whose Masters too often feed them with stincking fish and ye poorest sort of white people, buy for cheapness Stinking beef and pork and its to be feared rich masters too: To prevent wch it is to be wished ye the Goverment there, would order all bad or Corrupt beef, pork fish &c not to be brought on shore but carrid out and sunk in ye Sea, and ye beds burnt, and the poor only payed for ym

3) The Nastiness of ye Streets are supposed not to be one of ye Least Causes, which every houskeep or ower of an house

Figure 4. CO 28/4, Barbados original correspondence, bundles C and D, 1699–1701, number 46, fo. 170. Original paper concerning causes of 'Pestelentiall fevours' in Barbados.

should note that the listing of the Board of Trade correspondence first under the letters A–Z and subsequently under Aa, Bb, Cc, etc. simply follows the lettering of the registers themselves. It is done purely to enable identification of a particular item of correspondence from a register entry. It has no other significance and certainly does not indicate, as sometimes assumed, that a bundle listed as 'D' covers only correspondents or subjects starting with that initial letter.

As noted above there are no registers in CO 326 for the years between 1782 and 1810. During the period in which the secretary of state for home affairs was responsible for the colonies, and the early years of the War and Colonial Department, no parallel system of registration appears to have been used. Correspondence about the colonies which passed between the Home Office and other government departments is entered in Home Office entry books (HO 29) but these do not appear to include references to despatches from the colonies. The so-called 'précis books' do continue into the period, and can be found in a number of 'CO' record series. These and the indexes to correspondence compiled in the Colonial Office library during the 19th century are described in chapter 6, pp. 78–82. Many other record series commence in this early period and continue into the 19th century. Appendix 1 lists relevant record series for each dependency, and the various categories, for example 'acts' or 'sessional papers', are described in chapter 6.

5. Administration of the colonies from 1801

War and Colonial Department

In 1801 colonial business was transferred to the third secretary of state, formerly responsible solely for war. The emphasis of the work of his department, usually known as the War and Colonial Department, was inevitably on the conduct of war until the peace of 1815, and the colonies were initially neglected although some improvements were made on the colonial side from 1806 onwards. With the return of peace colonial responsibilities were enlarged. Treaties then entered into gave Britain new colonial territories: Ceylon, the Cape of Good Hope, Mauritius, Seychelles, the Ionian Islands, Heligoland, Malta, three provinces of Dutch Guiana (thereafter British Guiana) and the three Caribbean islands of St Lucia, Trinidad and Tobago. Since the loss of the American colonies Britain had also acquired possession of New South Wales, Van Diemen's Land (Tasmania), Norfolk Island and Sierra Leone.

The internal organisation of the colonial side of the War and Colonial Department is not entirely clear, but from at least 1825 it was divided into four exclusively geographical departments: the North American, West Indian, Australian, and African and Mediterranean Departments.[1] By 1828 the Australian department had been renamed the Eastern Department in recognition of its responsibilities for Ceylon and Mauritius.

Certain duties, such as financial and establishment matters, were handled by the chief clerk and eventually, in the 1840s, this lead to the creation of a separate Chief Clerk's Department. The department did not last, although the role did.[2] A new General Department was created in 1870.

Responsibility for colonial administration in this period was fragmented. The Treasury, Board of Customs, General Post Office and Board of Ordnance were represented by their own officials in many if not most of the colonies. A major concern of the Colonial Department was to consolidate its authority, and to insist that other departments should act according to its advice, and comply with local laws and the wishes of local governments. This was, however, to be a lengthy, and in some cases incomplete, process.

[1] See R. B. Pugh, 'The Colonial Office', in *The Cambridge History of the British Empire*, vol. 3, ed. E. A. Benians, Sir James Butler and C. E. Carrington (Cambridge, 1959), for a detailed discussion of the organisation and staffing of the office from 1801 to 1925.

[2] As Pugh has noted 'the Trevelyan-Northcote Committee did not like this department' (R. B. Pugh, *The Records of the Colonial and Dominions Offices* (London, HMSO, 1964), p. 10).

Although most of the records from this period have been placed in Colonial Office 'CO' and War Office 'WO' series according to subject, there is some overlap and misplacing. For example, part of CO 323 (Colonies, General: Original Correspondence) concerns the War Department. Recent cataloguing of CO 301, Turks and Caicos correspondence, revealed a number of examples of military papers which are not included in the volumes but for which there is a 'dummy' sheet noting that they have been 'bound military' or are 'with the War Department'. In these cases references in WO 1 have been identified and provided, but this has rarely been done. There is also a good deal of non-military material relating to the colonies in WO records, as can be seen from a published indexed guide.[3] Under Sierra Leone, for example, there are references to the transfer of government to the Crown (WO 1/352 and WO 6/120). Much of the colonial material in WO 1 is, in fact, in bound volumes clearly marked 'CD' for Colonial Department. See p. 177 for more details of War Office records relating to the dependencies.

Establishment of the Colonial Office

Following the outbreak of the Crimean War in 1853, an additional post of secretary of state was created, and the dual functions of the formerly united War and Colonial Department were split in 1854. It is only from this date therefore that there can be said to be a Colonial Office proper. As Jeffries has stressed, the relationship between a colony and London was centred upon two individuals – the secretary of state and the governor. Officially all communication was between these two (although we will see some exceptions to the rule later in this volume). The Colonial Office was, in fact, simply the secretary of state's secretariat, 'the tool with which he does his work'.[4]

Initially the machinery of the office was little affected by its separation from the War Office, although its staffing and details of its administrative processes were inevitably affected by the general reforms of the UK Civil Service in this period.[5] Its largely geographical organisation continued, although the number of departments and the arrangement of their responsibilities varied from time to time.[6] From 1862, when the *Colonial Office List*[7] was first published, there is a readily available breakdown of the business of the departments together with the names of the officials working within each one. It is not usually necessary to understand the organisation of the geographical departments because the arrangement of the records in the 19th and early 20th centuries is almost entirely specific to the colony concerned (as it is for the earlier period). For example, and to use an extreme case, in 1862 the Falkland Islands were the responsibility

[3] *An Alphabetical Guide to Certain War Office and Other Military Records Preserved in the Public Record Office* (London, HMSO, Public Record Office Lists & Indexes, 53, 1931).

[4] Jeffries, p. 37.

[5] The Trevelyan-Northcote reforms, which *inter alia* introduced recruitment based on competitive examination rather than patronage (see Stafford Henry Northcote, *Papers on the Re-organisation of the Civil Service: Presented to both Houses of Parliament by Command of Her Majesty* (London, HMSO, 1855)).

[6] For the organisation of the geographical departments from *c.*1860 onwards, see figure 5.

[7] See appendix 4.

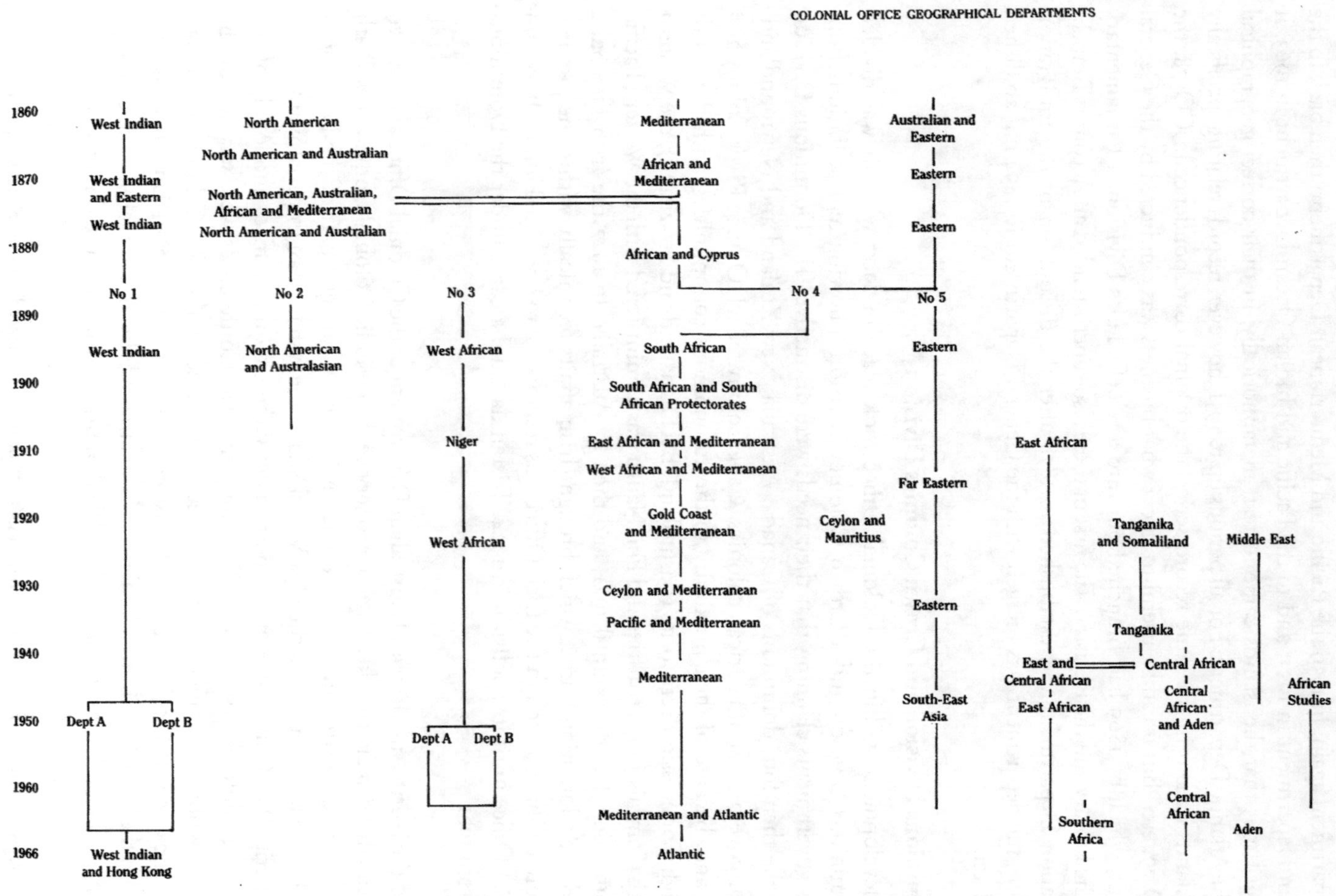

Figure 5. 'Line chart of geographical department development'.
Source: A. Thurston, *Sources for Colonial Studies in the Public Record Office, vol. 1: Records of the Colonial Office, Dominions Office, Commonwealth Relations Office and Commonwealth Office* (HMSO, 1995), p. 161.

of the North American Department; in 1878 they came under the Eastern and West Indian Department; in 1901 under the North American and Australasian Department; in 1929 the West Indian Department again; in 1939 the Pacific and Mediterranean Department; then back to the West Indian Department in 1957; and to the Pacific and Indian Ocean Department in 1963. It was not until 1965 that the islands came to rest, metaphorically, in their correct geographical location: the Atlantic Department. For all periods up to 1951, however, records relating specifically to the Falklands remain in the same record series: the original correspondence in CO 78, the acts in CO 79, etc.[8] But it can be useful to know what business was conducted by the General Department, which by 1869 had branched out into a Chief Clerk's Division, a Parliamentary Division, the Library and the Registry. The first of these also superintended an Accounts Branch. An Emigration Department was established in 1878 after the dissolution of the Emigration Commission; the department was merged with the General Department in 1894 but abolished two years later.[9]

1907: Dominions Division and Crown Colonies Division

A major development within the Colonial Office took place in 1907 when it was divided into a Dominions Division and a Crown Colonies Division following representations from dominions governments claiming that their needs were distinctive. The Dominions Division dealt with the then four dominions of Canada, Australia, New Zealand and Newfoundland, the four self-governing South African colonies (Cape Colony, Natal, Orange River Colony and Transvaal) and, because of their proximity to the autonomous communities, with the South African High Commission Territories (Basutoland, Bechuanaland and Swaziland), the Western Pacific High Commission Territories and Fiji. Nauru was administered with the Western Pacific High Commission Territories until 1921, and then by Australia. In 1922 the Irish Free State was created with dominion status, which brought Irish affairs technically within the purview of the Colonial Office, although the Irish Office was responsible to both the Home Office and the Colonial Office until its abolition in 1924. Tristan da Cunha came under the Dominions Division from 1921.

Before 1907 the North American and Australian Department of the Colonial Office and the two South African departments worked together to service the periodic Colonial Conferences. With the 1907 reorganisation the conference secretariat became an integral part of the Dominions Division. The development during the First World War of the system of an Imperial War Cabinet and an Imperial War Conference ended permanently the Colonial Office's monopoly of the provision of the conference secretariat. Then only the War Conferences were serviced by the Dominions Division; the Imperial War Cabinet was serviced by the War Cabinet Secretariat, assisted by the head of the Dominions Division. In 1921 the four-man United Kingdom contingent on the Inter-Dominion Conference Secretariat was led by the Cabinet secretary and had only one Colonial Office representative. The dominant position of the Cabinet Secretariat

[8] Changes in registry systems after 1951 are noted in chapter 6; post-1951 record series are included in the list in appendix 1.

[9] See appendix 2 for further details and records relating to migration.

was maintained for the 1923 conference and all subsequent conferences of prime ministers until the establishment of the Commonwealth Secretariat in 1965.[10]

With the establishment of the new division there began to be separate 'dominions' series of correspondence, although it is not until 1922 that the country series of original correspondence for the dominions come to an end (see chapter 7). The division of responsibility for the colonies and for the dominions was completed in 1925 when the Dominions Office was established as a separate department of government. The Dominions Office did not, however, take over all the functions of the former Dominions Division; the Colonial Office retained responsibility for the Western Pacific High Commission Territories, Fiji and Tristan da Cunha. Nor were the two offices separated in every respect; they remained in the same premises, continued to use certain common support services and shared a secretary of state from 1925 to June 1930, and for brief periods in 1931 and 1938/9. See below for further details.

Mandated territories

After the First World War, certain former enemy territories granted as mandated territories to Britain by the League of Nations were administered by the Colonial Office. In these cases there was a dual responsibility between the Colonial Office, responsible for day-to-day administration, and the Foreign Office, responsible, through Parliament, to the League of Nations (and subsequently the United Nations) for the good government of the territories. Mandated territories concerned were: Iraq, Palestine, Transjordan (Jordan), Nauru and, in Africa, Tanganyika (part of the former German East Africa) and parts of the Cameroons and Togoland. Although these territories were not British colonies, they were essentially treated in the same way as colonies and the same types of record exist. South West Africa (now Namibia) was administered by South Africa; the former German territory of New Guinea was administered by Australia.

The inclusion in the Colonial Office's responsibilities of Iraq, Palestine and Transjordan, in a part of the world for which the office had no expertise, led to the establishment in 1921 of a new geographical department, the Middle East Department (later Division). T. E. Lawrence ('of Arabia') was political adviser to the department for a short period. There is some evidence that it was originally intended to transfer Aden from the responsibility of the India Office at this time, but this was not actually done until 1937.

Subject departments

The period between the two world wars saw a new emphasis on the development of subject expertise within the Colonial Office. Before 1928 most business of the office was dealt with by the geographical departments, and correspondence from the governor of, for example, Jamaica will almost always be found in the series of Jamaica original correspondence. If it is not, that is if it was subsequently referred to another department, the pre-1927 registers will provide cross-references. There were, at various times, departments dealing with finance, emigration,

[10] For records of conferences held in both TNA and the Secretariat, see *Imperial and Commonwealth Conferences* (London, List and Index Society, 280, 2000).

appointments, honours and military matters, with dedicated correspondence series. The only long-standing record series is CO 323, the correspondence of the General Department, and some closely related departments, which dealt with matters concerning a group of colonies or the empire as a whole. Details of the responsibilities of these departments can be found, from 1862 onwards, in the annual *Colonial Office List*. In 1901, for example, the General Department was responsible for 'General and Miscellaneous Correspondence, including Questions affecting the Establishment of the Colonial Office and the Crown Agents' Office, Postal, Copyright, Telegraph, and Commercial Treaties and Conventions, University Examinations, Replies to Circulars, Governors' Pensions and Passage Allowances, Naval Cadetships, and General Correspondence respecting Colonial Defences'.[11]

In 1927–8 a departmental committee, appointed by L. S. Amery, secretary of state from 1924 to 1929, reviewed the internal organisation of the office.[12] His committee found that there was no adequate means of co-ordinating the work of the geographical departments and relating it to the needs of the colonies as a whole, or of securing the necessary technical advice. It therefore recommended that a 'subject' side should be established to take over matters of interest to a multiplicity of territories. This happened slowly, largely because many senior Colonial Office officials opposed the change, believing that it was more important to have internal expertise on, for example, Nigeria or Malaysia, than on subject areas such as sugar production or education.[13] As a first step, however, the General Department was split into two in 1928: one part dealt with personnel matters, the other with the remainder of the subjects which had previously belonged to the General Department. In 1930 a Personnel Division was created. The following year the responsibilities of the General Department were described as

> All general questions relating to the Colonies except those connected with personnel. The list of subjects dealt with includes defence, finance, economic questions, international and inter-imperial relations, mandates, League of Nations matters, merchant shipping, labour, medical and public health matters, education, aviation, surveys, films, liquor traffic, legal and judicial matters, postal, telegraph and wireless matters, railway and transport developments etc.[14]

In 1934 the General Department was renamed the General Division and split into two departments. Early in 1938 the first of these was handling defence, international relations, mandates, labour, education, public health, communications and currency; the second, called the Economic Department, dealt with the marketing and development of colonial products and with trade relations. The following year a third department, the Social Services Department, was added to the General Division, and took over responsibility for labour, health and medical

[11] *Colonial Office List* (1901), p. xiv.

[12] CO 885/30/5, Miscellaneous No. 391, 'Colonial Office Organisation Committee interim and final reports', 1927–8.

[13] In 1945 Sir Cosmo Parkinson, a former permanent under-secretary, wrote: 'Subject departments have doubtless come to stay … But it will be a sad day if these upstarts get out of control and bring about the elimination of the geographical departments' (Sir Cosmo Parkinson, *The Colonial Office from Within, 1909–1945* (London, 1947), p. 55).

[14] *Colonial Office List* (1931), p. xvi.

matters, education and penal administration.[15] Subject departments continued to proliferate thereafter. A diagram showing the development of such departments from 1934 is at figure 6. Details of the records of such departments can be found in appendix 2, and the *Colonial Office List* provides information about the functions and responsibilities of each department year by year.[16] Relations between the various departments were not always harmonious. Arguments about which was responsible for what may sometimes be found among the internal minutes filed with correspondence, as, for example in the early 1930s when the General Department refused to continue its earlier co-ordinating role in the area of labour policy and pushed work back to the geographical departments.

The development and proliferation of specialist departments is of major importance for users of the records. A great deal of material which would previously have been found in the individual colony series of original correspondence begins to appear elsewhere, although it is always sensible to check the colony series as well as that of the relevant subject department.

Specialist advisers and advisory committees

Alongside the subject departments there developed a network of specialist advisers to the secretary of state for the colonies, and advisory committees comprised of informed outsiders and representatives of other government departments as well as Colonial Office officials. This was not an entirely new initiative. A legal adviser had been appointed as early as 1866, and an advisory network was subsequently developed to deal with technical matters. It included specialist committees as well as organisations separate from the office such as the Imperial Institute, the Bureau of Hygiene and Tropical Diseases and the Imperial Agricultural Bureau. There were also long established links with experts in institutions such as the Royal Botanic Gardens and the London and Liverpool Schools of Tropical Medicine. After the First World War this informal system was considered no longer to meet the needs of the office and in 1926 Amery proposed the appointment of additional technical advisers. By 1932, in addition to the legal advisers, there were medical, financial, agricultural, fisheries and animal health advisers. A labour adviser was added in 1938, and education and business advisers in 1940.[17] By 1961 45 advisers were in post, although the number dropped sharply thereafter with the establishment of the Department of Technical Co-operation which assumed most of the Colonial Office's work in technical and advisory areas (see pp. 49–50).

Members of advisory committees were appointed by the secretary of state and included UK authorities on a wide range of scientific and social subjects including health, education, welfare,

[15] The establishment of the Social Services Department was a compromise solution designed to counter the demands of the Trades Union Congress for a separate labour department within the office; officials were violently opposed, but eventually agreed that a department covering labour, medical, nutritional and educational questions might be useful (see CO 859/23/1).

[16] See also A. Thurston, *Sources for Colonial Studies in the Public Record Office* (2 vols., The Stationery Office, London, 1995–8), vol. 1.

[17] Hans Vischer, one of the joint-secretaries of the Advisory Committee on Education and its predecessor the Advisory Committee on Native Education in Tropical Africa, is often regarded as the first education adviser, but it was not his formal title.

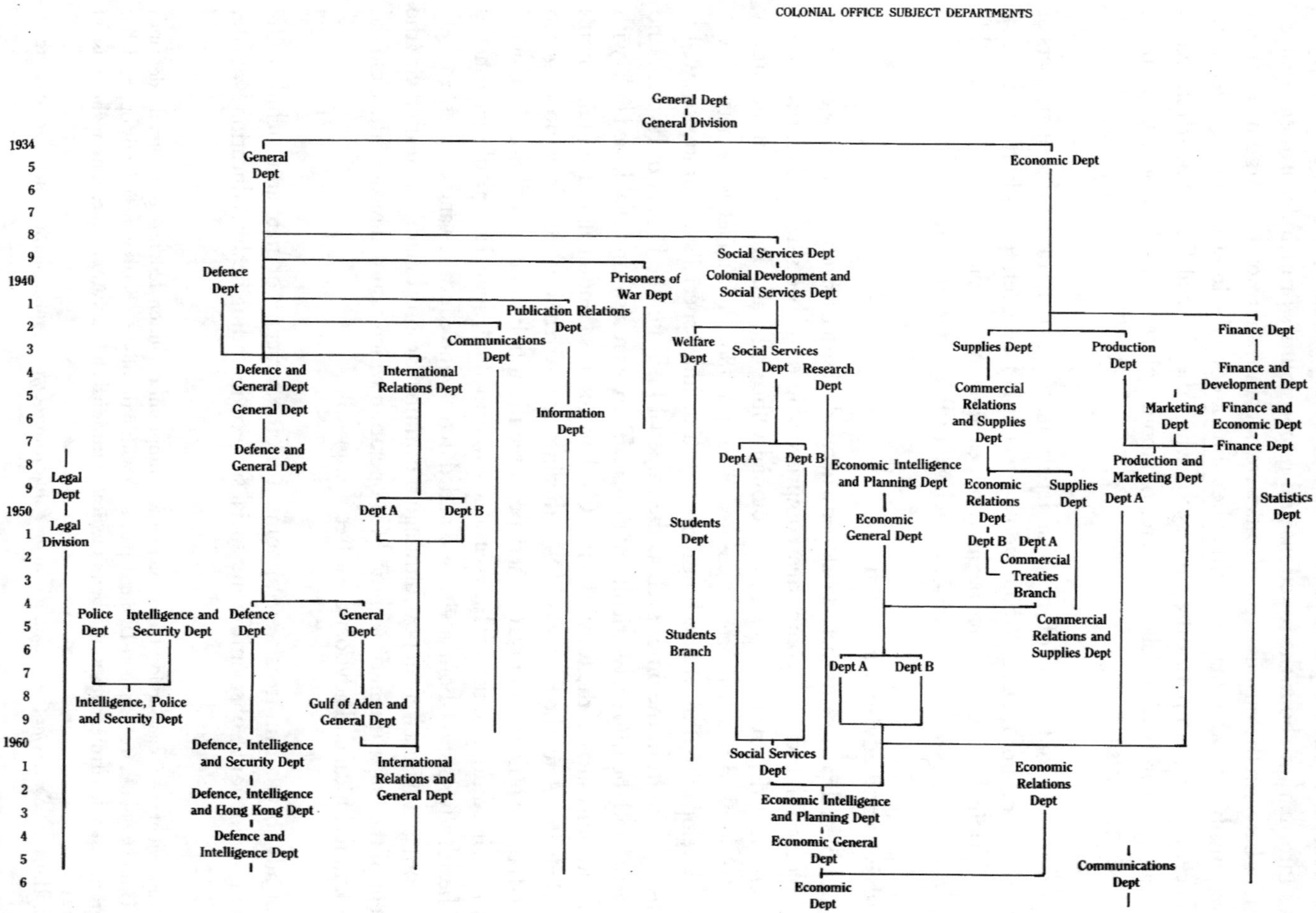

Figure 6. 'Line chart of subject department development'.
Source: A. Thurston, *Sources for Colonial Studies in the Public Record Office, vol. 1: Records of the Colonial Office, Dominions Office, Commonwealth Relations Office and Commonwealth Office* (HMSO, 1995), p. 313.

agriculture, labour and economic development. The secretary of state was not obliged to refer matters to the advisory committees nor to accept their recommendations. Nevertheless, the establishment of the committees was part of a more general move towards central planning, and they grew in number and importance, particularly from the latter stages of the Second World War. In 1961 most of the committees were also transferred to the Department of Technical Co-operation.

A list of Colonial Office advisory committees for which there are discrete record series is included in the subject based listing of records at appendix 2. Where there is no specific series for committee papers they should be sought in the most relevant correspondence series, for example papers of the Colonial Veterinary Services Organisation Committee are in CO 323, and can be identified through the online catalogue.[18] In some cases papers can be found in both locations, for example records of the Colonial Labour Committee and its successor the Colonial Labour Advisory Committee are in CO 888, but there is also material in CO 323, General Department, and CO 859, Social Services Department.

Advisers used the files of the relevant Colonial Office departments to record their comments and to contribute more substantial memoranda, but they also amassed their own papers which were deemed to be personal. TNA has only the papers of Sir Christopher Cox, the education adviser from 1940 (in CO 1045; see p. 113–15). The papers of the first labour adviser, Major G. St J. Orde Browne, are among the Commonwealth and African Collections at the Bodleian Library, University of Oxford (formerly at Rhodes House Library). Others should be sought through the National Register of Archives database, now incorporated into TNA's catalogue (see appendix 9).

By the 1960s, with fast-moving decolonisation and the loss of its advisory responsibilities to the new Department of Technical Co-operation, the Colonial Office declined in importance. In July 1962 ministerial responsibilities for colonial affairs were added to the duties of the secretary of state for Commonwealth relations. Amalgamation of the Colonial Office and the Commonwealth Relations Office was discussed over the next three years, but they continued as separate bodies. Where a matter was consider to be of common interest officials conferred and decided which office should take the lead. In October 1964 the incoming Labour government again appointed separate secretaries of state for the colonies and for Commonwealth relations, although with only one minister reporting to both. The two offices were finally merged in 1966 to form the short-lived Commonwealth Office (see below).

The Colonial Office Journal

In June 1907 the Colonial Office published the first issue of *The Colonial Office Journal*, which was to be continued quarterly. An editorial note states that the main purpose of the journal was to review recent books and reports relating to the colonies, and to discuss administrative questions.

[18] There is sometimes doubt about the official name of a committee, with different versions being given even within the minutes and papers of the committee itself. In this example a search of the catalogue on the term 'colonial veterinary committee' might be sensible.

The journal was unofficial, but approved by the secretary of state. It continued to 1920, with a change of name to *The Colonial Journal* from volume 10 (1917). There are no copies at TNA, but a set is held at the British Library.

The Dominions Office

As noted above, the Dominions Office developed from the Dominions Division of the Colonial Office and became a separate government department in 1925. It assumed responsibility for UK diplomatic relations with the 'autonomous communities within the British Empire', that is Canada, Australia, New Zealand, the Union of South Africa (created in 1910) and Newfoundland. It was also responsible for Southern Rhodesia, annexed to the Crown in 1923 following a period of British South Africa Company administration, and the South Africa High Commission Territories of Basutoland, Bechuanaland and Swaziland, and for relations with the Irish Free State. The Western Pacific High Commission Territories, Fiji and Tristan da Cunha, formerly dealt with by the Dominions Division of the Colonial Office, remained with the Colonial Office.

Despite the separation of the two offices, relations remained very close. The posts of secretary of state for the colonies and secretary of state for dominions affairs were initially held by the same individual; L. S. Amery, Lord Passfield (Sidney Webb), J. H. Thomas and Malcolm MacDonald all held the two offices concurrently.

The Colonial Office and Dominions Office also shared accommodation, and they were linked by a common administrative establishment and by common services such as the Accounts Branch, the Telegraph Section, the Library and the Printing Unit. Each department did, however, have its own registry, and incoming letters and telegrams went from a central opening section to the appropriate registry. The former *Colonial Office List* became *The Dominions Office and Colonial Office List* in 1926, but reverted to covering the Colonial Office only from 1946.

The Commonwealth Relations Office

The Dominions Office was renamed the Commonwealth Relations Office in July 1947, and the secretary of state for dominions affairs became the secretary of state for Commonwealth relations. The following month responsibility for relations with newly independent India and Pakistan was transferred to the Commonwealth Relations Office. The India Office was abolished, and its staff transferred to the CRO. The Indian Records Section (later the India Office Records) and the India Office Library, however, continued to exist as distinct entities. They were administered by, consecutively, the Commonwealth Relations Office, the Commonwealth Office and the Foreign and Commonwealth Office.[19] In 1948 the Burma

[19] In 1982 the India Office Library and Records were placed on deposit at the British Library, where they are now held in the Asia, Pacific and Africa Collections (formerly Oriental and India Office Collections).

Office[20] was abolished, and its staff were also absorbed into the CRO, although as Burma did not join the Commonwealth matters concerning Britain's relations with the independent territory were transferred to the Foreign Office.

Most colonies did join the Commonwealth upon independence, and each subsequently became the responsibility of the CRO rather than the Colonial Office. For the period around independence material relating to an individual territory may be expected to be found among the records of both departments, and some important constitutional material is in the records of the Cabinet Office (see pp. 159–60). With decolonisation the responsibilities of the Colonial Office were gradually diminished, as those of the Commonwealth Relations Office increased, which led to the amalgamation of the two, as the Commonwealth Office, in 1966 (see below).

The internal organisation of the Dominions Office/Commonwealth Relations Office is less important to the researcher than that of the Colonial Office in the same period since it does not so closely inform the arrangement of the records until at least the early 1950s. Details can, however, be found in the *List* (for 1926–40 only) and a detailed breakdown is provided by Thurston.[21] Departmentally arranged record series are listed in appendices 1 and 2 as appropriate.

Department of Technical Co-operation and successors

The UK government's responsibility for the development of its colonies on a continuing basis was first recognised in 1929 by the Colonial Development Act, and expanded under the Colonial Development and Welfare Act of 1940.[22] In 1961 a Department of Technical Co-operation (DTC) was established to deal with the technical co-operation side of the aid programme. It assumed many of the specialist and technical advisory functions of the Colonial Office, together with relevant staff.[23] Responsibilities for overseas aid work were also transferred from the Foreign Office, the Commonwealth Relations Office and the Ministry of Labour, along with specialist staff.

The new department was made responsible for a number of organisations previously the responsibility of the Colonial Office, such as the Crown Agents for Oversea Governments and Administrations, the Anti-Locust Research Centre, the Overseas Services Resettlement Bureau, the Directorate of Overseas (Geodesic and Topographical) Surveys and the Overseas Geological Surveys. It took over the Colonial Office's role in sponsoring the Council for Overseas Colleges

[20] The Burma Office had been established only in 1937 as a result of constitutional and administrative changes which led to the separation of Burma from British India during that year. The India Office and Burma Office shared a secretary of state and office accommodation; the records of the Burma Office are held with those of the India Office at the British Library.

[21] Thurston, vol. 1, pp. 351–98.

[22] Although it has since been argued that the purpose behind the first initiative had more to do with boosting the British economy than developing the colonies (see, for example, S. Constantine, *The Making of British Colonial Development Policy 1914–1940* (London, 1984)).

[23] Sir Christopher Cox, the Colonial Office education adviser, was one of those who transferred to DTC; his records in CO 1045 cover his Colonial Office, DTC, and later service.

of Arts, Science and Technology, the Inter-University Council for Higher Education Overseas and the Colonial University Grants Committee.[24]

The department was subsequently renamed the Ministry of Overseas Development (1964–70 and 1974–9), the Overseas Development Administration (1970–4 and 1979–97) and the Department for International Development (1997 onwards). In November 1970 the Overseas Development Administration ceased to be a separate government department. It was absorbed into the Foreign and Commonwealth Office, and the former office of minister of overseas development became that of a junior minister of the FCO. The ODA remained a distinct element within the Foreign and Commonwealth Office, however, and its organisation was largely unaltered. In June 1974 it became a separate department once more, reverting to the name Ministry of Overseas Development. In 1979 it was re-established as the Overseas Development Administration. In 1997 the ODA became the Department for International Development.

The organisation of the various development ministries and departments was primarily on subject lines in areas such as education, social services, natural resources and economics. There were also a number of geographical departments covering Asia and the Pacific, Africa and the Mediterranean, and America, the Caribbean and the Atlantic. Details of record series are not generally included in appendices 1 and 2; they are all held under the 'OD' departmental code, and can be readily identified by use of TNA's online catalogue.

Central African Office

The Central African Office was established on 19 March 1962 with responsibility for relations with the Federation of Rhodesia and Nyasaland and the territories of Northern Rhodesia, Southern Rhodesia and Nyasaland, but it was created mainly to supervise the dismantling of the federation. The office was initially under the control of the then home secretary, R. A. Butler, later Lord Butler. It was transferred to the newly designated secretary of state for Commonwealth relations and for the colonies in October 1963, and in April 1964 it was absorbed into the Commonwealth Relations Office, which had been the responsible department prior to March 1962.

Commonwealth Office and Foreign and Commonwealth Office

By 1965 there was a high degree of liaison between the Commonwealth Relations Office and the Foreign Office. In January of that year, as part of a scheme to unite responsibility for all external affairs within one department, a common Diplomatic Service and Diplomatic Service Administration Office was established jointly between the two. In June 1965 the creation of the Commonwealth Secretariat relieved the Commonwealth Relations Office of its responsibility

[24] Records of the Inter-University Council are held at TNA in the British Council series BW 90; those of the Council for Overseas Colleges of Arts, Science and Technology are in BW 91. See also p. 157–9.

for overall management of the Commonwealth. In August 1966 the Colonial Office and the Commonwealth Relations Office were merged to form the Commonwealth Office under a secretary of state for Commonwealth affairs. What remained of the Colonial Office became the Dependent Territories Division, and the post of secretary of state for the colonies disappeared a few months later. The scheme was completed on 17 October 1968 by the amalgamation of the Foreign Office, the Commonwealth Office and the Diplomatic Service Administration Office to form a single Foreign and Commonwealth Office. Plans for this series of mergers had begun as early as 1962, when a Committee on Representational Services Overseas, chaired by Lord Plowden, was appointed to review the purpose, structure and operation of the UK's overseas services.[25] The creation of a single ministry to handle all the UK's external affairs was identified as an ultimate aim by the committee, although it was not a specific recommendation.

The Foreign and Commonwealth Office (FCO) was a large and complex body from its inception, and a guide intended to introduce the researcher to records of colonial administration is not the place to attempt a history of its internal organisation. Brief details are given in the annual *Diplomatic Service List*, published from 1966, and a little more is said in chapter 8.

Details of the records of the departments described above are in chapters 6 and 7.

[25] Papers of the committee are in FO 366, and a copy of its report is at FO 953/2166. It was printed for Parliament as Miscellaneous No. 5 (1964): report of the Committee on Representational Services Overseas appointed by the Prime Minister under the chairmanship of Lord Plowden, 1962–3.

6. The records of the Colonial Office

As noted in chapter 4, records held at TNA under the 'CO' departmental code include much material pre-dating the establishment of the War and Colonial Department in 1801. They also include some dated later than 1966 when the Colonial Office merged with the Commonwealth Relations Office. Their overall covering dates are currently 1570–1990. Although many new series of records were introduced in the period covered by this guide, others span the administrative changes described in chapters 4–5. For example the series of 'original correspondence' for Barbados and for Jamaica cover the years 1689–1951. The majority of the record series are devoted to individual dependencies, and typically fall into the following categories, each described in this chapter, although not all exist for the entire period:

- 'Original correspondence'
- Registers of correspondence
- Entry books
- Registers of out-letters
- Acts
- Sessional papers
- Government gazettes
- Miscellanea

Other correspondence, together with associated finding aids, is held in general or subject-based series, and this becomes increasingly common from the 1930s with the new emphasis on subject expertise within the office described at pp. 43–7; the later correspondence series may be described in the catalogue as 'registered files' rather than 'original correspondence'. The collections of acts, sessional papers, gazettes and miscellanea continue in a territorial arrangement. Correspondence and its registers and indexes are described in this chapter, and full listings are provided in appendices 1 and 2. Acts, sessional papers, gazettes and miscellanea are described at pp. 117–32.

Other records held within the 'CO' collection are as follows:

- Confidential print (described in this chapter)
- Records of committees, commissions and other temporary bodies (listed in appendices 1 and 2 where discrete record series exist)
- Three collections of maps (see chapter 10)
- Two collections of photographs (see chapter 11)

- Private and private office collections (see chapter 9)
- Locally created records (see chapter 3)
- A collection of Empire Marketing Board posters, and other records of the board and of the Colonial Empire Marketing Board (see pp. 161–3)
- Four series of Board of Trade records pre-dating the establishment of the War and Colonial Department in 1801 (see chapter 4 for the role of the board in this period).

Users of this guide should bear in mind that changes in practice and subsequent format of the records is inevitable over the long period covered here, and detail may change.

Original correspondence

For the majority of researchers 'original correspondence' is likely to be the most important material held among the Colonial Office records. The original correspondence series consist primarily of correspondence coming in to the Colonial Office, for most of our period with draft replies, but also include outgoing correspondence initiated by the Colonial Office, other than circular despatches which are described below. Much of the correspondence is arranged by colony, for example Barbados, by group of colonies, for example Windward Islands, or by region. Some is arranged by subject function, and this becomes increasingly common from the 1930s onwards with the expansion of subject departments within the office as described above. Lists of colony and subject series of correspondence are given in appendices 1 and 2.

The correspondence is chronologically arranged, and until 1926/7 it is usually bound in volumes and often divided into three categories, as follows:

1. Official letters – called '**despatches**' – from the governor of a colony, or group of colonies, or from a deputy acting on his behalf, to the secretary of state for the colonies. Telegrams from governors are included in this category.

   The primary channel of official communication between a colonial government and the UK government ran directly from the governor to the secretary of state, although general or individual instructions issued to governors might allow them to deal directly with, for example, the defence departments in the UK.[1] Where a number of colonies were grouped in a federal arrangement, for example the Leeward Islands and Windward Islands in the Caribbean, despatches from the administrator of a constituent colony would go first to the governor-in-chief for forwarding to London with his comments on the matters under discussion. An exception could be made if the governor-in-chief was absent. This rule was occasionally ignored, for example during a period when communications between the Turks and Caicos Islands and the superintending governor in Jamaica were so unreliable that the

[1] During the period of the joint War and Colonial Department (1801–54) 'military' despatches are found sometimes in Colonial Office and sometimes in War Office records series. See also pp. 39–40.

president of the Turks and Caicos sometimes found it expedient to communicate directly with London. Detailed instructions issued in 1825 when the office recognised the 'want of some uniform mode in which all official communications should be addressed to this Department',[2] included in the 'rules and regulations'[3] first compiled in 1837, and amended from time to time thereafter, regulated the conduct of official correspondence.[4] From 1862 to 1940 they are printed in the annual *Colonial Office List*,[5] and the 1878 version is copied at appendix 5 together with a summary of the much briefer 1825 instructions. As well as setting out requirements for the layout of despatches (a ruling that does not often appear to have been complied with) and their numbering, the instructions also explain the use of classifications such as 'secret' and 'confidential'.

It is important to note that if a governor was away from his colony, whether on leave or on official business, any correspondence from him will be filed under 'individuals' (see below) not under 'despatches'. At such periods correspondence from the nominated deputy in the colony, known as the 'officer administering the government' (o.a.g.), will be found under 'despatches'. The same is true if no governor was in post and the outgoing and/or incoming official was in the UK and in correspondence with the Colonial Office.

2. Correspondence from UK government departments ('**offices**') and other organisations (referred to usually as '**miscellaneous offices**' or '**miscellaneous institutions**') to the Colonial Office on subjects relating to the colony or subject in question.

Although Colonial Office ministers and officials were sometimes reluctant to consult other government departments, and resented the delays caused – for which, of course, they were always blamed – consultation was often unavoidable. Essential military support required close liaison with the War Office and Admiralty; any matter touching on relations with a foreign state must be discussed with the Foreign Office, and, similarly, the Foreign Office would alert the Colonial Office if diplomacy was likely to impinge on colonial affairs, or if a problem arose concerning British colonial subjects resident in a foreign state or a dependency of such a state. The Treasury must be involved if additional finances were required, certain locally enacted legislation might need to be cleared with another department, and the Privy Council Office was responsible for implementing royal confirmation of appointments or locally enacted statutes. Queries and demands also came in the other direction; for example in the late 19th and early 20th centuries the India Office often had questions about the use of Indian indentured labourers in the colonies. Among the many other organisations

[2] CO 854/1, circular despatch of 26 July 1825.

[3] *Rules and Regulations for the Information and Guidance of the Principal Officers and Others in His Majesty's Colonial Possessions.* No copy of this publication has been found among the records of the Colonial Office; one is held in the Archives of the London School of Economics under the reference OX1837/5 (microform copy in TNA Library).

[4] Seven years earlier the Colonial Office had suggested that Foreign Office guidelines should be used, see CO 854/1 ff. 56–7; further instructions issued in September 1823 are in CO 854/1 ff. 172–6.

[5] The 'yearbook' of the Colonial Office (see appendix 4 for details).

which corresponded with the Colonial Office were missionary societies, pressure groups, international organisations and institutions on the fringe of government such as the Royal Botanic Gardens at Kew.

This category also includes correspondence from the London-based agents appointed by colonial governments to act as their representatives – the predecessors of the formally constituted Crown Agents for Oversea Governments and Administrations (see chapter 12) and of the high commissioners.

3. Correspondence from '**individuals**' in the UK to the Colonial Office on subjects relating to a particular colony or subject.

   A good proportion of such correspondence is from serving or retired colonial civil servants, sometimes providing expert opinion but more commonly seeking promotion or transfer, or discussing pension arrangements. There are also letters from private individuals seeking employment, enquiring about family members overseas, making claims on the estates of deceased persons, expressing opinions on current controversies, extolling their latest inventions, etc., etc. As noted above the 'individuals' category also includes correspondence from serving governors away from their dependencies. The 'individuals' sections often also include correspondence from commercial companies which one might expect to find under 'offices'. Filing practice is not always consistent; CO 111/470 (British Guiana, 1893), for example, includes two letters from the archbishop of Canterbury – one filed under 'offices', the other under 'individuals'.

Individuals and organisations within a colony were not officially permitted to write directly to the Colonial Office; all correspondence had to be channelled through the governor.[6] Hence, correspondence listed under '**offices**' and '**individuals**' is generally from within the UK, or if from overseas not from the colony in question. Some colonial organisations, for example the major commercial interests, were able to circumvent this ruling by corresponding through agents based in the UK, bodies such as the West India Committee[7] or local chambers of commerce in the major UK manufacturing centres. Inevitably the rule was sometimes broken, whether by design or through ignorance; in such cases the usual Colonial Office practice was to return a copy of the correspondence to the governor with a request for his report on the matter.

[6] See appendix 5, paragraphs 217–28, for the regulations on this point.

[7] The West India Committee, which is still in existence, was formed in the 18th century by a permanent association of London merchants engaged in the West Indian trade, and absentee owners of West Indian estates. It acted as a pressure group for West Indian interests. The archives of the West India Committee are held at the Institute of Commonwealth Studies, Senate House Library, University of London. The earlier records, 1769–1924, are held there on microfilm; the originals are held by the University of the West Indies in Trinidad and Tobago. The West India Committee Library is also currently deposited at the Institute of Commonwealth Studies. The Library collections are, however, likely to be returned to the committee. For further information see http://commonwealth.sas.ac.uk/library/ [accessed 22 Oct. 2014].

What does the original correspondence contain?

This is a very difficult question to answer; the subject matter varies so much from time to time, and from colony to colony. It may be helpful to remember that individual governors had considerable (but varying) authority to run the overseas territories as they saw fit, subject to instructions issued on their appointment, the agreement of their legislatures and pressure from other local interests.[8] Thus events which are now considered important to the history of a particular territory may hardly be mentioned, whereas matters which now seem quite trivial may give rise to extensive correspondence because the governor needed to seek approval from the home government for a suggested course of action or wished to deflect potential censure. For example, a researcher seeking information about a major East African famine found only a brief despatch from the governor asking for permission to spend money on famine relief. On the other hand, local criticism of a governor or the conduct of his government is likely to be vigorously defended, minor queries about leave or pension arrangements for individual colonial civil servants may be covered in some detail, and any incidence of misconduct by an official often results in voluminous paperwork. More detailed information about the current state of a territory is likely to be found when it is a new responsibility for the Colonial Office rather than a dependency with which officials in London have a long familiarity. Detailed information will also usually be included when significant new policies are proposed and implemented (or rejected), when major expenditure is proposed or, of course, if things are going badly wrong. Another point to bear in mind is that before the introduction of the telegraph during the second half of the 19th century it was impossible for the governor of a distant colony to seek guidance or approval before taking action on any urgent matter; it could be many weeks before his despatch reached London and many more before he received a reply. It would be interesting to know if governors saw the technological innovation as limiting their autonomy.[9]

This may suggest an overall content of dry, formal and high level policy mixed with minor administrative matters, but there is also much of local and personal detail. Complaints of officials and other residents, whether in the form of correspondence with the governors, petitions and memorials addressed to the secretary of state or the sovereign, or contained in the reports of the stipendiary magistrates appointed to supervise the emancipation process, are among the type of material likely to present a vivid picture of colonial life.

Outside his own dependency, or group of dependencies, a governor had very little authority, if any. Many of his concerns may have fallen into the arena of diplomatic relations – the responsibility of the Foreign Office rather than the Colonial or Dominions Offices. Such matters are too numerous to list in any detail, but just a few examples follow: the appointment, recognition and taxation of

[8] For a brief summary of the workings of colonial governments, see chapter 2.

[9] The development was not always welcomed by officials in London. In 1858 Edmund Hammond, permanent under-secretary at the Foreign Office, noted: 'I confess I dislike the telegraph very much. In the first place nothing is sufficiently explained by it. It tempts hasty decision. It is an unsatisfactory record for it gives no reason'. *The Permanent Under-Secretary of State: a brief history of the office and its holders* (FCO Historians, Records and Historical Department, Jan. 2002, p. 41).

foreign consuls; issues relating to foreign nationals resident in British colonies; trade with foreign states or the dependencies of such states; boundary questions, such as the ongoing disputes concerning the borders between British Guiana and its neighbours Venezuela, Brazil and Suriname; the alleged ill-treatment of British nationals in foreign states; relations with neighbouring territories at time of war between the metropolitan powers; and existing or proposed treaties, such as those concerning extradition or commerce (including slave trading) or dealing with the aftermath of war. In matters of this type it was essential for a governor to liaise with the Colonial Office, although as such business was primarily the concern of the Foreign Office the most significant papers may be held among the records of that department. In other cases the Colonial Office may have been alerted to a particular incident or problem not directly by the relevant governor, but by the Foreign Office subsequent to information received from its local diplomatic or consular representative. In 1879, for example, the Foreign Office notified the Colonial Office of the involvement of British West Indians in labour riots in the Danish colony of St Croix, and of the opinion of the British consul at the neighbouring island of St Thomas, shared by local naval officers, that they should be evacuated.[10] In other cases army or naval officers may have reported matters to the War Office or Admiralty which were taken up by those departments with the Colonial Office.[11]

Individuals occasionally persisted in ongoing 'nuisance' correspondence, as in the case of one Charles Phipps who pressed his claim to a government post in Barbados in the late 1830s and 1840s on the basis of services (which are not described) rendered by his mother to the duke of Kent at the capture of Martinique in 1793–4. There are also occasional references to letters from 'lunatics'. Although those sent directly to the Colonial Office appear not to have been kept, there are occasional examples sent under cover of governors' despatches. In 1893, for example, the governor of Trinidad forwarded a memorial from Thomas McGrath, a patient at the Colonial Hospital, with a printed pamphlet entitled 'Impediments to the Prosperity of the British West Indies caused by the crimes of the Fraudulent Clerks in the Colonial Office which they have made the Devil's Workshop...' The medical superintendent of the Lunatic Asylum describes McGrath as 'a garrulous old gentleman with his mental faculties impaired by senile decay' who will probably always need hospital care, but who does not need to be confined in a lunatic asylum.[12] Five years later the governor of Jamaica forwarded correspondence from William Kelly Smith whom he described as 'a respectable old African, but a harmless lunatic'.[13] Perhaps surprisingly the Colonial Office did sometimes take note of correspondence from anonymous correspondents – signing their letters as 'a lover of justice' or 'a voice', etc. – although clearly officials could not respond.

[10] See correspondence in CO 318/273 and 274. The first correspondence from the Foreign Office on the subject is a letter to the Colonial Office dated 12 Oct. 1878 forwarding a despatch from the British Legation at Copenhagen (CO 318/273/40). The first, printed, copies of correspondence from the British consul at St Thomas were forwarded to the Colonial Office on 19 Nov. 1878 (CO 318/273/44). They are not included in CO 318/273, but as 'prints' will be found in the Foreign Office series of confidential print (FO 881/4087, 'Insurrection at St Croix and claims arising therefrom'). A 'case' volume of Foreign Office papers on the subject is in the series of correspondence for Denmark (FO 22/435, Case, Labourers at Ste Croix (1879–80)).

[11] For example the correspondence from Capt. Gambier to the Admiralty reporting his refusal to give up a naval rating claimed as an escaped slave which is noted at pp. 78–81.

[12] CO 295/345/44, 15 June 1893.

[13] CO 137/592/48, 16 Aug. 1898.

How the correspondence is arranged

As noted above, correspondence dated earlier than 1926/7 is usually bound in volumes, although some early correspondence is contained in boxes of loose papers. Within the volumes of correspondence, despatches or letters are arranged in chronological order, i.e., in the order in which they were written, not the order in which they were received. A contents list is often provided listing them in this order (from the 1870s onwards the contents list is at the front of each bound volume; before that date it is at the end and is described as an 'index' – which it is not). These contents lists, especially those dated earlier than the 1870s, should be used with some care. A recent cataloguing project of West Indian material has discovered examples of correspondence omitted from the indexes, or not described in a manner which clearly indicates its contents. For most of our period the correspondence will be accompanied by the comments of Colonial Office officials and a draft reply, or notes indicating what that reply would be. From 1868 separate minute sheets were introduced; before that date comments will be found written onto the correspondence itself (often on a folded-back corner (see figure 7), on the 'docket' which noted the date, writer and subject of a despatch (see figure 8) and sometimes even on the face of a letter (see figure 9)) or on attached blank sheets. Examples of a minute sheet, a despatch and a draft reply are given as figures 10, 11 and 12.[14] Telegrams were sometimes sent in code or cipher; fortunately a decoded version is always provided, sometimes written onto the telegram itself, sometimes on a separate sheet and sometimes on both (see figures 13 and 14; figure 15 shows a draft reply put into code).

Minute sheets and other less formal notes record the internal discussion within the Colonial Office about the content of the despatch or letter and the action to be taken. As the authors of previous guides to Colonial Office records have noted, 'The minutes, which are sometimes quite extensive, reveal the main formulators of office policy and how their minds were working, or a least the opinions they wished their colleagues to attribute to them. In this respect Colonial Office records are far richer than most departmental records of the nineteenth century'.[15] Minutes are not reproduced in the correspondence printed for the use of the Colonial Office or for Parliament (see pp. 101 and 104), which tends to obscure the internal workings of the office. As a 20th-century official was to note, outsiders (including in this case members of Parliament) might be concerned with the decisions of the secretary of state but they should not be concerned 'with the office deliberations that may precede his decisions'.[16] Historians may not agree. Fortunately a recommendation that all internal minutes should be disposed of, and only despatches retained, was rejected by a Colonial Office committee in 1903. See p. 104.

As is shown in figure 10, a range of administrative detail is also recorded on the first page of the minute sheets. The governor's name is given (although not legible in this example), together with

[14] The first minute sheets used were plain pieces of blue paper with the printed heading 'Minute papers' rather than the more elaborate form shown here. There were other changes in format over the years.

[15] Thurston, vol. 1, p. 39.

[16] CO 323/1169/4, J Shuckburgh, 8 March 1932.

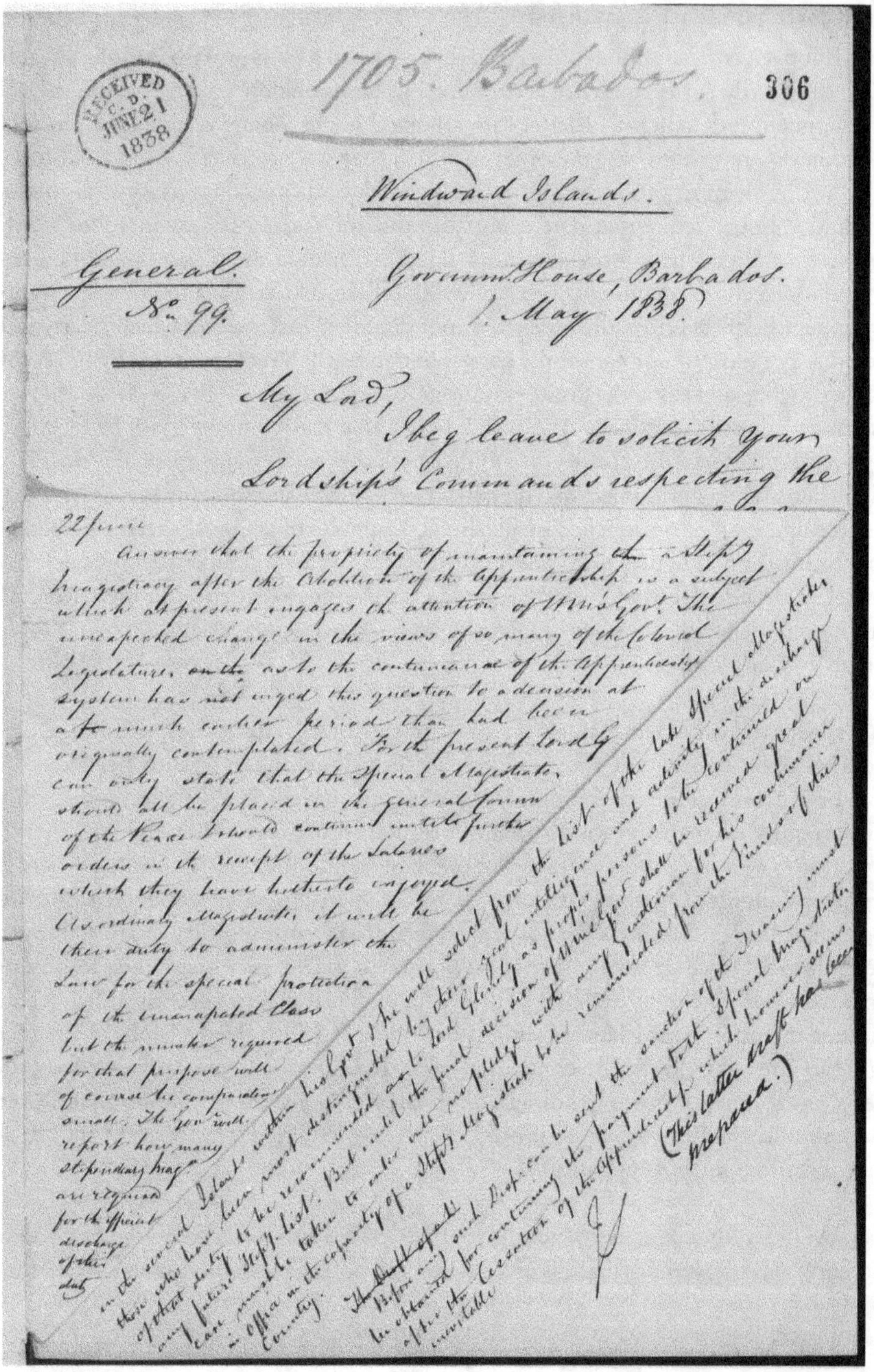
1705. Barbados. 306

RECEIVED C.O. JUNE 21 1838

Windward Islands.

General. No. 99.

Government House, Barbados. 1 May 1838.

My Lord,

I beg leave to solicit Your Lordship's Commands respecting the

22 June

Answer that the propriety of maintaining the Stipy Magistracy after the Abolition of the Apprenticeship is a subject which at present engages the attention of H.M.'s Govt. The unexpected change in the views of so many of the Colonial Legislatures as to the continuance of the Apprenticeship system has not urged this question to a decision at a much earlier period than had been originally contemplated. For the present Lord G. can only state that the Special Magistrates should all be placed in the general Comm of the Peace & should continue until further orders in the receipt of the Salaries which they have hitherto enjoyed. As ordinary Magistrates it will be their duty to administer the Law for the special protection of the emancipated Class but the number required for that purpose will of course be comparatively small. The Govr will report how many Stipendiary Magis are required for the efficient discharge of their duty in the several Islands within his Govt, & he will select from the list of the late Special Magistrates those who have been most distinguished by their zeal intelligence and activity in the discharge of that duty to be recommended to Lord Glenelg as proper persons to be continued on any future Stipy List. But until the final decision of HM's Govt shall be received great care must be taken to enter into no pledge with any Gentleman for his continuance in Office in the capacity of a Stipy Magistrate to be remunerated from the funds of the Country.

~~The Draft ought~~ Before any such Desp. can be sent the sanction of the Treasury must be obtained for continuing the payment to the Special Magistrates after the Cessation of the Apprenticeship which however seems inevitable. (This latter draft has been prepared.)

J

Figure 7. CO 28/122, fo. 306. Despatch with bottom right-hand corner folded back to record Colonial Office minutes on the reverse. Minutes are continued, written diagonally, on the following folio.

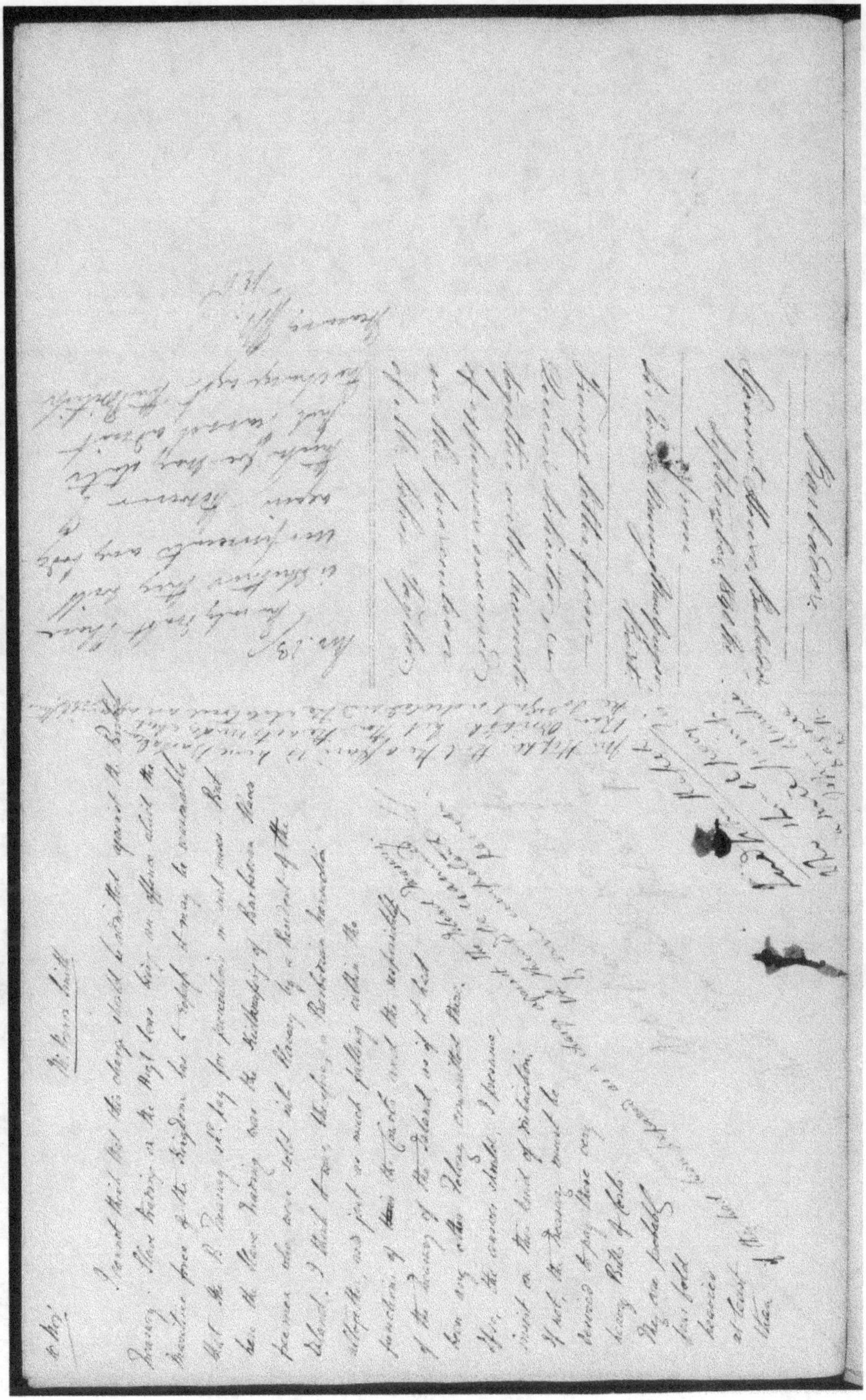

Figure 8. CO 28/135, fo. 40v. Docket sheet recording name of writer, date and subject of despatch and annotated with Colonial Office minutes.

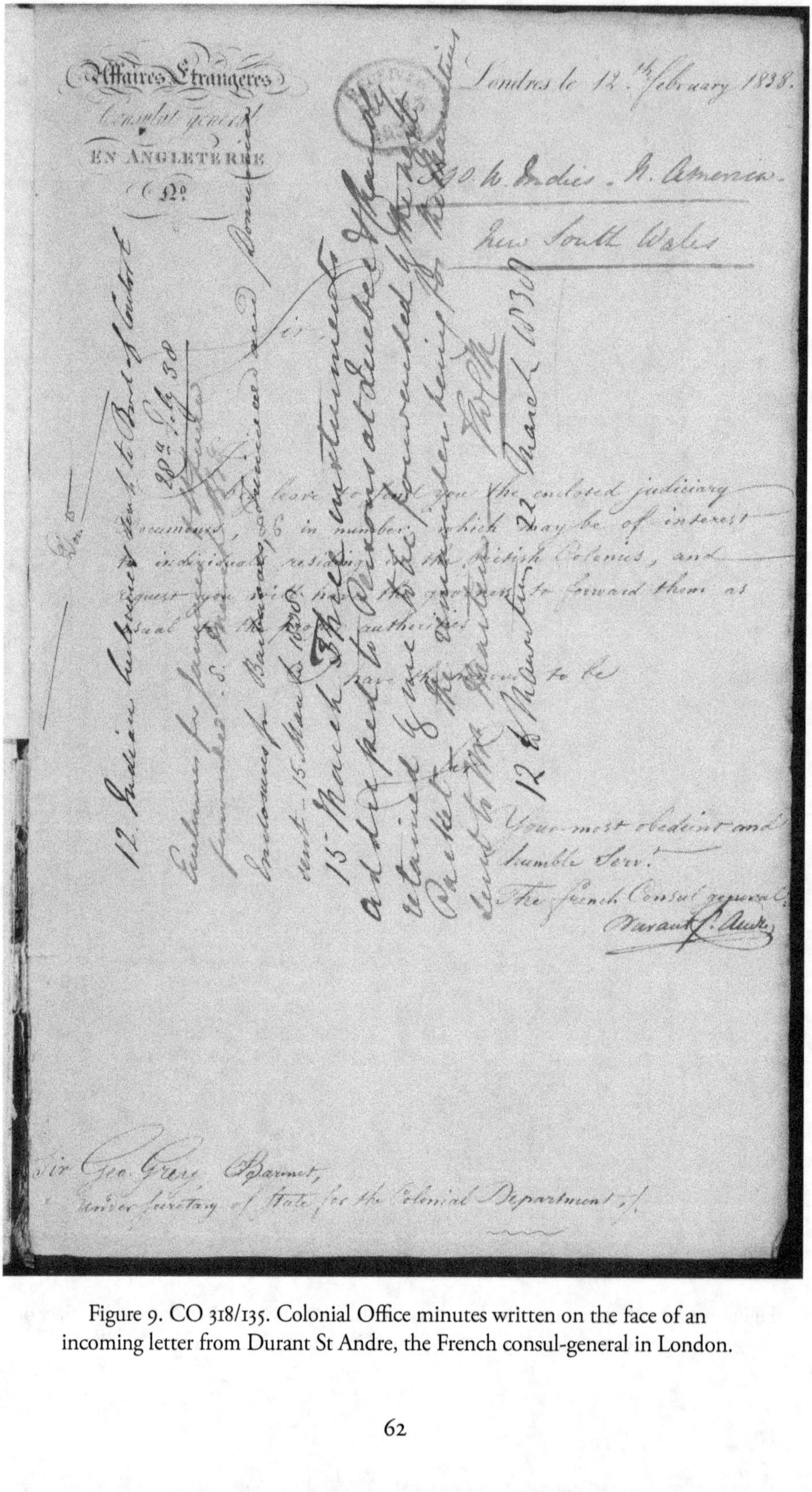

Figure 9. CO 318/135. Colonial Office minutes written on the face of an incoming letter from Durant St Andre, the French consul-general in London.

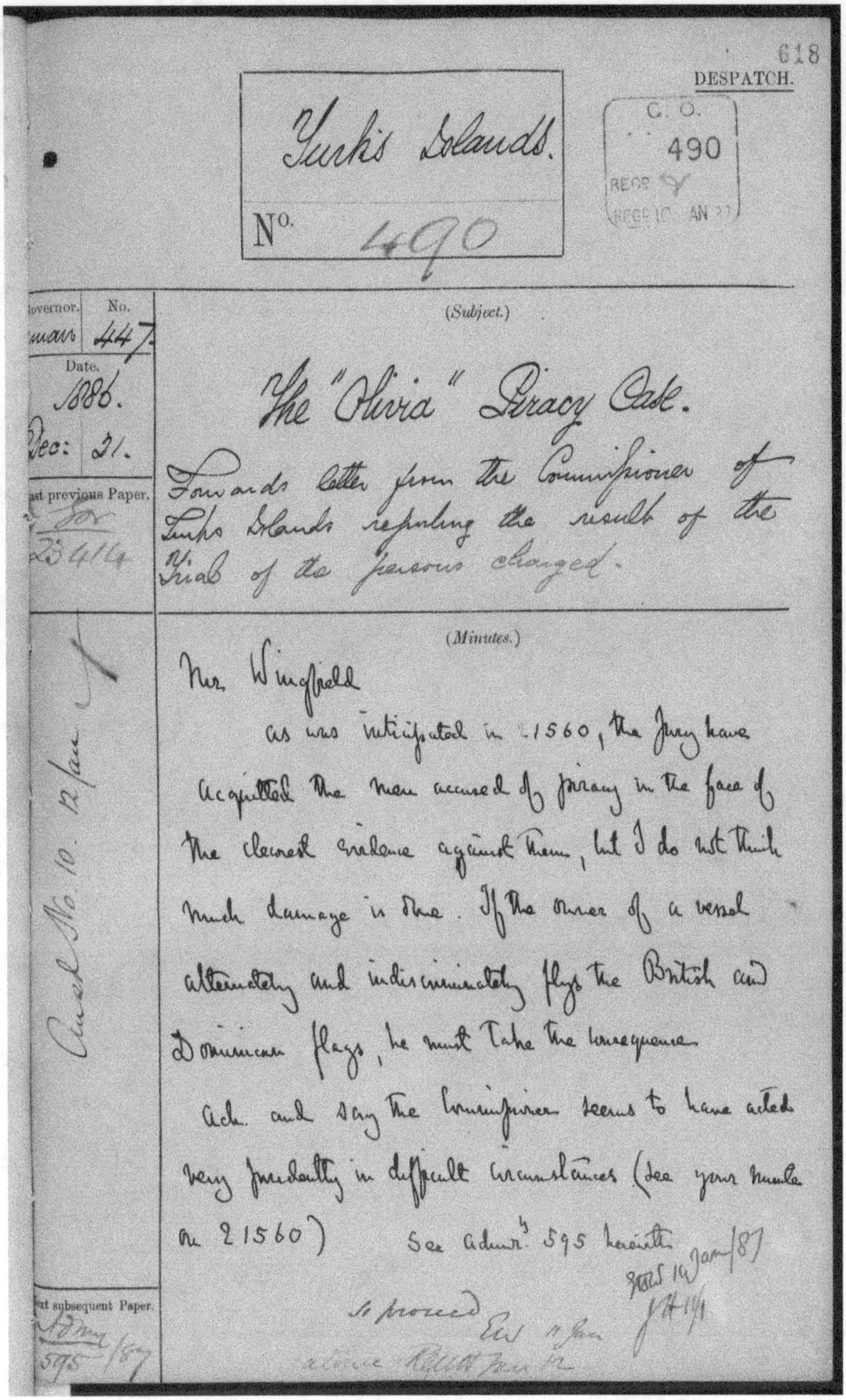

618

DESPATCH.

Turks Islands.

No. 490

C.O. 490

(Subject.)

The "Olivia" Piracy Case.

Forwards letter from the Commissioner of Turks Islands reporting the result of the trial of the persons charged.

Governor. No. 447.

Date. 1886. Dec: 21.

Last previous Paper. 23414

(Minutes.)

Mr. Wingfield

As was anticipated in 21560, the Jury have acquitted the men accused of piracy in the face of the clearest evidence against them, but I do not think much damage is done. If the owner of a vessel alternately and indiscriminately flys the British and Dominican flags, he must take the consequence.

Ack. and say the Commissioner seems to have acted very prudently in difficult circumstances (see your minute on 21560)

See Admy. 595 herewith. 14 Jan/87

So proceed. EW 14 Jan. JH 14/1

Ansd No. 10. 12/Jan

Next subsequent Paper. Admy 595/87

Figure 10. CO 137/528, fo. 618. A minute sheet recording details of a despatch which reports the result of a piracy trial [see figure 11] and comments on that report.

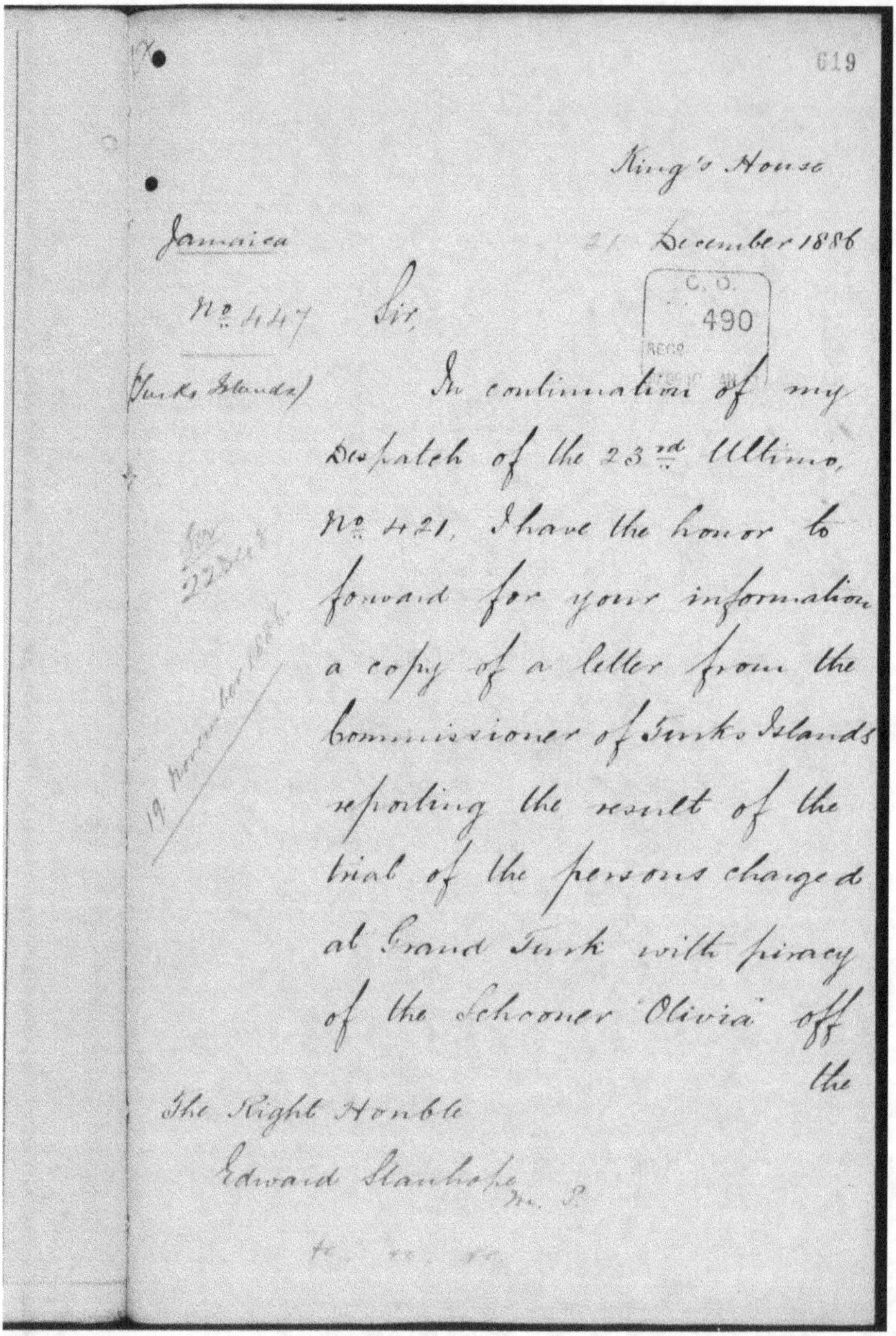

619

King's House

Jamaica

21 December 1886

No. 447

Sir,

C.O. 490

(Turks Islands)

Gov 22348

19 November 1886

In continuation of my despatch of the 23rd Ultimo, No. 421, I have the honor to forward for your information a copy of a letter from the Commissioner of Turks Islands reporting the result of the trial of the persons charged at Grand Turk with piracy of the Schooner 'Olivia' off the

The Right Honble

Edward Stanhope M.P.

&c. &c. &c.

Figure 11. CO 137/528, fo. 619. The first page of a despatch from the governor of Jamaica, 21 December 1886, covering a report of a recent piracy trial received from the commissioner of the Turks Islands. Annotations in the left-hand margin give the Colonial Office registered number of the governor's previous despatch on the subject (Gov 22348), and the date of the enclosure with a diagonal line noting its presence.

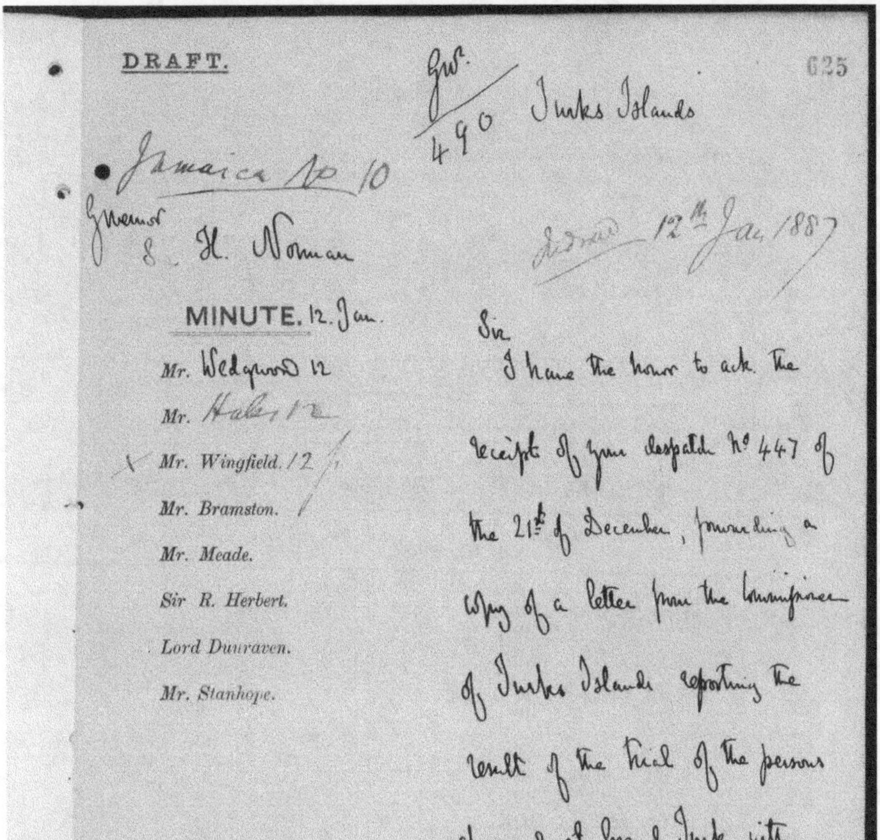

DRAFT. 625

Gov. 490 Turks Islands

Jamaica No 10

Governor S. H. Norman

Issued 12th Jan 1887

MINUTE. 12. Jan.

Mr. Wedgwood 12

Mr. Hales 12

Mr. Wingfield. 12 fs

Mr. Bramston.

Mr. Meade.

Sir R. Herbert.

Lord Dunraven.

Mr. Stanhope.

Sir

I have the honor to ack. the receipt of your despatch No 447 of the 21st of December, forwarding a copy of a letter from the Commissioner of Turks Islands reporting the result of the trial of the persons charged at Grand Turk with piracy in the case of the Schooner "Olivia" off the coast of St Domingo.

The Commissioner appears to have acted very prudently in difficult circumstances throughout this matter.

I have &c

Adm. 595 to Governor (Done) £7

Figure 12. CO 137/528, fo. 625. The first page of a draft reply to the despatch shown at figure 11; with names of officials approving the draft. Wingfield has followed the date (given just as '12') with the abbreviation 'fs' – for signature – indicating final approval.

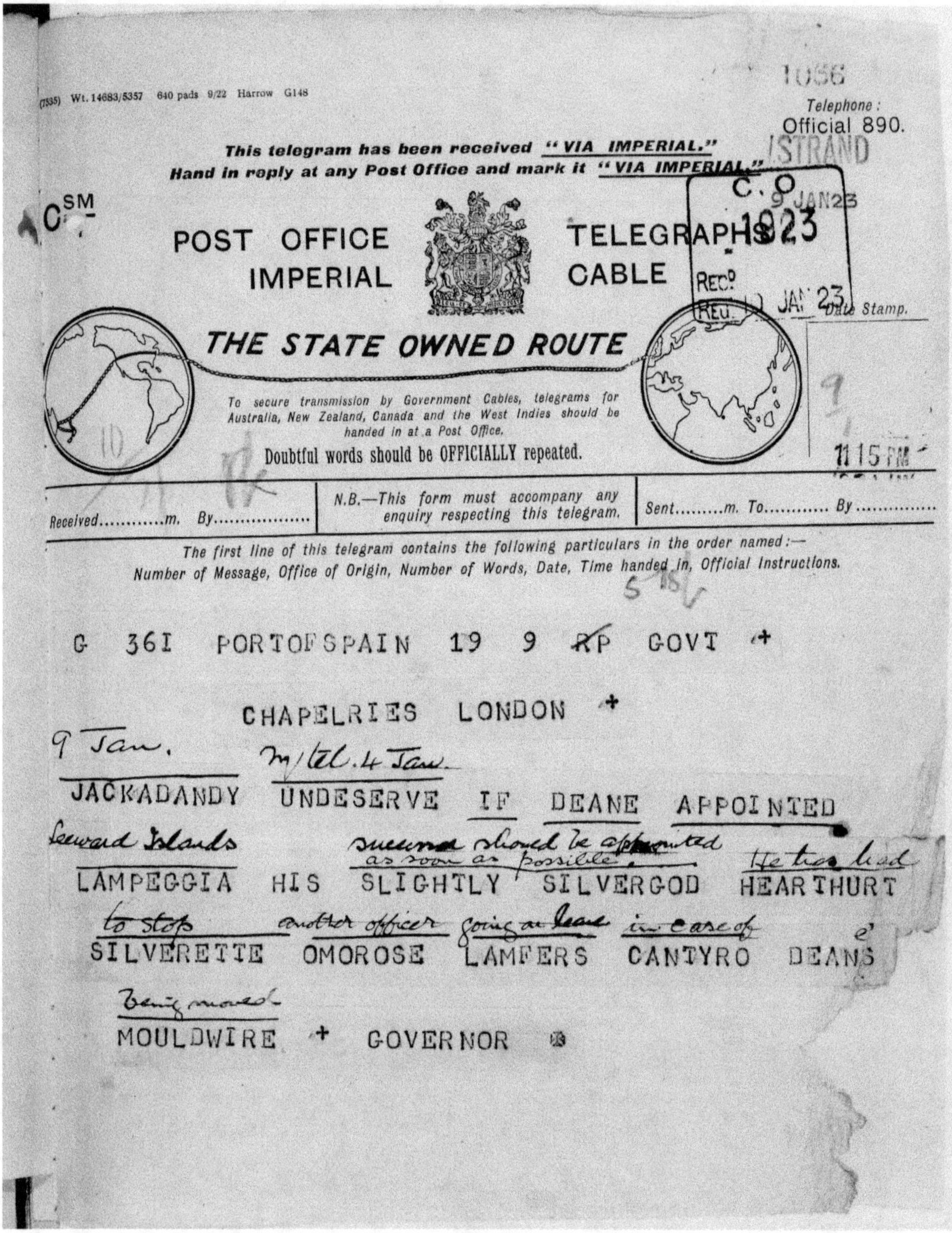

(7535) Wt. 14683/5357 640 pads 9/22 Harrow G148

1056

Telephone: Official 890.

This telegram has been received "VIA IMPERIAL."
Hand in reply at any Post Office and mark it "VIA IMPERIAL."

STRAND

C.O. 9 JAN 23 1923

REC^{D} 10 JAN 23

POST OFFICE TELEGRAPHS
IMPERIAL CABLE

THE STATE OWNED ROUTE

To secure transmission by Government Cables, telegrams for Australia, New Zealand, Canada and the West Indies should be handed in at a Post Office.

Doubtful words should be OFFICIALLY repeated.

Date Stamp.

11 15 PM

Received.........m. By.................. | N.B.—This form must accompany any enquiry respecting this telegram. | Sent.........m. To........... By...............

The first line of this telegram contains the following particulars in the order named:— Number of Message, Office of Origin, Number of Words, Date, Time handed in, Official Instructions.

G 361 PORTOFSPAIN 19 9 RP GOVT +

CHAPELRIES LONDON +

9 Jan. My tel. 4 Jan.

JACKADANDY UNDESERVE IF DEANE APPOINTED

Leeward Islands successor should be appointed as soon as possible. He has had

LAMPEGGIA HIS SLIGHTLY SILVERGOD HEARTHURT

to stop another officer going on leave in case of

SILVERETTE OMOROSE LAMFERS CANTYRO DEANS

being moved

MOULDWIRE + GOVERNOR

Figure 13. CO 295/546. Telegram from the governor of Trinidad sent in code, with the decoding added in manuscript.

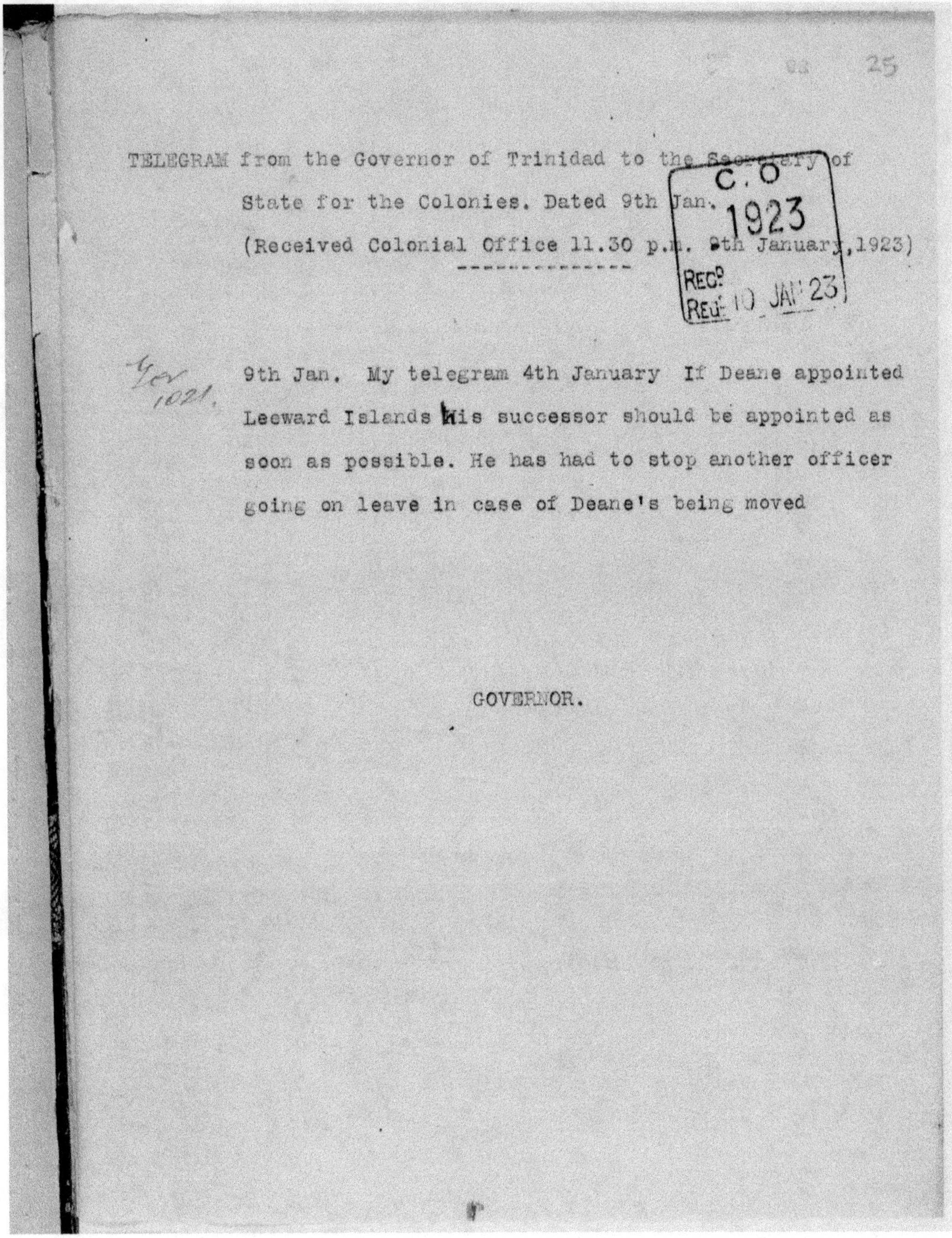

25

TELEGRAM from the Governor of Trinidad to the Secretary of State for the Colonies. Dated 9th Jan.
(Received Colonial Office 11.30 p.m. 9th January, 1923)

C.O 1923 RECD 10 JAN 23

9th Jan. My telegram 4th January If Deane appointed Leeward Islands his successor should be appointed as soon as possible. He has had to stop another officer going on leave in case of Deane's being moved

GOVERNOR.

Figure 14. CO 295/546. Typescript copy of the text of the decoded telegram shown in figure 13.

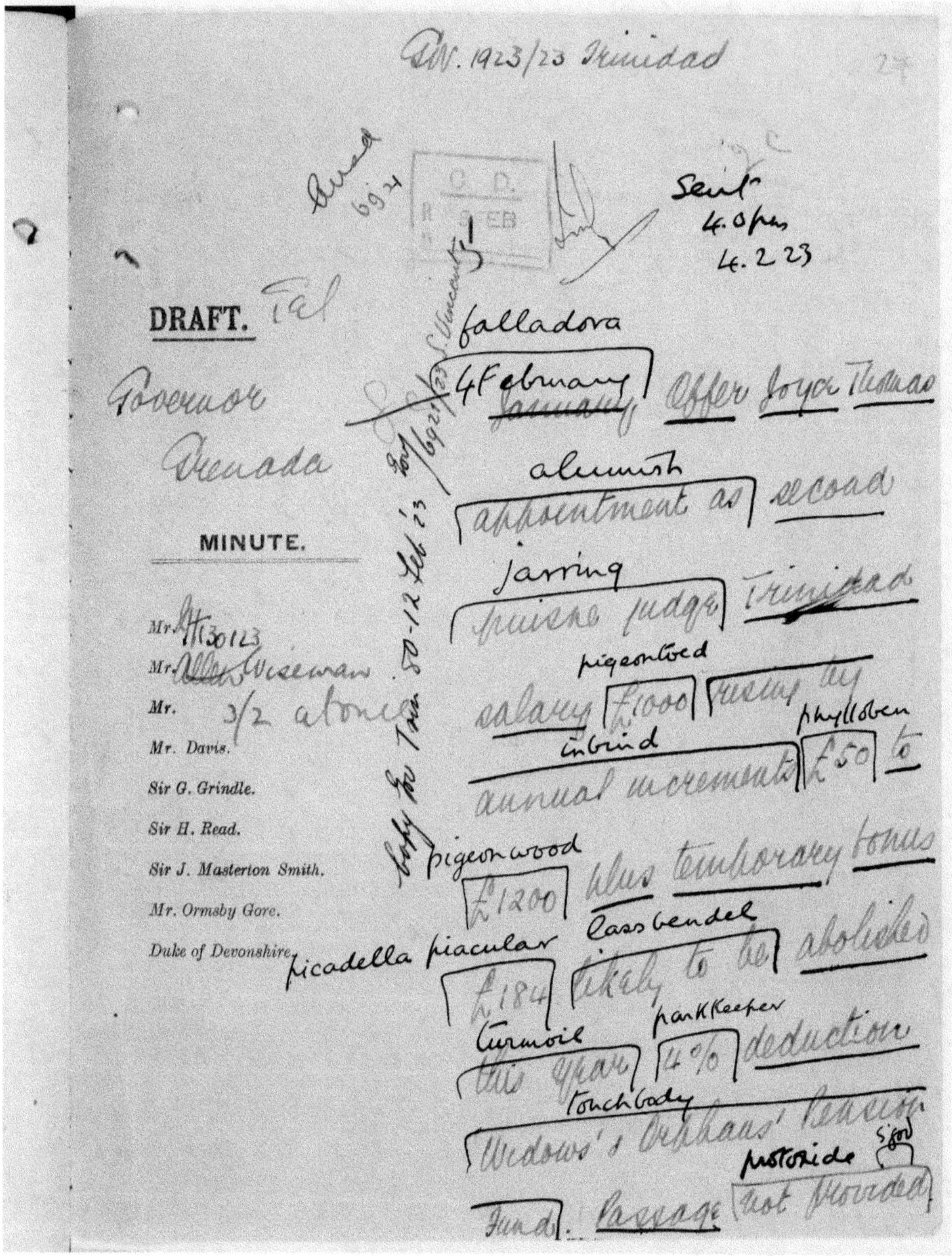

Figure 15. CO 295/546. Draft telegraphic instruction to the governor of Grenada with coding added.

the date and number of his despatch.[17] A box at the top of the page gives the colony name, in this case Turks Islands, but might give a subject classification; it also records the 'unique identifier' taken from the daily register (see pp. 87–92). The stamp to the right repeats this number and gives the date of receipt and/or registration within the Colonial Office. The subject matter of the despatch is noted. To the left of the page references to previous and subsequent correspondence on the same subject are given in the form used in the registers of correspondence (see pp. 92–100), while between those two references is a note of the 'disposal' of the correspondence – in this case that it was answered on 12 January [1887] by Colonial Office despatch no. 10.

Two points in particular should be noted about the minuting system:

1. Officials commonly initialled their minutes rather than signing them in full. Other notes on the minute sheets may help to identify officials, for example someone passing papers to a colleague may start his note with that person's name. In figure 16, for instance, because the minutes start with the names of Flood, Harding and Ellis it is (just about) possible to decipher their initials. Harding is AJH and Ellis WDE. Flood's full initials were JEWF – virtually unrecognisable here and not even clearly four separate letters, although there are certainly four full stops. Ellis follows his initials and the date with the words 'at once', being an instruction for the matter to be dealt with immediately as agreed. In other cases there may be no such clues within the minutes. From 1862, when the *Colonial Office List* first appears, it is usually quite straightforward to identify an individual from his initials.[18] The *List* describes the division of responsibility between the Colonial Office departments and gives names of officials within each department. In the example in figure 10, therefore, the illegible initials of the official who wrote the minute of 10 January 1887 addressed to Mr Wingfield become clear once you know that the only four officials working in the West Indian Department at the time were J. Hales, E. H. Wedgwood, C. A. Harris and S. Olivier (see figure 17). These can only be the initials of Wedgwood. The minute sheet is subsequently initialled by Hales; Wingfield, assistant under-secretary, whose name appears above the departmental organisation, adds 'so proceed'; and the final 'at once' is added by R. G. W. Herbert, permanent under-secretary, whose name appears almost at the top of the page shown in the image. Before 1862 it can be much more difficult to identify officials. The annual *Imperial Calendar* and *Royal Kalendar* (the predecessors of the *Civil Service Yearbook*) may help; copies are available on open access at Kew.

2. Until the 1830s decision-making within the office was generally by personal discussion, which left no paper trail. Comments may be added to correspondence, and there is occasionally a detailed memorandum on a particular subject, but often there is nothing. A formal system of minuting was subsequently introduced, and further developed over time. Initially correspondence went first to the senior clerk of the appropriate department, who

[17] Names of British governors are given in the annual *Colonial Office List*. For a more comprehensive listing see D. P. Henige, *Colonial Governors from the Fifteenth Century to the Present* (Madison, Wis., 1970).

[18] The problem of identification should not be overstated. Most researchers are likely to be reading comments from the same group of officials and will quickly come to recognise their initials however badly written.

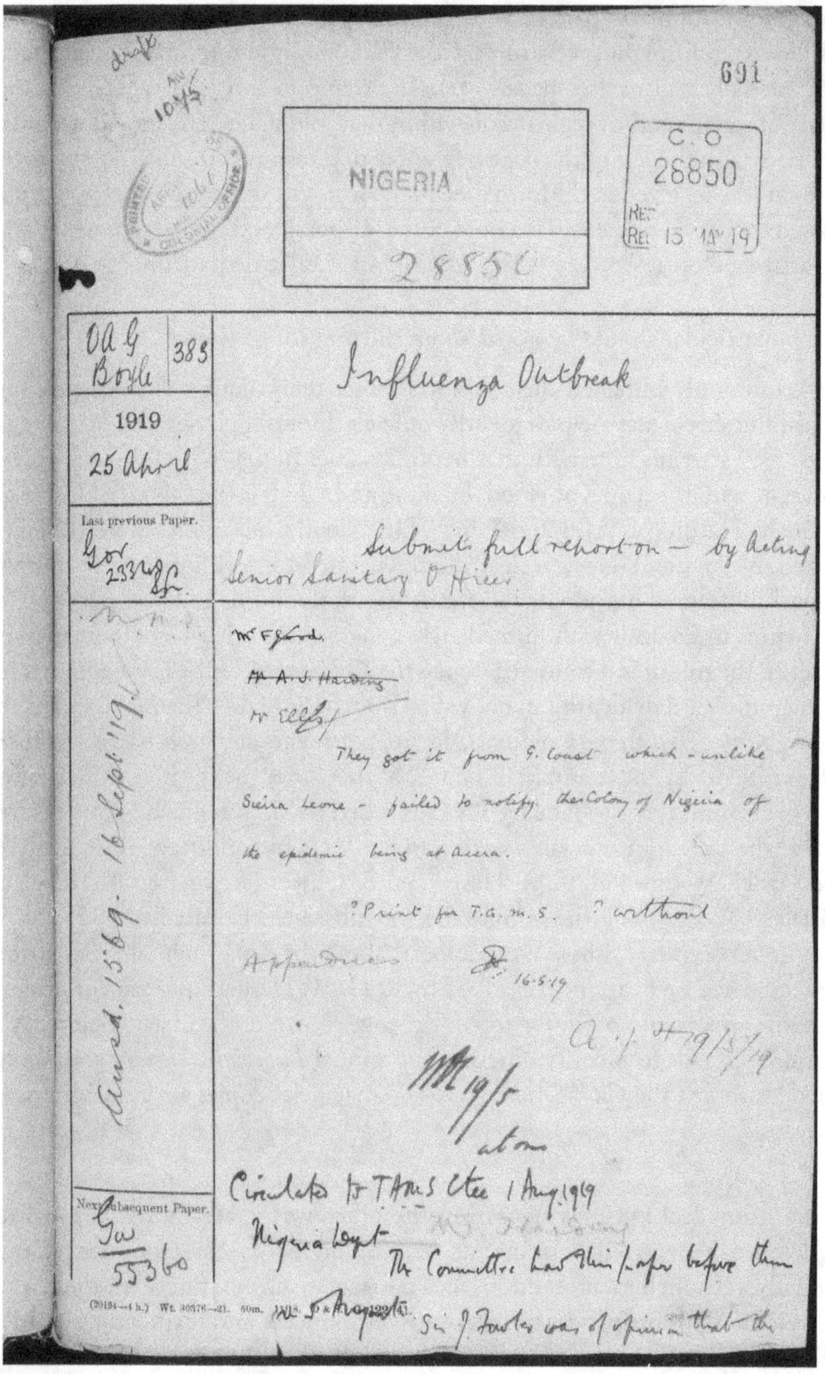

691

NIGERIA

28850

C.O
28850
REC 15 MAY 19

OAG Boyle 383

1919
25 April

Last previous Paper.

Influenza Outbreak

Submits full report on – by Acting Senior Sanitary Officer

Mr Flood
~~Mr A. J. Harding~~
Mr Ellis

They got it from G. Coast which – unlike Sierra Leone – failed to notify the Colony of Nigeria of the epidemic being at Accra.

? Print for T.A.M.S. ? without Appendices 16.5.19

Next Subsequent Paper.

Circulated to T.A.M.S. Ctee 1 Aug. 1919

Nigeria Dept

The Committee had this paper before them Sir J. Fowler was of opinion that the

Figure 16. CO 583/74, fo. 691. Minute sheet showing referral of report on an outbreak of influenza to Flood, Harding and Ellis, Colonial Office officials, with Flood's comments and the dated initials of all three. Stamped entries at the top left of the minute sheet indicate that the correspondence and draft reply were to be printed as 'confidential print'.

COLONIAL OFFICE LIST. 13

DISTRIBUTION OF BUSINESS IN THE COLONIAL OFFICE.

Secretary of State:—RT. HON. SIR H. T. HOLLAND, G.C.M.G., M.P.

Private Secretaries:—Mr. W. A. Baillie Hamilton and Mr. H. W. Just.

Parliamentary Under-Secretary:—EARL OF DUNRAVEN.

Private Secretary:—Mr. F. Graham.

Permanent Under-Secretary:—SIR ROBERT G. W. HERBERT, K.C.B.

Private Secretary:—Mr. C. P. Lucas.

Political and Constitutional Questions, General Supervision, Papers on all subjects before submission to the Secretary of State.

Assistant Under-Secretaries:—

THE HON. R. H. MEADE, C.B.:—Colonial Estimates, Finance, Currency, Public Works, Pensions, Military Questions, Requisitions for Supplies, and other business with Crown Agents, Accounts, miscellaneous Business of General Department, and Office Arrangements, Business connected with Ceylon, Hong Kong, Labuan, Straits Settlements, West Africa, and Cyprus.

MR. JOHN BRAMSTON, C.B.:—General Legal Business, Settlement of Commissions, Warrants, Charters, Orders in Council, &c., Postal and Telegraphic Business, Naturalization, Education, and Ecclesiastical Questions, Business connected with North American, Australasian and South African Colonies, Fiji, and Western Pacific High Commission.

MR. EDWARD WINGFIELD:—Colonial Laws and Ordinances, and other Legal Business, Land and Immigration, Correspondence on Merchant Shipping and Mercantile Marine Questions, Quarantine Prisons, Hospitals, and Lunatic Asylums, Circulars, Business connected with West Indian Colonies Mauritius, Malta, Gibraltar, St. Helena, Falkland Islands, and Heligoland.

Chief Clerk:—MR. R. P. EBDEN (Head of General Department).

Departments:—

WEST INDIAN. Jamaica, Turks Islands, British Honduras, British Guiana, Bahamas, Trinidad, Windward Islands (Barbados, St. Vincent, Grenada, Tobago, St Lucia), Leeward Islands (Antigua, Montserrat, St. Kitts, Nevis, Virgin Islands, Dominica), Bermuda, Falklands, and Heligoland.	Mr. J. Hales. „ E. H. Wedgwood.	Mr. C. A. Harris. „ S. Olivier.
NORTH AMERICAN AND AUSTRALIAN. Canada (Ontario, Quebec, Nova Scotia, New Brunswick, Manitobia, North-West Territories, British Columbia, and Prince Edward Island), Newfoundland, New South Wales, Victoria, South Australia, Queensland, Western Australia, Tasmania, New Zealand, Fiji, New Guinea, and Western Pacific High Commission.	Mr. E. B. Pennell, C.M.G. „ F. W. Fuller.	Mr. W. H. Mercer. „ G. V. Fiddes.
AFRICAN AND MEDITERRANEAN. Cape of Good Hope, Natal, Zululand, Bechuanaland, St. Helena, Sierra Leone, Gambia, Gold Coast, Lagos, Malta, Gibraltar, and Cyprus.	Mr. A W. L. Hemming. C M.G. „ E. Fairfield, C.M.G.	Mr. R. L. Antrobus. „ J. Anderson. „ S. Webb.
EASTERN. Ceylon, Hong Kong, Labuan, Straits Settlements (Singapore, Penang, Malacca), Mauritius and Seychelles.	Mr. G. W. B. De Robeck. „ A. A. Pearson.	Mr. G. W. Johnson.
GENERAL. General and Miscellaneous Correspondence, including Replies to Circulars, Governors' Pensions, Naval Cadetships, Precedence, and Civil Service Uniform, Correspondence respecting Colonial Defence, and the Passing of Charters, Letters Patent, Commissions, Warrants, &c.	Mr. R. P. Ebden (Chief Clerk) „ F. O. Adrian.	Mr. W. F. Westbrook. „ M. J. Drayson.

Registry:—Mr. J. C. Braddon (Superintendent), Mr. C. H. Niblett, Mr. T. Wilson, Mr. W. A. Harding, Mr. G. Attrill, and Mr. R. M. C. Esdale.

Printing Branch:—Mr. W. J. MacGee (Superintendent) and Mr. W. Baines; Mr. E. D. Rockett.

Library:—Mr. C. Atchley (Superintendent) and Mr. J. Russell; Mr. H. Watts, and Mr. W. Scott.

Copying Branch:—Mr. E. J. Jennings (Superintendent) and Writers.

FINANCIAL. Preparation of Parliamentary Estimates, Accounting for Parliamentary Votes Administered by Colonial Department, and correspondence relating to these and similar matters; Cash Receipts and Payments, Colonial Pensions, &c.	Mr. F. R. Round. „ A.H. H. Engelbach.	Mr. A. Browne. „ W. H. Eggett.
EMIGRATION - - - - - - - -	Mr. R. P. Ebden.	Mr. W. R. Pownall. „ J. B. Gill.

Order of St. Michael and St. George:—MR. CHARLES COX (Chancellor).

Figure 17. Extract from *Colonial Office List* of 1887 showing membership of the West Indian Department and the Colonial Office hierarchy above that department.

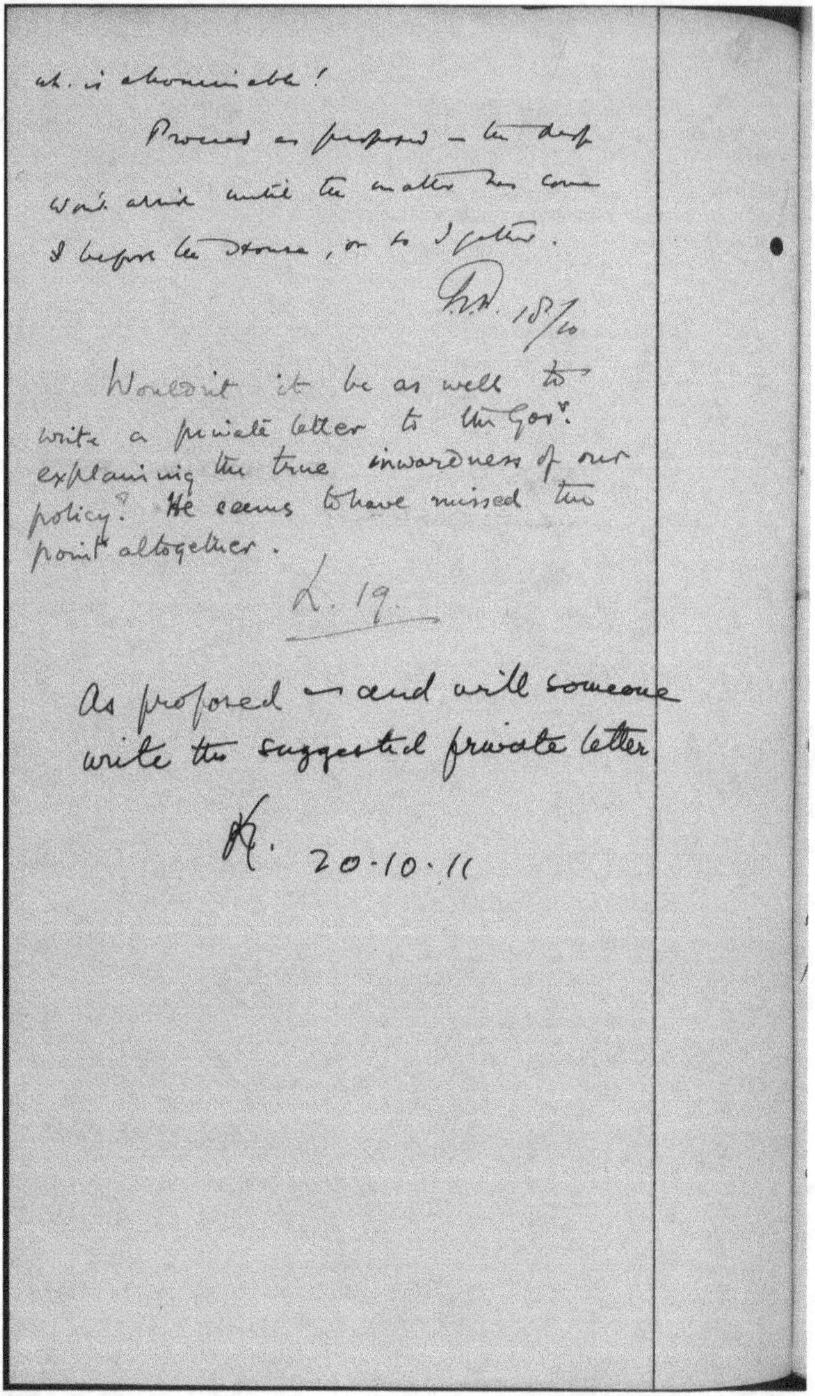
wh. is abominable!

Proceed as proposed – the desp. won't arrive until the matter has come before the House, or so I gather.

18/10

Wouldn't it be as well to write a private letter to the Govr. explaining the true inwardness of our policy? He seems to have missed the point altogether.

L. 19.

As proposed – and will someone write the suggested private letter

H. 20.10.11

Figure 18. CO 37/249, fo. 125v. Minute sheet showing initialled comments by Lord Lucas, parliamentary under-secretary of state, and Lewis Harcourt, secretary of state. Although not apparent in this reproduction Harcourt's comment is in red ink.

suggested a reply or method of dealing with the matter and passed the correspondence to his superiors. This system was inefficient in that minor matters took up the time of senior officials, but it did have the advantage of ensuring that such officials maintained a broad overview of business. Following the introduction of minute sheets in the late 1860s the exact progress of paperwork within the office can be more easily seen, and it was then often a relatively junior official within the appropriate department who received and read the incoming correspondence and appended his recommendation, and sometimes a draft reply, before referring it to his superior. At other times the draft reply was prepared after the initial circulation of papers. Clearly the exact procedure is likely to depend on the ability of individuals and the willingness of more senior officials to delegate. The final comments on a minute sheet usually come from an official empowered to make a final decision and, as noted above, commonly conclude with the words 'at once', although there are many cases, as in figure 16, when that 'final' instruction is followed by later comments.[19] Sometimes a minute sheet will simply bear the initialled words 'put by', meaning that no action is required and the papers can simply be filed away. Following receipt of uncontroversial, locally enacted legislation the comments on a minute sheet may read simply: 'sanction?' and 'at once'.

Over the years it became increasingly uncommon for any other than the most important matters to be referred to ministers; most correspondence could be dealt with at an official level, i.e., by civil servants.[20] Figure 18, however, gives an example of correspondence going right to the top – to parliamentary under-secretary of state Lord Lucas and secretary of state Lewis Harcourt.[21] Lucas, as a member of the House of Lords, uses the single initial 'L'.[22] Harcourt's instruction and initials are written in red ink, in theory the convention for secretaries of state although not always followed. The secretary of state was also the only person whose instructions did not have to be followed by the words 'at once'.[23]

At certain periods incoming telegrams have not been placed in the volumes; instead their text is recorded in a minute sheet. Any enclosures sent by a correspondent will be referred to in the

[19] In response to scathing recommendations made by Sydney Olivier on a supplementary vote of the Financial Board of Tobago for the upkeep of roads, C P Lucas added 'put it gently' to his 'at once'. CO 295/382/15, December 1897.

[20] Researchers should, therefore, be careful of attributing a policy to a particular secretary of state personally. It may have been issued under his name, but did he actually see the file?

[21] In this case correspondence was referred to the secretary of state because it concerned the thorny issue of how to persuade the attorney-general of Bermuda, whose work was considered unsatisfactory, to retire. The private letter referred to, the draft of which is included, was sent out under the name of G. Grindle, a principal clerk in the West Indies Department, and appears to have been drafted by him.

[22] It was usual for the parliamentary under-secretary of state to be a member of the House of Lords when the secretary of state sat in the Commons, and vice versa.

[23] Parkinson, p. 29. Parkinson's book is a very personal and anecdotal account of his years at the Colonial Office but it includes a detailed description of the way in which correspondence was handled when he joined the office and praises the efficiency of the registries. He is less complimentary about their work during the Second World War: 'however willing temporary staff may be, how can a registry function as a registry should, if in fact it is a sort of human kaleidoscope?' (p. 129).

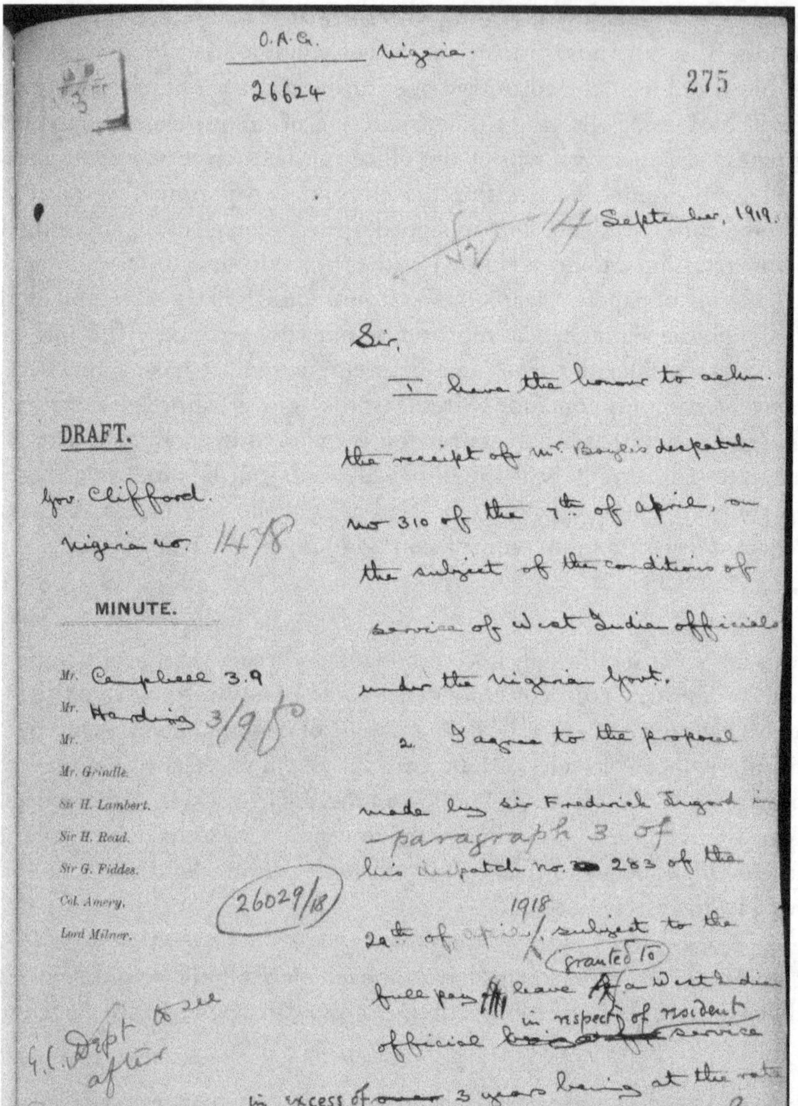
O.A.G. Nigeria.
26624
275

14 September, 1919.

DRAFT.

Gov. Clifford.
Nigeria no. 1478

MINUTE.

Mr. Campbell 3.9
Mr. Harding 3/9
Mr.
Mr. Grindle.
Sir H. Lambert.
Sir H. Read.
Sir G. Fiddes.
Col. Amery.
Lord Milner.

26029/18

Sir,

I have the honour to ackn. the receipt of Mr. Boyle's despatch no 310 of the 7th of April, on the subject of the conditions of service of West Indian officials under the Nigeria Govt.

2. I agree to the proposal made by Sir Frederick Lugard in paragraph 3 of his despatch no. 283 of the 29th of April 1918, subject to the full pay leave granted to a West Indian official in respect of resident service in excess of 3 years being at the rate only of 20 days for each completed year in excess of three.

3. I assume that the officer is to be given at the beginning of each tour the option between three years tour without a passage for his

G.C. Dept to see after

Figure 19. CO 583/74, fo. 275. Draft reply to an incoming despatch showing the difficulty of reading some amended drafts.

text of a letter or despatch, and that reference clearly indicated by a diagonal line in the left-hand margin (see figures 11, 22 and 35). If such enclosures are not in the volume, a note on the covering communication or a minute sheet will usually record their destination – returned to the correspondent; passed to another government department, organisation or individual for information, action or advice; deposited in the Colonial Office library. Copying of enclosures could, of course, be done only by hand for much of our period and was so labour intensive that it was not usually undertaken merely for a file copy to be retained. Sometimes there was a request for papers to be returned, but if that happened they were not always re-united with associated correspondence. Statutes, blue books, gazettes, sessional papers and annual departmental reports referred to in correspondence which are noted as 'to library' should be found in the record series for the appropriate colony entitled 'acts', 'miscellanea', 'gazettes' or 'sessional papers' now held in TNA and described at the end of this chapter. The same is true of newspapers for the period around the middle of the 19th century.[24] Other missing enclosures, together with the correspondence itself (or extracts from the correspondence), may have been printed for the use of the Colonial Office or for Parliament (see pp. 101–4). Yet others have not found their way to TNA.[25]

For much of this period there are no 'fair copies' of Colonial Office replies to despatches and other correspondence. Up to 1872, the final version of a response should be found in the 'entry books', which are listed for each colony in appendix 1 and described below. Thereafter (until typed carbon copies begin to appear) the draft bound up with the incoming correspondence is the only version. The initial draft may have been much amended by officials before it was finally approved. Some drafts can, therefore, be quite difficult to read (see figure 19) and one can only assume that the final version was exactly as the draft unless one has access to it in the national archives of the former colony, the records of another UK government department or a collection of private papers. The draft in figure 19 also shows, following Harding's name, the letters 'fs' – 'for signature' – meaning that the draft was approved. From 1872 to 1925 there are registers of out-letters (arranged by colony or subject in the same way as the registers of correspondence described below, and the original correspondence itself). It is not often necessary to consult these, but they will, if nothing else, provide the reference number and exact date of the out-letter.

[24] See appendix 3. Later newspapers were passed to the British Museum and should now be sought at the British Library. Following the closure of the Newspaper Library at Colindale in November 2013 the British Library has posted updates about future access to the collections on its website at http://www.bl.uk.

[25] The Colonial Office Library was incorporated into the library of the Foreign and Commonwealth Office, which has disposed of its historical holdings over the years. TNA has the Colonial Office Library's map collections (see chapter 10) and the bulk of a collection of photographs (in CO 1069; see chapter 11)'. The historical library collection of the FCO was transferred to King's College London on permanent loan in 2007 (see http://www.kcl.ac.uk/library/collections/archivespec/collections/fco.aspx [accessed 8 Oct. 2014]. The collection of statutes from the former FCO Legal Library is held at the Institute of Advanced Legal Studies, School of Advanced Study, University of London (see p 116). A collection of pamphlets from the FCO Library is now at the University of Manchester John Rylands University Library (see http://www.library.manchester.ac.uk/searchresources/guidetospecialcollections/atoz/foreignandcommonwealthoffice/ [accessed 8 Oct. 2014].

'Case' volumes

As well as the volumes described above, which contain papers on a variety of different subjects, and sometimes from several correspondents, the original correspondence series include a number of 'case' volumes, i.e., bound volumes devoted to a particular topic. They vary considerably in their subject matter, and just a few examples are given here:

CO 42/181 (Canada) Mr Coltman's mission to the Indian Territory. Disputes between the Hudson Bay and North West Companies, 1818–19

CO 54/94 (Ceylon) Testamentary jurisdiction of the Supreme Court, 1826

CO 167/35 (Mauritius) Accounts: relief afforded to the sufferers by the fire and drought, 1817

CO 201/114 (New South Wales) Report of commissioners of inquiry into state of New South Wales: convicts, part 1, 1822

CO 267/11 (Sierra Leone) Reports on Dutch African forts, 1804

Case volumes are described by subject matter in the catalogue – even those in series which have not otherwise been fully catalogued. They are more common in the 19th century, but do not appear in every series.

Entry books

'Entry books', as the name implies, are books in which certain information was entered, usually as a record of correspondence sent out from the office. They are also often known as 'letter books'. They can be found among the Colonial Office records in individual series relating to the colonies, as listed in appendix 1. There are also general series, and a small number of subject-based series, both listed in appendix 2. The series CO 324 includes entry books of out-letters to government departments and other organisations. Some of these are described in the catalogue as 'domestic', meaning within the UK, rather than the more usual 'offices'.[26]

The dates at which the entry books commence are usually close to the start dates of the related correspondence; all the entry books series come to an end in 1872. Their format varies over time. Early books often contain copies of both incoming and outgoing correspondence, but the practice of copying in-letters was abandoned during the 18th century. By the mid 19th century the entry books include contents lists showing 'to whom sent', date, number and subject. As noted above, the entry books can be particularly useful for locating the final version of an outgoing despatch. In addition they often include copies of other documents sent out, such as warrants or instructions to governors, which may be referred to in the volumes of incoming 'original correspondence' but not detailed. It should be noted that, although entries are usually in strict chronological order, this is not always the case; it can only be assumed that a clerk given a number of items to copy into an entry book sometimes copied them as they came to hand rather than sorting them into date order first. It appears that entry books do not necessarily include all outgoing communications. For example, CO 29/29, the entry book for Barbados dated 1801–13, does not, although there are occasional marginal notes – in red – referring to additional material sent out but not copied.

[26] That is, more usual in the Colonial Office context; the Foreign Office favoured 'domestic'.

Finding aids

Registration of correspondence before 1849

The National Archives' online catalogue is continually enhanced to improve or add descriptions of individual documents. At the time of writing, however, only a tiny proportion of the many thousands of volumes of Colonial Office original correspondence is adequately described for the period before 1927.[27] For the bulk of this material it is essential to use the contemporary registers and indexes of correspondence to identify documents relating to specific subjects or events. Do, of course, check the catalogue first to see if the relevant series has been catalogued in detail – whether in full or in part – for the period with which you are concerned. If, however, you are interested in only a very brief period in the history of one colony, or a single event for which you have a date, it is probably sensible to go straight to the correspondence itself, which is listed by date in the catalogue within each territorial, regional or subject record series.

The first series of registers of correspondence is CO 326 (1623–1849). The series contains registers compiled in the office of the Board of Trade, as well as later ones maintained in the War and Colonial Department (see chapters 4 and 5 for brief administrative histories of the departments responsible for colonial affairs). They vary considerably in arrangement and format, and it has been suggested that some of the earlier volumes cannot really be called registers, but are simply shelf lists of surviving papers.[28] Descriptions of some of the earlier registers (to 1782) are given in chapter 4.

After the abolition of the Board of Trade and the third post of secretary of state in 1782 there are gaps in CO 326, notably between 1783 and 1809, and again from 1818 to 1820. During those two periods the only finding aids available are the indexes and précis books (see below), which are not comprehensive for all territories, nor for the entire period. Furthermore, the volumes in CO 326 for the years 1810–17 are of little practical use. Described as journals of 'letters received and despatched' (with the exception of the last, CO 326/83, which covers just letters despatched) they record incoming correspondence on the left-hand side of the double-page spread, and outgoing on the right, with a brief note of the subject matter. They often provide cross-references between communications on the same or related subjects by use of an item number recorded in a column confusingly headed 'page'. Unfortunately, however, only the name of the correspondent is provided for each item; no indication is given of that person's position, whether the correspondence comes from a colony or from another government department, etc., or to what dependency it relates. It is, therefore, virtually impossible to use these journals to locate the correspondence itself.

From 1822 the registers in CO 326 are reasonably standard. Each covers a number of different colonies, reflecting the internal organisation of the office, and it is clear from the catalogue which is included in each, for example CO 326/101, Despatches: Ceylon, Mauritius, New South Wales, Tasmania (1825); CO 326/209, Despatches: Jamaica, Bahamas, Honduras, Guiana, St

[27] For examples of some recently enhanced catalogue entries see appendix 9.

[28] Thurston, vol. 1, p. 33.

Lucia, Mauritius (1834–5); and CO 326/212, Offices and Individuals: North America, Bermuda, Colonies General (1834–5). Each section within a register, i.e., the section for an individual colony, for a particular government department or for names of individuals, is contained within a 'cut' (as, for example, in a modern, indexed address book). The volume in figure 20 (CO 326/118) covers 'Offices and Individuals: West Indies' for 1826. Figure 21 shows a page from the cut for the Admiralty. Looking in the 'colony' column for 'Barbados' we find a reference to the refusal of Captain Gambier to hand over a member of his crew claimed as an escaped slave. Reference to appendix 1 shows that the Barbados correspondence for the period is in CO 28, and by using the online catalogue (or the paper version shelved at Kew) we can identify CO 28/99 as the volume containing 'offices and individuals' correspondence for 1826. In this volume also there is a cut for the Admiralty; within the cut, correspondence is arranged in date order (figure 22).[29]

Figure 21 also shows a number, on the extreme left, as allocated to each registered item of correspondence; a number which was also recorded on the communication itself. This appears to have been the practice from 1823,[30] but no complete numerical listing of incoming correspondence is held in TNA before 1849 (see 'daily registers' below).

Some registers in CO 326 contain references to countries for which there are no Colonial Office series of correspondence, e.g. CO 326/185 (1834-5), described in the catalogue as 'Africa, Mediterranean', includes Algiers, Morocco, Tripoli and Tunis. From 1804 to 1836 the War and Colonial Department was responsible for the supervision of British consuls in the Barbary States. Responsibility, together with related entry books and correspondence, was then transferred to the Foreign Office.[31]

The statistics of correspondence received recorded in the later 'daily registers' (see page 82) are not included in CO 326, but such statistics were sometimes compiled. CO 854/1, ff. 187–212, for example, gives numbers of letters received and sent in the years 1806, 1816 and 1824, together with numbers of clerks employed, as an indication of the increase of business within the department.

Indexes

The record series CO 714 contains indexed 'précis' of incoming correspondence dating overall from 1795 to 1874 but for most territories not starting until at least 1815. They are far from complete but can be extremely useful, especially if the researcher is looking for material on a particular subject over a period of time, or if the precise date of an event is unknown. Generally there are two types of document for each colony within the series: the collections of précis of correspondence, which are in fact copies of the so-called 'indexes' – in fact lists of correspondence

[29] Gambier's original letter to the Admiralty is in ADM 1/1866. In this period in-letters to the Admiralty in the series ADM 1 are arranged first by admirals' correspondence, and then by captains'. Knowing that Gambier is a captain allows one to go straight to the 1826 volume for 'Letters from captains, surnames G'. Indexes and digests of the papers in ADM 1 can be found in ADM 12, the contemporary finding aids.

[30] Thurston, vol. 1, p. 33

[31] See Michael Roper, *The Records of the Foreign Office, 1782–1968* (Public Record Office, 2002).

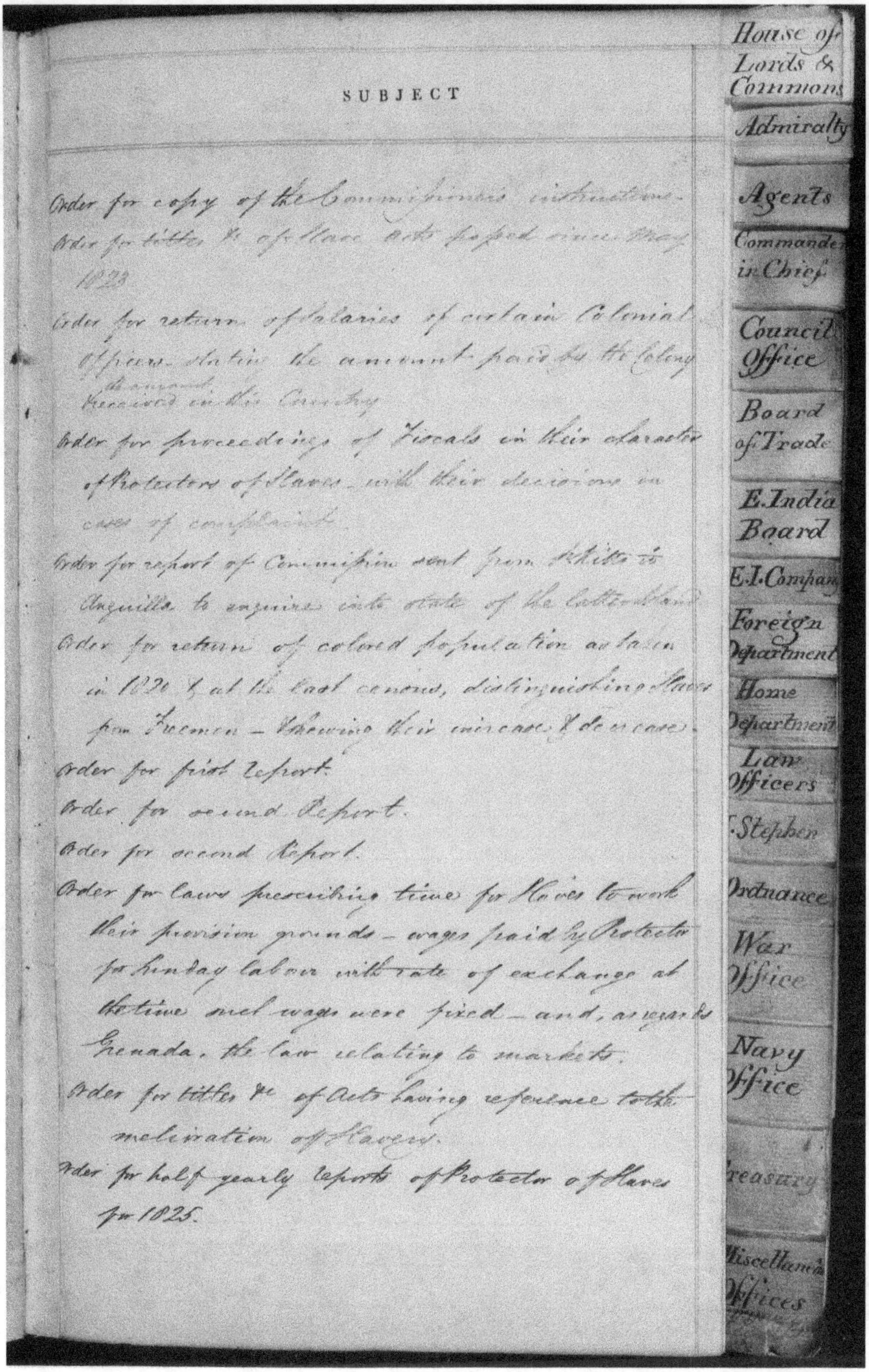

SUBJECT

Order for copy of the Commissioners' instructions.
Order for titles &c of Slave Acts passed since May 1823
Order for return of salaries of certain Colonial Officers stating the amount paid by the Colony & amount Received in this Country
Order for proceedings of Fiscals in their character of Protectors of Slaves with their decisions in cases of complaint.
Order for report of Commission sent from St Kitts to Anguilla to enquire into state of the latter Island
Order for return of colored population as taken in 1821 & at the last census, distinguishing Slaves from Freemen – shewing their increase & decrease.
Order for first Report.
Order for second Report.
Order for second Report.
Order for Laws prescribing time for Slaves to work their provision grounds – wages paid by Protector for Sunday labour with rate of exchange at the time such wages were fixed – and, as regards Grenada, the law relating to markets.
Order for titles &c of Acts having reference to the melioration of Slavery.
Order for half yearly Reports of Protector of Slaves for 1825.

House of Lords & Commons
Admiralty
Agents
Commander in Chief
Council Office
Board of Trade
E. India Board
E.I. Company
Foreign Department
Home Department
Law Officers
Stephen
Ordnance
War Office
Navy Office
Treasury
Miscellaneous Offices

Figure 20. CO 326/118, General Register: Offices and Individuals, West Indies, 1826. Showing the arrangement of the volume in 'cuts' for government departments and other organisations and officials.

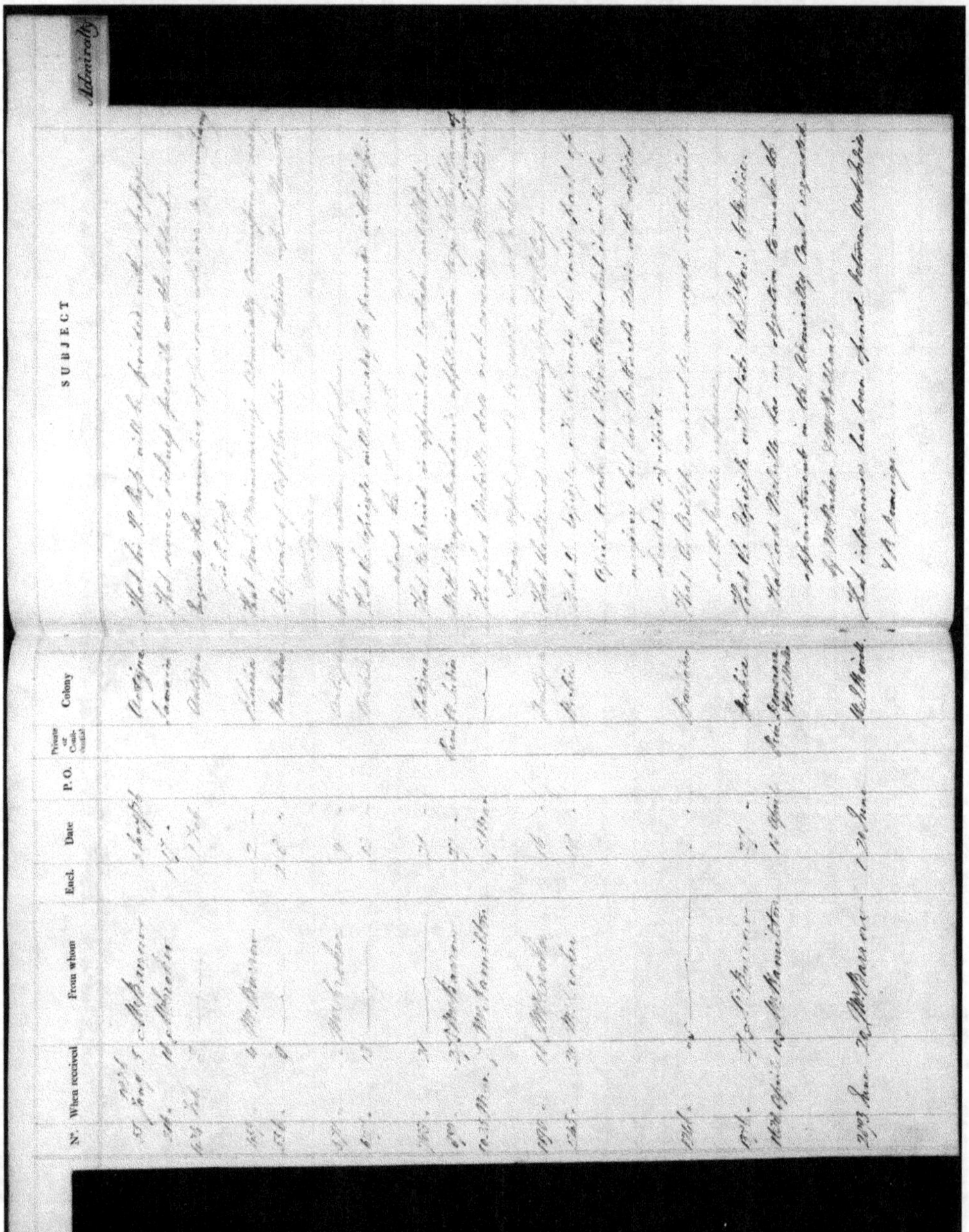

Figure 21. CO 326/118, General Register: Offices and Individuals, West Indies, 1826.
'Cut' for the Admiralty including entry (no. 556) referring to 'Refusal of Capt. Gambier to deliver up a Slave to Mr Tyne'.

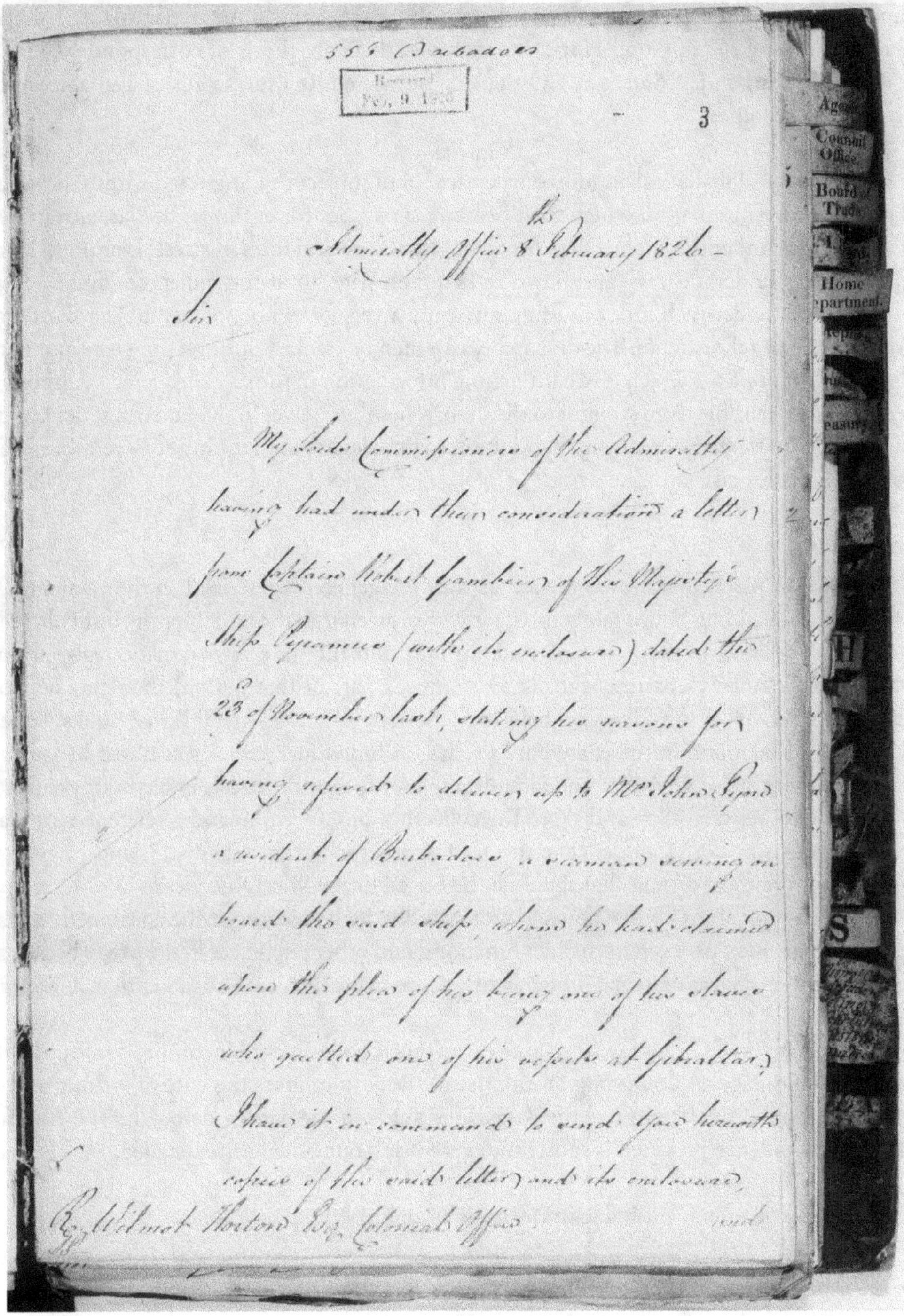

55? Barbadoes

Received Feb. 9 1826

3

Admiralty Office 8 February 1826 –

Sir

My Lords Commissioners of the Admiralty having had under their consideration a letter from Captain Robert Gambier of His Majesty's Ship Pyramus (with its enclosures) dated the 23rd of November last, stating his reasons for having refused to deliver up to Mr John Lynd a resident of Barbadoes, a seaman serving on board the said ship, whom he had claimed upon the plea of his being one of his slaves who quitted one of his vessels at Gibraltar, I have it in command to send you herewith copies of the said letter and its enclosures, and

R. Wilmot Horton Esq. Colonial Office

Figure 22. CO 28/99, fo. 3. Letter from the Admiralty forwarding and commenting on copies of correspondence from Captain Robert Gambier, Royal Navy, reporting his refusal to hand over an ordinary seaman, John Williams, claimed as an escaped slave.

– found in each volume of correspondence before about 1874; and an 'analytical' or 'alphabetical' index. So for the Cape of Good Hope, for example, there are précis of correspondence in CO 714/36–9 (1815–66) and an index in CO 714/40. See appendix 1 for details of available indexes for individual colonies.

The 'analytical' or 'alphabetical' indexes start with a list of subject headings used within the volume and give the page number on which each heading starts. So, for example, the Jamaica index in CO 714/ 89 lists under the letter 'D': debts, drought, duties and taxes, distress, Domingo St. and divorce; entries under 'distress' are shown as being on page 39 of the index (see figures 23 and 24). The entries under each index heading give only a very brief note of the subject matter and the date of relevant despatches. The despatches can then be tracked through the 'correspondence' volumes in CO 714/85–8 which give a little more information in the so-called 'précis', although it is perhaps more sensible to go straight to the despatches themselves in the Jamaica series CO 137. Figures 25 and 26 show the précis entry and the despatch described in the index as 'reimbursement of relief to 5 distressed Natives'.

Précis books

Précis books, or 'précis of correspondence' as they are generally described in the catalogue, are rarely referred to, and no doubt rarely used. However, given that they exist for the difficult period between the abolition of the Board of Trade in 1782 and the start of systematic registration in the War and Colonial Department in 1822 (or at least part of that period) they may be worth investigating. As well as the collection held in the series CO 324 (General Entry Books, Series I) they are also to be found in the entry books series for individual colonies as noted in appendix 1. Although there are some earlier and later examples, most of the précis books start about 1789 and continue to between 1807 and 1814. The collection in CO 324 includes references to places for which there is no correspondence in the 'CO' series, such as the Channel Islands, Egypt and Bengal, and it is almost certain that these can be traced to the War Office series WO 1. As noted elsewhere it did not always prove possible neatly to divide the records of the combined War and Colonial Department between its distinct functions, and other references in the précis books, and indeed in registers such as those in CO 326, may refer to material in a 'WO' rather than 'CO' series.

Like the 'journals' in CO 326 described above, the précis books record incoming correspondence on the left-hand page and outgoing on the right. The former gives the date of writing and the date of receipt, and the latter gives the date of writing and the date of despatch. The summary of the correspondence provided is sometimes very brief, but often quite detailed.

Précis books are readily identifiable in the online catalogue.

Registration of original correspondence 1849–1925

A new system of registration of correspondence was introduced in 1849/50 when a registrar was re-appointed and a central registry established as part of the general reforms taking place in the government service. It was a two stage system:

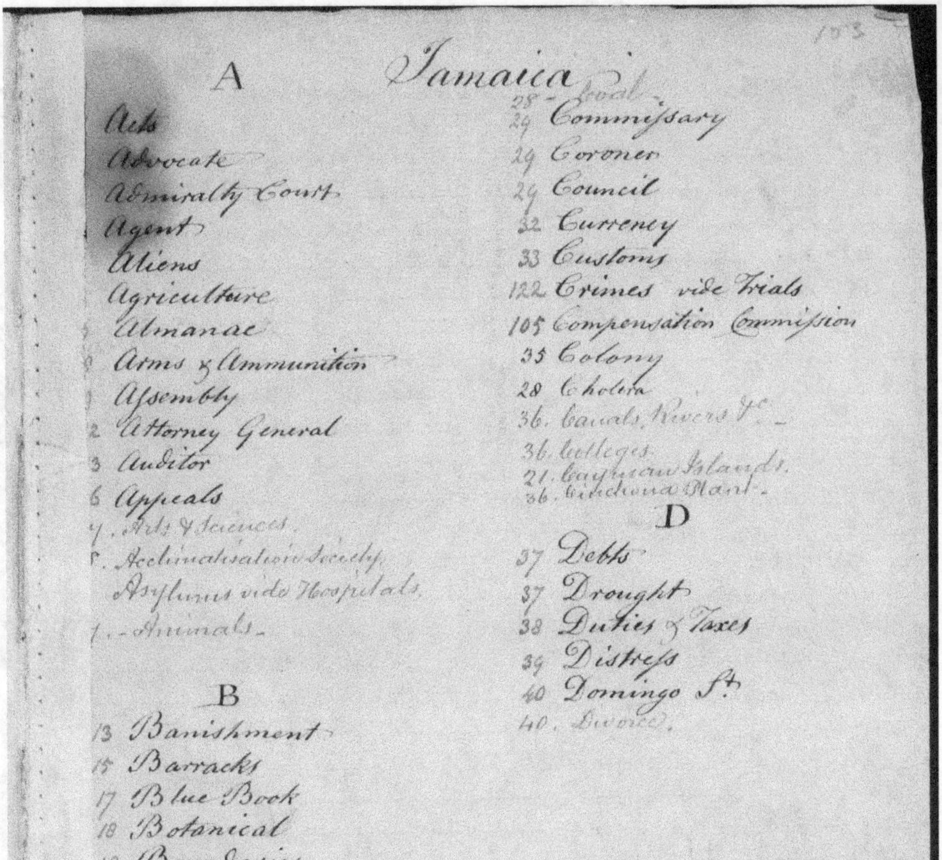
Jamaica

A
Acts
Advocate
Admiralty Court
Agent
Aliens
Agriculture
Almanac
Arms & Ammunition
Assembly
2 Attorney General
3 Auditor
6 Appeals
7. Arts & Sciences
8. Acclimatisation Society
Asylums vide Hospitals
1. Animals

B
13 Banishment
15 Barracks
17 Blue Book
18 Botanical
10 Boundaries
14 Banks
20 Buildings
16. Births & Deaths
20. Bavarians
20. Bridges

C
22 Chancery Court
22 Claims
23 Clergy
26 Clerk of the Crown
26 Coffee
27 Colonial Office
Consuls
Columbia

28 Coal
29 Commissary
29 Coroner
29 Council
32 Currency
33 Customs
122 Crimes vide Trials
105 Compensation Commission
35 Colony
28 Cholera
36. Canals, Rivers &c.
36. Colleges
21. Cayman Islands
36. Cinchona Plant

D
37 Debts
37 Drought
38 Duties & Taxes
39 Distress
40 Domingo St.
40. Divorce

E
42 Emigration & liberated Africans
117 Engineer vide Surveyor
43 Escheats
44 Estates & Plantations
45 Exports & Imports
44. Electors
44. Exhibition

Figure 23. CO 714/89, Jamaica: alphabetical index, 1815–70. Contents page showing subjects included under the letters 'A' to 'E'. Entries under 'Distress' are noted as being recorded on page 39.

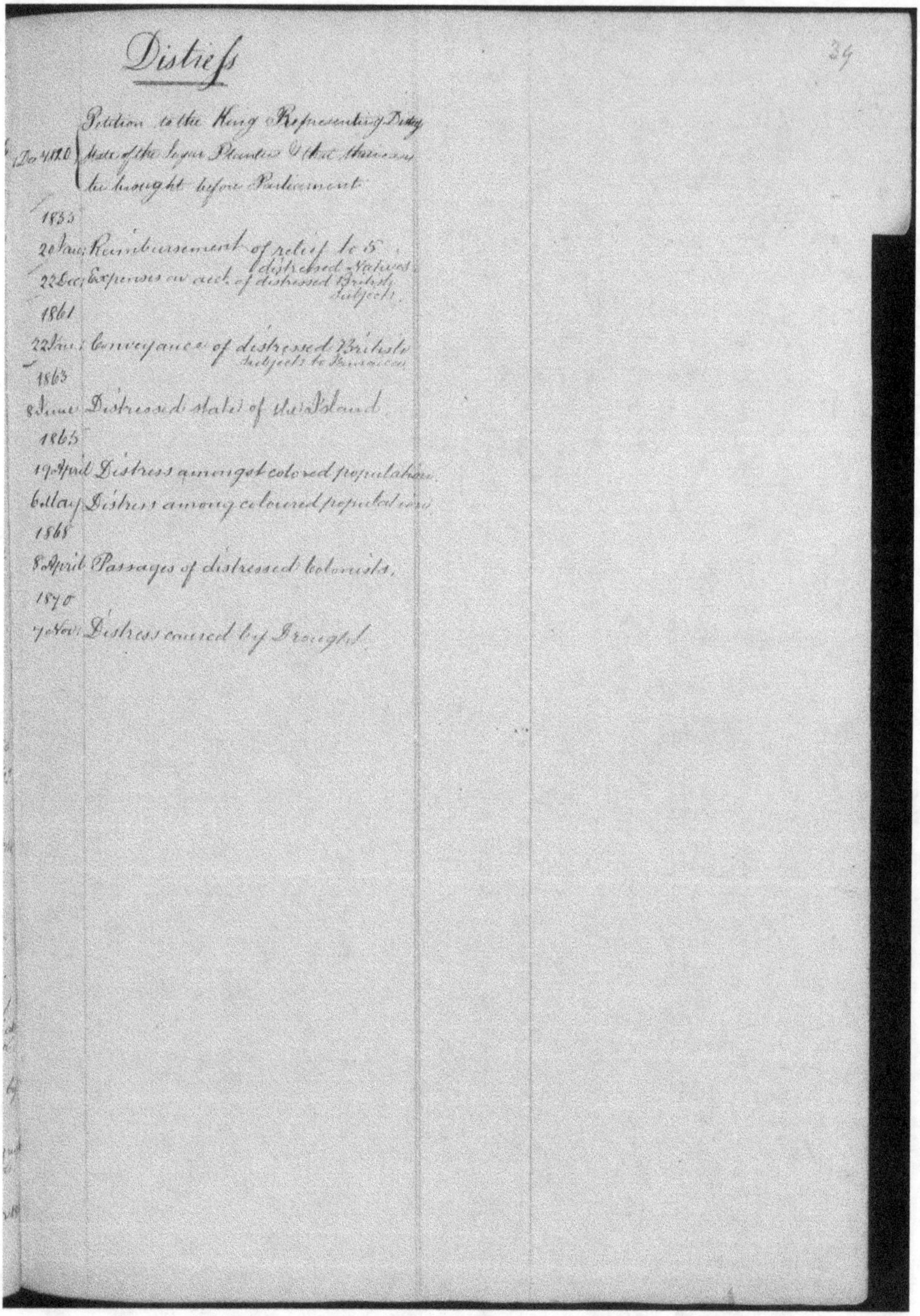

Distress

39

Dec 4 1820 Petition to the King Representing Distressed State of the Sugar Planters & that the same be brought before Parliament

1855

20 Jan. Reimbursement of relief to 5 distressed Natives

22 Dec. Expenses on acct. of distressed British subjects.

1861

22 Jan. Conveyance of distressed British subjects to Jamaica

1863

8 June Distressed state of the Island.

1865

19 April Distress amongst colored population.

6 May Distress among coloured population

1868

8 April Passages of distressed colonists.

1870

7 Nov. Distress caused by Drought.

Figure 24. CO 714/89, Jamaica: alphabetical index, 1815–70, p. 39.
Entries under the heading 'Distress' including reference to a despatch on the 'Reimbursement of relief to 5 distressed Natives' dated 20 January 1855.

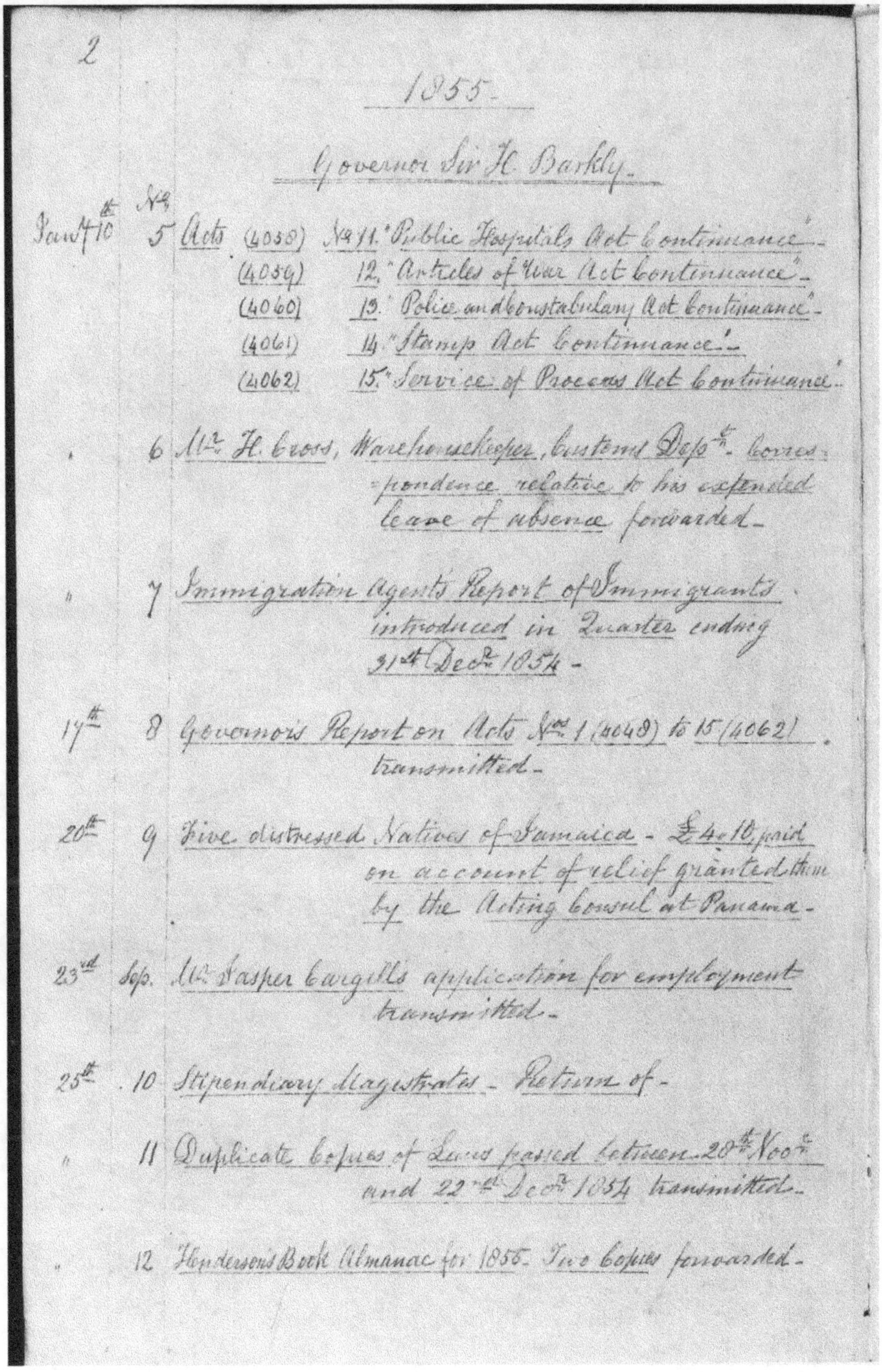

2

1855.

Governor Sir H. Barkly.

	No.			
Jan 4/10th	5	Acts	(4058)	No 11. "Public Hospitals Act Continuance".
			(4059)	12. "Articles of War Act Continuance".
			(4060)	13. "Police and Constabulary Act Continuance".
			(4061)	14. "Stamp Act Continuance".
			(4062)	15. "Service of Process Act Continuance".
"	6	Mr H. Cross, Warehousekeeper, Customs Dept. Correspondence relative to his extended leave of absence forwarded.		
"	7	Immigration Agent's Report of Immigrants introduced in Quarter ending 31st Decr 1854.		
17th	8	Governor's Report on Acts Nos 1 (4048) to 15 (4062) transmitted.		
20th	9	Five distressed Natives of Jamaica – £4.10 paid on account of relief granted them by the Acting Consul at Panama.		
23rd	Sep.	Mr Jasper Cargill's application for employment transmitted.		
25th	10	Stipendiary Magistrates – Return of.		
"	11	Duplicate Copies of Laws passed between 20th Novr and 22nd Decr 1854 transmitted.		
"	12	Henderson's Book Almanac for 1855. Two Copies forwarded.		

Figure 25. CO 714/87, Jamaica, Governor's correspondence, 1849–59. 'Précis' of the item concerning relief granted to five 'distressed Natives of Jamaica' as referred to in figures 24 and 26.

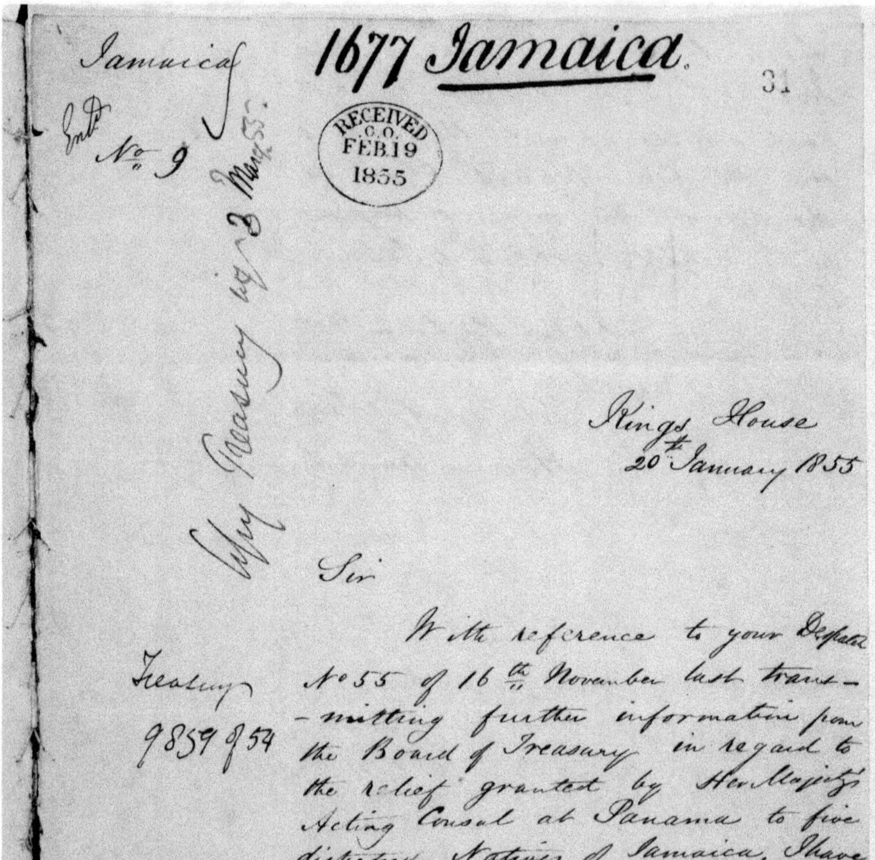

Jamaica

1677 Jamaica.

31

Entd

No 9

RECEIVED C.O. FEB 19 1855

Copy Treasury 27 March 55

Kings House
20th January 1855

Sir

With reference to your Despatch No 55 of 16th November last transmitting further information from the Board of Treasury in regard to the relief granted by Her Majesty's Acting Consul at Panama to five distressed Natives of Jamaica, I have the honor to state that my Executive Committee being satisfied that they were proper objects for relief, and that due caution will be observed in respect to [illegible] return Passages for those who go down to work on the Railway, advised me to pay the sum claimed – £4.10 – out of the Contingencies of the Civil List, secured by the Act for the better Government of the Island, in preference to renewing my application of last

Treasury 9859 of 54

The Right Honble Sir George Grey Bart G.C.B. &c &c

Figure 26. CO 137/326. Despatch concerning relief granted by the acting British consul at Panama to five 'distressed Natives of Jamaica' as referred to in figures 24 and 25.

1. 'Daily registers' or 'registers of daily correspondence' (CO 382, 1849–1929)

All incoming items of correspondence were recorded in these registers. Each item was given a running number, starting with '1' for the first item opened and registered on the first working day of January each year. This number was stamped or written onto the letter or despatch, any accompanying minute sheet, and often the enclosures too. It acts as a 'unique identifier' for the item, and cross-references to it among other papers will appear as 'number 26 of 1867' (or 26/67, or some similar form). As noted above, some system of general numbering was in existence from the 1820s, but no corresponding daily registers are held in TNA for the earlier period.

Figures 27 and 28 give examples of entries in the daily register. The column headed 'colony' in fact denotes the series of registers in which the item is to be registered at the second stage. It may be a subject series, rather than a colony series.

Inevitably the daily registers vary in format over the 75 or so years during which they were used. Two are described here.

CO 382/8, the register for 1855, is arranged in columns giving registered number, date (of writing), 'from whom', 'colony' and subject, plus additional columns showing the 'distribution' by Colonial Office department, i.e., the number of items of correspondence handled by each department. The printed distribution columns on each page are headed Australian, Mediterranean, North American, West Indian and Military, although a handwritten total at the end of the entries gives the final column as 'miscellaneous' rather than military.

11,918 letters were received during that year, divided between the departments as follows:

Departments	Number registered
Australian	2,628
Mediterranean	2,974
North American	2,926
West Indies	3,094
Miscellaneous	296
Total	11,918

In addition to the straight chronological and numerical listing of items received, at the end of the volume there are 'cuts' for government departments where entries repeat the information provided in the daily registration at the beginning of the volume, and use the numbers allocated in that first section. This would enable one to identify quickly correspondence received from the Admiralty on matters relating to Mauritius or St Helena, for example. Similarly there is a section indexing correspondence from individuals. Paradoxically, in this system it initially appears more

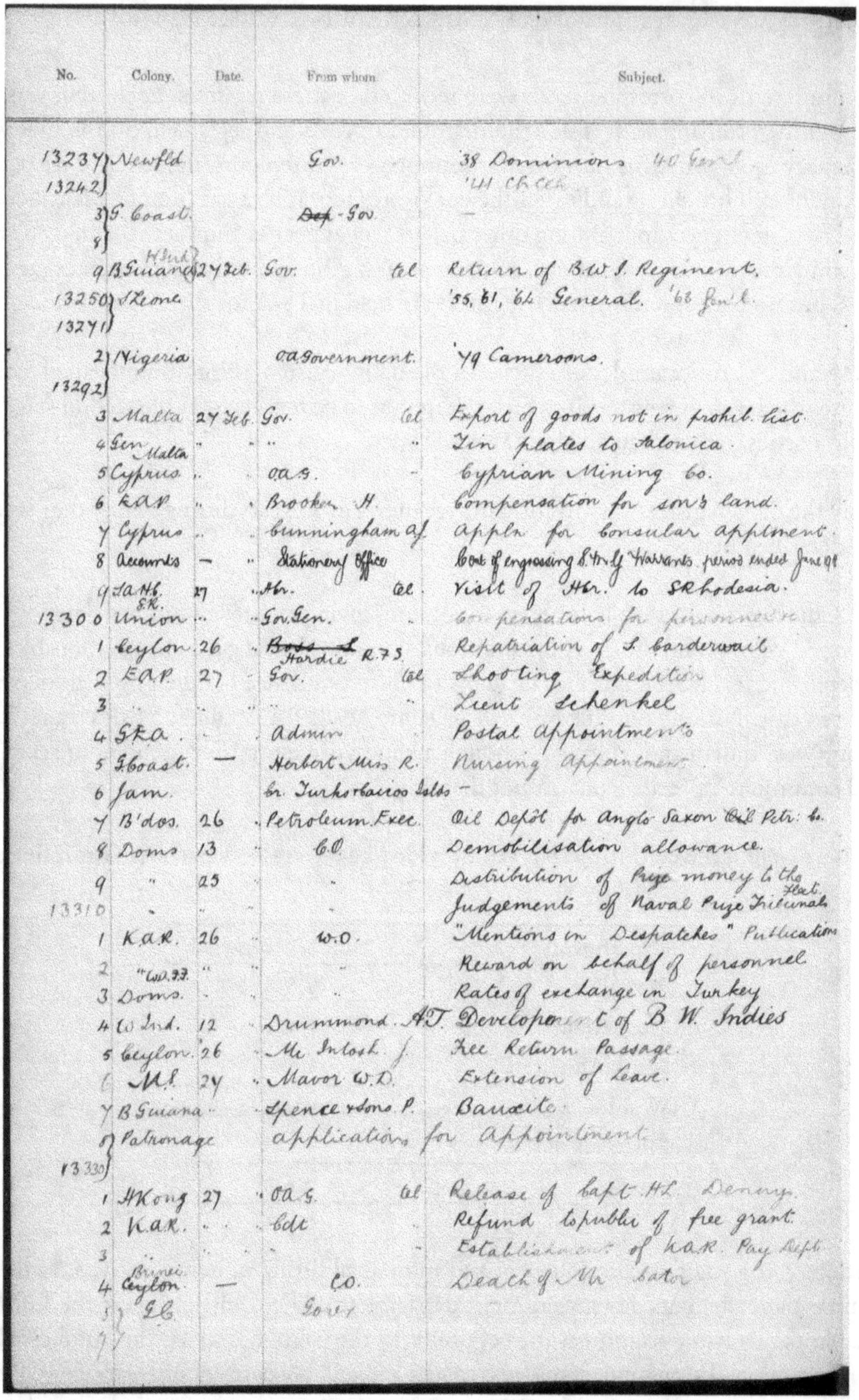

No.	Colony.	Date.	From whom.	Subject.
13237 / 13242	Newfld		Gov.	'38 Dominions '40 Genl '41 Chce
3 / 8	G. Coast		Dep.-Gov.	—
9	B Guiana (W Ind)	27 Feb.	Gov. tel	Return of B.W.I. Regiment.
13250 / 13271	S Leone			'55, 61, '64 General. '68 Genl.
2 / 13292	Nigeria		OA Government.	'79 Cameroons.
3	Malta	27 Feb.	Gov. tel	Export of goods not in prohib. list
4	Gen Malta	"	" "	Tin plates to Salonica.
5	Cyprus	"	OAG.	Cyprian Mining Co.
6	EAP	"	Brooke H.	Compensation for son's land.
7	Cyprus	"	Cunningham A.J.	Appln for Consular applmt
8	Accounts	—	Stationery Office	Cost of engrossing &c. of Warrants period ended June 1918
9	SA HC	27	Hr. tel	Visit of Hr. to S Rhodesia.
13300	Union S.K.	"	Gov. Gen.	Compensations for personnel &c
1	Ceylon	26	~~Boss~~ Hardie R.7.S.	Repatriation of S. Carderwail
2	EAP.	27	Gov. tel	Shooting Expedition
3	"	"	"	Lieut Schenkel
4	SKA.		Admin	Postal Appointments
5	G Coast	—	Herbert Miss R.	Nursing Appointment
6	Jam.		Cr. Turks & Caicos Islds	—
7	B'dos.	26	Petroleum Exec.	Oil Depot for Anglo Saxon Oil Petr: Co.
8	Doms	13	C.O.	Demobilisation allowance.
9	"	25	"	Distribution of Prize money to the Fleet.
13310	"	"	"	Judgements of Naval Prize Tribunals
1	K.A.R.	26	W.O.	"Mentions in Despatches" Publication
2	" W.A.F.F.	"	"	Reward on behalf of personnel
3	Doms.	"	"	Rates of exchange in Turkey
4	W Ind.	12	Drummond A.T.	Development of B.W. Indies
5	Ceylon	26	Mc Intosh J.	Free Return Passage.
6	M.S.	24	Mavor W.D.	Extension of Leave.
7	B Guiana		Spence & Sons P.	Bauxite
8 / 13330	Patronage		application for	Appointment.
1	H Kong	27	OAG. tel	Release of Capt H.L. Denny.
2	K.A.R.	"	Cdt	Refund to public of free grant.
3			"	Establishment of KAR Pay Dept
4	Brunei Ceylon	—	CO.	Death of Mr [illegible]
5	EC		Gov.	

Figure 27. CO 382/73. Layout of a page from the daily register, or register of daily correspondence, for 1919.

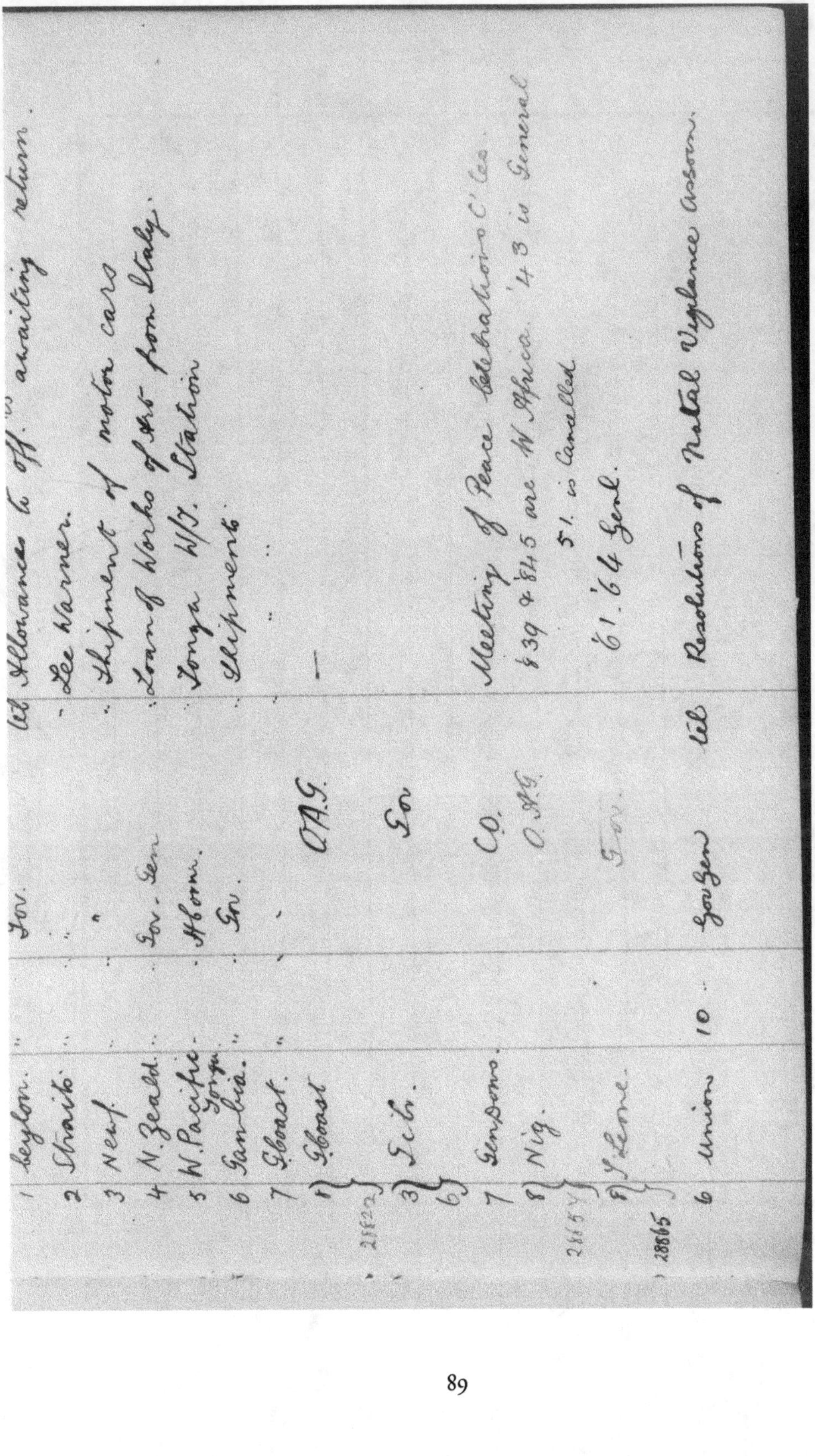

Figure 28. CO 382/73. Extract from the 1919 daily register showing items of correspondence received from Nigeria but subsequently registered under 'West Africa' and 'General'.

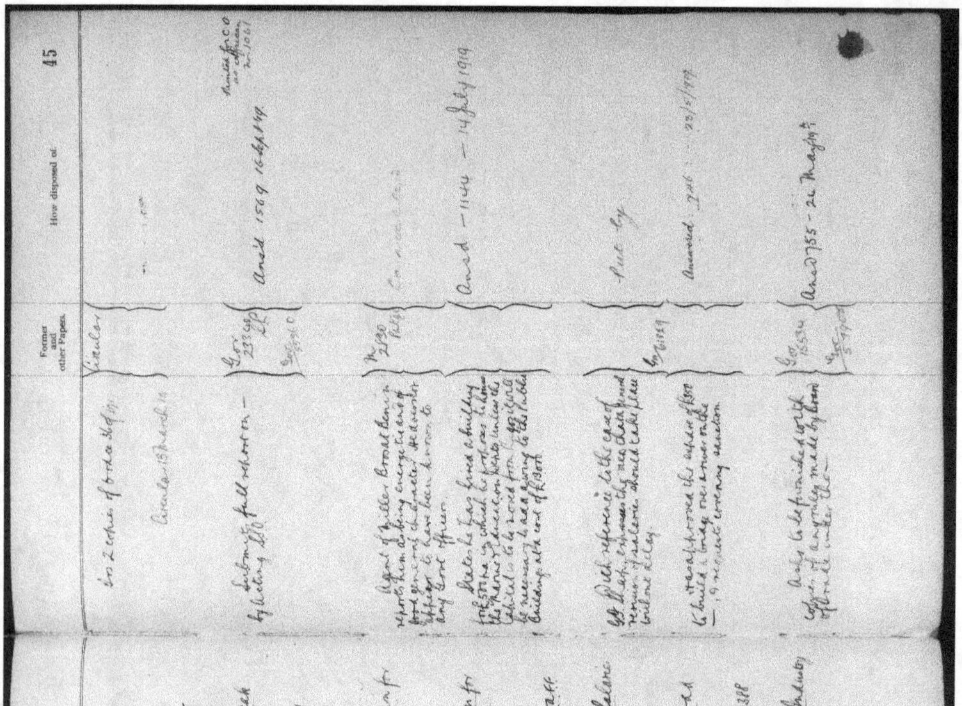

Figure 29. CO 763/7, Nigeria register of correspondence, 1919.
Showing double-page layout in the type of register of correspondence used from 1849/50 to 1926.

difficult to locate correspondence from governors which is recorded only in the first section and is not indexed. The reason for the emphasis on indexing correspondence from 'offices' and individuals is clear, however, when one considers that correspondence from the governor of, say, Sierra Leone, is most likely to be found in the series for that colony (and if it is not, a cross-reference will be provided in the registers of correspondence described below). A letter from the Disabled Men's Fund or from Mrs Jane Smith could be anywhere.

CO 382/73, the daily register for 1919, is similarly arranged in columns giving number, 'colony', date (of writing), 'from whom' and subject. The 'distribution' columns no longer appear on each page, but that information is provided as 'statistics of registration' at the end of the first part of the register where a page is allocated for each month with total numbers recorded for each day. The distribution columns used by this date are: West Africa, Nigeria, West Africa Frontier Force, King's African Rifles, Military, East Africa, Mediterranean, Eastern, West Indies, South Africa, North America, Australasia, Dominions, Accounts, Chief Clerk, Honours, General and Patronage, reflecting the increased complexity of the office's internal organisation. In this year the total number of items received had increased to 74,060.

The index of correspondence from government departments described above for 1855 is not included in the 1919 volume, although cuts for 'other government offices' and 'miscellaneous' are. The first includes departments with which the Colonial Office had little correspondence – for example, during this year, the Air Ministry and the Ministry of Food – and the second includes organisations such as the Anti-Slavery Society, the Disabled Men's Fund, the Norwegian Whaling Commission and the Liverpool Chamber of Commerce (to take a few examples at random). The alphabetical index for individuals continues as before.

Indexes to CO 382 for the years 1901–10 can be found separately in CO 668, rather than within the daily registers themselves.

It is rarely necessary to use the daily registers, but it is helpful to be aware of their existence and to know that they give rise to the registered number of each item of correspondence. An example of when they *are* needed is if you know that a despatch or letter was sent to the Colonial Office from a particular colony, organisation or individual on, or about, a certain date, but have not been able to locate it in the obvious series of correspondence. For example, in the example shown in figure 28 the Nigeria (Nig.) entries 28,828–57 have been bracketed together; a comment to the right notes that 28,839 has been treated as of more general 'West Africa' relevance, and 28,843 as falling within the responsibilities of the General Department. These would need to be tracked through the appropriate registers (CO 555 and CO 378 respectively) and the correspondence, if it has survived, would be in CO 554 and CO 323. The daily registers may also be of help if cross references within the correspondence cannot be interpreted. For example, a researcher using Southern Nigeria correspondence for 1908 was unable to follow up the cross reference 'T.32070 W.Afr'. Logically this would appear to refer to a paper in the 'individuals' section of the West Africa correspondence for 1908, but that series does not commence until 1911. Reference to the daily register for 1908 showed that the correspondence was in the Gold Coast series. Or, of course, you may wish to use the daily registers to analyse the type of queries coming from individuals, or the volume of correspondence dealt with.

2. Registers of correspondence

The second part of the registration procedure introduced in 1849 involved entering details of all incoming items of correspondence into an appropriate 'register of correspondence'. These registers are arranged in record series devoted to correspondence from, or relating to, an individual colony or region, or to a particular subject such as 'Honours' (CO 728) or 'Overseas Settlement' (CO 791), i.e., they usually match the individual correspondence series. Sometimes this is not the case; for example the correspondence for St Vincent (CO 260) is registered in the Windward Islands register (CO 376). Every attempt has been made to explain such exceptions in appendices 1 and 2, which list all registers of correspondence under the appropriate colony or subject heading.

Each register (which may cover one year or more depending on the amount of correspondence to be registered) is arranged in three sections following the division of correspondence into 'despatches', 'offices' and 'individuals'. The first section is arranged in chronological order by date of receipt in the Colonial Office. The second section is divided into a number of 'cuts' for correspondence from government departments and other organisations, for example Foreign Office, Treasury, 'miscellaneous offices' or 'miscellaneous institutions'. These 'cuts' are not standard; for example one register may have a separate cut for the Admiralty, whereas in another there may be so little correspondence from that department that it is described in the 'miscellaneous offices' cut, or, of course, there may be none at all. The third section is arranged in alphabetical order by surname of correspondent.

Figure 29 shows the layout of the registers of correspondence for the period 1849–1926. One entry covers the double-page spread. Columns, from left to right, provide the following information:

1. Date of receipt in Colonial Office
2. Colonial Office registered number (i.e., number taken from daily register)
3. Name of correspondent
4. Date on which the despatch or letter was written
5. Reference allocated by the governor or other correspondent (governors' ordinary despatches are numbered; secret despatches, confidential despatches, 'separate' despatches and telegrams are not)
6. Subject of correspondence (this column is itself divided into two; the brief description of the subject given on the left is usually, but not always, expanded on the right)
7. Cross-references to previous and subsequent papers on the same or a closely related subject (see below for an explanation of this system)
8. A note of the action taken, i.e., whether answered (if so, date and reference number of the reply), re-registered in another series, referred elsewhere or 'put away' as no action was required.

We saw above examples in the daily register (figure 28) of despatches from the governor of Nigeria being registered under 'West Africa' or 'General'. Such correspondence is sometimes first registered in the more obvious colony series, i.e., in this case 'Nigeria'. Figure 30 shows an item which has initially been registered under 'Nigeria', but subsequently re-registered under 'Cameroon' where the cross-references and disposal will be shown.

Indexed registers

The third section of each register – 'individuals' – was initially intended, as its name implies, simply to record correspondence to the Colonial Office from individuals. After 1868 this section also became, at least in principle, an index to individuals and subjects mentioned in correspondence. As an index it is certainly not complete, and it appears that practice varied between the registries, or perhaps between individual clerks. For example, the Jamaica register for 1912–15 (CO 351/21) indexes only names of individuals referred to elsewhere in the volume, whereas the Nigeria register for 1915 (CO 763/3) also indexes subject matter such as loan requirements, light dues, Lagos waterworks, Lands Committee, locomotive drivers, Legislative Council, Lagos harbour works and Lokoja Native Council. The indexes may, however, assist in searching. As can be seen in the example (figure 31), if an entry in the 'individuals' section extends across the double page it does indeed refer to a letter from an individual. If, however, the entry is intended as an index to another part of the register it will cover only the first five columns, i.e., date, number, name, date and subject, with the first column indicating the section within the register in which the full entry will be found, for example 'Gov.' (Governor) or 'C.A.' (Crown agents) rather than the date of receipt; the second column gives the 'unique identifier' taken from the daily register.

Registers of non-registered letters

These registers, described in the catalogue as 'registers of un-registered correspondence' (CO 652, three volumes, 1886–1927), were used to record letters from individuals in cases where it was not initially clear how they should be treated. They give name of correspondent, date received, colony (if stated), subject, 'when disposed of' and 'how disposed of'. Many correspondents wrote on subjects not within the remit of the Colonial Office, and their letters were referred to other UK or overseas departments or institutions as appropriate. Others asked for information such as the addresses of named officials, and were answered. A note at the beginning of CO 652/2 refers to an instruction that non-registered items 'can be torn up'. It should be assumed therefore that they have not survived.

A fourth volume in the series, CO 652/4 (1909–12), relates specifically to correspondence concerning personnel of the West Africa Frontier Force and King's African Rifles.

How to find the 'original correspondence'

Examples in this section come from the Nigeria register for 1919 (CO 763/7) as shown in figure 32. As it proved impossible to find a double-page spread in a register which included examples of all the various types of entry requiring explanation, this is a compilation of scattered entries.

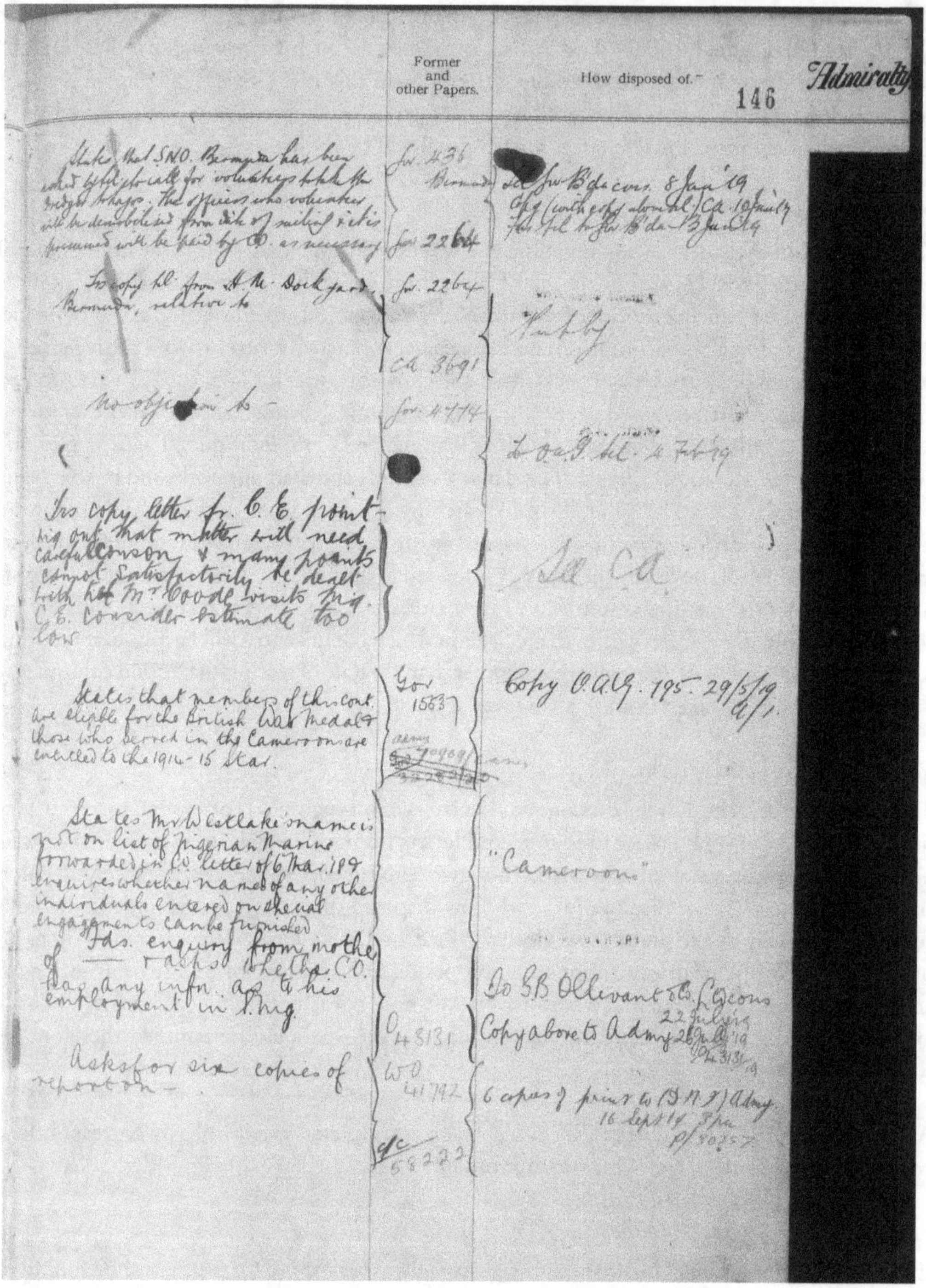

Figure 30. CO 763/7, Nigeria register of correspondence, 1919.
Including entry for correspondence concerning a Mr Westlake which was initially registered in the Nigeria register, but subsequently re-registered under 'Cameroon'.

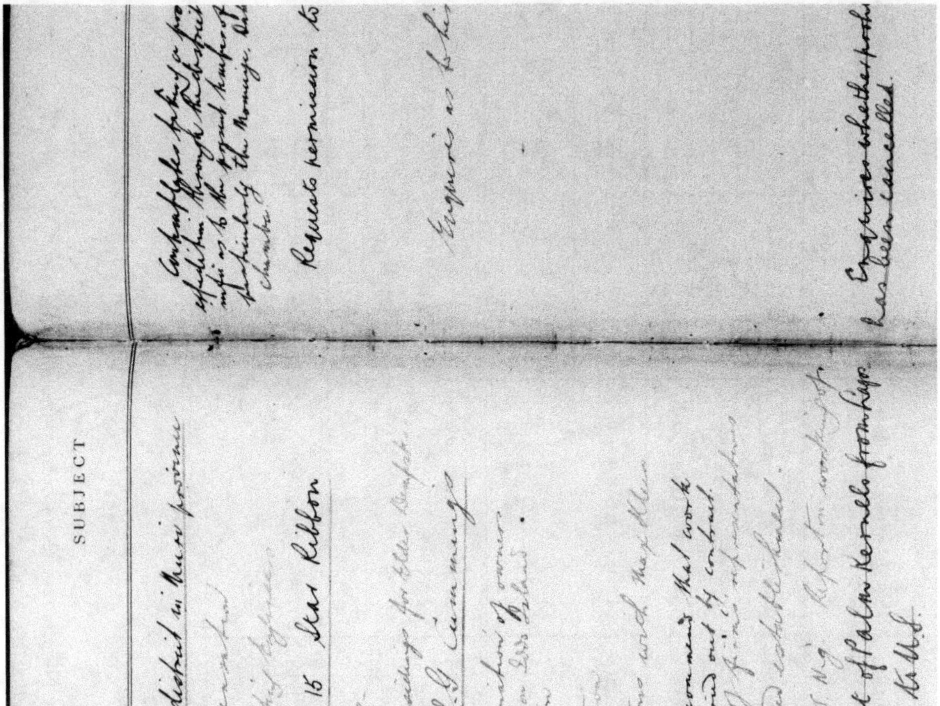

Figure 31. CO 763/7, Nigeria register of correspondence, 1919. Showing the way in which the 'individuals' section of the registers of correspondence was sometimes used as an index to other entries within the same register. Such cross-references are not carried over to the right-hand page; entries for correspondence from individuals are.

Registry		Name	Date	No.	SUBJECT		Former and other papers	*How disposed of*
Date 1919	No.							
28 Feb " "	13285	O.A.G. Moorhouse	[8 Feb.] 9 "	143 144	late C. Ungebauer R. Nicol 4026 W.A.	Fds. copy of proceedings ~~at~~ inquest on –	MI 863 MGO/32153	To P. of W. Dept. 10 Mch '19 **+ 44446/14**
3 May	26743	S. [O.A.G. Boyle]	31 Mch.	Secret	Civil Disturbances Scheme of Organisation	Trs. report of committee apptd. to consider a scheme of organisation for use in civil disturbances Secret Circular 11 Nov 1918	Circular Gov/45224/20	Ans'd Sec. 4 Dec '19
13 May	28850	[Boyle] PRINTED FOR USE OF *AFRICAN No. 1061* COLONIAL OFFICE	25 Apl.	383	Influenza Outbreak	Submits full report on – by Acting S.S.O.	Gov 23340 SL Gov/55360	Ans'd 1569 16 Sept'19 Printed for C.O. as African no. 1061
5 Aug	45205	D. C. Cameron for O.A.G. **// DESTROYED UNDER STATUTE //**	10 July	637	Naval Ratings buried in Lagos	Steps are being taken to erect crosses over the graves	Circ of 15 May Gov/46727/18 MO/35231/24 Nig	Copy to Admy. – 22 Aug '19 (Gov/45479/19 L'wds)
3 Dec.	68883	[Gov. Clifford]	31 Oct.	1001	Report on the Blue Book, 1918	Trs. –	Gov/37804 (B.B.) Gov/23331 (B.B. Report) Gov/61971/20	PRINTED FOR PARLIAMENT Colonial Reports. Annual 1030 Put by

Figure 32. A compilation of entries from the Nigeria register of correspondence for 1919, CO 763/7, selected to illustrate particular points in using the registers.

Once you have found a reference in the register to an item of correspondence you wish to see, two key pieces of information from the register are required to locate it: first, the category of correspondence, i.e., whether it is from a governor (a despatch), from a government department or other organisation ('office' or 'institution') or from an individual; second, the date on which the despatch or letter was *written* (i.e., the date given in column 4, *not* the date given in column 1 which is the date of receipt in the Colonial Office).

With this information, go to the catalogue for the relevant correspondence series (if the series is not known, consult appendix 1). Using the examples shown in figure 32 despatches and letters can be traced to CO 583, Nigeria Original Correspondence, as follows. Figure 33 is an extract from the former catalogue entry for CO 583 showing volumes dated 1919; the new catalogue presents this information in a slightly different format. Note that the correspondence is divided into despatches, offices and institutions, and individuals. Where these categories are further divided because of the bulk of correspondence the different volumes are identified by date in the case of despatches, by name or category in the case of offices and institutions, and by initial letter in the case of individuals. The numbers on the left-hand side under 'reference' are the individual volume numbers required, with the series number, for ordering; for example CO 583/72 for the first 1919 volume shown. Using the online catalogue rather than the paper copies housed at Kew you can use the advanced search facility to search on 'despatches' (or 'offices' or 'individuals'), restricting your search, in this example, to 1919 and to CO 583.

Note that 'despatches' in particular are often arranged in a number of volumes – in the case of Nigeria there are nine for the year 1919. For this reason it is essential to make careful note of the date of the despatch given in the register. Using figure 32 again, the despatch concerning an outbreak of influenza was written on 25 April. Look for it in CO 583/74 which covers 22 March to 30 April 1919. See figure 34, part of the contents list, and figure 35, the first page of the despatch itself.[32] A common mistake is to use the date of receipt, in this case 13 May. This would result in requesting CO 583/75, and not finding the despatch.

The contents list within each volume of correspondence will help in locating an individual despatch or letter, although it may be necessary to spend some time trawling through the volume. The process is much easier after the introduction of standard minute sheets in the late 1860s as they provide a clear marker between items. Note that the contents lists use the despatch numbers allocated by the governors' staffs – as noted in column 4 of the register – rather than the registered numbers allocated in the Colonial Office.

Cross-references in the registers of correspondence

To find the first reference to the subject matter sought it is often necessary simply to trawl through the register (although see note above on the partial indexes sometimes provided in the 'individuals' section).

[32] The despatch is marked up for printing. See pp. 101–4.

Catalogue Reference	Title/Scope and Content	Covering Dates
CO 583/72	Despatches.	1919 Jan. 1 - 21
CO 583/73	Despatches.	1919 Jan. 22 - Mar. 21
CO 583/74	Despatches.	1919 Mar. 22 - Apr. 30
CO 583/75	Despatches.	1919 May 1 - June 14
CO 583/76	Despatches.	1919 June 15 - Aug. 21
CO 583/77	Despatches.	1919 Aug. 22 - Sept. 30
CO 583/78	Despatches.	1919 Oct.
CO 583/79	Despatches.	1919 Nov. 1-24
CO 583/80	Despatches.	1919 Nov. 25- Dec. 31
CO 583/81	Offices.	1919
CO 583/82	Individuals, A - K.	1919
CO 583/83	Individuals, L - Z.	1919

Figure 33. Extract from TNA's catalogue showing volumes (pieces) of CO 583, Nigeria original correspondence, for 1919. The new version of the catalogue displays the same information in a different format.

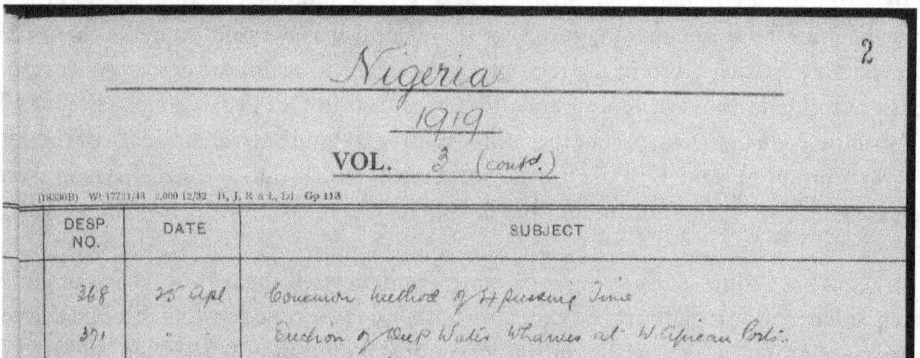

Nigeria
1919
VOL. 3 (contd.)
2

(18330B) Wt 17771/43 2,000 12/32 H, J, R & L, Ltd Gp 113

DESP. NO.	DATE	SUBJECT
368	25 Apl	Common method of expressing Time
371	"	Erection of Deep Water Wharves at W. African Ports.
375	"	Through Booking &c with E. D. & Co
376	"	Port Harcourt: Harbour Works
383	"	Influenza Outbreak
387	"	Office accommodn for Govt Depts in Lagos
390	"	Gen. Revision of Salaries in the Civil Service
Conf. A	"	Upper Transport Service
" B	"	Pay of West African Civil Officials attd to W.A.F.F.
403	30	Deficiencies in Railway Stores at Port Harcourt.

Figure 34. CO 583/74, Nigeria original correspondence, despatches, March to April 1919. Part of the contents list including reference to the despatch on the influenza outbreak referred to in figure 35.

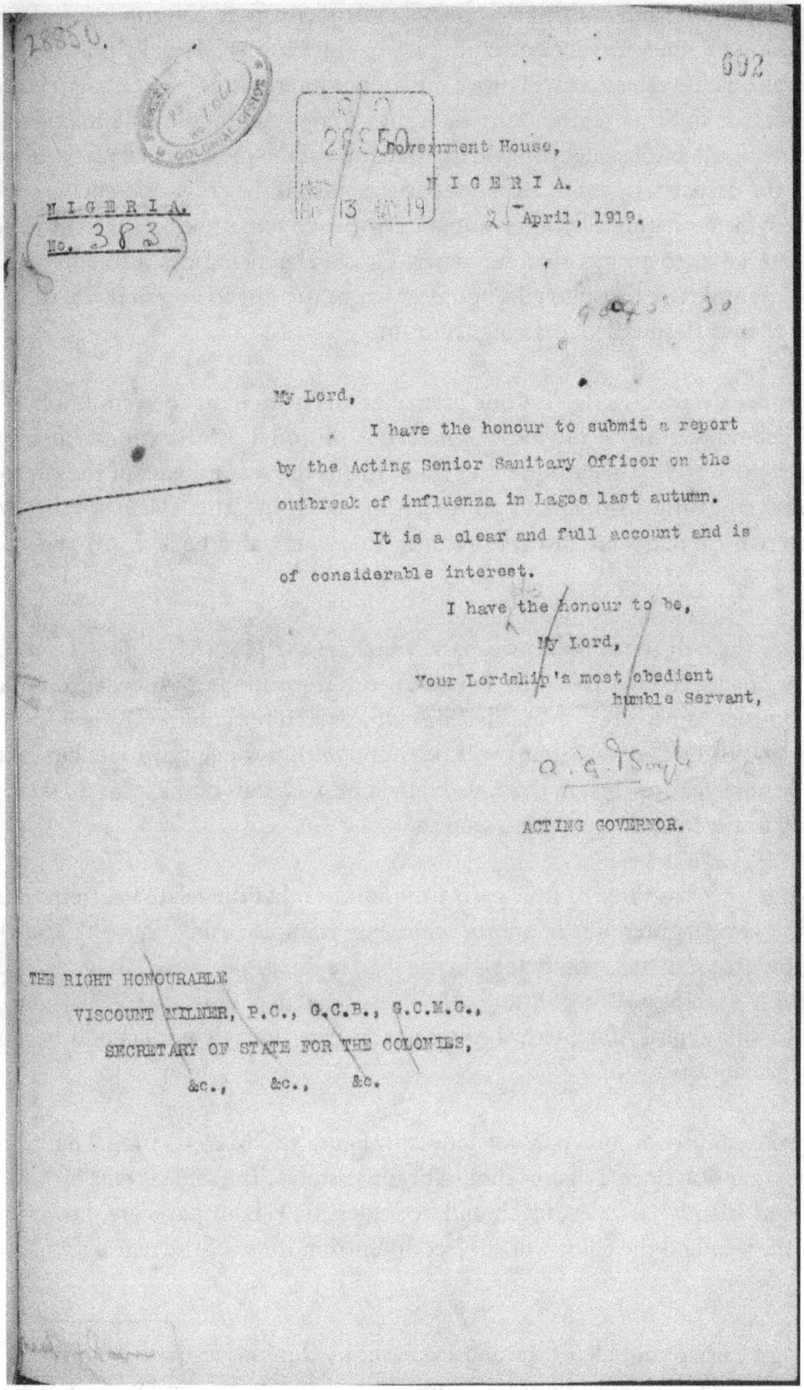

28850.

692

28850

Government House,

NIGERIA.

13 MAY 19

NIGERIA.

No. 383

25 April, 1919.

My Lord,

I have the honour to submit a report by the Acting Senior Sanitary Officer on the outbreak of influenza in Lagos last autumn.

It is a clear and full account and is of considerable interest.

I have the honour to be,

My Lord,

Your Lordship's most obedient humble Servant,

A. G. Boyle

ACTING GOVERNOR.

THE RIGHT HONOURABLE

VISCOUNT MILNER, P.C., G.C.B., G.C.M.G.,

SECRETARY OF STATE FOR THE COLONIES,

&c., &c., &c.

Figure 35. CO 583/74, fo. 692. Despatch from the acting governor of Nigeria covering report of an influenza outbreak. The diagonal line in the left-hand margin indicates the presence of an enclosure. The despatch is marked up for the printer.

Once a first reference is found, use of the 'former and other papers' column in a register will allow the identification of other relevant correspondence. This process is usually quite straightforward although occasionally a reference will prove difficult to interpret. It is essential to remember that cross-references are to other register entries. It may sometimes be possible to go straight to the correspondence itself, but usually you will not have one of the most crucial pieces of information – the date of the despatch or letter. Experience suggests that the cross-referencing was done very efficiently, but in the nature of things human error may sometimes have led to the omission of related material or to an incorrect reference. Cross-referencing can also cover quite lengthy periods. For example the first entry in figure 32 (from the Nigeria register for 1919) includes a cross-reference to correspondence dating from 1914.

Cross-references always give the 'unique identifier' of the item of correspondence referred to (i.e., the number taken from the daily register). Additional information is also provided to narrow down the search. The 'unique identifier' forms the second part of the cross-reference. The first part takes the form of an abbreviation denoting the writer of the despatch or letter. These two elements are always present. There may also be a third, and sometimes a fourth.

Figure 32 gives three of the simple, two-part references: MI/863, MGO/32153 and Gov/55360. The abbreviations stand respectively for 'Miscellaneous Institutions', 'Miscellaneous Government Offices' (an unusual form; 'MO', 'Miscellaneous Offices', is more common) and 'Governor'. More information about the first two items will be found within the appropriate cut in the second section of the same register, i.e., in this case Nigeria 1919. Details of the item marked 'Governor' will be found in the first, 'Despatches', section.

If the cross-reference has three or four parts this indicates that the related correspondence is not entered in the same register, but in another one. For example (using figure 32 again) the cross-reference 'Gov/45224/20' tells you to look in the 1920 register for Nigeria; 'Nigeria' is understood because there is nothing to the contrary. The cross-reference 'Gov/23340/SL' is an instruction to look in the 1919 register for Sierra Leone; in this case '1919' is understood because there is nothing to the contrary.

There are two examples of four-part references in figure 32. 'MO/35231/24/Nig.' is, in fact, an unnecessary expansion since 'Nigeria' should be understood. The same is true of 'Gov/45479/19/L'wds [Leeward Islands]' since '1919' should be understood. Four parts are, however, necessary where both the year and the colony or subject differ from those of the register you are currently using.

Most, although perhaps not all, of the abbreviations used in the registers are given at the end of this section. A single letter, for example 'B' or 'W', refers to correspondence from an individual whose name begins with that letter, and the papers should of course be traced in the 'individuals' section of both the register and the volume of correspondence.

Confidential and secret correspondence

From about 1872 until 1926, and again from the mid 1940s, much correspondence classified as confidential or secret was removed from the main series of original correspondence and put into the series CO 537, Confidential General and Confidential Original Correspondence.[33] It is not clear at what stage, or by whom, the decision was taken that a despatch classified as confidential or secret by a governor or other correspondent should be filed separately. There is certainly a substantial quantity of both types of despatch among the main colony and subject series of correspondence. Thurston notes that by 1888, 'Any paper that reached the registry in an envelope marked confidential was taken unopened to a private secretary, who decided whether it was to be registered in the open register or secretly'. She notes also that the former meaning of the words 'secret' and 'confidential' were reversed in that year.[34] An example of a secret despatch which was removed to CO 537 is shown among the register items in figure 32 – the secret despatch on the subject of civil disturbances which now has the reference CO 537/842. Between 1926 and the early 1940s, however, secret correspondence has been placed in the appropriate colony or subject record series rather than being extracted to CO 537. CO 537 is fully listed in the catalogue; you should remember its existence if you are failing to find papers in the relevant country or subject series as it often contains material of particular importance. For example the series includes over 100 files relating to Palestine in the periods 1921–6 and 1942–9, covering subjects such as illegal immigration, arms trafficking, 'colonial renegades' and the Anglo-American Committee on Palestine.

CO 537 also contains a collection of correspondence relating to the construction of the Uganda Railway (CO 537/50–88, 1895–1905); its presence here is unexplained. Other records relating to the railway are in CO 614; both collections are registered in CO 615.

Registers of correspondence relating to CO 537 are held by TNA for the period 1865–1938 only in CO 694; later volumes have not yet been transferred. They are described as 'secret', rather than the 'confidential' used for the related series of correspondence.

Printing of correspondence

Looking again at the example of register entries provided in figure 32, you will see stamped items indicating that correspondence has been printed. There are two examples here, 'Printed for use of Colonial Office', and 'Printed for Parliament'.[35]

The first refers to the Colonial Office 'confidential print'. Important papers were printed for ease of circulation within the Colonial Office, or for the information of the Cabinet or other government departments as appropriate. This particular item, 'African no. 1061', can be found in CO 879/118/15. If confidential print exists it is sensible to consult it as it often brings together a variety of papers from different Colonial Office sources and thus provides a good shortcut into a particular subject.

[33] As is explained in the rules governing correspondence in appendix 5, a regulation of 1871 laid down that 'confidential' was a more restricted classification than 'secret'.

[34] Thurston, vol. 1, p. 50.

[30] The actual appearance of the stamps used in the Colonial Office can be seen in figures 29 and 35.

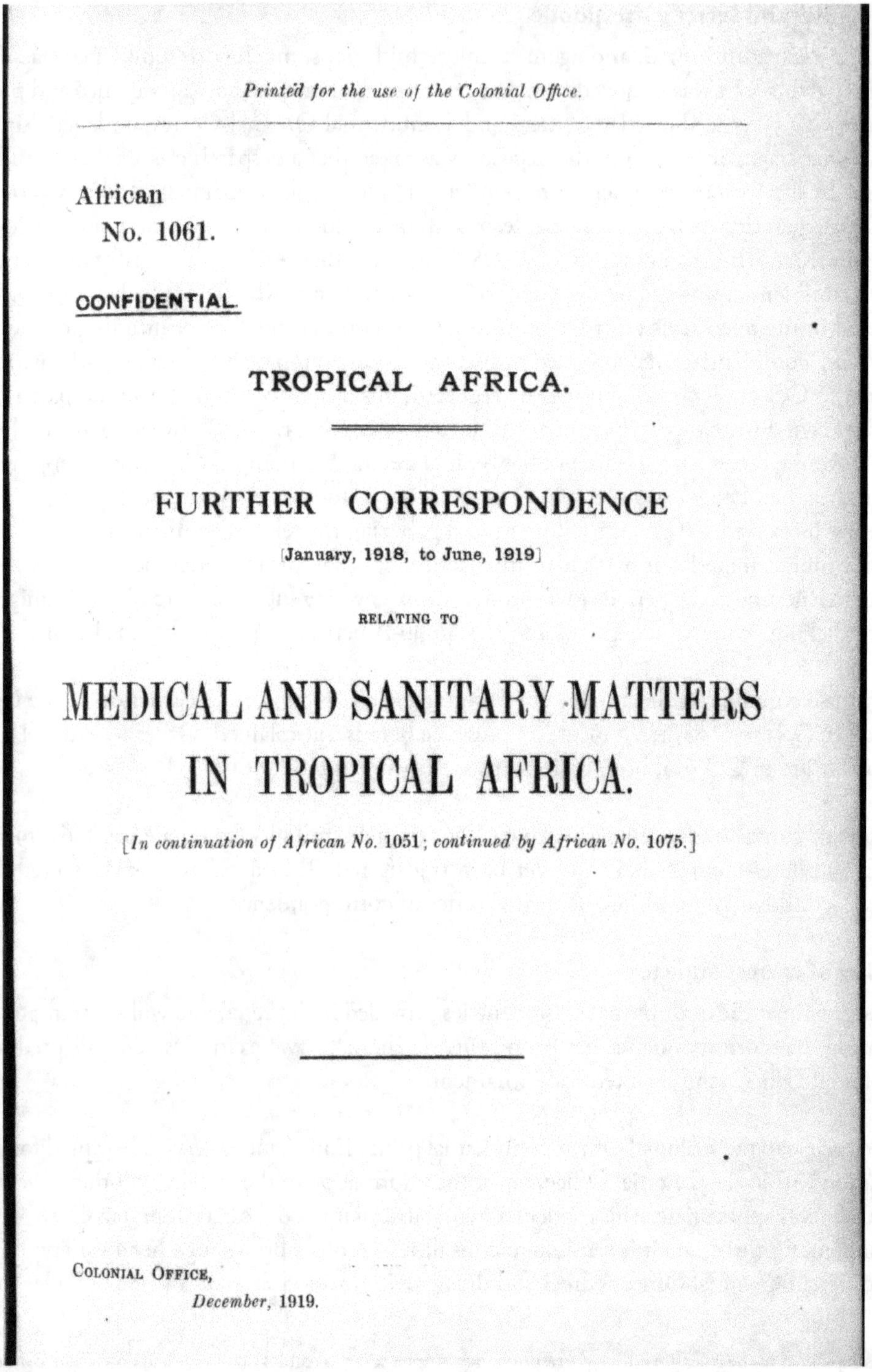

Printed for the use of the Colonial Office.

African
No. 1061.

CONFIDENTIAL.

TROPICAL AFRICA.

FURTHER CORRESPONDENCE

[January, 1918, to June, 1919]

RELATING TO

MEDICAL AND SANITARY MATTERS IN TROPICAL AFRICA.

[*In continuation of African No.* 1051; *continued by African No.* 1075.]

COLONIAL OFFICE,
December, 1919.

Figure 36. CO 879/118. Title page of Confidential Print African no. 1061, Medical and Sanitary Matters in Tropical Africa, which includes the despatch and report on influenza referred to in figure 35.

In this example the item of correspondence concerning the impact of the influenza pandemic in Nigeria is included in a 409-page print entitled 'Medical and sanitary matters in tropical Africa; further correspondence, 1918 January–1919 June' (see figure 36). You may still need to use the originals as some papers, particularly internal minutes, will be omitted completely from the prints, and correspondence and other papers may have been cut. Many lengthy despatches marked up for printing have long sections crossed through; in the example shown at figure 35 the brief text has been preserved and only peripheral detail removed. In some cases you may, however, find that the originals of correspondence so printed are not in the bound volumes or files of original correspondence, where only the internal minute sheets are present. It is not clear if this was deliberate, or if papers were simply not returned from the printer and put back. By 1989/90 a decision had been made by the Public Record Office and the Foreign and Commonwealth Office that no further accessions should be made into the confidential print series. Although the production of confidential print continued until the late 1970s far fewer were issued and those that were produced were very heavily edited.

The confidential print series, which are now fully described by subject in the catalogue,[36] are as follows:

- Africa, CO 879, 1848–1961
- North America, CO 880, 1839–1914
- Australia (including New Zealand and Western Pacific), CO 881, 1833–1923
- Eastern, CO 882, 1843–1952
- Mediterranean, CO 883, 1844–36
- West Indies, CO 884, 1833–1961
- Miscellaneous (subjects affecting colonies generally), CO 885, 1839–1966
- Dominions, CO 886, 1907–25
- Ireland, CO 903, 1885–1919
- Western Pacific, CO 934, 1914–60
- Middle East, CO 935, 1920–56

Prints relating to Australia, South Africa and the dominions generally are continued in DO 115, DO 116 and DO 114 respectively (see p. 135).

Because the arrangement of the prints follows the internal organisation of the Colonial Office rather than being on strict geographical lines, the Africa series also includes prints on Gibraltar, the Ionian Islands, Malta and St Helena (although other prints relating to the first three will be found in the Mediterranean series). The Australia series includes Fiji, New Guinea and the Western Pacific. The Eastern series includes Mauritius, and there is one print on Bermuda in the North America collection.[37]

[36] A published catalogue for part of the series is also available as Public Record Office, *List of Colonial Office Confidential Print to 1916* (London, HMSO, 1965).

[37] Despite its geographical location Bermuda is usually associated in the records with the West Indies in the period covered by this volume, and other prints are in CO 884.

The second register stamp indicates that papers were printed for Parliament. Again these do not include internal minutes, and the despatches and their enclosures are likely to have been edited – sometimes quite severely. Printed or microform sets of UK parliamentary papers, or access to the online full-text collection, will be found in many reference or university libraries. Researchers working at TNA have free access to the online papers. For details of this subscription service see http://parlipapers.chadwyck.co.uk/.

Destroyed papers

Items included in the registers which are stamped 'destroyed under statute' have, indeed, been destroyed. The statute in question is the Public Record Office Act of 1877 which sanctioned the destruction of 'valueless' documents.[38] In 1880 the Treasury circulated government departments with suggestions for systematic disposal, but it was not until 1903 that a Colonial Office committee reported on 'the custody of official correspondence and the selection and destruction of valueless documents in the Colonial Office'.[39] From 1927 it may be the entire file that has been destroyed, or just one or more individual items within the file. In both cases the register should be specific, and in the case of individual items the minute sheets in the file should also note destroyed papers. It is pointless to attempt to explain why correspondence which appears to be of importance to an individual researcher has suffered this fate. Fashions in historiography change and many of us may be researching topics which an earlier age considered to be obscure in the extreme. The register entry does at least supply basic information. And, of course, you should employ lateral thinking. Has this item been destroyed because the matter was primarily the responsibility of, for example, the Foreign Office or the Admiralty? Is it worth searching the records of that department? Do copies of the papers survive in the national archives of the former colony, or among private papers?[40]

The 1877 Act also allowed for documents of 'insufficient value' to be preserved in the PRO to be disposed of other than by destruction. Rules made in 1890 for the administration of the Act allowed for such documents to be transferred to libraries in Great Britain or Ireland, and by an Order in Council of 1908 certain Colonial Office documents were transferred to colonial governments. However, in 1912 the Royal Commission on Public Records noted only eight cases of documents being transferred overseas, and regretted that no steps had been taken to explore other possibilities.[41]

Circular despatches

Looking again at figure 32 you will see references to 'circulars' (one abbreviated to 'circ'). When the Colonial Office wished to convey information to all colonies, or a particular group of colonies, or

[38] Or, in full, 'not of sufficient public value to justify their preservation in the Public Record Office' (40 & 41 Vic., c. 55).

[39] CO 885/8, Miscellaneous No. 155, 'Public records in Colonial Office: report of departmental committee and schedule of valueless documents for destruction'.

[40] Philip Murphy's article 'Censorship, declassification and the history of end of empire in central Africa', *African Research & Documentation*, 92 (2003), pp. 3–26, is concerned with closed or retained material rather than destroyed papers, but it provides some interesting examples of such lateral thinking.

[41] Royal Commission on Public Records (1912) Cd. 6361, 1st Report, page 19, section 3, paragraph 67.

to seek information, it did so by issuing a standard despatch. Copies of these despatches, arranged in chronological order but after 1886 in separate sub-series for ordinary circular despatches and for secret and confidential circular despatches, are in CO 854 (1808–1966). Indexes are in CO 949, Colonies General Indexes to Circular Despatches, 1808–1956. Earlier circulars are in CO 324 and as CO 324/103 overlaps in date with the first volume of CO 854 it is worth checking for items which may be missing from the latter. Replies to circular despatches are, however, to be found in the original correspondence series for the individual colonies, usually clearly marked as being responses to circulars, unless they were secret in which case they may have been filed in CO 537 (as has the reply to the circular concerning civil disturbances included in this example). Presumably such replies were kept together while the matter was current; as noted on p. 44 the General Department of the Colonial Office was responsible for replies to circulars, at least temporarily. A register of replies to circular despatches (1862–1931 only) is in CO 862.

Replies to circulars may be obscure, perhaps referring only to the date of the circular and noting that the instructions will be followed or that a committee will be set up to examine the matter as requested, but reference to the circular itself will provide the context. The register entries shown in figure 32 include a despatch about naval ratings buried in Lagos which reports simply 'Steps are being taken to erect crosses over the graves'. In this case the correspondence itself has been destroyed, but the register entry gives the date of the circular as 15 May [1919], and the circular itself can be found in CO 854/55. It gives detailed instructions for the temporary marking of war graves.[42]

Original correspondence 1927–51 and its registration

For the period 1927–51, Colonial Office original correspondence and the corresponding registers of correspondence continue in the same record series used before 1927, but correspondence is now filed by subject rather than bound in chronologically arranged volumes. The format of the registers also changes.

From 1910 the Colonial Office had been experimenting with the use of a file system, initially for personal records of European officers serving in West Africa.[43] In 1925 a Colonial Office Registration Committee[44] recommended the increased use of the file system and during 1926 there was a major transition to subject file registration.

Subject file registration was extended to all correspondence from 1 January 1927; thereafter every communication received was registered to a file on a specific subject, rather than being bound up in a volume arranged solely by date. Daily registers were no longer used. Files were frequently divided into sub-files so as to include several cases similar in nature but having no direct relation.

[42] Despite the reference to 'crosses' it includes instructions for the appropriate marking of graves of Jews and those of other religions.

[43] The second entry of the register example at figure 32, 'R Nicol 4026 W.A.', is a reference to such a file; they have not survived. Make sure, however, that a reference in this format does not refer to a paper in the 'individuals' section of the original correspondence.

[44] The report of the committee is in the confidential print CO 885/28/7.

Questions from Parliament were attached to separate folders marked 'Parliamentary question' and bearing the title of the subject file to which the question related with its number and the next sub-number. (Parliamentary question files were, in fact, often destroyed, apparently on the grounds that the questions and answers can be found in the printed reports of debates in Parliament, *Hansard*, – unfortunately, of course, any discussion about the drafting of an answer is lost.)

Files generally ran for one-year periods, although some opened at the end of one year were allowed to run on through the next. During the Second World War files often ran on for longer periods as part of a drive to save paper, and by the early 1950s three-year files are standard.

File numbers

Blocks of subject file numbers were allocated for each series of correspondence (see appendix 6). Details of this allocation enable the researcher quickly to identify a file described only as '64501, 1929' as belonging to the series of Mauritius original correspondence and therefore to be sought in the series CO 167. Cross-references in this or a similar form are often found within the documents.

The allocation of blocks of numbers varies between 1927 and 1934, but thereafter is standardised. Thus from 1935 to 1951 inclusive the block 85,001–86,000 is always allocated to Fiji original correspondence.

Arrangement of files

Files are arranged with the earliest communication at the back and the minute sheets together at the front; papers are held in place with a treasury tag. Correspondence is held on the right-hand side of the opened file, and the minute sheets usually on the left, see figure 37, although this is by no means always the case. Each communication is numbered; the first item placed on a file will be no. 1 and so on. The minute sheets list the item number and date of each piece of correspondence (in and out) in consecutive order, followed by the comments of officials. If a particular item originally placed on the file has subsequently been destroyed, or moved to another file, this will be indicated on the minute sheet. See figure 38.[45]

File covers

Original file covers (also known as jackets) are marked with the file title, the reference number and year of the file, and the numbers of previous and subsequent files on the same subject. The TNA document reference has been added at transfer. File titles were, of course, allocated when the file was opened; although they give a good indication of the contents it is possible that coverage has developed into related subject areas and the original title may not be entirely comprehensive. This is particularly significant given that many catalogue descriptions of files have been taken solely from the file titles, although more recent cataloguing has often expanded those basic descriptions.[46] File covers also record the circulation of files between officials. Some

[45] CO 129/535/3. The Nguyen-ai-Quoc referred to is better known as Ho Chi Minh.

[46] See J. Rush and M. Banton, 'Improving access to modern African sources at The National Archives of the United Kingdom', *African Research & Documentation*, 93 (2003), pp. 39–46.

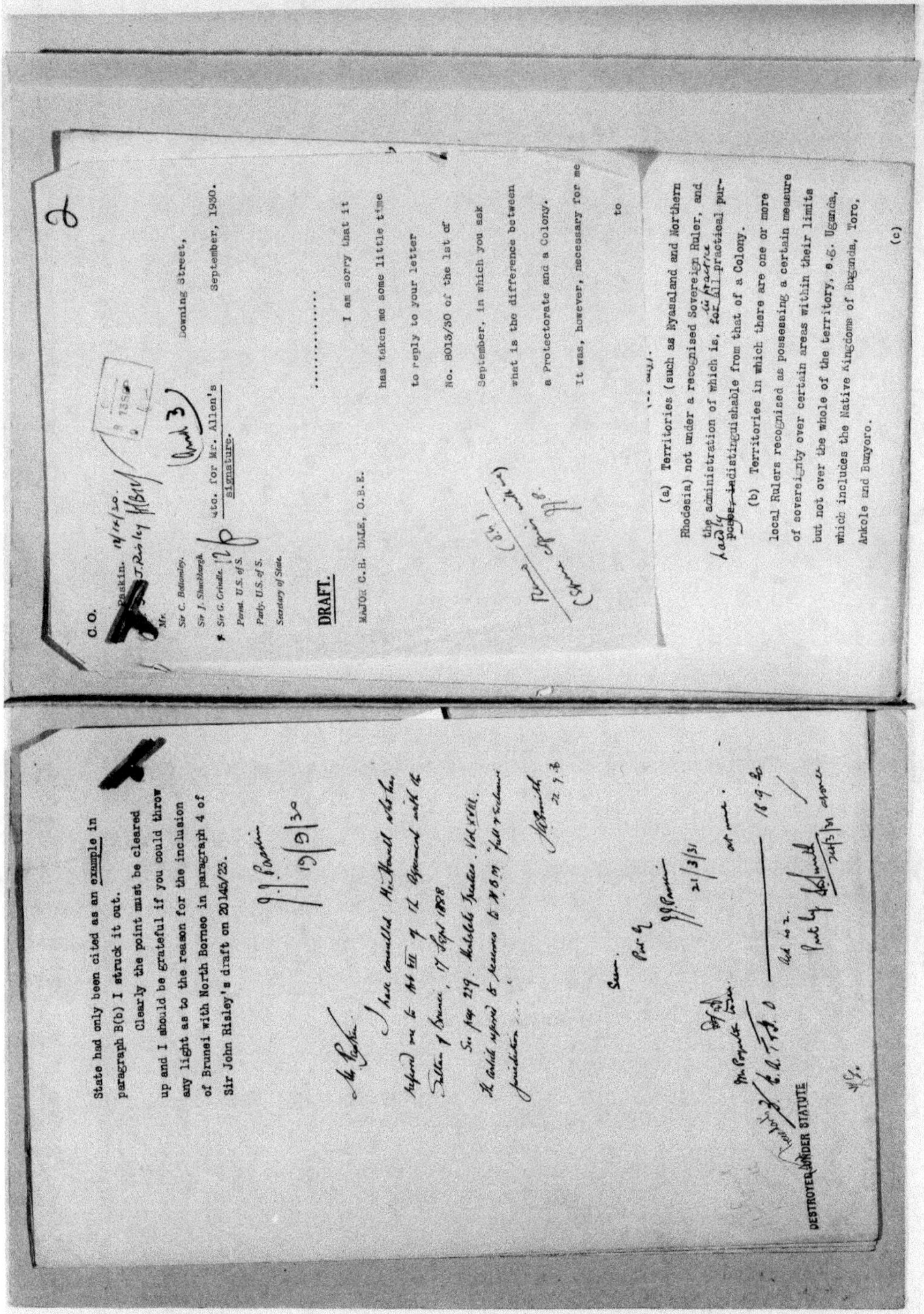

State had only been cited as an example in paragraph B(b) I struck it out.

Clearly the point must be cleared up and I should be grateful if you could throw any light as to the reason for the inclusion of Brunei with North Borneo in paragraph 4 of Sir John Risley's draft on 20145/23.

DESTROYED UNDER STATUTE

C.O.

Mr. Paskin.
Sir C. Bottomley.
Sir J. Shuckburgh.
Sir G. Grindle.
Perm. U.S. of S.
Parly. U.S. of S.
Secretary of State.

Qto. for Mr. Allen's signature.

DRAFT.

MAJOR C.H. DALE, O.B.E.

Downing Street,
September, 1930.

I am sorry that it has taken me some little time to reply to your letter No. 8013/30 of the 1st of September, in which you ask what is the difference between a Protectorate and a Colony.

It was, however, necessary for me to

(a) Territories (such as Nyasaland and Northern Rhodesia) not under a recognised Sovereign Ruler, and the administration of which is, for all practical purposes indistinguishable from that of a Colony.

(b) Territories in which there are one or more local Rulers recognised as possessing a certain measure of sovereignty over certain areas within their limits but not over the whole of the territory, e.g. Uganda, which includes the Native Kingdoms of Buganda, Toro, Ankole and Bunyoro.

(c)

Figure 37. CO 323/1105/6. Opened file showing typical arrangement of correspondence on the right-hand side and minutes on the left.

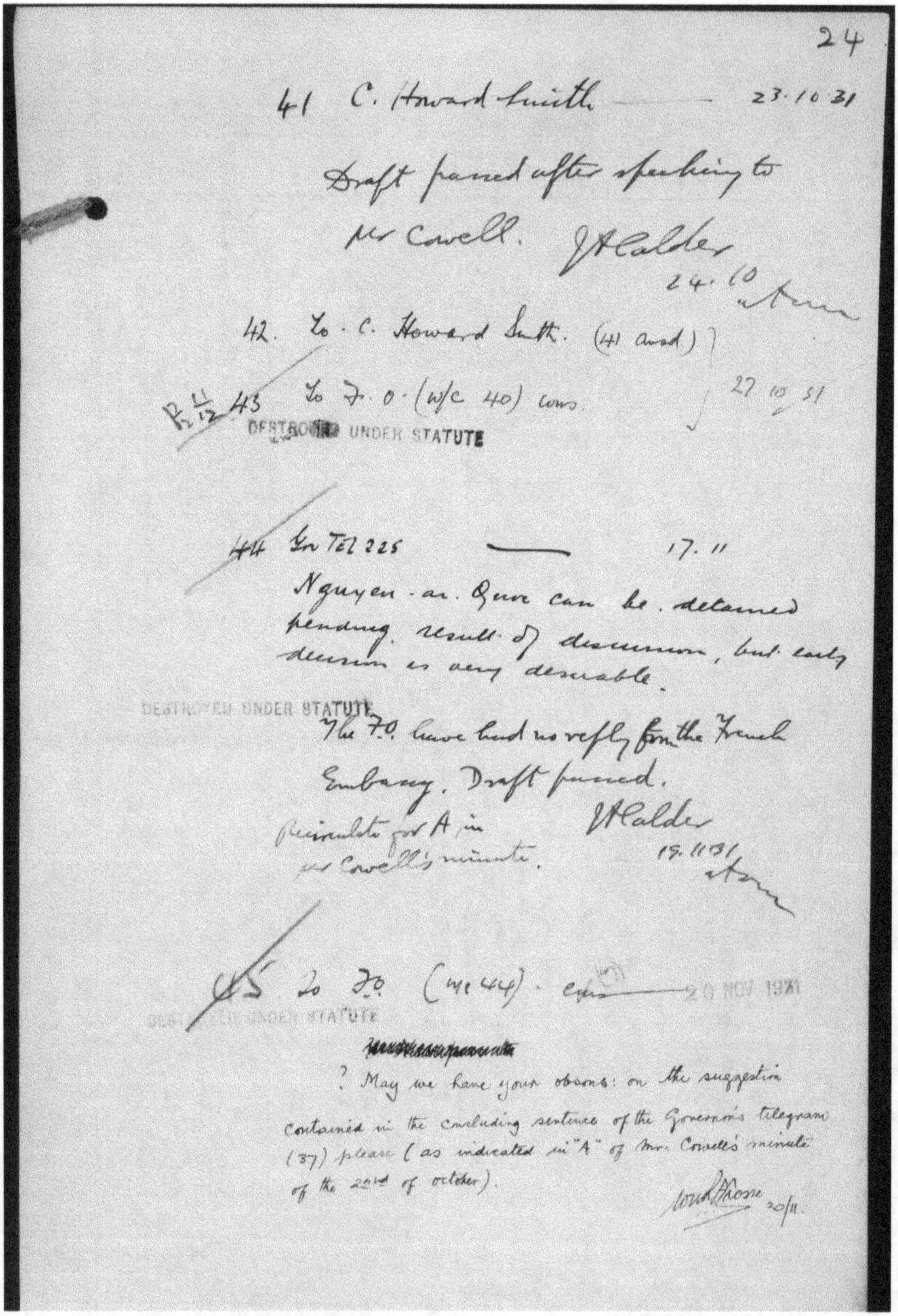
24

41 C. Howard Smith — 23.10.31

Draft passed after speaking to Mr Cowell. JHCalder 24.10

42. To C. Howard Smith. (41 ansd.)

43 To F.O. (w/c 40) cons. 27.10.31

DESTROYED UNDER STATUTE

44 Gov Tel 225 — 17.11

Nguyen-ai-Quoc can be detained pending result of discussion, but early decision is very desirable.

DESTROYED UNDER STATUTE

The F.O. have had no reply from the French Embassy. Draft passed. JHCalder 19.11.31

Recirculate for A in Mr Cowell's minute.

45 To F.O. (w/c 44) cons. — 20 NOV 1931

DESTROYED UNDER STATUTE

? May we have your obsns: on the suggestion contained in the concluding sentence of the Governor's telegram (37) please (as indicated in "A" of Mr. Cowell's minute of the 22nd of October). 20/11.

Figure 38. CO 129/535/3. Minute sheet noting destruction of individual items previously included in the file. The Nguyen-ai-Quoc referred to is better known as Ho Chi Minh.

have been replaced with plain file covers as the originals became damaged, but circulation can still be traced by use of the minute sheets which record the comments – or at least the initials or signature – of each official who saw the file.

Registers of correspondence

In 1926 the type of register used for the 1849–1925 period continues. Transition to the file system may cause difficulties in using the 1926 records and requires explanation. At the beginning of that year incoming papers received numbers in the normal sequence (i.e., as recorded in the daily register in CO 382). A second or subsequent item of correspondence received on a given subject was not entered in the daily register and did not receive a unique number, but was entered directly into the appropriate colony or subject register. The register entry for the new paper was cross-referenced to the earlier paper and marked with its number (plus, usually, the number 2, 3, etc. to indicate that it was a second or third item on that subject), while the entry for the original paper was marked with a red 'F' to signify that it now represented a file. The correspondence was then transferred to a file jacket. As 1926 progressed, more and more correspondence was placed on files. Single papers which did not develop into files were later bound chronologically as in previous practice. Tracing papers of the 1926 transition period can be complex not only because there are both bound volumes and files, but also because the registers have not been marked up to show destroyed items as consistently as was usually the case. Files of 1926 are adequately described in the catalogue. Volumes from this year, however, are listed as before simply as 'despatches', 'offices' or 'individuals'. A card index first introduced in 1909 must have been an indispensable aid to Colonial Office clerks operating this system, but it has not been selected for permanent preservation.[47]

A further point to note is that there are three separate daily registers for 1926 (CO 382/80, 81 and 82). These were maintained by three separate sub-registries, known as the 'C', 'X' and 'dominions' sub-registries. Sub-registry 'C' dealt with the Far Eastern, Middle East, West Indian and General Departments, while 'X' dealt with the West African, East African and Mediterranean Departments and the Military Section. The 'dominions' sub-registry became the Dominions Office registry and CO 382/82 relates to correspondence in 'DO' series. This detail of administrative arrangement would hardly be worth mentioning here were it not for the fact that the letters 'C' and 'X' were prefixed to the file numbers allocated by the two registries, which may cause confusion. For all practical purposes now this distinction is irrelevant.

From 1927 onwards although the registers of correspondence continue in the same record series, the register volumes are smaller, and a separate page is started for each file. There is almost always a full list of all files at the beginning of each volume. An example of a register page is provided as figure 39. The page records, on the left, each item of incoming correspondence, and, on the right, the action taken. The system of cross-referencing is much simplified. As each file is concerned with a distinct subject there is no longer any need to cross-reference individual items of correspondence; it is sufficient to provide cross-references to other relevant files. This is

[47] An associated card index providing information about individuals interned in Hong Kong during the Second World War is in CO 1070 (see appendix 1 under Hong Kong).

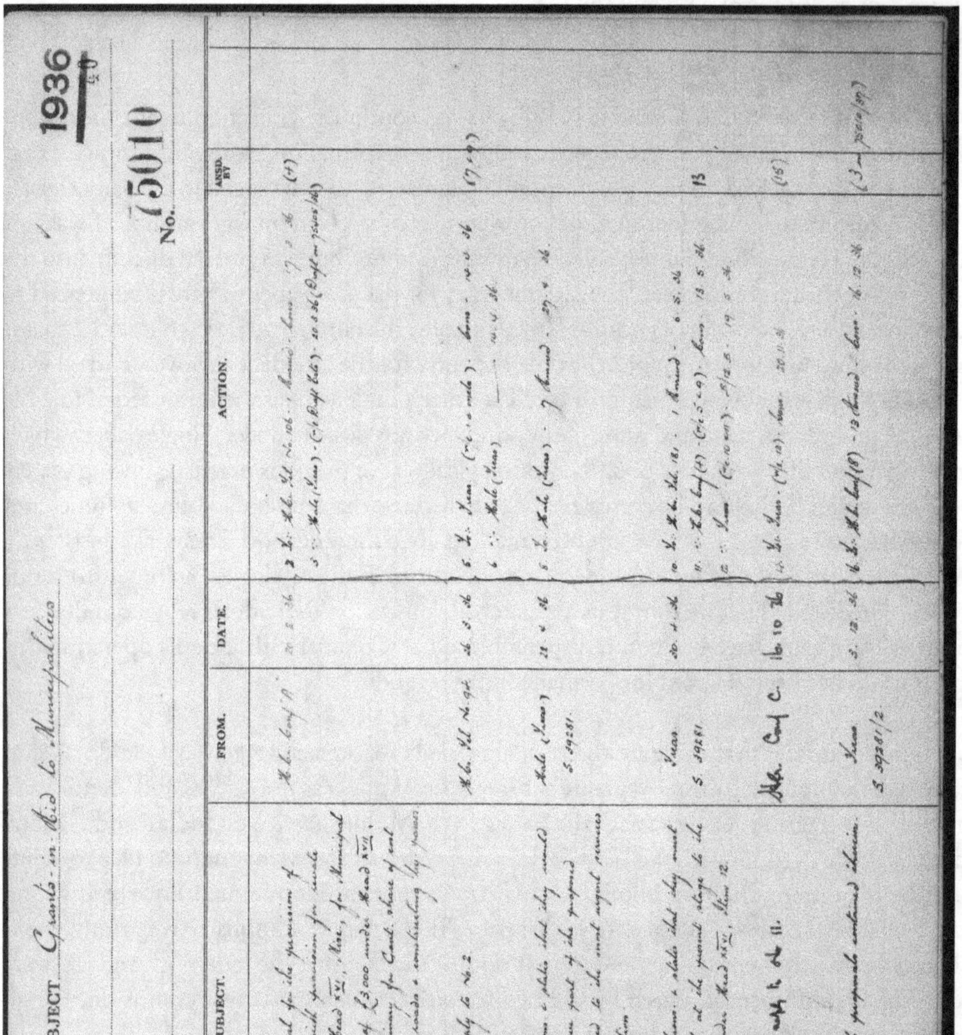

Figure 39. CO 792/26, Palestine register of correspondence, 1936. Example of a page of the type of register used from 1927–51. The numbers recorded in the first column and at the beginning of the 'action' were noted on the correspondence and on related minute sheets within the file.

done by use of the two boxes at top left marked 'previous' and 'subsequent'. If either, or both, of these entries gives only a year, rather than a file number, this indicates that the previous and/or subsequent file bears the same number. If another file number is given, the assumption is that it is a file of the same year unless another year is indicated.

When do you need to use the registers?

Almost all series of original correspondence are now catalogued in full for the 1927–51 period (as indeed are those series which continue into the post-1951 period), i.e., descriptions are provided in the online catalogue for all files which have been selected for permanent preservation and transferred to TNA. The catalogue does not, of course, include descriptions of destroyed files, and may not include descriptions of files that are closed or retained, although this is now unusual. The registers provide brief details of destroyed files, or destroyed items within a file, and can thus go some way towards filling gaps in the surviving records. Unfortunately no registers dated later than 1951 are available, and the full range of files which once existed is hidden.

Only five series now appear to be partially unlisted in TNA's catalogue. These are CO 158, Malta Original Correspondence, 1927–51 (152 boxes of files, pieces 439–590); CO 167, Mauritius Original Correspondence, 1926–28 (4 boxes, pieces 857–860); CO 247, St Helena Original Correspondence, 1927–51 (60 boxes, pieces 202–261); CO 448, Honours Original Correspondence, 1932, 1938–52 (89 boxes, pieces 37 and 52–139); and CO 866, Establishment and Organisation Department, 1926-46 (55 boxes, pieces 3–57). The only means of identifying relevant material is by using the registers in CO 355, CO 356, CO 366, CO 728, and CO 867 respectively, ensuring that the file you want is not marked as destroyed, and then ordering the appropriate box of files. For example, using CO 355/33, the Malta register for 1942, one might select file number 89623 entitled 'Evacuation of Maltese and Cypriots from Levant States' which can be traced through the catalogue to CO 158/536, Malta Original Correspondence, Files 89000 – 89024/3, 1941–43. Incidentally this description indicates that the box contains surviving files within this range of numbers, not that all are there.

It should be noted that the original correspondence series have been gradually catalogued since they were transferred to TNA (or, rather, to its predecessor the Public Record Office). Many secondary sources cite documents using the old style of reference, i.e., series/box/file number. As a rough rule of thumb any five-part reference, or a four-part reference with a fourth part of more than two digits, is likely to be in an obsolete format and un-orderable using that reference. In such cases the first three parts of the reference, representing the series and box, can be entered into the catalogue and the 'browse from here' facility then used to identify the current reference. For example, CO 691/167/42191/10 is the now obsolete format for sub-file 42191/10, contained in box number 167 of the Tanganyika correspondence series CO 691. The catalogue reference is now CO 691/167/3, indicating that this file is the third within the box. Alternatively, the 'advanced search' facility within the online catalogue can be used, and the number 42191/10 entered into the 'search for or within references' field, selecting 'Search The National Archives' under 'Held by'.[48]

[48] In some cases the whole box of files may be the producible item, in which case it is sufficient to request, using these examples, CO 447/125 and CO 691/167.

Secret registers

Files which are now closed or retained, as well as many which are open, may have been registered as secret. In this case, although a page giving the file number in the normal sequence will have been opened in the register for the appropriate colony or subject series, this will generally give no details of the contents of the file, and the page will be stamped 'Secret'. Further registration, retaining the same file number but giving details of contents, was in the secret registers. As noted above TNA holds such registers for the period 1865–1938 only in the series CO 694; they were originally closed for a period of 50 years, and a small number are still unavailable.

Re-organisation of the Colonial Office in the 20th century and its effects on the arrangement of the records

The Dominions Division

The split of the Colonial Office into a Crown Colonies Division and a Dominions Division in 1907 as described at pp. 42–3 initially had limited impact on the arrangement of the records. A new series was created for 'Dominions original correspondence' (CO 532), but until 1922 although this includes some 'despatches' it consists primarily of correspondence with other government departments, miscellaneous organisations and individuals on matters relating to the dominions as a whole or to more than one of them. The existing series for individual territories continue. From 1923, however, CO 532 replaces the individual correspondence series for Australia, Canada, Newfoundland, New Zealand and the Union of South Africa. It includes correspondence relating to the Irish Free State (1924–5 only) and to the individual Australian states. The series comes to an end with the establishment of the Dominions Office. It is registered in CO 708. Printed correspondence and papers are in Dominions, Confidential Print (CO 886, 1907–25).

Other record series relating specifically to the dominions in this period are concerned with the First World War, and are as follows:

- Dominions (War of 1914–18): Original Correspondence (CO 616) 1914–19 (with registers of correspondence in CO 752 and registers of out-letters in CO 753)
- Dominions (War of 1914–18): Prisoners Original Correspondence (CO 693) 1917–19 (with registers of correspondence in CO 754 and registers of out-letters in CO 755)
- Dominions (War of 1914–18): Trade Original Correspondence (CO 687) 1916–19 (with registers of correspondence in CO 756 and registers of out-letters in CO 757)

Subject departments

The development of the subject side of the Colonial Office, described in chapter 5, with its separate record series for each department, complicates the work of the researcher. One can no longer be certain that everything relating to Jamaica, for example, will be in CO 137, and it is not always obvious which department would have been responsible for a particular matter. Again, the *Colonial Office List* will help.[49] At the same time, the geographical departments should not be neglected; it is quite possible for a question relating to, for example, labour in Tanganyika to be addressed in CO 323 (General Department original correspondence) before 1939 or CO 859 (Social Services original correspondence) thereafter if it has a more general application, and also in the Tanganyika series CO 691. Fortunately the more detailed cataloguing of correspondence in this period makes the search not insurmountable.

Advisory committees

As well as subject departments the office came increasingly to use advisory committees, with outside representation, in specialist areas such as health, agriculture and education. Minutes and papers of these committees are often to be found in separate record series. A list of those Colonial Office advisory committees for which there are discrete record series is included in the subject based listing in appendix 2. Where there is no discrete record series for the minutes and papers of a committee they should be sought in the appropriate subject department correspondence series, which may also include duplicates and related correspondence. In other cases a discrete collection may not cover the entire life of a committee, for example records of the Advisory Committee on Education in the Colonies are in CO 987 from 1941 to 1961, but earlier papers can be found among the records of the General Department (CO 323) and (from 1939) in CO 859, the Social Services correspondence series. Some papers of the committee's predecessor, the Advisory Committee on Native Education in Tropical Africa, can be found in the confidential print series CO 879. Yet others are in the Uganda series (CO 536) although it is probable that these are copies of material to be found elsewhere.

For interdepartmental committees see p. 156.

Advisers

In this same period the Colonial Office began to appoint specialist advisers as described in chapter 5. The comments of these advisers, and sometimes fuller papers, can be found in the files of the geographical and subject departments as appropriate. They also amassed their own records which have been considered to be private papers. Only the papers of Sir Christopher Cox, education adviser from 1940 to 1961, are in TNA, in the series CO 1045.[50] Others should be sought through the National Register of Archives in the same way as other private papers. The records of Major G. St J. Orde Browne, the first labour adviser, are among the Commonwealth and African Collections at the Bodleian Library, University of Oxford (formerly at Rhodes House Library).

Cox's papers merit a brief description since they are so different from the majority of Colonial Office records, although they do include internal official material such as papers of the Advisory Committee on Education. Cox maintained correspondence with colonial directors of education, missionary societies and individual missionaries, and other professionals in the field of education.

[49] See appendix 4.

[50] Cox was subsequently an adviser to the Department of Technical Co-operation and then the Ministry of Overseas Development until his retirement in 1970. CO 1045 includes his papers from the post-Colonial Office periods.

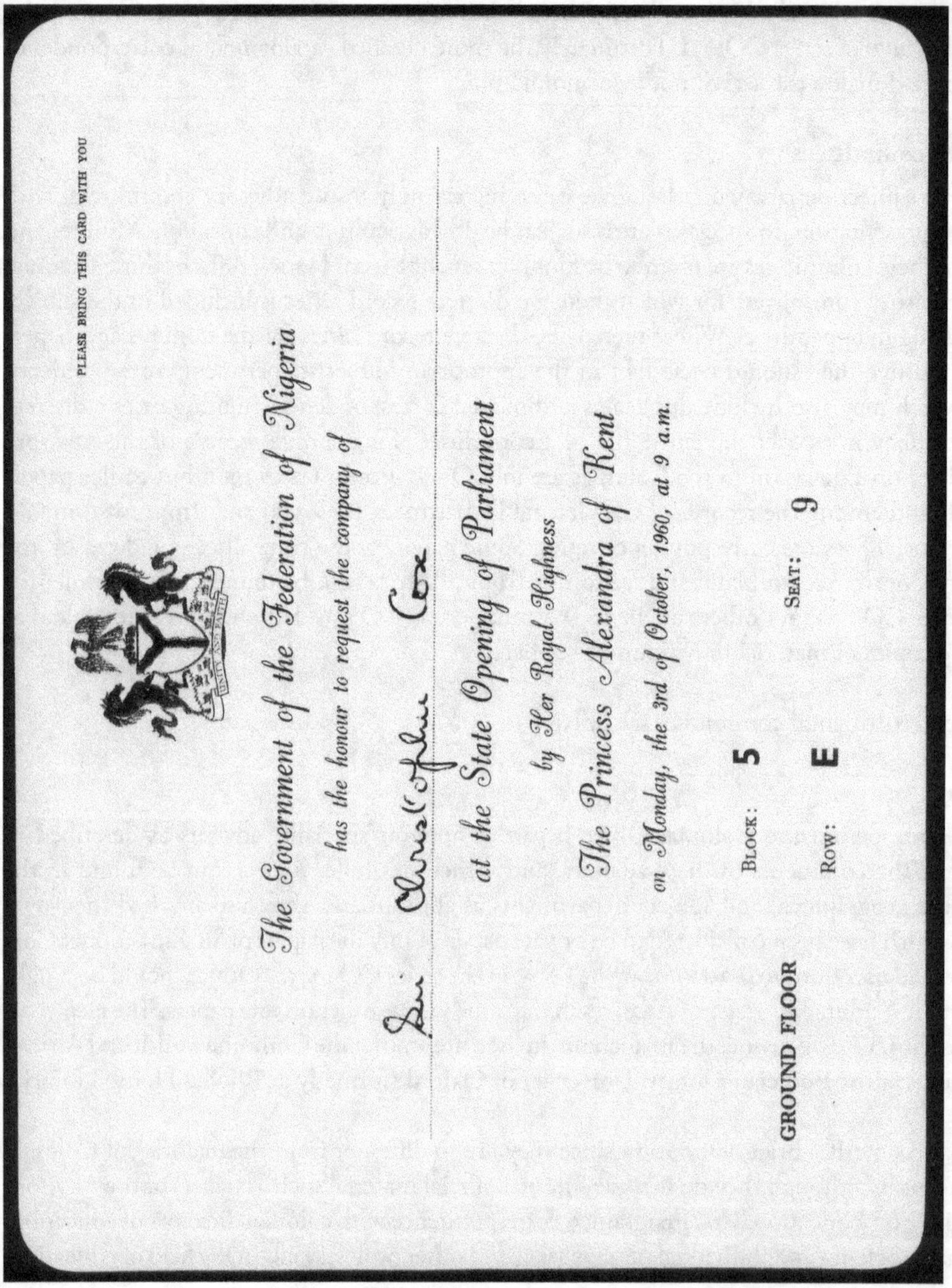

Figure 40. CO 1045/718. Sir Christopher Cox's invitation to the opening of the Nigerian Parliament; an example of the ephemera found among his papers. (By kind permission of the Federal Ministry of Information, Federal Republic of Nigeria.)

There is correspondence with Dutch officials, and files on Scottish education, the pay of educated Africans, juvenile delinquency, private schools, the School of Oriental and African Studies, simplified spelling, educational problems of Colonial Service parents, Rhodes scholarships, overseas universities and colleges, and numerous other topics. He travelled widely and collected a range of published and other material concerning education and related matters, making this a rich collection that is unlikely to be duplicated elsewhere. There is also a good deal of ephemera, such as his invitations and souvenir booklets from the Nigerian independence celebrations of 1960 (see figure 40). For a more detailed outline of Cox's life, his work in Whitehall and his papers, and the wider subject of British colonial education policy, see the publications of Clive Whitehead, who contributed much of the cataloguing of CO 1045.[51]

Geographically arranged correspondence series after 1951

The territorial series of original correspondence come to an end in 1951 and the remaining geographically arranged records are continued in regional series as noted in appendix 1. In some cases these are series created before 1951. For example, the West Africa series (CO 554), which commences in 1911 and was initially concerned with matters relating to the region as a whole or to more than one colony, continues into the post-1951 period and then replaces the separate series for Gambia, Gold Coast, Nigeria and Sierra Leone; similarly with the East Africa series (CO 822) which runs from 1927. In other cases new series were created for the post-1951 correspondence; for example correspondence relating to the West Indian colonies is not continued in the existing West Indies series (CO 318) but is placed in the new series CO 1031. During this period files are generally arranged in three-year cycles, following the introduction of a new registration system in June 1951. The subsequent file periods were: 1951 (nominally) – 1953; 1954–6; 1957–9; 1960–2; and 1963–5. A 1966–8 file cycle was begun but only ran until July 1966. The following month the Colonial Office merged with the Commonwealth Relations Office to form the Commonwealth Office whose first file cycle ran from August to December 1966. No registers for the correspondence of this period have been transferred to TNA from the Foreign and Commonwealth Office. The individual files are adequately described in the catalogue but there is of course no continuing detail of material that has not been selected for permanent preservation and transferred to TNA, or even evidence of its existence.

Some abbreviations used in the registers of correspondence

ADM or Admy.	Admiralty
A.G.	Agents general
A.M.	Air Ministry
B. of C. & E.	Board of Customs and Excise
B.I.R.	Board of Inland Revenue

[51] C. Whitehead, 'Sir Christopher Cox: an imperial patrician of a different kind', *Journal of Educational Administration and History*, 21 (1989), pp. 28–42; C. Whitehead, *Colonial Educators: the British Indian and Colonial Education Service 1858–1983* (London, 2003).

B.O.	Burma Office
B.S.A.C.	British South Africa Company
B.T.	Board of Trade
C. or C'cl.	Council [i.e., Privy Council]
C.A. or C.Ags.	Crown agents
Cab. or Cab.O.	Cabinet Office
C.O.	Colonial Office
D.O.	Dominions Office
D.O.T.	Department of Overseas Trade
F.O.	Foreign Office
G.G.	Governor-general
Gov.	Governor
G.P.O.	General Post Office
H.Cr.	High commissioner
H.O.	Home Office
H. of C.	House of Commons
H. of L.	House of Lords
I.O	India Office
L.O.	Law Officers
M. Agric.	Ministry of Agriculture
M.C.A.	Ministry of Civil Aviation
M.G.O.	Miscellaneous Government Offices
M.I.	Miscellaneous Institutions
M.O.	Miscellaneous Offices
Min. A. & F.	Ministry of Agriculture and Fisheries
Min. F. & P. or M.F.P.	Ministry of Fuel and Power
Min. Trans. or M/T	Ministry of Transport
O.A.G.	Officer administering the government
O.S.D.	Overseas Settlement Department
Parl.	Parliament
P. of W. Dept.	Prisoners of War Department
P.O.	Post Office
R. Cr.	Resident commissioner
Treas., Trsy., or Ty.	Treasury
T.W.E.D.	Trading with the Enemy Department
W.C.O.	War Cabinet Offices
W.O.	War Office

Printed and statistical material provided by the colonial governments

The Colonial Office required governors of British dependencies to send a variety of publications and returns to London. In 1817 governors were instructed to forward annual returns of civil and military offices in their territories, with names and salaries of office-holders. Five years later they were asked to submit various types of statistical data entered into blank books ('blue books'),[52] with printed headings, supplied from London.

Colonial regulations first issued in 1837 required the half-yearly transmission to the Colonial Office of proceedings of local legislatures, lists of council members, copies of acts passed, new compilations or corrected editions of laws, government gazettes and 'generally such books or pamphlets issuing from the colonial press as may be useful'. By this date all dependencies with printing presses were printing their own standard returns of revenue and expenditure. Acts, ordinances and proclamations – the terminology differed according to the constitutional arrangements of each colony – sessional papers and government gazettes had always formed a constituent part of the office's records relating to each dependency, but the 1837 regulation systematised formerly haphazard arrangements for their transmission.

Of the publications and other returns required by London, the sessional papers, statutes, government gazettes and blue books of statistics have found their way into The National Archives, together with the internal records of the Colonial Office itself. Other publications of the colonial governments may sometimes be found among the 'original correspondence' but, as noted above, they were often detached from the governors' correspondence and sent directly to the Colonial Office library.

The Colonial Office did recognise the problems of producing multiple copies of some of the items they required. Revised colonial regulations specified that if a colony printed its statutes, 18 copies should be supplied. If not, only six were required. Statutes, incidentally, were very widely circulated. By at least 1878 copies were required not only for the Colonial Office, but also for the House of Lords, the Treasury, the Board of Trade, the attorney-general and solicitor-general, the emigration commissioners, the British Museum, the Law Society, the Faculty of Advocates of Scotland, the four London Inns of Court and the King's Inns, Dublin.[53]

As noted above, systematic collections of four categories of printed or published material from the colonies were maintained by the Colonial Office. These are now held in discrete series of records for each colony under the headings 'acts', 'sessional papers', 'government gazettes' and 'miscellanea' (consisting primarily of the blue books of statistics but sometimes with additional items as noted below). Descriptions of these types of record follow, and series references for each colony can be found in appendix 1.

[52] Not, of course, to be confused with the various other official publications, including Parliamentary papers, also known as 'blue books'.

[53] 'Rules and regulations for Her Majesty's Colonial Service', as printed in the *Colonial Office List* (1878).

Acts, ordinances and proclamations

Among the records of the Colonial Office and related departments there are separate series known simply as 'Acts' for each dependency (see appendix 1 for the relevant record series for each territory). According to the constitution of an individual colony these statutes may technically be 'Acts', 'Ordinances' or 'Proclamations'. They are *locally enacted* statutes. Acts and ordinances were drafted by the colonial attorney-general or other legal officer, often with the input of other local official or unofficial interests. They passed through the local legislatures, and were approved or 'assented to' by the governor.[54] 'Proclamations' were issued in the name of the governor alone in territories without a legislature, for example the Cape of Good Hope before 1825 or Northern Nigeria in the early years of the 20th century.

Statutes in the 'Acts' series are usually printed and authenticated copies bound into volumes, although early statutes may be handwritten. Later volumes often have a contents list; earlier ones do not. No lists are provided in TNA's catalogue, so although it is a fairly simple matter to locate a statute if you know its date it is difficult to find all statutes enacted in a particular colony on a particular subject without that information. The indexes in CO 714 (see pp. 78–82) may help, but although they generally include references to acts these may be described merely by number and/or date rather than subject. Published compilations of the laws were produced in many dependencies, and may be available in specialist libraries; there are none in TNA. Acts, ordinances and proclamations are usually referenced by use of the year and a running number within each year's collection, for example Bahamas no. 36 of 1835, 'An Act for Reclaiming the Swamps and Low Grounds in the Town of Nassau'. Occasionally the regnal year is used rather than the calendar year, but acts so cited in the correspondence will frequently be found to be imperial (i.e. UK) acts rather than colonial ones. In some other cases a running number is used irrespective of year of enactment, for example Barbados no. 531, 'to remove certain restrictions affecting the Testimony of Slaves' (1831).

The legislative framework of British colonies depended on the processes by which they had been acquired. In a 1774 judgment the chief justice of England, Lord Mansfield, ruled that the laws of a conquered or ceded country remained in force until altered by the conqueror. English common law did not apply unless expressly introduced. His ruling remained in force. So in the Cape of Good Hope, for example, the Roman Dutch law of the previous Dutch administration stayed on the statute books of the new British possession until amended or replaced. And as late as 1873 the law officers of the Crown considered Spanish law when providing an opinion on the power of the governor of Trinidad to commute death sentences. Trinidad had been British since 1802. However, in colonies by settlement, for example Sierra Leone, it was held that English common law arrived as part of the 'luggage' of the settlers, together with all statutes passed in affirmation of the common law before the setting up of the colony. An imperial statute passed after the establishment of a settlement colony did not apply to it unless that colony, or the empire as a whole, was specifically mentioned or the statute was introduced into the colony by an act of the imperial Parliament or the local legislature. For UK legislation enacted for the colonies see below.

[54] See under Sessional Papers below for records relating to enactment of legislation.

During the first half of the 19th century commissions were set up to enquire into the conditions of newly acquired colonies such as the Cape of Good Hope, Ceylon (Sri Lanka), Mauritius, Trinidad and Guiana (Guyana) and particular attention was given to existing legal frameworks and judicial practices. Reports and selected papers of these commissions are noted in appendix 1. The work of the Commission of Enquiry into the Administration of Civil and Criminal Justice in the West Indies was subsequently extended to the region as a whole; its records are in the West India correspondence series CO 318. Reports of the commissions were also published for Parliament (see pp. 101 and 104).

For legislation to be imposed by Britain was a comparatively rare occurrence, but some well known examples – perhaps most famously the legislation to abolish slavery – have served to obscure this fact and have led to a widespread belief that the imposition of legislation from London was the norm. In fact, although model legislation might be circulated when entirely new provisions were sought (for example the introduction of workmen's compensation schemes in the early 1930s), or when an international standard was required (as, for example, in copyright), it was generally believed that the diverse requirements of individual colonies made conformity inappropriate. Standardised legislation was, however, required to implement international treaties or conventions. In 1860, for example, the law officers of the Crown drafted a British Guiana ordinance for the extradition of convicts escaped from the French penal colony at Cayenne.[55] And in the 20th century UK ratification of international labour conventions required the enactment of appropriate legislation throughout the British empire. The introduction of such legislation was not a straightforward process; it required the approval not only of the governors but also of the local legislatures. Such approval was not always readily forthcoming.[56]

The vast majority of statutes were, then, drafted in the colonies and, according to constitutional niceties, either discussed with the Colonial Office (and other government departments as required) at draft stage, or enacted locally and passed to London for formal approval.[57] In cases where legislation was already formally enacted, and assented to by the governor, it was usual for the secretary of state to reserve the power of veto within a given period. The governor's covering despatch, usually accompanied by a report from the colony's attorney-general or other legal officer, will be found in the relevant series of 'original correspondence', although the statute itself will usually have been removed to the 'Acts' series. The reports of attorneys general are often detailed, but may be brief and formulaic, e.g. 'This Ordinance was drafted in obedience to the instructions of the Secretary of State's despatch of April 13th 1898. This Ordinance is

[55] CO 111/329.

[56] In 1947, for example, the Colonial Office was forced to admit that the constitutions of many colonies made it impossible to impose the application of international conventions (CO 537/5223, draft joint Colonial Office and Ministry of Labour paper to Cabinet).

[57] For details of the machinery for the review of colonial legislation during the 19th century, see D. B. Swinfen, *Imperial Control of Colonial Legislation 1813–1865: a Study of British Policy towards Colonial Legislative Powers* (Oxford, 1970); for a case study of Colonial Office handling of new and revised labour legislation, see M. K. Banton, 'The Colonial Office, 1820–1955', in *Masters, Servants, and Magistrates in Britain and the Empire, 1562–1955*, ed. D. Hay and P. Craven (Chapel Hill, NC, 2004).

sufficient for its purpose and I humbly conceive that there is no reason why Her Majesty the Queen should be advised to disallow it.'[58] Notes of the internal discussion within the Colonial Office will be included with the correspondence at most periods, although from 1784 to 1860 a separate collection of reports by the Colonial Office legal advisers on colonial acts can be found in CO 323/34–90. Approval was often given quickly and almost automatically by the Colonial Office. A brief exchange of comments by officials appended to the correspondence will often end with the recommendation, 'sanction?', and the words of agreement, 'at once'. Although formal approval was given by order in council in the name of the reigning monarch, and thus had to be processed by the Privy Council Office, this tended to be a formality only. It did, however, impose a restriction on the powers of local legislatures in that any amendment or repeal of provisions confirmed by order in council would be required to be confirmed in the same way.

In some other cases a colonial enactment might give rise to considerable discussion, and sometimes serious disagreement, within the Colonial Office. In yet others the office might need to consult another UK government department. Legislation concerned with the regulation of shipping and seamen would go to the Board of Trade; regulation and pricing of postal services must be discussed with the General Post Office; changes to local defence arrangements with the War Office or Admiralty, etc., etc. Sometimes entirely new and unfamiliar legislation was proposed and led to voluminously recorded debate within the Colonial Office and ongoing discussion with the relevant governor. In 1816, for example, the government of Sierra Leone saw a need to introduce legislation to regulate labour relations. Had it been based on contemporary English law, or existing legislation in another British colony, it may well have avoided close scrutiny within the office, but instead it imposed on African migrant workers a system of government described by the legal adviser as 'an imitation of the old English law of frankpledge'.[59] It was not approved by the Colonial Office, or, in the formal term used, it was 'disallowed'. 'Disallowance' became increasingly rare during our period, and when it was invoked there was sometimes an anxious discussion about the exact procedure to be used.

The 'official' or 'government' gazettes for each territory (see pp. 125–7) often include draft legislation, and also give details of regulations issued under such legislation. Regulations did not need to be approved by the secretary of state, and are rarely included or mentioned elsewhere in the records. They should not be neglected, however, as they can sometimes have the effect of significantly changing policies imbedded in the primary legislation. For example, labour legislation enacted in Tanganyika in 1923 limited contracts of employment to six months in an attempt to ensure that paid labour and subsistence agriculture might co-exist. Regulations issued in 1925 extended the maximum length of a contract to 12 months. Colonial Office officials commented negatively on the change, but did not feel they could interfere given that the secretary of state had never asked for regulations to be referred.

[58] CO 295/387/11, f. 64.
[59] CO 323/40, James Stephen, 11 July 1817.

Colonial statutes may occasionally be found among the records of other government departments. The Treasury volume T 64/411, 1908–30, for example, contains a collection of pension laws from the various dependencies together with the Pensions Report of the Colonial Office Committee on Pensions and Passage Expenses of Colonial Officers, 1922–4.

The Institute of Advanced Legal Studies (IALS), University of London now holds the collection of colonial and Commonwealth statutes previously held in the library of the Foreign and Commonwealth Office (see http://ials.sas.ac.uk/library/cwealth.htm). IALS also hosts the Foreign Law Guide (FLAG), an Internet gateway to foreign and commonwealth statute, case law and treaty collections held in nearly 60 UK libraries. It includes details of the active and historic collections in over 50 universities including Oxford, Cambridge, London, Manchester, Edinburgh, Glasgow and Cardiff. It also features the vast collections of foreign and international law held by the British Library, the Advocates' Library (part of the National Library of Scotland) and the National Library of Wales (see http://ials.sas.ac.uk/library/flag/flag.htm).

Relevant national archives or libraries should hold copies of local statutes and proceedings of legislatures.

UK legislation enacted for the colonies or including the colonies

As explained above, colonial legislation was enacted by the local legislatures, although sometimes based on models provided by the Colonial Office; in general UK legislation enacted after the settlement of a colony did not apply. Some UK statutes did, however, cover the dependencies. An obvious example is the 1807 Act for the Abolition of the Slave Trade which covered the actions of 'any of His Majesty's Subjects, or any Person or Persons resident within this United Kingdom, or any of the Islands, Colonies, Dominions or Territories thereto belonging or in His Majesty's Possession or Occupation'.[60] Another example is the Colonial Laws Validity Act of 1865 which specifically included 'all of Her Majesty's possessions abroad in which there shall exist a Legislature, as hereinafter defined, except the Channel Islands, the Isle of Man, and such Territories as may for the Time being be vested in Her Majesty under or by virtue of any Act of Parliament for the Government of India'. The Foreign Enlistment Act of 1870, 'to regulate the conduct of Her Majesty's subjects during the existence of hostilities between foreign states with which Her Majesty is at peace', included a clause requiring the act to be proclaimed by governors as soon as possible after receipt of notice of the act, and that it should come into operation in each dependency on the day of such proclamation.

Other UK acts had limited territorial coverage: for example legislation enacted to bring about constitutional change such as the Commonwealth of Australia Constitution Act of 1900 or the Bermuda Constitution Act of 1967. UK legislation was also required to bring about the independence of individual colonies.

Printed copies of UK acts may be found in TNA's reference library, and in many other libraries in the UK and abroad. The original authoritative set of English and UK acts of Parliament

[60] 47 Geo. III, c. 36.

from 1497 is held by the Parliamentary Archives (formerly House of Lords Record Office) (see http://www.parliament.uk/business/publications/parliamentary-archives/).

Sessional papers

The sessional papers series among the records of the Colonial Office and related departments contain the proceedings of the local legislatures – the houses of assembly, executive councils and legislative councils – and much more. They are almost certainly under-used by researchers. The proceedings themselves are sometimes verbatim reports, like the UK *Hansard*, but more often much briefer minutes.[61] For example, the record of proceedings of the Sierra Leone House of Representatives for 29 January 1959 (CO 270/100) lists those present, and notes the start time and that prayers were said. It gives announcements by the speaker and lists papers laid before the House. The main business that day was discussion of two government bills concerning the diamond industry. The minutes note amendments and name members voting in favour of and against the bills. The opposition walked out twice during the day, on the grounds that the time limit imposed on speeches stifled discussion of matters of national importance.

A much earlier volume in this same series (CO 270/19), containing the minutes of the Sierra Leone Council and the Committee of Council, 1827–30, is in manuscript. Where legislation is discussed, a copy of the draft is usually included. A large number of petitions were considered by the council. These are often requests for grants of land, giving no details other than the names of petitioners, but on 12 November 1827 a petition was received from a Mrs Mary Mattop, asking that the land on which she and her children lived should be granted to her rather than to her estranged husband, who had also petitioned. It is perhaps unusual to find within these usually formal proceedings material of potential use to the family historians who now form such a high proportion of TNA's readership.

As well as being held in discrete series of records, copies or extracts of proceedings of the local legislatures are often to be found among the series of correspondence. In 1851, for example, the governor of Jamaica reported that the president of the Turks and Caicos Islands, a colony beset with shortages of labour, had proposed that 250 'immigrant African labourers' should be recruited at the cost of £1,500. The governor forwarded a copy of a petition signed by 43 'inhabitants and Proprietors of the Salt Ponds at Turks Islands' detailing their need for labourers, and extracts from minutes of the Legislative Council (CO 301/6/17). On this occasion Colonial Office officials agreed that 'liberated Africans' could not be supplied, that employers should cover costs of recruitment and that some Maltese migrants might be procured.

The sessional papers series for each dependency also contain a variety of reports submitted to the councils. There are usually annual reports of departments of the colonial governments, for example forestry, public works and education departments, although these are by no means comprehensive collections. TNA's catalogue describes these annual reports simply as 'departmental reports' or

[61] Researchers occasionally ask for colonial *Hansards*, but it is unclear if such verbatim reports exist for individual dependencies.

'administration reports', and gives covering dates; the catalogue does not indicate the contents of the volumes, so it is necessary to requisition them to check; many have a contents list. They date usually from the latter part of the 19th century, and are particularly useful for students of subjects such as public health, railways, 'native administration', etc. Other published reports are included. For the self-governing colonies in particular there are complex sets of sessional papers, generally running from the mid 19th century and probably reaching their high point around 1870–1905. As well as departmental annual reports, they include reports and evidence of commissions of enquiry and select committees, and commissioned reports on a range of topics reflecting economy and society. While not complete (only printed papers are included), they present a rich account of government activity. The series CO 633, Union of South Africa Sessional Papers, has been catalogued in detail and may give an indication of the type of material held in other series.[62]

Sessional papers in the Cape of Good Hope series, for example, include statistical returns from a census taken on the night of Sunday 7 March 1875 (CO 51/185-186), which give details of housing, ages, educational standards, 'conjugal conditions', religion, health, land and production, pastoral wealth, machines and industries. The cost of enumeration was £10,854 9*s* 8*d* (noted as being 'very great'), and the overall population was described as falling into two classes: the European or White, numbering 236,783, and the 'Coloured', numbering 484,201.

Three years later the Cape sessional papers include a lengthy report of a commission on the railways, looking at public expenditure on railways completed or under construction; the expediency or otherwise of any alteration in management and control of railways during construction; and what should be the principle of management to be adopted after completion (CO 51/203).

Similar printed papers published by the South African Republic (Transvaal) from 1884 to 1899 are also held. These are primarily in Afrikaans, although where they include correspondence or reports written in English the original is retained with an Afrikaans translation. The green books, as they are called, cover a variety of subjects: statistical data from census returns, and reports concerning Asian immigrants, the railways and the Jameson Raid.[63]

TNA also has, for a few years at the start of the 20th century, minutes of the Town Council of Johannesburg and of the Town Council and Municipal Commission of Pretoria (CO 610 and CO 611). At its second meeting in February 1902 the Pretoria Town Council agreed standing orders which included the provision that all meetings should be open to the press and the public, but there is no indication that minutes would be circulated more widely than to council members. Registered newspapers might, however, apply for copies of the weekly reports of committees submitted to the council. The minutes are in typescript; TNA has carbon copies.

[62] Hong Kong Sessional Papers are available online through the Hong Kong University Libraries at http://sunzi.lib.hku.hk/hkgro/ [accessed 9 March 2015].

[63] See the specimen search in appendix 7.

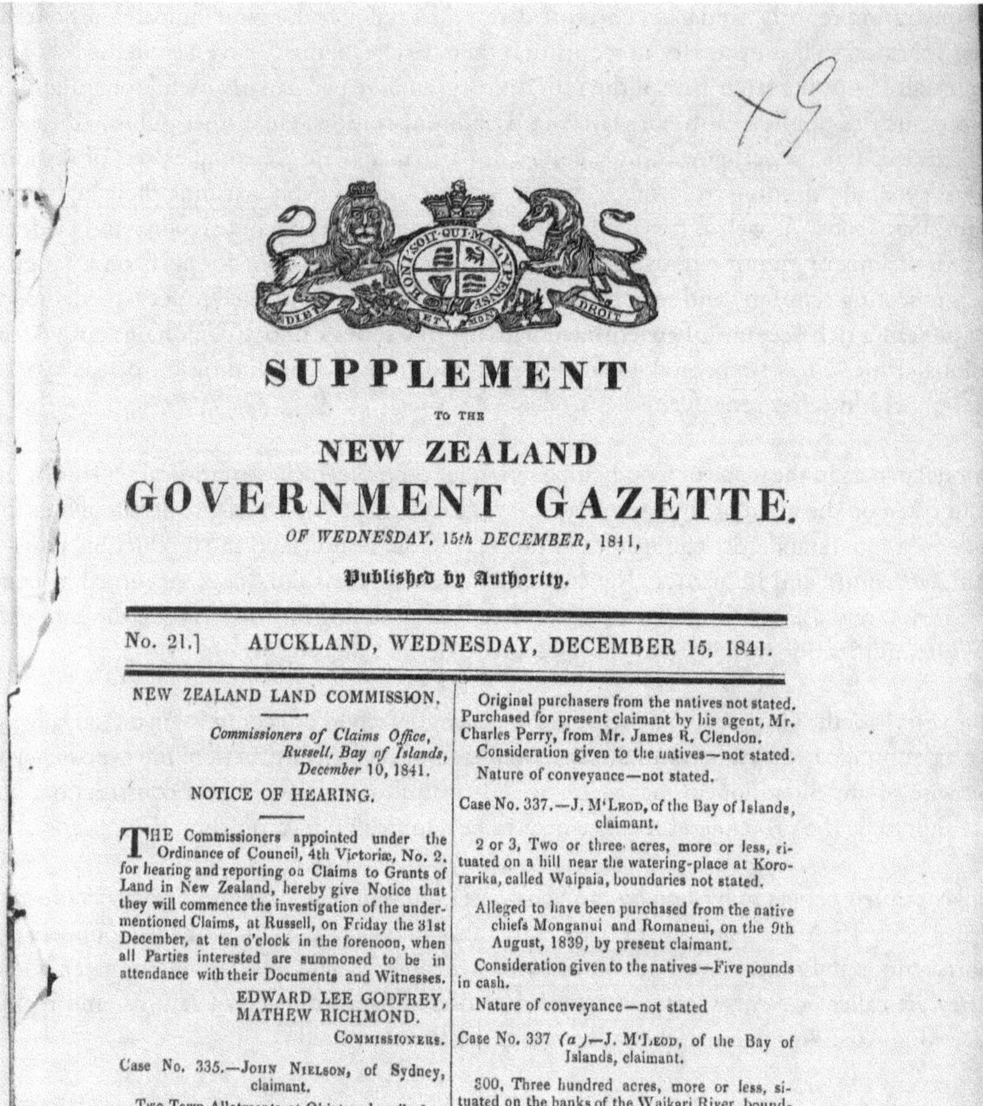

×9

SUPPLEMENT

TO THE

NEW ZEALAND

GOVERNMENT GAZETTE.

OF WEDNESDAY, 15th DECEMBER, 1841,

Published by Authority.

No. 21.] AUCKLAND, WEDNESDAY, DECEMBER 15, 1841.

NEW ZEALAND LAND COMMISSION.

Commissioners of Claims Office, Russell, Bay of Islands, December 10, 1841.

NOTICE OF HEARING.

THE Commissioners appointed under the Ordinance of Council, 4th Victoriæ, No. 2, for hearing and reporting on Claims to Grants of Land in New Zealand, hereby give Notice that they will commence the investigation of the undermentioned Claims, at Russell, on Friday the 31st December, at ten o'clock in the forenoon, when all Parties interested are summoned to be in attendance with their Documents and Witnesses.

EDWARD LEE GODFREY,
MATHEW RICHMOND.
COMMISSIONERS.

Case No. 335.—JOHN NIELSON, of Sydney, claimant.

Two Town Allotments at Okiato, described as Nos. 53 and 54, in the Township of Kent, bounded on the east by an intended street, called Thomas-street, 214 feet; on the north by Lo, 52; and an intended street, called Oxford-street, 66 feet; on the west by Lot 56, and on south-west and south by the Sea Beach, 214 feet.

Original purchasers from the natives not stated. Purchased for present claimant by his agent, Mr. Charles Perry, from Mr. James R. Clendon.

Consideration given to the natives—not stated.

Nature of conveyance—not stated.

Case No. 337.—J. M'LEOD, of the Bay of Islands, claimant.

2 or 3, Two or three acres, more or less, situated on a hill near the watering-place at Kororarika, called Waipaia, boundaries not stated.

Alleged to have been purchased from the native chiefs Monganui and Romaneui, on the 9th August, 1839, by present claimant.

Consideration given to the natives—Five pounds in cash.

Nature of conveyance—not stated

Case No. 337 *(a)*—J. M'LEOD, of the Bay of Islands, claimant.

300, Three hundred acres, more or less, situated on the banks of the Waikari River, boundaries not stated.

Alleged to have been purchased of the native chiefs Yakie, Tokey, Wykattio, and others, on the 26th November, 1839, by claimant, in conjunction with Edmund Powell and William Dodds.

Figure 41. CO 212/1. Title page of the Supplement to the *New Zealand Government Gazette* of 15 December 1841.

Sessional papers are listed in TNA's catalogue simply by date. Many of them have internal indexes. In some cases there are consolidated indexes, see, for example, under Ceylon and New South Wales in appendix 1, but this has not been checked for all series. Series of sessional papers for each dependency are included in the geographical listing in appendix 1.

Government gazettes

The gazette is the official 'newspaper' of the colonial government, comparable to the *London Gazette*. Some may initially have been established as commercial ventures. The first volume of the *Royal Gazette and Sierra Leone Advertiser* held in TNA includes a copy of the prospectus, which states:

> 'The objects of the Publication now proposed are, to provide the Colony with a Journal, not only free from just grounds of Censure, but especially intended to encourage Virtue and Industry among the Colonists and our Neighbouring Brethren; to offer to the Poor the best and wisest counsel within our scope; to give our Readers the earliest and most authentic information of all important transactions in distant Countries, and most particularly in Great Britain; being impressed with the conviction that our very Existence as a Colony, is interwoven with the Parent Country, and that as we participate in her Glory and Prosperity so shall we rise or fall with her.'[64]

The content of the gazettes varies widely, generally including official, commercial and news items. The first official notice in the first issue of the Sierra Leone gazette is a proclamation by the governor regarding foreign imports. There are then local and overseas news items, letters to the editor, advertisements, shipping news and obituaries. The issue of 24 January 1818 is devoted almost entirely to reports of the death of the princess of Wales – in contrast the gazette of the British South Africa Company for 25 January 1901 devotes only two brief paragraphs in a black-bordered issue to the death of Queen Victoria.[65] The Sierra Leone gazette of 1 April 1820 prints the results of a census of Europeans in the colony – excluding the military – which lists 98 men, 14 'ladies, maid servants, etc.' and five unnamed children. Annotations show that some have left the colony since the census was taken – most by ship, a few by death. The Cape of Good Hope *Government Gazette* of 1856 also reads like a local newspaper. As well as official notices concerning bills and government notices there are announcements of births, marriages and deaths; advertisements for farms, livestock, timber, stationery, perfume and ointment; lists of ships arriving at and departing Table Bay; notices of escaped prisoners, and strayed and found horses, cattle and dogs; a plea for people who have left their guns for repair to collect them; tenders for police uniforms; returns of lands granted and sold; and details of forthcoming horse races.[66] A supplement to the New Zealand gazette of 15 December 1841 gives notice of forthcoming investigations into land claims (see figure 41).

The Trinidad gazette of 29 October 1833 includes a notice of the forthcoming sale of the property of a deceased resident on behalf of his creditors. The property consists of 68 enslaved persons.

[64] CO 271/1, 1817–20.
[65] CO 455/2.
[66] CO 52/19.

The same issue carries an advertisement: 'For hire. Four valuable NEGROES, adapted for the Field, three of whom are Masons.'[67] The issue of 6 May 1834 includes a return of 18 runaway slaves, giving just their names rather than any other details. A supplement to the Jamaica gazette of 15–22 May 1813 includes a list of 127 runaways who have been apprehended and are held in the various workhouses. In this case names, descriptions and ownership, where known, are included: 'Prudence, a Mundingo [*sic*], 5 feet 3 inches, marked B. within a circle, and a diamond, to Roslin Castle estate or the Hon. John Cunningham, Esq.'. Another individual is described as: 'Anthony Ballantine, born at Curaçoa [*sic*], 5 feet 9 inches, says he is free, but has no document thereof'.[68]

An example of the type of overseas news item often found is included in the same Jamaica gazette volume: 'European intelligence, London, Dec. 18–23, 1812. A gentleman who left Hamburgh [*sic*] 14 days ago states, that the dreadful situation of Bonaparte's army in Russia was known there; but that the Police was so severe, that several persons, who only dared to hint at it, were arrested by gens d'armes. He asserts that the North of Germany is ripe for a general insurrection against the French.'

The contents of gazettes vary not only from time to time, but also from colony to colony. The gazette of the East Africa and Uganda Protectorate for 1901 was quite possibly the only published local news source available to the British expatriate community.[69] It gives results of local cricket matches as well as providing the latest news from the South African war in the form of copies of Reuters' telegrams. In contrast, the British South Africa Company gazette of the same period refers to the war only in the context of official notices – for example that the Cape government railways will accept consignments to, from or through martial law areas only at the owner's risk.[70]

Later gazettes tend to be more formal. The South West Africa *Official Gazette* of 1968, for example, publishes draft ordinances, proclamations, government notices and general notices.[71] These are clearly important to anyone studying legislative development or the machinery of government, but they are largely devoid of human interest. Gazettes published in Sierra Leone in 1975 carry the usual official notices but also give lists of vacancies in the public service and of new appointees.[72] They carry details of UNESCO vacancies in countries as far flung as Afghanistan, Colombia and Hungary. There are lists of students passing examinations, and details of found and unclaimed property at police stations – among them various items of clothing, a refrigerator, 29 plastic spoons, a windscreen, a James Bond travelling bag, a mosquito net, a rear view mirror, a steel door and a gallon of palm oil. The only advertisements noted are, appropriately, for government publications on sale at the government bookshop in Freetown – including copies of the national anthem priced at three cents each.

[67] CO 299/1.
[68] CO 141/2.
[69] CO 457/2.
[70] CO 52/84.
[71] DO 78/53–6.
[72] CO 271/112–14. Note that in this case the gazettes continue in a 'CO' series although dated long after the establishment of the Foreign and Commonwealth Office.

In his guide to sources for Caribbean family history Guy Grannum has noted the wealth of information concerning individuals to be found in the gazettes. His examples are: 'birth, marriage and death notices, including occasional obituaries of notable people; notices of proceedings and sales of property in the courts of chancery and petty sessions; lists of people applying for liquor, dog and gun licences; lists of jurors, druggists (chemists or pharmacists), constables, voters, solicitors, nurses, medical practitioners and militia; notices of sales of land; public appointments, leave of absence and resumption of duty; notices relating to cases of intestacy, guardianship and wills; notices on applications for naturalisation; inquests into shipwrecks; ships entering and clearing port, sometimes with the names of first class passengers; lists of people paid parish relief; and tax lists.'[73]

An anomaly is the existence in TNA of government gazettes for Sudan (1907–17) in the Colonial Office series CO 675 – the Colonial Office had no responsibility for the administration of Sudan. The gazette, printed in English and Arabic, is another very official example including government notices, statutes, appointments and transfers in the public service, and the award of decorations. A fuller collection of Sudan gazettes is in the Foreign Office series FO 867.

Details of other holdings of gazettes, in original or microform, can be found via the website of the Center for Research Libraries, Global Resources Network (http://www.crl.edu).

'Miscellanea'

The series of records of each colony that are known simply as 'miscellanea' (listed in appendix 1) often consist only of the annual 'blue books of statistics' described below. But series commencing before about the middle of the 19th century – and primarily those for dependencies in the Americas – include a range of other material, most commonly shipping returns, newspapers and returns of stipendiary magistrates. For some colonies there are memoranda and truly miscellaneous papers on a variety of subjects. For example, the Trinidad series includes the journal of a medical officer of a migrant ship (1847); St Helena has returns of Crown lands; St Christopher (St Kitts), papers relating to losses incurred in the French invasion of 1708; North Borneo, a volume of rules for native courts; Labuan, a volume of court records; Heligoland, reports of the census of 1881 and appeal cases; Grenada, sales of lands in ceded islands; Gibraltar, a rent roll of government properties; Fiji, the instrument of cession to the British Crown; Dominica, grants and sales of land; Bermuda, military accounts. An indication of contents of miscellanea series is provided in the territorial listings in appendix 1.

Blue books of statistics

As noted above, governors were first asked to provide annual returns of local staffing in 1817 when a Commons select committee on finance requested returns of the various civil and military offices, salaries, methods of appointment, names of office-holders and dates of their appointments. In 1822 additional statistical data was required under the following five headings: abstract of net

[73] Grannum, p. 24.

revenue and expenditure; schedule of taxes, duties, etc.; military expenditure; establishment; schedule of fees, etc. By a circular despatch dated 30 April 1823[74] the Colonial Office added three more headings: population; exports and imports; and currency. By this date the Colonial Office was providing forms with printed headings for completion within the colonies, and requests for blank forms can occasionally be found among the governors' correspondence. Categories were as follows:

- Schedule of taxes, duties, fees and all other sources of revenue
- Schedule of the fees received by the several officers in the respective departments
- Abstract of the net revenue and expenditure
- Local revenues
- Military expenditure
- Return of militia
- Public works
- Schedule of all the laws, proclamations, orders in council, etc. promulgated during the year
- Councils and assemblies: return of members
- Civil establishment: list of officers of the civil and judicial departments and list of clergy
- Return of officers who have given security for the due discharge of their duties
- Pensions payable out of the revenues of the colony
- Return of foreign consuls
- Population (according to last census or other accessible information)
- Ecclesiastical return (listing churches, denomination, number of persons attending)
- Return of schools (with name of head teacher, number of scholars, how financed and expenses)
- Return of exchanges, moneys, weights and measures
- Imports and exports
- Return of ships (whether from British, British colonial, US or foreign states, and brief note of cargo)[75]
- Return of agricultural produce and stock
- Return of manufactures, mines and fisheries
- Grants of land
- Return of gaols and prisoners

[74] CO 854/1, f. 113.

[75] Blue book shipping returns appear to replace the shipping returns previously to be found in the miscellanea series, but they do not name ships or masters, simply numbers of ships under each category and total tonnage.

Colonial Office instructions were regularly amended and reissued. The colonial governments sometimes added other material considered to be of interest. The Hong Kong blue book for 1844, for example, includes a meteorological table giving daily weather conditions over a nine-month period (CO 133/1).

It is fairly certain that the office experienced regular problems in collecting the statistics required. Among the Barbados correspondence, for example, there are despatches from five successive governors apologising for late transmission of the blue books and for omissions and imperfections, complaining about the difficulty of collecting information and about officials who refused to provide returns, and even recommending legislation to enforce compliance. In 1835 the governor of Bermuda reported the refusal of customs officers to supply information required in the prescribed form. Although the term 'blue book' appears to be widely used by 1821, the format and content of early returns does vary. For example a volume for Mauritius covering the long period 1810–28 is described just as 'revenue and expenditure' and does not use the standard forms. The content of the blue books was gradually improved under pressure from London, but in some dependencies they evolved in a non-standard form. For example the Canadian compilations from 1925 consist of the *Commercial Intelligence Journal*, which includes articles on commercial topics as well as the usual statistical information.[76] There were complaints about the accuracy and completeness of information provided. In 1838 Robert Montgomery Martin, a founding member of the Statistical Society of London, complained of the 'very unsatisfactory manner' in which some blue books had been compiled and emphasised 'the very great importance of having these Returns filled up with the utmost precision and exactitude'.[77]

The hand-written completed forms which initially comprised the blue books were gradually replaced by printed returns in colonies with use of printing presses, and instructions were periodically issued from London requesting the inclusion of alternative or additional information. In 1837 governors were asked to accompany their annual returns with reports 'exhibiting generally the past and present state of the Colony and its prospects, in every political Branch'.[78] References to the transmission of such reports – usually described as 'the report on the blue book' but generally becoming known as annual reports – can be regularly seen in governors' despatches and manuscript copies are sometimes included. There are very occasional examples of printed reports within correspondence files[79] but TNA held no discrete collection until 2014 when a set of annual reports from the Foreign and Commonwealth Office Library was accessioned into CO 1071. Early colonial annual reports were printed for Parliament, but it is not clear if this collection is comprehensive and they come to an end in the 1920s.

[76] Thurston, vol. 1, p. 52.

[77] Quoted in CO 854/2, circular despatch, 29 Jan. 1839

[78] Report of Select Committee on Colonial Receipt and Expenditure, quoted in Pugh, *Records of the Colonial and Dominions Offices*, p. 41.

[79] CO 525/125/9 includes a corrected proof of the Nyasaland Annual Report for 1927 together with a May 1927 report of an Annual Colonial Reports Committee appointed by the secretary of state to examine the contents and form of the reports and to make recommendations on possible improvements.

Amendment of blue book information continued. In 1918, for example, a committee appointed to review their content and use recommended the inclusion of information concerning industry, labour, wages and cost of living – possibly as the result of a request from the Ministry of Labour which had been established two years earlier.[80] The compilation of blue books was discontinued during the 1940s.

Blue books are of interest to the biographer or family historian in that they provide some information about the careers of individuals employed by the colonial governments, although this is admittedly very limited. Figure 42 shows part of an entry for senior officials in New South Wales.

Some blue books of statistics are available through British Online Archives (http://www.britishonlinearchives.co.uk), as are some of the shipping returns described below. British Online Archives is a subscription service which may be available through university and other major libraries.

Shipping returns

Shipping returns taken at colonial ports, also known as naval officers' returns, give details of vessels entering inwards and clearing outwards. They vary considerably in the information recorded. For example returns for the port of Quebec dated 1801–8 (CO 47/81) are entered on printed forms giving the date, ship's name, the names of the master and the owners, rig, tonnage, when and where built and registered, and where from and where bound. Details of cargoes are recorded under headings for: spirits, wine, beer, coffee, sugar, molasses, gunpowder, tobacco and salt. Other printed headings record type of packaging: chests, bales, trunks, boxes and cases, casks, jugs and jars, kegs, baskets, stove pieces, iron pots, bars iron [*sic*] and crates. A further column provides space for 'packages and contents of other goods'. In contrast the volume of Gibraltar returns for 1804–6 (CO 95/1) gives undated entries in a handwritten ledger. Headings are: 'nation' (i.e., nationality), 'quality' (i.e., type of vessel), vessel's name, master's name, 'from whence', 'where bound', 'where belonging' and 'lading' (giving very brief details of cargo, for example 'sugars and hides', 'bricks' or 'sundry merchandise'). A final column, 'supposed value', has not been completed. The subsequent volume for Gibraltar (CO 95/2, 1825) provides even less information. It is arranged in national sections – English, Gibraltar, American, Swedish, Dutch, Sardinian, etc. – recording tonnage, lading (for example 'oil, currants, silk, steel'), 'from whence' and 'where bound'. Names of individual ships are not recorded. This latter type of return is common for the later period; shipping returns detailing individual ships come to an end between about 1814 and 1825. Thereafter the information is presented in statistical form only within the blue books.

The presence of shipping returns within the 'miscellanea' series is noted for each dependency in appendix 1.

Newspapers

The colonial 'rules and regulations' first issued in 1837 requested the transmission to London of 'such books or pamphlets issuing from the colonial press as may be useful', and it is presumably

[80] CO 854/54, circular despatch, 28 Aug. 1918.

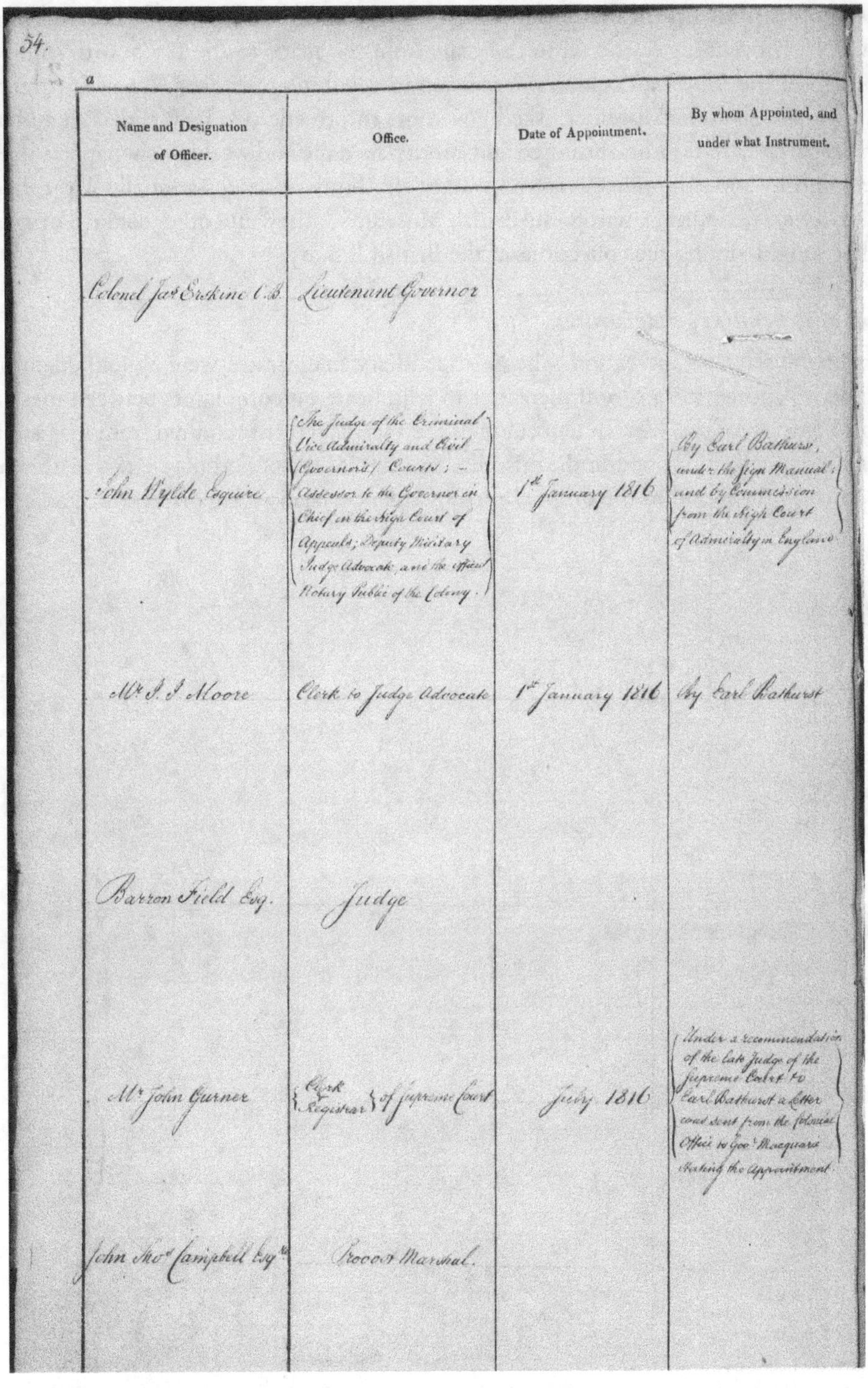

54.

a

Name and Designation of Officer.	Office.	Date of Appointment.	By whom Appointed, and under what Instrument.
Colonel Jas Erskine C.B.	Lieutenant Governor		
John Wylde Esquire	The Judge of the Criminal Vice Admiralty and Civil (Governor's) Courts; — Assessor to the Governor in Chief in the High Court of Appeals; Deputy Military Judge Advocate, and the official Notary Public of the Colony.	1st January 1816	By Earl Bathurst, under the Sign Manual; and by Commission from the High Court of Admiralty in England
Mr J. J. Moore	Clerk to Judge Advocate	1st January 1816	By Earl Bathurst
Barron Field Esq.	Judge		
Mr John Gurner	Clerk / Registrar of Supreme Court	July 1816	Under a recommendation of the late Judge of the Supreme Court to Earl Bathurst a Letter was sent from the Colonial Office to Govr Macquarie stating the Appointment.
John Thos Campbell Esqre	Provost Marshal.		

Figure 42. CO 206/63. Extract from a New South Wales 'blue book' listing senior officials. The right-hand page, not shown here, gives further details.

as a result of this instruction that local newspapers began to be supplied.[81] The collection now held at TNA is primarily restricted to the years from the 1820s to the 1850s, with some earlier examples from the American colonies. It is listed in detail in appendix 3. It was apparently not until 1870 that the Colonial Office asked governors to provide two newspapers in addition to the official gazette; 'in 1872 one hundred and twenty-six daily and weekly newspapers were being received, and by 1904 the office received twenty-six thousand issues annually. Up to 1891 the older issues were periodically sent to the British Museum'.[82] They, and other colonial newspapers, should be sought among the collections at the British Library.[83]

Returns of stipendiary magistrates

As part of the slave emancipation scheme stipendiary magistrates were appointed to oversee the period of 'apprenticeship' and thereafter to adjudicate on complaints between masters and servants. For most of the West Indian colonies the various returns required from magistrates are held in discrete collections within the miscellanea series for the period 1845–*c.*1853. Other returns and reports can be found in the original correspondence. Many were printed for Parliament.

81 Thurston, vol. 1, p. 52.

82 Thurston, vol. 1, p. 52.

83 Following the closure of the Newspaper Library at Colindale in November 2013 the British Library has posted updates about future access to the collections on its website at http://www.bl.uk.

7. Records of the Dominions Office and Commonwealth Relations Office

Records of the immediate predecessor of the Dominions Office – the Dominions Division of the Colonial Office established in 1907 – are described under Colonial Office in chapter 6.

Many of the new record series created on the formation of the Dominions Office in 1925 simply continue pre-existing Colonial Office series. This is true particularly of the discrete series of acts, government gazettes, sessional papers and 'miscellanea'. So, for example, Canadian sessional papers are in CO 45 up to 1925, and in DO 28 thereafter. A total of 113 of the 230 series within the 'DO' departmental code consist of this type of material. These new series are included in the geographical listing provided in appendix 1, and descriptions of the various types of documents are in chapter 6.

The Dominions Office made the decision to continue with a general 'dominions' series of correspondence as used by the Dominions Division of the Colonial Office rather than adopting a system of separate record series for individual territories and subject areas. So from 1926 until the late 1950s the vast majority of correspondence will be found in the series DO 35, Dominions Office and Commonwealth Relations Office: Original Correspondence. The overall covering dates of this series are 1915–71, but only four documents pre-date 1926 and only 20 are dated later than 1960. Running alongside DO 35 for a brief period from 1926 to 1929 is the series DO 117, Supplementary Original Correspondence, which comprises papers originally classified as secret or confidential and is the equivalent of the Colonial Office series CO 537 described at pp. 101. Later papers of this type have been placed in DO 35 or its successor series. There are no Dominions Office registers of secret correspondence.

The main correspondence series DO 35 was initially registered using the two-part system in use in the Colonial Office (see pp. 87–93). First registration was in the 'daily registers', using the Colonial Office register designated 'dominions' (CO 382/82, 1926–9) which continues in the overlapping Dominions Office series DO 6 (three volumes, 1928–9 only). The second stage of registration was in registers of correspondence similar to those in use in the Colonial Office, the main difference being that the Dominions Office registers are all in the one series – DO 3 (1927–42 only). The registers provide the subject of each despatch or letter, a note of the action taken and cross-references to other correspondence on the same subject. They are marked up to show destroyed papers. The four volumes for 1927 are described simply as 'registers of correspondence', but those for 1928 and 1929 are arranged by 'despatches', 'offices' and 'individuals' using the system with which we are familiar from the Colonial Office. From 1930 the registers are divided by the range of file numbers covered in each volume, and according to subject matter, following the division of work within the office. For example: DO 3/21, Files 4001–75: Constitutional Affairs, Imperial Conferences, Irish Free State; DO 3/28, Files 6501–908: Foreign Affairs, League of Nations, Treaties; DO 3/37, Files 10001–352: Canada, Australia, New Zealand, South Africa, S. Rhodesia, South Africa High Commission. These three registers cover the years 1930–2. Registers of out-letters are in DO 4 (1927–9 only).

In addition, the Dominions Office maintained a card index recording file reference numbers and subjects of the correspondence; this card index is available at TNA (DO 230). The card index is not complete, and includes references only to papers that were considered at the time to be particularly significant. Until 1936 the card index is arranged alphabetically by subject, but from 1937 it is arranged under broader subject headings.[1] As the correspondence in DO 35 is now catalogued in full it is debatable whether use of the registers and card index is necessary. But as noted for comparable records of the Colonial Office, they can be useful in providing brief details of correspondence which has not been selected for permanent preservation. The registers were abandoned in 1943, and the card index, which continues to 1946, does not record the action taken on correspondence. Neither has it been marked up to record if papers have been destroyed. File references given in the registers and card index can be traced in the catalogue of DO 35; if a file number cannot be found it must be assumed that the file has not survived unless it has been placed in the supplementary series DO 117 (1926–9 only). It is common for a number of small files to be tagged together to form one orderable document.

Ongoing amendments to the system of registration did not affect the placing of correspondence in DO 35 until more significant changes were introduced in the 1950s. Before the implementation of those changes, files within DO 35 begin to be arranged more clearly under the names of the internal departments responsible for the varied functions, for example the Constitutional Department or the Defence Department, rather then simply being arranged by the file numbers allocated to internal departments. This innovation led to the decision that the huge and unwieldy DO 35 should be gradually superseded by separate series for the records of the individual departments such as, to use the examples given above, Constitutional Department and Successors: Registered Files (CON series) (DO 161) 1953–67, and Defence: Registered Files (DEF series) (DO 164) 1957–67. By this period, of course, the Dominions Office had been reconstituted as the Commonwealth Relations Office (see p. 48–9) but the records continue under the 'DO' departmental code.

Although DO 35 holds almost all the Dominions Office/Commonwealth Relations Office correspondence until the development of separate departmental series in the 1950s there are a few exceptions, as follows:

High Commission for South Africa: Original Correspondence (DO 9) 1926–9 (with registers in DO 1 and DO 2)

[1] The research guide 'Dominions Office' providing information on the use of the card index and referred to in the first edition of this guide is no longer available in hard copy at TNA, but can be found in TNA's web archive at http://webarchive.nationalarchives.gov.uk/20091205113115/http://www.nationalarchives.gov.uk/catalogue/RdLeaflet.asp?sLeafletID=75&j=1 [accessed 7 Jan. 2015].

Honours (Dominions): Original Correspondence (DO 36) 1927–9
Overseas Settlement Department: Original Correspondence (DO 57) 1926–36 (with registers in DO 5 and DO 6)
Southern Rhodesia: Original Correspondence (DO 63) 1926–9 (registers in DO 7 and DO 8)
Imperial Service Order (Dominions): Original Correspondence (DO 81) 1927–9
Order of St Michael and St George (Dominions): Original Correspondence (DO 89) 1927–8

Later papers on these subjects were absorbed into DO 35.

A rather different case is that of the Private Office Papers in DO 121. These unregistered files cover a wide range of subjects including correspondence with British government representatives overseas, records of meetings held by the secretary of state, minutes to the prime minister and papers about the appointment of British government representatives in Commonwealth countries. The series includes a distinct collection of papers of Sir Eric Machtig, permanent under-secretary of state from 1940 to 1948. There is an account of the Ottawa Conference of 1932, and a file on the visit of King George VI and Queen Elizabeth to Canada and the USA in 1939. Files dating from after the Second World War include a number relating to Central Africa and the formation of the Central African Federation, and some on Bechuanaland (Botswana) and the Khama family. Three files include papers pre-dating the establishment of the Dominions Office: one relates to East Africa and covers the long period 1911–28; one relates to the appointment of Prince Arthur of Connaught as governor-general of South Africa (1920); and the third consists of correspondence relating to the establishment of the Dominions Office (1924–5).

The Commonwealth Relations Office correspondence series which gradually replace DO 35 from the early 1950s are arranged in both geographical and subject-related series. For example: India: Registered Files (DO 142); Far East and Pacific Department: Registered Files (FE series) (DO 169); Economic Policy: Registered Files (EC and EP series) (DO 165); Education: Registered Files (ED series) (DO 167). They are included as appropriate in the geographical or subject-based lists in appendices 1 and 2.

The Dominions Office, like the Colonial Office, printed some correspondence for ease of circulation within the office and for the information of the Cabinet and other government departments as required. There are three series: DO 114, Dominions, 1924–51; DO 115, Dominions (Australia) 1928–36; and DO 116, Dominions (South Africa) 1913–44. DO 201, accessioned in 2010, contains 53 volumes of Commonwealth Relations Office confidential printed dated 1946–66.

Another important grouping of records, which does not have an equivalent in the Colonial Office, is the collection of locally created records of British high commissioners to Commonwealth countries.[2] Following the Imperial Conference of 1926 a network of British

[2] In some cases, for example DO 154, Southern Rhodesia, these series include papers from the offices of the governors in the period immediately preceding independence.

high commissioners was gradually established in dominion capitals to provide a channel of communication between the British and dominion governments. They were able to deal directly with the government departments of the dominions to which they were posted, not being restricted, as was the case with ambassadors, to contacts with departments of external affairs. The dominion governments already maintained high commissioners in London, the direct descendants of the colonial agents. Governors-general remained in existence in the dominions to represent the monarch. Correspondence between the high commissioners and the Dominions Office and Commonwealth Relations Office will be found in DO 35 and the other series of correspondence and registered files. The number of series of high commissioners' records expanded as former colonies achieved independence and high commissioners were appointed to the newly independent countries. So, for example, a series of registered files from the High Commission in Malta (DO 203) commences in 1962, the year in which a new constitution gave Malta internal self-government. Malta attained full independence two years later. Series of high commissioners' records are included in the territorial listing in appendix 1.

None of the high commissioners' series is voluminous. At the time of writing the series for India is the largest with 232 files, followed by Canada with 144 and Eire/Republic of Ireland with 134. Some are very small indeed; the Sierra Leone series has seven files, and that for Trinidad and Tobago just two. It should be noted that because these are the local records of overseas diplomatic posts there have often been delays in their return to London and transfer to TNA.

One series of high commissioners' records is rather different from the others, and considerably bigger. DO 119 holds some of the records of the high commissioner for South Africa, a post dating from 1845 and holding wide responsibilities for relations with British colonies and independent states in the region and with adjacent German and Portuguese territories. Other records from the high commissioner's office were deposited with the Central African Archives in 1949 and are understood to be now in the National Archives of Botswana and of Zimbabwe. The records in DO 119 date from 1843 to 1965 but are held in a Dominions Office/Commonwealth Relations Office record series because the CRO was the responsible department for Southern Africa at the time of their transfer to the Public Record Office. Earlier correspondence with the High Commission and related records will be found in a number of Colonial Office record series as listed in appendix 1. For the very brief period 1926–9 Dominions Office correspondence with the High Commission is in the series DO 9 (it is registered in DO 1 and DO 2); thereafter correspondence is in DO 35.

Lastly, there are within the 'DO' records a small number of miscellaneous collections which do not fit into the arrangement adopted above. They are:

Commonwealth of Australia: Public Service Lists (DO 18) 1926–7

Colonial Office and Successors: Agreements, Treaties and Miscellaneous Documents (DO 118) 1856–1969. Material in this series which pre-dates the establishment of the Dominions Office relates primarily to the grant and surrender of licences for the economic exploitation of resources such as guano, copra and coconuts. However the series also contains the Anglo-Irish Treaty of 1921.

Southern Rhodesia Seals (DO 122) 1952–65 (containing two steel matrices for the seal of Southern Rhodesia, with copper counterparts)

Children's Overseas Reception Board (DO 131) 1940–59. The board (CORB) was responsible for co-ordinating the evacuation of children overseas during the Second World War. As well as general administrative and establishment files and minutes of meetings of advisory panels, the series includes a small selection of case files of children sent overseas and their escorts, registers of child applicants, unregistered lists of children considered by CORB and a history of the board.

British Phosphate Commissioners (DO 140) 1873–1983. The British Phosphate Commission was a board of Australian, British, and New Zealand representatives who managed extraction of phosphate from Christmas Island, Nauru and Ocean Island (Banaba). The series consists of minutes, memoranda, annual, general and technical reports, correspondence, and papers relating to a legal action brought by Banaban plaintiffs against the commissioners. Other records of the Australian and New Zealand commissioners are deposited in the National Archives of Australia.

South Africa High Commission: Agreements and Treaties (DO 141) 1881–1920

William Bankes Amery: Papers (DO 190) 1925–31. This series consists of an assortment of papers collected by William Bankes Amery between 1925 and 1931, all relating to the work of the Oversea Settlement Department of the Dominions Office in promoting emigration to Australia in accordance with the terms of the Empire Settlement Act 1922. It includes correspondence with his successor as British government representative in Australia for migration, E. T. Crutchley.

Imperial Economic Committee and Commonwealth Economic Committee: Records (DO 222) 1924–68

Two TNA record series were created for material relating to the India Office Library (DO 144) and the Indian Records Section (DO 184). Records intended for those series were subsequently deposited in the British Library, which, as noted elsewhere, holds the records and library collection of the India Office and its predecessors.

From 1926 the former *Colonial Office List* includes details of the Dominions Office, and is renamed the *Dominions Office and Colonial Office List* until 1940. The *List* was not published during the remaining years of the Second World War, and when it reappeared in 1946 it covered only the Colonial Office. The Commonwealth Relations Office published its own yearbook, the *Commonwealth Relations Office List*, only from 1953 to 1966. It includes details of the internal organisation of the office, which can be useful in identifying the correspondence series which succeed DO 35.

8. Records of the Commonwealth Office and the Foreign and Commonwealth Office

The Commonwealth Office, created by the merger of the Colonial Office and the Commonwealth Relations Office in August 1966, existed only for a little over two years until October 1968 when it joined with the Foreign Office to form the Foreign and Commonwealth Office (see pp. 50–1). Amalgamation was gradual over this period, and as part of the preparations for the smooth implementation of the merger the Foreign Office and Commonwealth Office operated a joint registry system from January 1967. When the offices were finally merged all files were closed, and a completely new set of files with new subject filing codes was begun on 17 October 1968. Some confusion was caused when the first records of the new office were transferred to TNA. The Foreign Office had previously run annual file cycles and regular users of the records were accustomed to a corresponding annual release of new material. In 1998, however, there was no such release because the decision had been made that a single initial file cycle should cover the period from January 1967 to October 1968, and be released in 1999. The subsequent file cycle therefore covers a period of just over a year, from October 1968 to December 1969. Thereafter files are in annual cycles.

The gradual period of merger further dictates the arrangement of the records in that for the years 1966–8 file series inevitably include material from the predecessor departments, as noted in the catalogue and in appendix 1. No separate departmental letter code was created for records of the Commonwealth Office which are found in CO, DO and FCO series. So, for example, the list of geographically arranged record series which include papers relating to the Bahamas reads as follows:

Colonial Office and Commonwealth Office: West Indian Department: Registered Files (WIS series) (CO 1031) 1948–67

Foreign Office and Foreign and Commonwealth Office: American and Latin American Departments: Registered Files (A and AL series) (FCO 7) 1967 onwards

Commonwealth Office: Atlantic Department: Registered Files (G series) (FCO 23) 1966–8

Commonwealth Office: West Indian Department 'B' and Foreign and Commonwealth Office, West Indian Department: Registered Files, Smaller Commonwealth West Indian Territories (WB and HW series) (FCO 44) 1967 onwards

Foreign and Commonwealth Office: North American and Caribbean Department and Caribbean Department: Registered Files (AN series) (FCO 63) 1968 onwards

Such information is included in appendix 1, whether or not the territory in question has achieved independence, in order to assist researchers working on the period from the late 1960s to the mid 1970s. All records of the Foreign and Commonwealth Office held at TNA are adequately described in the online catalogue; there are no original finding aids.

As noted in chapter 3, the collection of 'migrated archives' removed from former dependencies at independence has been transferred into the TNA series FCO 141. Recommendations made prior to that transfer have resulted in the compilation of an inventory of 'out of time' records held by the FCO; that is, records which have not been assessed for transfer to TNA in accordance with public records legislation. This collection is divided into two categories: 'departmental files' – annual files of the FCO only – which are late in being assessed for transfer, and 'special collections'. The latter is a highly miscellaneous collection, estimated at c. 600,000 items, including documentation from the Colonial Office and other of FCO's predecessor departments, some of which dates back many decades. The inventory, in the form of a spreadsheet, can be found at https://www.gov.uk/government/publications/foreign-offices-archive-inventory [accessed 7 January 2015]. A timetable for preparing 1980 to 1984 departmental files for release is also available (https://www.gov.uk/transfer-of-1981-and-1982-fco-files-to-the-national-archives).

To take just one example of Colonial Office material held among the 'special collections', there are 158 registered files from the Intelligence and Security Department, dated 1963–8. At time of writing these are being reviewed in preparation for transfer into the TNA series CO 1035 which currently includes files from the same series dated 1954–65.

Other records of the Foreign and Commonwealth Office cannot be covered here. The FCO series noted in appendix 1 are those of the primary geographical departments dealing with the individual territories; no attempt has been made to cover comprehensively the records of the myriad subject departments although a few references have been included in appendix 2. Record series from 1967 do, however, follow the internal organisation of the office which is described in the annual *Diplomatic Service List*, published from 1966 onwards and replacing the former *Foreign Office List*. A separate publication, the *Commonwealth Office Yearbook*, was published for 1967 and 1968, and continued thereafter as the *Yearbook of the Commonwealth*. This latter publication provides brief details of the individual Commonwealth countries, but given that it was published by the Commonwealth Secretariat (established in 1965) it says little about the Foreign and Commonwealth Office. The secretariat, based in London, maintains its own archive. A guide to its holdings can be found at http://thecommonwealth.org/library-and-archives/.

In addition to the registered file series created by the various geographical and subject departments within FCO there are a small number of other categories of records, most of which continue collections previously held in the records of the Foreign Office, Colonial Office and Commonwealth Relations Office. These include government gazettes of dependent territories;

records of embassies, high commissions, consulates and other British overseas representatives; protocols and ratifications of treaties;[1] and Private Office papers.

Readers interested in the detailed organisation of FCO records, and policy concerning the current and future selection of those records for permanent preservation, are advised to consult TNA's Operational Selection Policies (OSP) no. 13, 'Britain's diplomatic relations, 1973–96' and no. 23, 'Records of Britain's overseas representation, 1973–', available at http://www.nationalarchives.gov.uk/information-management/manage-information/selection-and-transfer/selecting-records/osp-number/.

[1] The series FCO 85 overlaps with the Foreign Office series FO 93, FO 94, FO 949 and FO 974 which continue, and are open, into the 1990s or the early years of the twenty-first century.

9. Private papers and private office papers relating to colonial affairs held in the records of the Colonial Office and of other government departments

Papers from the private offices of the secretaries of state for the colonies and other ministers can be found in the Colonial Office record series CO 967. This series contains private office papers on various subjects including the appointment of governors and other officials, visits to and development of the colonies, and the functions and organisation of the Colonial Office. There are also files relating to the League of Nations, the International Tin Agreement and the Imperial Communications Advisory Committee, together with correspondence with various governors and semi-official correspondence. Though the papers are unregistered many of those files originating with Sir Thomas Lloyd, permanent under-secretary for the colonies from 1947 to 1956, do retain departmental references. Papers in this series are arranged by subject or colony, or by the name of the minister or official whose private office papers they were.

Private office papers from the Dominions Office and Commonwealth Relations Office are in DO 121 (see p. 135). Later private files from the Foreign Office and Foreign and Commonwealth Office are in FCO 73.[1]

A certain amount of non-public correspondence created in the Colonial Office (as in other government departments) was removed by ministers, especially before the 20th century, and is now in libraries, record offices or private hands, but some is in TNA. Private correspondence and letter books of Earl Bathurst, secretary of state from 1812 to 1827, are in CO 323/142A, 142B and 143, and CO 324/73–5. Similar collections for R. W. Hay, permanent under-secretary of state 1825–36, are in CO 323/144–75 and CO 324/76–94. Private letter books of Sir R. J. Wilmot Horton, parliamentary under-secretary from 1821 to 1828, concerning North America and the West Indies, are in CO 324/95–100; and of William Huskisson, secretary of state from 1827 to 1828, in CO 324/101–2. Private correspondence of Lord Stanley as secretary of state is in CO 537/140–3, and concerns Canada, 1842–5.

As the place of deposit for the records of UK government departments, TNA does not collect private papers, but in the past certain such collections were deposited with its predecessor, the Public Record Office. These are held primarily in a number of PRO 30 series of original records acquired as gifts or on deposit, and include papers of four politicians who served as secretaries of state for the colonies during their varied careers, as follows:

[1] Earlier Foreign Office private office papers are in the series FO 800.

PRO 30/22, Lord John Russell: Papers. Russell was secretary for war and colonies from 30 August 1839 to 3 September 1841.

PRO 30/48, Viscount Edward Cardwell: Papers. Cardwell was secretary of state for the colonies from April 1864 to July 1866.

PRO 30/6, Henry Herbert, 4th earl of Carnarvon: Papers. Carnarvon was secretary of state for the colonies from July 1866 to March 1867, and from February 1874 to February 1878.

PRO 30/29, Leveson-Gower, 1st Earl Granville and predecessors and successors: Papers. Granville was secretary of state for the colonies from December 1868 to July 1870

The Colonial Office series CO 959, Various Private Collections, includes correspondence of Sir Bartle Frere, governor of Cape Colony, 1877–80; correspondence, reports and miscellaneous papers of Captain H. L. Norton Traill, resident in Northern Nigeria, 1909–22; private correspondence of Sir Robert Herbert, permanent under-secretary of state, concerning the abortive Lourenço Marques Treaty of 1879; a draft agreement regarding the future status of Transjordan, 1922; personal correspondence of E. V. G. Day (Malayan Civil Service), 1942–8 and 1952–3; and working papers of Louis Branney (land tenure expert in the African Studies Branch) relating to land tenure in Africa 1880–1950. Private papers of Sir Christopher Cox, education adviser to the secretary of state for the colonies, are in CO 1045 (see also under Advisers in chapter 6). The working papers of Lord Hailey in preparing *Native Administration in the British African Territories* are in CO 1018. Papers of W. B. Amery covering part of his period of service in the Oversea Settlement Department of the Dominions Office (1925–31) are in DO 190.

The Colonial Office records include papers of only one other colonial governor, Lord Aylmer, who was a governor of Lower Canada (CO 387, 1830–7).

Papers of a rather different type are the 'student files' maintained in the Welfare and Students Department of the Colonial Office. A total of 139 of these files have been selected for permanent preservation (CO 981, 1941–74); they include material on Hastings Banda, Julius Nyerere and Seretse Khama, subsequently presidents of Malawi, Tanzania and Botswana respectively.

The Foreign Office series FO 1109, Lord Butler of Saffron Walden: Private Office Papers, includes some papers from R. A. Butler's period as head of the Central African Office.

Material relating to colonial affairs will also be found in the following series: Amherst Papers (WO 34), Brownrigg Papers (WO 133), Buller Papers (WO 132), Chartwell Trust Papers (PRO 31/19), Codrington Papers (PRO 30/31), Anglo-American Committee of Enquiry on Palestine, 1946: Papers (PRO 30/78), Kitchener Papers (PRO 30/57), Lowry Cole Papers (PRO 30/43), Milner Papers (PRO 30/30), Murray Papers (WO 80), General Sir Charles Napier Papers (PRO 30/64), Northcote Papers (PRO 30/65), Roberts Papers (WO 105), Shaftesbury Papers (PRO 30/24), Harry Smith Papers (WO 135). The papers of Clement Attlee as secretary of state for the dominions are in CAB 118.

10. Maps and plans*

TNA does not hold a discrete map collection, but it does hold a huge accumulation of maps and related material estimated to amount to at least six million items. For British colonial history the most significant are the collections amassed for reference purposes by the Colonial Office library, and the maps extracted from Colonial Office records or still held in files, bound volumes of correspondence and other documents. On 1 January 1827 the Colonial Office circulated governors referring to want of geographical information and mapping and requesting half-yearly reports of progress in geographical and topographical knowledge.[1] These collections represent a vast area of the world, and are relevant for research into the history of topics such as exploration, boundary delimitation, the development of urban centres, plantations and extractive industries, postal and electoral districts, and many more. It should be stressed, however, that coverage is more comprehensive for some territories than for others.

The Colonial Office library collections have been deposited in TNA as follows:

CO 700, Colonial Office and Predecessors: Maps and Plans: Series I, 1595–1927, 2,975 flat sheets and volumes

CO 1047, Colonial Office: Maps and Plans: Series II, 1779–1947, 1,101 flat sheets

As the Colonial Office library provided a resource for both the Colonial Office and the Dominions Office there is no separate collection for the latter department, although there are maps in Dominions Office files.

CO 1054, Colonial Office and Successors: Maps and Plans: Post-1940 Collection, 1897–1984, 305 flat sheets. This collection includes maps from the Commonwealth Relations Office, Commonwealth Office and Foreign and Commonwealth Office. Other maps from this collection, together with a card index, were transferred to the Royal Geographical Society library.[2]

At time of writing no records have been transferred into the newly created TNA series CO 1072, Colonial Office: Registers and Indexes of Maps and Plans, 1900–1940.

Maps extracted from Colonial Office records (primarily for conservation reasons) can be found in the following series:

MPG 1, Maps and plans extracted to flat storage from various series of records of the Colonial Office and its predecessors, [1612]–1949, 1,240 portfolios

* I am grateful to Rose Mitchell, map archivist at TNA, for her contributions to this section.

[1] CO 854/1, f. 253.

[2] Royal Geographical Society (http://www.rgs.org/OurWork/Collections/Collections.htm [accessed 8 Oct. 2014]).

MPGG 1, Public Record Office: Maps and plans extracted to extra large flat storage from various series of records of the Colonial Office and its predecessors, 1715–1946, 127 portfolios

They can also be found in the general series of extracted flat maps (MF 1 and MFQ 1) and rolled maps (MR 1 and MRQ 1).

Where maps and plans (and other, usually oversized, items) have been extracted from documents, dummy sheets have been inserted in their place giving the new reference. However, this is often in an obsolete form and needs a very minor amendment before the item can be ordered: the insertion of the number '1' after the letter code. References were originally given in a two-part form, for example MPG 875. When TNA's catalogue was computerised it became necessary to introduce a series number, and this document should now be ordered as MPG 1/875.[3] Maps and plans contained in the Colonial Office library and extracted maps series are generally well catalogued, but many others remain undiscovered in bound volumes and files of correspondence, and in other documents. Cataloguing and serendipitous discoveries gradually uncover these.

As will be seen from the date ranges cited above, the library and extracted map collections precede our period by many years. TNA holds possibly the earliest English map of part of North America based on direct observation; a map probably made in 1585 and showing the location of the experimental colony of King's Island [Roanoke].[4] In 1676 colonial governors were instructed to procure and send home maps of the territories for which they were responsible. The Board of Trade acquired manuscript maps and plans, and purchased commercially printed maps and charts.[5] It also commissioned surveys, such as those of de Brahms and Samuel Holland in North America.

Similar library collections of maps and plans from the Foreign Office and the War Office have also been deposited in TNA in the series FO 925 and WO 78. Both are important for British dependencies. For example, a search for maps of, or including, Jamaica finds eight in FO 925 and over 40 in WO 78. For Gibraltar there are 20 in FO 925 and almost 50 in WO 78. These collections, especially FO 925, are also important for mapping of the dependencies of other European powers. Other War Office map series include those relating to campaigns of the First World War in Africa, Mesopotamia (Iraq) and Palestine (WO 300, WO 302 and WO 303 respectively), and Second World War campaigns in North Africa and the Mediterranean (WO

[3] Two items extracted from CO 273/165: (1) Plan of the waterfront at Singapore from Cavenagh Bridge to Middle Road, showing Town Hall, Cathedral, Raffles Monument, Raffles Hotel and other buildings. Scale: 1 inch to 4 chains. Compass indicator; (2) Plan of the Singapore River from Ord Bridge to Coleman Bridge, showing sea-wall. Scale: 1 inch to 1 chain. Compass indicator. Signed by H. E. McCullum, Major, RE, 10 Jan. 1890. Dimensions: (1) 34 cm × 52.3 cm; (2) 77 cm × 86.4 cm).

[4] MPG 1/584, extracted from CO 1/1.

[5] Until the British Navy set up its own Hydrographic Office in 1795 captains were reliant upon commercially published charts. In August 2014 the Hydrographic Office reported that part of its historical archive is in process of transfer to TNA. The transfer is concentrating on surveys dated before 1830 and supporting documentation before 1950.

234).[6] Yet other maps have been extracted from correspondence of the Foreign Office and the War Office, or remain with that correspondence.[7] An example of a map extracted from a Foreign Office document is David Livingstone's map of the Zambezi shown at figure 48.

Admiralty charts show the development of knowledge of colonial waters; significant numbers are included in the series CO 700, CO 1047, CO 1054, FO 925 and WO 78 described above, as well as in a number of Admiralty series.[8] Maps will also be found among other records of the Admiralty, such as the station records where they are sometimes appended in support of written records (see figures 43, 44 and 45).

Published guides to TNA maps include:

Maps and Plans in the Public Record Office, vol. 2: *America and West Indies*, ed. P. A. Penfold (London, 1974)

Maps and Plans in the Public Record Office, vol. 3: *Africa*, ed. P. A. Penfold (London, 1982)

Maps and Plans in the Public Record Office, vol. 4: *Europe and Turkey*, ed. G. Beech (London, 1998).

Two useful TNA research guides are:

'Maps and plans of lands abroad' (http://www.nationalarchives.gov.uk/records/research-guides/maps-plans-overseas-relations.htm)

'International boundaries in maps, surveys and other records' (http://www.nationalarchives.gov.uk/records/research-guides/maps-documents-international-boundaries.htm)

International boundaries

Maps of British and foreign dependencies are included among the public records for many reasons; they are especially important in the accurate depiction of international boundaries. A simple catalogue search on 'boundar*' (to pick up both 'boundary' and 'boundaries'), restricted to the departmental codes CO, DO and FCO, pulls up well over 1,000 references. The majority of the Colonial Office references come from the series CO 111, British Guiana original correspondence, which has recently been partially catalogued; they relate to ongoing disputes with Venezuela, Brazil and Suriname. Other boundary issues are recorded for British Honduras/Guatemala; British and Italian Somaliland; Northern Rhodesia/Belgian Congo; Nyasaland/Portuguese East Africa; Saudi Arabia/Aden, and many others.

[6] More information about military mapping of the First and Second World Wars can be found in TNA's research guides 'Military maps of the First World War' and 'Military maps of the Second World War'. Both are available via TNA's website (http://www.nationalarchives.gov.uk/records/research-guides/maps-military-first-world-war.htm and http://www.nationalarchives.gov.uk/records/research-guides/maps-military-second-world-war.htm [accessed 28 Nov. 2014]).

[7] Maps extracted from Foreign Office documents are in MPK 1 and MPKK 1; maps extracted from War Office documents are in MPH 1 and MPHH 1.

[8] See the research guide 'Admiralty charts (maps)' (http://www.nationalarchives.gov.uk/records/research-guides/admiralty-charts.htm [accessed 28 Nov. 2014]).

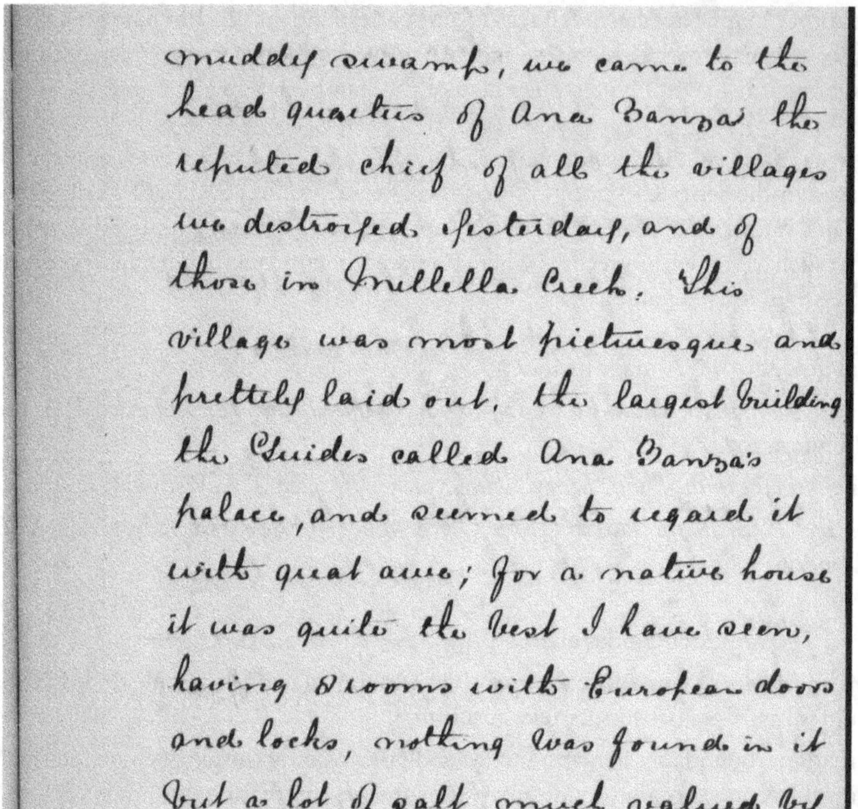

muddy swamp, we came to the head quarters of Ana Banza's the reputed chief of all the villages we destroyed yesterday, and of those in Mullella Creek. This village was most picturesque and prettily laid out, the largest building the Guides called Ana Banza's palace, and seemed to regard it with great awe; for a native house it was quite the best I have seen, having 8 rooms with European doors and locks, nothing was found in it but a lot of salt much valued by the natives, and as the "Geraldine's" cargo was partly salt it may fairly be presumed, that this was some of it. The village was set on fire, everything consumed, and the crops destroyed.

6.— The Natives, I feel certain never thought we should

penetrate

Figure 43. ADM 123/121, The expedition against the Congo pirates, 1875–6. Extract from the report of a punitive naval expedition against alleged pirates on the River Congo describing the destruction of villages and crops.

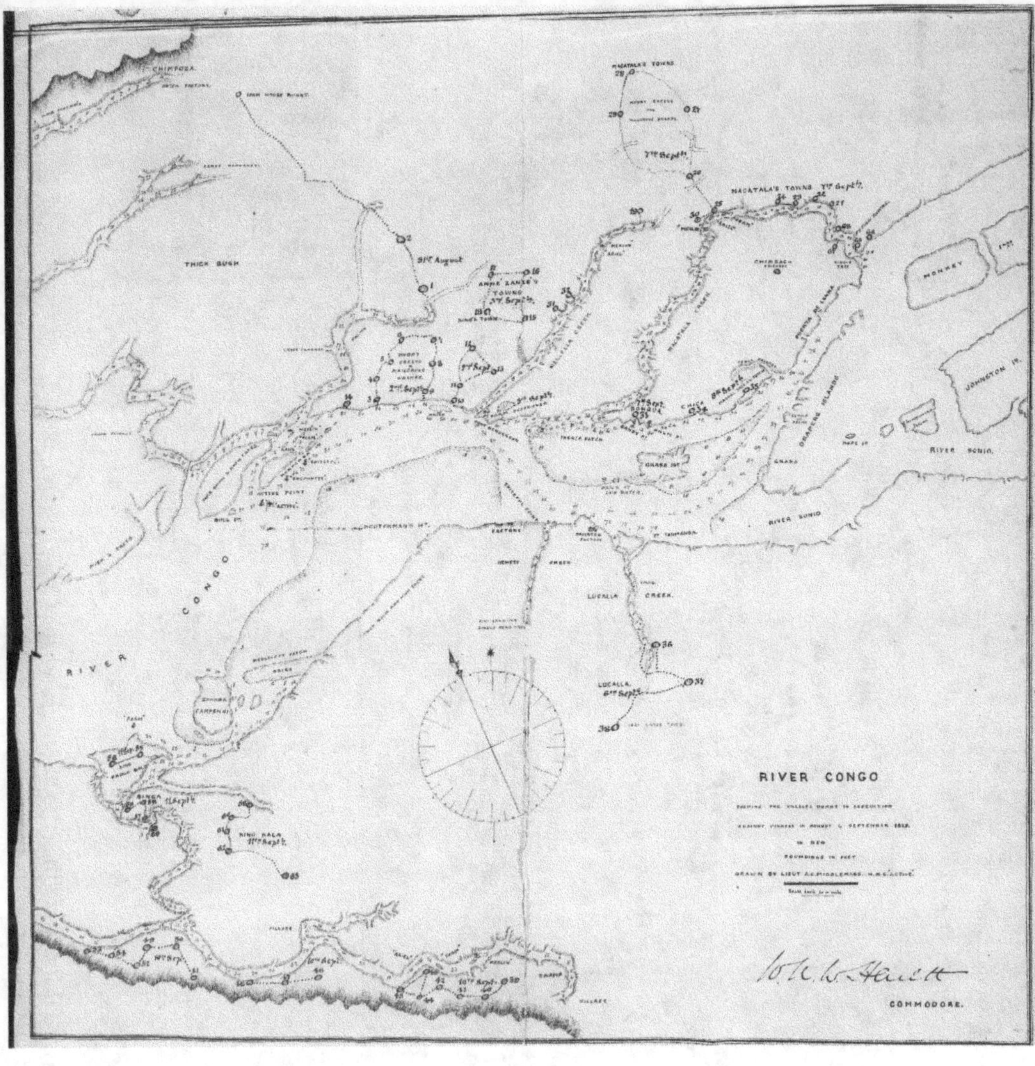

Figure 44. ADM 123/121. The expedition against the Congo pirates, 1875–6.
Map of part of the River Congo showing villages destroyed during a naval expedition against alleged pirates. No key to numbers used is included in the document.

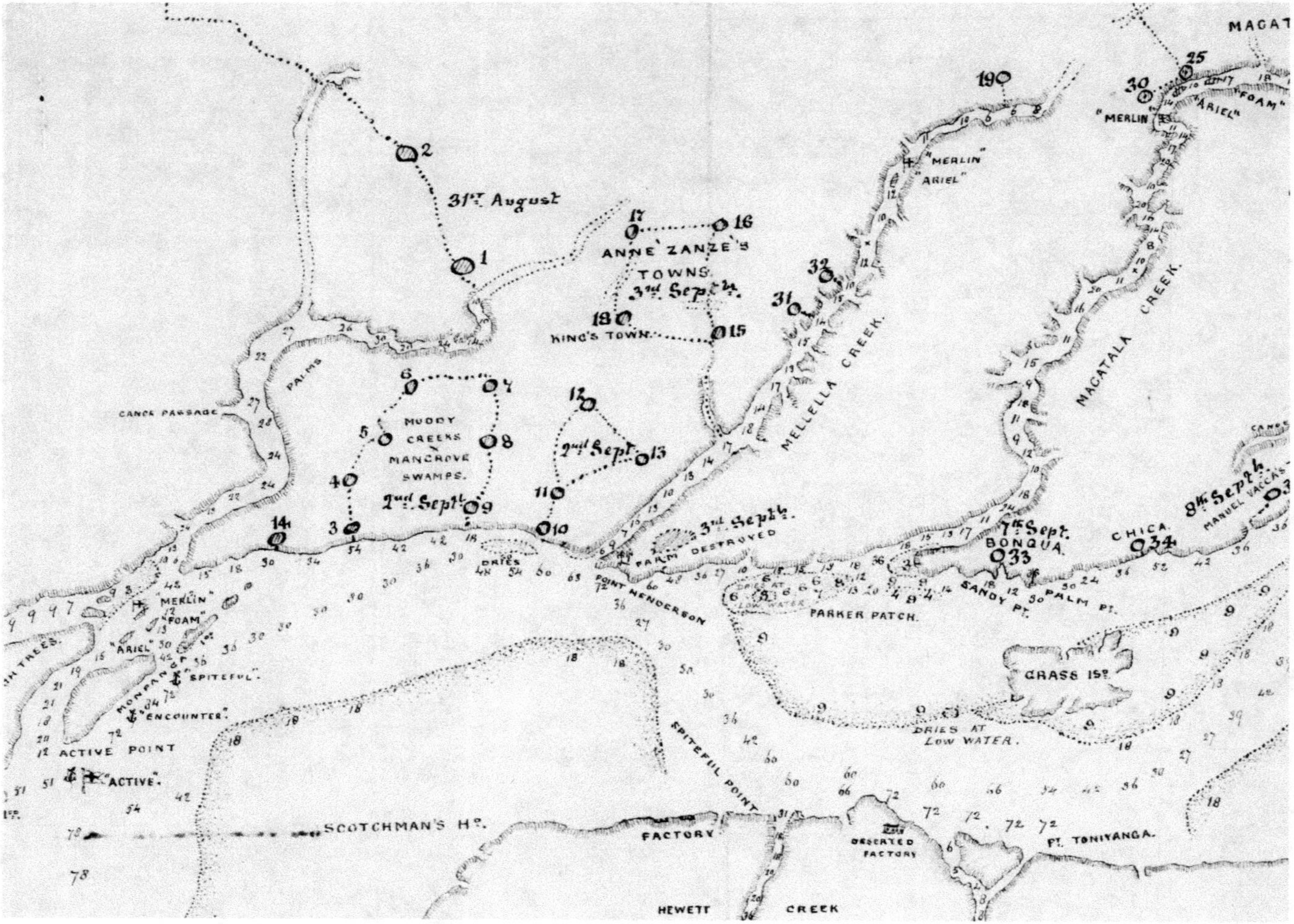

Figure 45. ADM 123/121. The expedition against the Congo pirates, 1875–6.
Enlargement of part of the map shown in figure 44 showing the location of the 'picturesque' village described in figure 43.

Again, a specific research guide is available: 'International boundaries: maps and other documents', Overseas Records Information 37 (http://nationalarchives.gov.uk/catalogue/RdLeaflet.asp?sLeafletID=387).

Directorate of Overseas Surveys

Systematic colonial surveys were first proposed in the aftermath of the Crimean War, when the War Office suggested that they might be a useful means of occupying military surveyors in peacetime. Disagreements between the military and the Ordnance Survey meant, however, that the proposal was not taken up. It was discussed again when the lack of adequate mapping was revealed during the South African War, but a programme was not established until the 1930s, and was then interrupted by the Second World War. A Directorate of Colonial Surveys was finally set up within the Colonial Office in 1946, with finance provided under the Colonial Development and Welfare Acts. Although systematic programmes of survey and mapping were envisaged to remedy the widespread lack of survey frameworks and topographical mapping in the colonies, these were almost immediately affected by urgent requirements for mapping to meet the need for development projects. An important element of the directorate's work was providing development assistance for local survey departments. The directorate, renamed the Directorate of Overseas Surveys in 1957, was transferred to the new Department of Technical Co-operation in 1961. In 1964 it became a special unit of the new Ministry of Overseas Development, and in 1970 it was transferred to the Overseas Development Administration on the creation of that department. In 1984/5 the directorate merged with the Ordnance Survey, and was renamed the Overseas Directorate; in 1992 the title of OS International was adopted; the organisation was finally wound up in 2002. Throughout these changes its functions remained largely constant and included field survey, mapping, aerial photography and the provision of technical advice and training for surveyors and associated personnel in developing countries.

Papers of and about the directorate will be found among the records of the Colonial Office and the Commonwealth Relations Office. From its transfer to the Department of Technical Co-operation in 1961 registered files are in OD 6, director's files in OD 5 and library records in OD 70. The latter consist primarily of tour briefs and reports, many of which date into the 1980s and 1990s and are not yet open. Material from the Ordnance Survey, known as the Ordnance Survey International Collection, was no longer required for operational purposes after 2002 and has been deposited at a number of institutions. The Royal Geographical Society has a full set of maps produced by the Directorate of Overseas Surveys and allied bodies; the Air Photograph Archive Library went initially to the British Empire and Commonwealth Museum, and subsequently, in 2012, to the National Collection of Aerial Photography in Edinburgh. Cambridge University Library and other bodies have taken remaining parts of the collection.[9] TNA will take the International Boundary Archive, selected registered files and survey records, and map production samples.

[9] For details see http://www.ordnancesurvey.co.uk/resources/historical-map-resources/international-collection.html [accessed 22 March 2015].

11. Photographs

Colonial Office

In 2008 an important collection of photographs was transferred to TNA from the Foreign and Commonwealth Office Library. It is now in the series CO 1069, Colonial Office and successors: Photographic Collection, 1815–2005, 920 photographs and volumes, and is estimated to comprise about 35,000 images. CO 1069/920 is an index to the collection, compiled in the FCO Library in 1986, which includes useful notes on the collection and on photographers.

The collection is formed from a core of the old Colonial Office collection, which began to come together when the secretary of state for the colonies asked governors, in 1869, to arrange for the taking of photographs of 'noteworthy buildings and scenery...together with individuals of various races peculiar to the colony'. The photographs were to be sent to the Colonial Office. The practice developed and over the next 100 years a collection was amassed consisting of a varied and eclectic set of images from all the dependencies. Some earlier images, including drawings and sketches, were added. After 1966 the collection was widened to include miscellaneous photographs from Commonwealth and Foreign sources, but the core of the collection remains the colonial element. Most photographs relating to India, Pakistan and Burma were separated out and now form part of the India Office collections at the British Library.

In February 2011, images from CO 1069 relating to Africa were digitised and uploaded to the photograph sharing website, Flickr, as a collection entitled 'Africa Through a Lens'. This was extended in June 2012 to Americas and Island Territories; in September 2012 to Asia; and in January 2013 to Australia. Links from TNA's online catalogue entry for CO 1069 provide access to the digitised images stored on Flickr, giving researchers an opportunity to add information about individual images, together with a range of background material about the content of the collection. It is important to note that the references used on the Flickr site are not necessarily the citable references which appear in TNA's catalogue. A small number of the images in CO 1069 have not been uploaded to Flickr for data protection and other reasons.

At the time of writing the album showing 'behind the scenes at the Colonial Office' which includes the photograph of Miss Heritage, reproduced as the frontispiece of this guide, has not been transferred into CO 1069 but is still with the FCO.[1]

Other photographs can be found among many Colonial Office records series, specifically the original correspondence. Recent cataloguing of such series will usually have identified any

[1] See CO 875/17/14 for details of this external photographic project and lists of subjects.

photographs included, but in most cases photographs are found by comprehensive searching or serendipity.

From the 1970s onwards the Public Record Office created the CN record series, an artificial accumulation to cater for photographic material extracted from records following transfer to the PRO, primarily as a preservation and/or security measure. A description of the photographs, including cross-references to the parent documents from which the material has been extracted, is included in the online catalogue. Extractions from Colonial Office records can be found in the CN 3 record series. They include the photograph of a durbar at Kumasi reproduced as figure 58 in this volume.

Central Office of Information

The British Empire Collection of Photographs is a collection of 8,472 photographs, dated 1945 to 1965, brought together by the Central Office of Information and illustrating the geography and way of life in colonial and Commonwealth territories. The photographs are arranged topographically by colony or dominion in albums with broad themes such as agriculture and food production; associations and societies; education; occupations and services; social conditions etc. They are held in the series INF 10 and are described individually in the catalogue.

Other government departments and private papers

Many other record series held at TNA include photographs on colonial and Commonwealth themes. Some may be identifiable through the catalogue; others may not. Clearly those of related government departments such as the Dominions Office, Foreign Office, and Foreign and Commonwealth Office must be considered. To take just three examples from other departments and private collections, the War Office file WO 32/17208 includes 10 photographs depicting riots in Singapore in 1956; the Admiralty document ADM 137/268 includes 66 photographs taken during the 1916 Lake Tanganyika expedition; the papers of James Ramsay MacDonald in PRO 30/69 include photographs taken during his visits to Australia, Canada, and South Africa. Further information is provided in the research guide 'Photographs' available at http://www.nationalarchives.gov.uk/records/research-guides/photographs.htm.

12. Records of other government departments

Some idea of the range of British government departments with an interest in colonial affairs can be derived from a basic search in TNA's catalogue for records relating to an individual dependency. Using 'Fiji' as a search term, for example, 2,310 results are found, grouped by department.[1] First comes the Colonial Office with 1,292 hits, followed by the Foreign and Commonwealth Office with 268 and the Foreign Office with 123. This is as might be expected. But records held in TNA from another 40 departments or closely related organisations are also included. In many cases contents may be insignificant; a total of 11 departments have only one document each relating to Fiji, and another 15 have results in single figures. But if you are looking for correspondence relating to the charter of the University of the South Pacific at Fiji or the establishment of a meteorological service there you will find material among these search results. If you are interested in the copra industry in Fiji you will certainly find material among the records of the Colonial Office, but there are additional papers among the records of the Ministry of Agriculture. Another fifteen departments have between 10 and 64 hits, the largest number being from the Admiralty. A search of this type also identifies maps, photographs and other items extracted from departmental files and volumes and no longer held under the departmental code of the originating body, as well as records of organisations such as the General Post Office, the Royal Botanic Gardens and the Natural History Museum which hold their own records rather than depositing them in TNA.

Only the briefest information about other government departments is given here, with an equally brief indication of those of their records which may be of use for research into colonial and Commonwealth affairs. A detailed introduction concentrating on the period from 1925 to 1957 is provided in the second volume of Thurston's guide.[2] A number of relevant research guides are available via TNA's website, its online catalogue provides short administrative histories of the departments, and some specific reference works are noted here.

Many government departments had some involvement in colonial affairs. The Air Ministry (AIR) maintained a liaison role with Commonwealth air forces, and provided some assistance in areas such as training. At an earlier period it was involved in the development of imperial air communications, as was the Ministry of Aviation (AVIA). The Royal Mint provided coinage, and there are a number of relevant 'MINT' record series. The Office of Works and its successors had responsibilities for British public buildings overseas, and although the discrete series in

[1] Search made on 12 Sept. 2007. The same search made on 8 October 2014, and not detailed here, gave the vastly increased total of 6,178. This indicates in some cases an actual increase in numbers of documents held, but in others is accounted for by refinements to the cataloguing which have revealed documents not previously identified.

[2] Thurston, vol. 2.

WORK 10 (registered files), WORK 40 (plans and drawings) and WORK 55 (photographs) are concerned primarily with buildings such as embassies and consulates in foreign countries, there is some colonial and Commonwealth content. Records of the Ministry of Labour (LAB) include correspondence and reports from labour attachés overseas, papers relating to international trades union federations, and some files concerning labour migration to the UK. The Board of Agriculture (MAF) and its successors clearly had ongoing interests in colonial produce. Records of the Medical Research Council (FD series) include much on tropical medicine and on research into diseases such as malaria, Trypanosomiasis, leprosy and bilharzia. There are many other examples. During the period when the empire was at the heart of British public life, rather than being of peripheral interest, many, if not all, government departments had at least a minor concern with colonial affairs.

Interdepartmental committees should also be mentioned here. Where an issue was not clearly the responsibility of a single government department such committees might be established to allow interdepartmental discussion and decision. Thurston lists a large number of interdepartmental committees concerned with some aspect of colonial affairs which sat during the period 1925–57.[3] Overall, however, papers of such committees are sometimes difficult to find; they are likely to be held among the records of the department which provided the committee's secretary, but who that person was is often unclear.

Admiralty

The importance of the Royal Navy in exploration, the expansion and defence of empire, and long distance trade hardly needs stating. It had a role in supporting British diplomacy in time of peace, it provided protection to merchant ships travelling in convoy at time of war, it patrolled the seas in search of illegal slavers after British Parliamentary abolition of the trade in 1807, and it provided ships and personnel for the Niger expeditions of the mid 19th century. Many of its personnel came from British colonies.[4] The story of one of them, subsequently claimed to be an escaped slave, is referred to at pp. 78–81. Many other matters reported by the Admiralty to the Colonial Office can be traced in more detail in the correspondence of naval officers to the Board of Admiralty, in the logs and journals of ships, captains and surgeons, and in the records of the naval stations.[5] As noted in appendix 1, one British dependency, Ascension, even had the status of a Royal Navy ship in the period during which it was administered by the Admiralty.

[3] Thurston, vol. 2, pp. 397–432.

[4] For example, the 'find your Trafalgar ancestor' database, available through TNA's website and searchable by place of birth, identifies 25 individuals who fought at Trafalgar and were born at Malta, 11 born in each of the West Indies and Africa, eight at Gibraltar, two in Canada and one in Newfoundland. Service records of ratings who joined the Royal Navy between 1853 and 1923 can also be searched online by place of birth (see http://www.nationalarchives.gov.uk/records/royal-naval-seamen.htm [accessed 9 March 2015]).

[5] An example of the latter is shown at figures 43–5 – an account of a punitive expedition against alleged pirates on the River Congo. Related material, including lieutenants' logs, is held at the National Maritime Museum (http://collections.rmg.co.uk [accessed 8 Oct. 2014]).

The records of the Admiralty are too vast even to be outlined here; two excellent and recent guides exist.[6] However particular note should be made of the series ADM 101, Admiralty and predecessors: Office of the Director General of the Medical Department of the Navy and predecessors: Medical Journals which has been recently re-catalogued in some detail. Previously catalogued only by ships' names and covering dates its contents were obscured. The journals contain not only accounts of the diseases and accidents befalling the crews, and their treatment, but sometimes details of places, peoples and events, for example in the case of journals of ships involved in the Niger Expedition.[7]

Board of Trade

The responsibilities of the Board of Trade for colonial affairs before 1782, and its records, are described in chapter 4. Because of the board's supervisory or regulatory role in areas such as shipping, patents, designs and trademarks and copyright, weights and measures, merchandise marks, companies, bankruptcy, insurance, the distribution of industry, films, and enemy property it continued to play an important role in ensuring legislative conformity throughout the empire, and a regular exchange of correspondence with the Colonial Office will be found in the CO original correspondence series. Records of the board itself include not only correspondence and papers relating to the responsibilities mentioned above but also service records of merchant seamen who, of course, came from all over the empire, records concerning the registration of shipping, and passenger lists for ships arriving from or leaving for destinations outside Europe in the period from about 1890 to 1960. TNA research guides covering these functions can be found through TNA's website.

British Council[8]

The British Committee for Relations with Other Countries was established in 1934, and soon renamed the British Council. Its initial purpose was to counter cultural propaganda by the Axis powers; more generally its functions were to promote wider appreciation of Great Britain and the English language abroad and to develop closer cultural and commercial links with other countries. Since the Second World War, the British Council has been represented overseas – both within the Commonwealth and in foreign states – and its activities have included the promotion of English language teaching and British studies in foreign educational institutions, the maintenance of British libraries and cultural centres abroad and the general fostering of contacts in educational, scientific and professional fields. The council is not a government department, and its records are not public records, but they have been deposited at TNA. They

[6] *A Guide to the Naval Records in The National Archives of the UK*, ed. R. Cock and N. A. M. Rodger (London, 2006), the coverage of which is wider than just the records of the Admiralty; B. Pappalardo, *Tracing your Naval Ancestors* (Public Record Office, London, 2003), which also has a wider application than is suggested by its title.

[7] See especially the medical journal of HMS *Albert*, ADM 101/82/2, 1840–2.

[8] For a history of the council, see F. Donaldson, *The British Council: the First Fifty Years* (London, 1984).

APPENDIX (Refce. 602/49)

Revised

CONFIDENTIAL

THE SITUATION AT MAKERERE

1. Introduction

It is difficult to form a clear picture as reports reaching the IUC are at times contradictory and in any case correspondence is subject to censorship. The last first-hand account received is from a member of staff who left Makerere on 24 October.

Events have unfortunately clouded Makerere's Jubilee Celebrations held in early October.

2. Academic Situation

1. The Vice-Chancellor, Mr. Frank Kalimuzo, was apparently arrested by the army on 5 October durin the period of the Jubilee Celebrations. Members of staff are said to have made contact with him for a time when he was in custody but there are now fears in Makerere that he is no longer alive. On the other hand, there are other recent, more hopeful, reports to the contrary. His arrest meant that at a critical stage Makerere lacked the authority of a Vice-Chancellor on the spot. Professor Wandira (Professor of Education and at one time Registrar) who has been appointed Acting Vice-Chancellor, was away in Europe.

2. Another senior African member of staff, the Librarian, is reported as having disappeared.

3. Two British members of staff who served in Uganda for many years have been required to leave - Sir Ian McAdam (Professor of Surgery) and Professor R. R. Trussell (Professor of Obstetrics and Gynaecology) - together with a senior Government Medical Consultant from the Teaching Hospital. Professor Trussell has now arrived in the United Kingdom and is in touch with the IUC. He has reported that he met with no physical harassment.

4. There have been reports of up to 80 resignations over the University as a whole and it is said that the 20 or so Asians on the staff have resigned. As the majority of expatriate staff held short-term contracts it is difficult to assess the significance of this figure since the number may include those who intend to stay only until their contracts run out in order to ~~secure~~ avoid losing any of the ~~full~~ contract benefits.

Figure 46. BW 90/1384, 1972, Inter-University Council: Makerere University and the present Uganda situation. Extract from correspondence and papers outlining events under the regime of Idi Amin.

include papers from the council's London headquarters, including committee papers, and from its overseas offices. Two educational organisations amalgamated with the British Council in 1981, the Inter-University Council for Higher Education Overseas and its advisory body the Technical Education and Training Organisation for Overseas Countries. Figure 46 shows an extract from an I-UC report about the situation at Makerere University, Uganda, during the regime of Idi Amin. In December 1993 the British Council became the corporate trustee of the Central Bureau for Educational Visits and Exchanges and in effect absorbed its functions, though the bureau retained its distinct organisation.

The Cabinet Office

The Cabinet Office was established in 1916 to act as the secretariat for the Cabinet and its committees. As will be seen from the catalogue, however, a number of the 'CAB' record series pre-date 1916; these include records of the Committee of Imperial Defence and its sub-committees, and copies of prime ministers' letters to the sovereign, held in the Royal Archives at Windsor, reporting proceedings at Cabinet meetings. Minutes of the full Cabinet, known as 'conclusions', are in the record series CAB 23 (1916–39), CAB 65 (1939–45) and CAB 128 (1945 onwards). Associated 'memoranda', the papers presented to the Cabinet on the matters under discussion, are in CAB 24, CAB 66 and CAB 129. At the time of writing only CAB 65 and CAB 66 are listed in detail in the catalogue; reference to the other series is through contemporary indexes held at TNA. However, Cabinet papers, including minutes and memoranda dated from 1915 onwards, have been digitised by TNA in a project funded by the Joint Information Systems Committee (JISC). The papers are available to search and download at http://www.nationalarchives.gov.uk/cabinetpapers/ [accessed 8 October 2014].[9] A published guide to the work and records of the Cabinet (to 1945 only) is available.[10]

Numerous committees and sub-committees of the Cabinet were relevant to colonial affairs, for example the Africa Committee, the Committee on the Ceylon Constitution, the Colonial Affairs Committee, the Colonial Policy Committee, the Committee on Colonial Immigrants, the Committee on Copper Production in Northern Rhodesia, the Committee on Judicial Appeals from Malaya, the Committee on Palestine and many others. A full listing for the period 1925–57 is provided by Thurston.[11] Others can be identified through the catalogue.

The series CAB 133, Commonwealth and International Conferences and Ministerial Visits to and from the UK: Minutes and Papers, 1944 onwards, is particularly important for the decolonisation period. It includes records of conferences and related meetings to consider the constitutions of Nigeria, the Federation of Malaya, Singapore, Fiji, the Federation of Rhodesia and Nyasaland, the Leeward and Windward Islands, Malta, Mauritius, Northern Rhodesia, Southern Rhodesia,

[9] Images of documents in CAB 128 and CAB 129 from the period of Harold Macmillan's premiership have been made available by Adam Matthew Publications (http://www.amdigital.co.uk [accessed 8 Oct. 2014]).

[10] S. S. Wilson, *The Cabinet Office to 1945* (London, HMSO, 1975).

[11] Thurston, vol. 2, pp. 15–260.

Zanzibar, Antigua, Barbados, British Guiana, Kenya, Nyasaland, Sierra Leone, the West Indies, St Christopher (St Kitts)-Nevis-Anguilla and St Vincent. It also contains records of meetings of Commonwealth prime ministers and other politicians and officials.[12]

Registered files of the Cabinet Office in the series CAB 21 contain some miscellaneous papers relating to the dependencies. For example a search for material concerning New Zealand identifies 39 files relating primarily to defence, trade and visits by prime ministers and members of the royal family.

Central Office of Information

A Ministry of Information existed for a brief period towards the end of the First World War, but was dissolved late in 1918. The Foreign Office was subsequently responsible for overseas information and publicity services. On 5 September 1939 a Ministry of Information was again created; it became the Central Office of Information in April 1946. As well as the correspondence series of the Ministry and the Central Office, which contain material on overseas information, publicity, press and propaganda, there are collections of photographs, posters and original artwork, and film production documents. INF 2 includes publicity material produced in or for India, Burma, Africa and the dominions during the Second World War. INF 3 is a collection of original paintings and drawings produced for propaganda and publicity purposes during the Second World War; it includes some material designed for the colonies. INF 10 is a collection of about 8,000 photographs representing the geography and way of life in British colonies and the Commonwealth and dating from 1945 to 1965 (see chapter 11). INF 6 includes film production documents from the Colonial Film Unit; TNA does not hold the films themselves.[13]

Civil Service Commission[14]

The Civil Service Commission, established in 1855, regulated the admission of candidates to the UK Civil Service and conducted competitive examinations, including, sometimes, for posts in the colonies. CSC 10, for example, includes tables of marks and results from examinations for 'Eastern cadetships' (in Ceylon, the Straits Settlements and Hong Kong) and for sub-inspectors of police in British Guiana. A small collection of individual case files relating to people who were, or became, famous or infamous have been transferred to TNA. They include files on Sydney Olivier (CSC 11/206) and Sidney Webb (CSC 11/262).[15]

[12] See also *Imperial and Commonwealth Conferences* (London, List and Index Society, 280, 2000)

[13] Copies are likely to be held by the British Film Institute National Archive or the Imperial War Museum.

[14] For a history, see R. A. Chapman, *The Civil Service Commission, 1855–1991: a Bureau Biography* (London, 2004).

[15] Olivier and Webb were contemporaries in the Colonial Office in the late 19th century. Olivier, who remained in the colonial service and was governor of Jamaica from 1907 to 1913, became secretary of state for India in the short-lived Labour government of 1924. Webb, who soon left the Colonial Office to concentrate on his political work, became secretary of state for the colonies in 1929 (as Lord Passfield).

Crown agents

The difficulties experienced by early colonists in maintaining control of their affairs in the UK led to their appointing 'agents' to handle their affairs.[16] This came to be a system also adopted for the transaction of official business. There were three types of official agents: colonial agents, appointed by colonial governments; king's agents, appointed by the Crown with a duty to aid and protect merchants and trade in the colonies; and Crown agents, appointed on the recommendation of the Treasury to receive and account for moneys issued by the Treasury. The first regular appointment of a Crown agent, for Nova Scotia, was made in 1749, and between then and 1835 there were 25 more appointments. In 1830 commissioners recommended that the agents be established as a consolidated agency, rather than there being a separate agent for each colony. Subsequently all agents were dismissed, and two of their number, both former Colonial Office clerks, were re-appointed as the joint agents-general for the Crown colonies in 1833. A further re-organisation took place between 1858 and 1863. Very few of the records of the Crown agents before 1863 survive, but there is a considerable amount of correspondence from them in the Colonial Office correspondence series. The agents assumed responsibilities in areas such as procurement – for example the supply of uniforms and equipment for the King's African Rifles and the West Africa Frontier Force, and the issuing of postage stamps – the raising of loans, recruitment to posts in colonial governments, and construction projects such as the development of railway networks and harbours. In 1954 their name was changed to Crown Agents for Oversea Governments and Administrations. Not all of the agents' records are public records; those that are are held at TNA in 'CAOG' record series. For a timeline of the Crown Agents history and responsibilities see http://www.crownagents.com/about-us/our-history [accessed 25 January 2015].

Empire Marketing Board

The Empire Marketing Board was a government department established in 1926 to administer the Empire Marketing Fund. As Stephen Constantine has noted, it was a constitutional oddity: 'Technically, the Board was an advisory committee of the Secretary of State for the Dominions. But as he was *ex officio* chairman and authorised its activities, the Board possessed executive authority.'[17] Its work was of three types, each supervised by one of its committees: it gave research grants for the investigation of problems affecting food production; it supervised investigations into such problems and those affecting food distribution; and it attempted to influence consumer choice and promote colonial products. A prominent part of its activities was its poster campaign. One of the most famous images of that campaign is the map 'Highways of Empire' by MacDonald Gill (see figure 47).[18]

[16] See L. M. Penson, *The Colonial Agents of the British West Indies* (London, 1924).

[17] S. Constantine, *Buy and Build: the Advertising Posters of the Empire Marketing Board* (London, HMSO, 1986), p. 3.

[18] EMB posters held by TNA in the series CO 956 are supplemented by collections held at the Victoria & Albert Museum, the Manchester City Galleries and Birmingham City University.

Figure 47. CO 956/537A. Empire Marketing Board poster 'Highways of Empire'; artist: Macdonald Gill

The board was wound up in 1933, a victim of government hostility and financial restraints. Its records are:

Dominions Office: Empire Marketing Board: Original Correspondence (CO 758) 1922–34, 107 boxes

Dominions Office: Empire Marketing Board: Card Index (CO 759) 1922–34, 134 bundles (an index to correspondence)

Colonial Office: Empire Marketing Board: Posters (CO 956) 1926–39, 734 flat sheets

The Colonial Empire Marketing Board was established in 1937 by the secretary of state for the colonies, acting as chairman, following the recommendations of an interdepartmental committee, to promote the marketing of colonial produce in the United Kingdom and overseas. It included MPs and representatives of commercial and shipping interests as well as members from the Department of Overseas Trade and the Imperial Institute. It was financed through, and worked closely with, the Colonial Office. Its operations were cut short by the outbreak of the Second World War.

Colonial Office: Colonial Empire Marketing Board: Original Correspondence (CO 868) 1938–9, 7 boxes

Foreign Office

Records of the Foreign Office are, in general, included in the territorial listings in appendix 1 only where that office had administrative responsibility for territories – usually protectorates – before the Colonial Office became the lead department, or in the case of countries which did not join, or subsequently left, the Commonwealth after achieving independence. Researchers should be aware, however, that the Foreign Office, as the government department with formal responsibility for managing the external relations of the United Kingdom and its dependencies, had an ongoing and significant role in colonial affairs. It was, for example, responsible for diplomatic relations with Spain concerning the British dependency of Gibraltar, and for relations with China concerning Hong Kong. It was concerned with boundary questions between British dependencies and their foreign neighbours. It was responsible for British colonial subjects in foreign territories, and for foreign subjects resident in British colonies. British diplomats and consular agents in foreign states or the dependencies of such states were often involved in questions relating to the British empire; they reported to the Foreign Office. The Foreign Office was also responsible for Britain's relations with international organisations such as the League of Nations and the United Nations, and with their specialist agencies. In the case of mandated territories, although the Colonial Office was responsible for the day-to-day administration of, for example, Palestine and Tanganyika, it was the Foreign Office that reported to the mandatory powers on that administration. The Foreign Office was also responsible for those countries which were never British dependencies, but which formed part of the 'informal' empire (see pp. 5–6).

Comprehensive guides to the records of the Foreign Office and its predecessors exist, and should be consulted by researchers wishing to make much use of those records.[19] Briefly, however, the records of the Foreign Office commence in or about 1782.[20] From that date until 1905 the main series of correspondence between the Foreign Office, British diplomats and consuls overseas, and foreign diplomatic representatives in the UK are arranged by country, for example FO 27, France; FO 72, Spain. British interests in matters concerning French or Spanish colonial dependencies are likely to be covered in those series. From 1906 when the Foreign Office reorganised its registry systems all these geographic series continue in FO 371 and some closely related series.

Another important category of Foreign Office records is the collection of Embassy and Consular Archives (also known as 'post' records), that is the internal records of British embassies and consulates ('posts') overseas. It should be noted, however, that there are substantial gaps in the embassy and consular archives, and for some posts no material survives. The Foreign Office Library map collection, now at TNA in the series FO 925, together with other maps extracted from correspondence, is also important for colonial studies and is described further in chapter 10. David Livingstone's 1859 map of the Zambezi, extracted from the series of correspondence with Portugal (FO 63) is shown at figure 48.

Like the Colonial Office the Foreign Office printed some of its correspondence. FO 881 is a virtually complete numerical series of confidential print covering the years 1827–1914; there are additional geographical series duplicating and continuing this collection. Figure 49 shows the first page of a letter from Livingstone describing his exploration of the Zambezi.[21]

Special mention should also be made of a small number of record series which have not been subject to the usual 30-year closure arrangements. One is FO 93, Protocols of Treaties, which continues to 2003 and is open. It includes, for example, an 'exchange of notes' between the UK and the USA concerning the construction of a monitoring facility on Diego Garcia (1999), and an Anglo-Dutch 'agreement concerning Air Services between and beyond the United Kingdom Overseas Territories of Anguilla, Bermuda, the British Virgin Islands, the Cayman Islands, Montserrat and Turks and Caicos Islands on one hand, and The Netherlands Antilles on the other' (2000). The treaty series FO 93 continues in FCO 85 after 2003. Other series which are open are FO 972, foreign policy papers, and FO 973, 'background briefs'. Both were prepared in the Research Department (later Research and Analysis Department) from 1978 to 1992 for general briefing purposes. They tend to be fairly short, but can be useful in presenting an account of a wide variety of contemporary topics such as the Brandt Commission

[19] M. Roper, *The Records of the Foreign Office, 1782–1968* (Public Record Office, 2002); L. Atherton, *'Never Complain, Never Explain': Records of the Foreign Office and State Paper Office 1500–c.1960* (Public Record Office, 1994).

[20] Earlier records of the secretaries of state concerned with diplomatic relations are in a number of State Papers, Foreign series

[21] Livingstone is best known as an explorer and missionary; he was also a British consul, as was Roger Casement whose work in exposing the conditions of British colonial and foreign workers in the Congo and South America is covered in his correspondence and reports to the Foreign Office.

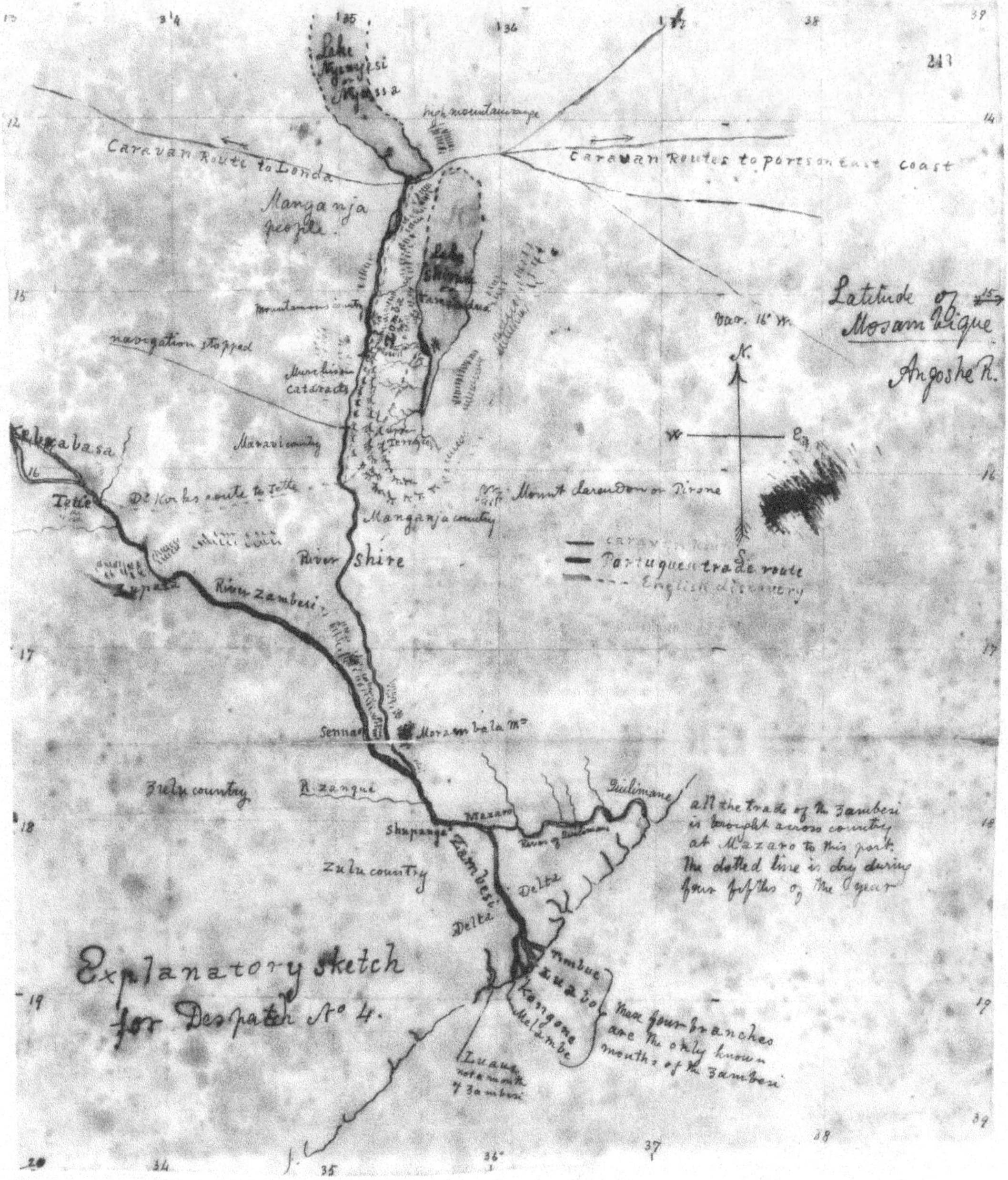

Figure 48. MPK 1/422(1). Sketch map, drawn by David Livingstone, of the area (now in Malawi) southwards from about 13° 20′ S as far as the Tete area, the Zambezi delta and Quelimane (now in Mozambique). Shows the Shire River, Lakes Chirwa and Nyasa, the mouths of the Zambezi River, and trade routes.

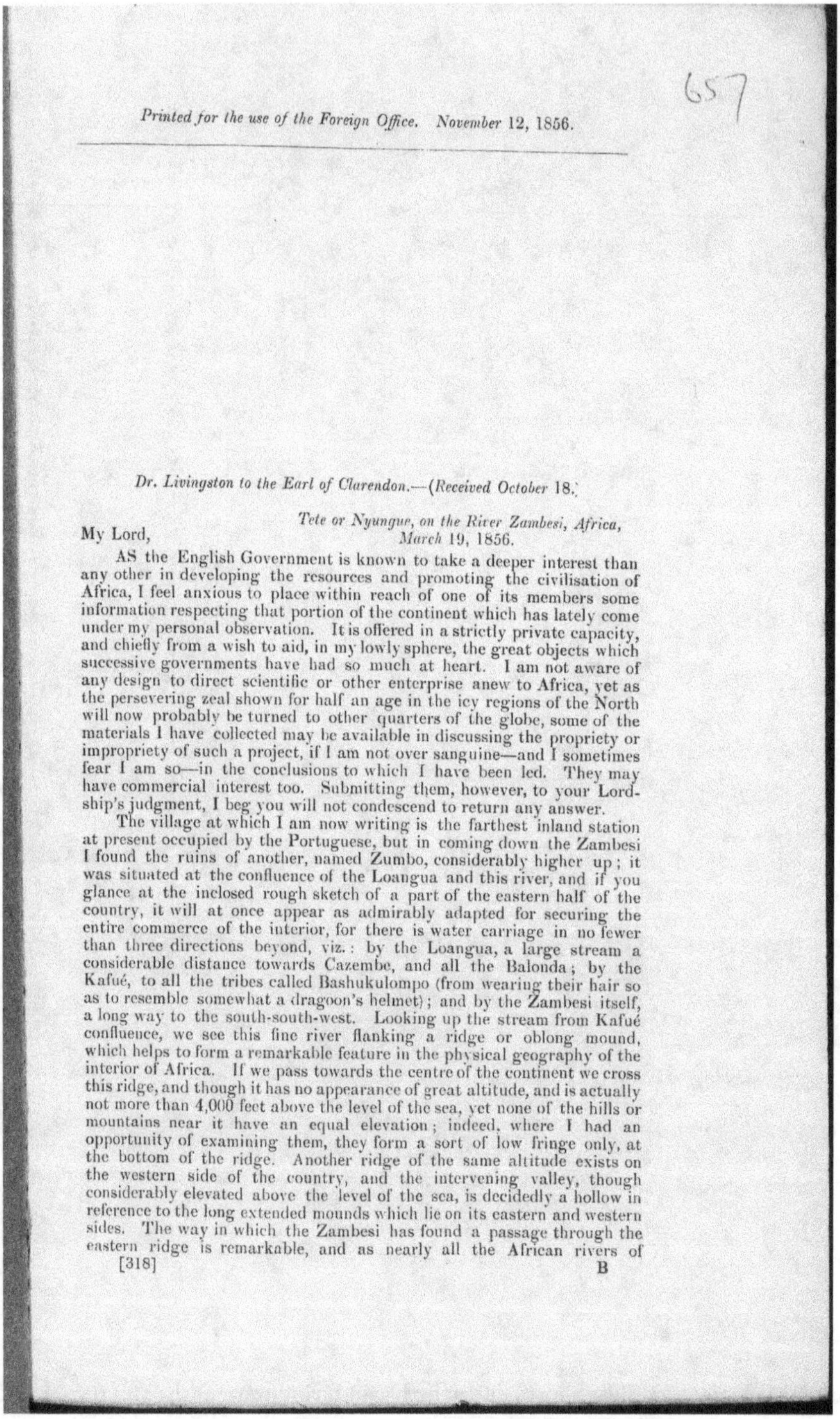

657

Printed for the use of the Foreign Office. *November* 12, 1856.

Dr. Livingston to the Earl of Clarendon.—(*Received October* 18.)

Tete or Nyungue, on the River Zambesi, Africa,
March 19, 1856.

My Lord,

AS the English Government is known to take a deeper interest than any other in developing the resources and promoting the civilisation of Africa, I feel anxious to place within reach of one of its members some information respecting that portion of the continent which has lately come under my personal observation. It is offered in a strictly private capacity, and chiefly from a wish to aid, in my lowly sphere, the great objects which successive governments have had so much at heart. I am not aware of any design to direct scientific or other enterprise anew to Africa, yet as the persevering zeal shown for half an age in the icy regions of the North will now probably be turned to other quarters of the globe, some of the materials I have collected may be available in discussing the propriety or impropriety of such a project, if I am not over sanguine—and I sometimes fear I am so—in the conclusions to which I have been led. They may have commercial interest too. Submitting them, however, to your Lordship's judgment, I beg you will not condescend to return any answer.

The village at which I am now writing is the farthest inland station at present occupied by the Portuguese, but in coming down the Zambesi I found the ruins of another, named Zumbo, considerably higher up; it was situated at the confluence of the Loangua and this river, and if you glance at the inclosed rough sketch of a part of the eastern half of the country, it will at once appear as admirably adapted for securing the entire commerce of the interior, for there is water carriage in no fewer than three directions beyond, viz.: by the Loangua, a large stream a considerable distance towards Cazembe, and all the Balonda; by the Kafué, to all the tribes called Bashukulompo (from wearing their hair so as to resemble somewhat a dragoon's helmet); and by the Zambesi itself, a long way to the south-south-west. Looking up the stream from Kafué confluence, we see this fine river flanking a ridge or oblong mound, which helps to form a remarkable feature in the physical geography of the interior of Africa. If we pass towards the centre of the continent we cross this ridge, and though it has no appearance of great altitude, and is actually not more than 4,000 feet above the level of the sea, yet none of the hills or mountains near it have an equal elevation; indeed, where I had an opportunity of examining them, they form a sort of low fringe only, at the bottom of the ridge. Another ridge of the same altitude exists on the western side of the country, and the intervening valley, though considerably elevated above the level of the sea, is decidedly a hollow in reference to the long extended mounds which lie on its eastern and western sides. The way in which the Zambesi has found a passage through the eastern ridge is remarkable, and as nearly all the African rivers of

[318] B

Figure 49. FO 881/657, 1856. Foreign Office 'confidential print' reproducing a report from David Livingstone.

Report (1980) and 'Haiti: before and after Aristide' (1992). There is occasional coverage of historical subjects such as the 1820 Settlers in South Africa. Reports in these two latter series are, of course, those of the Foreign and Commonwealth Office rather than the Foreign Office, although held in FO series.

A little more information about Foreign Office records is given in the specimen search at appendix 7.

Home Office

As noted elsewhere, the Home Office was responsible for colonial affairs from 1782 to 1801. This has not significantly affected the arrangement of the surviving records although it has left a gap in the series of registers of correspondence. Thereafter, however, the Home Office is significant in that it had responsibilities for immigration, nationality and for colonial peoples in the UK. Its records collection includes certificates of the registration as British nationals of colonial people resident in the UK (HO 334), and service records of men who served in the Royal Irish Constabulary.

Intelligence agencies

Special Branch

The Metropolitan Police Special Irish Branch was formed in March 1883 to counter Irish 'Fenian' terrorism on mainland Britain. Over the years, Special Branch took on responsibility for combating a wide range of extremist and terrorist activity and the term 'Irish' was dropped from its title. Special Branch had responsibility for gathering, collating and exploiting intelligence on extremist political and terrorist activity, disseminating intelligence for operational use and assisting other government agencies to counter threats to the security of the United Kingdom. It was also responsible for the protection of VIPs.

In 2006 the government announced that Special Branch was to merge with Scotland Yard's anti-terrorist branch to form the Counter-Terrorism Directorate. The key reform of the restructuring was to combine the intelligence-gathering activities of Special Branch with the investigatory functions of the Anti-Terrorist Branch.

To date only a small selection of Special Branch files have been released to TNA (in MEPO 38). Among those with relevance to colonial affairs are a file relating to Nancy Cunard and the Negroes Welfare Association (1932–47); a report on the history of communism in Ireland (1925); reports on the International African Service Bureau (1937–65); a report on possible extremist associations of Vengalil Krishnan Krishna Menon, appointed Indian high commissioner in London, 1947 (1928–73); and reports on Kwame Nkrumah, ex-president of Ghana, with regard to an international arrest warrant for extradition from Britain on charges of extortion and theft (1949–91). See figures 50 and 51.

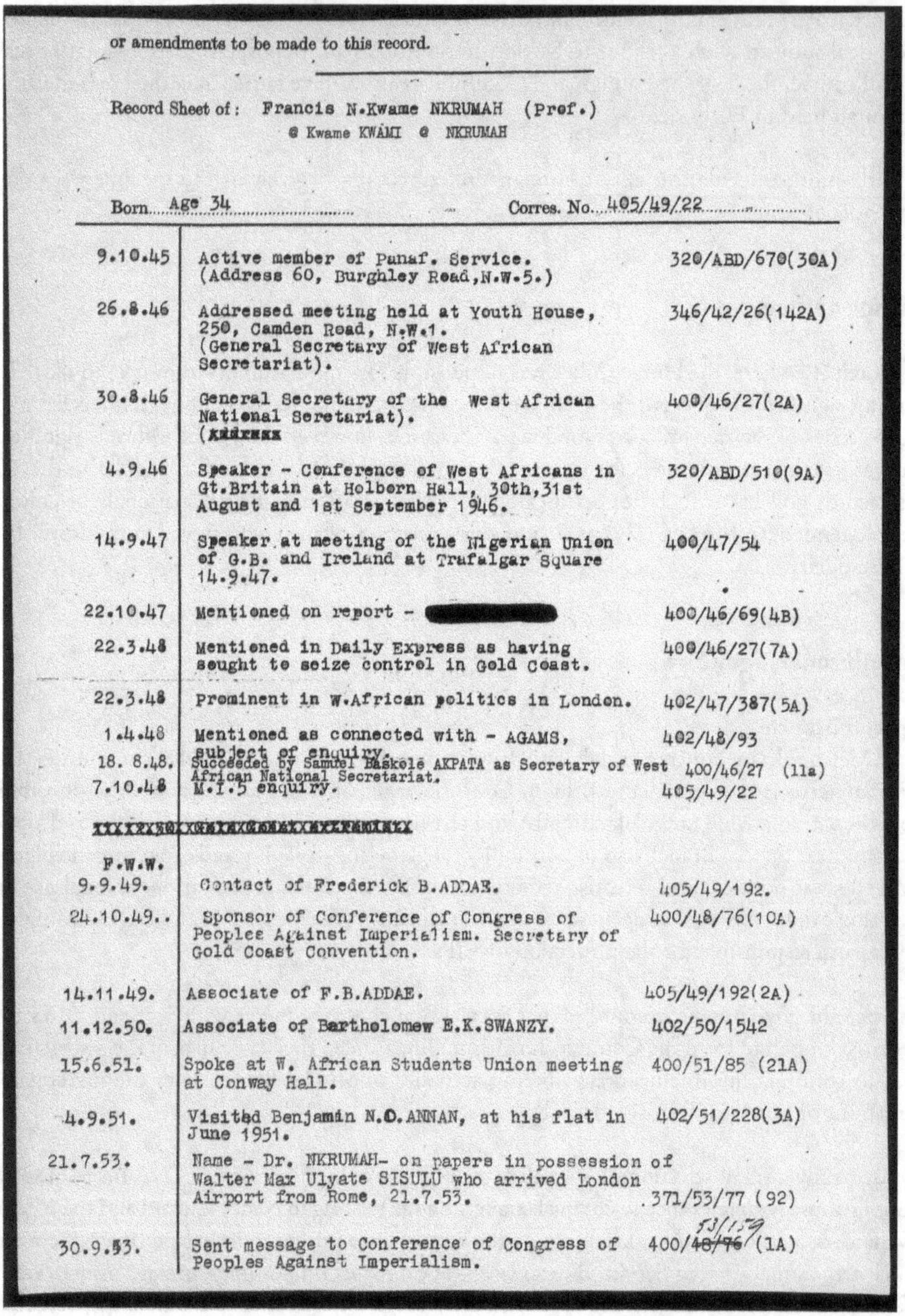

or amendments to be made to this record.

Record Sheet of: Francis N.Kwame NKRUMAH (Prof.)
@ Kwame KWAMI @ NKRUMAH

Born Age 34 Corres. No. 405/49/22

9.10.45	Active member of Panaf. Service. (Address 60, Burghley Road, N.W.5.)	320/ABD/670(30A)
26.8.46	Addressed meeting held at Youth House, 250, Camden Road, N.W.1. (General Secretary of West African Secretariat).	346/42/26(142A)
30.8.46	General Secretary of the West African National Seretariat). (~~Address~~	400/46/27(2A)
4.9.46	Speaker - Conference of West Africans in Gt.Britain at Holborn Hall, 30th, 31st August and 1st September 1946.	320/ABD/510(9A)
14.9.47	Speaker at meeting of the Nigerian Union of G.B. and Ireland at Trafalgar Square 14.9.47.	400/47/54
22.10.47	Mentioned on report - [redacted]	400/46/69(4B)
22.3.48	Mentioned in Daily Express as having sought to seize control in Gold Coast.	400/46/27(7A)
22.3.48	Prominent in W.African politics in London.	402/47/387(5A)
1.4.48	Mentioned as connected with - AGAMS, subject of enquiry.	402/48/93
18. 8.48.	Succeeded by Samuel Haskelé AKPATA as Secretary of West African National Secretariat.	400/46/27 (11a)
7.10.48	M.I.5 enquiry.	405/49/22

~~xxxxxxxxxxxxxxxxxxxxxxxxxxxxxxxx~~

F.W.W. 9.9.49.	Contact of Frederick B.ADDAE.	405/49/192.
24.10.49..	Sponsor of Conference of Congress of Peoples Against Imperialism. Secretary of Gold Coast Convention.	400/48/76(10A)
14.11.49.	Associate of F.B.ADDAE.	405/49/192(2A)
11.12.50.	Associate of Bartholomew E.K.SWANZY.	402/50/1542
15.6.51.	Spoke at W. African Students Union meeting at Conway Hall.	400/51/85 (21A)
4.9.51.	Visited Benjamin N.O.ANNAN, at his flat in June 1951.	402/51/228(3A)
21.7.53.	Name - Dr. NKRUMAH- on papers in possession of Walter Max Ulyate SISULU who arrived London Airport from Rome, 21.7.53.	371/53/77 (92)
30.9.53.	Sent message to Conference of Congress of Peoples Against Imperialism.	400/~~48/76~~ 53/159 (1A)

Figure 50. MEPO 38/181, 1949–1991. Extract from a Special Branch file on Kwame Nkrumah detailing his activities in London.

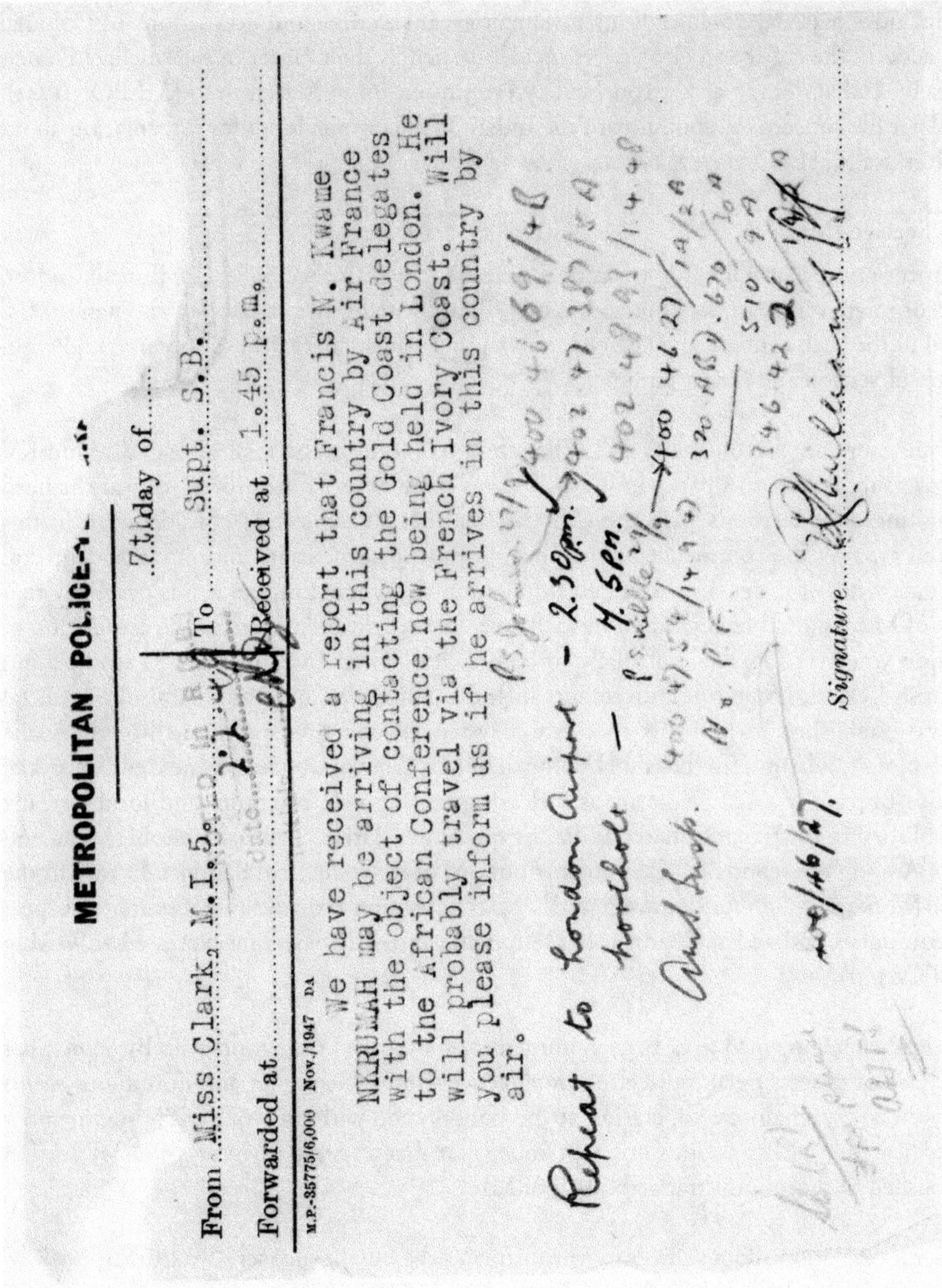

METROPOLITAN POLICE

From Miss Clark, M.I.5. To Supt. S.B. 7th day of

Forwarded at Received at 1.45 p.m.

M.P.-35775/6,000 Nov./1947 DA

We have received a report that Francis N. Kwame NKRUMAH may be arriving in this country by Air France with the object of contacting the Gold Coast delegates to the African Conference now being held in London. He will probably travel via the French Ivory Coast. Will you please inform us if he arrives in this country by air.

Repeat to London Airport – 2.30pm.

Northolt – 4.5pm.

Signature

Figure 51. MEPO 38/181, 1949–1991. Memorandum from an MI5 officer concerning the possible arrival of Kwame Nkrumah in the United Kingdom.

The more mainstream records of the Metropolitan Police also have some interest. There are references to training provided for colonial police forces, such as a file on scholarships for Jamaican police officers, 1947–8 (MEPO 2/7925). MEPO 2/9288, 'Colonials in London: social conditions', 1950–3, includes material on conditions in Jamaica, ganja, crime and accusations of Colonial Office inaction. The collection also covers incidents such as the murder of Sir Michael Francis O'Dwyer by Udham Singh at Caxton Hall, Westminster, on 13 March 1940 (MEPO 3/1743). A much later file concerns a request from the Indian high commissioner for information about the revolver used (MEPO 26/182, 1972).

Security Service (MI5)

The Security Service began life in 1909 as the domestic arm of the Secret Service Bureau. In 1916 it was incorporated into a new Directorate of Military Intelligence, assuming the name MI5. For much of the 20th century, the key concerns of the Security Service, as it became known in 1931, were subversion and Soviet espionage.

The colonies were the responsibility of D Branch of MI5 during the First World War and KV 1/15–19 covers its activities. A paper in KV 1/19 states 'Even before the outbreak of war the need of establishing close relations with the Colonies had been a subject of consideration in this Office, and as, after the commencement of hostilities, it became more and more evident that the secret activities of the enemy extended throughout the whole Empire, it was necessary that the work of M.I.5 should be organised in such a way as to provide means for the acquisition of information wherever mischief was likely to be brewing'. German influence was seen behind Sinn Féin in Ireland, home rule movements in India and Egypt and Pan-Islamism. A central bureau was established in July 1915 to create a system of counter-espionage throughout the British empire. In July 1916 this became D Branch of MI5, known overseas as the Central Special Intelligence Bureau. It acted primarily as a clearing-house for information and local bureaux were established in Australia, Canada, India, Egypt, South Africa, Cyprus, Nairobi, Malta and Gibraltar. Among the reports in KV 1 are attributions of strikes in Trinidad in July 1917 to the Industrial Workers of the World movement (KV 1/15 paragraph 313), and 1918 reports on suspect Indian seditionists, Indian Pan-Islamists in Detroit and anti-British feeling expressed at Woking mosque (KV 1/51).

It is not clear what happened to D Branch immediately after the First World War. By September 1939, the task of processing and directing intelligence from the colonies and dominions seems to have been a very small-scale operation at the London end with only one part-time member of staff dedicated to it. It was not until September 1941 that a special 'Overseas control' section was established in the administrative branch of MI5.

For further information about sources for the history of the intelligence services see: http://www.nationalarchives.gov.uk/records/looking-for-subject/securityhistory.htm.

The illustration in figure 51 from the Special Branch file on Nkrumah clearly shows that some surveillance activity was taking place which would also have been recorded in MI5 records.

Secret Intelligence Service (MI6)

It is not the policy of MI6 to release its records to the public. For further information see its website, particularly https://www.sis.gov.uk/our-history/archive.html.

Ministry of Defence

A minister for the co-ordination of defence was appointed in 1936 to assist the prime minister. The post was abolished in April 1940, and when Churchill became prime minister the following month he assumed the additional title of minister of defence. A minister of defence was again appointed on 21 December 1946, to be responsible to Parliament for the inter-relation of the three armed services and their supply, and the Ministry was formally constituted on 1 January 1947. In 1964 the Ministry of Defence, Admiralty, War Office and Air Ministry were amalgamated, and arrangements were made for collaboration with the Ministry of Aviation. Records of the Ministry, in 'DEFE' series, include papers on Second World War combined operations in South East Asia, the Middle East and Africa. Post-war records include a considerable amount of material concerning the colonies and the Commonwealth, on subjects such as defence schemes and agreements, military assistance and the supply of arms and equipment.

Prime Minister's Office

The office of the prime minister did not officially exist until December 1905, and very few of the records in PREM record series pre-date 1919. Thereafter they are an important source for policy-making for the colonies and Commonwealth, especially regarding constitutional change and independence and crisis situations such as the Kenyan emergency and the Nigerian civil war. They include details of visits of the prime minister and other ministers overseas, and of overseas ministers to the UK, together with meetings of Commonwealth prime ministers and heads of government. Papers about royal tours and visits are also included. As noted in Chapter 1, footnote 16, it is a Prime Minister's Office file which records the disagreement between Attlee and Churchill over whether the Atlantic charter applied to 'coloured races' (see figure 52).

In addition TNA holds some private papers of prime ministers: the Chatham Papers, comprising papers of William Pitt (the 'Elder'), First Earl of Chatham and his son William Pitt (the 'Younger') in PRO 30/8; the Russell Papers relating to John, First Earl Russell and his family in PRO 30/22; and papers of James Ramsay MacDonald and his family in PRO 30/69.

Privy Council

The primary role of the Privy Council in colonial affairs before the establishment of the War and Colonial Department in 1801, and the inclusion of its records in 'CO' series, is described at

Downing Street,

20th November, 1941.

My dear Martin,

With reference to Miss Malleson's letter to you enclosing a copy of telegram No. 1129 which we have received from the Governor of Nigeria containing a message for the Prime Minister, I enclose, as requested, the draft of a reply which my Secretary of State thinks the Prime Minister might send to the West African Pilot. I also enclose the report which appeared in "West Africa" of the speech which Mr. Attlee made at the West African Students' Union to which reference is made in the message.

Lord Moyne appreciates that the Prime Minister may see some difficulty in the terms of paragraph 2 of this draft. But he feels that Mr. Churchill should know that the West African Pilot is as widely read in Nigeria as any other newspaper and particularly so amongst the native intelligentsia. This being so he feels that any attempt to gloss over the fact - and there has in fact been some inconsistency between the references to the Charter by the Prime Minister and by Mr. Attlee - would very likely be used by the Editor of the "Pilot", who is an astute and rather unscrupulous person, to suggest that H.M.G. are insincere in their professed intentions towards the Colonies. This might be further exploited in the Gold Coast and in the Colony of Sierra Leone where the people are even more politically minded than in Nigeria. Lord Moyne has tried to find some way of reconciling these two statements but has been forced to the conclusion that any attempt to do so would fail to convince the senders of the message who, it must be remembered, have at times shown themselves suspicious of the good faith of H.M.G.

I should add that Lord Moyne has not consulted Mr. Attlee in this matter. You will no doubt take such

action

J.M. Martin, Esq.

Figure 52. PREM 4/43A/3, Application of Atlantic Charter to coloured races, 1941. Letter from the Colonial Office to the Prime Minister's Office.

p. 29. The colonial right of appeal to its Judicial Committee is referred to at p. 20. The legislative role of the Privy Council continued to consist, and still consists, of making orders in council and issuing royal proclamations. Orders in council are of two kinds: prerogative, such as those relating to the constitutions or currency of overseas territories; and statutory, made under the authority of an act of Parliament.

The registers of the Privy Council (in PC 2) comprise the minutes of its proceedings, its orders, certain proclamations and the reports of committees with the papers accompanying them, sometimes entered at length, sometimes in abstract only. Material in the Privy Council registers relating to colonial affairs is calendared in the *Acts of the Privy Council of England, Colonial Series*, ed. W. L. Grant, J. Munro (London, 1908–12), I–VI. It includes summaries of the entries in the registers relating to colonial affairs, 1613–1783, and is indexed. It also includes colonial business which was referred to various council committees after 1660. The Privy Council unbound correspondence in PC 1 (1481–1946) is a useful source for colonial policy, and includes some minutes of the Committee for Plantation Affairs. The series includes papers concerning colonial regulation and policy towards the American colonies before and during the War of American Independence. After the mid 19th century, however, its coverage appears to be almost entirely UK-based.

Treasury

The huge amount of correspondence from the Treasury found among the Colonial Office records clearly indicates its major role in colonial affairs – it held the purse strings. Although we are often told that colonies were required to pay for themselves, the reality was not, and could not be, so simple. Revenue based primarily on taxation, mining receipts, customs and harbour dues, etc., was bound to fluctuate and grants-in-aid and/or loans from the British government were often required, especially in the face of demands for improved services and capital development.[22] Careful financial planning was, however, expected and estimates of revenue and expenditure from the colonies are perhaps one of the most regularly submitted items to be found in the Colonial Office correspondence. Unplanned and ad hoc expenditure was usually frowned upon however. In the St Croix case described at p. 58, although both the Foreign Office and the Admiralty, who had information from their 'men on the spot', urged the evacuation of British West Indian workers, it was the Treasury that declared that expenditure from imperial funds was unjustified.[23]

Unfortunately there is no guide to the records of the Treasury and it is probable that they are under-used. Some of its records are calendared, but only for an earlier period.[24] Apart from the

[22] See the chapter on 'Public finances' (chapter 20, iv, pp. 1432–65) in Hailey, *An African Survey*, for a discussion of the situation in African colonies in the inter-war years.

[23] CO 318/373/24.

[24] *Calendar of Treasury Books, 1660–[1718], Preserved in the Public Record Office* (32 vols. in 64, London, HMSO, 1904–62); *Calendar of Treasury Books and Papers, 1729–[1745], Preserved in Her Majesty's Public Record Office* (5 vols., London, HMSO, 1897–1903).

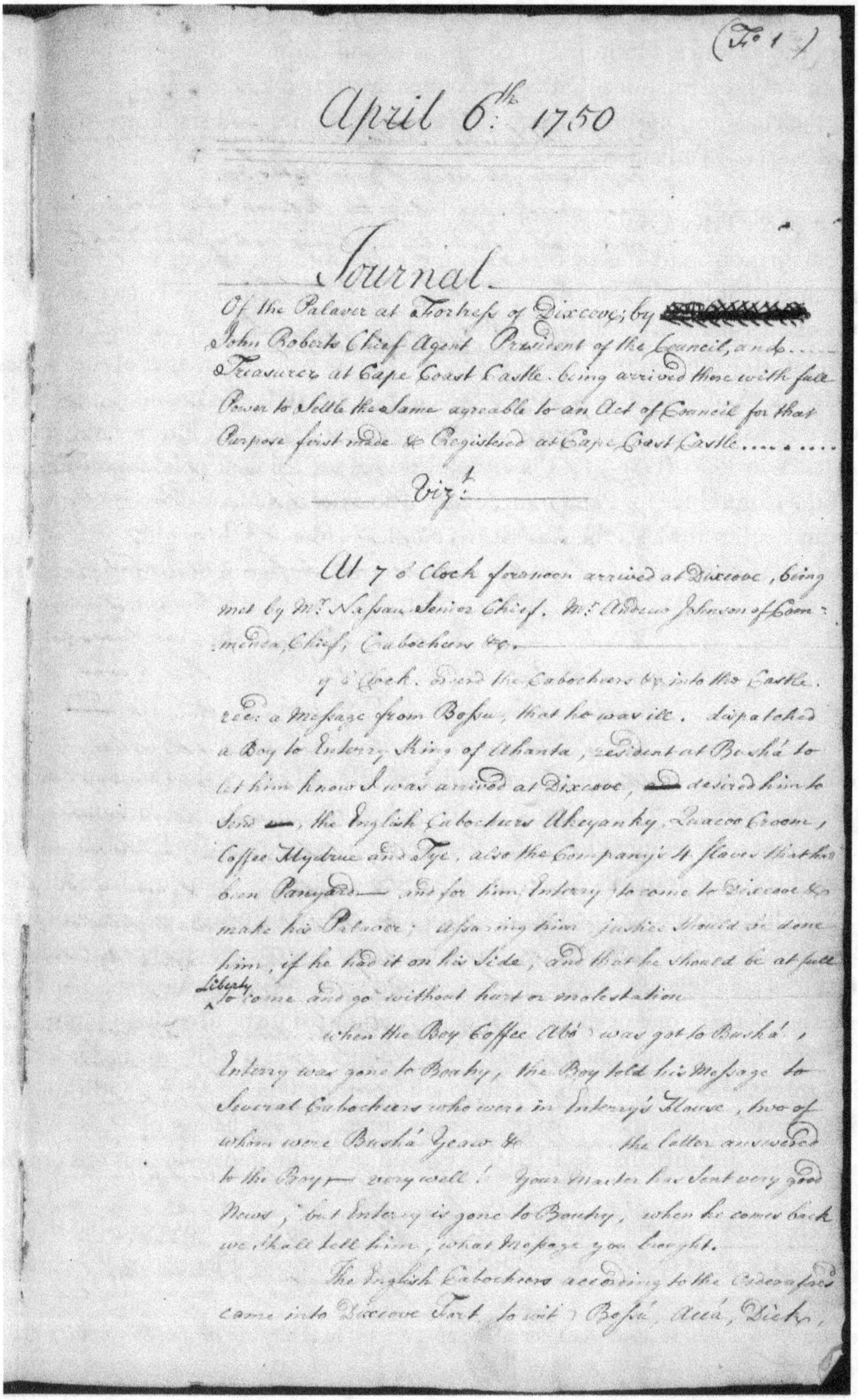

(Fo 1)

April 6th 1750

Journal

Of the Palaver at Fortress of Dixcove; by John Roberts Chief Agent President of the Council, and Treasurer at Cape Coast Castle being arrived there with full Power to Settle the Same agreable to an Act of Council for that Purpose first made & Registered at Cape Coast Castle..........

Viz.t

At 7 o'Clock forenoon arrived at Dixcove, being met by Mr. Nassau Senior Chief, Mr. Andrew Johnson of Commenda, Chief, Caboceers &c.

9 o'Clock. rec'd the Caboceers &c into the Castle. rec'd a Message from Bossu, that he was ill. dispatched a Boy to Interry King of Ahanta, resident at Busha to let him know I was arrived at Dixcove, desired him to send, the English Caboceers Akeyanky, Quacoo Croom, Coffee Mydrue and Tye, also the Company's 4 slaves that had been Panyarred — and for him, Interry to come to Dixcove to make his Palaver; assuring him justice should be done him, if he had it on his Side, and that he should be at full Liberty to come and go without hurt or molestation

when the Boy Coffee Abo was got to Busha, Interry was gone to Boahy, the Boy told his Message to Several Caboceers who were in Interry's House, two of whom were Busha Yeaw & the latter answered to the Boy — very well! your Master has sent very good News, but Interry is gone to Boahy, when he comes back we shall tell him, what Message you brought.

The English Caboceers according to the Order aforesaid came into Dixcove Fort to wit, Bossu, Acca, Dick,

Figure 53. T 70/1467, 1750: Journal of palaver at Dixcove (with letters). Extract from a journal written by an agent of the Royal African Company.

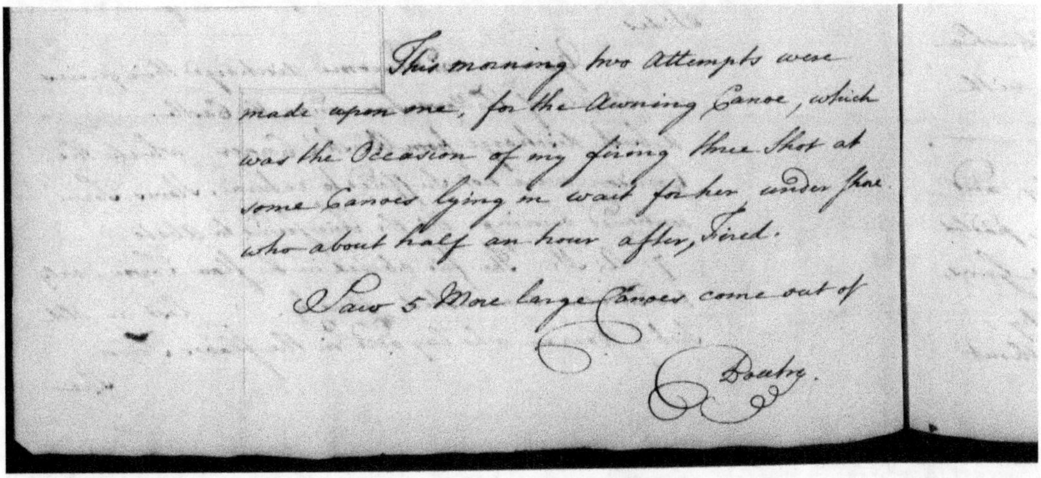

This morning two Attempts were made upon me, for the Awning Canoe, which was the Occasion of my firing three Shot at some Canoes lying in wait for her, under shore who about half an hour after, Fired.

Saw 5 More large Canoes come out of

Boatry.

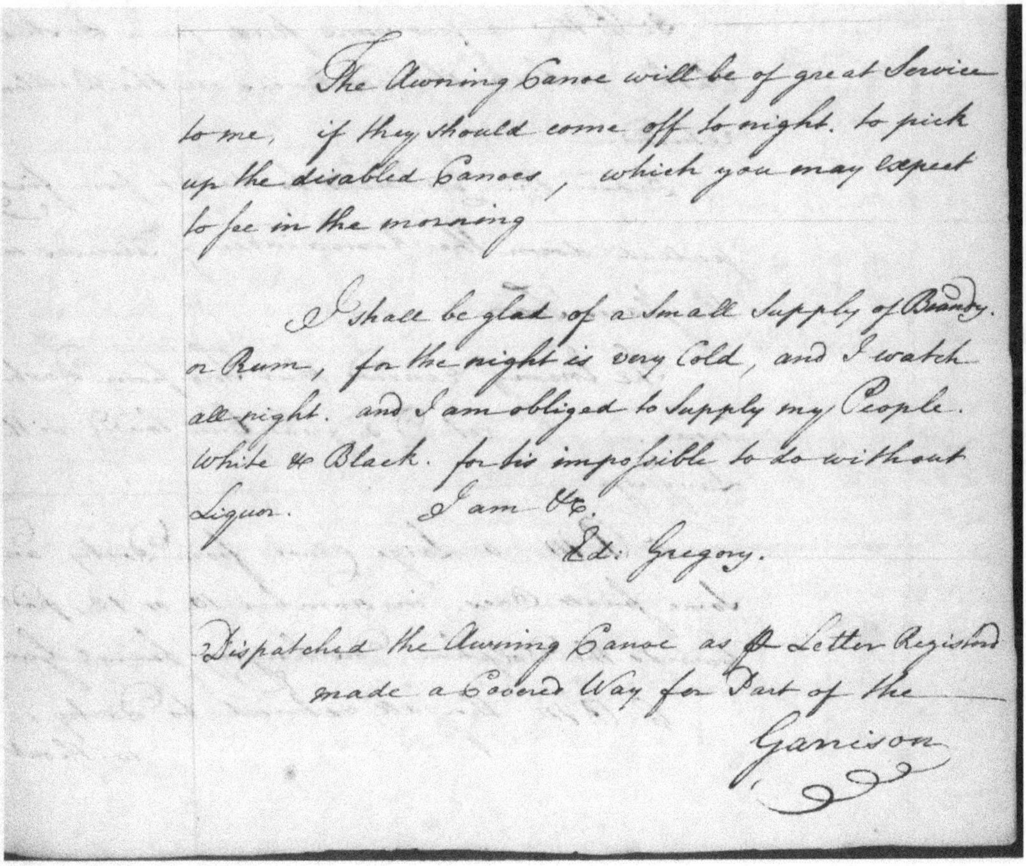

The Awning Canoe will be of great Service to me, if they should come off to night. to pick up the disabled Canoes, which you may expect to see in the morning

I shall be glad of a Small Supply of Brandy. or Rum, for the night is very Cold, and I watch all night. and I am obliged to Supply my People. White & Black. for tis impossible to do without Liquor. I am &c.

Ed: Gregory.

Dispatched the Awning Canoe as ℘ Letter Registerd

made a Covered Way for Part of the Garrison

Figure 54. T 70/1467, 1750: Journal of palaver at Dixcove (with letters). Extracts of a letter from Edward Gregory, an agent of the Royal African Company, reporting skirmishes with local people and requesting a 'Small Supply of Brandy or Rum'.

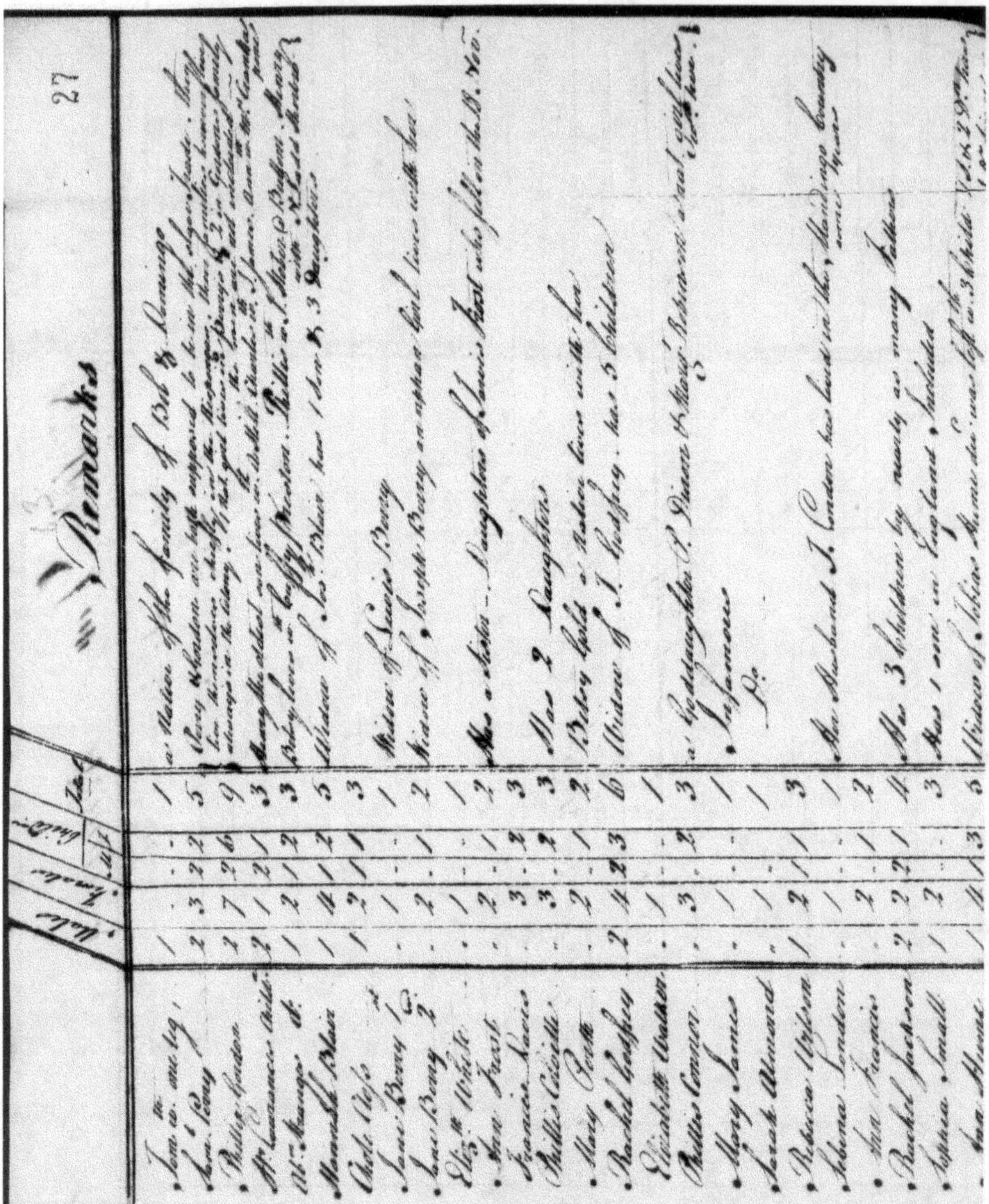
27

Remarks

Figure 55. WO 1/352, War Department in-letters and papers, 1800–7. Extract from a list of 'Nova Scotians' at Sierra Leone.

more mainstream records, the collection includes two series of major importance for colonial studies. These are the records of the Company of Royal Adventurers of England Trading with Africa and its successors (T 70), and the records of the Office of Registry of Colonial Slaves and Slave Compensation Commission (T 71).[25] Examples from the first of these are shown at figures 53 and 54. Records relating to the proceedings of the Committee for the Relief of the Black Poor, 1786–7, and the campaign to encourage London's black poor to volunteer to be re-settled in Sierra Leone, which is referred to at p. 2, are among the Treasury in-letters (T 1/631–8 and T 1/641–7).

War Office

As noted in chapter 5, responsibility for both colonial affairs and for war was vested in one secretary of state between 1801 and 1854. Although records relating to the two functions have in theory been divided between CO and WO record series respectively there is a certain amount of overlap, and the guide to War Office and other military records provides some references to colonial affairs.[26] One of these relates to migrants from Nova Scotia resident at Sierra Leone (see figure 55). The in-letters and miscellaneous papers in WO 1 and the registered files in WO 32 are perhaps of particular interest for military campaigns within the empire, including as they do material concerning the French Revolutionary and Napoleonic wars and the Ashanti, Zulu and South African wars, to give just a few examples. There are also headquarters records for some of these campaigns, and TNA holds unit war diaries not only for the First and Second World Wars, but also for peacetime operations in Shanghai, India, Ethiopia, Egypt and Palestine. Service records include not only those of regular British Army units (although not those of the Indian Army which are held at the British Library) but also musters and pay lists for the British West India Regiments (see under West Indies in appendix 1) and nominal rolls and enrolment forms for those who served in locally raised units in the South African (Boer) War. There is a handbook to records of the War Office,[27] as well as TNA research guides, available through the website, relating to operational and service records.

[25] For more information about the contents of T 71 see G. Grannum, *Tracing your Caribbean Ancestors* (London, 2012) pp. 97-100. Many of the registers have been digitised and made available through the subscription service hosted by Ancestry (see http://search.ancestry.co.uk/search/db.aspx?htx=List&dbid=1129&offerid=0%3a7858%3a0 [accessed 9 March 2015]). See also details of the Legacies of British Slave-ownership project based at University College London (http://www.ucl.ac.uk/lbs/ [accessed 9 March 2015]) and Catherine Hall et al, *Legacies of British Slave-ownership: colonial slavery and the formation of Victorian Britain* (Cambridge, 2014).

[26] *An Alphabetical Guide to Certain War Office and Other Military Records Preserved in the Public Record Office* (Public Record Office Lists & Indexes, 53, London, HMSO, 1931).

[27] M. Roper, *The Records of the War Office and Related Departments 1660–1964* (Public Record Office, 1998).

Appendix 1
Records relating to individual dependencies and regions

This appendix provides an alphabetical listing of territories which have been British dependencies, usually with brief details of their constitutional histories under British administration, and with details of relevant geographically arranged record series. The country names given are those used during the colonial period; cross-references from and to modern names have been provided as appropriate.

Descriptions of the various types of record listed, for example 'original correspondence' or 'register' or 'sessional papers' may be found elsewhere in this guide. Where a record series is devoted exclusively to the individual dependency (or sometimes group of dependencies), and is not accruing, the number of documents within that series is noted. Lists of record series arranged by subject rather than territorial unit may be found in appendix 2. The records noted here are primarily those of the Colonial Office and the Dominions Office, but in most cases records of the Commonwealth Relations Office, Commonwealth Office and/or Foreign and Commonwealth Office have been included for the period immediately following independence. Some cross-references are provided to records of the Foreign Office, where that department had a responsibility for the administration of a particular territory, and there are occasional references to the records of other departments such as the Admiralty and War Office. Information about the records of these latter departments is far from comprehensive, and researchers should consult the published guides where available (see bibliography) or the online catalogue. See also chapter 12. The series of original correspondence or registered files, considered to be of most interest to the majority of researchers, are in bold.

The main sources used in the compilation of the brief administrative histories of the territories have been the *Colonial Office List* (see appendix 4), the guides written by R. B. Pugh[1] and Anne Thurston,[2] David P. Henige's list of colonial governors,[3] and the Foreign and Commonwealth Office website.[4] In some cases details vary from one source to another, especially for the early periods of British annexation or settlement, and users of this guide may consequently find some factual or dating errors.

[1] Pugh, *Records of the Colonial and Dominions Offices.*

[2] Thurston, vol. 1

[3] D. P. Henige, *Colonial Governors from the Fifteenth Century to the Present* (Madison, Wis., 1970).

[4] Foreign and Commonwealth Office (https://www.gov.uk/government/organisations/foreign-commonwealth-office/ [accessed 22 Oct. 2014]).

Aden, Aden Protectorate, Protectorate of South Arabia (South Yemen)

The strategic port of Aden was seized by the British from the sultan of Lahej in 1839 and administered by the East India Company. Little Aden was purchased by Britain in 1868 and Perim Island, first occupied by France in 1738 and temporarily by Britain in 1799, was finally occupied by Britain in 1857. The territory continued to be administered as part of British India; the Colonial Office had some responsibility from 1921, and assumed administration in 1937 when Aden became a colony. Between 1839 and 1914 rulers whose territories adjoined Aden Colony made protective treaty arrangements with the British. These territories formed the Aden Protectorate, known later as the Protectorate of South Arabia. The protectorate was never directly administered by the United Kingdom, but from 1921 relations with the constituent states were conducted by the secretary of state for the colonies. Colonial Office records before 1937 mainly concern the protectorate. In 1959 a number of the protectorate states formed the Federation of Arab Emirates of the South, later called the Federation of South Arabia. The Yemen Arab Republic (YAR), also known as North Yemen, came into being on 26 September 1962 following a military coup. In 1963 Aden Colony joined the Federation of South Arabia but remained a colony until 1967. The People's Republic of South Yemen (later known as the People's Democratic Republic of Yemen) was formed on 30 November 1967 from the territory of the former Federation of South Arabia and the Aden Protectorate. The two countries of North Yemen and South Yemen united on 22 May 1990 to form the Republic of Yemen (ROY). See also under Middle East.

East India Company and India Office

Records at the British Library

Colonial Office

Aden: Original Correspondence (CO 725) 1921–51, 106 volumes and boxes of files. Correspondence continues in **Central Africa and Aden: Original Correspondence (CO 1015)** 1950–62 and **Aden Department: Registered Files (ADN series) (CO 1055)** 1962–6, 307 files. See also Colonies General: Supplementary Original Correspondence (CO 537).

Aden: Register of Correspondence (CO 773) 1921–51, 19 volumes

Aden: Register of Out-letters (CO 774) 1921–6, 1 volume

Aden: Acts (CO 858) 1937–67, 10 volumes

Aden: Sessional Papers (CO 846) 1924–66, 31 volumes

Aden: Government Gazettes (CO 853) 1932–67, 41 volumes

Aden: Miscellanea (CO 817) 1926–50, 29 volumes, comprising trade and navigation reports and blue books of statistics

Commonwealth Relations Office

Commonwealth Relations Office: Western and Middle East Department and Successors: Registered Files, Middle East (ME series) (DO 174) 1957–66

Foreign Office/Foreign and Commonwealth Office

Foreign Office and Foreign and Commonwealth Office: Arabian Department and Middle East Department: Registered Files (B and NB series) (FCO 8) 1967 onwards

Foreign and Commonwealth Office and predecessors: Records of Former Colonial Administrations: Migrated Archives (FCO 141)

Africa

The Colonial Office record series listed below deal with questions relating to foreign states and dependencies as well as British possessions. For earlier records relating to British relations with Africa in the pre-colonial period see Foreign Office records, the most relevant series of which are also listed. In 1947 the Colonial Office set up an African Studies Branch, a small specialist section closely associated with the African departments, to collect and disseminate information on administrative and social questions. It produced the *Journal of African Administration*, organised periodic conferences on African administration, and provided a secretariat for the Land, Law and Local Government Panels. There are some early papers on the work of the branch in CO 847. The branch was dissolved in 1961 and most of its staff transferred to the new Department of Technical Co-operation. See also Central Africa, East Africa, West Africa and individual countries.

Foreign Office

General Correspondence before 1906, Africa (FO 2)

Slave Trade Department and Successors: General Correspondence before 1906 (FO 84)

Colonial Office and predecessors

Africa: Exploration, etc. (CO 2) 1794–1843, 25 volumes

Africa: Exploration, Entry Books (CO 392) 1825–44, 4 volumes

Africa: Original Correspondence (CO 847) 1932–65, 105 files

Africa: Register of Correspondence (CO 917) 1932–51, 9 volumes

African Studies Branch: Original Correspondence (CO 955) 1950–9, 86 files

Confidential Print: Africa (CO 879) 1848–1961, 190 volumes

Hailey Papers (CO 1018) 1946–55, 88 files. This series consists of the working papers of Lord Hailey in preparing *Native Administration in the British African Territories*. The papers include replies to questionnaires, records of meetings and miscellaneous publications.

The series CO 959, Various Private Collections, includes working papers of Louis Branney, land tenure expert in the African Studies Branch, relating to land tenure in Africa, 1880–1950.

Alberta

In 1882 Canada's Northwest Territory was divided into four districts: Athabasca, Alberta, Saskatchewan and Assiniboia (where the capital, Regina, was located). Constitutional change coupled with demands for increased autonomy and provincial status resulted, in 1905, in the creation of the new provinces of Alberta and Saskatchewan which formed part of the Dominion of Canada.

Colonial Office
Alberta: Sessional Papers (CO 643) 1906–9, 1 volume
Alberta: Government Gazettes (CO 556) 1905–24, 15 volumes
Dominions Office/Commonwealth Relations Office
Alberta: Sessional Papers (DO 95) 1937–65, 36 volumes
Alberta: Government Gazettes (DO 14) 1925–80, 144 volumes

For correspondence and other records see under Canada

Amatongaland

Amatongaland became a British protectorate in 1895. In 1897 it was incorporated into Zululand which was annexed to Natal in the same year.

Colonial Office
Amatongaland: Proclamations (CO 4) 1896–7, 1 volume

America and West Indies

The main series for records relating to the British colonies in what was to become the United States of America is CO 5, Board of Trade and Secretaries of State: America and West Indies, Original Correspondence, 1606–1822. This is an artificial series formed during the reorganisation of Colonial Office records undertaken in the Public Record Office in the 19th and early 20th centuries. It includes the original correspondence and entry books of the Board of Trade and the secretaries of state, together with acts, sessional papers and miscellanea arranged under the following sub-series: Carolina (Propriety), North Carolina, South Carolina, Connecticut, East Florida, West Florida, Georgia, Maryland, Massachusetts, New England, New Hampshire, New Jersey, New York, Pennsylvania, Rhode Island, Vermont, Virginia, and Proprieties. The last comprises the Bahamas, Carolina, Connecticut, Maryland, East and West New Jersey, Pennsylvania and Rhode Island. As can be seen from this list, although the series has been named 'America and West Indies' the only West Indian colony covered is the Bahamas. Earlier papers relating to the Americas may be found in the series CO 1, Privy Council and Related Bodies: Colonial Papers (General Series) 1574–1757. This series relates to the American and West Indian colonies and includes some records of the Board of Trade. It ends virtually in 1688, after which date most of the American papers are to be found in CO 5, and the West Indian ones in CO 318 and under the various islands and mainland territories. Transcripts or précis of documents in CO 1 and CO 5, for the period to 1739 only, are included in the *Calendar of State Papers, Colonial Series* (HMSO, London, 1858–1994). In 2000 a CD-ROM edition of the *Calendar* was published by Routledge, in association with the Public Record Office, under the title *Calendar of State Papers, Colonial: North America and the West Indies*, and in 2007 ProQuest published an online version which includes digitised images of documents in CO 1. Access to both is available at TNA. The Institute of Historical Research has published the *Calendar of State Papers, Colonial Series* as free content in its digital library, British History Online.

Documents for the period of the American War of Independence have been similarly calendared in K. G. Davies, *Documents of the American Revolution, 1770–1783* (Shannon, 1972–81). Documents relating to British relations with the newly independent United States of America can be found among the records of the Foreign Office, especially FO 4 and FO 5.

Anglo-Egyptian Sudan *see* Sudan

Anguilla

Colonised by English and Irish settlers in 1650, Anguilla was administered as part of the Leeward Islands. In 1882 it was united with St Christopher (St Kitts) and Nevis into one presidency. The islanders, believing their interests were being ignored and wishing to retain their direct links with Britain, sought separation from the federation in the 1960s. This disquiet culminated in the revolution of 1967. Anguilla came under direct British rule in the 1970s and eventually became a separate British dependent territory (later UK Overseas Territory) in 1980. See also under St Christopher (St Kitts).

Colonial Office and predecessors

Leeward Islands, Original Correspondence (CO 152) 1689–1816, 1872–1951 and **St Christopher (St Kitts), Nevis and Anguilla: Original Correspondence (CO 239)** 1702–1872 (with the exception of the first volume which includes papers dated between 1702 and 1812 this series commences in 1816). CO 152 continues in **West Indian Department: Registered Files (WIS series) (CO 1031)** 1948–67. Both CO 152 and CO 239 are registered in Leeward Islands: Register of Correspondence (CO 354) 1850–1951, 44 volumes (for registers before 1850 see CO 326).

St Christopher (St Kitts), Nevis and Anguilla: Acts (CO 240) 1672–1972, 37 volumes

St Christopher (St Kitts), Nevis and Anguilla: Sessional Papers (CO 241) 1704–1960, 69 volumes

St Christopher (St Kitts), Nevis and Anguilla: Government Gazettes (CO 242) 1879–1989, 53 volumes

St Christopher (St Kitts), Nevis and Anguilla: Miscellanea (CO 243) 1704–1887, 75 volumes

Commonwealth Office and Foreign and Commonwealth Office

Commonwealth Office: West Indian Department 'A' and Associated States Department: Registered Files, Antigua, Dominica, Grenada, St Christopher (St Kitts)-Nevis-Anguilla, St Lucia and St Vincent (WA series) (FCO 43) 1967–8

Commonwealth Office: West Indian Department 'B' and Foreign and Commonwealth Office, West Indian Department: Registered Files, Smaller Commonwealth West Indian Territories (WB and HW series) (FCO 44) 1967 onwards

Foreign and Commonwealth Office: North American and Caribbean Department, and Caribbean Department: Registered Files (AN series) (FCO 63) 1968 onwards

Foreign and Commonwealth Office and predecessors: Records of Former Colonial Administrations: Migrated Archives (FCO 141)

Antigua and Montserrat

Antigua and Montserrat were British from 1632 apart from two brief periods of French occupation in 1666–7 and (Montserrat only) 1782–3. Both islands formed part of the general government of the Caribbean Islands until 1671, then part of the new government of the Leeward Islands until 1816 when they became a separate governmental unit. They were reunited with the other Leeward Islands under a governor-in-chief in 1833. After 1871 Antigua was administered by the colonial secretary of the Leeward Islands; in 1936 the office of administrator was created. The Leeward Islands Federation was dissolved in 1956 when Antigua and Montserrat became colonies in their own right. They entered the Federation of the West Indies on its creation in 1958, but on the break-up of the federation in 1962 were again governed separately. Antigua became an independent state and part of the Commonwealth in November 1981 under the name of Antigua and Barbuda. Montserrat remains a British dependency (UK Overseas Territory). See also under Montserrat.

Colonial Office and predecessors

Leeward Islands: Original Correspondence (CO 152) 1689–1816, 1872–1951 and **Antigua and Montserrat: Original Correspondence (CO 7)** 1702–1872, 144 volumes (apart from the first volume which includes papers dated between 1702 and 1820 CO 7 commences in 1816). CO 152 continues in **West Indian Department: Registered Files (WIS series) (CO 1031)** 1948–67. See also Colonies General: Supplementary Original Correspondence (CO 537).

Both CO 7 and CO 152 are registered in Leeward Islands: Register of Correspondence (CO 354) 1850–1951, 44 volumes (for registers before 1850 see CO 326)

Index to Correspondence: Antigua (CO 714/2–4) 1815–70; Montserrat (CO 714/101) 1853–66

Antigua and Montserrat: Entry Books (CO 393) 1816–72, 15 volumes

Antigua and Montserrat: Miscellanea (CO 10) 1666–1887, 71 volumes, including accounts, shipping returns, blue books of statistics and newspapers (for a list of newspapers see appendix 3)

Antigua: Acts (CO 8) 1668–1967, 43 volumes (the first volume, 1668–1706, relates also to Nevis)

Antigua: Sessional Papers (CO 9) 1704–1966, 81 volumes

Antigua: Government Gazettes (CO 1049) 1967–89, 23 volumes

Commonwealth Office and Foreign and Commonwealth Office

Commonwealth Office: West Indian Department 'A' and Associated States Department: Registered Files, Antigua, Dominica, Grenada, St Christopher (St Kitts)-Nevis-Anguilla, St Lucia and St Vincent (WA series) (FCO 43) 1967–8

Commonwealth Office: West Indian Department 'B' and Foreign and Commonwealth Office, West Indian Department: Registered Files, Smaller Commonwealth West Indian Territories (WB and HW series) (FCO 44) 1967 onwards

Foreign and Commonwealth Office: North American and Caribbean Department and Caribbean Department: Registered Files (AN series) (FCO 63) 1968 onwards

Arabia

Responsibility for policy concerning Britain's relations with the Arab areas within British spheres of influence was transferred from the Foreign Office and the India Office to the Colonial Office in 1921. The series referred to below comprise despatches between the secretary of state for the colonies and the political resident in the Persian Gulf and other agents, together with associated domestic correspondence. Earlier Foreign Office records are held at TNA (see chapter 12); records of the India Office and its predecessors are at the British Library.[5] See also under Aden, Middle East and Persian Gulf.

Colonial Office

Arabia: Original Correspondence (CO 727) 1921–6, 14 volumes
Arabia: Register of Correspondence (CO 775) 1921–6, 2 volumes
Arabia: Register of Out-letters (CO 776) 1921–6, 1 volume

Asante *see* Ashanti

Ascension

Ascension was under British control from 1815 and administered by the Admiralty until 1922 when control was transferred to the Colonial Office. The island was then made a dependency of St Helena, receiving a resident magistrate. From the late 1990s discussions and consultations with residents explored the form of democratic government to be introduced and culminated in a plebiscite held on 22 and 23 August 2002. Ninety-five per cent of those who voted chose the establishment of an Island Council rather than an Inter-Island Council with St Helena which was the second option. A general election to select members of the Island Council took place on 1 November 2002. The status of Ascension as a dependent territory (UK Overseas Territory) was changed by a new constitution dated 1 September 2009 which created a single dependency of Saint Helena, Ascension and Tristan da Cunha giving the three islands equal status within the territory.

[5] In 2012 The British Library Qatar Foundation Partnership launched the Qatar Digital Library, a new, bilingual, online portal providing access to previously undigitised British Library archive materials relating to Gulf history and Arabic science. See http://www.bl.uk/qatar/ [accessed 25 Jan. 2015].

Admiralty

Records of the Admiralty relating to Ascension can be found in a variety of record series including: ADM 1, Admiralty, and Ministry of Defence, Navy Department: Correspondence and Papers (with indexes in ADM 12); ADM 116, Admiralty: Record Office: Cases; and ADM 123, Admiralty: Africa Station: Correspondence. As the island had the status of a ship, there are also ship's musters (ADM 37 and ADM 38), captains' logs (ADM 51), medical journals (ADM 101), hospital musters (ADM 102) and ship's ledgers (ADM 117)

Colonial Office

Ascension: Original Correspondence (CO 749) 1922–3, 1 volume
Ascension: Register of Correspondence (CO 823) 1922–3, 1 volume
For later Colonial Office correspondence see under St Helena

Commonwealth Office and Foreign and Commonwealth Office

Commonwealth Office and Foreign and Commonwealth Office: Gibraltar and South Atlantic Department: Registered Files (Y and HG series) (FCO 42) 1967 onwards
Foreign and Commonwealth Office, West Indian and Atlantic Department (FCO 44) 1972 onwards
Foreign and Commonwealth Office: Atlantic and Indian Ocean Department: Registered Files (FCO 83) 1970 onwards

Ashanti (Asante)

Following British conquest in 1896 the Ashanti Confederation, formed by the late 17th century, was broken up and King Prempeh I was exiled to Seychelles. In 1901 Ashanti territory was annexed to the Gold Coast under a resident administrator, who was replaced by a chief commissioner in 1902. The Ashanti Confederation was restored in 1935, and in 1945 the Ashanti were given representation in the Executive and Legislative Councils of the Gold Coast. With the granting of internal autonomy in the Gold Coast in 1951 the administrators of Ashanti were designated regional officers. Ashanti became part of the independent state of Ghana in 1957. For correspondence and other records see under Gold Coast; for material concerning the Anglo-Ashanti wars see the records of the War Office (WO series) especially WO 32, WO 33, WO 106 and WO 107. See also under West Africa

Colonial Office

Ashanti: Acts (CO 843) 1920–34, 2 volumes

Auckland Islands

The Auckland Islands were granted by Britain to Messrs Enderby as a whaling station in 1806 but were abandoned in 1852 and subsequently administered by New Zealand. The register in CO 330 relates to papers now in a volume of New Zealand correspondence (CO 209/134, 1846–55).

Colonial Office and predecessor

Auckland Island: Register of Correspondence (CO 330) 1850–3, 1 volume
Index to Correspondence (CO 714/5) 1846–55, 1 volume
Auckland Island: Entry Book (CO 394) 1850–3, 1 volume

Australia

A Federal Council of Australasia was established in 1885 with power to legislate on matters of common interest to the colonies in the region. South Australia, Western Australia, Fiji, Queensland, Tasmania and Victoria participated. From 1890 a succession of conventions was held among the Australian colonies, the outcome of which was the creation in 1901 of the Commonwealth of Australia. Apart from CO 11 the Colonial Office series below relate to these federal projects. See also under Australia and New Zealand, Commonwealth of Australia and under the individual colonies and states, i.e., New South Wales, Queensland, South Australia, Tasmania, Victoria and Western Australia. There are also minor references under Auckland Islands, Norfolk Island, North Australia and Northern Territory.

Colonial Office

Australia: Original Correspondence (CO 418) 1889–1922, 226 volumes
Australia: Register of Correspondence (CO 557) 1889–1900, 1 volume (for registers after 1900 see under Australia and New Zealand)
Australia: Memoranda (CO 11) 1842–58, 1 volume
Australia: Acts (CO 12) 1886–97, 1 volume
Australia: Sessional Papers (CO 433) 1886–99, 8 volumes

Australia and New Zealand

The registers of correspondence for the separate Australian colonies, later states, and for New Zealand cease in 1900, the year before Australian federation, as does the Australia general series of registers (CO 557, see under Australia) which is devoted to correspondence about the colonies collectively. The registers noted below relate to CO 418, Australia Original Correspondence, and CO 209, New Zealand Original Correspondence. They are succeeded by two separate series, each running until 1922: New Zealand (CO 361), which is a resumption of the old New Zealand series, and Commonwealth of Australia (CO 706). The registers, so far as they concern Australia, include despatches from the governors of the states as well as from the governor-general. See also under Australia, Commonwealth of Australia, New Zealand and the individual colonies and states.

Colonial Office

Australia and New Zealand: Register of Correspondence (CO 644) 1901–8, 4 volumes
Australia and New Zealand: Register of Out-letters (CO 645) 1901–8, 3 volumes

Bahamas (The Bahamas)

After a long period of sporadic occupation by the Spanish, English settlements were established on New Providence from 1629 and Eleuthera from 1646. The islands were granted to successive proprietors by Charles I in 1629, Parliament in 1649 and Charles II in 1670 (when civil government was first introduced under six of the lords proprietors of South Carolina). The British government assumed control in 1717. In 1776 the Bahamas surrendered to American forces; they were captured by Spain in 1782, but recaptured by the British in 1783. The Turks and Caicos Islands were annexed to the Bahamas in 1799 but separated in 1848. The Bahamas became an independent state within the Commonwealth on 10 July 1973.

Colonial Office and predecessors

Board of Trade and Secretaries of State: America and West Indies, Original Correspondence (CO 5). For further details see under America and West Indies.

Bahamas: Original Correspondence (CO 23) 1696–1951, 899 volumes and boxes of files, continued in **West Indian Department: Registered Files (WIS series) (CO 1031)** 1948–67. See also Colonies General: Supplementary Original Correspondence (CO 537).

Bahamas: Register of Correspondence (CO 333) 1850–1951, 25 volumes (for registers before 1850 see CO 326)

Index to Correspondence (CO 714/16–19) 1815–70

Bahamas: Entry Books (CO 24) 1717–1872, 34 volumes, including précis books

Bahamas: Register of Out-letters (CO 508) 1872–1926, 9 volumes

Bahamas: Acts (CO 25) 1729–1973, 53 volumes

Bahamas: Sessional Papers (CO 26) 1721–1956, 184 volumes

Bahamas: Government Gazettes (CO 564) 1894–1965, 32 volumes

Bahamas: Miscellanea (CO 27) 1721–1941, 139 volumes, including shipping returns, returns of stipendiary magistrates, blue books of statistics and newspapers (for a list of newspapers see appendix 3)

Colonial Office and Successors: Governor, The Bahamas: Registered Files (CO 1067) 1964 onwards, 10 files

Foreign Office/Commonwealth Office/Foreign and Commonwealth Office

Foreign Office and Foreign and Commonwealth Office: American and Latin American Departments: Registered Files (A and AL series) (FCO 7) 1967 onwards

Commonwealth Office: Atlantic Department: Registered Files (G series) (FCO 23) 1966–8

Commonwealth Office: West Indian Department 'B' and Foreign and Commonwealth Office, West Indian Department: Registered Files, Smaller Commonwealth West Indian Territories (WB and HW series) (FCO 44) 1967 onwards

Foreign and Commonwealth Office: North American and Caribbean Department and Caribbean Department: Registered Files (AN series) (FCO 63) 1968 onwards

Foreign and Commonwealth Office and predecessors: Records of Former Colonial Administrations: Migrated Archives (FCO 141)

Bahrain

Bahrain became a British protectorate as a result of several 19th-century treaties. In 1900 a political agent was appointed to preserve British interests; the agent was appointed by and reported to the government of India. For records see under Persian Gulf.

Bangladesh

Before the independence of India and Pakistan, the territory which became Bangladesh formed part of the Indian provinces of Bengal and Assam. Following partition in 1947, East Bengal, with a Muslim majority population, emerged as the eastern wing of Pakistan. The new independent state of Bangladesh was created on 16 December 1971. For records before that date see under India and Pakistan.

Commonwealth Office/Foreign and Commonwealth Office

Commonwealth Office and Foreign and Commonwealth Office: South Asia Department: Registered Files (S and FS series) (FCO 37) 1967 onwards

Foreign and Commonwealth Office: Bangladesh: Government Gazettes (FCO 2) 1972–5

Barbados

Barbados was occupied by England in 1625 and settled by 1627; it was privately governed by successive proprietors until 1652. In 1662 the Crown assumed direct control. From 1833 to 1885 the governor of Barbados was also governor-in-chief of the Windward Islands. Barbados was a member of the short-lived Federation of the West Indies (1958–62) and became an independent state within the Commonwealth on 30 November 1966. From 1874 to 1885 Barbados original correspondence is in the Windward Islands series CO 321. See also under West Indies.

Colonial Office and predecessors

Barbados: Original Correspondence (CO 28) 1689–1873, 1886–1951, 343 volumes and boxes of files, and **Windward Islands: Original Correspondence (CO 321)** 1874–85. CO 28 is continued in **West Indian Department: Registered Files (WIS series) (CO 1031)** 1948–67. See also Colonies General: Supplementary Original Correspondence (CO 537).

Barbados: Register of Correspondence (CO 565) 1886–1951, 16 volumes. From 1833 to 1885 Barbados correspondence in both CO 28 and CO 321 is registered under Windward Islands (CO 326, and CO 376 from 1850).

Index to Correspondence (CO 714/20–3) 1815–69

Barbados: Entry Books (CO 29) 1627–1872, 41 volumes, including précis books

Barbados: Register of Out-letters (CO 501) 1872–1926, 8 volumes

Barbados: Acts (CO 30) 1643–1966, 62 volumes

Barbados: Sessional Papers (CO 31) 1660–1965, 156 volumes

Barbados: Government Gazettes (CO 32) 1867–1989, 269 volumes
Barbados: Miscellanea (CO 33) 1678–1947, 156 volumes, including shipping returns, accounts, returns of stipendiary magistrates, court returns and newspapers (for a list of newspapers see appendix 3)

Commonwealth Relations Office/Commonwealth Office

Commonwealth Relations Office and Commonwealth Office: West Indies Department and Atlantic Department: Registered Files, Commonwealth West Indies (WID series) (DO 200) 1961–7
Commonwealth Office: Atlantic Department: Registered Files (G series) (FCO 23) 1966–8

Foreign and Commonwealth Office

Foreign and Commonwealth Office: North American and Caribbean Department, and Caribbean Department: Registered Files (AN series) (FCO 63) 1968 onwards

Barotseland *see under* Northern Rhodesia

Basutoland (Lesotho)

The territory of the Basotho was declared a British protectorate in 1868. In 1871 Basutoland was annexed to Cape Colony, but with legislative provisions to ensure its autonomy. In 1884 the territory was handed over to the British government and a resident commissioner was appointed under the direction of the high commissioner for South Africa. Basutoland became an independent state within the Commonwealth on 4 October 1966 under the name of Lesotho. Basutoland, Bechuanaland and Swaziland are sometimes known as the 'South Africa High Commission Territories' (or simply 'High Commission Territories') and may be described in the records under those terms.

Colonial Office and predecessor

Cape of Good Hope (Cape Colony), Original Correspondence (CO 48) 1807–910
Basutoland: Sessional Papers (CO 646) 1903–21, 3 volumes
Basutoland: Miscellanea (CO 566) 1903–25, 23 volumes of blue books of statistics
Dominions: Original Correspondence (CO 532), 1907–25

Colonial Office and Commonwealth Office

Colonial Office and Commonwealth Office: Southern Africa Department: Original Correspondence (CO 1048) 1960–8, 966 files

Dominions Office/Commonwealth Relations Office/Commonwealth Office/Foreign and Commonwealth Office

High Commissioner for South Africa, and High Commissioner for Basutoland, the Bechuanaland Protectorate and Swaziland, and UK High Commissioner for the Union of South Africa: Correspondence (DO 119) 1843–1965

Dominions Office and Commonwealth Relations Office: Original Correspondence (DO 35) 1915–71
Basutoland (Lesotho): Sessional Papers (DO 92) 1921–65, 50 volumes
Basutoland: Miscellanea (DO 25) 1926–46, 18 volumes of blue books of statistics
Basutoland and Lesotho; Bechuanaland Protectorate and Botswana; and Swaziland: Government Gazettes (DO 145) 1961–75, 56 volumes
Commonwealth Relations Office: South Africa High Commission Territories: Registered Files (BBS series) (DO 157) 1959–63, 66 files
Commonwealth Office: East Africa Department: Registered Files, Botswana, Lesotho and Swaziland (BLS, SAB, SAR and SAS series) 1966–7, 14 files
Commonwealth Office and Foreign and Commonwealth Office: Central African Department and Predecessors: Registered Files (NR and CA series) (FCO 29) 1967–9
Commonwealth Office and Foreign and Commonwealth Office: Central African Department and Predecessors: Registered Files (NR and CA series) (FCO 45) 1967 onwards
Foreign and Commonwealth Office and predecessors: Records of Former Colonial Administrations: Migrated Archives (FCO 141)

Bay Islands

After brief periods of British settlement in Ruatan[6] in the 17th and 18th centuries, immigration from the Cayman Islands after 1838 was followed by British claims to the islands from 1841. The Bay Islands were constituted a British colony in 1852 with a lieutenant-governor representing the governor of Jamaica, and an elective Assembly. The islands were ceded to the Republic of Honduras in 1859.

Colonial Office and predecessor

Bay Islands: Original Correspondence (CO 34) 1852–61, 10 volumes
Bay Islands correspondence is registered in the Jamaica register of correspondence (CO 351) from 1852 to 1854, and then in the British Honduras register (CO 348)
Index to Correspondence (CO 714/24) 1852–61
Bay Islands: Acts (CO 35) 1852–9, 1 volume
Bay Islands: Miscellanea (CO 36) 1855–9, 5 volumes of blue books of statistics

Bechuanaland Protectorate (Botswana)

Northern Bechuanaland was treated as part of British Bechuanaland until 1895, after which it was administered as a separate territory by a resident commissioner under the high commissioner for South Africa. Its constitutional position was regulated largely by orders in council and proclamations issued by the high commissioner. The tribal administrations and courts were

6 Now Roatan; often cited within the documents as Rattan.

formally recognised and their powers defined by various proclamations. In 1960 a new constitution was introduced, and on 27 September 1963 the territory was made independent of High Commission rule, the resident commissioner becoming Her Majesty's commissioner and being directly responsible to the secretary of state for the colonies. A revised constitution, which came into effect on 3 March 1965, established internal self-government based on universal adult suffrage and a ministerial form of government. Botswana became a republic on 30 September 1966. Bechuanaland, Basutoland and Swaziland are sometimes known as the 'South Africa High Commission Territories' (or simply 'High Commission Territories') and may be described in the records under that collective term. See also British Bechuanaland.

Colonial Office

Bechuanaland Protectorate Miscellanea (CO 567) 1896–1925, 19 volumes of blue books of statistics

Dominions: Original Correspondence (CO 532) 1907–25

Colonial Office and Commonwealth Office

Colonial Office and Commonwealth Office: Southern Africa Department: Original Correspondence (CO 1048) 1960–8, 966 files

Dominions Office/Commonwealth Relations Office/Commonwealth Office/Foreign and Commonwealth Office

High Commissioner for South Africa, and High Commissioner for Basutoland, the Bechuanaland Protectorate and Swaziland, and UK High Commissioner for the Union of South Africa: Correspondence (DO 119) 1843–1965

Dominions Office and Commonwealth Relations Office: Original Correspondence (DO 35) 1915–71

Bechuanaland Protectorate: Miscellanea (DO 26) 1926–47, 22 volumes of blue books of statistics

Bechuanaland Protectorate: Sessional Papers (DO 102) 1921–65, 41 volumes

Basutoland and Lesotho; Bechuanaland Protectorate and Botswana; and Swaziland: Government Gazettes (DO 145) 1961–75

Commonwealth Relations Office: South Africa High Commission Territories: Registered Files (BBS series) (DO 157) 1959–63, 66 files

Commonwealth Office: East Africa Department: Registered Files, Botswana, Lesotho and Swaziland (BLS, SAB, SAR and SAS series) 1966–7, 14 files

Basutoland, Bechuanaland and Swaziland: Acts (DO 150) 1961–6

Commonwealth Office and Foreign and Commonwealth Office: Central African Department and Predecessors: Registered Files (NR and CA series) (FCO 29) 1967–9

Commonwealth Office and Foreign and Commonwealth Office: East Africa and East and Southern Africa Departments: Registered Files (P and JE series) (FCO 31) 1967 onwards

Commonwealth Office and Foreign and Commonwealth Office: Southern African Department and Predecessors: Registered Files (SAD and CS series) (FCO 45) 1967 onwards

Foreign and Commonwealth Office and predecessors: Records of Former Colonial Administrations: Migrated Archives (FCO 141)

Belize *see* British Honduras

Berbice *see under* British Guiana

Bermuda

The Bermuda islands (also known as the Somers Islands) were first settled in 1609 following the shipwreck there of British settlers bound for Virginia. In 1612 the charter of the Virginia Company was extended to include the islands but the company sold its rights to the Somers Islands Company in 1615. Representative government was introduced in 1620. In 1684 the charter, which had been taken over by the Bermuda Company of London, was annulled and the colony passed to the Crown. Bermuda remains a British dependency (UK Overseas Territory).

Colonial Office and predecessors

Bermuda: Original Correspondence (CO 37) 1689–1951, 303 volumes and boxes of files, continued in **West Indian Department: Registered Files (WIS series) (CO 1031)** 1948–67. See also Colonies General: Supplementary Original Correspondence (CO 537).

Bermuda: Register of Correspondence (CO 334) 1850–1951, 22 volumes (for registers before 1850 see CO 326)

Index to Correspondence (CO 714/25–8) 1815–69

Bermuda: Entry Books (CO 38) 1615–1872, 38 volumes, including précis books

Bermuda: Register of Out-letters (CO 499) 1872–1925, 6 volumes

Bermuda: Acts (CO 39) 1690–1989, 102 volumes

Bermuda: Sessional Papers (CO 40) 1687–1965, 166 volumes

Bermuda: Government Gazettes (CO 647) 1902–89, 35 volumes

Bermuda: Miscellanea (CO 41) 1715–1950, 144 volumes, including shipping returns, military accounts, blue books of statistics and newspapers (for a list of newspapers see appendix 3)

Commonwealth Office/Foreign and Commonwealth Office

Commonwealth Office: West Indian Department 'B' and Foreign and Commonwealth Office, West Indian Department: Registered Files, Smaller Commonwealth West Indian Territories (WB and HW series) (FCO 44) 1967 onwards

Foreign and Commonwealth Office: North American and Caribbean Department and Caribbean Department: Registered Files (AN series) (FCO 63) 1968 onwards

Biafra

The short-lived Republic of Biafra (1967–70) ceded from Nigeria some years after Nigerian independence, and was not recognised by the British government. For these and other reasons there are no discrete record series, but there is a considerable amount of relevant material. Most of this will be found in the Foreign and Commonwealth Office series listed under Nigeria, but because of international interest there is much in the records of other government departments. Other aspects of British government interest in the matter can be found in records of the Cabinet, Prime Minister's Office, British Council, Ministry of Defence, Treasury, etc. Topics covered include sale and smuggling of arms, concerns of the UN Security Council, humanitarian aid, mercenaries, illegal procurement of UK aircraft, visits by British parliamentarians, BBC news reporting, French military support, and many others.

Bioko *see* Fernando Po

Botswana *see* Bechuanaland Protectorate

British Antarctic Territory

Originally administered as a dependency of the Falkland Islands, the British Antarctic Territory became an Overseas Territory of the United Kingdom in its own right by order in council of 3 March 1962. It is administered by the Foreign and Commonwealth Office and the commissioner for the British Antarctic Territory is the head of the Foreign and Commonwealth Office Overseas Territories Department. See also under Falkland Islands.

Colonial Office/Commonwealth Office/Foreign and Commonwealth Office

Falkland Islands, St Helena, Tristan da Cunha and British Antarctica: Original Correspondence (FST series) (CO 1024) 1951–68

Commonwealth Office: West Indian Department 'B' and Foreign and Commonwealth Office, West Indian Department: Registered Files, Smaller Commonwealth West Indian Territories (WB and HW series) (FCO 44) 1967 onwards

British Antarctic Territory: Government Gazettes (FCO 5) 1962–90, 1 volume

British Bechuanaland

The British government appointed a deputy commissioner to the Bakswana people of Bechuanaland in 1884. The following year, with the concurrence of Chief Khama III and principal chiefs, the whole of Bechuanaland was placed under British protection. The southern part of the country was constituted a Crown colony called British Bechuanaland and was annexed to Cape Colony in 1895. See also under Bechuanaland Protectorate.

Colonial Office

British Bechuanaland: Government Gazettes (CO 451) 1887–95, 1 volume

British Cameroons

The Cameroons, German (as Kamerun) since 1888, were conquered by British and French troops in 1916. In 1919 they were divided between Britain and France, and assigned to those countries under League of Nations mandates in 1922. The British Cameroons were administered as part of Nigeria until 1960 when Nigeria became independent. A plebiscite was held in February 1961 to decide whether the British Cameroons should join Nigeria or the newly independent Republic of Cameroon. Northern Cameroons voted to become part of Nigeria and formally joined the federation on 1 June 1961. The Southern Cameroons opted to join the Republic of Cameroon and did so on 1 October 1961.

Colonial Office

Cameroons: Original Correspondence (CO 649) 1915–26, 13 volumes
Cameroons: Register of Correspondence (CO 750) 1915–26, 5 volumes
Cameroons: Register of Out-letters (CO 751) 1915–26, 4 volumes
After 1926 see under Nigeria

Foreign and Commonwealth Office and predecessors

Records of Former Colonial Administrations: Migrated Archives (FCO 141)

For records relating to the 1961 plebiscite see the Foreign Office series FO 371, Political Departments: General Correspondence 1906–66

British Central Africa Protectorate *see* Nyasaland

British Columbia

British Columbia is an amalgamation of four colonial jurisdictions. Vancouver Island, formerly part of the Hudson's Bay Company territory, became a Crown colony in 1849; British Columbia, formerly known as New Caledonia, was settled from Vancouver Island and in 1858 became a Crown colony comprising roughly the southern half of its present mainland area. In 1862 the northern half of the area, including part of the present Yukon Territory, was established as the Territory of Stikine. In 1863 the Queen Charlotte Islands, British Columbia and the Stikine Territory were united under the name of British Columbia, and in 1866 Vancouver Island joined this composite colony. In 1871 British Columbia became a province of the Dominion of Canada. For correspondence from 1871 and other later records see under Canada.

Colonial Office

British Columbia: Original Correspondence (CO 60) 1858–71, 44 volumes
British Columbia: Register of Correspondence (CO 338) 1858–71, 3 volumes
Index to Correspondence (CO 714/49) 1858–67
British Columbia: Entry Books (CO 398) 1858–71, 7 volumes
British Columbia: Acts (CO 61) 1858–87, 10 volumes

British Columbia: Sessional Papers (CO 62) 1864–1925, 121 volumes
British Columbia: Government Gazettes (CO 63) 1863–1925, 101 volumes
British Columbia: Miscellanea (CO 64) 1860–70, 11 volumes of blue books of statistics

Dominions Office/Commonwealth Relations Office

British Columbia: Sessional Papers (DO 33) 1926–65, 127 volumes
British Columbia: Government Gazettes (DO 34) 1926–75, 167 volumes

British Guiana (Guyana)

The Dutch West India Company occupied Berbice, Demerara and Essequibo from 1621, Demerara and Essequibo being united in 1784. The territories were captured by Britain in 1796, restored to the Dutch in 1802, recaptured in 1803 and formally ceded to Britain in 1814. All three were united in 1831 as British Guiana. The territory became independent under the name of Guyana on 26 May 1966, and a republic within the Commonwealth on 23 February 1970. Some records of the Dutch West India Company relating to the administration of Essequibo, Demerara and Berbice between 1686 and 1792 are in the miscellanea series (CO 116) listed below. They were surrendered to Britain by The Netherlands in 1819 on the grounds that they would be needed for the effective British administration of the territories. Remaining records are in the National Archives (Nationaal Archief) of The Netherlands at The Hague (http://en.nationaalarchief.nl). See also under West Indies.

Colonial Office and predecessors

British Guiana: Original Correspondence (CO 111) 1781–1951, 825 volumes and boxes of files, continued in **West Indian Department: Registered Files (WIS series) (CO 1031)** 1948–67. See also Colonies General: Supplementary Original Correspondence (CO 537).
British Guiana: Register of Correspondence (CO 345) 1850–1951, 39 volumes (for registers before 1850 see CO 326)
Index to Correspondence (CO 714/71–7) 1815–67
British Guiana: Entry Books (CO 112) 1797–1872, 42 volumes, including précis books
British Guiana: Register of Out-letters (CO 502) 1872–1926, 10 volumes
British Guiana: Acts (CO 113) 1837–1965, 32 volumes
British Guiana: Sessional Papers (CO 114) 1805–1965, 304 volumes
British Guiana and Guyana: Government Gazettes (CO 115) 1838–1975, 322 volumes
British Guiana: Miscellanea (CO 116) 1681–1943, 312 volumes, including grants of land, registers of legal instruments, court records, taxation returns, reports of protectors of slaves, Venezuelan Boundary Commission papers, magistrates' returns, blue books of statistics and newspapers (for a list of newspapers see appendix 3). As noted above, this series also includes papers of the Dutch West India Company, 1686–1792, relating to the Dutch administration of Berbice, Demerara and Essequibo.
British Guiana: Sugar Industry Commission (Venn Commission, 1948–9) (CO 946) 1948–9, 4 pieces
British Guiana: Constitutional Commission (CO 951) 1950–1, 70 files

British Guiana: Constitutional Commission (CO 891) 1954, 10 volumes
Commission of Inquiry into Disturbances in British Guiana in February 1962 (CO 887) 1962, 13 volumes

Commonwealth Office

Commonwealth Office: Atlantic Department: Registered Files (G series) (FCO 23) 1966–8

Foreign and Commonwealth Office

Foreign and Commonwealth Office: North American and Caribbean Department, and Caribbean Department: Registered Files (AN series) (FCO 63) 1968 onwards

British Honduras (Belize)

English settlements appeared on the Central American coast from 1638, and increased after 1660. From 1740 to 1782 the settlements were administered by the superintendent of the Mosquito (or Moskito) Coast. From 1862 the superintendent was replaced by a lieutenant-governor and British Honduras was placed under the nominal superintendence of Jamaica until 1884 when it was given its own governor. Internal self-government was attained in 1964, and on 1 June 1973 the name of the territory was changed to Belize. In March 1981 Britain and Guatemala signed an agreement providing the basis for a full negotiated settlement which would terminate Guatemala's claim to Belize and assure Belize's future security. Subsequent negotiations ended without agreement on a formal treaty. Belize became an independent state within the Commonwealth on 21 September 1981.

The British Honduras register of correspondence (CO 348) also covers correspondence relating to the Bay Islands (1854–61) and the Turks and Caicos Islands (1855–67). For Foreign Office records relating to the Mosquito (or Moskito) Coast see Foreign Office: Political and Other Departments: General Correspondence before 1906, Mosquito (FO 53) 1845–95.

Colonial Office and predecessors

British Honduras: Original Correspondence (CO 123) 1744–1951, 409 volumes and boxes of files, continued in **West Indian Department: Registered Files (WIS series) (CO 1031)** 1948–67. See also Colonies General: Supplementary Original Correspondence (CO 537).
British Honduras: Register of Correspondence (CO 348) 1855–1951, 27 volumes (for registers before 1850 see CO 326)
Index to Correspondence (CO 714/79–81) 1815–70
British Honduras: Entry Books (CO 124) 1630–1872, 9 volumes
British Honduras: Register of Out-letters (CO 503) 1872–1926, 9 volumes
British Honduras and Belize: Acts (CO 125) 1855–1977, 25 volumes
British Honduras: Sessional Papers (CO 126) 1848–1965, 83 volumes
British Honduras and Belize: Government Gazettes (CO 127) 1861–1975, 94 volumes
British Honduras: Miscellanea (CO 128) 1807–1943, 117 volumes, comprising shipping returns and blue books of statistics

Commonwealth Office/Foreign and Commonwealth Office

Commonwealth Office: West Indian Department 'B' and Foreign and Commonwealth Office, West Indian Department: Registered Files, Smaller Commonwealth West Indian Territories (WB and HW series) (FCO 44) 1967 onwards

British Indian Ocean Territory

The British Indian Ocean Territory (BIOT) was established by order in council in 1965 for UK and USA defence purposes and included islands formerly administered by Mauritius and Seychelles. The settled inhabitants were subsequently relocated to those two countries. Since then, the only inhabitants have been UK and US military personnel and civilian contract employees, all living on Diego Garcia. After the independence of Mauritius and Seychelles the territory was redefined in 1976 as comprising only the islands of the Chagos Archipelago, including Diego Garcia, and the islands which had been detached from Seychelles were returned. Successive Mauritian governments have asserted a claim to the Chagos Islands. Chagos islanders are engaged in a long-running legal battle for permission to return. BIOT remains a British dependency (UK Overseas Territory).

Commonwealth Relations Office/Commonwealth Office/Foreign and Commonwealth Office

British Indian Ocean Territory: Acts (DO 151) 1965–81, 1 volume

British Indian Ocean Territory Official Gazette (FCO 4) 1965–90, 7 volumes

Commonwealth Office and Foreign and Commonwealth Office: Pacific and Indian Ocean Department and Pacific Dependent Territories Department: Registered Files (Q and HP series) (FCO 32) 1967 onwards

Commonwealth Office and Foreign and Commonwealth Office: Hong Kong Departments: Registered Files, Hong Kong, British Honduras, British Indian Ocean Territories and Seychelles (HW and HK series) (FCO 40) 1965 onwards

Foreign and Commonwealth Office: Atlantic and Indian Ocean Department: Registered Files (HG series) (FCO 83) 1970–2

Foreign and Commonwealth Office and predecessors: Records of Former Colonial Administrations: Migrated Archives (FCO 141)

British Kaffraria

British Kaffraria was established as a separate colony in 1847, but annexed to the Cape in 1866. There are no separate series of records for the territory; the first volume of the records of the high commissioner for South Africa (DO 119) concerns British Kaffraria, 1852–8, and there are references in the Africa confidential print series CO 879. See also under Cape of Good Hope.

British Malaya *see also under* individual territories, Malayan Union *and* Malaysia

By 'British Malaya' is meant the area comprising the settlements of Singapore, Penang, Labuan, Christmas Island and the Dindings (see Straits Settlements), the Federated Malay States and the states of Johore, Kedah and Perlis, Kelantan and Trengganu.

Colonial Office

British Malaya: Miscellanea (CO 740) 1921–37, 15 volumes of annual returns of imports and exports

British New Guinea (Papua)

In 1883 that part of New Guinea not claimed by The Netherlands was annexed to Queensland. In 1884 a British protectorate was proclaimed and a special commissioner appointed; in 1888 the territory was annexed to the British Crown. In 1901 it was assigned to the Commonwealth of Australia for five years, and in 1906 it was proclaimed a territory of Australia under the name Papua. From 1945 to 1946 Papua was united with the former German Territory of New Guinea as a single territory under the name of Papua New Guinea. Papua New Guinea became a fully independent state within the Commonwealth on 16 September 1975.
See also New Guinea and Papua New Guinea.

Colonial Office

British New Guinea (Papua): Original Correspondence (CO 422) 1884–1900, 15 volumes. Printed correspondence is in the Australia confidential print series CO 881.
British New Guinea (Papua): Register of Correspondence (CO 578) 1884–1900, 2 volumes
British New Guinea (Papua): Register of Out-letters (CO 579) 1884–1900, 1 volume
British New Guinea (Papua): Acts (CO 200) 1888–1906, 2 volumes
British New Guinea (Papua): Sessional Papers (CO 436) 1888–1925, 7 volumes
British New Guinea (Papua): Government Gazettes (CO 453) 1888–1921, 4 volumes

Dominions Office/Commonwealth Relations Office/Commonwealth Office/Foreign and Commonwealth Office

Dominions Office and Commonwealth Relations Office: Original Correspondence (DO 35) 1915–71
Papua: Sessional Papers (DO 97) 1910–41, 3 volumes
Papua: Government Gazettes (DO 86) 1922–49, 2 volumes
Commonwealth Relations Office and Commonwealth Office: Far East and Pacific Department: Registered Files (FE series) (DO 169) 1960–7
Commonwealth Office, Far East and Pacific Department and Foreign and Commonwealth Office, South West Pacific Department: Registered Files (H and FW series) (FCO 24) 1967 onwards

British North America

The earlier part of the original correspondence series (CO 6) concerns the boundary between British North America and the United States (1816–40), and the North West Expedition (1819–50). The later part (1857–68) consists of domestic correspondence, i.e., correspondence between the Colonial Office, other British government departments, miscellaneous organisations and individuals, concerning the North American colonies collectively. The emigration registers (CO 327) were combined with the general registers of correspondence (CO 328) after 1863. See also under Canada.

Colonial Office and predecessor

British North America: Original Correspondence (CO 6) 1816–68, 43 volumes. See also Colonies General: Supplementary Original Correspondence (CO 537).
British North America: Emigration Registers (CO 327) 1850–63, 2 volumes
British North America: General Registers (CO 328) 1850–68, 4 volumes (for registers before 1850 see CO 326)
Index to Correspondence (CO 714/1) Governor's Despatches (Military) 1845
British North America: Registers of Out-letters (CO 329) 1872–80, 2 volumes
Confidential Print: North America (CO 880) 1839–1914, 32 volumes

British North Borneo *see under* North Borneo

British Solomon Islands Protectorate

The southern Solomon Islands were declared a British protectorate in 1893, and other outlying islands were added from 1898 to 1900. By a convention of 14 November 1899 several islands in the northern group were transferred from Germany; those not transferred were administered by Australia under the mandate for New Guinea. The protectorate was administered through the Western Pacific High Commission; a resident commissioner was appointed in 1896, and a nominated advisory council established in 1921. The central Solomon Islands were occupied by the Japanese in 1942. In 1952 the headquarters of the High Commission for the Western Pacific was moved from Fiji to Honiara, the capital of the Solomon Islands, and the high commissioner took over responsibility for the direct administration of the protectorate from the acting resident commissioner. The Solomon Islands became a fully independent state within the Commonwealth on 7 July 1978.

Colonial Office

British Solomon Islands Protectorate: Acts (CO 907) 1935–65, 9 volumes
British Solomon Islands Protectorate: Sessional Papers (CO 856) 1921–65, 13 volumes
British Solomon Islands Protectorate: Miscellanea (CO 723) 1920–42, 22 volumes of blue books of statistics

For correspondence relating to the Solomon Islands see **Western Pacific Original Correspondence (CO 225)** 1878–1951, continued in Hong Kong and Pacific Department: Original Correspondence (CO 1023) 1946–55 and Pacific and Indian Ocean Department: Registered Files (CO 1036) 1952–67

Western Pacific Register of Correspondence (CO 492) 1878–1951

Western Pacific Register of Out-letters (CO 493) 1879–1926

Commonwealth Office/Foreign and Commonwealth Office

Commonwealth Office and Foreign and Commonwealth Office: Pacific and Indian Ocean Department and Pacific Dependent Territories Department: Registered Files (Q and HP series) (FCO 32) 1967 onwards

Foreign and Commonwealth Office and predecessors: Records of Former Colonial Administrations: Migrated Archives (FCO 141)

British Somaliland (Somalia)

Egypt claimed Somaliland in 1875; when it withdrew in 1884 Somaliland became a British protectorate. It was administered by the resident political agent at Aden as a dependency of the government of India until 1898, when it was transferred to the control of the Foreign Office and the political agent became consul-general. In 1905 control was transferred to the Colonial Office and an administrator was appointed; the post became that of commissioner in 1914, and governor in 1919. British Somaliland was occupied by the Italians from 1940 to 1941; the territory was then under British military administration until 1948. In 1960 British Somaliland became independent and joined with its neighbour, the former Italian colony and United Nations trust territory, to form an enlarged and independent Somalia. Somaliland declared independence after the overthrow of the Somali military dictator Siad Barre in 1991. Although internationally recognised as an autonomous region within Somalia, the territory continues to lobby to win support for its claim to be a sovereign state under the name of the Republic of Somaliland.

Records relating to the military administration are in War Office and Foreign Office series, especially WO 230 and FO 1015, and material relating to unification and independence and to ongoing boundary questions and other international matters is in FO 371, Political Departments: General Correspondence 1906–66.

India Office

Records at the British Library

Foreign Office

Foreign Office: Political and Other Departments: General Correspondence before 1906, Africa (FO 2)

Colonial Office

Somaliland: Original Correspondence (CO 535) 1905–51, 152 volumes and boxes of files, continued in the series **Central Africa and Aden: Original Correspondence (CO 1015)**

1950–62. See also Colonies General: Supplementary Original Correspondence (CO 537).
Somaliland: Register of Correspondence (CO 713) 1905–51, 18 volumes
Somaliland: Register of Out-letters (CO 769) 1905–26, 2 volumes
Somaliland: Acts (CO 673) 1900–60, 6 volumes
Somaliland: Sessional Papers (CO 830) 1925–61, 26 volumes
Somaliland: Government Gazettes (CO 922) 1941–60, 8 volumes
Somaliland: Miscellanea (CO 607) 1901–38, 38 volumes of blue books of statistics

Commonwealth Relations Office/Commonwealth Office/Foreign and Commonwealth Office

Commonwealth Relations Office and Commonwealth Office: East Africa Departments: Registered Files, East Africa (EA series) (DO 213) 1963–7
Commonwealth Office and Foreign and Commonwealth Office: East Africa Departments: Registered Files (P and JE series) (FCO 31) 1967 onwards
Foreign Office and Foreign and Commonwealth Office, North and East African Department and Successors: Registered Files (V and NA series) (FCO 39) 1967 onwards

British South Africa Company

In 1889 the British South Africa Company was granted a royal charter to develop and administer the Rhodesias. The charter was abrogated in 1923, and in the following year the company surrendered the last of its administrative rights. The two series listed here are continued by CO 671 and CO 815 under Southern Rhodesia, while the company's government gazettes for North-Eastern and Northern Rhodesia will be found in CO 669 and CO 670. The series CO 468 under Rhodesia consists of the company's reports on the administration of Rhodesia. Correspondence with or relating to the company will be found in CO 417 under South Africa High Commission. The National Archives does not hold records of the company itself.[7]

Colonial Office

British South Africa Company: Ordinances (CO 3) 1891–9, 1 volume
British South Africa Company: Government Gazettes (CO 455) 1894–1923, 8 volumes

British Virgin Islands

The English expelled the Dutch from some of the Virgin Islands in 1666 and from Tortola, the most important of the islands, in 1672, and thereafter the islands were included in the government of the Leeward Islands. When this federation broke up in 1816, the Virgin Islands,

[7] Some reports, minutes, papers and correspondence of the company, 1888–1911, are held in the Commonwealth and African Collections at the Bodleian Library, University of Oxford (formerly at Rhodes House Library). Minutes, accounts, correspondence etc. are among the papers of P. L. Gell, a director of the company, at the Derbyshire Record Office. It is understood that the main body of the official correspondence of the company is held at the National Archives of Zambia and of Zimbabwe.

St Christopher (St Kitts) and Nevis formed a separate governmental unit, but in 1833 they were reunited with the other Leeward Islands under a governor-in-chief. When the Leeward Islands were de-federated in July 1956 the British Virgin Islands were established as a separate colony. The islands continued to be administered by the governor of the Leeward Islands until January 1960 when the office was abolished and the administrator (later governor) of the British Virgin Islands became directly responsible to the Colonial Office. The British Virgin Islands remain a British dependency (UK Overseas Territory). See separate entries for St Croix and St Thomas. See also under Leeward Islands and West Indies.

Colonial Office and predecessors

Virgin Islands: Original Correspondence (CO 314) 1711–1872, 24 volumes (apart from the first volume, which includes papers dated 1711–91, the series commences in 1854). Before 1854 and after 1872 correspondence is in **Leeward Islands, Original Correspondence (CO 152)** which is continued after 1951 in **West Indian Department: Registered Files (WIS series) (CO 1031)** 1948–67. Both CO 314 and CO 152 are registered in Leeward Islands: Register of Correspondence (CO 354) 1850–1951 (for registers before 1850 see CO 326).

Index to Correspondence (CO 714/164) 1854–66

Virgin Islands: Acts (CO 315) 1774–1965, 17 volumes

Virgin Islands: Sessional Papers (CO 316) 1773–1965, 22 volumes

Virgin Islands: Miscellanea (CO 317) 1784–1896, 67 volumes of shipping returns and blue books of statistics

Commonwealth Office/Foreign and Commonwealth Office

Commonwealth Office: West Indian Department 'B' and Foreign and Commonwealth Office, West Indian Department: Registered Files, Smaller Commonwealth West Indian Territories (WB and HW series) (FCO 44) 1967 onwards

Brunei

The Sultanate of Brunei included Sarawak, Labuan and North Borneo until their cession to Britain (for details see under those territories). Brunei itself was placed under British protection by a treaty of 1888. From 1906 the sultan acted on the advice of a British resident, who reported to the governor of the Straits Settlements, and a nominated advisory council. Brunei was occupied by the Japanese from 1941 to 1945. From 1946 the governor-general for South East Asia acted as the channel of communication between the secretary of state and the resident, but in 1948 the governor of Sarawak was appointed high commissioner for Brunei. In 1963 Brunei decided not to become part of the new Federation of Malaysia. It became a fully independent sovereign state in 1983.

Colonial Office

Brunei: Original Correspondence (CO 943) 1946–51, 2 boxes of files, continued in **Far Eastern Department and Successors: Registered Files (FED series) (CO 1030)** 1941–67.

See also Colonies General: Supplementary Original Correspondence (CO 537).
Brunei: Sessional Papers (CO 824) 1906–65, 6 volumes
Brunei: Government Gazettes (CO 985) 1951–75, 25 volumes
See also:
Federated Malay States: Original Correspondence (CO 717) 1920–51
Borneo Territories: Original Correspondence (CO 954) 1946–51
North Borneo, Brunei and Sarawak: Registers of Correspondence (CO 992) 1942–51

Commonwealth Office and Foreign and Commonwealth Office

Foreign and Commonwealth Office and Predecessors: British Residency and High Commission, Brunei: Registered Files (DO 229) 1952 onwards
Commonwealth Office, Far East and Pacific Department and Foreign and Commonwealth Office, South West Pacific Department: Registered Files (H and FW series) (FCO 24) 1967 onwards
Foreign and Commonwealth Office and predecessors: Records of Former Colonial Administrations: Migrated Archives (FCO 141)

Burma (Myanmar)[8]

Burma came under the control of the British raj in 1885. It was administered first through the India Office, and then from 1937 by the newly established Burma Office. Records of both offices are held at the British Library with the exception of part of the Foreign Office series Burma Office, Burma Secretariat, and Foreign Office, Embassy, Rangoon, Burma: General Correspondence (FO 643) 1942–62, 163 volumes and boxes of files. Burma achieved independence in 1948, but did not subsequently join the Commonwealth. Records relating to Britain's relations with the newly independent country are, therefore, also in Foreign Office series, particularly FO 371, Political Departments: General Correspondence 1906–66. Records after 1966 are in the series Foreign Office and Foreign and Commonwealth Office: South East Asian Department: Registered Files (D and FA series) (FCO 15) 1967 onwards.

Caicos Islands *see* Turks and Caicos Islands

Cameroon *see* British Cameroons

Canada

French Canada was conquered by Britain during the Seven Years' War (the French and Indian War) and ceded in 1763. From 1763 until 1774 there was a military administration under a governor,

[8] Although the two names 'Burma' and 'Myanmar' are recognised internationally, the policy of the British government is to use 'Burma'.

but in 1774 a nominated council was established. By the Canada Act of 1791 Canada was divided into two provinces, Upper Canada (now Ontario) and Lower Canada (now Quebec). In 1867 the British North America Act united the provinces of Ontario, Quebec, New Brunswick and Nova Scotia as the Dominion of Canada. Other provinces were added later: Manitoba in 1870, British Columbia in 1871, Prince Edward Island in 1873, Alberta and Saskatchewan in 1905, and Newfoundland in 1949. See also under British North America and the individual colonies and provinces.

Colonial Office and predecessors

Canada: Original Correspondence (CO 42) 1700–1922, 1,045 volumes, continued in **Dominions: Original Correspondence (CO 532)** 1907–25. See also Colonies General: Supplementary Original Correspondence (CO 537).

Canada: Register of Correspondence (CO 335) 1850–1922, 31 volumes, continued in Dominions Register of Correspondence (CO 708) 1907–26 (for registers before 1850 see CO 326)

Index to Correspondence (CO 714/29–35) 1815–70

Canada: Entry Books (CO 43) 1763–1873, 158 volumes

Canada: Register of Out-letters (CO 340) 1872–1922, 14 volumes (continued in CO 709, Dominions Register of Out-letters)

Canada: Acts (CO 44) 1764–1925, 219 volumes

Canada: Sessional Papers (CO 45) 1764–1925, 1,428 volumes

Canada: Government Gazettes (CO 46) 1825–1925, 172 volumes

Canada: Miscellanea (CO 47) 1764–1925, 213 volumes, including shipping returns, declarations as to ownership of Canadian paper money, accounts, memoranda on various subjects, blue books of statistics and newspapers (for a list of newspapers see appendix 3)

Canada: Civil Service List (CO 569) 1887–1910, 6 volumes

Papers of Lord Aylmer, governor of Lower Canada 1830–35 (CO 387), 1830–7, 11 volumes

Dominions Office/Commonwealth Relations Office/Commonwealth Office

Original Correspondence (DO 35) 1915–71

Canada: Acts, Orders in Council (DO 27) 1926–42, 16 volumes

Canada: Sessional Papers (DO 28) 1926–66, 337 volumes

Canada: Government Gazettes (DO 29) 1926–78, 272 volumes

Canada: Miscellanea (DO 30) 1926–46, 38 volumes of Commercial Intelligence Journals

High Commission and Consular Archives, Canada: Correspondence (DO 127) 1928 onwards

Commonwealth Relations Office and Commonwealth Office: Western and Middle East Department and Successors: Registered Files, Canada, Ireland and International Western Organisations (WES series) (DO 182) 1960–6

Commonwealth Office: Atlantic Department: Registered Files (G series) (FCO 23) 1966–8

Foreign Office and Foreign and Commonwealth Office

Foreign Office and Foreign and Commonwealth Office: American and Latin American Departments: Registered Files (A and AL series) (FCO 7) 1967 onwards

Foreign and Commonwealth Office: North American and Caribbean Department and Caribbean Department: Registered Files (AN series) (FCO 63) 1968 onwards

Foreign and Commonwealth Office: North America Department: Registered Files (AM series) (FCO 82) 1971 onwards

Cape Breton *see* Nova Scotia and Cape Breton, *and under* Canada

Cape Colony *see* Cape of Good Hope

Cape of Good Hope (Cape Colony)

Following earlier Portuguese interest in the territory and a brief English annexation in 1620, the Dutch East India Company took possession of the Cape of Good Hope in 1652. Britain occupied it in 1795, restored it to the Batavian Republic in 1803 under the terms of the Treaty of Amiens, recaptured it in 1806 and finally received it by cession in 1814. In 1910 it became a province of the Union of South Africa. After the close of the Napoleonic wars the British government set up several commissions of inquiry into the new British possessions. An inquiry into Cape Colony was carried out during the period from 1823 to 1826, the records of which are held mainly in CO 414, with some commissioners' reports in CO 48. For records before 1807 see War Office correspondence in WO 1. For correspondence and other records from 1910 see under Union of South Africa. See also under South Africa High Commission.

Colonial Office and predecessors

Cape of Good Hope (Cape Colony): Original Correspondence (CO 48) 1807–1910, 606 volumes. See also Colonies General: Supplementary Original Correspondence (CO 537).
Cape of Good Hope (Cape Colony): Register of Correspondence (CO 336) 1850–1910, 17 volumes (for registers before 1850 see CO 326)
Index to Correspondence (CO 714/36–40) 1815–70
Cape of Good Hope (Cape Colony): Entry Books (CO 49), 1795–1872, 62 volumes
Cape of Good Hope (Cape Colony): Register of Out-letters (CO 462) 1872–1910, 7 volumes
Cape of Good Hope (Cape Colony): Acts (CO 50) 1825–1910, 11 volumes
Cape of Good Hope (Cape Colony): Sessional Papers (CO 51) 1825–1925, 418 volumes
Cape of Good Hope (Cape Colony): Government Gazettes (CO 52) 1823–1925, 120 volumes
Cape of Good Hope (Cape Colony): Miscellanea (CO 53) 1799–1909, 147 volumes, including accounts, reports of protectors of slaves, blue books of statistics and newspapers (for a list of newspapers see appendix 3)
Commissioners of Eastern Inquiry, Cape of Good Hope (Cape Colony) (CO 414) 1805–30, 15 volumes, etc.
The series CO 959, Various Private Collections, includes correspondence of Sir Bartle Frere, governor of Cape Colony 1877–80

Dominions Office

Cape of Good Hope: Sessional Papers (DO 31) 1926–61, 45 volumes
Cape of Good Hope: Government Gazettes (DO 32) 1926–61, 68 volumes

Carolina *see under* America and West Indies

Carriacou *see under* Grenada

Cayman Islands

The Cayman Islands were ceded to England by Spain (which claimed but did not occupy them) in 1670 and settled by British colonists from Jamaica from 1734. From then until 1959 they were a dependency of Jamaica and under its legislature, but with a partly elective local Legislative Assembly from 1832. In 1959 the islands, no longer a dependency of Jamaica, became a part of the Federation of the West Indies. With the dissolution of the federation in 1962, the Cayman Islands became a Crown colony under a new constitution. The islands remain a British dependency (UK Overseas Territory). See also under West Indies.

Colonial Office and predecessors

For correspondence see **Jamaica Original Correspondence (CO 137)**, continued after 1951 in **West Indian Department: Registered Files (WIS series) (CO 1031)** 1948–67
Cayman Islands: Acts (CO 650) 1898–1966, 8 volumes
Cayman Islands: Sessional Papers (CO 857) 1908–65, 8 volumes
Cayman Islands: Government Gazettes (CO 1019) 1956–90, 67 volumes
Cayman Islands: Miscellanea (CO 651) 1912–47, 35 volumes of blue books of statistics

Commonwealth Office/Foreign and Commonwealth Office

Commonwealth Office: West Indian Department 'B' and Foreign and Commonwealth Office, West Indian Department: Registered Files, Smaller Commonwealth West Indian Territories (WB and HW series) (FCO 44) 1967 onwards

Central Africa

Before 1950 papers relating to the region as a whole, or to more than one of the dependencies, are in the record series relating to the individual territories. For a brief period in 1950 and 1951 papers on subjects common to Northern Rhodesia and Nyasaland or relating to the Central African Council and Rhodesia Railways are in CO 952. See also under individual territories and Federation of Rhodesia and Nyasaland.

Colonial Office

Central Africa: Original Correspondence (CO 952) 1950–1, 16 files, continued in **Central Africa and Aden: Original Correspondence (CO 1015)** 1950–62

Central Africa: Register of Correspondence (CO 1014) 1950, 1 volume

Central African Federation *see* Federation of Rhodesia and Nyasaland

Ceylon (Sri Lanka)

Britain occupied Dutch possessions in Ceylon in 1796 and annexed them to the presidency of Madras under military rule. In 1798 a governor was appointed by the Crown, but subject to the East India Company. In 1802 Ceylon became a separate colony, and a Council of Government was set up in 1810. In 1815 the Kandyan kingdom of the interior was overcome and the whole island came under British rule. After the close of the Napoleonic wars the British government set up several commissions of inquiry into the new British possessions. An inquiry into Ceylon was carried out from 1829 to 1830, the records of which are held mainly in CO 416, with some in CO 54. Ceylon became an independent member of the Commonwealth on 4 February 1948. On 22 May 1972 it adopted a new constitution as the Republic of Sri Lanka, remaining within the Commonwealth. From 1887 until 1948 Ceylon included the British protected state of Maldive Islands, which became independent as the Republic of Maldives on 26 July 1965.

Colonial Office and predecessors

Ceylon: Original Correspondence (CO 54) 1798–1949, 1,004 volumes. See also Colonies General: Supplementary Original Correspondence (CO 537).

Ceylon: Register of Correspondence (CO 337) 1849–1948, 46 volumes (for registers before 1849 see CO 326)

Index to Correspondence (CO 714/41–8) 1813–70

Ceylon: Entry Books (CO 55) 1794–1872, 121 volumes

Ceylon: Register of Out-letters (CO 488) 1872–1926, 17 volumes

Ceylon: Acts (CO 56) 1835–1947, 24 volumes

Ceylon: Sessional Papers (CO 57) 1831–1946, 283 volumes. CO 57/283 is an index to papers laid before the Legislative Council of Ceylon, 1855–1939

Ceylon: Government Gazettes (CO 58) 1813–1946, 314 volumes

Ceylon: Miscellanea (CO 59) 1795–1945, 161 volumes, including memoranda on various subjects, blue books of statistics and newspapers (for a list of newspapers see appendix 3)

Commissioners of Eastern Inquiry, Ceylon (CO 416) 1829–30, 32 volumes

Special Commission on the Constitution of Ceylon (Donoughmore Commission): Reports and Papers (CO 1041) 1927–8, 15 volumes

Dominions Office/Commonwealth Relations Office/Commonwealth Office/Foreign and Commonwealth Office

Dominions Office and Commonwealth Relations Office: Original Correspondence (DO 35) 1915–71
Ceylon: Sessional Papers (DO 109) 1947–65, 121 volumes
Ceylon and Sri Lanka: Government Gazettes (DO 104) 1947–75, 230 volumes
Ceylon: Miscellanea (DO 111) 1946–9, 1 volume of customs returns
Commonwealth Relations Office and Commonwealth Office: South Asia Department: Registered Files (SEA series) (DO 196) 1960–8
Commonwealth Relations Office and Successors: High Commission and Consular Archives, Ceylon: Registered Files (DO 225) 1955–67, 25 files
Commonwealth Office and Foreign and Commonwealth Office: South Asia Department: Registered Files (S and FS series) (FCO 37) 1967 onwards
Foreign and Commonwealth Office and predecessors: Records of Former Colonial Administrations: Migrated Archives (FCO 141). Includes records of the Soulbury Commission on Constitutional Reform

Chagos Islands *see* British Indian Ocean Territory

Christmas Island *see* Straits Settlements

Cocos Islands *see* Straits Settlements

Commonwealth of Australia

The Commonwealth of Australia was constituted in 1901 by a federation of the colonies, thereafter states, of New South Wales, Victoria, South Australia, Queensland, Tasmania and Western Australia. Subsequently a governor-general, acting for the sovereign, an elective Senate and an elective House of Representatives formed the legislature, and the governor-general and Executive Council constituted the executive. Each state retained its own constitution, and records relating to them will also be found listed under their individual names. See also under Australia and under Australia and New Zealand.

Colonial Office

Australia: Original Correspondence (CO 418) 1889–1922, 226 volumes, continued in **Dominions: Original Correspondence (CO 532)** 1907–25. See also Colonies General: Supplementary Original Correspondence (CO 537). The correspondence in CO 418 is registered in, successively, Australia and New Zealand: Register of Correspondence (CO

644) 1901–8, 4 volumes, and Commonwealth of Australia: Register of Correspondence (CO 706) 1909–22, 9 volumes.

Australia and New Zealand: Register of Out-letters (CO 645) 1901–8, 3 volumes
Commonwealth of Australia: Register of Out-letters (CO 707) 1909–22, 7 volumes
Commonwealth of Australia: Acts (CO 558) 1901–25, 23 volumes
Commonwealth of Australia: Sessional Papers (CO 562) 1901–25, 88 volumes
Commonwealth of Australia: Government Gazettes (CO 559) 1901–25, 36 volumes
Commonwealth of Australia: Miscellanea (CO 560) 1903–25, 28 volumes of statistical returns and summaries
Commonwealth of Australia: Public Service Lists (CO 561) 1902–25, 21 volumes
Confidential Print: Australia (CO 881) 1833 to 1923

Dominions Office/Commonwealth Relations Office

Original Correspondence (DO 35) 1915–71
Commonwealth of Australia: Acts (DO 15) 1926–66, 66 volumes
Commonwealth of Australia: Sessional Papers (DO 79) 1926–66, 126 volumes
Commonwealth of Australia: Government Gazettes (DO 16) 1926–87, 282 volumes
Commonwealth of Australia: Miscellanea (DO 17) 1925–50, 39 volumes, comprising statistical returns, summaries and surveys
Commonwealth of Australia: Public Service Lists (DO 18) 1926–7, 2 volumes
Confidential Print: Dominions (Australian) (DO 115) 1928–36, 3 volumes
High Commission and Consular Archives, Australia: Correspondence (DO 126) 1932 onwards

Commonwealth Office/Foreign and Commonwealth Office

Commonwealth Office, Far East and Pacific Department and Foreign and Commonwealth Office, South West Pacific Department: Registered Files (H and FW series) (FCO 24) 1967 onwards
Australian Royal Commission into United Kingdom Nuclear Weapons Testing in Australia: Photocopies of Documents Made Available to the Commission by the Foreign and Commonwealth Office (FCO 1) 1950–79

Connecticut *see under* America and West Indies

Cook Islands

The Cook Islands were declared to be under British protection in 1888. From 1890 to 1900 British authority was represented by a resident who reported to the government of New Zealand. The islands were formally annexed to New Zealand on 7 October 1900. There are no discrete series of records at TNA; scattered references can be found through the online catalogue and it is likely that additional material may be held in the series relating to New Zealand.

Corsica

Formerly held by the Genoese, Corsica became French in 1769. In 1794 it was occupied by Britain, but it was evacuated and retaken by France in 1796. Britain recaptured it in 1814, but it was returned to France in 1815. The following records are précis of despatches from Sir Gilbert Elliott, the civil administrator.

State Paper Office
Corsica: Entry Books (CO 65) 1794–6, 2 volumes

Cosmoledo Islands *see* Mauritius

Cuba *see* Havana

Curaçao

Curaçao was occupied in 1597 by the Spanish and captured in 1634 by the Dutch. During the years from 1800 to 1802 and 1807 to 1816 it was in British hands after being captured, but was then restored to the Dutch. Further records relating to Curaçao for the period 1800–16 will be found among the War Office records, especially in WO 1/97–117 and 145.

Colonial Office and predecessors
Curaçao: Entry Books (CO 66) 1800–16, 4 volumes

For later records see Foreign Office, especially FO 37, Foreign Office and Predecessor: Political and Other Departments: General Correspondence before 1906, Holland (later Netherlands), which includes correspondence from British consuls at Curaçao, and FO 371, Foreign Office: Political Departments: General Correspondence 1906–66

Cyprus

Held by Venice from 1489 until it was incorporated into the Ottoman empire by conquest in 1570–1, Cyprus was handed over to Britain by Turkey for administrative purposes in 1878, although not formally ceded. At the outbreak of war with Turkey in 1914 Cyprus was annexed to the British Crown. The annexation was recognised by Greece and Turkey under the Treaty of Lausanne and in 1925 Cyprus became a Crown colony. Cyprus became an independent republic on 16 August 1960 and a member of the Commonwealth on 13 March 1961. Under the terms of the London Agreement of 1959 Britain retained sovereign rights in two areas of the island to ensure their effective use as military bases. Following independence, tension between Greek and Turkish Cypriots increased and a UN force was established in 1964. In 1974 Turkish troops landed in northern Cyprus following a coup on the island which has since been effectively partitioned. At the time of writing the northern part of the island uses the name 'Turkish Republic of Northern Cyprus' (TRNC), but it is not internationally recognised.

Some of the records listed below for the years 1878–89 are records of the Foreign Office; for earlier records of the Foreign Office relating to Cyprus see FO 78, Foreign Office and Predecessor: Political and Other Departments: General Correspondence before 1906, Ottoman Empire, which includes correspondence from British consuls there. See also under Mediterranean.

Colonial Office

Cyprus: Original Correspondence: (CO 67) 1878–1951, 373 volumes and boxes of files, continued in **Mediterranean Department, Predecessor and Successors: Registered Files, Mediterranean Colonies (MED series) (CO 926)** 1938–66. See also Colonies General: Supplementary Original Correspondence (CO 537).
Cyprus: Register of Correspondence (CO 512) 1878–1951, 33 volumes
Cyprus: Register of Out-letters (CO 516) 1878–1926, 7 volumes
Cyprus: Acts (CO 68) 1878–1960, 16 volumes
Cyprus: Sessional Papers (CO 69) 1878–1965, 80 volumes
Cyprus: Government Gazettes (CO 70) 1878–1965, 59 volumes
Cyprus: Miscellanea (CO 456) 1878–1946, 68 volumes of blue books of statistics

Commonwealth Relations Office/Commonwealth Office

Commonwealth Relations Office: Mediterranean Department: Registered Files (MED series) (DO 220) 1963–6
Commonwealth Relations Office and Successors: High Commission and Predecessor, Cyprus: Registered Files (DO 204) 1960 onwards
Commonwealth Office: Middle East, Western and United Nations Department and Mediterranean Department: Registered Files (M series) (FCO 27) 1967–8

Foreign Office/Foreign and Commonwealth Office

Foreign Office, Central Department and Foreign and Commonwealth Office, Southern European Department: Registered Files (C and WS series) (FCO 9) 1967 onwards
Foreign and Commonwealth Office and predecessors: Records of Former Colonial Administrations: Migrated Archives (FCO 141)

Demerara *see under* British Guiana

Diego Garcia *see under* British Indian Ocean Territory

Dindings *see under* Straits Settlements

Dominica

Dominica was granted with other Caribbean islands to the earl of Carlisle in 1627, but was first settled by the French in 1632. It was captured by Britain in 1761 and ceded in 1763. France recaptured it in 1778, but it was restored to Britain in 1783. It was made part of the Windward Islands Federation in 1763, became a separate colony in 1771, was put under the governor-in-chief of the Leeward Islands in 1833, and rejoined the Windward Islands Federation in 1940. Between 1958 and 1962 Dominica was a member of the Federation of the West Indies. On 3 November 1978 the island became an independent republic under the name of the Commonwealth of Dominica. See also under Leeward Islands, Windward Islands and West Indies.

Colonial Office and predecessors

Dominica: Original Correspondence (CO 71) 1730–1872, 144 volumes. For later correspondence see **Leeward Islands: Original Correspondence (CO 152)** to 1940 and **Windward Islands: Original Correspondence (CO 321)** 1940–51; for correspondence after 1951 see **Colonial Office and Commonwealth Office: West Indian Department: Registered Files (WIS series) (CO 1031)** 1948–67. See also Colonies General: Supplementary Original Correspondence (CO 537). The correspondence in both CO 71 and CO 152 is registered in Leeward Islands Register of Correspondence (CO 354) 1850–1951 (for registers before 1850 see CO 326). The correspondence in CO 321 is registered in Windward Islands Register of Correspondence (CO 376).

Index to Correspondence (CO 714/50–2)

Dominica: Entry Books (CO 72) 1770–1872, 18 volumes, including précis books

Dominica: Acts (CO 73) 1768–1965, 32 volumes

Dominica: Sessional Papers (CO 74) 1767–1965, 63 volumes

Dominica: Government Gazettes (CO 75) 1865–1975, 57 volumes

Dominica: Miscellanea (CO 76) 1763–1940, 78 volumes, including shipping returns, returns of stipendiary magistrates, grants and sales of land, blue books of statistics and newspapers (for a list of newspapers see appendix 3)

Commonwealth Office

Commonwealth Office: West Indian Department 'A' and Associated States Department: Registered Files, Antigua, Dominica, Grenada, St Christopher (St Kitts)-Nevis-Anguilla, St Lucia and St Vincent (WA series) (FCO 43) 1967–8

Foreign and Commonwealth Office

Foreign and Commonwealth Office: North American and Caribbean Department and Caribbean Department: Registered Files (AN series) (FCO 63) 1968 onwards

Dominican Republic *see under* Santo Domingo

Ducie Island *see under* Pitcairn

East Africa

Records in these series deal with matters relating to the region as a whole and especially to the question of 'closer union' and the administration of the common services of the four territories of Kenya, Tanganyika, Uganda and Zanzibar. From 1951 the separate territorial series of correspondence come to an end, and CO 822 becomes the main geographical series for the whole region. A Governors' Conference was established in 1926; records of its proceedings are in CO 962. From 1943 there are also Governors' Conference records in CO 822. The East Africa High Commission, consisting of the governors of Kenya, Tanganyika and Uganda, was established in January 1948 to replace the Governors' Conference. It administered inter-territorial services such as the East African Posts and Telegraphs, the East African Inter-Territorial Languages Committee, the Lake Victoria Fisheries Board, the East African Literature Bureau and the East African Veterinary Research Organisation. In addition, a central Legislative Assembly was set up to advise on and agree legislation passed by the High Commission on matters within its sphere of responsibility; such legislation had effect throughout the British East African territories. The East Africa Royal Commission was set up in 1953 to examine measures necessary to achieve economic and social development in the region. In 1961 the High Commission was replaced by the East African Common Services Organisation which was independent of the British government. See also under individual territories in the region.

Colonial Office

East Africa: Original Correspondence (CO 822) 1927–64, 1,201 volumes and boxes of files. See also Colonies General: Supplementary Original Correspondence (CO 537).
East Africa: Register of Correspondence (CO 869) 1927–51, 22 volumes
East Africa Conference of Governors (CO 962) 1926–43, 16 volumes
East Africa High Commission: Gazettes (CO 921) 1948–66, 16 volumes
East Africa High Commission: Acts (CO 924) 1948–63, 5 volumes
East Africa High Commission: Sessional Papers (CO 942) 1948–65, 23 volumes
East Africa Royal Commission (Dow Commission) (CO 892) 1953–5, 17 files
East Africa Economic and Fiscal Commission (CO 893) 1960, 8 files
East Africa Common Services Organisation and East African Community: Government Gazettes (CO 1050) 1967–77, 5 volumes

East Africa Protectorate *see* Kenya

East Florida *see under* America and West Indies *and* Florida

East Indies

The series noted below contains original correspondence and entry books relating to the East Indies, and includes documents concerning Persia and China, some from the embassy to

China of 1793–4. CO 77 also includes volumes on Bengal, Bombay and Madras. CO 77/64 is a meteorological journal for Canton and Macao. The earlier records are described in *The Calendar of State Papers Colonial, East Indies, 1513–1634* (London, 1862–92) which also covers records of the East India Company held at the British Library. From 1811 to 1816 Java and other parts of the Netherlands East Indies were under the control of the British, and some records of the period can be found in War Office series (WO).

Colonial Office and predecessors

East Indies Original Correspondence, Entry Books, etc. (CO 77) 1570–1856

Egypt

Egypt was formally a British protectorate only from 1914 to 1922, although British interests in the country extended over a much longer period. The Foreign Office retained responsibility, but there is also substantial Colonial Office material, especially among the records of the General Department (CO 323) and the Middle East Department (CO 732), as well as in series relating to neighbouring territories. See also pp. 5–6.

Ellice Islands (Tuvalu) *see under* Gilbert and Ellice Islands

Essequibo *see under* British Guiana

Falkland Islands and Dependencies

The Falkland Islands were settled by both British (at Port Egmont) and French colonists in 1764; in 1767 the French sold their claim to Spain, which knew the islands as the Islas Malvinas. In 1770 Spain expelled the British from Port Egmont. It was restored to Britain the following year but abandoned in 1774. In 1833 Britain finally took possession of the islands, whose dependencies were South Georgia and South Sandwich, both annexed by Captain Cook in 1775; South Shetlands, annexed in 1819; South Orkney, annexed in 1821; and Graham Land, annexed in 1832. In 1842 a lieutenant-governor (later governor) took over from the naval officer who had formerly administered the islands. In 1962 that part of the Falkland Islands Dependencies lying south of latitude 60° south, including the South Orkney and South Shetland Islands, became a separate British dependency – the British Antarctic Territory. Argentina, whose version of this history differs somewhat, continues to claim the Falkland Islands (or Islas Malvinas). The first edition of this guide noted that very little material relating to the Argentine invasion of 1982 and subsequent hostilities had been transferred to The National Archives. With the thirtieth anniversary of the conflict and the opening of records under the 30-year rule there is now a mass of material from various government departments, covering British policy, planning and military operations as well as reactions from the international community. The Falkland Islands remain a British dependency (UK Overseas Territory).

Colonial Office and predecessor

Falkland Islands: Original Correspondence (CO 78) 1831–1951, 269 volumes and boxes of files, continued in **Falkland Islands, St Helena and Tristan da Cunha: Original Correspondence (CO 1024)** 1951–68. See also Colonies General: Supplementary Original Correspondence (CO 537).

Falkland Islands: Register of Correspondence (CO 339) 1849–1951, 24 volumes (for registers before 1849 see CO 326)

Index to Correspondence (CO 714/54–5) 1841–70

Falkland Islands: Entry Books (CO 399) 1832–70, 7 volumes

Falkland Islands: Register of Out-letters (CO 500) 1865–1926, 8 volumes

Falkland Islands: Acts (CO 79) 1846–1965, 9 volumes

Falkland Islands: Sessional Papers (CO 80) 1845–1965, 23 volumes

Falkland Islands: Government Gazettes (CO 458) 1891–1965, 40 volumes

Falkland Islands: Miscellanea (CO 81) 1846–1944, 99 volumes of blue books of statistics

Foreign Office/Commonwealth Office/Foreign and Commonwealth Office

Foreign Office and Foreign and Commonwealth Office: American and Latin American Departments: Registered Files (A and AL series) (FCO 7) 1967 onwards

Commonwealth Office and Foreign and Commonwealth Office: Gibraltar and South Atlantic Department: Registered Files (Y and HG series) (FCO 42) 1967 onwards

Commonwealth Office: West Indian Department 'B' and Foreign and Commonwealth Office, West Indian Department: Registered Files, Smaller Commonwealth West Indian Territories (WB and HW series) (FCO 44) 1967 onwards

Foreign and Commonwealth Office: Atlantic and Indian Ocean Department: Registered Files (HG series) (FCO 83) 1971 onwards

Far East/South East Asia

The earliest correspondence for the region is in CO 77 (see under East Indies). The other record series listed here relate to the region as a whole, or to more than one territory. They sometimes also cover Ceylon, Mauritius, Seychelles, Fiji and the Western Pacific High Commission Territories. A special commissioner with the status of an ambassador, and responsible to the Foreign Office, was appointed in October 1945 to co-ordinate British activities in the Far East and Pacific. The post was combined in 1948 with that of governor-general of Malaya and commissioner general for the United Kingdom in South East Asia. Records of the commissioner general are in the Foreign Office series Commissioner General for the United Kingdom in South East Asia, and United Kingdom Commissioner for Singapore and South East Asia: Registered Files (FO 1091) 1950–63, 114 files.

Colonial Office

Eastern: Original Correspondence (CO 825) 1927–51, 90 boxes of files continued in **South East Asia Department: Original Correspondence (CO 1022)** 1950–6, 494 files, and **Far East Department: Original Correspondence (CO 1030)** 1948–67, 906 files. See also Colonies General: Supplementary Original Correspondence (CO 537).

Eastern: Register of Correspondence (CO 872) 1927–51, 12 volumes

Far Eastern Reconstruction: Original Correspondence (CO 865) 1942–5, 86 files

Far Eastern Reconstruction: Registers of Correspondence (CO 975) 1942–4, 1 volume

Far Eastern Economic and Supplies Committee: Minutes and Papers (CO 1008) 1944–5, 2 folders

Confidential Print: Eastern (CO 882) 1843–1952, 32 volumes

Federated Malay States

British control of states of the Malaya peninsula spread from the Straits Settlements after 1826. British officials ('residents') were introduced into Pahang, Perak and Selangor in 1874, and into Negri Sembilan in 1889. In 1895 a treaty of federation was signed by the rulers of the four states. The federation was at first executive and judicial only under a resident responsible to the high commissioner for the Federated States, a post held by the governor of the Straits Settlements. From 1942 to 1945 the states were under Japanese occupation. After a period of British military administration (1945–6, see WO 203) the federation was not revived and in 1946 all four states joined the short-lived Malayan Union and, in 1948, the new Federation of Malaya. See also under the individual states.

Colonial Office and predecessor

Until 1920 correspondence is found in the series **Straits Settlements: Original Correspondence (CO 273)** 1838–1946, and thereafter in **Federated Malay States: Original Correspondence (CO 717)** 1920–51, 210 volumes and boxes of files, which also relates to the unfederated Malay states, the Malayan Union and the Federation of Malaya

Straits Settlements: Register of Correspondence (CO 426) 1867–1945, and Federated Malay States: Register of Correspondence (CO 786) 1919–51, 19 volumes

Federated Malay States: Register of Out-letters (CO 787) 1920–6, 3 volumes

Federated Malay States: Acts (CO 828) 1925–48, 5 volumes

Federated Malay States: Sessional Papers (CO 576) 1896–1948, 79 volumes

Federated Malay States: Government Gazettes (CO 574) 1909–48, 96 volumes

Federated Malay States: Miscellanea (CO 575) 1904–49, 38 volumes of manuals of statistics

Federation of Malaya

The Federation of Malaya was constituted on 1 February 1948 under the Federation of Malaya Agreement, 1948, between the British Crown and the rulers of Malay states. It comprised the states of Johore, Pahang, Negri Sembilan, Selangor, Perak, Kedah and Perlis, Kelantan, Trengganu and the two British Settlements of Penang and Malacca. The federation became an independent member of the Commonwealth on 31 August 1957. In 1963 it joined with other territories to form Malaysia. See also under Federated Malay States, Malayan Union, Malaysia, Far East/South East Asia and individual states.

Colonial Office

For correspondence see **Federated Malay States: Original Correspondence (CO 717)** 1920–51, 210 volumes and boxes of files, continued in **South East Asia Department: Original Correspondence (CO 1022)** 1950–6, and **Far Eastern Department and Successors: Registered Files (FED series) (CO 1030)** 1941–67. See also Colonies General: Supplementary Original Correspondence (CO 537).
Federated Malay States: Register of Correspondence (CO 786) 1919–51, 19 volumes
Federation of Malaya: Acts (CO 923) 1948–57, 9 volumes
Federation of Malaya: Sessional Papers (CO 941) 1946–65, 87 volumes
Federation of Malaya (Malaysia): Government Gazettes (CO 930) 1948–80, 181 volumes
Federation of Malaya Constitutional Commission (1956) (CO 889) 1956, 9 volumes

Federation of Rhodesia and Nyasaland

Closer political union between Northern Rhodesia, Southern Rhodesia and Nyasaland was considered for some years. In 1951 a conference of officials recommended the formation of a federation under which the federal government should have specified powers to deal with matters common to all three territories, leaving residual matters with the territorial governments. In January 1953 a conference of ministers produced a draft scheme setting out the details of a federal constitution, which was approved by the Legislative Councils of Northern Rhodesia and Nyasaland, and by a referendum in Southern Rhodesia. The Federation of Rhodesia and Nyasaland came into being on 3 September 1953. The Commonwealth Relations Office became responsible for relations with the federal government, while Northern Rhodesia and Nyasaland remained the responsibility of the Colonial Office. In March 1962 the Central African Office was set up and assumed responsibility for both the federation and its constituent parts. It was placed under R. A. Butler, then home secretary, until October 1963, and then under the newly designated secretary of state for Commonwealth relations and the colonies. The federation came to an end on 31 December 1963, and the Central African Office was absorbed by the Commonwealth Relations Office in April 1964. See also under Central Africa and the constituent territories.

Colonial Office

Commission on the Constitution of Rhodesia and Nyasaland, the Monckton Commission (CO 960) 1960, 50 files

Commonwealth Relations Office/Central African Office

Dominions Office and Commonwealth Relations Office: Original Correspondence (DO 35) 1915–71, **Central Africa: Registered Files (CA series) (DO 158)** 1953–63 and **Central**

African Office and Commonwealth Relations Office: Central Africa: Registered Files (CAO series) (DO 183) 1962–6. See also Private Office Papers (DO 121). Butler's private office papers (Lord Butler of Saffron Walden: Private Office Papers, FO 1109, 1946–64) include a small amount of relevant material.

Dominions Office and Successors: Governor, Southern Rhodesia and High Commission, Southern Rhodesia, Federation of Rhodesia and Nyasaland and Rhodesia: Correspondence (DO 154) 1946–66

Federation of Rhodesia and Nyasaland: Acts (DO 129) 1954–63, 10 volumes

Federation of Rhodesia and Nyasaland: Sessional Papers (DO 123) 1953–63, 28 volumes

Federation of Rhodesia and Nyasaland: Government Gazettes (DO 125) 1953–63, 27 volumes

Federation of the West Indies

The Federation of the West Indies came into being in January 1958. It comprised Barbados, Jamaica (including the Cayman Islands and the Turks and Caicos Islands), the Leeward Islands (Antigua, Montserrat and St Christopher (St Kitts)-Nevis-Anguilla), Trinidad and Tobago, and the Windward Islands (Grenada, Dominica, St Lucia and St Vincent). It did not include British Guiana, British Honduras or the British Virgin Islands. The federation came to an end in 1962 with the decision of Jamaica to withdraw. In May 1962 a London conference agreed the formation of a new West Indies Federation to consist of Barbados, the Leeward Islands and the Windward Islands, with a federal capital in Barbados. This arrangement was abandoned in 1966. Other correspondence regarding the federation is in the main West Indies regional and territorial original correspondence series.

Colonial Office/Commonwealth Office

West Indian Department: Registered Files (CO 1031) 1948–67

Commonwealth Relations Office

Federation of the West Indies: Government Gazettes (DO 136) 1958–61, 6 volumes

Federation of the West Indies: Acts (DO 139) 1958–62, 2 volumes

Fernando Po (Bioko)

From 1827 to 1843 the British leased bases at Fernando Po for their anti-slave trade naval patrols. Spain, which had briefly settled the island in the 18th century, then re-established its rule. The last British superintendent continued as Spanish governor until his death in 1854. For records concerning Fernando Po before 1828 and after 1842 see under Sierra Leone. For Foreign Office correspondence with British consuls at Fernando Po see FO 2 and FO 84.

Colonial Office and predecessor

Fernando Po: Original Correspondence, Entry Books, etc. (CO 82) 1818–44, 12 volumes

Fiji

Fiji was ceded to Britain on 10 October 1874. In 1879 immigration of indentured labourers from India was authorised. The system of local government established in 1876, and known as the Fijian Administration, was based on indigenous institutions and had jurisdiction over all Fijian affairs. At the apex was the council of chiefs and executive control was through the Fijian Affairs Board. In 1952 the office of governor was separated from that of the high commissioner for the Western Pacific with which it had been joined since 1877. Fiji became an independent state within the Commonwealth on 10 October 1970. It left the Commonwealth in 1987, but rejoined in 1997; its membership has been suspended twice since. Records of the Fiji office of the British representatives to the South Pacific Commission are in CO 1009 (see also under South Pacific).

Foreign Office

For Foreign Office correspondence with British consuls in Fiji, 1858–76, see Foreign Office: Political and Other Departments: General Correspondence before 1906, Pacific Islands (Fiji, Hawaii, Rarotonga, Samoa, Tahiti and Tonga) (FO 58) 1822–1905

Colonial Office

Fiji: Original Correspondence (CO 83) 1860–1951, 261 volumes and boxes of files, continued in **Hong Kong and Pacific Department: Original Correspondence (CO 1023)** 1946–55, and **Pacific and Indian Ocean Department: Registered Files (PAC series) (CO 1036)** 1952–67. See also Colonies General: Supplementary Original Correspondence (CO 537). Printed correspondence is in the Australia confidential print series CO 881.

Fiji: Register of Correspondence (CO 419) 1860–1951, 26 volumes

Fiji: Entry Books (CO 400) 1859–62, 1 volume

Fiji: Register of Out-letters (CO 515) 1873–1926, 9 volumes

Fiji: Acts (CO 84) 1875–1965, 22 volumes

Fiji: Sessional Papers (CO 85) 1875–1965, 79 volumes

Fiji: Government Gazettes (CO 86) 1874–1975, 71 volumes

Fiji: Miscellanea (CO 459) 1874–1940, 66 volumes, comprising the instrument of cession to the British Crown (10 October 1874) and blue books of statistics

Commonwealth Office/Foreign and Commonwealth Office

Commonwealth Office, Far East and Pacific Department and Foreign and Commonwealth Office, South West Pacific Department: Registered Files (H and FW series) (FCO 24) 1967 onwards

Foreign and Commonwealth Office and predecessors: Records of Former Colonial Administrations: Migrated Archives (FCO 141)

Florida

The Spanish colony of Florida was ceded to Britain at the end of the Seven Years' War (the French and Indian War) in 1763, and was divided into West Florida and East Florida. At the Treaty of

Paris in 1783 both were returned to Spain, which had already reoccupied West Florida in 1780/1. There are no Colonial Office series for Florida although some references can be found, particularly among records relating to British West Indian colonies. There is, however, a considerable amount of material in the Treasury correspondence series T 1, and papers and reports of the East Florida Claims Commission are in another Treasury series, T 77. See also under America and West Indies.

Gambia (The Gambia)

In 1651 an English colony was established on St Andrew's Island; it was taken over by the African Company and renamed James Island in 1661. The British occupied the French territory of Senegal in 1758, and incorporated it into the colony of Senegambia in 1765, but Senegal was recaptured by the French in 1778 and formally ceded in 1783, at which time Senegambia formally came to an end. Following the dissolution of the African Company, Gambia was placed under the administration of Sierra Leone in 1821. From 1816 to 1822 it was administered by a military commandant, assisted by a board of merchants called the Settlement Court, and from 1822 to 1829 the commandant governed alone. In 1829 a lieutenant-governor was appointed and in 1843, when Gambia became a separate colony, it was given an administrator and nominated Executive and Legislative Councils. It was part of the West African Settlements administered from Freetown, Sierra Leone, from 1866 to 1888, but retained its own Legislative Council during that period. It became a separate colony again in 1888, when the 1843 constitution was resumed. The Gambia Protectorate area first came under British administration in 1894. The title of administrator was changed to that of governor in 1901. By 1902 only Bathurst (Banjul) and its environs were governed as a Crown colony; the remainder of the territory, the protectorate, was administered through the existing traditional chiefdoms. The Gambia became an independent state within the Commonwealth in February 1965 and a republic on 24 April 1970. In October 2013 the Government of the Gambia announced its decision to leave the Commonwealth. The Gambia's relationship with Senegal has always been an important factor in political and economic policy. In February 1982 the Senegambian Confederation was formally instituted based on certain joint institutions and integration of policies, but each country remained sovereign and independent. For records before 1828 see the records series listed under Sierra Leone; records of the Africa Companies are in the Treasury series T 70. See also under West Africa.

Colonial Office and predecessor

Gambia: Original Correspondence (CO 87) 1828–1951, 270 volumes and boxes of files, continued in **West Africa Original Correspondence (CO 554)** 1911–65. See also Colonies General: Supplementary Original Correspondence (CO 537).

Gambia: Register of Correspondence (CO 341) 1849–1951, 23 volumes (for registers before 1849 see CO 326

Index to Correspondence (CO 714/56–8) 1828–70

Gambia: Entry Books (CO 401) 1827–72, 16 volumes

Gambia: Register of Out-letters (CO 481) 1872–1926, 8 volumes

Gambia: Acts (CO 88) 1843–1966, 18 volumes

Gambia: Sessional Papers (CO 89) 1843–1965, 46 volumes
Gambia: Government Gazettes (CO 460) 1883–1974, 46 volumes
Gambia: Miscellanea (CO 90) 1822–1945, 110 volumes, comprising an abstract of 'Net Revenue, Expenditure and Establishment, St Mary's' (1822) and blue books of statistics

Commonwealth Relations Office/Commonwealth Office/Foreign and Commonwealth Office
Commonwealth Relations Office and Commonwealth Office: West and General Africa Department and Successors: Registered Files (WA series) (DO 195) 1960–7
Commonwealth Office: West and General Africa Department: Registered Files, Commonwealth Africa, General African Affairs and the Organisation of African Unity (T series) (FCO 38) 1967–8
Foreign and Commonwealth Office: West African Department: Registered Files (JW series) (FCO 65) 1968 onwards
Foreign and Commonwealth Office and predecessors: Records of Former Colonial Administrations: Migrated Archives (FCO 141)

Georgia *see under* America and West Indies

Ghana *see* Gold Coast

Gibraltar

Gibraltar was captured from Spain in 1704 during the War of the Spanish Succession and formally ceded to Britain by the Treaty of Utrecht in 1713. It withstood a combined French and Spanish force during the siege of 1779–83. Work began in 1894 to convert Gibraltar into a naval base. In 1940 the entire civilian population (16,700) was evacuated to Britain. They returned between 1944 and 1951. Gibraltar remains a British dependency (UK Overseas Territory).

Colonial Office and predecessors
Gibraltar: Original Correspondence (CO 91) 1705–1951, 545 volumes and boxes of files, continued in **Colonial Office: Mediterranean Department, Predecessor and Successors: Registered Files, Mediterranean Colonies (MED series) (CO 926)** 1938–66. See also Colonies General: Supplementary Original Correspondence (CO 537).
Gibraltar: Register of Correspondence (CO 342) 1850–1951, 34 volumes (for registers before 1850 see CO 326)
Index to Correspondence (CO 714/59–63) 1815–65
Gibraltar: Entry Books (CO 92) 1794–1872, 33 volumes
Gibraltar: Register of Out-letters (CO 517) 1872–1926, 8 volumes
Gibraltar: Acts (CO 93) 1832–1965, 16 volumes
Gibraltar: Sessional Papers (CO 832) 1909–65, 17 volumes

Gibraltar: Government Gazettes (CO 94) 1839–1965, 182 volumes
Gibraltar: Miscellanea (CO 95) 1704–1947, 130 volumes, comprising shipping returns, a historical abstract (1704–26), rent roll of government properties etc. (1830–3) and blue books of statistics
Confidential Print: Mediterranean (CO 883). Other printed correspondence relating to Gibraltar can be found in the Africa confidential print series CO 879.

For records relating to UK/Spanish relations concerning Gibraltar, and for later records, see the records of the Foreign Office and the Foreign and Commonwealth Office, especially:
Foreign Office and Predecessor: Political and Other Departments: General Correspondence before 1906, Spain (FO 72) 1781–1905
Foreign Office: Political Departments: General Correspondence 1906–66 (FO 371)
Foreign Office, Central Department and Foreign and Commonwealth Office, Southern European Department: Registered Files (C and WS series) (FCO 9) 1967 onwards
Commonwealth Office and Foreign and Commonwealth Office: Gibraltar and South Atlantic Department: Registered Files (Y and HG series) (FCO 42) 1967–71
Foreign and Commonwealth Office: Atlantic and Indian Ocean Department: Registered Files (HG series) (FCO 83) 1970–2
Foreign and Commonwealth Office: Gibraltar and General Department and Predecessors: Registered Files (HX series) (FCO 86) 1970 onwards

Gilbert and Ellice Islands (Kiribati, Tuvalu)

The Gilbert and Ellice Islands were brought under the jurisdiction of the high commissioner for the Western Pacific in 1877. They became a British protectorate in 1892, and a British resident was appointed in 1893. They were formally annexed in 1915 and became a colony the following year. The Gilbert Islands were occupied by the Japanese from 1941 to 1943. After the war, administration was again by a resident commissioner under the Western Pacific High Commission. The Ellice Islands separated from the Gilbert Islands in 1975 and became an independent state within the Commonwealth on 1 October 1978 under the name Tuvalu. The Gilbert Islands became an independent republic within the Commonwealth on 12 July 1979 under the name Kiribati. For correspondence see under Western Pacific

Colonial Office
Gilbert and Ellice Islands: Acts (CO 826) 1916–65, 9 volumes
Gilbert and Ellice Islands: Sessional Papers (CO 860) 1922–65, 6 volumes
Gilbert and Ellice Islands: Government Gazettes (CO 1051) 1968–74, 5 volumes
Gilbert and Ellice Islands: Miscellanea (CO 833) 1930–41, 11 volumes of blue books of statistics

Commonwealth Office/Foreign and Commonwealth Office
Commonwealth Office and Foreign and Commonwealth Office: Pacific and Indian Ocean Department and Pacific Dependent Territories Department: Registered Files (Q and HP series) (FCO 32) 1967 onwards

Foreign and Commonwealth Office and predecessors: Records of Former Colonial Administrations: Migrated Archives (FCO 141)

Gold Coast (Ghana)

The Gold Coast was occupied from 1600 by the English, Danes, Dutch, Germans and Portuguese, but by 1750 only British, Dutch and Danish settlements remained. From 1664 the British settlements were under the control of the African Company until its abolition in 1821 when the British government assumed control. They were initially placed under the government of Sierra Leone but from 1828 to 1843 their administration was entrusted to a committee of London merchants. Sierra Leone then resumed control until 1850 when the British Gold Coast possessions became separate; they were again put under Sierra Leone in 1866. The last Danish and Dutch settlements were ceded to Britain in 1850 and 1867/72 respectively. In 1874 the Gold Coast and Lagos became the Gold Coast Colony, but Lagos was separated in 1886. In 1896 treaties of trade and protection were concluded with several tribes north of Ashanti and a protectorate over the area subsequently known as the Northern Territories was established in 1898. Ashanti was annexed to the Gold Coast in 1901. In 1922 a part of the adjoining German Territory of Togoland was placed under British control by a League of Nations mandate and subsequently administered as part of the Gold Coast. The Gold Coast became an independent state within the Commonwealth under the name of Ghana on 6 March 1957, and a republic on 19 June 1960. For correspondence before 1843 see under Sierra Leone and West Africa. For records of the African Companies see T 70. See also under Ashanti.

Colonial Office and predecessors

Gold Coast: Original Correspondence (CO 96) 1753–1951, 830 volumes and boxes of files (with the exception of the first volume, which contains correspondence between the English authorities at Cape Coast Castle and the Dutch authorities at Elmina dated 1753–6, the series starts in 1843). Correspondence continues in **West Africa Original Correspondence (CO 554)** 1911–65. See also Colonies General: Supplementary Original Correspondence (CO 537).

Gold Coast: Register of Correspondence (CO 343) 1849–1951, 56 volumes (for registers before 1849 see CO 326)

Index to Correspondence (CO 714/64–7) 1843–74

Gold Coast: Entry Books (CO 402) 1843–72, 13 volumes

Gold Coast: Register of Out-letters (CO 482) 1872–1926, 22 volumes

Gold Coast: Acts (CO 97) 1852–1957, 20 volumes

Gold Coast: Sessional Papers (CO 98) 1829–1956, 102 volumes

Gold Coast: Government Gazettes (CO 99) 1872–1957, 103 volumes

Gold Coast: Miscellanea (CO 100) 1845–1946, 96 volumes of blue books of statistics

Commission of Inquiry into Disturbances in the Gold Coast (Watson Commission) (CO 964) 1948, 32 files

Dominions Office/Commonwealth Relations Office

Dominions Office and Commonwealth Relations Office: Original Correspondence (DO 35) 1915–71

Ghana: Government Gazettes (DO 132) 1957–75, 75 volumes

Ghana: Sessional Papers (DO 138) 1956–65, 14 volumes

High Commission and Consular Archives, Ghana (Gold Coast): Correspondence (DO 153) 1954 onwards

Commonwealth Relations Office: Ghana: Registered Files (GHA series) (DO 171) 1958–62, 1 file

Commonwealth Office

Commonwealth Office: West and General Africa Department: Registered Files, Commonwealth Africa, General African Affairs and the Organisation of African Unity (T series) (FCO 38) 1967–8

Foreign and Commonwealth Office

Foreign and Commonwealth Office: West African Department: Registered Files (JW series) (FCO 65) 1968 onwards

Gold Coast Northern Territories

The territories north of Ashanti were formed into a separate district in 1896, declared a protectorate and placed under a commissioner. In 1901 the protectorate came under the control of the government of the Gold Coast and was administered by a chief commissioner. From 1923 the northern section of the British sphere of the former German colony of Togoland was administered as part of the Northern Territories.

Colonial Office

Correspondence relating to the protectorate can be found among the Gold Coast correspondence in CO 96.

Gold Coast, Northern Territories: Acts (CO 849) 1920–33, 1 volume

Grenada

Grenada was temporarily and unsuccessfully settled by the English in 1609 but became French in 1650. It was captured by the British in 1762, and ceded the following year. It became part of the Windward Islands government in 1776. Captured by France in 1779 it was restored to Britain in 1783 and reoccupied by Britain in 1784. When the post of governor of the Windward Islands was abolished in 1960 a new constitution was introduced. Grenada was a member of the Federation of the West Indies from 1958 to 1962. It became a fully independent state within the Commonwealth on 7 February 1974. Records of the UK government response to the United States invasion of Grenada in October 1983 can be found among the records of the Cabinet and the Prime Minister's Office.

Colonial Office and predecessors

Grenada: Original Correspondence (CO 101) 1747–1873, 135 volumes. For later correspondence to 1951 see **Windward Islands Original Correspondence (CO 321)**, which is continued in **West Indian Department: Registered Files (WIS series) (CO 1031)** 1948–67. See also Colonies General: Supplementary Original Correspondence (CO 537). Both CO 101 and CO 321 are registered in Windward Islands: Register of Correspondence (CO 376) 1850–1951 (for registers before 1850 see CO 326), except between 1872 and 1882 when CO 101 is registered in the Grenada Register of Correspondence (CO 504) 1872–82, 3 volumes.

Index to Correspondence (CO 714/68–70) 1815–70

Grenada: Entry Books (CO 102) 1763–1872, 25 volumes, including précis books

Grenada: Register of Out-letters (CO 504) 1872–82, 3 volumes

Grenada: Acts (CO 103) 1766–1965, 36 volumes

Grenada: Sessional Papers (CO 104) 1766–1965, 75 volumes

Grenada: Government Gazettes (CO 105) 1834–1975, 75 volumes

Grenada: Miscellanea (CO 106) 1764–1938, 132 volumes, comprising shipping returns, sales of lands in the ceded islands, returns of stipendiary magistrates and blue books of statistics

Grenada: Administrator, Registered Files (CO 1061) 1962–6, 2 files

Commonwealth Office

Commonwealth Office: West Indian Department 'A' and Associated States Department: Registered Files, Antigua, Dominica, Grenada, St Christopher (St Kitts)-Nevis-Anguilla, St Lucia and St Vincent (WA series) (FCO 43) 1967–8

Foreign and Commonwealth Office

Foreign and Commonwealth Office: North American and Caribbean Department and Caribbean Department: Registered Files (AN series) (FCO 63) 1968 onwards

Grenadines *see under* St Vincent

Griqualand West

Possession of Griqualand West was disputed between the Cape of Good Hope and the Transvaal Republic following the discovery of diamonds there in 1867. Most of the territory was awarded to Great Britain by arbitration in 1871, and the governor of the Cape was made *ex officio* governor. Griqualand West was then given a nominated Executive Council and a partly elective Legislative Council. These were abolished in 1880 when the territory was annexed to the Cape.

Colonial Office

Griqualand West: Original Correspondence (CO 107) 1875–80, 9 volumes

Griqualand West: Register of Correspondence (CO 344) 1875–80, 1 volume

Griqualand West: Register of Out-letters (CO 522) 1876–80, 1 volume

Griqualand West: Sessional Papers (CO 108) 1873–80, 3 volumes
Griqualand West: Government Gazettes (CO 109) 1876–80, 1 volume
Griqualand West: Miscellanea (CO 461) 1873, 1 blue book of statistics

Guadeloupe

Guadeloupe, otherwise a French dependency, was occupied by the British from 1759 to 1763, from 1810 to 1814, and from 1815 to 1816. The records in CO 110 include entry books, public accounts and vouchers, and shipping returns.

War and Colonial Department and predecessors
Guadeloupe: Original Correspondence, etc. (CO 110) 1758–1816, 25 volumes

For periods of French administration see Foreign Office, especially FO 27, Foreign Office and Predecessor: Political and Other Departments: General Correspondence before 1906, France, which includes correspondence from British consuls at Guadeloupe, and FO 371, Foreign Office: Political Departments: General Correspondence 1906–66.

Guyana *see* British Guiana

Havana

The province of Havana, founded in 1514 by Spain, was captured by Britain in 1762 but restored to Spain in 1763. The following series consists of correspondence between the secretary of state and military, naval and civil authorities concerning the expedition against Havana, a campaign of the Seven Years' War (the French and Indian War) and related matters.

State Paper Office
Havana: Original Correspondence (CO 117) 1762–3, 2 volumes

For later records concerning Cuba see Foreign Office, especially FO 72, Foreign Office and Predecessor: Political and Other Departments: General Correspondence before 1906, Spain, which includes correspondence from British consuls, and FO 371, Foreign Office: Political Departments: General Correspondence 1906–66.

Heligoland

Heligoland was captured from the Danes in 1807 and formally ceded to Britain in 1814. In 1890 it was ceded to Germany under the terms of the Heligoland-Zanzibar Treaty which redefined certain Anglo-German interests in Africa. See also FO 36, Foreign Office: Political and Other Departments: General Correspondence before 1906, Heligoland, 1808–17.

Colonial Office and predecessor

Heligoland: Original Correspondence (CO 118) 1807–94, 64 volumes. See also Colonies General: Supplementary Original Correspondence (CO 537).

Heligoland: Register of Correspondence (CO 346) 1850–1910, 6 volumes (for registers before 1850 see CO 326)

Index to Correspondence (CO 714/78) 1842–66

Heligoland: Entry Books (CO 119) 1807–77, 7 volumes

Heligoland: Register of Out-letters (CO 347) 1874–1910, 2 volumes

Heligoland: Acts (CO 120) 1883–9, 1 volume

Heligoland: Sessional Papers (CO 121) 1881–90, 1 volume

Heligoland: Miscellanea (CO 122) 1834–90, 36 volumes, comprising blue books of statistics, return of a census taken in 1881 (giving name, age, sex and profession of 2,001 inhabitants), one volume of appeal cases, town clerk's accounts and minutes and memoranda from the governor's office

Henderson Island *see under* Pitcairn

Hong Kong

Hong Kong became a British colony in 1841 and was formally ceded by China in 1842. For the relevant treaties see FO 93/23/1B and FO 93/23/2. The Kowloon peninsula was ceded to Britain in 1860 (FO 93/23/6) and the New Territories were leased to it for 99 years in 1898 (FO 93/23/18). From 1941 to 1945 Hong Kong was occupied by the Japanese. Sovereignty over Hong Kong reverted to China on 1 July 1997. There are no records from Hong Kong among the 'migrated archives' described in chapter 3, but a large accumulation is included in the 'special collections' still held by the Foreign and Commonwealth Office. The FCO reported in 2014 that it needed to undertake a further assessment of the content of these records, partly because of their volume and partly because so many are held in microform.[9]

Colonial Office and predecessor

Hong Kong: Original Correspondence (CO 129) 1841–1951, 629 volumes and boxes of files, continued in **Hong Kong and Pacific Department: Original Correspondence (CO 1023)** 1946–55, and **Far Eastern Department and Successors: Registered Files (FED series) (CO 1030)** 1941–67. See also Colonies General: Supplementary Original Correspondence (CO 537).

[9] See https://www.gov.uk/fco-special-collections/ [accessed 6 March 2015].

Hong Kong: Register of Correspondence (CO 349) 1849–1952, 43 volumes (for registers before 1849 see CO 326)
Index to Correspondence (CO 714/82–4) 1843–69
Hong Kong: Entry Books (CO 403) 1843–72, 21 volumes
Hong Kong: Register of Out-letters (CO 489) 1872–1926, 15 volumes
Hong Kong: Acts (CO 130) 1844–1965, 24 volumes
Hong Kong: Sessional Papers (CO 131) 1844–1966, 178 volumes
Hong Kong: Government Gazettes (CO 132) 1846–1990, 714 volumes
Hong Kong: Miscellanea (CO 133) 1844–1940, 111 volumes, comprising blue books of statistics, and trade and shipping returns
Prisoners of War and Civilian Internees Department: Nominal Index of Allied Internees (CO 1070) *c.*1941–*c.*1947, primarily concerned with Hong Kong but including some references to Malaya.

Foreign Office/Commonwealth Office/Foreign and Commonwealth Office
Foreign Office and Foreign and Commonwealth Office: Far Eastern Department: Registered Files (F and FE series) (FCO 21) 1967 onwards
Commonwealth Office and Foreign and Commonwealth Office: Hong Kong Departments: Registered Files, Hong Kong, British Honduras, British Indian Ocean Territories and Seychelles (HW and HK series) (FCO 40) 1965 onwards
For British relations with China concerning Hong Kong see also FO 17, Political and Other Departments: General Correspondence before 1906, China, and FO 371, Political Departments: General Correspondence 1906–66.

Hudson's Bay

The lands draining into Hudson's Bay, which Henry Hudson had explored in 1610, were assigned to the Hudson's Bay Company on its creation by royal charter in 1670. In 1820 the company amalgamated with the North-West Company, which had been formed after 1763 to exploit the North-West Territories not covered by the 1670 charter. In 1869 the Hudson's Bay Company sold its territorial rights to the new Dominion of Canada.

Colonial Office and predecessors
Hudson's Bay: Original Correspondence (CO 134) 1675–1759, 3 volumes
Hudson's Bay: Entry Books (CO 135) 1670–1789, 4 volumes
See also BH 1 (1667–1991), microfilm copies of records held in the Hudson's Bay Company Archives, a division of the Archives of Manitoba (http://www.gov.mb.ca/chc/archives/hbca/)

Île de France *see* Mauritius

Imperial British East Africa Company *see under* Kenya *and* Uganda

India

The records of the East India Company and the India Office, successively responsible for the British administration of India, are held separately in the Asia, Pacific and Africa Collections of the British Library. After independence in 1947 British relations with India became the responsibility of the Commonwealth Relations Office (a new department bringing together the former Dominions Office and India Office) whose records are at The National Archives with the exception of the series India Office Library (DO 144) and Indian Records Section (DO 184) which were transferred to the British Library.

Dominions Office/Commonwealth Relations Office/Commonwealth Office

India: Registered Files (DO 142) 1912–58, 605 files (with the exception of one document, DO 142/581, the series starts in 1947)

India: Sessional Papers (DO 148) 1960–5, 22 volumes

India: Government Gazettes (DO 105) 1948–79, 469 volumes

India: Miscellanea (DO 112) 1946–50, 5 volumes of statistical abstracts

Dominions Office and Commonwealth Relations Office: Original Correspondence (DO 35) 1915–71

Commonwealth Relations Office and Successors: High Commission and Consular Archives, India: Registered Files (DO 133) 1946–71, 232 files

Commonwealth Relations Office and Commonwealth Office: South Asia Department: Registered Files (SEA series) (DO 196) 1960–8

Commonwealth Office/Foreign and Commonwealth Office

Commonwealth Office and Foreign and Commonwealth Office: South Asia Department: Registered Files (S and FS series) (FCO 37) 1967 onwards

Ionian Islands

The Ionian Islands consist of Kerkyra (listed in the catalogue of CO 136 as Corfu), Paxi (Paxo), Lefkada (Santa Maura), Kefalonia (Cephalonia), Ithaki (Ithaca), Zakynthos (Zante) and Kythira (Cerigo). They were held by Venice from 1388 to 1797, when they were captured by France. In 1799 they were taken by Russia and in 1800 made a Russo-Turkish protectorate. The Treaty of Tilsit of 1807 restored them to France, but they were occupied by the British in 1809/10 and made a British protectorate in 1814. In 1864 Britain ceded the islands to Greece. CO 136 includes the local records of the islands – many of them in Italian – which were returned to Britain following surrender of the protectorate, together with entry books, sessional papers, government gazettes and blue books. Printed correspondence is included in the Africa confidential print series (CO 879) as well as in the Mediterranean series (CO 883). Records relating to the Order of St Michael and St George, originally created for Malta and the Ionian Islands, are listed under 'honours' in appendix 2. For Foreign Office records relating to the Ionian Islands see Political and Other Departments: General Correspondence before 1906, Ionian Islands (FO 42) 1778–1820, and for records relating to Greece see FO 32 (1827–1905) and FO 78 (Turkey) before 1827. See also under Mediterranean.

Colonial Office and predecessor

Ionian Islands: Original Correspondence, etc. (CO 136) 1802–73, 1,433 volumes. See also Colonies General: Supplementary Original Correspondence (CO 537).

Ionian Islands: Register of Correspondence (CO 350) 1849–1910, 6 volumes (for registers before 1849 see CO 326)

Index to Correspondence (CO 714/168–71) 1815–64

Iraq

Iraq, formerly Mesopotamia, came under British control during the First World War. Although Turkey did not formally renounce sovereignty until 1923, Britain was selected as mandatory power in 1920, and the terms of the mandate were approved by the League of Nations in 1922. The first Iraq parliament opened in 1925, and Iraq was virtually independent during this period although a high commissioner 'advised' the king, and British advisers were also attached to the various ministries. The British mandate came to an end in 1932 and thereafter British relations were conducted by the Foreign Office. A British military presence continued under treaty until 1955. For records of the Ottoman period see Foreign Office, especially FO 78 Foreign Office and Predecessor: Political and Other Departments: General Correspondence before 1906, Ottoman Empire and FO 371 Foreign Office: Political Departments: General Correspondence 1906–66. See FO 371 also for the post-1932 period. For military records of the First World War and the immediate post-war period see records of the War Office (WO series). See also under Middle East.

Colonial Office

Iraq: Original Correspondence (CO 730) 1921–32, 178 volumes.[10] See also Colonies General: Supplementary Original Correspondence (CO 537).

Iraq: Register of Correspondence (CO 781) 1921–32, 17 volumes

Iraq: Register of Out-letters (CO 782) 1921–6, 5 volumes

Iraq: Sessional Papers (CO 696) 1917–31, 7 volumes

Iraq: Government Gazettes (CO 813) 1921–32, 5 volumes

Iraq: Civil Commissioner's Staff Lists (CO 731) 1919–20, 1 volume

Records of the Baghdad High Commission, 1921–33, are included in the Foreign Office series Embassy, High Commission and Consulate, Iraq: General Correspondence (FO 624) 1921–64

[10] Selected records from CO 730 and CO 935 (Middle East confidential print), together with documents relating to Iraq from Cabinet, Foreign Office and Foreign and Commonwealth Office series, have been made available online by Gale Cengage as part of *The Middle East Online* series (see http://gale.cengage.co.uk/product-highlights/history/iraq-1914--1974.aspx [accessed 13 Oct. 2014]). It can be accessed free of charge at TNA.

Ireland

Between the Act of Union of 1800 and the Anglo-Irish Treaty of 1921 Ireland was an integral part of the United Kingdom. The lord lieutenant and the chief secretary of Ireland were members of the UK administration and conducted their official business from Dublin Castle. The Dublin Castle records in CO 904 below relate mainly to the measures planned or taken to combat the efforts of the nationalist organisations to secure independence. CO 906 contains the more routine correspondence of the Irish Office, the department responsible for liaison between Dublin Castle and the UK government. The Irish Grants Committee, records in CO 762, was created in 1923 to replace the Irish Distress Committee formed the previous year. Its role was to recommend what grants or loans should be made to refugees from Ireland, and what advances should be under the Criminal and Malicious Injuries Acts of the Irish Free State. It ceased to sit in 1926. The correspondence and records of claims made to the Compensation (Ireland) Commission are held separately in CO 905. Reports of political and criminal activities in Ireland, including accounts of the United Irish League and Sinn Féin, were printed for restricted circulation to ministers and government departments and are held in the confidential print series CO 903.

The transfer of British power in Ireland to the provisional government of the Irish Free State was effected by the Irish Free State (Agreement) Act 1922. The department of the chief secretary to the lord lieutenant was then abolished, and the Irish Office became jointly responsible to the Home Office for the affairs of Northern Ireland and to the Colonial Office (Dominions Division) for the affairs of the Irish Free State. The Irish Office, or the Irish Branch as it had then become, was in turn abolished in 1924. Responsibility for relations with the Free State (later Eire/Republic of Ireland) was transferred to the Dominions Office in 1925, and it was treated as a dominion until the Republic of Ireland Act of 1948 severed the formal association of the republic with the Commonwealth. The title of UK representative to Ireland was changed to ambassador in 1950, but the post continued to be responsible to the Commonwealth Relations Office.

For earlier records relating to Ireland see the State Papers series, which include eight series of 'State Papers Ireland'. For other records relating to Ireland see especially Home Office (HO) series, including records of the Royal Irish Constabulary in HO 184, and War Office (WO) series. For records relating to activities of the Fenian Brotherhood in the United States of America see FO 5.

Colonial Office and predecessors

Ireland Criminal Injuries and Irish Grants Committee: Files and Minutes (CO 762) 1922–30, 212 boxes and volumes

Ireland: Confidential Print (CO 903) 1885–19, 19 volumes

Ireland: Dublin Castle Records (CO 904) 1795–1926, 216 boxes [the registers of which remain in Dublin at the National Archives of Ireland]

Ireland: Claims for Compensation Registers, Indexes, etc. (CO 905) 1922–30, 22 registers, indexes and papers

Irish Office Records (CO 906) 1795–24, 31 volumes and files

See also General Registers (CO 326)

Irish Free State: Original Correspondence (CO 739) 1922–4, 27 volumes. Continued in CO 532/277–8 and 314 (1924–5)

Irish Free State: Register of Correspondence (CO 783) 1922–4, 4 volumes

Irish Free State: Register of Out-letters (CO 784) 1922–3, 2 volumes

Irish Free State: Dublin Gazettes (CO 785) 1923–5, 5 volumes

Dominions Office, Commonwealth Relations Office/Commonwealth Office/Foreign and Commonwealth Office

Dominions Office and Commonwealth Relations Office: Original Correspondence (DO 35) 1915–71

Irish Free State and Republic of Ireland: Government Gazettes (DO 37) 1926–75, 84 volumes

Irish Free State and Republic of Ireland: Sessional Papers (DO 99) 1922–65, 47 volumes

Irish Free State and Republic of Ireland: Miscellanea (DO 100) 1925–52, 10 volumes of trade and shipping statistics, and statistical abstracts

Dominions Office and Successors: United Kingdom Representative to Eire, and Embassy, Republic of Ireland: Archives, Correspondence (DO 130) 1939 onwards

Commonwealth Relations Office and Commonwealth Office: Western and Middle East Department and Successors: Registered Files, Canada, Ireland and International Western Organisations (WES series) (DO 182) 1960–6

Foreign Office, Western Department and Foreign and Commonwealth Office, Western European Department: Registered Files (R and WR series) (FCO 33) 1967 onwards

Foreign and Commonwealth Office: Republic of Ireland Department: Registered Files (WL series) (FCO 87) 1972 onwards

Jamaica

Jamaica was originally settled by Spain but frequently raided by the English from 1596. It was occupied by Britain in 1655 and recognised as British by Spain in 1670. It had a British governor from 1657 and a mainly elective council from 1661. A new constitution in 1662 comprised a governor with a nominated Legislative Council and an elective House of Assembly. In 1853 a nominated Privy Council and Executive Committee were added. In 1866, following the Morant Bay 'rebellion', the House of Assembly was abolished, and a Legislative Council was established. From 1958 to 1962 Jamaica was part of the Federation of the West Indies, which broke up after Jamaica withdrew to seek independence alone. Jamaica became a fully independent state within the Commonwealth on 6 August 1962. For brief periods the Jamaica registers cover Bay Islands, British Honduras and Turks and Caicos Islands correspondence. The Cayman Islands were administered from Jamaica until 1959. See also under West Indies.

Colonial Office and predecessors

Jamaica: Original Correspondence (CO 137) 1689–1951, 906 volumes and boxes of files, continued in **West Indian Department: Registered Files (CO 1031)** 1948–67. See also Colonies General: Supplementary Original Correspondence (CO 537).

Jamaica: Register of Correspondence (CO 351) 1850–1951, 42 volumes (for registers before 1850 see CO 326)
Index to Correspondence (CO 714/85–9) 1815–70
Jamaica: Entry Books (CO 138) 1661–1872, 83 volumes, including précis books
Jamaica: Register of Out-letters (CO 494) 1872–1926, 12 volumes
Jamaica: Acts (CO 139) 1662–1962, 133 volumes
Jamaica: Sessional Papers (CO 140) 1661–1965, 369 volumes
Jamaica: Government Gazettes (CO 141) 1794–1968, 156 volumes
Jamaica: Miscellanea (CO 142) 1658–1945, 155 volumes, including shipping returns; returns and memoranda on various subjects including gaols, landholdings and the Maroons; blue books of statistics; and newspapers (for a list of newspapers see appendix 3)

Commonwealth Relations Office/Commonwealth Office

Commonwealth Relations Office and Commonwealth Office: West Indies Department and Atlantic Department: Registered Files, Commonwealth West Indies (WID series) (DO 200) 1961–7

Foreign and Commonwealth Office

Foreign and Commonwealth Office: North American and Caribbean Department and Caribbean Department: Registered Files (AN series) (FCO 63) 1968 onwards
Foreign and Commonwealth Office and predecessors: Records of Former Colonial Administrations: Migrated Archives (FCO 141)

Jelebu *see* Negri Sembilan

Johore (Johor)

Johore became a British protected state in 1885, and received a British agent, with consular functions, in 1895. A British adviser, responsible to the governor of the Straits Settlements, was appointed in 1910. Between 1941 and 1945 Johore was occupied by the Japanese; it was under British military administration from 1945 to 1946 (see WO 203). Johore became a member of the short-lived Malayan Union in 1946, and the Federation of Malaya in 1948. In 1963 the federation, independent since 1957, joined with other territories to form Malaysia. See also under Unfederated Malay States.

Colonial Office

For correspondence see under Straits Settlements
Johore: Sessional Papers (CO 715) 1910–40, 6 volumes
Johore: Government Gazettes (CO 653) 1911–79, 66 volumes

Jordan *see* Transjordan

Kedah and Perlis *see also* Perlis

Kedah was under Portuguese rule from 1654 until 1711. Penang, to the south of Kedah State, was brought under British East India Company rule in 1786 and Province Wellesley in 1800. In 1821 the Siamese took possession of Kedah, but in 1843 they allowed its sultan to resume government. A Siamese adviser was sent to Kedah in 1905, but he was replaced by a British adviser in 1909 when Kedah became a British protected state. Perlis was subject to Kedah until the Siamese occupation of 1821. It became an independent state under a rajah in 1841. In 1909 it became a British protected state and a British adviser replaced the Siamese adviser. After 1909 the sultan of Kedah and the rajah of Perlis were both assisted by nominated state councils which included the British advisers. Both states were under Japanese occupation from 1942 to 1945, and under British military administration from 1945 to 1946 (see WO 203) when they joined the Malayan Union. Kedah and Perlis became part of the Federation of Malaya in 1948, which in turn merged with other independent territories in 1963 to form Malaysia.

For correspondence relating to both states see under Straits Settlements. See also under Unfederated Malay States.

Colonial Office

Kedah and Perlis: Sessional Papers (CO 716) 1905–40, 4 volumes
Kedah and Perlis: Government Gazettes (CO 819) 1925–79, 38 volumes
Perlis: Government Gazettes (CO 931) 1948–77, 10 volumes

Keeling Islands *see* Straits Settlements

Kelantan

Formerly under Siamese suzerainty, Kelantan received a British adviser in 1903 by agreement with Siam. In 1909 it formally became a British protected state, and an advisory state council was established. It was under Japanese occupation from 1942 to 1945 and British military administration from 1945 to 1946 (see WO 203), when it joined the Malayan Union. For subsequent developments and for other relevant records see under Federation of Malaya. See also under Unfederated Malay States.

Colonial Office

Kelantan: Sessional Papers (CO 827) 1909–40, 2 volumes
Kelantan: Government Gazettes (CO 928) 1948–79, 21 volumes

Kenya

An Anglo-German agreement of 1886 designated the area which was to become Kenya as part of a British sphere of influence; it was administered by the Imperial British East Africa Company from 1891. In 1895 the Foreign Office assumed control of the territory which was now known as the East Africa Protectorate. A commissioner was appointed who was also, until 1904, the consul-general in Zanzibar. In 1905 control was transferred to the Colonial Office, and a governor was appointed. In 1920 the coastal strip originally leased from the sultan of Zanzibar became the Protectorate of Kenya, and the remaining territory became Kenya Colony. Kenya became an independent member of the Commonwealth on 12 December 1963, and a republic the following year.

For Foreign Office correspondence relating to the Imperial British East Africa Company, and the region more generally, see FO 2 and FO 84. The records of the company itself are not known to survive. For records relating to the emergency of 1952–60 (the Mau Mau 'rebellion') see also records of the War Office, especially WO 216 and WO 276. See also comments on the 'migrated archives' in chapter 3.

Colonial Office

East Africa and Uganda Protectorate: Original Correspondence (CO 519) 1904–5, 1 volume

Kenya: Original Correspondence (CO 533) 1905–51, 764 volumes and boxes of files, continued in **East Africa: Original Correspondence (CO 822)** 1927–64. See also Colonies General: Supplementary Original Correspondence (CO 537).

Kenya: Register of Correspondence (CO 628) 1904–51, 44 volumes

Kenya: Register of Out-letters (CO 629) 1904–25, 9 volumes

Kenya: Acts (CO 630) 1901–63, 30 volumes

Kenya: Sessional Papers (CO 544) 1903–65, 111 volumes

Kenya: Government Gazettes (CO 542) 1908–75, 103 volumes

Kenya: Miscellanea (CO 543) 1901–46, 35 volumes of blue books of statistics

Kenya Coastal Strip Commission (Robertson Commission): Correspondence and Papers (CO 894) 1961, 14 files

Kenya Constituencies Delimitation Commission (Foster-Sutton Commission): Papers (CO 895) 1962, 7 files

Kenya Northern Frontier District Commission (CO 896) 1962, 5 files

Kenya Regional Boundaries Commission (Foster-Sutton Commission): Papers (CO 897) 1962, 9 files

Kenya Information Service: Photographs (CO 1066) 1952–61, 17 folders of photographs

Commonwealth Relations Office/Commonwealth Office/Foreign and Commonwealth Office

Commonwealth Relations Office: East and General Africa: Registered Files (EGA series) (DO 168) 1961–3

Commonwealth Relations Office and Commonwealth Office: East Africa Departments: Registered Files, East Africa (EA series) (DO 213) 1963–7

Commonwealth Relations Office and Commonwealth Office: East Africa Economic Department and Development Policy and East and West Africa Economic Department: Registered Files, East Africa Economic (EAE series) (DO 214) 1964–6
Commonwealth Relations Office and Successors: High Commission and Consular Archives: Kenya: Registered Files (DO 226) 1963 onwards
Commonwealth Office and Foreign and Commonwealth Office: East Africa Departments: Registered Files (P and JE series) (FCO 31) 1967 onwards
Foreign and Commonwealth Office and predecessors: Records of Former Colonial Administrations: Migrated Archives (FCO 141)

King's African Rifles

In 1902 the armed forces of the East African dependencies (Uganda, the East Africa Protectorate, Somaliland and the British Central Africa Protectorate) were reorganised as one regiment, the King's African Rifles. In 1927 the administration of the unit was brought together with that of the West African Frontier Force within the military branch of the Colonial Office. For operational and other military records see records of the War Office (WO series).

Colonial Office

King's African Rifles: Original Correspondence (CO 534) 1905–26, 63 volumes
King's African Rifles: Register of Correspondence (CO 623) 1905–26, 8 volumes
King's African Rifles: Register of Out-letters (CO 624) 1905–26, 7 volumes
See also:
Military: Original Correspondence (CO 820) 1927–51, 77 volumes and boxes of files
Military: Register of Correspondence (CO 871) 1927–52, 25 volumes
Defence Department and Successors: Original Correspondence (CO 968) 1941–67

Kiribati *see* Gilbert and Ellice Islands

Kuria Muria Islands

The five Kuria Muria islands were ceded to Britain in 1854 by the sultan of Oman for use as a cable station. They were administered from Aden until 1963 when control passed to the political resident in the Persian Gulf, although legislative powers remained with the authorities in Aden. In 1967 the islands were returned to the Sultanate of Oman.

Colonial Office

Kuria Muria Islands: Original Correspondence (CO 143) 1857–8, 1 volume. The correspondence in CO 143 is registered in the Mauritius register CO 356.

Kuwait

Kuwait was nominally under the authority of the Ottoman empire until it became a British protectorate in 1904. A political agent was then appointed who reported to the British resident in the Persian Gulf, himself responsible to the government of India. For records see under Persian Gulf.

Labrador

Formerly part of the French domain in North America, Labrador came under British control in 1763 and was incorporated into the government of Newfoundland. In 1964 the name of the territory, which had become a province of Canada in 1949, was changed to Newfoundland and Labrador. For records see under Newfoundland.

Labuan

Labuan was ceded to Britain in 1846 by the sultan of Brunei. It was given a nominated Legislative Council under a governor in 1848 and was a separate colony until 1890, when administration was entrusted to the British North Borneo Company. Its Borneo representative became governor of Labuan with legislative powers, and the Legislative Council was abolished. In 1906 the Colonial Office resumed responsibility and the governor of the Straits Settlements was appointed governor of Labuan, which was annexed to the Straits Settlements in 1907 as part of Singapore. It was constituted as a separate settlement in 1912. It was under Japanese occupation during the Second World War and in 1946 it was united with North Borneo.

Colonial Office and predecessor

Labuan: Original Correspondence (CO 144) 1844–1906, 81 volumes
Labuan: Register of Correspondence (CO 352) 1849–1914, 7 volumes (for registers before 1849 see CO 326)
Index to Correspondence (CO 714/90) 1850–66
Labuan: Entry Books (CO 404) 1847–72, 5 volumes
Labuan: Register of Out-letters (CO 487) 1871–1914, 4 volumes
Labuan: Acts (CO 145) 1849–1906, 9 volumes
Labuan: Sessional Papers (CO 434) 1849–89, 1 volume
Labuan: Government Gazettes (CO 573) 1890–1906, 1 volume
Labuan: Miscellanea (CO 146) 1848–1906, 60 volumes, comprising blue books of statistics, and one volume of minutes of the High Criminal Court and the General Court 1850–67
For later records see under Straits Settlements and North Borneo.

Lagos

A British consul was appointed to Lagos in 1852 and in 1861 Lagos was ceded to Britain by its king. In 1862 it became a colony with a governor and nominated Executive and Legislative Councils. In 1866 it became part of the West African Settlements, subject to the governor-in-chief at Sierra Leone, but with a lieutenant-governor and its own nominated Legislative Council. From 1874 to 1886 it was part of the Gold Coast Colony, under first an administrator (until 1883) and then a lieutenant-governor, but retaining the legislative council. It became a separate colony again in 1886 with a governor and nominated Executive and Legislative Councils. In the same year Lagos Protectorate was created from bordering territories. In 1906 the colony and protectorate amalgamated with the Protectorate of Southern Nigeria to form the Colony and Protectorate of Southern Nigeria.

Colonial Office

Lagos: Original Correspondence (CO 147) 1861–1906, 179 volumes
Lagos: Register of Correspondence (CO 421) 1861–1906, 10 volumes (Lagos correspondence for 1883–6 is registered in the Gold Coast registers CO 343)
Lagos: Entry Books (CO 420) 1861–1901, 6 volumes
Lagos: Register of Out-letters (CO 483) 1872–1906, 8 volumes
Lagos: Acts (CO 148) 1862–1905, 3 volumes
Lagos: Sessional Papers (CO 149) 1872–1906, 7 volumes
Lagos: Government Gazettes (CO 150) 1881–1906, 12 volumes
Lagos: Miscellanea (CO 151) 1862–1905, 43 volumes of blue books of statistics
For later records see under Southern Nigeria

Leeward Islands

Until 1671 the Leeward Islands were part of the general government of Montserrat, the Virgin Islands and Nevis under a governor-in-chief. From 1671 a federal legislature gradually grew up. In 1816 the Leeward Islands administration broke into two: Antigua and Montserrat forming one division and St Christopher (St Kitts), Nevis and the Virgin Islands the other. In 1833 they were reunited under one governor-in-chief, and Dominica was added, but it was transferred to the Windward Islands in 1940. The Leeward Islands Federation was dissolved in 1956 and separate colonies were established under one governor. In 1960 the post of governor of the Leeward Islands was abolished.

See also under the separate islands and West Indies.

Colonial Office and predecessors

Leeward Islands: Original Correspondence (CO 152) 1689–1951, 547 volumes and boxes of files, continued in **West Indian Department: Registered Files (CO 1031)** 1948–67. See also Colonies General: Supplementary Original Correspondence (CO 537).

Leeward Islands: Register of Correspondence (CO 354) 1850–1951, 44 volumes (for registers before 1850 see CO 326). Correspondence from and about Antigua, Dominica, Montserrat, Nevis, St Christopher (St Kitts) and the Virgin Islands is registered from 1850 in the Leeward Islands register of correspondence (CO 354).
Leeward Islands: Entry Books (CO 153) 1670–1816, 34 volumes, including précis books
Leeward Islands: Register of Out-letters (CO 507) 1872–1926, 11 volumes
Leeward Islands: Acts (CO 154) 1644–1956, 17 volumes
Leeward Islands: Sessional Papers (CO 155) 1680–1956, 29 volumes
Leeward Islands: Government Gazettes (CO 156) 1683–1945, 60 volumes
Leeward Islands: Miscellanea (CO 157) 1683–1945, 57 volumes, comprising shipping returns and blue books of statistics.

Lesotho *see* Basutoland

Lower Canada *see* Quebec

Malacca (Melaka)

Malacca was occupied by the Portuguese from 1511, and by the Dutch from 1641. It was occupied by the British between 1795 and 1818, and ceded to Britain in 1824. It became part of the Straits Settlements in 1826. When the Straits Settlements administration was dissolved at the end of 1946 Malacca was incorporated into the short-lived Malayan Union and then into the Federation of Malaya in 1948. For correspondence see under Straits Settlements.

Colonial Office

Malacca: Sessional Papers (CO 944) 1946–50, 2 volumes
Malacca: Government Gazettes (CO 929) 1948–79, 18 volumes

Malawi *see* Nyasaland

Malayan Union

In January 1946 the British government set out proposals for the unification of the four Federated Malay States, the five unfederated Malay states and the settlements of Penang and Malacca, but excluding Singapore, Labuan, Christmas Island and the Cocos (Keeling) Islands, under a governor with a strong unitary government. The Malayan Union was established on 1 April 1946, but was soon abandoned because of local opposition. In its place the Federation of Malaya, consisting of the same territories as the Malayan Union, was established on 1 February 1948.

Colonial Office

Correspondence will be found in the original correspondence series relating to the Federated Malay States (CO 717) and Singapore (CO 953). See also under Far East/South East Asia.

Malayan Union and Singapore: Registers of Correspondence (CO 991) 1946–51, 8 volumes

Malaysia

On 9 July 1963 Britain, the Federation of Malaya, North Borneo, Sarawak and Singapore signed the Malaysia Agreement, and Britain relinquished sovereignty over the colonies of North Borneo and Sarawak and the state of Singapore. These territories then joined the existing states of the Federation of Malaya as the states of Sabah, Sarawak and Singapore to form the federation thereafter called Malaysia, which came into being on 16 September 1963 as a member of the Commonwealth. On 9 August 1965 Singapore separated from Malaysia and became an independent sovereign state within the Commonwealth. Correspondence relating to the setting up of the federation will be found in the correspondence series for the Federated Malay States (CO 717) and Singapore (CO 953). In the mid 1960s a Malaysia/Indonesia Department was set up jointly by the Foreign Office and the Commonwealth Relations Office to handle the situation known as 'confrontation'. Its records are in the Foreign Office series FO 371. See also under Malayan Union and Far East/South East Asia.

Colonial Office

Commission of Enquiry in North Borneo and Sarawak Regarding Malaysian Federation (Cobbold Commission, 1962) (CO 947) 1962, 61 files

Commonwealth Relations Office/Commonwealth Office/Foreign and Commonwealth Office

Commonwealth Relations Office and Successors: High Commission, Federation of Malaya and Malaysia: Records (DO 187) 1954 onwards

Commonwealth Relations Office and Commonwealth Office: Far East and Pacific Department: Registered Files (FE series) (DO 169) 1960–7

Foreign Office and Foreign and Commonwealth Office: South East Asian Department: Registered Files (D and FA series) (FCO 15) 1967 onwards

Commonwealth Office, Far East and Pacific Department and Foreign and Commonwealth Office, South West Pacific Department: Registered Files (H and FW series) (FCO 24) 1967 onwards

Foreign and Commonwealth Office and predecessors: Records of Former Colonial Administrations: Migrated Archives (FCO 141)

Maldives

On 16 December 1887 the sultan of Maldives signed an agreement with the British governor of Ceylon making the islands a British protectorate. Maldives gained independence on 26 July 1965, became a republic on 11 November 1968, and joined the Commonwealth in 1982. For records relating to the pre-independence period see under Ceylon.

Commonwealth Relations Office/Commonwealth Office/Foreign and Commonwealth Office

Dominions Office and Commonwealth Relations Office: Original Correspondence (DO 35) 1915–71

Commonwealth Relations Office: High Commission, Maldive Islands: Registered Files (DO 188) 1960–3

Commonwealth Relations Office and Commonwealth Office: South Asia Department: Registered Files (SEA series) (DO 196) 1960–8

Commonwealth Office and Foreign and Commonwealth Office: South Asia Department: Registered Files (S and FS series) (FCO 37) 1967 onwards

Malta

Malta was ceded by Rome to the Knights of St John of Jerusalem in 1530 and captured from them by France in 1798. It was surrendered to Britain in 1800 and was ceded to her in 1814 by the Treaty of Paris. Malta became an independent member state of the Commonwealth on 21 September 1964, and a republic in December 1974. The order of St Michael and St George was created in 1818 for the inhabitants of Malta and the Ionian Islands and for other British subjects holding high position there or in the British naval forces serving in the Mediterranean. It was extended in 1868 to all colonies, and from 1879 persons connected with the conduct of foreign affairs were admitted. For records relating to the order see under 'honours' in appendix 2. Printed correspondence is included in the Africa confidential print series (CO 879) as well as in the Mediterranean series (CO 883).

Colonial Office and predecessors

Malta: Original Correspondence (CO 158) 1801–1951, 590 volumes and boxes of files, continued in **Mediterranean: Original Correspondence (CO 926)** 1936–66. See also Colonies General: Supplementary Original Correspondence (CO 537).

Malta: Register of Correspondence (CO 355) 1850–1951, 40 volumes (for registers before 1850 see CO 326)

Index to Correspondence (CO 714/91–4) 1815–70

Malta: Entry Books (CO 159) 1799–1872, 32 volumes, including précis books

Malta: Register of Out-letters (CO 518) 1872–1926, 9 volumes

Malta: Acts (CO 160) 1839–1962, 23 volumes

Malta: Sessional Papers (CO 161) 1835–1965, 155 volumes

Malta: Government Gazettes (CO 162) 1818–1975, 199 volumes

Malta: Miscellanea (CO 163) 1816–1938, 157 volumes, including memoranda and returns on various subjects, blue books of statistics and newspapers (for a list of newspapers see appendix 3)

Malta Royal Commission (CO 945) 1911–12, 86 files
Governor and Commander-in-Chief's Office, Malta: Records (CO 1053) [not transferred to TNA at the time of writing]
Malta: Governor: Registered Files (CO 1062) 1958–69, 8 files (this small series relates to the Bailey Dockyard case)

Commonwealth Relations Office
Malta Department: Registered Files (MTA series) 1964–9, 71 files
Commonwealth Relations Office and Successors: High Commission, Malta: Registered Files (DO 203) 1962 onwards

Foreign Office/Commonwealth Office/Foreign and Commonwealth Office
Foreign Office, Central Department and Foreign and Commonwealth Office, Southern European Department: Registered Files (C and WS series) (FCO 9) 1967 onwards
Commonwealth Office: Middle East, Western and United Nations Department and Mediterranean Department: Registered Files (M series) (FCO 27) 1967–8
Foreign Office, Western Department and Foreign and Commonwealth Office, Western European Department: Registered Files (R and WR series) (FCO 33) 1967 onwards
Foreign and Commonwealth Office and predecessors: Records of Former Colonial Administrations: Migrated Archives (FCO 141)

Manitoba

Manitoba was formed from the territory, including the Red River Colony which was part of Rupert's Land, granted to the Hudson's Bay Company by royal charter in 1670. It became a province of the Dominion of Canada on 15 July 1870. At first the province extended over only a small area south of Lake Winnipeg but in 1912 it was increased to its present size of 251,000 square miles. For correspondence and other records see under Canada. See also under Hudson's Bay.

Colonial Office
Manitoba: Acts (CO 164) 1867–86, 6 volumes
Manitoba: Sessional Papers (CO 165) 1875–1924, 39 volumes
Manitoba: Government Gazettes (CO 577) 1905–25, 21 volumes

Dominions Office and Successors
Manitoba: Government Gazettes (DO 38) 1926–75, 83 volumes
Manitoba: Sessional Papers (DO 96) 1938–65, 64 volumes

Martinique

Martinique has been French since 1635 except from 1762 to 1763, from 1794 to 1802 and again from 1809 to 1815 when it was in British hands. During the latter two periods it retained its old institutions but was given a British governor with executive powers aided by a consultative council. The records referred to below include entry books, précis of correspondence, and shipping returns. Other correspondence relating to the island will be found in the War Office series In-letters (WO 1), and among the records of the Admiralty (ADM series). For records relating to French administration see Foreign Office, especially FO 27, Foreign Office and Predecessor: Political and Other Departments: General Correspondence before 1906, France, which includes correspondence from British consuls at Martinique, and FO 371, Foreign Office: Political Departments: General Correspondence 1906–66.

War and Colonial Department and predecessors

Martinique: Original Correspondence, etc. (CO 166) 1693–1815, 7 volumes

Maryland *see under* America and West Indies

Massachusetts *see under* America and West Indies

Mauritius

Mauritius was first settled by the Dutch in 1598, abandoned by them in 1710 and claimed by France in 1715. In 1721/2 it was settled from Réunion, placed under the administration of the Compagnie des Indes and its name changed to Île de France; in 1767 it was transferred to the French Crown. Because of its use as a base for privateering raids against British shipping during the Napoleonic wars it was seized by Britain in 1810. The former name of Mauritius was then restored and with its dependencies, including Rodrigues, it was ceded to Britain in 1814 by the Treaty of Paris. Reunion, also captured by the British in 1810, was returned to France in 1814. Records of the five years of British administration are in the Archives départementales de la Réunion. After the close of the Napoleonic wars the British government set up several commissions of inquiry into the new British possessions. An inquiry into Mauritius was carried out from 1826 to 1828, the records of which are held mainly in CO 415, with some in CO 167. From 1810 Mauritius and Seychelles were administered as a single unit, but they became separate colonies in 1903. On 12 March 1968 Mauritius became an independent state within the Commonwealth.

Colonial Office and predecessors

Mauritius: Original Correspondence (CO 167) 1778–1951, 959 volumes and boxes of files (printed correspondence is in the Eastern confidential print series CO 882). CO 167 is continued in **Hong Kong and Pacific Department: Original Correspondence (CO 1023)** 1946–55, and **Pacific and Indian Ocean Department: Registered Files (PAC series) (CO 1036)** 1952–67. See also Colonies General: Supplementary Original Correspondence (CO 537).

Mauritius: Register of Correspondence (CO 356) 1850–1950, 42 volumes (for registers before 1850 see CO 326)

Index to Correspondence (CO 714/95–100) 1809–66
Mauritius: Entry Books (CO 168) 1810–72, 63 volumes
Mauritius: Register of Out-letters (CO 490) 1873–1926, 13 volumes
Mauritius: Acts (CO 169) 1833–1967, 50 volumes
Mauritius: Sessional Papers (CO 170) 1825–1965, 422 volumes
Mauritius: Government Gazettes (CO 171) 1823–1975, 173 volumes
Mauritius: Miscellanea (CO 172) 1810–1947, 172 volumes, including reports of protectors of slaves, blue books of statistics and newspapers (for a list of newspapers see appendix 3)
Commissioners of Eastern Inquiry, Mauritius (CO 415) 1826–8, 19 volumes
Mauritius Electoral Boundary Commission (CO 890) 1957, 15 files
Commission on the Constitution of Mauritius (Banwell Commission) (CO 961) 1965–6, 49 files
Mauritius: Registrar General: Registers of Births (CO 1068) 1921–2, 2 volumes

Commonwealth Relations Office/Commonwealth Office/Foreign and Commonwealth Office
Commonwealth Relations Office and Commonwealth Office: East Africa Departments: Registered Files, East Africa (EA series) (DO 213) 1963–7
Commonwealth Office and Foreign and Commonwealth Office: East Africa Departments: Registered Files (P and JE series) (FCO 31) 1967 onwards
Commonwealth Office and Foreign and Commonwealth Office: Pacific and Indian Ocean Department and Pacific Dependent Territories Department: Registered Files (Q and HP series) (FCO 32) 1967 onwards
Foreign and Commonwealth Office and predecessors: Records of Former Colonial Administrations: Migrated Archives (FCO 141)

Mediterranean

The record series CO 173 contains despatches from Mediterranean naval commanders Horatio Nelson (1803–4) and Cuthbert Collingwood (1808); entry books of letters relating to the occupation of Toulon (1793) and to military affairs; précis of letters from Tangier, Algiers, Tunis, Tripoli, Gibraltar and Malta; and civil, military, ecclesiastical and commercial returns from Gibraltar, Malta and the Ionian Islands. Further Mediterranean despatches of 1805 from Nelson are in CO 537/151. CO 926 contains registered files of the Pacific and Mediterranean Department and its successors relating to Cyprus, Gibraltar and Malta; a very small number of files concern Palestine and the Middle East.

Colonial Office and predecessors
Mediterranean: Despatches and Entry Books (CO 173) 1793–1828, 6 volumes (registered in CO 326). See also Colonies General: Supplementary Original Correspondence (CO 537).
Mediterranean: Original Correspondence (CO 926) 1936–66, 1127 volumes
Confidential Print: Mediterranean (CO 883) 1844–1936, 10 volumes (the Africa confidential print series CO 879 also includes papers on Gibraltar, the Ionian Islands and Malta)

Melaka *see* Malacca

Mesopotamia *see* Iraq

Middle East

The League of Nations allocated mandates over the former Turkish territories of Palestine, Iraq and Transjordan (Jordan) to Britain following the First World War, and the Colonial Office became responsible for their administration. This led to the establishment of a separate Middle East Department, later Division. British relations with Egypt remained the responsibility of the Foreign Office, and those with Aden initially (until 1937) of the India Office. The mandate in Iraq came to an end in 1932 and the Foreign Office took over responsibility for British relations. In July 1941 a minister of state for the Middle East was appointed with headquarters at Cairo, seat of the Middle East Supply Centre. His sphere included, among other areas in the large region, Palestine and Transjordan, British Somaliland, Cyprus and Aden. His office was linked to the Cabinet Office rather than to the Colonial Office, and information about his role can be found in a number of Cabinet (CAB) and Foreign Office (FO) record series. The mandate over Transjordan came to an end in 1946, and that over Palestine in 1948. The Colonial Office Middle East Division was then abolished. For later material see records of the Foreign Office, particularly FO 371, Political Departments: General Correspondence 1906–66. See also under the individual territories and under Arabia and Mediterranean.

Colonial Office

Middle East: Original Correspondence (CO 732) 1921–49, 89 volumes and boxes of files (see also Colonies General: Supplementary Original Correspondence (CO 537))
Middle East: Register of Correspondence (CO 788) 1921–44, 15 volumes
Middle East: Register of Out-letters (CO 789) 1921–6, 2 volumes
Confidential Print: Middle East (CO 935) 1920–56, 25 volumes

Minorca

Britain captured Minorca, one of the Balearic Islands, from Spain in 1708 and it was ceded by Spain in 1713 under terms of the Treaty of Utrecht. Captured by France in 1756, it was restored to Britain in 1763. Again captured by France and Spain in 1782, it was ceded to Spain in 1783, was reoccupied by Britain in 1798 and finally restored to Spain by the Treaty of Amiens in 1802. While it was in British hands legislative and executive authority was vested in the governor. CO 174 includes entry books of instructions to governors and précis of correspondence.

War and Colonial Department and predecessors

Minorca: Original Correspondence and Entry Books (CO 174) 1711–1802, 21 volumes

Montserrat

Montserrat was closely linked with Antigua, and details of the two islands and the joint record series are given under Antigua and Montserrat. Montserrat came under English control in 1632 when it was settled by a group of Irish people initially transported to Nevis; it was held by the French during 1667 and from 1782 to 1783. In 1956 Montserrat became a separate colony on the dissolution of the Leeward Islands. It became a member of the Federation of the West Indies in 1958 and a separate dependency again when the federation broke up in 1962. It remains a British dependency (UK Overseas Territory). See also under West Indies and under Leeward Islands.

Colonial Office and predecessors

Montserrat: Original Correspondence (CO 175) 1726–1872, 21 volumes. Apart from the first volume which includes papers dated from 1726 to 1787 the series commences in 1853. Correspondence continues in **Leeward Islands Original Correspondence (CO 152)** and, after 1951, in **West Indian Department: Registered Files (CO 1031)** 1948–67. Both CO 175 and CO 152 are registered in the Leeward Islands registers (CO 354).

Index to Correspondence (CO 714/101) 1853–66

Montserrat: Acts (CO 176) 1668–1960, 24 volumes

Montserrat: Sessional Papers (CO 177) 1704–1965, 44 volumes

Montserrat: Miscellanea (CO 178) 1829–87, 57 volumes of blue books of statistics

Colonial Office/Commonwealth Office/Foreign and Commonwealth Office

Commonwealth Office: West Indian Department 'A' and Associated States Department: Registered Files (WA series) (FCO 43) 1967–8

Commonwealth Office: West Indian Department 'B' and Foreign and Commonwealth Office, West Indian Department: Registered Files, Smaller Commonwealth West Indian Territories (WB and HW series) (FCO 44) 1967 onwards

Foreign and Commonwealth Office: Montserrat: Government Gazettes (FCO 6) 1967–89

Mosquito (or Moskito) Coast

Following cession of lands to Great Britain by a local ruler, a superintendent was appointed in 1740 to supervise logging settlements. In 1782 the office was abolished as British interests in Central America focused on Belize to the north. However, a shadowy protectorate was maintained by Great Britain over the area until 1860 when these rights were transferred to Nicaragua. See also under British Honduras.

Foreign Office

Foreign Office: Political and Other Departments: General Correspondence before 1906, Mosquito (FO 53) 1844–95

Myanmar *see* Burma

Namibia *see* South West Africa

Natal

In 1844 Natal was annexed to Cape Colony, under which it was given a lieutenant-governor and Executive Council in 1845 and an official Legislative Council for advisory purposes in 1847. In 1856 it was separated from the Cape and the Legislative Council became partly elective. Natal received responsible government in 1893, an elective Legislative Assembly being added to the Legislative Council. In 1910 it became a province of the Union of South Africa. See also under Cape of Good Hope and South Africa High Commission. For correspondence and other records after 1910 see also under Union of South Africa.

Colonial Office and predecessor

Natal: Original Correspondence (CO 179) 1846–1910, 256 volumes
Natal: Register of Correspondence (CO 357) 1849–1910, 15 volumes
Index to Correspondence (CO 714/102–3) 1849–70
Natal: Entry Books (CO 405) 1852–72, 7 volumes
Natal: Register of Out-letters (CO 480) 1872–1910, 6 volumes
Natal: Acts (CO 180) 1848–1910, 12 volumes
Natal: Sessional Papers (CO 181) 1846–1924, 73 volumes
Natal: Government Gazettes (CO 182) 1858–1925, 59 volumes
Natal: Miscellanea (CO 183) 1850–1908, 58 volumes, including blue books of statistics and newspapers (for a list of newspapers see appendix 3)

Dominions Office/Commonwealth Relations Office

Natal: Sessional Papers (DO 39) 1925–60, 34 volumes
Natal: Government Gazettes (DO 40) 1926–61, 48 volumes

Nauru

The phosphate-rich atoll of Nauru was annexed by Germany in 1888 and surrendered to Australian forces in 1914. At Australia's request it was administered by the high commissioner for the Western Pacific from then until 1921. A mandate to administer the island was conferred jointly upon Britain, New Zealand and Australia by the League of Nations in 1920. The governments of the United Kingdom, the Commonwealth of Australia and New Zealand agreed that it should be governed by Australia, which from that time appointed the administrator, in whom executive and legislative powers were vested. Nauru was occupied by the Japanese from 1942 to 1945. It became an independent republic within the Commonwealth on 31 January 1968. See also under Western Pacific.

Dominions Office/Commonwealth Relations Office

Nauru: Government Gazettes (DO 83) 1926–65, 15 volumes. See also

British Phosphate Commissioners (DO 140) 1873–1983, 853 files, maps, photographs, etc. For further details see p. 137.

Negri Sembilan (Negeri Sembilan), Sungei Ujong and Jelebu

Negri Sembilan, the 'Nine States', was formerly part of the kingdom of Malacca. A confederation known as 'the old Negri Sembilan', which did not include Sungei Ujong and Jelebu, was established in 1889 and received a British resident. Sungei Ujong and Jelebu had received British residents in 1874 and 1883 respectively. They both joined the modern Negri Sembilan which was constituted in 1895 and had a single resident. In the same year this new federation was included in the Federated Malay States. In 1898 the Negri Sembilan Federation was made a unitary state and supreme authority was vested in the yam tuan of Sri Menati who presided over the state council. The federation was under Japanese occupation from 1942 to 1946. It joined the Malayan Union in 1946 and the Federation of Malaya in 1948. See also under Sungei Ujong and Federated Malay States.

Colonial Office and successors

Negri Sembilan, Sungei Ujong and Jelebu: Sessional Papers (CO 435) 1888–1929, 4 volumes

Negri Sembilan, Sungei Ujong and Jelebu: Government Gazettes (CO 463) 1896–1980, 26 volumes

Nevis

Nevis was colonised by the English from St Christopher (St Kitts) in 1628. It was part of the general government of the Caribbean Islands until 1671, when it was made part of the Leeward Islands. Nevis was briefly occupied by the French in 1706, and from 1782 to 1784. When the Leeward Islands government broke up in 1816 Nevis, St Christopher (St Kitts) and the Virgin Islands formed a separate governmental unit, but in 1833 they were reunited with the other Leeward Islands under a governor-in-chief and in 1871 the federal legislature was reconstituted. In 1882 Nevis joined with St Christopher (St Kitts) and Anguilla to form one presidency. On the dissolution of the Leeward Islands Federation in 1956, St Christopher (St Kitts)-Nevis-Anguilla became a separate colony with the capital in St Christopher. From 1958 the colony was a member state of the Federation of the West Indies. In 1967 it became a self-governing state in association with Great Britain. Anguilla seceded later that year and remains a British dependency. The Federation of St Christopher (St Kitts) and Nevis attained full independence on 19 September 1983. See also under St Christopher.

Colonial Office and predecessors

Nevis: Original Correspondence (CO 184) 1703–1872, 20 volumes (with the exception of the first volume, which covers the years 1703–87, the series starts in 1854; for earlier and later periods see under Leeward Islands)

Index to Correspondence (CO 714/104) 1854–66

Nevis: Acts (CO 185) 1664–1882, 15 volumes (the first volume of Antigua Acts, CO 8/1) also relates to Nevis)

Nevis: Sessional Papers (CO 186) 1721–1882, 22 volumes

Nevis: Miscellanea (CO 187) 1704–1882, 56 volumes, comprising shipping returns and blue books of statistics

Commonwealth Office/Foreign and Commonwealth Office

Commonwealth Office: West Indian Department 'A' and Associated States Department: Registered Files, Antigua, Dominica, Grenada, St Christopher (St Kitts)-Nevis-Anguilla, St Lucia and St Vincent (WA series) (FCO 43) 1967–8

Foreign and Commonwealth Office: North American and Caribbean Department and Caribbean Department: Registered Files (AN series) (FCO 63) 1968 onwards

New Brunswick

New Brunswick was part of the French province of Acadia and was ceded to Britain in 1713. It was colonised by British subjects from New England in 1761, and in 1783 it received a large body of loyalists from the thirteen colonies. In 1784 it was separated from Nova Scotia, of which it had been part, and given a separate governor and Assembly. In 1854 responsible government was established and in 1867 New Brunswick became a province of the Dominion of Canada. For later correspondence and other records see under Canada.

Colonial Office and predecessors

New Brunswick: Original Correspondence (CO 188) 1784–1876, 206 volumes

New Brunswick: Register of Correspondence (CO 358) 1850–67, 4 volumes (for registers before 1850 see CO 326)

Index to Correspondence (CO 714/105–8) 1815–57

New Brunswick: Entry Books (CO 189) 1769–1867, 21 volumes, including précis books

New Brunswick: Acts (CO 190) 1786–1897, 26 volumes

New Brunswick: Sessional Papers (CO 191) 1786–1924, 156 volumes

New Brunswick: Government Gazettes (CO 192) 1842–1923, 26 volumes

New Brunswick: Miscellanea (CO 193) 1786–1865, 48 volumes, including shipping returns, miscellaneous memoranda and papers, and blue books of statistics

Dominions Office/Commonwealth Relations Office

New Brunswick: Sessional Papers (DO 137) 1956–65, 19 volumes

New Brunswick: Government Gazettes (DO 43) 1924–68, 18 volumes

New England *see under* America and West Indies

New Guinea

New Guinea was declared a German protectorate in 1884. From 1885 until 1899 it was controlled by the German New Guinea Company and then placed under the Imperial German government. It was captured by Australian forces in 1914 and was under military administration from 1914 to 1921. In 1920 New Guinea was assigned to Australia under a League of Nations mandate and legislative authority was vested in the governor-general of Australia. In 1932 nominated Executive and Legislative Councils were set up. New Guinea was occupied by the Japanese in 1942, but partly recaptured by 1945. In 1945/6 it was united with British New Guinea (Papua) as a single territory of the Commonwealth of Australia. See also British New Guinea (Papua)

Colonial Office
New Guinea (Former German Territory): Government Gazettes (CO 667) 1914–25, 2 volumes
Dominions Office/Commonwealth Relations Office/Foreign and Commonwealth Office
New Guinea and Papua New Guinea: Government Gazettes (DO 85) 1926–75, 37 volumes

New Hampshire *see under* America and West Indies

New Hebrides (Vanuatu)

New Hebrides was the source of heavy labour recruiting for Fiji, New Caledonia and Queensland during the 19th century. In 1877 the islands were put under the jurisdiction of the high commissioner for the Western Pacific through whom all communications were channelled. In 1887 a joint Anglo-French naval commission was established for the protection of British and French nationals and in 1902 British and French resident commissioners were appointed. In 1906 an Anglo-French condominium was proclaimed and three administrations were created – the British national, the French national and the condominium. New Hebrides, renamed Vanuatu, became an independent republic within the Commonwealth on 30 January 1980. For correspondence see under Western Pacific.

Because of the nature of the joint Anglo-French administration the Foreign Office had a close involvement, and relevant records of that department are also listed below.

Colonial Office and successors
New Hebrides: Sessional Papers (CO 983) 1934–65, 2 volumes
New Hebrides: Government Gazettes (CO 829) 1927–69, 5 volumes
New Hebrides: Miscellanea (CO 718) 1920–3, 4 volumes of blue books of statistics
New Hebrides: Joint Regulations (CO 914) 1907–23, 1 volume

New Hebrides: British Resident Commissioner, Registered Files (CO 1060) 1957–73, 2 files

Foreign Office

Political and Other Departments: General Correspondence before 1906, France (FO 27) 1781–1905

Political Departments: General Correspondence from 1906 to 1966 (FO 371) 1906–66

Confidential Print: Pacific Islands (FO 534) 1822–1923

Confidential Print (Numerical Series) (FO 881) 1827–1914

Protocols of Treaties (FO 93) 1695–2003

Commonwealth Office/Foreign and Commonwealth Office

Commonwealth Office and Foreign and Commonwealth Office: Pacific and Indian Ocean Department and Pacific Dependent Territories Department: Registered Files (Q and HP series) (FCO 32) 1967 onwards

Foreign and Commonwealth Office and predecessors: Records of Former Colonial Administrations: Migrated Archives (FCO 141)

New Jersey *see under* America and West Indies

New South Wales

New South Wales was first settled in 1788 when a penal colony was established at Botany Bay. Initially it administered much of the eastern part of Australia. Tasmania was separated in 1825, Victoria in 1851 and Queensland in 1859. New Zealand was also administered through New South Wales until 1841. New South Wales became an original state of the Commonwealth of Australia in 1901. For other records relating to the penal colony and to transportation more generally see the research guides 'Looking for records of a criminal transportee' (http://www.nationalarchives.gov.uk/records/looking-for-person/transportees.htm) and 'Criminal transportees: further research' (http://www.nationalarchives.gov.uk/records/research-guides/transportation-australia.htm). For later correspondence and other records see under Commonwealth of Australia.

Colonial Office and predecessors

New South Wales: Original Correspondence (CO 201) 1783–1900, 629 volumes

New South Wales: Register of Correspondence (CO 360) 1849–1900, 16 volumes (for registers before 1849 see CO 326)

Index to Correspondence (CO 714/113–18) 1812–70

New South Wales: Entry Books (CO 202) 1786–1873, 78 volumes

New South Wales: Register of Out-letters (CO 369) 1873–1900, 4 volumes

New South Wales: Acts (CO 203) 1829–1925, 85 volumes

New South Wales: Sessional Papers (CO 204) 1825–1925, 621 volumes, with consolidated indexes to minutes of proceedings and printed papers at DO 45/153 (1894–1913) and DO 45/154 (1914–34)

New South Wales: Government Gazettes (CO 205) 1832–1925, 309 volumes
New South Wales: Miscellanea (CO 206) 1803–1925, 187 volumes, including memoranda on various subjects, blue books of statistics and newspapers (for a list of newspapers see appendix 3)
New South Wales: Public Service Lists (CO 580) 1895–1916, 21 volumes
New South Wales: Entry Books Relating to Convicts (CO 207/9–11) 1788–1868, 3 reels of microfilm (copies of records of the superintendent of convicts in New South Wales; the originals, formerly in CO 207/1–8, were transferred to the Archives Authority of New South Wales in 1973)

Dominions Office/Commonwealth Relations Office

New South Wales: Acts (DO 44) 1926–66, 71 volumes
New South Wales: Sessional Papers (DO 45) 1925–65, 219 volumes
New South Wales: Government Gazettes (DO 46) 1926–80, 206 volumes
New South Wales: Miscellanea (DO 47) 1925–51, 27 volumes of statistical registers

New York *see under* America and West Indies

New Zealand

New Zealand was settled by Britain from 1814 but was under the jurisdiction of New South Wales until 1841. In 1840 the local leaders ceded sovereignty over North Island to the British Crown by the Treaty of Waitangi. In the same year Britain proclaimed its sovereignty over South Island by right of settlement. In 1841 the islands became a separate colony and from 1841 to 1850 they were administered by the New Zealand Company (see separate entry). Responsible government was established in 1856. In 1907 New Zealand obtained dominion status under a governor-general.

Colonial Office and predecessor

New Zealand: Original Correspondence (CO 209) 1830–1922, 313 volumes, continued in **Dominions: Original Correspondence (CO 532)** 1907–25. See also Colonies General: Supplementary Original Correspondence (CO 537).
New Zealand: Register of Correspondence (CO 361) 1849–1922, 21 volumes (for registers before 1849 see CO 326)
Index to Correspondence (CO 714/119–22) 1840–70
New Zealand: Entry Books (CO 406) 1837–72, 28 volumes
New Zealand: Register of Out-letters (CO 365) 1873–1922, 9 volumes
New Zealand: Acts (CO 210) 1841–1925, 43 volumes
New Zealand: Sessional Papers (CO 211) 1841–1925, 347 volumes
New Zealand: Government Gazettes (CO 212) 1841–1925, 115 volumes
New Zealand: Miscellanea (CO 213) 1840–1925, 107 volumes, including blue books of statistics and newspapers (for a list of newspapers see appendix 3)
New Zealand: Public Service Lists (CO 719) 1916–20, 2 volumes

Dominions Office

Dominions Office and Commonwealth Relations Office: Original Correspondence (DO 35) 1915–71

New Zealand: Acts (DO 48) 1926–47, 14 volumes

New Zealand: Sessional Papers (DO 49) 1926–65, 195 volumes

New Zealand: Government Gazettes (DO 50) 1926–80, 165 volumes

New Zealand: Miscellanea (DO 51) 1925–51, 51 volumes, comprising statistical reports and blue books of statistics

High Commission and Consular Archives, New Zealand: Correspondence (DO 128) 1955 onwards, 6 files

Commonwealth Office/Foreign and Commonwealth Office

Commonwealth Office, Far East and Pacific Department and Foreign and Commonwealth Office, South West Pacific Department: Registered Files (H and FW series) (FCO 24) 1967 onwards

New Zealand Company

The New Zealand Company was a chartered company which was formed as a joint stock company in 1839 and incorporated in 1841. It was empowered to buy, sell, settle and cultivate lands in New Zealand, and to advance money on the security of such lands in order to promote their cultivation. It did not prove a satisfactory agency for colonising New Zealand and was induced to surrender its charters in 1850. It was finally dissolved in 1858. After the surrender, its records were handed over to the Colonial Office. They now form the series CO 208, which consists of in-letters and out-letters, registers, minute books, and accounts and registers of emigrants and land transfers. Correspondence between the company and the Colonial Office is in CO 209 (see above under New Zealand).

Colonial Office and predecessor

New Zealand Company: Original Correspondence, etc. (CO 208) 1837–61, 309 volumes, etc.

Newfoundland

Newfoundland was incorporated into the realm of England in 1583, but not effectively colonised until well into the next century when English and French settlers arrived. In 1713 British sovereignty was finally acknowledged, and in 1729 a civil government was instituted and a governor appointed. Governors were naval officers until 1818 when the first resident governor was appointed. In 1763 Labrador, ceded by France under terms of the Treaty of Paris, was incorporated into the government of Newfoundland. Newfoundland remained a separate dependency, acquiring dominion status in 1918, until in a 1948 referendum a majority of the electorate voted in favour of confederation with Canada, rather than responsible government and independence. Newfoundland accordingly joined Canada on 31 March 1949. In 1964 the name of the province was changed to Newfoundland and Labrador. Because of the territory's close links with Canada the Dominions Division of the Colonial Office became the responsible department on its establishment in 1907, and the Dominions Office in 1925. For correspondence and other records after 1949 see under Canada.

Colonial Office and predecessors

Newfoundland: Original Correspondence (CO 194) 1696–1922, 303 volumes, continued in **Dominions: Original Correspondence (CO 532)** 1907–25. See also Colonies General: Supplementary Original Correspondence (CO 537).

Newfoundland: Register of Correspondence (CO 359) 1850–1922, 16 volumes (for registers before 1850 see CO 326)

Index to Correspondence (CO 714/109–12) 1815–70

Newfoundland: Entry Books (CO 195) 1623–1867, 23 volumes, including précis books

Newfoundland: Register of Out-letters (CO 363) 1868–1922, 8 volumes Newfoundland: Acts (CO 196) 1833–1925, 18 volumes

Newfoundland: Sessional Papers (CO 197) 1825–1925, 194 volumes

Newfoundland: Government Gazettes (CO 198) 1844–1923, 13 volumes

Newfoundland: Miscellanea (CO 199) 1677–1903, 98 volumes, including various reports and returns, blue books of statistics and newspapers (for a list of newspapers see appendix 3)

Dominions Office

Dominions Office and Commonwealth Relations Office: Original Correspondence (DO 35) 1915–71

Newfoundland: Acts (DO 84) 1926–48, 7 volumes

Newfoundland: Sessional Papers (DO 41) 1924–63, 49 volumes

Newfoundland: Government Gazettes (DO 42) 1924–68, 17 volumes

Niger and West Africa Frontier Force *see* West Africa Frontier Force

Niger Coast Protectorate

From 1849 British consuls, responsible to the Foreign Office, were appointed to the eastern part of what is now the coast of Nigeria. The Niger Districts Protectorate was declared in 1885, and renamed the Oil Rivers Protectorate in 1891 when a commissioner and consul-general replaced the consul at Old Calabar. In 1893 the protectorate was extended and named the Niger Coast Protectorate. In 1899 responsibility was transferred from the Foreign Office to the Colonial Office, and in 1900 the protectorate was united with the southern portion of the territories of the Royal Niger Company to form the Protectorate of Southern Nigeria.

Foreign Office

Foreign Office: Political and Other Departments: General Correspondence before 1906, Africa (FO 2)

Foreign Office: Slave Trade Department and Successors: General Correspondence before 1906 (FO 84)

Colonial Office

Niger Coast Protectorate: Original Correspondence (CO 444) 1899, 4 volumes (registered in the Southern Nigeria Register of Correspondence, CO 589)

Niger Coast Protectorate: Miscellanea (CO 464) 1896–1900, 4 volumes of blue books of statistics

Nigeria

The Colony and Protectorate of Nigeria was formed in 1914 by the amalgamation of Southern Nigeria and Northern Nigeria. Nigeria became an independent state within the Commonwealth on 1 October 1960, and a federal republic on 1 October 1963.

Colonial Office

Nigeria: Original Correspondence (CO 583) 1912–51, 318 volumes and boxes of files, continued in **West Africa Original Correspondence (CO 554)** 1911–65. See also Colonies General: Supplementary Original Correspondence (CO 537).

Nigeria: Register of Correspondence (CO 763) 1912–51, 43 volumes

Nigeria: Register of Out-letters (CO 764) 1912–26, 8 volumes

Nigeria: Acts (CO 656) 1914–60, 26 volumes

Nigeria: Sessional Papers (CO 657) 1912–66, 157 volumes

Nigeria: Government Gazettes (CO 658) 1914–76, 273 volumes

Nigeria: Miscellanea (CO 660) 1913–45, 35 volumes, including blue books of statistics and trade statistical abstracts

Nigeria Railway (CO 741) 1912–22, 2 volumes (minutes of official meetings relating to the railway)

Nigeria: Customs and Trade Journal (CO 659) 1911–16, 3 volumes

Commission on Minority Groups in Nigeria (Willink Commission) (CO 957) 1957–8, 41 files

Nigeria: Council of Ministers: Papers (CO 1039) 1952–9, 123 files

Commonwealth Relations Office/Commonwealth Office/Foreign Office/Foreign and Commonwealth Office

Dominions Office and Commonwealth Relations Office: Original Correspondence (DO 35) 1915–71

Commonwealth Relations Office and Successors: High Commission, Nigeria: Registered Files (DO 186) 1958 onwards

Commonwealth Relations Office: Africa Economic: Registered Files (ECA series) (DO 166) 1961–2

Commonwealth Relations Office: Nigeria: Registered Files (NIG series) (DO 177) 1961

Commonwealth Relations Office and Commonwealth Office: West and General Africa Department and Successors: Registered Files (WA series) (DO 195) 1960–7

Commonwealth Relations Office and Commonwealth Office: West and General Africa Department: Registered Files, General Africa (GA series) (DO 216) 1963–6
Commonwealth Relations Office and Commonwealth Office: West Africa Economic Department and Successors: Registered Files, West Africa Economic (WAE series) (DO 221) 1964–7
Commonwealth Office: West and General Africa Department: Registered Files, Commonwealth Africa, General African Affairs and the Organisation of African Unity (T series) (FCO 38) 1967–8
Foreign Office: West and Central African Department: Registered Files (J series) (FCO 25) 1967–8
Foreign and Commonwealth Office: West African Department: Registered Files (JW series) (FCO 65) 1968 onwards
Foreign and Commonwealth Office and predecessors: Records of Former Colonial Administrations: Migrated Archives (FCO 141)

Norfolk Island

Norfolk Island was settled by Britain from 1788 to 1815 and again from 1825 to 1855. It was used as a convict settlement by New South Wales from 1788 to 1844, and by Tasmania from 1844 to 1856. In 1856 the convict establishment was dissolved, the island was handed over to settlers from Pitcairn, and it became a separate colony under the administration of, first, New South Wales and, subsequently, the Commonwealth of Australia. Norfolk Islanders have continued to claim self-determination, holding that the island has not been ceded to, or annexed by, the Commonwealth of Australia. For other records see under New South Wales and Commonwealth of Australia.

Commonwealth Relations Office
Norfolk Island: Government Gazettes (DO 135) 1956–60, 1 volume

North America *see* British North America

North Australia

A colony of North Australia existed briefly from 17 February 1846, and consisted of the land in the Northern Territory and Queensland lying north of 26° south. It was intended for use as a penal colony, but the charter establishing it and the governor's letters patent were revoked in December of the same year.

War and Colonial Department
North Australia: Entry Books (CO 395) 1846, 2 volumes

North Borneo (Sabah)

British North Borneo was part of the Sultanate of Brunei until ceded to a British syndicate in 1878. In 1882 the British North Borneo Company assumed charge of the territory under a charter of 1881 and continued to govern it until it fell to the Japanese in 1942. When liberated in 1945 it was placed under military administration (WO 203). In 1946 North Borneo became a Crown colony, to which Labuan was joined. During the post-war period matters common to North Borneo, Sarawak and Brunei were dealt with by the UK commissioner for South East Asia. The British North Borneo Company, the last of the chartered companies to administer British territory, wound up its affairs in 1952 and transferred its surviving records to TNA's predecessor the Public Record Office. Following the findings of the Cobbold Commission into possible political association with Malaya, the colony of North Borneo became the state of Sabah in July 1963 on joining Sarawak, Singapore and the Federation of Malaya to form the independent federation thereafter called Malaysia. For other records before 1907 see under Labuan. See also under Far East/South East Asia.

Colonial Office

British North Borneo Company Papers (CO 874) 1865–1952, 1,114 volumes and files

British North Borneo: Original Correspondence (CO 531) 1907–51, 50 volumes and boxes of files, continued in **South East Asia Department: Original Correspondence** (CO 1022) 1950–6. See also Colonies General: Supplementary Original Correspondence (CO 537).

British North Borneo: Register of Correspondence (CO 777) 1915–41, 4 volumes (North Borneo original correspondence and out-letters for 1907–14 are registered under Labuan in CO 532 and CO 487 respectively)

British North Borneo: Register of Out-letters (CO 778) 1915–26, 1 volume

British North Borneo: Acts (CO 986) 1951–63, 6 volumes

British North Borneo (Sabah): Sessional Papers (CO 648) 1908–65, 47 volumes

British North Borneo and Sabah: Government Gazettes (CO 855) 1883–1980, 108 volumes

British North Borneo: Miscellanea (CO 966) 1907–41, 1 volume of rules for Native Courts in the interior

Borneo Territories: Original Correspondence (CO 954) 1946–51, 8 boxes of files

North Borneo, Brunei and Sarawak: Register of Correspondence (CO 992) 1942–51, 6 volumes

Commission of Enquiry in North Borneo and Sarawak Regarding Malaysian Federation (Cobbold Commission, 1962) (CO 947) 1962, 61 files

North Carolina *see under* America and West Indies

North-Eastern Rhodesia

North-Eastern Rhodesia was separated from North-Western Rhodesia in 1895, but reunited in 1911 to form Northern Rhodesia. The territories were administered by the British South Africa

Company from 1889 to 1923; the following are publications of the company. See also under Rhodesia and Northern Rhodesia.

Colonial Office

North-Eastern Rhodesia: Government Gazettes (CO 669) 1903–11, 1 volume

Northern Nigeria

The Royal Niger Company[II] gradually extended its administration into the area that was to become Northern Nigeria from 1886 onwards. Legislative power was vested in the governor and council of the company in London. In 1899 the company's charter was surrendered to the Crown, and in 1900 Northern Nigeria was proclaimed a protectorate under a high commissioner, in whom legislative authority was vested. In 1908 the post of high commissioner was replaced by that of governor. In 1914 Northern Nigeria was amalgamated with Southern Nigeria to form the Colony and Protectorate of Nigeria. For later records see under Nigeria.

Colonial Office

Northern Nigeria: Original Correspondence (CO 446) 1898–1913, 114 volumes
Northern Nigeria: Register of Correspondence (CO 584) 1898–1913, 7 volumes
Northern Nigeria: Register of Out-letters (CO 585) 1898–1913, 6 volumes
Northern Nigeria: Acts (CO 587) 1900–13, 3 volumes
Northern Nigeria: Government Gazettes (CO 586) 1900–13, 4 volumes
Northern Nigeria: Miscellanea (CO 465) 1900–13, 14 volumes of blue books of statistics
The series CO 959, Various Private Collections, includes reports and miscellaneous papers of Captain H. L. Norton Traill, the British resident in Northern Nigeria from 1909 to 1922.

Northern Rhodesia (Zambia)

In 1899 the British South Africa Company was granted a royal charter to develop and administer the Rhodesias. Barotseland and North-Western Rhodesia were separated from North-Eastern Rhodesia in 1895 and jointly received a British resident, who became the administrator in 1900. In 1899 North-Western Rhodesia was placed under the high commissioner for South Africa. In 1911 North-Western and North-Eastern Rhodesia were united to form Northern Rhodesia under a single administrator and a resident commissioner reporting to the high commissioner for South Africa. In 1924 the British South Africa Company surrendered the administration of the territory to the Crown, and with the appointment of a governor, Executive Council and partly elective Legislative Council the high commissioner in Cape Town ceased to have any jurisdiction.

[II] Records of the Royal Niger Company are held at the Unilever Archives and Records Management, PO Box 69, Port Sunlight, CH62 4ZD, England; and in the Commonwealth and African Collections at the Bodleian Library, University of Oxford (formerly at Rhodes House Library).

After a series of conferences on the closer political association of Northern Rhodesia, Southern Rhodesia and Nyasaland, the Federation of Rhodesia and Nyasaland came into existence on 3 September 1953. It was dissolved on 31 December 1963. On 24 October 1964 Northern Rhodesia became a fully independent state within the Commonwealth under the name of the Republic of Zambia. See also under British South Africa Company, Rhodesia, Federation of Rhodesia and Nyasaland, and Central Africa.

Colonial Office

Northern Rhodesia: Original Correspondence (CO 795) 1924–51, 170 volumes and boxes of files, continued in **Central Africa and Aden: Original Correspondence (CO 1015)** 1950–64. See also Colonies General: Supplementary Original Correspondence (CO 537).

Northern Rhodesia: Register of Correspondence (CO 796) 1924–51, 23 volumes

Northern Rhodesia: Register of Out-letters (CO 797) 1924–6, 1 volume

Northern Rhodesia: Proclamations (CO 743) 1911–64, 16 volumes

Northern Rhodesia and Zambia: Sessional Papers (CO 799) 1923–65, 50 volumes

Northern Rhodesia and Zambia: Government Gazettes and Acts (CO 670) 1911–70, 56 volumes

Northern Rhodesia: Miscellanea (CO 798) 1924–48, 25 volumes of blue books of statistics

See also Union of South Africa: Miscellanea (CO 553) 1910–25, comprising statements of trade and shipping which include material on Northern and Southern Rhodesia

Dominions Office/Central African Office/Commonwealth Relations Office

Dominions Office and Commonwealth Relations Office: Original Correspondence (DO 35) 1915–71

Dominions Office and Successors: Governor, Southern Rhodesia and High Commission, Southern Rhodesia, Federation of Rhodesia and Nyasaland and Rhodesia: Correspondence (DO 154) 1946 onwards, 98 files

Commonwealth Relations Office: Central Africa: Registered Files (CA series) (DO 158) 1953–63

Central African Office and Commonwealth Relations Office: Central Africa: Registered Files (CAO series) (DO 183) 1962–6

High Commission and Consular Archives, Zambia: Records (DO 206) 1964–70, 20 files

Commonwealth Relations Office: Malawi and Zambia Department: Registered Files, Zambia (ZCA series) (DO 209) 1965–6, 133 files

Foreign Office/Commonwealth Office/Foreign and Commonwealth Office

Foreign Office: West and Central African Department: Registered Files (J series) (FCO 25) 1967–8

Commonwealth Office and Foreign and Commonwealth Office: Central African Department and Predecessors: Registered Files (NR and CA series) (FCO 29) 1967–8

Commonwealth Office and Foreign and Commonwealth Office: Southern African Department and Predecessors: Registered Files (SAD and CS series) (FCO 45) 1967 onwards

Foreign and Commonwealth Office and predecessors: Records of Former Colonial Administrations: Migrated Archives (FCO 141)

Northern Territory

The Northern Territory was part of New South Wales from 1825 to 1863, except for a brief period from 1 February 1846 until December of the same year when it was included in the short lived colony of North Australia, and part of South Australia from 1863 to 1911. On 1 January 1911 it was separated from South Australia and transferred to Commonwealth control. Between 1927 and 1931 it was divided into North Australia and Central Australia. The northern part of the territory, known as the Top End, was under military government during the Second World War. In 1978 the territory was granted responsible government, but it has not attained full statehood. See also under Australia, Commonwealth of Australia and New South Wales.

Commonwealth Relations Office/Foreign and Commonwealth Office
Australia, Northern Territory: Government Gazettes (DO 108) 1948–74, 13 volumes

Northwest Territories

In 1870 the Hudson's Bay Company transferred Rupert's Land and the North-Western Territory to the government of Canada, and these became the Northwest Territories. The territories subsequently lost land to the creation of Manitoba, and to the further extension of Manitoba, Ontario and Quebec, but gained substantially from the addition of the Arctic islands in northern Canada. In 1898 the Yukon was made a separate territory, and in 1905 the provinces of Alberta and Saskatchewan were created. In 1912 the Northwest Territories were divided into the districts of Mackenzie, Keewatin and Franklin. In 1999 the territory of Nunavut was created to the north and west of Hudson's Bay as a result of the Nunavut Land Claims Agreement. For correspondence and other records see under Canada.

Colonial Office
Northwest Territories: Acts (CO 214) 1878–81, 1 volume
Northwest Territories: Sessional Papers (CO 215) 1877–1904, 4 volumes
Northwest Territories: Government Gazettes (CO 216) 1883–1905, 4 volumes

Nova Scotia and Cape Breton

Acadia – comprising roughly Nova Scotia, New Brunswick and part of the state of Maine – was colonised by the French in 1598 and remained French until 1713 except that from 1621 to 1632 there was a Scottish colony called Nova Scotia on Cape Breton Island and part of the mainland, and that between 1654 and 1667 Acadia was held by the English. In 1713 Acadia was ceded to Britain, but the French retained Cape Breton (known as Île Royale) until 1758. The old name of Nova Scotia was resumed for the ceded territory. In 1786 Cape Breton and New Brunswick were formed into separate colonies, the former being reunited with Nova Scotia in 1819. Nova Scotia became an original province of the Dominion of Canada in 1867.

Colonial Office and predecessors

Nova Scotia and Cape Breton: Original Correspondence (CO 217) 1710–1867, 242 volumes
Nova Scotia and Cape Breton: Register of Correspondence (CO 362) 1850–67, 5 volumes (for registers before 1850 see CO 326)
Index to Correspondence (CO 714/123–6) 1815–66
Nova Scotia and Cape Breton: Entry Books (CO 218) 1710–1867, 37 volumes, including précis books
Nova Scotia and Cape Breton: Acts (CO 219) 1749–1899, 81 volumes
Nova Scotia and Cape Breton: Sessional Papers (CO 220) 1725–1923, 206 volumes
Nova Scotia and Cape Breton: Government Gazettes (CO 593) 1905–25, 17 volumes
Nova Scotia and Cape Breton: Miscellanea (CO 221) 1730–1866, 76 volumes, including memoranda on various subjects, blue books of statistics, and newspapers (for a list of newspapers see appendix 3)

Dominions Office/Commonwealth Relations Office

Nova Scotia: Government Gazettes (DO 52) 1926–75, 74 volumes
Nova Scotia: Sessional Papers (DO 124) 1954–65, 19 volumes

Nunavut *see under* Northwest Territories

Nyasaland (Malawi)

A British consul was appointed to the area around Lake Nyasa in 1883 following missionary activities from 1874, and a protectorate was declared over a limited area in 1889. The geographical area was extended to cover the entire western shore of the lake in 1891, and in 1893 the territory was named the British Central Africa Protectorate. Until 1904 the protectorate was under a commissioner and a consul-general, but the latter office was then abolished and responsibility for the territory was transferred from the Foreign Office to the Colonial Office. In 1907 the name Nyasaland Protectorate was adopted, the commissioner became governor, and nominated Executive and Legislative Councils were established. Nyasaland was part of the Federation of Rhodesia and Nyasaland set up in 1953 and dissolved ten years later. On 6 July 1964 Nyasaland became an independent state within the Commonwealth under the name of Malawi. See also under Central Africa and Federation of Rhodesia and Nyasaland, and under King's African Rifles. Before 1904 see records of the Foreign Office, especially FO 2 and FO 84.

Colonial Office

Nyasaland: Original Correspondence (CO 525) 1904–51, 221 volumes and boxes of files, continued in **Central Africa and Aden: Original Correspondence (CO 1015)** 1950–64. See also Colonies General: Supplementary Original Correspondence (CO 537).
Nyasaland: Register of Correspondence (CO 703) 1904–51, 28 volumes
Nyasaland: Register of Out-letters (CO 704) 1904–26, 5 volumes

Nyasaland: Acts (CO 625) 1901–64, 14 volumes
Nyasaland (Malawi): Sessional Papers (CO 626) 1907–65, 43 volumes
Nyasaland (Malawi): Government Gazettes (CO 541) 1894–1975, 65 volumes
Nyasaland: Miscellanea (CO 452) 1897–1941, 45 volumes of blue books of statistics

Central African Office/Commonwealth Relations Office/Commonwealth Office/Foreign and Commonwealth Office

Central African Office and Commonwealth Relations Office: Central Africa: Registered Files (CAO series) (DO 183) 1962–6
Commonwealth Relations Office and Successors: High Commission and Consular Archives, Malawi: Registered Files (DO 224) 1945 onwards (apart from DO 224/13 which includes papers dating from 1945 the series begins in 1964)
Commonwealth Relations Office: Malawi and Zambia Department: Registered Files, Malawi (MCA series) (DO 208) 1965–7, 43 files
Commonwealth Office and Foreign and Commonwealth Office: Central African Department and Predecessors: Registered Files (NR and CA series) (FCO 29) 1967–9
Commonwealth Office and Foreign and Commonwealth Office: Southern African Department and Predecessors: Registered Files (SAD and CS series) (FCO 45) 1967 onwards
Foreign and Commonwealth Office and predecessors: Records of Former Colonial Administrations: Migrated Archives (FCO 141)

Oeno Island *see under* Pitcairn

Oil Rivers Protectorate *see under* Niger Coast Protectorate

Ontario

In 1791 British North America was divided into two provinces, Upper Canada (now Ontario) and Lower Canada (now Quebec). In 1867 the British North America Act united the provinces of Ontario, Quebec, New Brunswick and Nova Scotia as the Dominion of Canada. For correspondence and other records see under Canada and British North America.

Colonial Office

Ontario: Acts (CO 222) 1867–86, 18 volumes
Ontario: Sessional Papers (CO 223) 1867–1925, 507 volumes
Ontario: Government Gazettes (CO 595) 1905–25, 34 volumes

Dominions Office/Commonwealth Relations Office/Commonwealth Office/Foreign and Commonwealth Office

Ontario: Sessional Papers (DO 53) 1926–65, 129 volumes
Ontario: Government Gazettes (DO 54) 1926–78, 161 volumes

Orange Free State

The territory between the Orange and Vaal Rivers was settled by Afrikaners (Boers) from the Cape during the Great Trek of 1836–7 and became a republic in 1842. In 1848 it was declared to be under British sovereignty and a British resident was appointed, but in 1854 the Orange Free State was recognised as independent. In 1899 it allied itself with the South African Republic and in 1900 it was annexed to Britain under the name of the Orange River Colony. In 1910 it became a province of the Union of South Africa and resumed its former name of Orange Free State. For correspondence between 1853 and 1856 and between 1901 and 1910 see under Orange River Colony; for later correspondence and other records see under Union of South Africa.

Colonial Office

Orange Free State: Sessional Papers (CO 661) 1911–24, 9 volumes
Orange Free State: Government Gazettes (CO 662) 1911–25, 10 volumes

Dominions Office/Commonwealth Relations Office

Orange Free State: Sessional Papers (DO 55) 1925–62, 29 volumes
Orange Free State: Government Gazettes (DO 56) 1926–61, 47 volumes

Orange River Colony

For the history of British administration and further records see under Orange Free State. The registers of correspondence for 1901–2 will be found under Transvaal and Orange River Colony.

See also under South Africa, and for later records under Union of South Africa.

Colonial Office

Orange River Colony: Original Correspondence (CO 224) 1853–6 and 1901–10, 33 volumes
Orange River Colony: Register of Correspondence (CO 663) 1903–10, 3 volumes
Orange River Colony: Register of Out-letters (CO 664) 1903–10, 2 volumes
Orange River Colony: Acts (CO 596) 1902–10, 5 volumes
Orange River Colony: Sessional Papers (CO 599) 1902–10, 19 volumes
Orange River Colony: Government Gazettes (CO 597) 1900–10, 13 volumes
Orange River Colony: Miscellanea (CO 598) 1905–6, 1 volume of blue books of statistics

Pacific Islands *see under* Western Pacific High Commission

Pahang

Once a vassal state of Malacca and then part of the Johore sultanate, Pahang was recognised as independent in 1882; in 1888 it came under British protection and received a British resident. In

1895 it was included in the Federated Malay States; supreme authority remained with the sultan, who presided over the state council. Pahang was under Japanese occupation from 1942 to 1945. After the British military occupation of 1945–6 (see WO 203) it joined the Malayan Union in 1946 and the Federation of Malaya in 1948 as a separate state. For correspondence and other records see under Federated Malay States.

Colonial Office
Pahang: Sessional Papers (CO 437) 1888–1939, 5 volumes
Pahang: Government Gazettes (CO 466) 1897–1977, 25 volumes

Pakistan

Records relating to the British administration of the Indian subcontinent are held separately in the Asia, Pacific and Africa collections of the British Library. Following independence in 1947 British relations with Pakistan were the responsibility of first the Commonwealth Relations Office and subsequently the Foreign and Commonwealth Office. Pakistan left the Commonwealth in 1972, but rejoined in 1989.

Commonwealth Relations Office
India: Registered Files (DO 142) 1912–58, 605 files (the series includes documents relating to Pakistan; with the exception of one document, DO 142/581, it starts in 1947)
Pakistan: Government Gazettes (DO 106) 1948–72, 107 volumes
Pakistan: Sessional Papers (DO 149) 1961–5, 3 volumes
High Commission and Consular Archives Pakistan: Correspondence (DO 134) 1948 onwards
Dominions Office and Commonwealth Relations Office: Original Correspondence (DO 35) 1915–71

Commonwealth Office/Foreign and Commonwealth Office
Commonwealth Office and Foreign and Commonwealth Office: South Asia Department: Registered Files (S and FS series) (FCO 37) 1967 onwards

Palestine

Formerly a Turkish province (since 1516), Palestine was conquered by Britain in 1917/18 and in 1920 was assigned to the UK under a League of Nations mandate which came into effect in 1923. A high commissioner was appointed in 1920 after an initial period of British military administration. Britain withdrew from Palestine in May 1948 when the greater part of the territory became the state of Israel. The remainder became part of the state of Jordan. Although the Foreign Office then took charge of British relations with those states, it was later found necessary to create a small Palestine section within the General Department of the Colonial Office.

For records of First World War military operations and subsequent military administration see records of the War Office, especially WO 32, WO 95, WO 106 and WO 191.

The Palestine land registers of the British mandate and the Ottoman 'Tabu' registers have not been transferred to the United Kingdom. Where they survive they are to be found in the local land registries or the lands or surveyor's departments of the successor governments of Jordan and Israel.[12] See also under Middle East and Mediterranean.

Colonial Office

Palestine: Original Correspondence (CO 733) 1921–49, 495 volumes and boxes of files. See also Colonies General: Supplementary Original Correspondence (CO 537).[13]

Palestine: Register of Correspondence (CO 793) 1921–48, 49 volumes

Palestine: Register of Out-letters (CO 794) 1921–5, 4 volumes

Palestine: Acts (CO 765) 1921–45, 10 volumes

Palestine: Sessional Papers (CO 814) 1921–48, 41 volumes

Palestine: Government Gazettes (CO 742) 1919–48, 26 volumes

Palestine: Miscellanea (CO 821) 1926–45, 20 volumes of blue books of statistics

Palestine: Custodian of Enemy Property: Registered Files (CO 1044) 1939–52, 6 files

Colonial Office: Committee on Palestine Public Service (Supplementary Grants) Trust: Minutes (CO 1064) 1949–60, 1 volume

Government of Palestine War Medal List (CO 1065) *c.*1945 [records not transferred to TNA at the time of writing]

Foreign and Commonwealth Office

Foreign and Commonwealth Office and predecessors: Records of Former Colonial Administrations: Migrated Archives (FCO 141)

Foreign Office

During the period of the British mandate a joint responsibility for the territory was held by the Colonial Office – responsible for general administration – and the Foreign Office which liaised with the mandatory authorities. Relevant Foreign Office records for the period are held primarily in the series Foreign Office: Political Departments: General Correspondence 1906–66 (FO 371), as are those relating to Israel in the period from 1948.

Papua *see under* Papua New Guinea *and* British New Guinea

[12] Following the destruction of the Jerusalem District Land Registry Office in July 1944 it was decided to safeguard the surviving registers and associated papers by photographing them. Film was processed in the UK, but no copies were retained here and the current location of the films is unclear. It is possible that the following organisations may be able to help: Israel State Archives, http://www.archives.gov.il; United Nations Archives and Records Management Section (https://archives.un.org/content/united-nations-archives-and-records-management-section [accessed 28 Nov. 2014]); Institute for Palestine Studies, Beirut (http://www.palestine-studies.org [accessed 28 Nov. 2014]); Department of Lands and Survey, Amman, Aradi and Masaha Street, PO Box 70, Amman 11118, Jordan; Negotiations Affairs Department, Palestinian National Authority (http://www.nad-plo.org [accessed 28 Nov. 2014]).

[13] *Arab-Israeli Relations 1917–1970: the Middle East Online Series I* (London, 2007) which draws on CO 733 and CO 537, is available free of charge at TNA.

Papua New Guinea

Papua New Guinea was formed in 1945–6 when British New Guinea, known since 1906 as Papua, was united with the former German colony of New Guinea as a single territory of the Commonwealth of Australia. Military control of the territory was progressively withdrawn from 1946 and the civil administration restored. A partly elective Legislative Council was established in 1951, and replaced by a House of Assembly with a majority of elected members in 1963. Papua New Guinea became a fully independent state within the Commonwealth on 16 September 1975. See also under British New Guinea.

Dominions Office/Commonwealth Relations Office

New Guinea and Papua New Guinea: Government Gazettes (DO 85) 1926–75, 37 volumes

Penang (Pulau Pinang)

Penang consists of the island of Penang and Province Wellesley on the mainland of the Malaysian peninsula. It was one of the Straits Settlements which were incorporated into the Federation of Malaya, formed in 1948, and which became part of Malaysia in 1963. For correspondence and other records see under Straits Settlements.

Colonial Office

Penang: Government Gazettes (CO 933) 1948–77, 27 volumes

Pennsylvania *see under* America and West Indies

Perak

Perak was placed under British protection and received a British resident in 1874. In 1895 it was included in the Federated Malay States; supreme authority was vested in the sultan, who presided over the state council. Perak was under Japanese occupation from 1942 to 1945. After the British military occupation of 1945–6 it joined the Malayan Union as a separate state. For correspondence and other records see under Federated Malay States.

Colonial Office

Perak: Sessional Papers (CO 438) 1888–1939, 5 volumes

Perak: Government Gazettes (CO 467) 1888–1980, 56 volumes

Perim *see under* Aden

Perlis *see also* Kedah and Perlis

Colonial Office

Kedah and Perlis: Sessional Papers (CO 716) 1905–40, 4 volumes
Perlis: Government Gazettes (CO 931) 1948–77, 10 volumes

Persian Gulf

The British residency in the Persian Gulf and the agencies at Muscat, Kuwait, Bahrain, Qatar and Sharjah, Abu Dhabi and Dubai (the Trucial States, later United Arab Emirates) were responsible to the India Office until 1948, and records will be found at the British Library. Some of the papers in the series noted below pre-date the transfer of responsibility to the Foreign Office.

India Office/Foreign Office and successor

India Office and Successors: Political Residencies and Agencies, Persian Gulf: Correspondence and Papers (FO 1016) 1917–72, 920 volumes and files. Papers will also be found in FO 371, Foreign Office: Political Departments: General Correspondence 1906–66

Pitcairn Island

Pitcairn was first settled in 1790 by some of the HMS *Bounty* mutineers and their Tahitian companions. The island was left uninhabited between 1856 and 1859 when the entire population was resettled on Norfolk Island. The present population is descended from two parties who, not wishing to remain on Norfolk Island, returned to Pitcairn in 1859 and 1864 respectively. Pitcairn became a British settlement under the British Settlements Act of 1887, although the islanders usually date their recognition as a British territory to a constitution of 1838 devised with the help of a visiting Royal Navy officer. Pitcairn was administered by the high commissioner for the Western Pacific until 1952 when responsibility was transferred to the governor of Fiji. When Fiji became independent in 1970 the Pitcairn Royal Instructions established the office of governor. The island remains a British dependency (British Overseas Territory) with the full name of Pitcairn, Henderson, Ducie and Oeno Islands. In practice, the British high commissioner to New Zealand is appointed concurrently as governor (non-resident) of Pitcairn and is assisted by the Pitcairn Island Administration Office in Auckland. Pitcairn Islanders manage their internal affairs through an Island Council. For other records see under Western Pacific.

Colonial Office/Commonwealth Office and Foreign and Commonwealth Office

Pitcairn, Henderson, Ducie and Oeno Islands: Ordinances (CO 1052) 1966–8
Commonwealth Office and Foreign and Commonwealth Office: Pacific and Indian Ocean Department and Pacific Dependent Territories Department: Registered Files (FCO 32) 1967 onwards
Foreign and Commonwealth Office: Office of the Governor of Pitcairn, Ducie, Henderson and Oeno Islands: Registered Files (FCO 94) 1973 onwards

Pondoland

Pondoland was annexed to the Cape in 1894. It became part of the Transkei in 1976, and part of the Eastern Cape in 1994. For records see under Cape Colony. See also High Commissioner for South Africa, and High Commissioner for Basutoland, the Bechuanaland Protectorate and Swaziland, and UK High Commissioner for the Union of South Africa: Correspondence (DO 119).

Prince Edward Island

Prince Edward Island, first settled by the French and known by them as Île Saint-Jean, was taken by the British in 1758 and ceded to Britain in 1763 when it was annexed to Nova Scotia. It became a separate colony in 1769, and a province of the Dominion of Canada in 1873.

Colonial Office and predecessors

- **Prince Edward Island: Original Correspondence (CO 226)** 1769–1873, 111 volumes
- Prince Edward Island: Register of Correspondence (CO 364) 1850–73, 5 volumes (for registers before 1850 see CO 326)
- Index to Correspondence (CO 714/127–9) 1815–66
- Prince Edward Island: Entry Books (CO 227) 1769–1872, 12 volumes, including précis books
- Prince Edward Island: Acts (CO 228) 1770–1888, 31 volumes
- Prince Edward Island: Sessional Papers (CO 229) 1770–1925, 131 volumes
- Prince Edward Island: Government Gazettes (CO 230) 1832–1925, 20 volumes
- Prince Edward Island: Miscellanea (CO 231) 1807–71, 54 volumes, including shipping returns, blue books of statistics and newspapers (for a list of newspapers see appendix 3)

Dominions Office/Commonwealth Relations Office

- Prince Edward Island: Sessional Papers (DO 58) 1926–65, 43 volumes
- Prince Edward Island: Government Gazettes (DO 87) 1926–68, 16 volumes

Protectorate of South Arabia *see under* Aden

Protectorate of Southern Nigeria *see* Southern Nigeria

Province Wellesley *see under* Straits Settlements

Pulau Pinang *see* Penang

Quebec

In 1791 British North America was divided into two provinces, Upper Canada (now Ontario) and Lower Canada (now Quebec). In 1867 the British North America Act united the provinces of Ontario, Quebec, New Brunswick and Nova Scotia as the Dominion of Canada. For other records see under British North America and Canada.

Colonial Office

Quebec: Acts (CO 232) 1867–83, 13 volumes
Quebec: Sessional Papers (CO 233) 1867–1924, 248 volumes
Quebec: Government Gazettes (CO 602) 1905–25, 41 volumes
Quebec: Miscellanea (CO 722) 1919–21, 3 volumes of statistical yearbooks

Dominions Office/Commonwealth Relations Office/Commonwealth Office/Foreign and Commonwealth Office

Quebec: Sessional Papers (DO 94) 1920–65, 37 volumes
Quebec: Government Gazettes (DO 59) 1926–73, 186 volumes

Queensland

Queensland was first settled in 1824 from New South Wales. It became a separate colony in 1859 and an original state of the Commonwealth of Australia in 1901. For earlier records see under New South Wales; for later records see under Commonwealth of Australia.

Colonial Office

Queensland: Original Correspondence (CO 234) 1859–1900, 71 volumes
Queensland: Register of Correspondence (CO 424) 1859–1900, 8 volumes
Index to Correspondence (CO 714/130) 1859–66
Queensland: Entry Books (CO 423) 1859–73, 4 volumes
Queensland: Register of Out-letters (CO 450) 1873–1900, 2 volumes
Queensland: Acts (CO 235) 1860–1924, 32 volumes
Queensland: Sessional Papers (CO 236) 1860–1925, 288 volumes
Queensland: Government Gazettes (CO 237) 1859–1925, 125 volumes
Queensland: Miscellanea (CO 238) 1859–1920, 62 volumes of blue books of statistics

Dominions Office/Commonwealth Relations Office

Dominions Office and Commonwealth Relations Office: Original Correspondence (DO 35) 1915–71
Queensland: Acts (DO 60) 1925–60, 62 volumes
Queensland: Sessional Papers (DO 61) 1926–65, 105 volumes
Queensland: Government Gazettes (DO 62) 1926–80, 269 volumes
Queensland: Miscellanea (DO 103) 1925–50, 10 volumes of statistics

Reunion *see under* Mauritius

Rhode Island *see under* America and West Indies

Rhodesia

In 1889 the British South Africa Company was granted a royal charter to develop and administer Northern and Southern Rhodesia, and in 1890 Northern Rhodesia was declared a British protectorate. From 1890 to 1895 Northern Rhodesia and Nyasaland were under the commissioner for Nyasaland. In 1895 North-Eastern and North-Western Rhodesia were separated, with North-Eastern Rhodesia remaining under the commissioner for Nyasaland. In 1910 North-Eastern Rhodesia was placed under the high commissioner for South Africa, but the company's administrator retained executive powers. In 1911 North-Eastern and North-Western Rhodesia were united to form Northern Rhodesia. The following series of records consists of British South Africa Company reports on the administration of Rhodesia. See also under British South Africa Company, Northern Rhodesia, Southern Rhodesia and Federation of Rhodesia and Nyasaland.

Colonial Office

Rhodesia: Sessional Papers (CO 468) 1889–1902, 3 volumes

Rodrigues Island *see under* Mauritius

Royal West Africa Frontier Force *see* West Africa Frontier Force

Sabah *see* North Borneo

St Christopher (St Kitts)

St Christopher (St Kitts) was first settled by the English in 1623. In 1625 French settlers arrived and the island was divided between the two nations. The French portion (Saint-Christophe) was captured by Britain in 1702 and formally ceded in 1713. Recaptured by France in 1782, it was restored to Britain in 1783. It was part of the general government of the Caribbean Islands until 1671, when it was made part of the new government of the Leeward Islands. When this broke up in 1816 St Christopher (St Kitts), Nevis and the Virgin Islands formed a separate governmental unit, but in 1833 they were reunited with the other Leeward Islands under a governor-in-chief, and in 1871 the federal legislature was reconstituted. In 1882 St Christopher (St Kitts), Anguilla and Nevis were united in one presidency. On the dissolution of the Federation of the Leeward

Islands in 1956, St Christopher (St Kitts)-Nevis-Anguilla became a separate colony with its capital in St Christopher. From 1958 to 1962 the colony was a member state of the Federation of the West Indies. Britain assumed direct administrative responsibility for Anguilla in 1971 following disturbances there, and the island became (and remains) a separate British dependent territory (now UK Overseas Territory). The Federation of St Christopher (St Kitts) and Nevis achieved independence in 1983.

Colonial Office and predecessors

St Christopher (St Kitts), Nevis and Anguilla: Original Correspondence (CO 239) 1702–1872, 126 volumes (with the exception of the first volume, which covers the period 1702–1812, the series commences in 1816; for later correspondence see the **Leeward Islands series, CO 152**, which continues after 1951 in **West Indian Department: Registered Files (CO 1031)** 1948–67). Both CO 239 and CO 152 are registered in the Leeward Islands Register of Correspondence, CO 354, 1850–1951 (for registers before 1852 see CO 326).

Index to Correspondence (St Christopher (St Kitts), Nevis, Virgin Islands and Tortola) CO 714/131–3) 1815–66

St Christopher (St Kitts): Entry Books (CO 407) 1816–72, 15 volumes

St Christopher (St Kitts), Nevis and Anguilla: Acts (CO 240) 1672–1972, 37 volumes

St Christopher (St Kitts), Nevis and Anguilla: Sessional Papers (CO 241) 1704–1960, 69 volumes

St Christopher (St Kitts), Nevis and Anguilla: Government Gazettes (CO 242) 1879–1989, 53 volumes

St Christopher (St Kitts), Nevis and Anguilla: Miscellanea (CO 243) 1704–1887, 75 volumes, including papers relating to losses incurred in the French invasion of 1708, returns of stipendiary magistrates, and blue books of statistics

Commonwealth Office/Foreign and Commonwealth Office

Commonwealth Office: West Indian Department 'A' and Associated States Department: Registered Files, Antigua, Dominica, Grenada, St Christopher (St Kitts)-Nevis-Anguilla, St Lucia and St Vincent (FCO 43) 1967–8

Foreign and Commonwealth Office: North American and Caribbean Department and Caribbean Department: Registered Files (FCO 63) 1968 onwards

St Croix

St Croix (or Santa Cruz), one of the Virgin Islands, was jointly occupied by the British and Dutch in 1625. About 1645 the Dutch were ousted by the British, who were shortly afterwards expelled by the Spaniards. In 1650 a French settlement was established and in 1651 the island became French. In 1653 Louis XIV gave it to the knights of Malta, and in 1733 Denmark purchased it. From 1801 to 1802, and again from 1808 to 1815, it was in British hands after being captured. In 1917 the United States of America acquired it from the Danes.

Other correspondence for the periods of British administration will be found in the War Office series WO 1. See also under British Virgin Islands.

Colonial Office and predecessor

St Croix: Entry Books of Correspondence (CO 244) 1808–15, 10 volumes, including précis of correspondence and public accounts

St Eustatius

St Eustatius was settled by the Dutch West India Company after 1636, together with the neighbouring islands of St Martin and Saba. Britons, from Jamaica, captured it in 1665, but in 1666 they were driven out by the French and the island was restored to the Dutch. It was again captured by the British in 1672, but recaptured by the Dutch the following year. In 1781 the British recaptured it, but later in the same year the French captured it for the Dutch. It was taken by France in 1795 and was in British hands from 1801 to 1802 and from 1810 to 1815, before being restored to the Dutch.

Colonial Office and predecessors

St Eustatius: Original Correspondence (CO 246) 1779–83, 1 bundle (a considerable part of which consists of intercepted commercial correspondence)

St Helena and Dependencies

St Helena was annexed by the Dutch in 1633 but occupied by them only from 1645 to 1651 when the English East India Company occupied it. It was briefly recaptured by the Dutch in 1665 and again in 1673; when the Dutch were driven out in that latter year the East India Company was granted a charter to govern the island. From 1815 to 1821, during the period of Napoleon's exile there, it was directly administered by the British government and in 1834 the charter was surrendered to the Crown. Ascension became a dependency of St Helena in 1922, but the formal link was broken in 2002. Tristan da Cunha became a dependency of St Helena in 1938 and remained so until a new constitution dated 1 September 2009 created a single dependency of Saint Helena, Ascension and Tristan da Cunha giving the three islands equal status within the territory. St Helena also remains a British dependency (UK Overseas Territory). For correspondence before 1805 see the War Office series WO 1. There is a small amount of printed correspondence relating to St Helena in the Africa confidential print series CO 879. Records of the East India Company are at the British Library.

Colonial Office and predecessors

St Helena: Original Correspondence (CO 247) 1805–1951, 251 volumes, and boxes of files, continued in **Falkland Islands, St Helena, Tristan da Cunha and British Antarctica: Original Correspondence (CO 1024)** 1951–68. See also Colonies General: Supplementary

Original Correspondence (CO 537).

St Helena: Register of Correspondence (CO 366) 1849–1951, 20 volumes (for registers before 1849 see CO 326)

Index to Correspondence (CO 714/134–6) 1836–66

St Helena: Entry Books (CO 248) 1815–72, 18 volumes

St Helena: Register of Out-letters (CO 491) 1872–1926, 5 volumes

St Helena: Acts (CO 249) 1837–1969, 10 volumes

St Helena: Sessional Papers (CO 250) 1836–1965, 24 volumes

St Helena: Government Gazettes (CO 251) 1845–1965, 11 volumes

St Helena: Miscellanea (CO 252) 1836–1941, 106 volumes, including returns of Crown property (1839) and blue books of statistics

Commonwealth Office/Foreign and Commonwealth Office

Commonwealth Office and Foreign and Commonwealth Office: Gibraltar and South Atlantic Department: Registered Files (FCO 42) 1967–71

Foreign and Commonwealth Office, West Indian and Atlantic Department (FCO 44) 1972 onwards

Foreign and Commonwealth Office: Atlantic and Indian Ocean Department: Registered Files (FCO 83) 1970–2

St Kitts *see* St Christopher

St Lucia

St Lucia was temporarily settled by the English in 1605, and its possession subsequently disputed between Britain and France until it was ultimately ceded to Britain in 1814. In 1838 it was incorporated within the Windward Islands government. In 1956 the government of the Windward Islands was abolished and four separate colonies, including St Lucia, were established under one governor. This post was abolished in 1960 and a new constitution was introduced in each of the territories, providing for a large measure of internal self-government. On 22 February 1979 St Lucia became a fully independent member state of the Commonwealth.

Colonial Office and predecessors

St Lucia: Original Correspondence (CO 253) 1709–1873, 150 volumes (with the exception of the first volume which includes papers dated from 1709 the series commences in 1798), continued in **Windward Islands: Original Correspondence (CO 321)** 1874–1951 and then in **West Indian Department: Registered Files (CO 1031)** 1948–67. See also Colonies General: Supplementary Original Correspondence (CO 537).

St Lucia: Register of Correspondence (CO 367) 1850–81, 5 volumes (for registers before 1850 see CO 326; registers after 1881 are in the Windward Islands series CO 376)

Index to Correspondence (CO 714/137–9) 1816–52

St Lucia: Entry Books (CO 254) 1794–1872, 19 volumes, including précis books
St Lucia: Register of Out-letters (CO 505) 1872–82
St Lucia: Acts (CO 255) 1818–1965, 25 volumes
St Lucia: Sessional Papers (CO 256) 1820–1965, 66 volumes
St Lucia: Government Gazettes (CO 257) 1857–1975, 125 volumes
St Lucia: Miscellanea (CO 258) 1722–1940, 136 volumes, including memoranda on various subjects, returns of protectors of slaves, returns of stipendiary magistrates, blue books of statistics and newspapers (for a list of newspapers see appendix 3)

Commonwealth Office/Foreign and Commonwealth Office

Commonwealth Office: West Indian Department 'A' and Associated States Department: Registered Files, Antigua, Dominica, Grenada, St Christopher (St Kitts)-Nevis-Anguilla, St Lucia and St Vincent (FCO 43) 1967–8
Foreign and Commonwealth Office: North American and Caribbean Department and Caribbean Department: Registered Files (FCO 63) 1968 onwards

St Thomas

St Thomas, one of the Virgin Islands, was captured by Britain in 1663, and recognised as British in 1667, but it was never fully settled and became Danish in 1671. It was in British hands again in 1801, and from 1807 to 1815. It was then restored to Denmark, from whom the United States of America purchased it in 1917. The following records include shipping returns and accounts of the Danish and Dutch loan commissioners. The accounts of the commissioners for liquidating the Danish and Dutch loans for St Thomas and the neighbouring island of St John are in the War Office series WO 1. See also under British Virgin Islands.

Colonial Office and predecessor

St Thomas: Entry Books of Correspondence, etc. (CO 259) 1808–15, 6 volumes

St Vincent

St Vincent remained a refuge of the Caribs long after the settlement of its neighbours. It was granted to a proprietor by Charles I in 1627, but remained unoccupied by Europeans. With French agreement it was declared neutral in 1660, but in 1672 it was granted to a proprietor by Charles II although still not settled. Later there were some French settlements, and disputes between Britain and France, until it was again declared neutral in 1748. It was captured by Britain in 1762, ceded to her in 1763 and thereafter settled. Captured by France in 1779, it was restored to Britain in 1783. From 1763 until 1776, and again from 1833, it formed part of the Windward Islands government. In 1956 the Windward Islands grouping was dissolved and four separate colonies, including St Vincent, were established under one governor. From 1958 to 1962 St Vincent was a member of the Federation of the West Indies. In 1960 the post of governor of the

Windward Islands was abolished, and St Vincent again became a separate colony. The territory of St Vincent, which includes the islands which make up the Northern Grenadines, became an independent member state of the Commonwealth on 27 October 1979 under the name of St Vincent and the Grenadines. See also under West Indies.

Colonial Office and predecessors

St Vincent: Original Correspondence (CO 260) 1668–1873, 118 volumes (with the exception of volume 3, which consists of papers dated between 1668 and 1812, the series commences in 1773). Correspondence from 1873 to 1951 will be found in the **Windward Islands Original Correspondence (CO 321)** and is continued thereafter in **West Indian Department: Registered Files (WIS series) (CO 1031)** 1948–67. See also Colonies General: Supplementary Original Correspondence (CO 537).

Correspondence dated to 1849 is registered in CO 326, and after that date in the Windward Islands Register of Correspondence (CO 376) 1850–1951.

Index to Correspondence (CO 714/140–2) 1815–70

St Vincent: Entry Books (CO 261) 1776–1872, 24 volumes, including précis books

St Vincent: Register of Out-letters (CO 506) 1872–82, 3 volumes

St Vincent: Acts (CO 262) 1768–1969, 37 volumes

St Vincent: Sessional Papers (CO 263) 1769–1965, 92 volumes

St Vincent: Government Gazettes (CO 264) 1831–1975, 82 volumes

St Vincent: Miscellanea (CO 265) 1763–1941, 121 volumes, including shipping returns, returns of stipendiary magistrates and blue books of statistics.

Commonwealth Office/Foreign and Commonwealth Office

Commonwealth Office: West Indian Department 'A' and Associated States Department: Registered Files, Antigua, Dominica, Grenada, St Christopher (St Kitts)-Nevis-Anguilla, St Lucia and St Vincent (WA series) (FCO 43) 1967–8

Commonwealth Office: West Indian Department 'B' and Foreign and Commonwealth Office, West Indian Department: Registered Files, Smaller Commonwealth West Indian Territories (WB and HW series) (FCO 44) 1967 onwards

Foreign and Commonwealth Office: North American and Caribbean Department and Caribbean Department: Registered Files (AN series) (FCO 63) 1968 onwards

Samoa *see* Western Samoa

Santa Cruz *see* St Croix

Santo Domingo (Dominican Republic)

The Spanish island of Hispaniola (Española) was divided into French Saint-Domingue (later Haiti) and Spanish Santo Domingo in 1697. In 1801 Haitian forces occupied Santo Domingo, but it was returned to Spain in 1808. In 1822 Haitians unified the whole island, but inhabitants of Santo Domingo claimed independence in 1844 and adopted a republican constitution. From 1793 to 1798 Santo Domingo had a British governor with executive powers, aided by a consultative council. The records in CO 245 include entry books, précis books, accounts and miscellanea. Other records relating to Santo Domingo will be found in the War Office series WO 1, and in the Treasury series T 81 (Santo Domingo Claims Committee, 1794–1812). Later records relating to the Dominican Republic are in Foreign Office series, mainly FO 23 and FO 140. In 2010 a visiting post-graduate researcher at TNA discovered a copy of the original Haitian declaration of independence (1804) in the Jamaica volume of correspondence CO 137/111 (for a copy, see http://www.nationalarchives.gov.uk/dol/images/examples/haiti/0001.pdf)

War and Colonial Department and predecessors

Santo Domingo: Original Correspondence, etc. (CO 245) 1693–1805, 10 volumes.

Sarawak

Sarawak was a province of the Sultanate of Brunei until 1839, when James Brooke put down a revolt and in return was made rajah in 1841. It was recognised as an independent state by Britain in 1864 and was granted British protection in 1888. It was under Japanese occupation from 1941 to 1945 and British military administration from 1945 to 1946 (see the War Office series WO 203), and became a British colony in 1946.

During the post-war period matters common to Sarawak, Brunei and North Borneo were dealt with by a UK commissioner for South East Asia appointed to ensure co-ordination of policy in the area under British control. These records are in CO 954 and CO 992 (see under Far East/South East Asia). Following the Cobbold Commission's enquiry into possible political association, Sarawak and North Borneo (Sabah) joined Singapore and the Federation of Malaya on 16 September 1963 to form the independent federation thereafter called Malaysia. For other records before 1946 see series listed under British North Borneo.

Colonial Office

Sarawak: Original Correspondence (CO 938) 1946–51, 12 files

Sarawak: Acts (CO 1020) 1958–63, 4 volumes

Sarawak: Sessional Papers (CO 802) 1900–65, 24 volumes

Sarawak: Government Gazettes (CO 604) 1903–80, 115 volumes

The Rajah of Sarawak Fund: Papers (CO 1040) [records not transferred to TNA at the time of writing]

See also:

Borneo Territories: Original Correspondence (CO 954) 1946–51, 8 boxes of files

North Borneo, Brunei and Sarawak: Registers of Correspondence (CO 992) 1942–51, 6 volumes

Commission of Enquiry in North Borneo and Sarawak Regarding Malaysian Federation (Cobbold Commission, 1962) (CO 947) 1962, 61 files

Foreign and Commonwealth Office and predecessors
Records of Former Colonial Administrations: Migrated Archives (FCO 141)

Saskatchewan

In 1882 Canada's Northwest Territory was divided into four districts: Athabasca, Alberta, Saskatchewan and Assiniboia (where the capital, Regina, was located). Constitutional change coupled with demands for increased autonomy and provincial status resulted, on 1 September 1905, in the creation of the new provinces of Alberta and Saskatchewan which formed part of the Dominion of Canada. For correspondence and other records see under Canada.

Colonial Office
Saskatchewan: Sessional Papers (CO 606) 1906–21, 9 volumes
Saskatchewan: Government Gazettes (CO 605) 1905–25, 19 volumes

Dominions Office/Commonwealth Relations Office
Saskatchewan: Sessional Papers (DO 90) 1923–65, 37 volumes
Saskatchewan: Government Gazettes (DO 66) 1926–66, 42 volumes

Selangor

Selangor, previously part of Perak, became independent early in the 18th century but came under Dutch suzerainty in 1782. In 1874 it was placed under British protection and received a British resident. In 1895 it was included in the Federated Malay States but supreme authority was vested in the sultan who presided over the state council. It was under Japanese occupation from 1942 to 1945. After the British military administration of 1945–6 (see WO 203) it joined the short-lived Malayan Union as a separate state and in 1948 it became part of the new Federation of Malaya. In 1963 the federation joined with Sabah, Sarawak and Singapore to form Malaysia.

Colonial Office
Selangor: Sessional Papers (CO 439) 1888–1941, 5 volumes
Selangor: Government Gazettes (CO 469) 1890–1975, 41 volumes

Senegambia *see under* Gambia

Seychelles

The Seychelles Islands were annexed by the French in 1756 and conquered by the British in 1794. They were reconquered for the sixth time by Britain in 1810 and formally annexed in

1814. From 1811 the islands were administered by an agent as a dependency of Mauritius, but the connection with Mauritius was gradually loosened and in 1903 Seychelles became a separate colony. On 29 June 1976 Seychelles became an independent republic within the Commonwealth. For correspondence between 1887 and 1903 see under Mauritius; see also under British Indian Ocean Territory, Western Pacific and Far East/South East Asia.

Colonial Office

Seychelles: Original Correspondence (CO 530) 1904–51, 782 volumes and boxes of files, continued in **Hong Kong and Pacific Department: Original Correspondence (CO 1023)** 1946–55, and **Pacific and Indian Ocean Department: Registered Files (PAC series) (CO 1036)** 1952–67. See also Colonies General: Supplementary Original Correspondence (CO 537).

Seychelles: Register of Correspondence (CO 712) 1904–48, 11 volumes

Seychelles: Register of Out-letters (CO 768) 1904–25, 2 volumes

Seychelles: Acts (CO 266) 1889–1965, 11 volumes

Seychelles: Sessional Papers (CO 440) 1889–1965, 40 volumes

Seychelles: Government Gazettes (CO 470) 1889–1976, 59 volumes

Seychelles: Miscellanea (CO 471) 1899–1939, 41 volumes of blue books of statistics

Commonwealth Office/Foreign and Commonwealth Office

Commonwealth Office and Foreign and Commonwealth Office: Pacific and Indian Ocean Department and Pacific Dependent Territories Department: Registered Files (Q and HP series) (FCO 32) 1967 onwards

Commonwealth Office and Foreign and Commonwealth Office: Pacific and Indian Ocean Department and Pacific Dependent Territories Department: Registered Files (Q and HP series) (FCO 40) 1965 onwards

Foreign and Commonwealth Office: Atlantic and Indian Ocean Department: Registered Files (HG series) (FCO 83) 1970–2

Foreign and Commonwealth Office and predecessors: Records of Former Colonial Administrations: Migrated Archives (FCO 141)

Sierra Leone

A British trading station was established on the coast of Sierra Leone in 1672. In 1788 part of the territory was sold and ceded to newly arrived British settlers, most of African descent, and additional territory was ceded to the colony from time to time by local rulers. From 1791 Sierra Leone was administered by the Sierra Leone Company and additional settlers arrived including Maroons from Jamaica and re-captives from slave ships. Sierra Leone became a colony in 1808. Its administrative responsibilities encompassed Gambia from 1821 to 1843, and the Gold Coast from 1821 to 1850. In 1866 the governor of Sierra Leone became governor-in-chief of the West African Settlements of Sierra Leone, Gambia, the Gold Coast and Lagos, with headquarters in Sierra Leone; each colony retained its own Legislative Council. In 1874 Lagos and the Gold Coast were separated, as was Gambia in 1888, leaving Sierra Leone a single colony again. In 1896 the hinterland was declared a protectorate. Sierra Leone became a fully independent member of the Commonwealth on 27 April 1961, and a republic on 19 April 1971.

Correspondence relating to Sierra Leone includes Fernando Po before 1828 and after 1842; Goree, Cape Coast Castle and Gambia before 1828; and the Gold Coast before 1843. Correspondence with the Sierra Leone Company, 1800–7, is in the War Office series WO 1. Documents relating to the Committee for the Relief of the Black Poor, which organised the first settlement, can be found in the Treasury series T 1. See also under West Africa and West African Settlements.

Colonial Office and predecessors

Sierra Leone: Original Correspondence (CO 267) 1664–1951, 702 volumes and boxes of files (with the exception of CO 267/5 which includes papers dating from 1664 to 1752 the series starts in 1753). After 1951 correspondence is in **West Africa Original Correspondence (CO 554)** 1911–65. See also Colonies General: Supplementary Original Correspondence (CO 537).

Sierra Leone: Register of Correspondence (CO 368) 1849–1951, 42 volumes (for registers before 1849 see CO 326)

Index to Correspondence (CO 714/143–7) 1815–66

Sierra Leone: Register of Out-letters (CO 484) 1872–1926, 13 volumes

Sierra Leone: Entry Books (CO 268) 1672–1872, 57 volumes

Sierra Leone: Acts (CO 269) 1801–1961, 21 volumes

Sierra Leone: Sessional Papers (CO 270) 1776–1965, 104 volumes

Sierra Leone: Government Gazettes (CO 271) 1817–1975, 114 volumes

Sierra Leone: Miscellanea (CO 272) 1819–1943, 120 volumes of blue books of statistics

Sierra Leone: Board of Education (CO 672) 1899–1900, 1 volume

Commonwealth Relations Office/Commonwealth Office/Foreign and Commonwealth Office

Commonwealth Relations Office and Commonwealth Office: West and General Africa Department and Successors: Registered Files (WA series) (DO 195) 1960–7

Commonwealth Relations Office and Commonwealth Office: West Africa Economic Department and Successors: Registered Files, West Africa Economic (WAE series) (DO 221) 1964–7

Commonwealth Relations Office and Successors: High Commission and Consular Archives, Sierra Leone: Registered Files (DO 223) 1961 onwards

Commonwealth Office: West and General Africa Department: Registered Files, Commonwealth Africa, General African Affairs and the Organisation of African Unity (T series) (FCO 38) 1967–8

Foreign and Commonwealth Office: West African Department: Registered Files (JW series) (FCO 65) 1968 onwards

Foreign and Commonwealth Office and predecessors: Records of Former Colonial Administrations: Migrated Archives (FCO 141)

Singapore

A British settlement was founded at Singapore in 1819 under an agreement with the sultan of Johore initiated by Sir Stamford Raffles. It became part of the Straits Settlements in 1826. Initially under the control of the East India Company and subsequently the India Office it became a Colonial Office responsibility in 1867. The colony of the Straits Settlements was dissolved in 1946, and Singapore, the Cocos (Keeling) Islands and Christmas Island were united to form the separate colony of Singapore. At the same time Labuan, which had been united with Singapore, was detached and became part of the colony of British North Borneo. The Cocos (Keeling) Islands and Christmas Island were later transferred to Australia in 1955 and 1958 respectively. After the end of the war with Japan, a short period of military administration (see the War Office series WO 203) was followed by the restoration of civil government. A new constitution conferring full internal self-government and the title State of Singapore was introduced in 1959. Singapore became a member state of Malaysia when the latter was formed on 16 September 1963, but separated from Malaysia on 9 August 1965 to become an independent sovereign state within the Commonwealth.

East India Company/India Office

Records at the British Library

Colonial Office

Singapore: Original Correspondence (CO 953) 1936–51, 53 boxes of files.

Earlier correspondence and some from 1946 relating to the then new colony of Singapore will be found in the original correspondence series of the Straits Settlements (CO 273) and the Federated Malay States (CO 717).

Singapore: Register of Correspondence (CO 1010) 1946–51, 5 volumes

Singapore: Acts (CO 925) 1946–59, 12 volumes

Singapore: Sessional Papers (CO 940) 1946–65, 175 volumes

Singapore: Government Gazettes (CO 932) 1945–70, 123 volumes

Singapore: Miscellanea (CO 939) 1946, 1 blue book of statistics

Commonwealth Relations Office/Commonwealth Office/Foreign and Commonwealth Office

Dominions Office and Commonwealth Relations Office: Original Correspondence (DO 35) 1915–71

Commonwealth Relations Office and Successors: High Commission, Singapore: Registered Files (DO 228) 1965–71

Commonwealth Relations Office and Commonwealth Office: Far East and Pacific Department: Registered Files (FE series) (DO 169) 1960–7

Foreign Office and Foreign and Commonwealth Office: South East Asian Department: Registered Files (D and FA series) (FCO 15) 1967 onwards

Commonwealth Office, Far East and Pacific Department and Foreign and Commonwealth Office, South West Pacific Department: Registered Files (H and FW series) (FCO 24) 1967 onwards

Foreign and Commonwealth Office and predecessors: Records of Former Colonial Administrations: Migrated Archives (FCO 141). This series includes files relating to the various Malay states.

Solomon Islands *see* British Solomon Islands Protectorate

Somalia *see* British Somaliland

Somaliland *see* British Somaliland

Somers Islands *see* Bermuda

South Africa

In 1889 a customs union was established between Cape Colony and the Orange Free State. It was joined by Natal in 1898, and by Transvaal, Southern Rhodesia, Basutoland and Bechuanaland in 1903. In the same year an Intercolonial Council representative of the Transvaal and the Orange River Colony (the former Orange Free State) was set up to oversee the financial administration of the railways and the constabulary, as well as other expenditure common to the two territories. CO 549 consists of the minutes of the Executive and Public Sessions and Railway Committees together with papers laid before them. The Board of Control for Railways was a financial body. The tour of South Africa by Joseph Chamberlain, secretary of state for the colonies, provided a stimulus for these developments towards complete union. As union approached, the Intercolonial Council was dissolved in 1908. From 1910 see under Union of South Africa; see also under individual colonies.

Colonial Office

South Africa: Customs Union (CO 547) 1906–9, 4 volumes
South African Constabulary: Original Correspondence (CO 526) 1902–8, 8 volumes
South African Constabulary: Register of Correspondence (CO 639) 1902–8, 2 volumes
South African Constabulary: Register of Out-letters (CO 640) 1902–8, 2 volumes
South Africa: Intercolonial Council: Original Correspondence (CO 527) 1904–8, 16 volumes
South Africa: Intercolonial Council: Register of Correspondence (CO 634) 1904–8, 2 volumes
South Africa: Intercolonial Council: Register of Out-letters (CO 635) 1904–8, 2 volumes
South Africa: Intercolonial Council, Transvaal and Orange River Colony (CO 549) 1903–8, 11 volumes
South Africa: Railways Original Correspondence (CO 528) 1902–3, 7 volumes
South Africa: Railways Register of Correspondence (CO 636) 1903, 1 volume
South Africa: Railways Register of Out-letters (CO 637) 1903, 1 volume
South Africa: Secretary of State's Tour Original Correspondence (CO 529) 1902–3, 1 volume
South Africa: Secretary of State's Tour Register of Correspondence (CO 638) 1902–3, 1 volume

South Africa High Commission

The British High Commission in southern Africa dates from 1845 when the governor of the Cape Colony was appointed as high commissioner with responsibility for relations with the territories in southern Africa not administered by Britain. The office continued to be held by the governor of the Cape until 1901 when it remained with Lord Milner on his move from the governorship of the Cape to that of the Transvaal. It was reorganised in 1878 under the title of high commissioner in and for South Africa. The incumbent was then formally charged with conducting relations with the South African Republic (the Transvaal) and the Orange Free State, when these states were independent, and with the African states and tribes, as they then were, that lay in southern Africa outside Cape Colony and Natal. At various times the high commissioner was responsible for British Bechuanaland, Pondoland, Basutoland, the Bechuanaland Protectorate and Swaziland, as well as relations with the British South Africa Company and the Portuguese and German territories. When the Union of South Africa became a republic in 1961 the High Commission's remaining responsibilities – for the so-called High Commission Territories of Basutoland, Bechuanaland and Swaziland – were transferred to the Colonial Office. Some of the internal records of the High Commission are in the record series DO 119; others remain in southern Africa.

Colonial Office

South Africa: Original Correspondence (CO 417) 1884–1925, 716 volumes, continued in Dominions: Original Correspondence (CO 532) 1907–25. See also Colonies General: Supplementary Original Correspondence (CO 537).
South Africa: Register of Correspondence (CO 545) 1884–1927, 27 volumes
South Africa: Register of Out-letters (CO 546) 1884–1928, 15 volumes
South Africa: Proclamations (CO 550) 1906–23, 7 volumes
South Africa: Government Gazettes (CO 548) 1901–22, 3 volumes
Colonial Office and Commonwealth Office: Southern Africa Department: Original Correspondence (CO 1048) 1960–8, 966 files. The series includes files from the BBS file series which are otherwise to be found in DO 157.

Dominions Office/Commonwealth Relations Office/Commonwealth Office

South Africa High Commission: Original Correspondence (DO 9) 1926–9, 15 volumes
South Africa High Commission: Proclamations (DO 10) 1924–61, 33 volumes
South Africa High Commission: Register of Correspondence (DO 1) 1928–9, 1 volume
South Africa High Commission: Register of Out-letters (DO 2) 1929, 1 volume
South Africa High Commission: Government Gazettes (DO 91) 1923–60, 8 volumes
South Africa High Commission: Agreements and Treaties (DO 141) 1881–1920, 17 files
Dominions Office and Commonwealth Relations Office: Original Correspondence (DO 35) 1915–71
High Commissioner for South Africa, and High Commissioner for Basutoland, the Bechuanaland Protectorate and Swaziland, and UK High Commissioner in the Union of South Africa: Correspondence (DO 119) 1843–1965, 1479 volumes and boxes of files

Commonwealth Relations Office: South Africa High Commission Territories: Registered Files (BBS series) (DO 157) 1959–63, 66 files
Commonwealth Office: East Africa Department: Registered Files, Botswana, Lesotho and Swaziland (BLS, SAB, SAR and SAS series) 1966–7, 14 files

South Africa High Commission Territories *see under* Basutoland, Bechuanaland Protectorate *and* Swaziland

South Arabia *see under* **Aden**

South Australia

South Australia was established as a colony in 1836 under a charter granted to the South Australian Association, but in 1841 the charter was suspended. South Australia then became a Crown colony. In 1901 it became an original state of the Commonwealth of Australia.

Colonial Office and predecessor

South Australia: Original Correspondence (CO 13) 1831–1900, 155 volumes
South Australia: Register of Correspondence (CO 331) 1849–1900, 12 volumes (for registers before 1849 see CO 326)
South Australia: Register of Out-letters (CO 514) 1873–1900, 2 volumes
Index to Correspondence (CO 714/7–10) 1835–66
South Australia: Entry Books (CO 396) 1834–73, 16 volumes
South Australia: Acts (CO 14) 1842–1925, 28 volumes
South Australia: Sessional Papers (CO 15) 1836–1925, 226 volumes
South Australia: Government Gazettes (CO 16) 1839–1925, 135 volumes
South Australia: Miscellanea (CO 17) 1836–1925, 101 volumes, including blue books and statistics and newspapers (for a list of newspapers see appendix 3)
South Australia: Public Service Lists (CO 695) 1918–20, 3 volumes

Dominions Office/Commonwealth Relations Office/Commonwealth Office/Foreign and Commonwealth Office

South Australia: Sessional Papers (DO 19) 1857–1966, 77 volumes
South Australia: Government Gazettes (DO 20) 1926–80, 135 volumes
South Australia: Miscellanea (DO 21) 1925–50, 17 volumes of blue books and statistical registers
South Australia: Acts (DO 80) 1926–65, 19 volumes

South Carolina *see under* America and West Indies

South East Asia *see under* Far East/South East Asia

South Pacific

A South Pacific Commission was established in 1947, by agreement between the governments of Australia, France, The Netherlands, New Zealand, the United Kingdom and the United States of America, to act as a consultative and advisory body in matters affecting the economic and social development of non-self governing territories in the South Pacific. Annual sessions of the commission were held at its headquarters in Noumea, New Caledonia; in framing its working programmes, it was assisted by annual meetings of a Research Council, and triennial meetings of a conference of territorial delegates. The governor of Fiji acted as first UK commissioner, and a full time official as second commissioner, with an office in Fiji. Since 1997 the commission has been known as the South Pacific Community.

Colonial Office

Fiji: South Pacific Office: Original Correspondence (CO 1009) 1940–70, 817 files. This series contains files of the British commissioners on the South Pacific Commission and includes records of the South Pacific Commission Research Council and the British Fiji Office.

South West Africa (Namibia)

A German protectorate from 1880, South West Africa was taken by forces from the Union of South Africa in 1915, and subsequently administered by South Africa under a League of Nations mandate. After the Second World War, South Africa's intention to incorporate South West Africa into the Union was challenged by the United Nations, which terminated the mandate in 1966. One year later, the name of the territory was changed to Namibia, and in 1971 the International Court of Justice ruled that South Africa's presence in the territory was illegal. South Africa ignored these rulings, and it was not until 21 March 1990 that Namibia became independent and joined the Commonwealth. For other records see under South Africa.

Colonial Office

South West Africa: Government Gazettes (CO 738) 1915–25, 2 volumes

Dominions Office/Commonwealth Relations Office

Dominions Office and Commonwealth Relations Office: Original Correspondence (DO 35) 1915–71

South West Africa: Government Gazettes (DO 78) 1926–68, 56 volumes

South West Africa Sessional Papers (DO 110) 1931–46, 1 volume

High Commissioner for South Africa, and High Commissioner for Basutoland, the Bechuanaland Protectorate and Swaziland, and UK High Commissioner for the Union of South Africa: Correspondence (DO 119)

Foreign Office/Commonwealth Office/Foreign and Commonwealth Office

Foreign Office: West and Central African Department: Registered Files (J series) (FCO 25) 1967–8

Commonwealth Office and Foreign and Commonwealth Office: Southern African Department and Predecessors: Registered Files (SAD and CS series) (FCO 45) 1967 onwards

Southern Nigeria

The Royal Niger Company was established in 1886 and was empowered to administer the Niger delta area; thereafter it gradually extended its jurisdiction northwards. In 1899 its charter was surrendered to the Crown and in 1900 the southern portion of its territories was united with the Niger Coast Protectorate to form the Protectorate of Southern Nigeria under a high commissioner.[14] In 1906 this territory was combined with Lagos to form the Colony and Protectorate of Southern Nigeria. In 1914 it was amalgamated with Northern Nigeria to form the Colony and Protectorate of Nigeria.

Colonial Office

Southern Nigeria: Original Correspondence (CO 520) 1900–13, 131 volumes
Southern Nigeria: Register of Correspondence (CO 589) 1899–1913, 8 volumes
Southern Nigeria: Register of Out-letters (CO 590) 1899–1913, 6 volumes
Southern Nigeria: Acts (CO 588) 1900–13, 4 volumes
Southern Nigeria: Sessional Papers (CO 592) 1906–13, 16 volumes
Southern Nigeria: Government Gazettes (CO 591) 1900–13, 12 volumes
Southern Nigeria: Miscellanea (CO 473) 1900–13, 16 volumes of blue books of statistics

Southern Rhodesia (Zimbabwe)

Southern Rhodesia came under British protection in 1888 and the following year the British South Africa Company was granted a charter to develop and administer the territory. In 1891 an administrator, nominated by the company, was appointed. His position was reinforced in 1896 by a resident commissioner appointed by the British government. In 1898 Southern Rhodesia was placed under the supervision of the high commissioner for South Africa, although retaining the post of resident commissioner. In 1923 the territory was annexed to the Crown. On 3 September 1953 Southern Rhodesia joined with Northern Rhodesia and Nyasaland to form the Federation of Rhodesia and Nyasaland; the federation was dissolved on 31 December 1963.

In 1965, after inconclusive discussions on independence, the Southern Rhodesia government made a unilateral and unconstitutional declaration of independence (UDI), and in 1970 declared

[14] Records of the Royal Niger Company are held at the Unilever Archives and Records Management, PO Box 69, Port Sunlight, CH62 4ZD, England; and among the Commonwealth and African Collections at the Bodleian Library, University of Oxford (formerly at Rhodes House Library).

the country a republic. No country in the world recognised Southern Rhodesia's self-asserted status and sanctions were invoked by the United Nations. Constitutional talks between the white minority government, the British government and the nationalist groups in the African National Council continued until 1975. They failed to agree proposals for a settlement that met all the requirements laid down by the British government for the grant of legal independence. A new government of Zimbabwe Rhodesia took office on 1 June 1979, but guerrilla activity by the main nationalist groups continued. Against this background the Commonwealth heads of government met in Lusaka, Zambia, in August 1979, and as a result of agreement reached there a constitutional conference was held at Lancaster House in London in September–December 1979. The Lancaster House agreements were signed on 21 December 1979 and Southern Rhodesia became independent as Zimbabwe on 18 April 1980. Zimbabwe was suspended from the Commonwealth in 2002 and withdrew voluntarily the following year. See also under British South Africa Company, Rhodesia, South Africa High Commission and Federation of Rhodesia and Nyasaland.

Colonial Office

Southern Rhodesia: Original Correspondence (CO 767) 1923–5, 5 volumes. See also Colonies General: Supplementary Original Correspondence (CO 537).
Southern Rhodesia: Register of Correspondence (CO 800) 1923–6, 1 volume
Southern Rhodesia: Register of Out-letters (CO 801) 1923–6, 1 volume
Southern Rhodesia: Acts (CO 671) 1901–25, 4 volumes
Southern Rhodesia: Sessional Papers (CO 603) 1896–1925, 30 volumes
Southern Rhodesia: Government Gazettes (CO 815) 1923–5, 1 volume

Dominions Office/Commonwealth Relations Office

Southern Rhodesia: Original Correspondence (DO 63) 1926–9, 6 volumes
Dominions Office and Commonwealth Relations Office: Original Correspondence (DO 35) 1915–71
Southern Rhodesia: Register of Correspondence (DO 7) 1927–9, 1 volume
Southern Rhodesia: Register of Out-letters (DO 8) 1927–9, 1 volume
Southern Rhodesia: Acts (DO 88) 1926–66, 26 volumes
Southern Rhodesia: Sessional Papers (DO 64) 1926–66, 102 volumes
Southern Rhodesia: Government Gazettes (DO 65) 1926–75, 109 volumes
Miscellaneous Seals (DO 122) 1952–65, 2 steel matrices for the seal of Southern Rhodesia, with copper counterparts
Commonwealth Relations Office: Rhodesia Department: Registered Files (RCA series) (DO 207) 1965–6, 345 files

Commonwealth Office/Foreign and Commonwealth Office

Commonwealth Office and Foreign and Commonwealth Office: Rhodesia Economic Department: Registered Files (RE and CM series) (FCO 35) 1967–73, 517 files
Commonwealth Office and Foreign and Commonwealth Office: Rhodesia Political Department: Registered Files (RP and CP series) (FCO 36) 1967 onwards
Many other series of FCO records include material relating to Rhodesia and UDI, reflecting the international dimensions of the debates on the constitutional development of the country. They can be easily identified through the online catalogue.

Foreign and Commonwealth Office and predecessors: Records of Former Colonial Administrations: Migrated Archives (FCO 141, 15 references only)

Sri Lanka *see* Ceylon

Straits Settlements

Penang was ceded to the East India Company in 1786 and Province Wellesley was acquired by the company in 1800. Malacca was captured from the Dutch in 1795, returned to them in 1818 and ceded to Britain in 1824. In the same year Singapore was recognised as British. In 1826 Singapore, Malacca and Penang (including Province Wellesley) became a Crown colony under the name Straits Settlements; they were transferred from the control of the India Office to that of the Colonial Office in 1867. The Cocos (Keeling) Islands joined them in 1886 (having been proclaimed a British possession in 1857 and placed under the governor of Ceylon in 1878), Christmas Island in 1900, and Labuan in 1907. The Straits Settlements were occupied by the Japanese from 1942 to 1945 and under British military administration from 1945 to 1946 (see WO 203). In 1946 they were dissolved: Malacca and Penang joined the Malayan Union; Singapore, the Cocos (Keeling) Islands and Christmas Island united to form the colony of Singapore; and Labuan joined the colony of North Borneo. See also under the individual settlements.

Colonial Office and predecessor

Straits Settlements: Original Correspondence (CO 273) 1838–1946, 680 volumes and boxes of files. The first six volumes consist of miscellaneous reports and correspondence transferred from the India Office to the Colonial Office in 1876. See also Colonies General: Supplementary Original Correspondence (CO 537).

Straits Settlements: Register of Correspondence (CO 426) 1867–1945, 42 volumes

Straits Settlements: Register of Out-letters (CO 486) 1873–1926, 17 volumes

Straits Settlements: Entry Books (CO 425) 1867–73, 8 volumes

Straits Settlements: Acts (CO 274) 1867–1949, 23 volumes

Straits Settlements: Sessional Papers (CO 275) 1855–1940, 155 volumes

Straits Settlements: Government Gazettes (CO 276) 1867–1942, 161 volumes

Straits Settlements: Miscellanea (CO 277) 1867–1939, 91 volumes of blue books of statistics

Sudan

Sudan was conquered by the khedive of Egypt in a series of campaigns culminating in 1821/2, and administered by Egypt until 1881 when the Mahdist forces drove out the Egyptians and their British supporters. In 1898 British and Egyptian forces reoccupied Sudan and an Anglo-Egyptian condominium was established the following year whereby Sudan was to be autonomous under a governor-general appointed by the khedive on the recommendation of Britain. Britain's relations with Sudan were the responsibility of the Foreign Office both before and after independence (in 1956) and the presence of a series of government gazettes among the Colonial Office records is unexplained. For records of military campaigns see War Office records, especially WO 32, WO 106 and the map series WO 78. For sources held in the Sudan Archive at Durham see https://www.dur.ac.uk/library/asc/sudan/.

South Sudan became independent on 9 July 2011 following an overwhelming Southern vote for secession in a referendum held in January 2011.

Colonial Office
- Sudan: Government Gazettes (CO 675) 1907–17, 2 volumes

Foreign Office
- General correspondence before 1906, Ottoman Empire (FO 78) 1780–1905 (continued in FO 371, Political Departments: General Correspondence 1906–66)
- Embassy and Consulates, Egypt: General Correspondence (FO 141) 1815 onwards
- Cromer Papers (FO 633)
- Foreign Office: Political Departments: General Correspondence 1906–66 (FO 371)
- Anglo-Egyptian Sudan (FO 867) 1903–71, comprising minutes of proceedings of the Governor-General's Committee, papers relating to the Darfur-Wadi boundary, and Sudan government gazettes

Sungei Ujong

In 1874 a British resident was appointed to Sungei Ujong. In 1895 the territory became part of the modern Negri Sembilan. For other records see under Negri Sembilan and Federated Malay States.

Colonial Office
- Sungei Ujong: Sessional Papers (CO 474) 1883–93, 1 volume
- Sungei Ujong: Government Gazettes (CO 475) 1893, 1 volume

Surinam (Suriname)

Surinam was settled by the English in 1630, but they left in 1645. In 1662 Charles II assigned it to Lord Willoughby and Lawrence Hyde, but in 1667 it was ceded to The Netherlands by the Treaty of Breda. Britain captured it in 1799, returned it to the Batavian Republic by the Treaty of Amiens in 1802, reconquered it in 1804 and finally restored it to The Netherlands in 1816. The following records include entry books, précis books and miscellanea such as shipping returns, accounts and returns of a population census taken in 1811.

War and Colonial Department and predecessors

Surinam: Original Correspondence, etc. (CO 278) 1667–1832, 28 volumes

Swaziland

From 1894 to 1899 Swaziland was administered by the government of the South African Republic. In 1902 a British special commissioner was appointed and in 1903 Swaziland was put under the high commissioner for South Africa who administered the territory through a resident commissioner. In 1964 a new post of Her Majesty's commissioner was created and a new constitution provided for a nominated Executive Council and a partly elective Legislative Council. However, the traditional Swazi political system was largely retained, with the Swazi paramount chief being advised by the two councils. In 1967 a new constitution, designed to take the country to independence, was introduced. Swaziland became a protected state, the paramount chief was recognised as king and head of state, and a parliament was established. Swaziland became a fully independent state within the Commonwealth on 6 September 1968. Basutoland, Bechuanaland and Swaziland are sometimes known as the 'South Africa High Commission Territories' (or simply 'High Commission Territories') and may be described in the records under those terms. See also under South Africa High Commission.

Colonial Office

Swaziland: Miscellanea (CO 608) 1906–24, 17 volumes of blue books of statistics

Swaziland: Proclamations (CO 609) 1904–6, 1 volume

Colonial Office and Commonwealth Office

Colonial Office and Commonwealth Office: Southern Africa Department: Original Correspondence (CO 1048) 1960–8, 966 files

Colonial Office and Commonwealth Office: Office of Her Majesty's Commissioner, Swaziland: Registered Files (CO 1063) 1966–8, 8 files

Dominions Office/Commonwealth Relations Office/Foreign Office/Commonwealth Office/Foreign and Commonwealth Office

Swaziland: Miscellanea (DO 67) 1925–47, 18 volumes of blue books of statistics

Swaziland: Sessional Papers (DO 93) 1921–65, 48 volumes

Commonwealth Relations Office: South Africa High Commission Territories: Registered Files (BBS series) (DO 157) 1959–63, 66 files

Commonwealth Office: East Africa Department: Registered Files, Botswana, Lesotho and Swaziland (BLS, SAB, SAR and SAS series) (DO 212) 1966–7, 14 files

Foreign Office: West and Central African Department: Registered Files (FCO 25) 1967–8

Commonwealth Office and Foreign and Commonwealth Office: Central African Department and Predecessors: Registered Files (FCO 29) 1967–9

Commonwealth Office and Foreign and Commonwealth Office: East Africa Departments: Registered Files (FCO 31) 1967 onwards

Commonwealth Office and Foreign and Commonwealth Office: Southern African Department and Predecessors: Registered Files (FCO 45) 1967 onwards

Foreign and Commonwealth Office and predecessors: Records of Former Colonial Administrations: Migrated Archives (FCO 141)

Tanganyika (Tanzania)

Tanganyika was under German control from 1884 until it was captured by British and Belgian forces in 1916/17. It was placed under British civil administration in 1917, and assigned by mandate to Britain in 1919. Ruanda-Urundi (Rwanda and Burundi), also formerly part of German East Africa, was assigned to Belgium. The administration of Tanganyika continued to be carried out under the terms of the mandate until its transfer to the trusteeship system under the United Nations. Before 1920 there was a British administrator. A governor was appointed in 1920 and was given an Executive Council; a nominated Legislative Council was established in 1926. On 1 May 1961 Tanganyika attained internal self-government, and on 9 December 1961 it became a fully independent member of the Commonwealth. It became a republic exactly one year later, and on 25 April 1964 it joined with Zanzibar to form the United Republic of Tanganyika and Zanzibar, which became the United Republic of Tanzania on 29 October 1964.

Colonial Office

Tanganyika: Original Correspondence (CO 691) 1916–51, 217 volumes and boxes of files, continued in **East Africa: Original Correspondence (CO 822)** 1927–64. See also Colonies General: Supplementary Original Correspondence (CO 537).
Tanganyika: Register of Correspondence (CO 746) 1916–26, 6 volumes
Tanganyika: Register of Out-letters (CO 747) 1916–51, 29 volumes
Tanganyika: Acts (CO 735) 1919–61, 15 volumes
Tanganyika: Sessional Papers (CO 736) 1918–63, 62 volumes
Tanganyika: Government Gazettes (CO 737) 1919–64, 72 volumes
Tanganyika: Miscellanea (CO 726) 1921–48, 30 volumes, including blue books of statistics, and trade and information reports

Commonwealth Relations Office/Commonwealth Office/Foreign and Commonwealth Office

Tanzania: Government Gazettes (DO 146) 1964–75, 29 volumes
Tanzania: Sessional Papers (DO 147) 1964–5, 2 volumes
Commonwealth Relations Office and Successors: High Commission, Tanganyika: Registered Files (DO 185) 1962 onwards
Commonwealth Relations Office and Commonwealth Office: East Africa Departments: Registered Files, East Africa (EA series) (DO 213) 1963–7
Commonwealth Relations Office and Commonwealth Office: East Africa Economic Department and Development Policy and East and West Africa Economic Department: Registered Files, East Africa Economic (EAE series) (DO 214) 1964–6
Commonwealth Office and Foreign and Commonwealth Office: East Africa Departments: Registered Files (P and JE series) (FCO 31) 1967 onwards
Foreign and Commonwealth Office and predecessors: Records of Former Colonial Administrations: Migrated Archives (FCO 141)

Tangier

Tangier was ceded to England by Portugal in 1661 as part of the dowry of Catherine of Braganza, the wife of Charles II. From 1661 to 1684 it was under a British governor, who had legislative authority and was at the head of a military administration until 1668 when a charter of incorporation established an elective council, headed by a mayor and aldermen. The following records include entry books and local records sent to London when Tangier was abandoned in 1684, including the court books of its municipal assemblies under English rule, local notarial documents, etc. See also under Mediterranean.

State Paper Office

Tangier: Original Correspondence, etc. (CO 279) 1661–1735, 49 volumes (apart from a very few papers in CO 279/33 the series covers the period 1661–86)

Tanzania *see* Tanganyika *and* Zanzibar

Tasmania

Britain took possession of Tasmania in 1803 for use as a penal colony and annexed it to New South Wales; it became a separate colony in 1825. It was called Van Diemen's Land until 1856. Tasmania became part of the Commonwealth of Australia in 1901.

Colonial Office and predecessor

Tasmania: Original Correspondence (CO 280) 1824–1900, 403 volumes

Tasmania: Register of Correspondence (CO 370) 1849–1900, 13 volumes (for registers before 1849 see CO 326)

Index to Correspondence (CO 714/148–53) 1820–66

Tasmania: Entry Books (CO 408) 1825–72, 46 volumes

Tasmania: Register of Out-letters (CO 371) 1873–1900, 2 volumes

Tasmania: Acts (CO 281) 1830–1924, 35 volumes

Tasmania: Sessional Papers (CO 282) 1825–1925, 204 volumes

Tasmania: Government Gazettes (CO 283) 1816–1925, 143 volumes

Tasmania: Miscellanea (CO 284) 1822–1925, 146 volumes, including blue books of statistics and newspapers (for a list of newspapers see appendix 3)

Dominions Office/Commonwealth Relations Office

Tasmania: Acts (DO 68) 1925–65, 24 volumes

Tasmania: Sessional Papers (DO 69) 1925–65, 71 volumes

Tasmania: Government Gazettes (DO 70) 1926–80, 118 volumes

Tasmania: Miscellanea (DO 71) 1925–50, 15 volumes of statistics

Teranggganu *see* Trengganu

The Gambia *see* Gambia

Tobago

Possession of Tobago was contested during the 17th and 18th centuries by the English, the Dutch, the Courlanders and the French. It was under British control from 1762 to 1783 when it was restored to France, and was finally ceded to Britain in 1814. It was within the Windward Islands government from 1763 to 1783, and again from 1833 to 1889 when it was annexed to Trinidad.

Colonial Office and predecessors

- **Tobago: Original Correspondence (CO 285)** 1700–1873, 91 volumes (apart from the first two volumes which include papers dated between 1700 and 1808 the series commences in 1794), continued in **Windward Islands: Original Correspondence (CO 321)** and under Trinidad.CO 285 and CO 321 are registered in the Windward Islands Register of Correspondence (CO 376) 1850–1951. For registers before 1850 see CO 326.
- Tobago: Register of Out-letters (CO 498) 1872–82, 3 volumes (continued in the Windward Islands series CO 377)
- Index to Correspondence (CO 714/154–6) 1815–66
- Tobago: Entry Books (CO 286) 1793–1872, 11 volumes, including précis books
- Tobago: Acts (CO 287) 1768–1898, 15 volumes
- Tobago: Sessional Papers (CO 288) 1768–1898, 30 volumes
- Tobago: Government Gazettes (CO 289) 1872–98, 7 volumes
- Tobago: Miscellanea (CO 290) 1766–1892, 73 volumes, including shipping returns, returns of stipendiary magistrates and blue books of statistics

Togoland (Togo)

Togoland was general regarded as being under British suzerainty until 1885/6 when Britain and France formally recognised German influence. After capture by British and French troops in 1914, the territory was divided provisionally into British and French spheres. In 1922 the League of Nations approved this arrangement, and both parts became mandated territories. From 1923 the northern section of the British sphere was administered as part of the Northern Territories of the Gold Coast and the southern section as part of the Eastern Province of the Gold Coast Colony. The governor of the Gold Coast Colony was empowered to legislate for both sections of the British sphere. After a United Nations-sponsored referendum in 1956, the British sector merged with the Gold Coast to form Ghana, while the French part chose to become an autonomous republic. Togo was granted full independence in 1960.

Colonial Office

Togoland: Original Correspondence (CO 724) 1920–6, 4 volumes
Togoland: Register of Correspondence (CO 803) 1920–6, 1 volume
Togoland: Register of Out-letters (CO 804) 1920–6, 1 volume
For records from 1927 to 1960 see under Gold Coast

Tonga

Tonga became a British protected state in 1900 and was under the jurisdiction of the high commissioner for the Western Pacific until 1952 when the responsibility was transferred to the governor of Fiji. In 1965 the British commissioner and consul became responsible directly to the secretary of state for the colonies. On 4 June 1970 the Kingdom of Tonga became a fully independent member state of the Commonwealth. See also under Western Pacific High Commission.

Foreign Office

Foreign Office: Political and Other Departments: General Correspondence before 1906, Pacific Islands (Fiji, Hawaii, Rarotonga, Samoa, Tahiti and Tonga) (FO 58) 1822–1905

Colonial Office

Tonga: Sessional Papers (CO 861) 1914–65, 10 volumes of administration reports
Tonga: Government Gazettes (CO 676) 1905–75, 21 volumes

Tortola *see under* St Christopher

Transjordan (Jordan)

Formerly part of the Ottoman empire, Transjordan was captured by British troops in 1917/18, and was under British military administration until 1920. It was then assigned to Britain under a League of Nations mandate, which took effect in 1923. The mandate was terminated in 1946, when Transjordan became the independent state of Jordan. See also under Middle East.

Colonial Office

Transjordan: Original Correspondence (CO 831) 1928–46, 61 files
Transjordan: Register of Correspondence (CO 870) 1928–48, 7 volumes

For earlier records relating to the Ottoman empire, and later records relating to Jordan, see the records of the Foreign Office, especially FO 78, Political and Other Departments: General Correspondence before 1906, Ottoman Empire, and FO 371, Political Departments: General Correspondence 1906–66. Files of the British residency and the legation at Amman spanning the periods of the mandate and of independence are in Foreign Office and Foreign and Commonwealth Office: Legation and Embassy, Amman, Jordan (formerly Transjordan): General Correspondence (FO 816) 1920 onwards.

Transkeian Territories

From 1858 to 1865 the Transkeian Territories were neutral under the protection of Cape Colony, which then abandoned them. From 1879 to 1894 they were annexed to Cape Colony and legislative authority was vested in the governor of the Cape in council. In 1894 the Transkeian Territories General Council was established, which was extended to all the territories by 1903 and given considerable powers of local government. For other records see under Cape of Good Hope.

Dominions Office/Commonwealth Relations Office

Transkeian Territories: Sessional Papers (DO 101) 1931–63, 9 volumes

Transvaal

The Transvaal was occupied by Boers from the Cape in 1837 during the Great Trek. In 1852 it was recognised as independent, but it consisted of several separate communities until they were united as the South African Republic in 1858. In 1877 it was annexed to Britain, but its independence was restored in 1881. In 1899 it allied with the Orange Free State, the following year it was annexed to Britain, and in 1910 it became an original province of the Union of South Africa. The registers of correspondence for 1901–2 will be found under Transvaal and Orange River Colony. For other records from 1881 see under South Africa High Commission and South Africa, and after 1910 under Union of South Africa.

Colonial Office

Transvaal: Original Correspondence (CO 291) 1877–1910, 145 volumes

Transvaal: Register of Correspondence (CO 510) 1877–1910, 10 volumes. See also Transvaal and Orange River Colony: Register of Correspondence (CO 679) 1901–2, 2 volumes.

Transvaal: Register of Out-letters (CO 511) 1877–1910, 5 volumes. See also Transvaal and Orange River Colony: Register of Out-letters (CO 680) 1901–2, 1 volume.

Transvaal: Acts (CO 292) 1880–1910, 7 volumes

Transvaal: Sessional Papers (CO 293) 1880–1925, 70 volumes

Transvaal: Government Gazettes (CO 294) 1869–1925, 58 volumes

Transvaal: Miscellanea (CO 476) 1878–1909, 6 volumes, including blue books and abstracts of statistics

Transvaal: Municipality of Johannesburg (CO 610) 1901–6, 7 volumes (minutes of the Town Council of Johannesburg)

Transvaal: Municipality of Pretoria (CO 611) 1902–3, 4 volumes (minutes of the Town Council and Municipal Commission of Pretoria)

Transvaal Green Books (CO 477) 1884–99

Dominions Office/Commonwealth Relations Office

Transvaal: Sessional Papers (DO 72) 1925–60, 40 volumes

Transvaal: Government Gazettes (DO 73) 1926–64, 56 volumes

Trengganu (Terengganu)

Formerly under Siamese suzerainty, Trengganu became a British protected state in 1909 by agreement with Siam and received a British adviser. An advisory state council was established in 1911. Trengganu was under Japanese occupation from 1942 to 1945 and British military administration from 1945 to 1946 (see WO 203), when it joined the Malayan Union. For correspondence see under Federated Malay States and Straits Settlements.

Colonial Office

Trengganu: Sessional Papers (CO 840) 1910–40, 2 volumes

Trengganu: Government Gazettes (CO 909) 1939–75, 20 volumes

Trinidad (Trinidad and Tobago)

In 1797 Trinidad was captured by Britain from Spain, and it was ceded to Britain by the Treaty of Amiens in 1802. It was united with Tobago in 1889, and the colony was subsequently known as Trinidad and Tobago. From 1958 to 1962 Trinidad and Tobago was a member state of the Federation of the West Indies. On 31 August 1962 it became a fully independent member state of the Commonwealth, and in 1976 it became a republic. See also under Tobago, West Indies and Federation of the West Indies.

Colonial Office and predecessors

Trinidad: Original Correspondence (CO 295) 1783–1951, 656 volumes and boxes of files, continued in **West Indian Department: Registered Files (WIS series) (CO 1031)** 1948–67. See also Colonies General: Supplementary Original Correspondence (CO 537).

Trinidad: Register of Correspondence (CO 372) 1850–1951, 35 volumes (for registers before 1850 see CO 326)

Index to Correspondence (CO 714/157–9) 1797–1866

Trinidad: Register of Out-letters (CO 497) 1872–1926, 11 volumes

Trinidad: Entry Books (CO 296) 1797–1872, 31 volumes, including précis books

Trinidad: Acts (CO 297) 1832–1960, 42 volumes

Trinidad: Sessional Papers (CO 298) 1803–1965, 221 volumes

Trinidad: Government Gazettes (CO 299) 1833–1975, 193 volumes

Trinidad: Miscellanea (CO 300) 1804–1945, 156 volumes, including shipping returns, accounts, reports of protectors of slaves, a journal of the medical officer on an immigrant ship from Madras (1847), blue books of statistics and newspapers (for a list of newspapers see appendix 3)

Commonwealth Relations Office/Commonwealth Office/Foreign and Commonwealth Office

Commonwealth Relations Office and Commonwealth Office: West Indies Department and Atlantic Department: Registered Files, Commonwealth West Indies (WID series) (DO 200) 1961–7

Commonwealth Relations Office and Successors: High Commission, Trinidad and Tobago: Registered Files (DO 227) 1962 onwards

Commonwealth Office: Atlantic Department: Registered Files (G series) (FCO 23) 1966–8

Foreign and Commonwealth Office: North American and Caribbean Department and Caribbean Department: Registered Files (AN series) (FCO 63) 1968 onwards

Foreign and Commonwealth Office and predecessors: Records of Former Colonial Administrations: Migrated Archives (FCO 141)

Tristan da Cunha

Tristan da Cunha was discovered in 1506 by the Portuguese navigator Tristão da Cunha, but it was not claimed by any nation state until Britain garrisoned it in 1816 to prevent it from being used as a base from which to rescue Napoleon from St Helena. Tristan da Cunha was a dependency of St Helena until a new constitution dated 1 September 2009 created a single dependency of Saint Helena, Ascension and Tristan da Cunha giving the three islands equal status within the territory. For records see under St Helena.

Turks and Caicos Islands

The Turks Islands were occupied by the English from Bermuda from 1678, and the Caicos Islands were settled by loyalists from America after the War of Independence. They were both formally annexed to and administered from the Bahamas in 1799. In 1848 they were separated from the Bahamas and made a presidency under the governor of Jamaica; in 1874 they became a dependency of Jamaica. When Jamaica became independent in 1962 the Turks and Caicos Islands became a Crown colony with an administrator rather than a governor. In 1965 the powers of the governor of the Bahamas were extended to Turks and Caicos which received their own governor when the Bahamas became independent in 1973. Turks and Caicos remain a British dependency (UK Overseas Territory).

Colonial Office and predecessor

Turks and Caicos Islands: Original Correspondence (CO 301) 1848–82, 66 volumes (for correspondence before and after those dates see under Bahamas and Jamaica respectively)

Turks and Caicos Islands: Register of Correspondence (CO 495) 1868–82, 1 volume (for earlier and later registers see under Bahamas and Jamaica)

Index to Correspondence (CO 714/160) 1849–66

Turks and Caicos Islands: Register of Out-letters (CO 496) 1872–81, 2 volumes

Turks and Caicos Islands: Entry Books (CO 409) 1849–72, 5 volumes

Turks and Caicos Islands: Acts (CO 302) 1849–1965, 13 volumes
Turks and Caicos Islands: Sessional Papers (CO 303) 1849–1965, 16 volumes
Turks and Caicos Islands: Government Gazettes (CO 681) 1907–65, 13 volumes
Turks and Caicos Islands: Miscellanea (CO 304) 1852–1947, 95 volumes of blue books of statistics

Commonwealth Office/Foreign and Commonwealth Office

Commonwealth Office: West Indian Department 'B' and Foreign and Commonwealth Office, West Indian Department: Registered Files, Smaller Commonwealth West Indian Territories (FCO 44) 1967 onwards
Foreign and Commonwealth Office and predecessors: Records of Former Colonial Administrations: Migrated Archives (FCO 141)

Tuvalu *see under* Gilbert and Ellice Islands

Uganda

Uganda was claimed by Germany in 1885, but was ceded to the UK by an Anglo-German Agreement of 1 July 1890 and administered initially by the Imperial British East Africa Company. A protectorate over Buganda was declared in 1890 and over the rest of present-day Uganda when the Crown took over in 1896 and control passed to the Foreign Office. Construction of the Uganda Railway was commenced in 1896, and in 1903 responsibility for the railway's administration was transferred from the Foreign Office to the government of the East Africa Protectorate (see under Kenya). In 1905 control of the administration of Uganda was transferred from the Foreign Office to the Colonial Office. Uganda became an independent sovereign state and a member of the Commonwealth on 9 October 1962; it became a republic on 8 September 1967.

Colonial Office

East Africa and Uganda Protectorate: Original Correspondence (CO 519) 1904–5, 1 volume (registered in the Kenya register, CO 628)
Uganda: Original Correspondence (CO 536) 1905–51, 225 volumes and boxes of files, continued in **East Africa: Original Correspondence (CO 822)** 1927–64. See also Colonies General: Supplementary Original Correspondence (CO 537).
Uganda: Register of Correspondence (CO 682) 1905–51, 26 volumes
Uganda: Register of Out-letters (CO 683) 1905–51, 5 volumes
Uganda: Acts (CO 684) 1901–60, 12 volumes
Uganda: Sessional Papers (CO 685) 1907–65, 63 volumes
East Africa and Uganda Protectorate: Government Gazettes (CO 457) 1899–1907, 7 volumes
Uganda: Government Gazettes (CO 612) 1908–73, 74 volumes
Uganda: Miscellanea (CO 613) 1901–45, 45 volumes of blue books of statistics
Uganda Railway: Construction (CO 614) 1895–1904, 14 volumes

There are also 39 volumes of papers relating to the Uganda Railway in CO 537, which are registered in CO 615, as well as some unregistered papers about the railway.

Uganda Railway: Register of Correspondence (CO 615) 1895–1905, 7 volumes

Commonwealth Office/Foreign and Commonwealth Office

Commonwealth Relations Office: East and General Africa: Registered Files (EGA series) (DO 168) 1961–3

Commonwealth Relations Office and Commonwealth Office: East Africa Departments: Registered Files, East Africa (EA series) (DO 213) 1963–7

Commonwealth Relations Office and Commonwealth Office: East Africa Economic Department and Development Policy and East and West Africa Economic Department: Registered Files, East Africa Economic (EAE series) (DO 214) 1964–6

Commonwealth Office and Foreign and Commonwealth Office: East Africa Departments: Registered Files (P and JE series) (FCO 31) 1967 onwards

Foreign and Commonwealth Office and predecessors: Records of Former Colonial Administrations: Migrated Archives (FCO 141)

Unfederated Malay States

British advisers appointed to the Malay states of Kelantan in 1903, to Kedah and Perlis in 1909, and to Johore in 1910 were responsible to the governor of the Straits Settlements. These states had refused to join the Federation of Malay States, formed in 1896, and continued as independent Malay monarchies. Correspondence concerning the unfederated states is in the Straits Settlements series (CO 273) until 1920 when it is included in the new series for the Federated Malay States (CO 717). The unfederated states were occupied by the Japanese from 1942 to 1945, and under British military administration from 1945 to 1946 (see the War Office series WO 203). In 1946 the states joined the short-lived Malayan Union, and in 1948 the new Federation of Malaya. For sessional papers and government gazettes see under the individual states.

Union of South Africa

In 1910 Cape Colony, Natal, the Orange River Colony and the Transvaal were joined together in the Union of South Africa. The Colonial Office was responsible for relations with the Union until 1925 when the Dominions Office was established and assumed responsibility. On 1 December 1961 the Union of South Africa withdrew from the Commonwealth and became a republic, and responsibility passed to the Foreign Office. South Africa rejoined the Commonwealth in 1994. For earlier and related records see under South Africa, South Africa High Commission and individual colonies.

Colonial Office

Union of South Africa: Original Correspondence (CO 551) 1910–22, 157 volumes, continued in **Dominions: Original Correspondence (CO 532)** 1907–25, 335 volumes. See also Colonies General: Supplementary Original Correspondence (CO 537).

Union of South Africa: Register of Correspondence (CO 705) 1910–22, 9 volumes
Union of South Africa: Register of Out-letters (CO 748) 1910–22, 5 volumes
Union of South Africa: Acts (CO 632) 1910–25, 9 volumes
Union of South Africa: Sessional Papers (CO 633) 1910–25, 191 volumes
Union of South Africa: Government Gazettes (CO 552) 1910–25, 57 volumes
Union of South Africa: Miscellanea (CO 553) 1910–25, 20 volumes, comprising statements of trade and shipping, and statistical year books

Dominions Office/Commonwealth Relations Office

Dominions Office and Commonwealth Relations Office: Original Correspondence (DO 35) 1915–71
Commonwealth Relations Office: Southern Africa Department: Registered Files (SA series) (DO 180) 1960–1, 14 files
Union of South Africa: Sessional Papers (DO 11) 1926–60, 262 volumes
Union of South Africa: Government Gazettes (DO 12) 1926–78, 343 volumes
Union of South Africa: Miscellanea (DO 13) 1926–50, 26 volumes, comprising statements of trade and shipping, and commercial and industrial gazettes
Union of South Africa: Acts (DO 77) 1926–31, 2 volumes
Confidential Print: Dominions (South Africa) (DO 116) 1913–44, 8 volumes

Foreign Office/Foreign and Commonwealth Office

Foreign Office: Political Departments: General Correspondence 1906–66 (FO 371)
Foreign Office: West and Central African Department: Registered Files (J series) (FCO 25) 1967–8
Commonwealth Office and Foreign and Commonwealth Office: Southern African Department and Predecessors: Registered Files (SAD and CS series) (FCO 45) 1967 onwards

Upper Canada *see* Ontario

Vancouver Island

Vancouver Island, formerly part of the Hudson's Bay Company territory, became a Crown colony in 1849. It was united with British Columbia in 1866. See also under British Columbia and Canada.

Colonial Office and predecessor

Vancouver Island: Original Correspondence (CO 305) 1846–67, 30 volumes
Vancouver Island: Register of Correspondence (CO 373) 1853–67, 2 volumes
Vancouver Island correspondence from 1850 to 1853 is registered in the British North America registers (CO 328)
Index to Correspondence (CO 714/161) 1849–66
Vancouver Island: Entry Books (CO 410) 1849–67, 2 volumes
Vancouver Island: Acts (CO 306) 1853–66, 1 volume

Vancouver Island: Sessional Papers (CO 307) 1860–6, 2 volumes
Vancouver Island: Government Gazettes (CO 308) 1864–6, 1 volume
Vancouver Island: Miscellanea (CO 478) 1863–5, 3 volumes of blue books of statistics

Vanuatu *see* New Hebrides

Vermont *see under* America and West Indies

Victoria

Colonists from New South Wales established settlements at Victoria, which did not survive, in 1803 and 1825. In 1834 Victoria was colonised from Van Diemen's Land (Tasmania). It was, however, administered from New South Wales until 1851 when it was separated from New South Wales and named Victoria. In 1901 it became an original state of the Commonwealth of Australia.

Colonial Office and predecessor

Victoria: Original Correspondence (CO 309) 1851–1900, 150 volumes. For later correspondence see under Australia.
Victoria: Register of Correspondence (CO 374) 1852–1900, 14 volumes
Index to Correspondence (CO 714/162–3) 1851–66
Victoria: Entry Books (CO 411) 1851–72, 13 volumes
Victoria: Register of Out-letters (CO 513) 1873–1900, 4 volumes
Victoria: Acts (CO 310) 1851–1925, 89 volumes
Victoria: Sessional Papers (CO 311) 1851–1925, 312 volumes
Victoria: Government Gazettes (CO 312) 1838–1916, 96 volumes
Victoria: Miscellanea (CO 313) 1838–1916, 96 volumes, including blue books of statistics and newspapers (for a list of newspapers see appendix 3)
Victoria: Public Service Lists (CO 479) 1892–1910, 19 volumes

Dominions Office and Successors

Victoria: Acts (DO 74) 1926–64, 74 volumes
Victoria: Sessional Papers (DO 75) 1926–80, 170 volumes
Victoria: Government Gazettes (DO 76) 1926–80, 170 volumes

Virgin Islands *see* British Virgin Islands

Virginia *see under* America and West Indies

Wei-Hai-Wei

Wei-Hai-Wei was leased to Britain by China in 1898 for use as a naval harbour; administration was undertaken by the senior naval officer. In 1899 it was transferred to a military and civil commissioner appointed by the War Office. In 1901 control passed to the Colonial Office, and a civil commissioner was appointed in 1902. In 1930 Wei-Hai-Wei was returned to China under the terms of the lease. The civil commissioner's files were stored in the British Embassy at Peking (Beijing) from 1930 until 1961 when they were sent to the Colonial Office; they are now in CO 873. For earlier records of the Admiralty and the War Office see ADM 1, ADM 116, ADM 125, WO 32, WO 33 and WO 106. See also under Far East/South East Asia. For Foreign Office records see especially Foreign Office: Political and Other Departments: General Correspondence before 1906, China (FO 17) 1815–1905, and Foreign Office: Political Departments: General Correspondence 1906–66 (FO 371).

Colonial Office

Wei-Hai-Wei: Original Correspondence (CO 521) 1898–1933, 86 volumes and boxes of files
Wei-Hai-Wei: Register of Correspondence (CO 770) 1898–1931, 4 volumes
Wei-Hai-Wei: Register of Out-letters (CO 771) 1901–26, 4 volumes
Wei-Hai-Wei: Acts (CO 841) 1903–30, 1 volume
Wei-Hai-Wei: Government Gazettes (CO 744) 1908–30, 3 volumes
Wei-Hai-Wei: Wei-Hai-Wei Commissioner's Files (CO 873) 1899–1930, 779 files

West Africa *see also under* individual colonies, West African Settlements *and* West Africa Frontier Force

Records relating to the British West African colonies of Gambia, Gold Coast, Nigeria and Sierra Leone in general or to more than one colony in the region were, from 1911, registered separately and are found in the series CO 554 which also includes papers on the West African Inter-Territorial Conference. From 1951 the individual colony series of records disappear and CO 554 becomes the main geographical series for the whole region. The West African Governors' Conference, inaugurated in 1939 to facilitate meetings between the four West African governors, set up a permanent office in 1940 and a supply centre in 1941. This system was superseded in 1942, when the region had become an important staging post in the airlift of supplies to the armies in the western desert, by the creation of a new post of Cabinet minister resident in West Africa. It was his job to secure the effective co-operation of the territories in the prosecution of the war, and to consult French and Belgian territories. The resident minister's office was linked to the Cabinet through its Africa Committee, and the Colonial Office provided his London secretariat. When the office was abolished in 1945 the co-ordinating agency for West Africa became the secretariat of the West African Council in Accra. In 1951 it was replaced by the West African Inter-Territorial Council, which became a conference in 1953, with the governor of Nigeria as permanent president.

Colonial Office

West Africa: Original Correspondence (CO 554) 1911–65, 2654 volumes, boxes of files and files. See also Colonies General: Supplementary Original Correspondence (CO 537).

West Africa: Register of Correspondence (CO 555) 1911–51, 25 volumes

West African Currency Board (CO 984) 1880–1974, 58 files, volumes and a cash box of specimen currency

West Africa Frontier Force

The Niger and West Africa Frontier Force, known from 1900 as the West Africa Frontier Force and from 1928 as the Royal West Africa Frontier Force, was raised locally in 1897 to protect the frontiers of the British protectorates in West Africa. It was financed by the imperial government, and officered by the British Army. From 1927 the administration of the unit was brought together with that of the King's African Rifles under the Military Branch of the Colonial Office. Records relating to the two units were then registered and kept together.

Colonial Office

Niger and West Africa Frontier Force: Original Correspondence (CO 445) 1898–1926, 69 volumes

Niger and West Africa Frontier Force: Register of Correspondence (CO 581) 1898–9, 1 volume

West Africa Frontier Force: Register of Correspondence (CO 641) 1900–26, 10 volumes

Niger and West Africa Frontier Force: Register of Out-letters (CO 582) 1898–9, 1 volume

West Africa Frontier Force: Register of Out-letters (CO 642) 1900–26, 10 volumes

See also:

Military: Original Correspondence (CO 820) 1927–51, 77 volumes and files

Military: Register of Correspondence (CO 871) 1927–52, 25 volumes

Accounts Branch: Miscellanea (CO 701), includes accounts and notes on the European establishment

Colonies General: Supplementary Original Correspondence (CO 537)

West African Settlements

In 1865 it was decided that a central government of the British dependencies in West Africa should be established, with the seat of government at Sierra Leone. This change was effected by a charter of 19 February 1866, which constituted one government-in-chief comprising Sierra Leone, the Gambia, the Gold Coast and Lagos. Each of these territories had its own Legislative Council, and an Executive Council was established at Sierra Leone to advise and assist the governor-in-chief. The Gold Coast and Lagos were removed from this arrangement in 1874. For correspondence and other records see under the four constituent territories.

West Indies

Up to 1825 the original correspondence series CO 318 contains despatches, but they are mainly of a military character. After that year the series consists primarily of domestic correspondence between the Colonial Office and other British government departments, miscellaneous organisations and individuals, and includes material about relations between British colonies and foreign countries or foreign dependencies within the region. From 1843 to 1873 a section of the correspondence is devoted to the immigration into the West Indies of indentured labourers, a subject which is eventually resumed in the series Immigration, CO 571 (see under migration in appendix 2). The series also contains correspondence with the commissioners appointed in 1822 to enquire into the administration of civil and criminal justice in the West Indies, and with the commissioners, first reporting in 1825, appointed to consider the state of Africans confiscated by the Crown under the anti-slave trade acts and thereafter apprenticed or otherwise living in the West Indies. A West India Relief Commission was established by Act of Parliament in 1832 with power to grant loans for relief purposes. Its functions were transferred to the Public Works Loan Commissioners as from 1 January 1881. Records of the commission, consisting of mortgage indentures with supporting schedules of slaves, inventories of estates, proofs of ownership, and sometimes details of the projects to be financed, were made available in the TNA series PWLB 11 in June 2014. A royal commission was established in 1854 to investigate those landed estates in the West Indies whose owners had overburdened them with mortgages (the Incumbered Estates Commission). The commission was dissolved in 1886 and its records form the series CO 441 which includes private papers from a number of estates in Antigua, Dominica, Grenada, Jamaica, Montserrat, Nevis, St Christopher (St Kitts), St Vincent, Tobago and Tortola. The Imperial Department of Agriculture was established in 1898, with headquarters in Barbados, for research and experiment in tropical crops, especially sugar cane. In 1922 it was amalgamated with the Imperial College of Agriculture in Trinidad, which had been incorporated the previous year.

The West India Royal Commission, appointed under the chairmanship of Lord Moyne in 1938, investigated social and economic conditions and related matters in British colonies in the region. Its records, which include evidence presented by many individuals and organisations, are in CO 950. The commission's findings resulted in the establishment of the West Indies Development and Welfare Organisation, which was set up under a comptroller for development and welfare. After the Second World War it collaborated with local governments in working out long-term social reform programmes and development and welfare schemes for which United Kingdom grants were recommended. The comptroller also served as British co-chairman of the Caribbean Commission established by the United States and the United Kingdom and joined by the French and Netherlands governments in 1945 to strengthen economic and social co-operation and avoid duplication of research. With the creation of the Federation of the West Indies in January 1958 the Development and Welfare Organisation's functions were largely assumed by the federal government, and in March 1958 the organisation ceased to exist. See also under individual colonies.

Material on the British West India Regiments can be found among the records of the Colonial

Office and a number of other departments, especially the War Office, the records of which include muster books and pay lists for the regiments.[15]

Colonial Office and predecessors

West Indies: Original Correspondence (CO 318) 1624–1951, 515 volumes and boxes of files, continued in **West Indian Department: Registered Files (CO 1031)** 1948–67. See also Colonial Papers General Series (CO 1) 1574–1757, 69 volumes and Colonies General: Supplementary Original Correspondence (CO 537).

West Indies: Register of Correspondence (CO 375) 1849–1951, 30 volumes[16]

Index to Correspondence (CO 714/165) 1850–7

West Indies: Entry Books (CO 319) 1699–1872, 56 volumes

West Indies: Register of Out-letters (CO 509) 1872–1926, 5 volumes

West Indies: Miscellanea (CO 320) 1820–40, 10 volumes, consisting of memoranda on various subjects including the slave trade, abolition of slavery and the apprenticeship system.

Confidential Print: West Indies (CO 884) 1833–1961, 38 volumes

West Indian Incumbered Estates Commission (CO 441) 1770–1893, 25 boxes of correspondence, papers, deeds, plans and miscellanea

Imperial Department of Agriculture (CO 617) 1899–1923, 18 volumes

West India Royal Commission (CO 950) 1938–9, 961 volumes and files

West Indies, United States Bases: Original Correspondence (CO 971) 1941–51, 163 boxes of files

West Indies, United States Bases: Register of Correspondence (CO 972) 1940–51, 3 volumes

British West Indies: Governor's Office: Registered Files (CO 1043) 1939–59, 1 file

Colonial Office/Commonwealth Office

West Indies Development and Welfare Organisation: Registered Files (CO 1042) 1938–58, 404 files

Commonwealth Relations Office

Federation of the West Indies: Government Gazettes (DO 136) 1958–61

Federation of the West Indies: Government Acts (DO 139) 1958–62

Commonwealth Relations Office and Commonwealth Office: West Indies Department and Atlantic Department: Registered Files, Commonwealth West Indies (WID series) (DO 200) 1961–7

Commonwealth Relations Office and Commonwealth Office: Atlantic Department: Registered Files (AME series) (DO 210) 1964–6

Commonwealth Office/Foreign and Commonwealth Office

Commonwealth Office: West Indian Department 'A' and Associated States Department: Registered Files, Antigua, Dominica, Grenada, St Christopher (St Kitts)-Nevis-Anguilla, St Lucia and St Vincent (WA series) (FCO 43) 1967–8

Commonwealth Office: West Indian Department 'B' and Foreign and Commonwealth

[15] For details of a collaborative research project 'Africa's Sons Under Arms' running for four years from October 2014 see http://www2.warwick.ac.uk/fac/arts/history/research/projects/asua/ [accessed 6 March 2015].

[16] According to the catalogue, CO 375/4, 5 and 8 have been transferred to CO 694. This is misleading as the three volumes are not West Indies registers of correspondence; it appears that they were wrongly assigned to CO 375 initially.

Office, West Indian Department: Registered Files, Smaller Commonwealth West Indian Territories (WB and HW series) (FCO 44) 1967 onwards

Foreign and Commonwealth Office: North American and Caribbean Department and Caribbean Department: Registered Files (AN series) (FCO 63) 1968 onwards

Foreign and Commonwealth Office and predecessors: Records of Former Colonial Administrations: Migrated Archives (FCO 141)

Western Australia

In 1826 a group of officers and ten convicts were sent to Western Australia from New South Wales, but did not lay claim to the territory. The first settlement, which was not established as a colony, was at Albany. In 1829 a colony was established at Swan River. Nominated Executive and Legislative Councils were established in 1832; representative government with a partially elected Legislative Council in 1870; and responsible government in 1890. In 1901 the colony became a state of the Commonwealth of Australia.

Colonial Office and predecessor

Western Australia: Original Correspondence (CO 18) 1828–1900, 228 volumes

Western Australia: Register of Correspondence (CO 332) 1849–1900, 14 volumes

Western Australia: Register of Out-letters (CO 353) 1873–1900, 3 volumes

Western Australia: Entry Books (CO 397) 1828–73, 29 volumes

Western Australia: Acts (CO 19) 1844–1925, 31 volumes

Western Australia: Sessional Papers (CO 20) 1832–1925, 78 volumes

Western Australia: Government Gazettes (CO 21) 1836–1925, 74 volumes

Western Australia: Miscellanea (CO 22) 1833–1918, 95 volumes of blue books of statistics and newspapers (for a list of newspapers see appendix 3)

Western Australia: Public Service Lists (CO 563), 1909–14, 6 volumes

Dominions Office/Commonwealth Relations Office

Western Australia: Acts (DO 22) 1926–66, 39 volumes

Western Australia: Sessional Papers (DO 23) 1926–65, 100 volumes

Western Australia: Government Gazettes (DO 24) 1926–89, 243 volumes

Western Australia: Miscellanea (DO 98) 1925–51, 10 volumes

For later and related records see under Australia and Commonwealth of Australia

Western Pacific

The office of high commissioner in, over and for the Western Pacific islands was created in 1877 for the purpose of better carrying out the provisions of the Pacific Islanders' Protection Acts, 1872 and 1875, and to provide a Civil Court for the settlement of disputes between British subjects living in the region. Its jurisdiction extended over all the islands not within the limit of the colonies of Fiji, Queensland, New South Wales or New Zealand, and not within the jurisdiction of any other colonial power. These included the Gilbert and Ellice Islands Colony, British Solomon Islands Protectorate, Tonga, New Hebrides condominium and Pitcairn Islands. The post of high commissioner was abolished in 1976. As the high commissioner was the sole channel of communication with the Colonial Office there are no territorial series of original correspondence, although there are separate series of printed documents. The Colonial Office records listed below relate to the Western Pacific territories in general, or to more than one territory, and in certain periods also to Hong Kong, Ceylon, St Helena, Tristan da Cunha, Mauritius, Seychelles, the Falkland Islands and the Antarctic. The regulations in CO 665 had the force of law, and this series is the equivalent of one of acts or ordinances. See also under the constituent colonies.

Many of the internal records of the high commission were sent to the FCO in London after abolition of the post of high commissioner. They were transferred to the University of Auckland Library in 2002.[17]

Foreign Office

Foreign Office: Political and Other Departments: General Correspondence before 1906, Pacific Islands (Fiji, Hawaii, Rarotonga, Samoa, Tahiti and Tonga) (FO 58) 1822–1905

Colonial Office

Western Pacific: Original Correspondence (CO 225) 1878–1951, 375 volumes and boxes of files, continued in **Hong Kong and Pacific Department: Original Correspondence (CO 1023)** 1946–55, 242 files, and **Pacific Department: Original Correspondence (CO 1036)** 1952–67, 575 files. See also Dominions: Original Correspondence (CO 532) and Colonies General: Supplementary Original Correspondence (CO 537).

Western Pacific: Register of Correspondence (CO 492) 1878–1951, 29 volumes

Western Pacific: Register of Out-letters (CO 493) 1879–1926, 7 volumes

Western Pacific: Government Gazettes (CO 692) 1914–71, 30 volumes

Western Pacific: King's Regulations (CO 665) 1879–1934, 2 volumes

Confidential Print: Western Pacific (CO 934) 1914–60, 8 volumes (earlier printed correspondence is in the Australia confidential print series CO 881)

Commonwealth Office and Foreign and Commonwealth Office

Commonwealth Office and Foreign and Commonwealth Office: Pacific and Indian Ocean Department and Pacific Dependent Territories Department: Registered Files (Q and HP series) (FCO 32) 1967 onwards

Foreign and Commonwealth Office and predecessors: Records of Former Colonial Administrations: Migrated Archives (FCO 141)

[17] For details of the collections at Auckland see http://www.library.auckland.ac.nz/sites/public/files/documents/WPAGuide.pdf [accessed 7 Jan. 2015]

Western Samoa (Samoa)

Western Samoa became a German colony in 1899 following a 20-year period during which the Samoan Islands were jointly administered by Britain, the United States and Germany. Under the agreement which put an end to this arrangement the United States acquired islands in the eastern part of the Samoan group, and Britain received half of the Solomon Islands, a free hand in Tonga and certain other concessions. New Zealand assumed control following the outbreak of the First World War and the islands subsequently became a mandated territory of New Zealand and, after the Second World War, a United Nations trust territory. Under the name of Western Samoa the territory became the first fully independent Polynesian state on 1 January 1962. It was treated as a member of the Commonwealth until its formal admission on 28 August 1970. In 1997 Samoa changed its formal name from the Independent State of Western Samoa to the Independent State of Samoa. American Samoa remains a dependency of the United States.

Foreign Office

Foreign Office: Political and Other Departments: General Correspondence before 1906, Pacific Islands (Fiji, Hawaii, Rarotonga, Samoa, Tahiti and Tonga) 1822–1905

Dominions Office/Commonwealth Relations Office

Western Samoa: Government Gazettes (DO 107) 1920–73, 5 volumes

Western Samoa: Miscellanea (DO 113) 1916–50, 1 volume of trade, commerce and shipping statistics

Commonwealth Office and Foreign and Commonwealth Office

Commonwealth Office, Far East and Pacific Department and Foreign and Commonwealth Office, South West Pacific Department: Registered Files (FCO 24) 1967 onwards

Windward Islands

In 1763 Grenada, St Vincent, Dominica and Tobago were united under a single government called the government of the Southern Caribbee Islands. Dominica was separated in 1771, St Vincent in 1776 and Tobago on its cession to France in 1783. In 1833 Grenada, St Vincent, Tobago and Barbados were united under a single government, called the government of the Windward Islands, with a governor-in-chief, although the individual islands kept their own institutions, each under a lieutenant-governor or administrator. St Lucia was added in 1838, Barbados was separated in 1885, Tobago was separated and attached to Trinidad in 1889, and Dominica was added from the Leeward Islands in 1940. In 1956 the government of the Windward Islands was abolished, and four separate colonies were established under one governor. The post of governor of the Windward Islands was abolished in 1960 and a new constitution was introduced in each territory. See also under the constituent colonies and under West Indies.

Colonial Office and predecessor

Windward Islands: Original Correspondence (CO 321) 1874–1951, 444 volumes and boxes of files, continued in **West Indian Department: Registered Files (WIS series) (CO 1031)** 1948–67. See also Colonies General: Supplementary Original Correspondence (CO 537).

Windward Islands: Register of Correspondence (CO 376) 1850–1951, 42 volumes

Windward Islands: Register of Out-letters (CO 377) 1883–1926, 8 volumes

For original correspondence before 1874, and for series of entry books, acts, sessional papers, government gazettes and miscellanea, see under the individual islands.

Yemen *see under* Aden

Zambia *see* Northern Rhodesia

Zanzibar

Zanzibar was controlled by the Sultanate of Oman, which transferred its capital there from Muscat in 1840. In the same year the first British consul was posted to the island. Germany claimed control in 1885, but British influence continued and in 1890 the Heligoland-Zanzibar Treaty redefined certain Anglo-German interests in the region. At the same time Britain renounced claims to Madagascar in return for French recognition of British claims to Zanzibar. A protectorate was established in 1891 under a consul-general subject to the Foreign Office, and from 1906 the British ruled more directly. Control was transferred from the Foreign Office to the Colonial Office in 1913 with effect from 1914. Zanzibar achieved independence in 1963. The union of Tanganyika and Zanzibar took place in April 1964 and the name of the United Republic of Tanzania was adopted in October of the same year.

Foreign Office

General Correspondence before 1906, Africa (FO 2) 1825–1905

General Correspondence before 1906, Muscat (FO 54) 1834–1905 (which includes correspondence from British consuls at Zanzibar)

Slave Trade Department and Successors: General Correspondence before 1906 (FO 84) 1816–92

General Correspondence before 1906, Zanzibar and East Africa (FO 107) 1893–1905, continued in FO 371

Colonial Office

Zanzibar: Original Correspondence (CO 618) 1913–51, 88 volumes and boxes of files; after 1951 see **East Africa: Original Correspondence (CO 822)** 1927–64. See also Colonies General: Supplementary Original Correspondence (CO 537).

Zanzibar: Register of Correspondence (CO 772) 1913–50, 13 volumes

Zanzibar: Register of Out-letters (CO 805) 1913–26, 2 volumes

Zanzibar: Acts (CO 842) 1926–62, 11 volumes
Zanzibar: Sessional Papers (CO 688) 1909–63, 46 volumes
Zanzibar: Government Gazettes (CO 689) 1913–65, 67 volumes
Zanzibar: Miscellanea (CO 690) 1913–47, 35 volumes of blue books of statistics

Commonwealth Relations Office/Commonwealth Office/Foreign and Commonwealth Office

Commonwealth Relations Office and Successors: High Commission, Tanganyika: Registered Files (DO 185) 1962–73. This series contains registered files of the British High Commissions in Tanganyika and Zanzibar, and then in the united state of Tanzania.
Commonwealth Relations Office and Commonwealth Office: East Africa Departments: Registered Files, East Africa (EA series) (DO 213) 1963–7
Commonwealth Relations Office and Commonwealth Office: East Africa Economic Department and Development Policy and East and West Africa Economic Department: Registered Files, East Africa Economic (EAE series) (DO 214) 1964–6
Commonwealth Office and Foreign and Commonwealth Office: East Africa Departments: Registered Files (P and JE series) (FCO 31) 1967 onwards
Foreign and Commonwealth Office and predecessors: Records of Former Colonial Administrations: Migrated Archives (FCO 141)

Zimbabwe *see* Southern Rhodesia

Zululand

Zululand first came under British influence in 1879 when, after long conflicts with the Boers and the Natal government, a British resident was appointed as adviser to the thirteen Zulu chiefs holding office. In 1887 Zululand was declared British territory. The office of resident commissioner was continued under the governor of Natal, in whom legislative authority was vested. In 1897 Zululand was annexed to Natal.

For the Zulu War of 1878/9 see records of the War Office, especially WO 32.

Colonial Office

Zululand: Original Correspondence (CO 427) 1887–97, 28 volumes
Zululand: Register of Correspondence (CO 619) 1887–97, 2 volumes
Zululand: Register of Out-letters (CO 620) 1887–97, 1 volume
Zululand: Acts (CO 322) 1887–97, 1 volume
Zululand: Miscellanea (CO 472) 1889–96, 8 volumes of blue books of statistics

Appendix 2
Records arranged by subject

This appendix lists the record series of subject-based departments within the Colonial Office, Dominions Office, Commonwealth Relations Office and Commonwealth Office, together with other records of a general nature, i.e., those which are not geographically arranged, and some relating to common services. Later records of the Foreign and Commonwealth Office are occasionally referred to, but are not listed systematically.

In the case of the Colonial Office the gradual development of subject departments described at pp. 43–5 was matched by the creation of record series specific to each department; most subject-based functions had previously been the responsibility of the General Department and correspondence earlier than that listed can usually be found in its records (in CO 323). In other cases a department may have emerged from an earlier specialist department. For example, the Economic Department which first split off from the General Department in 1934 subsequently underwent a number of reorganisations, spawning departments responsible for supplies, production and marketing. As noted elsewhere the internal division of responsibility within the Colonial Office is given in the annual *Colonial Office List*, and an organisation chart showing the development of subject departments is at figure 6. The case of records of the Dominions Office/Commonwealth Relations Office is somewhat different. Although the Dominions Office also worked partly through specialist subject departments (which were inherited and developed by the Commonwealth Relations Office) these arrangements did not initially affect record-keeping practices. Until at least the early 1950s the records of subject departments will be found in DO 35, together with the geographically arranged collections.

Much specialist work of the Colonial Office and Commonwealth Relations Office was transferred to the newly created Department for Technical Co-operation in 1961, together with advisory staff and committees, and records from that period should be sought in 'OD' record series.

In an attempt to make this list as useful as possible entries have been provided for some subjects as well as for named departments, with cross-references as appropriate. It starts with a listing of various record series which are 'general' in their coverage, including but not limited to records of the Colonial Office General Department for which there is also a separate entry.

General

Colonial Office and predecessors

Colonies, General: Original Correspondence (CO 323) 1689–1952, 1,931 volumes and boxes of files

Colonial Office: General Register of Correspondence (CO 378) 1852–1952, 218 volumes (for registers before 1852, see CO 326)

General Entry Books, Series I (CO 324) 1662–1872, 176 volumes

General Miscellanea (CO 325) 1744–1909, 54 volumes

General Draft Letters Patent, Commissions, Royal Instructions, Warrants, etc. (CO 380) 1764–1925, 215 volumes

General Entry Books, Series II (CO 381) 1740–1872, 93 volumes. This series is arranged almost entirely by colony or region, and is 19th century with the exception of one volume dated 1740 and described as 'abstract of commissions and instructions'.

Register of Daily Correspondence (CO 382) 1849–1929, 82 volumes

Duplicates of Correspondence (CO 412) 1605–1863 (The presence of this collection of duplicates is explained by the practice of sending despatches from the colonies in duplicate or triplicate. Some of the duplicates originally allocated to this series have been returned to the Colonial Office or donated to overseas governments or to the Crown agents, as noted in the catalogue.)

Colonies General Register of General Miscellaneous Correspondence (CO 432) 1860–70, 2 volumes

Colonies General: Supplementary Original Correspondence (CO 537) 1759–1955, 7862 files and volumes

Colonies General Secret Entry Books and Register of Out-letters (CO 570) 1870–95, 2 volumes

Colonies General Register of 'Unregistered' Correspondence (CO 652) 1886–1927, 4 volumes

Index to Register of Daily Correspondence (CO 668) 1901–10, 9 volumes

Colonies General Register of Secret Correspondence (CO 694) 1865–1938, 42 volumes

Colonies General Circular Despatches (CO 854) 1808–1966, 231 volumes

Colonies General Indexes to Circular Despatches (CO 949) 1808–1956, 13 volumes

Colonies General Registers of Replies to Circular Despatches (CO 862) 1862–1931, 25 volumes

War and Colonial Department and Colonial Office: Subjects Affecting Colonies Generally, Confidential Print (CO 885) 1839–1966, 140 volumes

Register of Acts (CO 383) 1781–1892, 93 volumes

Defence and General Department: Coronation of Elizabeth II, Registered Files (COR series) (CO 1021) 1952–6, 13 files

Accounts

Colonial Office and predecessors

Accounts Branch and Successors: Original Correspondence (CO 431) 1868–1925, 152 volumes

Accounts Branch: Registers of Correspondence (CO 622) 1868–1921, 18 volumes
Accounts Branch: Entry Books and Register of Out-letters (CO 621) 1868–1908, 19 volumes
Accounts Branch: Miscellanea (CO 701) 1794–1954, 30 volumes and files (This series contains miscellanea from the Accounts Branch and successors, including: the Contingent Fund account of the Colonial and War Departments, 1795–1868; applications to the Treasury for money, 1794–1868; the Fee Fund, 1795–1848; estimates, 1794–1868; accounting documents connected with the West Africa Frontier Force, etc.)

Commonwealth Relations Office

Commonwealth Relations Office and Diplomatic Service Administration Office: Accountant-General's Department and Finance Department: Registered Files (AG series) (DO 156) 1951–67, 25 files

Administration *see under* Establishment

Aid *see* Development *and* Technical assistance

Appointments *see under* Personnel

Chief Clerk's Department

The chief clerk, first appointed in 1795, was the most senior of the permanent establishment of the Colonial Office. He was responsible for military work, the management of the common services of the office, including the library and registry, and for that work of the office which could not be fitted into the geographical framework but affected the colonies collectively. Between 1843 and 1849 his office achieved departmental status. Subsequently several new departments were established to take over his responsibilities, specifically the General Department. This series comprises the correspondence, mostly of a later date than 1901, of the Chief Clerk's Department and the General Department on such formal matters as precedence, seals, the consecration of colonial bishops, medals, titles, the coronations and the drafting of governors' instructions.

Chief Clerk: Original Correspondence (CO 523) 1843–1931, 92 volumes
General Department and Chief Clerk's Department: Registers of Correspondence (CO 863) 1902–31, 8 volumes
General Department and Chief Clerk's Department: Registers of Out-letters (CO 864) 1902–33, 4 volumes

Colonial Empire Marketing Board *see* Empire Marketing Board

Commercial Treaties Branch

The branch, formerly part of the Economic Relations Department, was established in 1952 when it took over the work of the former department. It was absorbed by the Economic General Department in 1954.

Original Correspondence (CO 1016) 1951–6, 115 files
Commonwealth Relations Office: Commercial Policy: Registered Files (CPD series) (DO 162) 1963–6, 101 files

Committees, Commissions and Panels

This is not a full listing of all committees, but only of those for which there are discrete series of records. Papers of, or relating to, other committees should be sought in the appropriate series of correspondence, or in the confidential print. Additional papers of the committees listed here, or their predecessors, may also be found in such series. The records of commissions and other temporary bodies whose work was devoted to a single dependency or group of dependencies are listed in appendix 1.

British Phosphate Commissioners (DO 140) 1873–1983, 853 files and photographs
Colonial Economic Research Committee: Minutes and Papers (CO 898) 1947–61, 8 volumes
Colonial Office: Advisory Committee on Colonial Colleges of Arts, Science and Technology: Minutes and Papers (CO 995) 1949–52, 5 files
Colonial Office: Advisory Committee on Education in the Colonies: Papers and Minutes (CO 987) 1941–61, 42 files
Colonial Office: Advisory Committee on Overseas Geology and Mineral Resources and Predecessor (CO 1001) 1949–61, 4 files
Colonial Office: Advisory Committee on Treatment of Offenders in the Colonies and Related Bodies: Minutes and Papers (CO 912) 1937–61, 23 volumes
Colonial Office: Colonial Advisory Council of Agriculture, Animal Health and Forestry: Minutes and Papers (CO 996) 1943–51, 15 files
Colonial Office: Colonial Advisory Medical Committee: Minutes and Papers (CO 994) 1940–52, 5 files
Colonial Office: Colonial Agricultural, Animal Health and Forestry Research Committee: Minutes and Papers (CO 908) 1944–61, 42 volumes
Colonial Office: Colonial Development Advisory Committee (CO 970) 1929–40, 3 volumes
Colonial Office: Colonial Economic Advisory Committee: Minutes and Papers (CO 990) 1943–6, 19 files
Colonial Office: Colonial Economic and Development Council: Minutes and Papers (CO 999) 1946–8, 5 files

Colonial Office: Colonial Fisheries Advisory Committee: Minutes and Papers (CO 910) 1943–61, 5 volumes
Colonial Office: Colonial Higher Education Commission (Asquith Commission, 1943–4) (CO 958) 1943–4, 3 volumes
Colonial Office: Colonial Housing Research Group: Minutes and Papers (CO 1005) 1944, 2 files
Colonial Office: Colonial Insecticides Committee and Colonial Pesticides Research Committee: Minutes and Papers (CO 911) 1947–61, 26 volumes
Colonial Office: Colonial Labour Committee and Colonial Labour Advisory Committee: Papers and Minutes (CO 888) 1931–66, 11 volumes
Colonial Office: Colonial Land Tenure Advisory Panel: Minutes and Papers (CO 993) 1945–52, 6 files
Colonial Office: Colonial Local Government Advisory Panel (CO 915) 1948–60, 3 volumes
Colonial Office: Colonial Medical Research Committee: Minutes and Papers (CO 913) 1945–60, 19 files and volumes
Colonial Office: Colonial Native Law Advisory Panel: Minutes and Papers (CO 1003) 1946–52, 4 files
Colonial Office: Colonial Primary Products Committee: Minutes and Papers (CO 1002) 1947–9, 8 files
Colonial Office: Colonial Social Welfare Advisory Committee: Minutes and Papers (CO 997) 1943–52, 17 files
Colonial Office: Colonial University Grants Advisory Committee: Minutes and Papers (CO 1004) 1950–1, 1 file
Colonial Office: Commission to Enquire into the Service, Salary Scales, etc. of Colonial Government Staff (CO 963) 1945–8, 230 files
Colonial Office: Committee on Mass Education (Community Development): Minutes and Papers (CO 1000) 1949–51, 4 files
Colonial Office: Committee on the Deportation of British Subjects from the Colonies (CO 916) 1932–3, 1 volume
Colonial Office: Committee on the Training of Nurses for the Colonies: Minutes and Papers (CO 998) 1943–5, 6 files
Colonial Office: Concessions and Finance Committees (CO 948) 1907–12, 2 volumes
Colonial Office: Office Committee on Co-operation in the Colonies: Minutes and Papers (CO 1007) 1944–6, 2 files
Colonial Office: Working Party on the Employment in the United Kingdom of Surplus Colonial Labour: Minutes and Papers (CO 1006) 1948, 2 files
Colonial Products Research Council and Colonial Products Council: Minutes and Papers (CO 899) 1943–59, 6 volumes
Colonial Research Committee and Colonial Research Council: Minutes and Papers (CO 900) 1943–59, 16 volumes
Colonial Social Science Research Council: Minutes and Papers (CO 901) 1944–61, 40 volumes
Imperial Economic Committee and Commonwealth Economic Committee: Records (DO 222) 1924–68, 41 volumes and files

Private Enterprise Committee (CO 766) 1923, 1 volume
Tsetse Fly and Trypanosomiasis Committee: Minutes and Papers (CO 902) 1944–61, 21 volumes

Common Market *see under* Economic Departments and International Relations

Communications

A Communications Department was established in the Colonial Office in 1943 with responsibility for subjects such as post and telecommunications, civil aviation, road transport, merchant shipping and meteorological services. It was transferred to the Department of Technical Co-operation in 1961 but re-established within the Economic Division of the Colonial Office in 1965 and absorbed by the Commonwealth Office in 1966. Before 1943 communications were the responsibility of the General Department (CO 323). A Communications Department was first set up in the Commonwealth Relations Office in 1953.

Colonial Office/Department of Technical Co-operation

Original Correspondence (CO 937) 1944–67, 605 boxes of files
Register of Correspondence (CO 973) 1944–52, 34 volumes
Department of Technical Co-operation and Colonial Office: Communications Department: Registered Files (CM series) (OD 23) 1961–6, 190 files

Commonwealth Relations Office/Commonwealth Office

Commonwealth Relations Office and Commonwealth Office: Communications Department and Successors: Registered Files (COM series) (DO 160) 1955–66, 68 files

For earlier records of the Dominions Office and Commonwealth Relations Office concerning communications, see DO 35. For later records, see FCO 19, Diplomatic Service Administration Office and Foreign and Commonwealth Office: Communications Department and successors, 1967 onwards.

Constitutional Policy and Constitutional Planning Departments

A Constitutional Planning Department was created in the Colonial Office in 1965 with responsibility for the co-ordination of constitutional developments in the emerging independent territories; the department was absorbed by the Commonwealth Office in 1966. A Constitutional Department existed in the Commonwealth Relations Office from 1953; it became the Constitutional and Protocol Department in 1965, and the Commonwealth Policy and Planning Department in 1966. The records noted below deal with subjects such as constitutional development in the Commonwealth, royal visits and honours, appeals to the Judicial Committee of the Privy Council, protocol matters, and the formation of the Commonwealth Secretariat.

Earlier Dominions Office/Commonwealth Relations Office records are in DO 35.

There are no comparable record series for earlier periods. Details of constitutional change should be sought in the original correspondence series for individual dependencies, in the government gazettes, and in general series such as CO 380, Colonial Office and Predecessors: General Draft Letters Patent, Commissions, Royal Instructions, Warrants, etc., 1764–1925.

Colonial Office/Commonwealth Relations Office/Commonwealth Office

Colonial Office and Commonwealth Office: Dependent Territories Constitutions Department and Predecessors: Registered Files (CNS series) (CO 1058) 1965–7, 42 files

Commonwealth Relations Office and Commonwealth Office: Constitutional Department and Successors: Registered Files (CON series) (DO 161) 1953–67, 493 files

Commonwealth Relations Office: Planning and Research Unit: Registered Files (PLA series) (DO 193) 1957–66, 91 files

Cultural Relations

This series contains files produced by the Cultural Relations Department of the Commonwealth Relations Office and Commonwealth Office dealing with educational and cultural relations within the Commonwealth. For earlier records of the department, see DO 35. For later records, see FCO 13, Foreign and Commonwealth Office and Predecessors: Cultural Relations Departments: Registered Files (CR, CU and PC series) (FCO 13) 1967 onwards. See also under British Council in chapter 12.

Commonwealth Relations Office and Commonwealth Office: Cultural Relations Department: Registered Files (CUL and CRD series) (DO 163) 1960–7, 119 files

Defence Department *see also under* Military

By 1940 a Colonial Office Defence Department had been established within the General Division; it dealt with all general defence questions including censorship, aviation, broadcasting, extradition and deportation. The Military Section, which dealt with the King's African Rifles and the West Africa Frontier Force, now became part of the Defence Department, and its staff was expanded to handle work in connection with the African colonial forces and the local forces of other dependencies. In 1948 the Defence Department became the Defence and General Department; in 1955 the Defence Department; in 1961 the Defence Department became the Defence, Intelligence and Security Department; in 1963 the Defence, Intelligence and Hong Kong Department; and in 1965 the Defence and Intelligence Department. It was absorbed by the Commonwealth Office in 1966. A Defence Department was established in the Commonwealth Relations Office in 1947; it became the Defence and Western Department in 1958; and the Defence Department in 1960.

Colonial Office/Commonwealth Office

Colonial Office and Commonwealth Office: Defence Department and Successors: Original Correspondence (CO 968) 1941–67, 913 boxes of files

Register of Correspondence (CO 974) 1941–51, 34 volumes

Colonial Office and Commonwealth Office: Defence and General Department and Successors: Registered Files, General Colonial Policy (GEN series) (CO 1032) 1950–68, 523 files

Colonial Office: Defence and General Department: Coronation of Elizabeth II, Registered Files (COR Series) (CO 1021) 1952–56, 13 files

Commonwealth Relations Office

Commonwealth Relations Office: Defence: Registered Files (DEF series) (DO 164) 1957–67, 136 files

For earlier records of the Commonwealth Relations Office Defence Department, see DO 35. For later records, see FCO 46, Foreign Office and Foreign and Commonwealth Office: Defence Department and Successors: Registered Files (ZD, DP and DT series) 1967 onwards.

Development *see also* Technical assistance

Records of the West Indies Development and Welfare Organisation are in the Colonial Office series CO 1042 (1938–58). They relate to the organisation's wide range of responsibilities in the fields of economic and social development, including projects arising from the Colonial Development and Welfare Act 1940. Subjects covered include agriculture, fisheries, industrial development, transport and employment, and the development of welfare services, health, education and housing, together with public administration and public relations. Much other material about development projects is included in geographically arranged record series and among the records of the Economic and Finance Departments. Dominions Office/Commonwealth Relations records relating to the Colonial Development Fund and the Colonial Development Corporation are mainly in DO 35. The Department of Technical Co-operation and its successors became the lead departments in the area from 1961 onwards; its records are in OD series.

Dominions General

The business of the Colonial Office was split between a Dominions Division and a Crown Colonies Division in 1907, and a separate government department, the Dominions Office, was established in 1925 (see p. 48). This section lists record series concerning the dominions generally; for records relating to individual territories, see appendix 1.

Colonial Office

Colonial Office: Dominions: Original Correspondence (CO 532) 1907–25, 335 volumes

Colonial Office: Dominions Register of Correspondence (CO 708) 1907–26, 37 volumes

Colonial Office: Dominions Register of Out-letters (CO 709) 1907–26, 12 volumes

Colonial Office: Dominions, Confidential Print (CO 886) 1907–25, 11 volumes

Colonial Office: Dominions (War of 1914–18): Original Correspondence (CO 616) 1914–19, 82 volumes
Colonial Office: Dominions (War of 1914–18): Register of Correspondence (CO 752) 1914–19, 8 volumes
Colonial Office: Dominions (War of 1914–18): Register of Out-letters (CO 753) 1914–19, 5 volumes
Colonial Office: Dominions (War of 1914–18): Trade Original Correspondence (CO 687) 1916–19, 68 volumes
Colonial Office: Dominions (War of 1914–18): Trade Register of Correspondence (CO 756) 1916–19, 4 volumes
Colonial Office: Dominions (War of 1914–18): Trade Register of Out-letters (CO 757) 1916–19, 4 volumes
Colonial Office: Dominions (War of 1914–18): Prisoners Original Correspondence (CO 693) 1917–19, 10 volumes
Colonial Office: Dominions (War of 1914–18): Prisoners Register of Correspondence (CO 754) 1917–19, 2 volumes
Colonial Office: Dominions (War of 1914–18): Prisoners Register of Out-letters (CO 755) 1917–19, 2 volumes

Colonial Office/Dominions Office/Commonwealth Relations Office

Dominions Office and Commonwealth Relations Office: Original Correspondence (DO 35) 1915–71, 10,914 files and volumes
Dominions Office: Register of Correspondence (DO 3) 1927–42, 184 volumes
Dominions Office: Register of Out-letters (DO 4) 1927–9, 3 volumes
Confidential Print: Dominions (DO 114) 1924–51, 120 volumes
Dominions Office: Supplementary Original Correspondence (DO 117) 1926–9, 189 files
Colonial Office and Successors: Agreements, Treaties and Miscellaneous Documents (DO 118) 1856–1969, 477 flat sheets, photographs and volumes

Economic Departments/Division

An Economic Section within the Colonial Office General Department, first established to deal with matters relating to the Ottawa Conference of 1932, became the Economic Department in 1934. It dealt with the marketing and development of colonial produce and with trade relations. In 1943 the department was split into a Supplies Department and a Production Department. A Marketing Department was established in 1946, and further reorganisation took place over the following two years. By 1949 the various economic departments had come together within an Economic Intelligence and Manning Division. In 1961 some of the division's functions were transferred to the Department of Technical Co-operation (records in 'OD' series). Similarly, the Commonwealth Relations Office included a number of economic departments during its history; earlier records of the Dominions Office relating to economic development and related matters can be found in DO 35. The series listed below cover a broad range of colonial economic policy including commerce, finance, industrial development, the supply and production of food and commodities, tariffs and taxation policy. Records relate to the Colonial Development Corporation, to international commercial relations, to American aid and associated questions, and to the United Nations. They include material on UK negotiations to enter the European Economic Community and related organisations and Commonwealth reactions to those negotiations, and papers of or relating to a number of internal or associated committees. The later economic work of the Foreign and Commonwealth Office is arranged under a number of economic general and economic geographical departments.

Colonial Office

Colonial Office: Economic General Department and Predecessors: Registered Files (CO 852) 1935–66, 2,447 boxes of files

Colonial Office: Economic General Department and Predecessors: Registers of Correspondence (CO 920) 1935–52, 266 volumes

Colonial Office: Economic Relations Department: Registered Files (ERD series) (CO 1056) 1962–6, 182 files

Commonwealth Relations Office/Commonwealth Office

Commonwealth Relations Office: Economic Policy: Registered Files (EC and EP series) (DO 165) 1960–7, 174 files

Commonwealth Relations Office and Commonwealth Office: Economic Relations Divisions I and II and Successors: Registered Files (ER and WED series) (DO 189) 1960–7, 704 files

Commonwealth Relations Office and Commonwealth Office: Economic General Department: Registered Files (EGD series) (DO 215) 1964–7, 321 files

Education

In the Colonial Office education was a responsibility of the Social Services Department, established in 1939, the records of which are in CO 859. General policy matters were previously the responsibility of the General Department, whose records are in CO 323. See also under committees, and under welfare and students. An Education Department was established in the Commonwealth Relations Office in 1960, but only for a brief period; the specialist work of both the Colonial Office and the Commonwealth Relations Office was subsequently transferred to the Department of Technical Co-operation (see OD series).

Commonwealth Relations Office

Commonwealth Relations Office: Education: Registered Files (ED series) (DO 167) 1960–1, 6 files. For earlier records see DO 35

Emigration *see under* Migration

Empire Marketing Board *see also under* Production and Marketing Departments in this appendix and pp. 161–3

Dominions Office: Empire Marketing Board: Original Correspondence (CO 758) 1922–34, 107 boxes of files
Dominions Office: Empire Marketing Board: Card Index (CO 759) 1922–34, 134 bundles
Dominions Office: Empire Marketing Board Minutes and Papers (CO 760) 1926–33, 39 volumes
Colonial Office: Colonial Empire Marketing Board: Original Correspondence (CO 868) 1938–9, 7 boxes
Colonial Office: Empire Marketing Board: Posters (CO 956) 1926–39, 734 flat sheets

Establishment

An establishment officer was appointed in the Colonial Office in 1922, and became part of the joint establishment after the creation of the Dominions Office three years later. Until 1930 the role came under the General Department, and thereafter under the Colonial Service Department within the Personnel Division. By 1945 a separate Establishment Department had been set up. The Establishment miscellanea series (CO 878) includes: office minutes, 1836–29; a set of Colonial Office bulletins, 1920–32; and a series of establishment notices, 1935–65. The papers contain instructions to staff, regulations, material relating to appointments, and other matters affecting the internal administration of the office. When the joint Colonial Office/ Dominions Office establishment broke up in 1947 a separate Establishment Department was created within the Commonwealth Relations Office. It became the Establishment and Organisation Department the following year, and was absorbed by the Commonwealth Office in 1966.

Colonial Office

Colonial Office and Predecessors: Establishment Miscellanea (CO 878) 1794–1965, 34 volumes
Colonial Office: Establishment and Organisation Department and Predecessors: Registered Files (EOD and other series) (CO 866) 1922–67, 176 volumes and boxes of files
Colonial Office: Establishment and Organisation Department and Predecessors: Registers of Correspondence (CO 867) 1922–51, 21 volumes

Commonwealth Relations Office

Commonwealth Relations Office: Establishment Department: Registered Files (DO 152) 1953–8, 3 files
Commonwealth Relations Office: Administration: Registered Files (ADM series) (DO 155) 1960–5, 54 files
Commonwealth Relations Office: Administration Department, Inspectorate: Registered Files, Inspection of Overseas Posts (INSP series) (CO 218) 1964, 2 files

Finance

A financial adviser was appointed in the Economic Department of the Colonial Office in 1939 to deal with taxation, exchange control, war loans and war damage. The post was converted to a Finance Department in 1942. It was called the Finance and Development Department in 1944 and the Finance and Economic Department in 1945 before resuming its original name in 1946. It handled all important questions of post-war investment from colonial development funds. The department existed until 1966 when it was absorbed by the Commonwealth Office. For earlier papers, see CO 852, Economic General Department and Predecessors: Registered Files.

Colonial Office

Colonial Office: Finance Department: Registered Files (FIN series) (CO 1025) 1951–66, 289 files

Commonwealth Relations Office

Commonwealth Relations Office and Diplomatic Service Administration Office: Accountant-General's Department and Finance Department: Registered Files (AG series) (DO 156) 1951–67, 25 files

French Relations Department

The department was created within the Colonial Office in 1940 to handle questions arising from the division of the former French colonial empire between the Vichy administration and the Free French. The papers of this department, which was closely associated with the Cabinet Committee on French Resistance, were never registered separately and are to be found in a large number of sub-files of the General Department (CO 323) and then in the Defence Department (CO 968) under file numbers 13076 and 13093. These files are registered in the General Secret Register (CO 694).

General Department/Division *see also under* 'General' at the start of this appendix

The responsibilities of the General Department varied quite considerably from time to time, but primarily it was concerned with matters relating to the empire as a whole, or to issues concerning more than one colony. Earlier records include: those formerly known as 'Plantations General' among the Board of Trade correspondence, 1689–1780; law officers reports on colonial acts; applications for passports and colonial appointments; private correspondence of Earl Bathurst, 1822–5, and R. W. Hay, 1825–35; and correspondence, including circular despatches, relating to the colonies generally. Between 1801 and 1854, when the departments of War and the Colonies were under the same secretary of state, much of the correspondence concerns both departments. In the early 20th century matters covered include many which were subsequently to become the responsibility of the new subject departments, for example relating to economic and social concerns, but the General Department and its successors retained responsibility for matters such as war graves and memorials in the colonies; war pensions; constitutional questions and colonial legislation; ceremonial matters, flags and precedence; consular matters; the deportation of UK and colonial citizens from foreign countries; passports and visas; colonial development; immigration into the UK and emigration; dangerous drugs; and a small amount of miscellaneous international business, including papers for Commonwealth Prime Ministers' Conferences. From 1862 full details of the responsibilities of the departments can be found in the annual *Colonial Office List*. Earlier records of the general departments of the Dominions Office and Commonwealth Relations Office can be found in DO 35.

Colonial Office

Colonies, General: Original Correspondence (CO 323) 1689–1952, 1931 volumes and boxes of files, continued in Defence and General Department and Successors: Registered Files, General Colonial Policy (GEN series) CO 1032, 1950–68, 523 files

Colonial Office: General Register of Correspondence (CO 378) 1852–1952, 218 volumes

Colonial Office: General Register of Out-letters (CO 379) 1871–1925, 24 volumes

Commonwealth Relations Office and Commonwealth Office

Commonwealth Relations Office and Commonwealth Office: General Department and Successors: Registered Files (GEN series) (DO 170) 1953–67, 128 files

Honours

Matters relating to the award of honours had traditionally been the responsibility of the Colonial Office Chief Clerk's Department. By at least 1901 an Honours Department was in existence, with responsibility also for charters, letters patent, commissions and warrants, etc. The Imperial Service Order was created in 1902 with one level of award – Companion – and a medal for civil servants. The award of Companion ceased to be used in the United Kingdom in 1993, but the Imperial Service Medal continues to be awarded to certain civil servants. The Order of St Michael and St George was created in 1818 for the inhabitants of Malta and the Ionian Islands and for other British subjects holding high position there or in the British naval forces serving in the Mediterranean. It was extended in 1868 to all colonies, and from 1879 persons connected with the conduct of foreign affairs were admitted.

The Dominions Office series DO 36 listed below is continued in DO 35 until 1953 when material is included in the records of the Constitutional Department of the Commonwealth Relations Office.

Colonial Office

Honours: Original Correspondence (CO 448) 1858–1952, 139 volumes and boxes of files

Honours: Register of Correspondence (CO 728) 1859–1952, 37 volumes

Honours: Register of Out-letters (CO 729) 1872–1934, 4 volumes

Imperial Service Order: Original Correspondence (CO 524) 1902–32, 14 volumes
Imperial Service Order: Register of Correspondence (CO 834) 1902–26, 2 volumes
Imperial Service Order: Register of Out-letters (CO 835) 1902–26, 2 volumes
Order of St Michael and St George: Original Correspondence (CO 447) 1836–1932, 129 volumes
Order of St Michael and St George: Register of Correspondence (CO 845) 1869–1930, 5 volumes (after 1930 correspondence is registered in the Honours register, CO 728)
Order of St Michael and St George: Entry Books and Register of Out-letters (CO 734) 1838–1934, 7 volumes
Order of St Michael and St George: Miscellanea (CO 745) 1818–1940, 5 volumes
Order of St Michael and St George: Original Warrants and Letters Patent (CO 844) 1852–99, 8 volumes
Order of St Michael and St George (Dominions): Original Correspondence (DO 89) 1927–8, 1 volume

Dominions Office/Commonwealth Relations Office/Commonwealth Office
Dominions Office: Honours (Dominions): Original Correspondence (DO 36) 1927–9, 2 volumes
Commonwealth Relations Office and Commonwealth Office: Constitutional Department and Successors: Registered Files (CON series) (DO 161) 1953–67
Dominions Office: Imperial Service Order (Dominions): Original Correspondence (DO 81) 1927–9, 1 volume
Order of St Michael and St George (Dominions): Original Correspondence (DO 89) 1927–8, 1 volume

Immigration *see under* Migration

Information

An acting public relations officer was appointed to the Colonial Office in July 1940, and a Public Relations Department was set up in 1942 to handle publicity about the colonies in Britain and other countries through publications, broadcasting and the supply of information to the press. It was renamed the Information Department in 1946. It was absorbed by the Commonwealth Office in 1966. Related records of the Dominions Office and Commonwealth Relations Office will be found in DO 35. See also under Central Office of Information in chapter 12.

Colonial Office
Public Relations Department, later Information Department: Registered Files (CO 875) 1940–52, 75 files
Public Relations and Information: Register of Correspondence (CO 978) 1941–52, 49 volumes
Information Department: Registered Files (INF series) (CO 1027) 1952–67, 758 files

Commonwealth Relations Office/Commonwealth Office

Commonwealth Relations Office and Commonwealth Office: Information Policy Department: Registered Files (IPD series) (DO 191) 1957–66, 267 files

Commonwealth Relations Office: Information Services Department: Registered Files (ISD series) (DO 192) 1960–6, 48 files

Commonwealth Relations Office and Commonwealth Office: News Department: Registered Files (NEW series) (DO 194) 1960–7, 79 files

See also Colonial Office and Commonwealth Office: Library: Registered Files (COL series) (CO 1059) 1966–7, 5 files

Intelligence

Establishment of a political intelligence section within the Colonial Office was considered in 1948, and discussed again in 1953, but intelligence, security and police matters continued to be handled by the Defence and General Department until 1955 when two new departments were formed. The Intelligence and Security Department provided guidance to colonial governments and liaised with intelligence services in the UK; the Police Department dealt with general colonial questions. The two departments merged in 1959 to become the Intelligence, Police and Security Department. There were subsequent reorganisations as the number of colonial territories decreased: responsibility passed to the Defence, Intelligence and Security Department in 1961; to the Defence, Intelligence and Hong Kong Department in 1963; and finally to the Defence and Intelligence Department in 1965. Records of the Dominions Office and Commonwealth Relations Office relating to intelligence and security can be found in DO 35, among the papers of the Defence Departments (see above) and also in series relating to individual territories. See also under Intelligence agencies in chapter 12.

Colonial Office

Intelligence and Security Departments: Registered Files (ISD series) (CO 1035) 1954–65, 195 files. At the time of writing a further 158 files from this series, dated 1963–8 and held amongst the 'special collections' at the FCO, are being assessed for transfer to TNA.

International Relations

The International Relations Department of the Colonial Office was set up in 1944. It co-ordinated work relating to relations with international organisations such as the UN Trusteeship Council, the International Labour Organisation, UNESCO and the Food and Agriculture Organisation. From 1950 to 1952 it was divided into Departments A and B. In 1961 it merged with the General Department to become the International Relations and General Department, which was absorbed by the Commonwealth Office in 1966. See also under French Relations Department. A comparable department to deal with the UN and its specialist agencies was established in the Commonwealth Relations Office in 1953; earlier records relating to international organisations are in DO 35.

Colonial Office/Commonwealth Office

Colonial Office and Commonwealth Office: International and General Department and Predecessors: Original Correspondence (CO 936) 1944–67, 979 files and boxes of files

Registers of Correspondence (CO 989) 1946–51, 14 volumes

Commonwealth Relations Office/Commonwealth Office

Commonwealth Relations Office: Common Market: Registered Files (CMD series) (DO 159) 1954–63, 83 files

Commonwealth Relations Office and Commonwealth Office: United Nations Department and Successors: Registered Files (UND series) (DO 181) 1940–66, 180 files

Commonwealth Relations Office and Commonwealth Office: Western and Middle East Department and Successors: Registered Files, Canada, Ireland and International Western Organisations (WES series) (DO 182) 1960–6, 185 files

Internees *see under* Prisoners of War and Civilian Internees

King's African Rifles *see under* Military

Legal Departments

Although there had always been a legal adviser in the Colonial Office (although not necessarily under that title) a separate Legal Department was not created until 1949. It was treated as a division from 1951. Its responsibilities (formerly dealt with by the General Department) concerned all legal matters affecting the colonies in general in areas such as matrimonial and family law, constitutional and procedural matters, questions of nationality and naturalisation, qualifications and appointment of lawyers. It was absorbed by the Commonwealth Office in 1966. Early Colonial Office papers on legal matters will be found among the territorial or subject series according to the subjects under discussion. In addition a collection of legal advisers' reports on colonial legislation and other matters is in CO 323/34–95, 1784–1860. As well as the small series of Commonwealth Relations Office legal adviser's papers listed below, there are files relating to legal matters in DO 35 and other geographically and subject-based records of the Dominions Office and Commonwealth Relations Office. Records of the Legal Departments of the Commonwealth Office and Foreign Office are in FCO 52, 1967 onwards.

Colonial Office

Colonial Office: Legal Department: Registered Files (LEG series) (CO 1026) 1951–67, 327 files

Colonial Office: Legal Department: Registers of Correspondence (CO 1013) 1951–2, 4 volumes

Dominions Office/Commonwealth Relations Office

Commonwealth Relations Office: Legal Adviser's Department: Registered Files (LEG series) (DO 219) 1964–6, 3 files

Maps and Plans

Three Colonial Office library collections of maps and plans have been transferred to TNA as follows. For further information about maps, see chapter 10.

Colonial Office and Predecessors: Maps and Plans: Series I (CO 700) 1595–1927, 2,975 flat sheets and volumes
Colonial Office: Maps and Plans: Series II (CO 1047) 1779–1947, 1,101 flat sheets
Colonial Office and Successors: Maps and Plans: Post-1940 Collection (CO 1054) 1897–1984, 305 flat sheets

Marketing *see under* Production and Marketing Departments, Empire Marketing Board

Migration

A variety of government departments and other agencies had a responsibility for migration within the British empire. A Colonial Land and Emigration Commission was created in 1840 to undertake the duties of two earlier and overlapping authorities which were both under the supervision of the secretary of state for the colonies. These were the colonisation commissioners for South Australia, established under an Act of 1834, and the agent general for emigration, appointed in 1837. The new commission dealt with land grants, the outward movement of settlers, the administration of the Passenger Acts of 1855 and 1863 and, from 1846 to 1859, the scrutiny of colonial legislation. Its records include copies of *The Colonial Gazette*, a weekly journal published in connection with the Colonial Society, for 1839–42 (CO 386/190-3). In 1855 it became the Emigration Commission. The commission's powers were gradually given up to the larger colonies as they attained self-government, and after 1873 it was responsible only for controlling the importation of Indian labour into sugar-producing colonies. In 1873 the administration of the Passenger Acts was transferred to the Board of Trade. The Emigration Commission was abolished in 1878 when an Emigration Department was set up within the Colonial Office. The new department merged with the General Department in 1894, and was abolished in 1896. Meanwhile in 1886 an Emigrants' Information Office had been established to provide impartial information about emigration. It was under Colonial Office supervision, but had a voluntary committee of management. After the First World War the British government saw a need for closer supervision of emigration, and the voluntary committee was replaced in 1918 by the Government Emigration Committee, which was renamed the Oversea Settlement Committee the following year. The committee operated as a sub-department of the Colonial Office, with responsibility for the movements of British subjects wishing to settle overseas. In 1925 it was transferred to the Dominions Office, and in 1935 it was replaced by the Oversea Settlement Board, which was responsible for advising the secretary of state for the Dominions on migration policy. Its activities were suspended during the Second World War, and it was not re-established thereafter. Minutes and papers of the board are in DO 35/665–70 and DO 114/89–90, and some related papers can be found in CO 323. Papers collected by William Bankes Amery between 1925 and 1931 relating to the work of the Oversea Settlement Department of the Dominions Office in promoting emigration to Australia in accordance with the terms of the Empire Settlement Act 1922 are in DO 190.

The Children's Overseas Reception Board was established in 1940 to co-ordinate the evacuation of children overseas following offers from governments and individuals within the empire. Records relating to more general schemes for the emigration of children can be found among records relating to the territories concerned.

See also under Welfare and Students Departments in this appendix.

Colonial Office

- Immigration: Original Correspondence (CO 571) 1913–20, 7 volumes (This series continues correspondence of the General Department (CO 323) concerning the entry of Indian indentured labour into the West Indies and Mauritius.)
- Immigration: Register of Correspondence (CO 780) 1913–20, 1 volume
- Emigration: Original Correspondence (CO 384) 1817–96, 193 volumes
- Emigration: Register of Correspondence (CO 428) 1850–96, 14 volumes
- Emigration: Entry Books (CO 385) 1814–71, 30 volumes
- Emigration: Register of Out-letters (CO 485) 1872–1903, 9 volumes
- Land and Emigration Commission, etc. (CO 386) 1833–94, 194 volumes
- Colonial Office: Oversea Settlement Department: Register of Correspondence (CO 791) 1918–26, 10 volumes
- Colonial Office: Oversea Settlement Department: Daily Register of Correspondence (CO 792) 1918–27, 4 volumes

Dominions Office/Commonwealth Relations Office/Commonwealth Office

- Overseas Settlement Department: Original Correspondence (DO 57) 1926–36, 189 boxes of files
- Overseas Settlement Department: Register of Correspondence (DO 5) 1927–36, 12 volumes
- Overseas Settlement Department: Daily Register of Correspondence (DO 6) 1928–9, 3 volumes
- Children's Overseas Reception Board (DO 131) 1940–59, 113 files
- Commonwealth Relations Office and Commonwealth Office: General Department and Successors: Registered Files, Migration (MIG series) (DO 175) 1954–67, 214 files

Military *see also under* Defence

In 1902 the armed forces of the east and central African dependencies (Uganda, the East Africa Protectorate, Somaliland and the British Central Africa Protectorate) were reorganised as one regiment, the King's African Rifles. The Niger and West Africa Frontier Force, known from 1900 as the West Africa Frontier Force and from 1928 as the Royal West Africa Frontier Force, was raised locally in 1897 to protect the frontiers of the British protectorates in west Africa against the French. It was paid by the imperial government, and officered by the British Army. From 1927 the administrative arms of the two units were brought together to form the Military Branch of the Colonial Office. Records relating to the two units were then registered and kept together.

Colonial Office

King's African Rifles: Original Correspondence (CO 534) 1905–26, 63 volumes
King's African Rifles: Register of Correspondence (CO 623) 1905–26, 8 volumes
King's African Rifles: Register of Out-letters (CO 624) 1905–26, 7 volumes
Niger and West Africa Frontier Force: Original Correspondence (CO 445) 1898–1926, 69 volumes
Niger and West Africa Frontier Force: Register of Correspondence (CO 581) 1898–9, 1 volume
West Africa Frontier Force: Register of Correspondence (CO 641) 1900–26, 10 volumes
Niger and West Africa Frontier Force: Register of Out-letters (CO 582) 1898–9, 1 volume
West Africa Frontier Force: Register of Out-letters (CO 642) 1900–26, 10 volumes
Military: Original Correspondence (CO 820) 1927–51, 77 volumes and boxes of files
Military: Register of Correspondence (CO 871) 1927–52, 25 volumes
See also Colonies General: Supplementary Original Correspondence (CO 537) and Accounts Branch: Miscellanea (CO 701), which includes some documents relating to the West Africa Frontier Force

Nationality

Questions relating to national status and naturalisation, and concerning both policy and individual cases, can be found among the records of the Colonial Office General Department (in CO 323, continued in CO 1032), and the Legal Department (CO 1026), as well as in the geographically arranged record series. Similar Dominions Office/Commonwealth Relations Office material is in DO 35 until the raising of the series listed below. See also under Home Office in chapter 12.

Commonwealth Relations Office and Commonwealth Office: Nationality and Consular Department and Predecessors: Registered Files, Commonwealth Nationality (NAT series) (DO 176) 1952–67, 122 files
Commonwealth Relations Office and Commonwealth Office: Nationality and Consular Department and Predecessor: Registered Files, Consular (CLR series) (DO 211) 1964–7, 48 files

News *see* Information

Overseas Settlement *see* Migration

Patronage *see under* Personnel

Personnel

Procedures for the appointment of staff to overseas posts varied considerably in our period, from old-fashioned 'patronage' to more modern recruitment methods. See appendix 8 for more detail of some of the records listed here.

Patronage Original Correspondence (CO 428) 1867–1919, 131 volumes
Patronage Register of Correspondence (CO 430) 1867–1918, 20 volumes. (This series includes lists of applicants, confidential applications and recommendations.)
Appointments Department: Registered Files (CO 877) 1920–52, 59 files
Appointments: Register of Correspondence (CO 918) 1920–52, 36 volumes
Personnel: Original Correspondence (CO 850) 1932–52, 267 boxes of files
Personnel Register of Correspondence (CO 919) 1932–52, 47 volumes
Colonies General: Original Letters Patent, Warrants, etc. (CO 816) 1834–82, 7 papers
Colonial Office and Successors: Colonial Service Division, later Overseas Service Division: Registered Files (CSA, CSB, OSA and BCD series) (CO 1017) 1948–66, 902 files
Training: Registers of Correspondence (CO 1011) 1948–52, 9 volumes
Colonial Office: Precedence Original Correspondence (CO 851) 1873–87, 31 files
Commonwealth Relations Office: Personnel Department: Registered Files (PER series) (DO 197) 1962–5, 52 files
Colonial Office: Governors' Pensions Original Correspondence (CO 449) 1863–1925, 10 volumes
The Governors' Pensions Act was passed in 1865. This series relates to negotiations leading to its enactment, its subsequent amendment and related matters. From 1926 to 1931 it appears to have been absorbed into CO 323, Colonies General: Original Correspondence. After that it forms part of the Personnel Original Correspondence series in CO 850. Up to 1932 correspondence is registered in the registers to general correspondence in CO 378.

Planning *see under* Research

Police Department

A Police Department existed within the Colonial Office during the brief period 1956–8. Policy issues relating to colonial police forces were subsequently handled by the Intelligence, Police and Security Department, 1959–61, the Defence, Intelligence and Security Department, 1961–3, the Defence, Intelligence and Hong Kong Department, 1963–5, and the Defence and Intelligence

Department, 1965–6. Thereafter the responsibility was absorbed into the International and General Department of the Commonwealth Office, 1966–8. Earlier general issues concerning the police were handled by the General Department (see CO 323) and the Defence Department (CO 968), and there is also a good deal of material among the records of the Personnel Division in CO 850. Most papers specific to individual local forces are held among the records of the geographical departments.

Records relating to the South African Constabulary (1902–8) are described under South Africa in appendix 1. Records of the Royal Irish Constabulary, including service records, are in the Home Office series HO 184 (1816–1922). Records of the Palestine Police previously held by the Department for International Development (DfID) were deposited at St Antony's College, Oxford, and at the British Empire and Commonwealth Museum. Following the closure of the museum in late 2012, those records were removed for safe keeping by DfID. At time of writing an assessment of the collection is underway. Once this is completed options for its future will be considered by DfID and TNA.

Relevant records of the Dominions Office and the Commonwealth Relations Office are primarily in DO 35.

Colonial Office/Commonwealth Office

Colonial Office and Commonwealth Office: Police Department and Successors: Registered Files (POL series) (CO 1037) 1953–68, 262 files

See also under Intelligence and Defence

Precedence *see under* Personnel

Printing

Documents printed by the Colonial Office were of two types: those printed as single papers, and those printed in 'slip' form and later combined into volumes of continuous correspondence. The registers in CO 600 give the date of receipt of the manuscript in the Printing Branch or Department, and of its despatch to the printer, the name of the printer, the date of return, the number of copies made, and the disposal of the print within the office. Papers printed as 'slips' were, from 1875, entered in separate registers within CO 600. The Printing Department was part of the shared services of the Colonial Office and Dominions Office after 1925. Although the printing of correspondence was much reduced after the First World War, it continued throughout the life of the Colonial Office and it is not known why no later registers and catalogues exist. There are no comparable records of the Dominions Office/Commonwealth Relations Office, but scattered references can be found in DO 35 and other series.

Lists of Colonial Office and Dominions Office/Commonwealth Relations Office confidential print series are given at p. 103 and p. 135.

Colonial Office: Printing Registers (CO 600) 1864–1914, 26 volumes (These are registers of confidential papers printed, papers printed for Parliament, and papers printed as slips.)
Colonial Office: Confidential Print Catalogues (CO 601) 1852–1934, 6 volumes

Prisoners of War and Civilian Internees

The Dominions Division of the Colonial Office dealt with matters relating to prisoners of war arising from the First World War. In December 1941 an Enquiries and Casualties Branch was set up in the General Department to deal with matters relating to aliens who were prisoners of war or civilian internees in British colonial territories, and to British subjects held in enemy and enemy-occupied territories. It was later renamed the Prisoners of War and Civilian Internees Department, and from October 1942 it included a statistical section. It disappeared as a separate department at the end of the war although the records continue into the 1950s. Records of the Dominions Office and Commonwealth Relations Office relating to prisoners of war and internees are mainly in DO 35.

Colonial Office

Colonial Office: Dominions (War of 1914–18): Prisoners Original Correspondence (CO 693) 1917–19, 10 volumes
Colonial Office: Dominions (War of 1914–18): Prisoners Register of Correspondence (CO 754) 1917–19, 2 volumes
Colonial Office: Dominions (War of 1914–18): Prisoners Register of Out-letters (CO 755) 1917–19, 2 volumes
Prisoners of War and Civilian Internees Department: Original Correspondence (CO 980) 1941–53, 240 files
Prisoners of War and Civilian Internees Department: Register of Correspondence (CO 1012) 1942–8, 15 volumes
Prisoners of War and Civilian Internees Department: Nominal Index of Allied Internees (CO 1070) *c.*1941–7. (This collection of cards records information about civilians and civilian volunteers who were, or were thought to be, interned or imprisoned in Hong Kong and Malaya. It includes details of British, dominions and colonial subjects, but not, for the most part, local colonial inhabitants. There are also cards relating to nationals of various allied states, principally The Netherlands, Norway, Russia and Czechoslovakia.)

Private Office

The series CO 967 contains papers of the private offices of ministers on various subjects including appointments of governors and other officials, visits to and development of the colonies, and the functions and organisation of the Colonial Office. There are also files relating to the League of Nations, the International Tin Agreement and the Imperial Communications Advisory Committee, together with correspondence with various governors and semi-official correspondence. The records are arranged by subject or colony or by the name of the minister or official whose private office papers they were. Private office papers of the Dominions Office and Commonwealth Relations Office are in DO 121. For later private office files, see FCO 73. See also chapter 9 for additional information about private office and private papers.

Colonial Office
Private Office Papers (CO 967) 1873–1966, 443 files
Dominions Office and Commonwealth Relations Office
Private Office Papers (DO 121) 1911–55, 224 files

Private Papers *see* chapter 9

Prize Court

CO 848 consists of Colonial Office records of appeals to the Prize Court relating to claims arising from losses in war, enemy debts and reparations, and includes correspondence with custodians of enemy property in the colonies. Earlier material is in CO 323, which is fully catalogued for the years 1914–26. The records in CO 836–9 are printed reports of Prize Court cases. Other material relating to prize causes is in the records of the High Court of Admiralty (HCA series). Dominions Office/Commonwealth Relations Office records relating to prize courts in the dominions and prize law are in DO 35.

Colonial Office
War of 1914–18 Claims: Original Correspondence (CO 848) 1920–38, 51 boxes
Naval Appeals (CO 836) 1916–21, 2 volumes
Overseas Appeals (CO 837) 1914–19, 2 volumes
United Kingdom Appeals (CO 838) 1914–21, 13 volumes
Naval Prize Tribunal (CO 839) 1918–21, 1 volume
Original Correspondence (CO 969) 1939–51, 314 files
Register of Correspondence (CO 988) 1941–51, 13 volumes

Production and Marketing Departments *see also under* Empire Marketing Board

A Production Department was created in the Colonial Office in 1943 to co-ordinate colonial wartime policy on commodity production; the Marketing Department was set up in 1946 to develop marketing organisation. They merged in 1947. In 1961 some of its functions were transferred to the Department of Technical Co-operation; the remainder were taken over by the Economic General Department.

Colonial Office
   Production and Marketing Department: Registered Files (PMD series) (CO 1029) 1949–63, 329 files

Protocol *see under* Constitutional Policy and Constitutional Planning Departments

Public Relations *see* Information

Research

A Research Department was set up in the Colonial Office in 1945 following an exploration of research needs which had led to the establishment of new advisory bodies such as the Colonial Social Science Research Council. The office also took an interest in scientific research organisations in the colonies, particularly in the field of agriculture, geology and surveying. The new department had an overall responsibility for research projects, but did not itself undertake research. By 1949 it had been incorporated into the Economic Division, and in 1961 it was transferred to the Department of Technical Co-operation. CO 927 contains material on all aspects of research in the sciences and social sciences, and includes minutes and papers of the Colonial Research Council and the Committee for Colonial Agriculture and other colonial research organisations, and files on the use of Colonial Development and Welfare (CDW) funds on research in colonial territories. For records of the African Studies Branch see under 'Africa' in appendix 1.

Colonial Office
   Colonial Office: Research Department: Original Correspondence (CO 927) 1944–62, 825 files and boxes of files
   Colonial Office: Research Department: Registers of Correspondence (CO 976) 1944–52, 28 volumes

Social Services

A Social Services Department was established in the Colonial Office in 1939. It took over and developed former responsibilities of the General Department for labour, nutrition, public health, education, housing and penal administration. In 1941 it also became responsible for the welfare of colonial people in Britain (see also under Welfare and Students Departments). The specialist work of the department was transferred to the Department for Technical Co-operation in 1961. The remaining responsibilities of the Colonial Office reverted to the General Department.

Original Correspondence (CO 859) 1939–63, 1,344 boxes of files
Register of Correspondence (CO 965) 1939–52, 54 volumes

Statistics Department

Created in the Colonial Office in 1948 when the economic departments were reorganised, the Statistics Department operated under a chief statistician until 1961 when it was transferred to the Department of Technical Co-operation. See under Economic Department for earlier correspondence, and records in the 'OD' series for later.

Colonial Statistical Tables Command Papers (CO 442) 1833–1912, 63 volumes of Board of Trade statistics of United Kingdom trade with overseas territories, and the revenue, population and commerce of the United Kingdom and its dependencies
Colonial Office: Statistics Department: Registered Files (STA series) (CO 1034) 1952–62, 39 files

Supplies Department

Created in 1943 when the Economic Department was divided. It co-ordinated colonial requirements and distribution and was represented in Washington by the British Colonies Supply Mission. Renamed the Commercial Relations and Supplies Department in 1945, it became the Supplies Department again in 1948, reverted to the name Commercial Relations and Supplies in 1954 and was abolished the same year.

Colonial Office: Supplies Department: Registered Files (SUP series) (CO 1033) 1951–6, 22 files

Students *see under* Welfare and Students Departments

Technical Assistance *see also* Development

Before the establishment of the Department for Technical Co-operation in 1961 material on the subject of British and international technical assistance for the dependencies and developing world can be found scattered through the geographically arranged records of the Colonial Office (see appendix 1). In addition, there is material among the records of the Social Services Department (CO 859) and the International and General Department (CO 936) which includes, for example, papers relating to the work of the Commission for Technical Co-operation in Africa South of the Sahara (CCTA). References to the CCTA and other international programmes will also be found among the records of the Foreign Office and its successor.

Commonwealth Relations Office/Commonwealth Office

Commonwealth Relations Office: Technical Assistance Department: Registered Files (TA series) (DO 198) 1960–1, 31 files

Commonwealth Office: Aid Department: Registered Files, Development, Aid and Finance Policy (AID series) (CO 1057) 1966–7, 5 files

See also records of the Department of Technical Co-operation and its successors in OD series

Telegraph Section

From 1923 to 1942, a distinct Telegraph Section existed within the General Department of the Colonial Office to deal with telegraphic communications. It was a shared service with the Dominions Office. This small series, however, deals almost entirely with a later period. It includes papers on cipher arrangements with Aden, cost of telegrams, co-ordination of common ciphers with the Commonwealth Relations Office and overseas posts, compensation to Cable and Wireless, and communications problems arising from the merger with the Commonwealth Relations Office.

Telegraph Section: Original Correspondence (CO 1038) 1936–66, 5 files and volumes

United Nations *see under* International Relations

Welfare and Students Departments

A Welfare Section was set up in the Social Services Department in 1941 to look after the interests of colonial people in Britain, particularly students. A separate Welfare Department was created in 1943 with responsibility for clubs and hostels and for UK race relations questions generally. In 1951 it was renamed the Students Department, and in 1956 the Students Branch. In 1961 it was transferred to the Department of Technical Co-operation.

Original Correspondence (CO 876) 1942–52, 276 files (CO 1028) 1952–62, 112 files

Registers of Correspondence (CO 977) 1942–52, 22 volumes

Selected Personal Files (CO 981) 1941–74, 139 files

Colonial Office: Students Department, later Students Branch: Registered Files (STU series) (CO 1028) 1952–62, 112 files

West Africa Frontier Force *see under* Military

Appendix 3
Newspapers

Colonial Office 'rules and regulations' issued from 1837 asked governors to send to London 'such books or pamphlets issuing from the colonial press that may be useful', and it is presumably as a result of this request that colonial newspapers began to be acquired. A circular despatch of 1870 asked governors to send two newspapers in addition to the official gazette. By 1872 126 daily and weekly newspapers were being received, and by 1904 the office received 26,000 issues annually. The newspapers listed below were retained in the Colonial Office and transferred to TNA as part of the 'miscellanea' series for individual colonies. The covering dates given in the list below do not indicate that complete runs of each title within those date ranges are present. There may be gaps. Later accumulations were sent periodically to the British Museum, and should now be sought in the British Library. Following the closure of the Newspaper Library at Colindale in November 2013 the British Library has posted updates about future access to the collections on its website at http://www.bl.uk. The official newspapers or 'gazettes' of colonial governments are held separately in designated series and are listed in appendix 1, although there may be some overlap between the official and commercial titles.

Copies of, or extracts from, local newspapers will sometimes also be found within the 'original correspondence' series.

America

Boston Gazette, 1736	CO 5/899
Connecticut Courant, 1778	CO 5/181
Connecticut Gazette and the Universal Intelligencer, 1782	CO 5/186
Continental Journal and Weekly Advertiser, 1778	CO 5/181
Freeman's Journal or the North American Intelligencer, 1783	CO 5/186
Massachusetts Gazette and Boston Post Boy and Advertiser, 1774	ADM 1/485; T 1/513
New Jersey Gazette, 1778	CO 5/181
New York Gazette and Weekly Mercury, 1776	CO 5/177
New York Gazette or Weekly Post Boy, 1765–6	CO 5/1221
Newport Mercury (Pennsylvania), 1765	CO 5/1233
Pennsylvania Journal and Weekly Advertiser, 1782	CO 5/186
Pennsylvania Packet or General Advertiser, 1778	CO 5/181
Royal Gazette, 1778	CO 5/181

Antigua

Antigua Free Press, 1827–35	CO 10/1

Antigua Messenger, 1836	CO 10/1
Weekly Register, 1827–38	CO 10/1

Bahamas

Argus, 1831–6	CO 27/6
Bahama Herald, 1849–55	CO 27/10–11
Nassau Guardian, 1850–6	CO 27/8–9
Nassau Guardian and Colonial Advertiser, 1847–9	CO 27/7
Royal Gazette and Bahama Advertiser, 1826–36, 1847–9	CO 27/1-2
Royal Gazette and Bahama Advertiser, Commercial Advertiser, 1850–6	CO 27/3–5

Barbados

Barbadian, 1833, 1836	CO 33/4
Barbados Globe and Colonial Advocate, 1833–6	CO 33/4
Barbados Globe Colonial Advocate, 1830–2	CO 33/1
Barbados Globe and Demerara Advocate, 1829–30	CO 33/1
Barbados Mercury and Bridgetown Gazette, 1833, 1836	CO 33/4
The Liberal, 1838–56	CO 33/5–12
The West Indian, 1833	CO 33/4

Bermuda

Bermuda Herald, 1847–51	CO 41/4
The Bermudian, 1847–51	CO 41/5
Royal Gazette and Bermuda Commercial and General Advertiser and Recorder, 1839–53	CO 41/1–3

British Guiana

The Colonist, 1848–56	CO 116/13–16
The Guiana Chronicle, 1835–40	CO 116/1–3
The Royal Gazette, 1838–56	CO 116/3–12

Canada

British Whig (Kingston), 1847–56	CO 47/71–3
The Chronicle and Gazette (Kingston), 1833–42	CO 47/68–70
The Globe (Toronto), 1847–56	CO 47/74–9
Kingston Herald, 1841–7	CO 47/59–60
Montreal Courier, 1850–1	CO 47/54
Montreal Gazette, 1827–57	CO 47/4–26
Montreal Herald, 1824–41	CO 47/1–3
Montreal Weekly Pilot, 1846–51	CO 47/55
Morning Courier, 1835–49	CO 47/42–53
The Patriot, 1829–39	CO 47/61–3
Quebec Gazette, 1829–55	CO 47/27–41

The Toronto Patriot, 1839–48	CO 47/63–7
Upper Canada Herald, 1826–41	CO 47/56–9

Cape of Good Hope

Anglo African (Grahamstown), 1855–7	CO 53/44
The Cape Colonist (Grahamstown), 1850–1	CO 53/38
Cape Frontier Times (Grahamstown), 1840–4, 1847–53	CO 53/18–20
Cape Monitor, 1850–6	CO 53/36–7
Cape of Good Hope and Port Natal Shipping and Mercantile Gazette, 1847–56	CO 53/24–5
Cape of Good Hope Exchange Gazette, 1851–2	CO 53/32
Cape of Good Hope Observer, 1849–51	CO 53/30–1
Cape Town Mail, 1841–52	CO 53/21–3
The Colonist, 1851–7	CO 53/38–9
Eastern Province Herald (Port Elizabeth), 1847–50, 1854–6	CO 53/26–7
Eastern Province News (Port Elizabeth), 1850–3	CO 53/34
Friend of the Sovereignty and Bloemfontein Gazette, 1850–3	CO 53/35
Graaff Reinet Herald, 1852–6	CO 53/43
Grahamstown Journal, 1832–53	CO 53/13–17
Port Elizabeth Mercury, 1850–3	CO 53/33
Port Elizabeth Telegraph and Mercantile Gazette, 1848–55	CO 53/28–9
South African Commercial Advertiser, 1824–51	CO 53/1–9
South African Commercial Advertiser (and Cape Town Mail), 1852–6	CO 53/10–12
De Zuid Afrikaan (Cape Town), 1851–6	CO 53/40–2

Ceylon

Ceylon Times, 1846–56	CO 59/3–10
Colombo Journal, 1832–3	CO 59/1–2
Colombo Observer, 1847–56	CO 59/20–5
The Examiner, 1846–56	CO 59/11–19

Dominica

The Dominican, 1842–56	CO 76/1–3

Jamaica

The Kingston Chronicle, 1835–7	CO 142/3
Morning Journal, 1838–54	CO 142/4–12
The Watchman and Jamaica Free Press, 1830–6	CO 142/1–2

Malta

Malta Mail, 1842–55	CO 163/29–32
Malta Times, 1840–55	CO 163/24–8
Il Mediterraneo, 1838–70	CO 163/7–23
Il Portafoglio Maltese, 1838–55	CO 163/1–6

Mauritius	
Commercial Gazette, 1850–6	CO 172/22–6
Le Cernéen, 1832–56	CO 172/1–10
Le Mauricien, 1848–56	CO 172/13–17
Mauritius Sentinel, 1854–5	CO 172/20–1
Mauritius Times, 1848–9	CO 172/12
Price Current and Shipping List, 1847–53	CO 172/11
Sentinelle de Maurice, 1850–3	CO 172/18–19
Natal	
Natal Independent, 1850–3	CO 183/1
Natal Witness, 1850–3	CO 183/2
New South Wales	
Australasian Chronicle, 1842–3	CO 206/58
Australian, 1824–47	CO 206/16–26
The Monitor, 1826–8	CO 206/27
Morning Chronicle, 1844–7	CO 206/59–60
Sydney Gazette, 1803–40	CO 206/1–15
Sydney Herald, 1831–42	CO 206/33–9
The Sydney Monitor, 1829–41	CO 206/28–32
Sydney Morning Herald, 1842–57	CO 206/39–57
New Zealand	
The Lyttleton Times, 1851–3	CO 213/25
Nelson Examiner and New Zealand Chronicle, 1848–55	CO 213/20–1
The New Zealand Journal, 1840–7	CO 213/1–7
The New Zealand Spectator, 1845–56	CO 213/16–19
The New Zealander, 1845–56	CO 213/11–15
Southern Cross and New Zealand Guardian, 1843–55	CO 213/8–10
The Wellington Independent, 1848–55	CO 22–4
Newfoundland	
Newfoundland Patriot, 1838–53	CO 199/1–3
The Public Ledger, 1838–55	CO 199/4–11
The Times, 1842–55	CO 199/12–15
Nova Scotia	
Acadian Recorder, 1850–5	CO 221/26
The British Colonist, 1848–56	CO 221/19–22
The British North American, 1850–5	CO 221/23–5
Halifax Daily Sun, 1852–6	CO 221/10–14
Halifax Sun, 1849–51	CO 221/8–9

The Morning Chronicle, 1848–56	CO 221/15–18
The Morning Journal, 1854–6	CO 221/27
The Nova Scotian or Colonial Herald, 1829–39	CO 212/1–3
The Nova Scotian (New Series), 1840–53	CO 212/4–6
The Sun, 1847–50	CO 221/7–8

Prince Edward Island

Colonial Herald, 1838–41	CO 231/1

St Lucia

The Palladium, 1838–56	CO 258/1–2

South Australia

Adelaide Observer, 1846–7, 1854–5	CO 17/8–9
Adelaide Times, 1848–56	CO 17/10
Adelaide Weekly Times, 1853–6	CO 17/11
Port Philip Gazette, 1851	CO 17/10
South Australia, 1844–9	CO 17/5–7
South Australian Gazette, 1836–41	CO 17/1
South Australian Register, 1836–52	CO 17/1–3
South Australian Weekly Despatch, with which is incorporated The Adelaide Weekly Times, 1853–4	CO 17/11
Southern Australian, 1838–44	CO 17/4–5
The Times (Melbourne) late the Port Philip Gazette, 1851	CO 17/10

Tasmania

Colonial Times and Tasmanian, 1847–55	CO 284/31–5
The Cornwall Chronicle, 1835–9, 1847–55	CO 284/7–14
The Courier, 1848–55	CO 284/36–40
The Hobart Town Advertiser, 1842–55	CO 284/24–30
The Hobarton Guardian, 1849–54	CO 284/41–2
The Hobarton Mercury, 1854	CO 284/42
The Launceston Advertiser, 1829–39	CO 284/5–6
The Launceston Examiner, 1842–54	CO 284/15–23
The Tasmanian, 1827–36	CO 284/1–3
The Tasmanian and Australasiatic Review, 1837–9	CO 284/4
The Tasmanian Colonist, 1851–4	CO 284/43

Trinidad

Port of Spain Gazette, 1830–55	CO 300/3–9
Trinidad Guardian, 1826–31	CO 300/1–3
Trinidad Spectator, 1845–8	CO 300/12–13

Trinidad Standard and West India Journal, 1837–42	CO 300/10–11
Trinidadian, 1848–53	CO 300/13–15

Victoria

Argus, 1850–6	CO 313/22–30
The Herald, 1855–6	CO 313/19–21
The Melbourne Daily News, 1849–51	CO 313/10–11
The Melbourne Morning Herald, 1849–55	CO 313/12–19
The Port Philip Gazette, 1838–46	CO 313/1–4
The Port Philip Herald, 1842–6	CO 313/8–9
The Port Philip Patriot, 1839–41, 1846–7	CO 313/5–7
The Times (Melbourne) late the Port Philip Gazette, 1851	CO 313/4

Western Australia

Inquirer, 1844–56	CO 22/6–9
Inquirer and Commercial News, 1855–6	CO 22/9
Perth Gazette and Independent Journal of Politics and News, 1848–55	CO 22/4–5
Perth Gazette and Western Australian Journal, 1838–47	CO 22/1–3
Swan River Guardian, 1836–8	CO 22/2

Appendix 4
The *Colonial Office List*

The annual *Colonial Office List* is referred to throughout this guide. Because it is such a useful reference tool a little more is said about it here. A set is available on open access at TNA.

The first edition of the *Colonial Office List* was published in 1862 under the full title *The Colonial Office List for 1862; or, General Register of the Colonial Dependencies of Great Britain*. The title page notes 'first publication – to be continued annually' and in their preface the editors, William C. Sargeaunt and Arthur N. Birch, state 'the present Number is submitted to Subscribers and the Public in fulfilment of promises made in a Circular Letter, dated the 8th November, 1860'. Its contents are:

1. List of secretaries of state from 1804; and under-secretaries from 1835
2. Current establishment of the Colonial Office [i.e., names of staff serving, with dates of appointment and promotion]
3. Organisation of the Colonial Office with lists of staff in each department
4. List of staff of the Colonial Land and Emigration Commission
5. List of emigration officers in the United Kingdom
6. Brief details of each colony – its geography, history under European rule, natural resources, etc. – with list of governors, current membership of the legislature, and the civil, judicial and ecclesiastical establishments
7. List of agents for the colonies residing in England
8. List of foreign consulates in British colonies, with names and dates of appointments of consuls
9. Rules and regulations for Her Majesty's colonial service [see appendix 5 for rules concerning correspondence]
10. Statement 'containing the Dates of the several Appointments, and further remarks respecting those Persons now Living who have served or are now serving under the Secretary of State, or in the Colonies' [These are often very brief notes of the careers of officials, for example 'Tickel, J. – appointed colonial engineer at the Gold Coast, Aug. 1857. Salary £400', but can be quite detailed for long-serving or senior officials.]
11. A final section called the 'Colonial Office List Advertiser', which as well as advertisements for guns, life assurance, books, etc. includes 'The London Wreck Register and Chart for 1860' from *The Times* of 26 September 1861. As there is nothing similar in any later edition this may be just an advertisement for the newspaper.

The 1863 edition is the first to include a map of the British empire. Maps of individual colonies are gradually included; by 1892 there are 26. It is clear from the introductions that the editors were dependent on colonial governments for the provision of these maps.

The introduction to the 1875 edition states that the List has 'passed under New Management' and that its arrangement is 'somewhat altered'. In addition to the information noted above, the new editor, Edward Fairfield, included the following:

- Details of arrangements for emigration to Australia, New Zealand, South Africa and Canada
- 'Regulations respecting admission to colonial appointments at Home and Abroad'
- Details of pension arrangements in various colonies
- A list of honours awarded, with information about the Order of St Michael and St George
- A 'synopsis' of Acts of the UK Parliament, passed in the previous session, affecting the colonies
- A list of Parliamentary papers on colonial affairs dating from 1864

The volume again ends with advertisements, including one for the *List* itself, then priced at six shillings.

The format of the *List* then remains much the same until after the Second World War. The only significant change is that from 1926 it includes details of the newly created Dominions Office, and is renamed the *Dominions Office and Colonial Office List*. It does, however, expand considerably, growing from 164 pages in 1862 to 932 in 1940. Much of this additional bulk is accounted for by the far more detailed entries for individual territories.

The *List* for 1923 includes 53 pages of advertisements – which clearly subsidised costs. Advertisements are for watches, uniforms and tropical outfits, trunks, hydraulic tools, guns, lorries, shipping lines, bankers, accommodation in the UK, ceramics, stationery, medical equipment and tents, and other items. The 1923 *List* is arranged as follows:

Part I

- Brief history of the Colonial Office and its predecessors
- List of secretaries of state responsible for administration of the colonies going back to 1768; permanent under-secretaries from 1825; parliamentary under-secretaries from 1830; and assistant under-secretaries from 1849
- Current establishment of the Colonial Office, listing names and dates of appointment. This appears to cover all levels of staff and includes temporary clerks, office keepers, messengers and the office porter

- Outline of the organisation of business within the office, giving responsibilities of each department and the names of staff working within those departments
- Brief details of closely related organisations and their staffing: Oversea Settlement Department; Order of St Michael and St George; Colonial Audit Department; the crown agents for the colonies; high commissioners and agents general in London; the Imperial Institute; Pacific Cable Board; Malay States Information Agency; Royal Botanic Gardens, Kew; the West Indian Agricultural College, Trinidad; London School of Tropical Medicine;[1] Liverpool School of Tropical Medicine; Overseas Nursing Association; Tropical Diseases Bureau; Tropical Diseases Research Fund; Colonial Advisory Medical and Sanitary Committee; Imperial Bureau of Entomology; Imperial Bureau of Mycology; Colonial Survey Committee; West African Currency Board; and East African Currency Board. Includes names and addresses of medical advisers and their consulting hours
- 'Colonial Associations' are then listed separately as follows: Royal Colonial Institute; the Society of Comparative Legislation; the Overseas League; the Ceylon Association in London; the Association of British Malaya; the West India Committee; and the West Indian Club
- List of currently serving governors with date of appointment, place of residence and salary
- Brief history of the Imperial Conference

Part II

- 'Historical and Statistical Account of the Dominions, Colonies and Protectorates, etc. (in alphabetical order) with public establishments'
- Appendix covering Iraq, North Borneo, Palestine, Sarawak and 'Miscellaneous Possessions or Protectorates not included in the above Historical and Statistical Account'

Part III

- Honours granted for services in and for the dominions and colonies
- Papers presented to Parliament relating to the dominions and colonies since 1877
- Information as to colonial appointments

Part IV

- Services of dominion and colonial officers

[1] The school amalgamated with the University of London teaching departments for the diploma in public health in 1929, and adopted the current name of London School of Hygiene and Tropical Medicine.

Part V

- The colonial regulations (with appendices)

The *List* was not published from 1941 to 1945, and it reappeared in 1946 as a much slimmer volume covering only the Colonial Office and omitting biographical notes and certain other material including lists of honours awarded and Parliamentary papers. Lists of staff employed by the colonial governments are given together at the end, rather than in the territorially arranged sections. The *List* was not published in 1947 because of a general paper shortage, but then appeared annually until 1966.

A compilation of biographical information from the lists for 1939–66 is available.[2]

[2] A. H. M. Kirk-Greene, *A Biographical Dictionary of the British Colonial Service 1939–1966* (London, 1991).

Appendix 5
Rules for the conduct of correspondence between governors and the Colonial Office

In a circular despatch to governors dated 26 July 1825 the Colonial Office noted the inconvenience caused by the 'want of some uniform mode in which all official communication should be addressed to this Department', and complained that the 'private directions' issued on the subject had not been 'permanently followed in many instances'.[1] It now instructed that despatches must be numbered and docketed, each despatch should be confined, so far as possible, to one subject, and that on 1 January each year the number of despatches and letters sent should be reported, together with copies of all dockets. The content of any enclosures should be stated in the covering despatch, and attention drawn to any points 'particularly deserving of notice'. 'Separate' despatches, that is those 'not immediately connected with the series of your official correspondence, but not of a private and confidential nature', should not be numbered. Any strictly private letters should be marked 'secret and confidential' and not numbered, but such marking should be used only for correspondence 'of so private a nature as to prevent their being deposited with propriety among the Archives of this Department'. It was stressed that these instructions should supersede any earlier ones, 'with the exception of those that have been given for the separate headings of the different subjects of your colonial correspondence and the regular transmission of duplicates'.

Instructions concerning correspondence were subsequently included in the *Rules and Regulations for the Information and Guidance of the Principal Officers and Others in His Majesty's Colonial Possessions* first issued in 1837, and amended from time to time thereafter. From 1862 onwards the 'rules and regulations' were printed in the annual *Colonial Office List.* By 1878 the section concerning correspondence had been much expanded, and reads as follows:

Chapter VII: Correspondence

§ I. *Mode in which Governors and Officers administering Colonial Governments (with certain exceptions in the West Indies and West Africa) are to conduct their Official Correspondence.*

165. Governors, or Officers administering Colonial Governments, must address the Secretary of State for the Colonial Department *alone* on all matters connected with their Government.

[1] CO 854/1, fo. 218. CO 854/1 also includes earlier circulars concerning the conduct of correspondence dated September 1823. In November 1829 governors were directed to paginate all despatches exceeding one sheet.

166. Every communication, therefore, to whatever Public Department in this Country it may more immediately relate, must in the first instance be addressed to the Secretary of State, with the exceptions hereafter mentioned; but in cases in which the Colonial Office is merely the channel of communicating with other Departments, the matter to be reported may be embodied in a memorandum addressed to the Department concerned, and forwarded to the Secretary of State in a covering despatch.
167. The Governor's Despatches should be written in a large and distinct hand, with dark ink, on folio paper of uniform size; and an inner margin of about one-third of the page should be left.
168. They are to be numbered in succession, commencing annually with a fresh series, without interruption from changes in Her Majesty's Government.
169. Each despatch should be confined as much as possible to a single subject. The paragraphs of each despatch should be numbered, and if it consists of two or more sheets the pages should be numbered.
170. When any Colonial or Imperial law, or any previous letters or despatches, are referred to, they must be described by their numbers and dates, either in the body of the despatch or in the margin.
171. Each despatch must be docketed. The docket should specify the date and place of which the despatch was written, the name of the writer, and of the Secretary of State to whom it is addressed, the subject of the despatch, and the number of its enclosures.
172. Its enclosures should be noted in the margin, and reference made, in the body of the despatch to such portions of them as may require particular attention.
173. The enclosures must be copied separately on folio paper, corresponding in size with the despatch transmitting them, and must also be written in a large and distinct hand, with dark ink; the paragraphs of each enclosure should be numbered. If an enclosure should be a copy of a despatch or letter, it should be preceded by a heading designating the person by whom, the person to whom, it is written, and the date. If it be a copy of a petition or memorial, a similar descriptive heading should be prefixed.
174. Should the enclosures be in any foreign language, translations of them, as well as copies, are to be forwarded.
175. The enclosures are also to be paged consecutively through the whole series; but each enclosure should be separately numbered and docketed like the despatch, and the docket should specify that the document is an "Enclosure in … despatch, No. … of …"
176. If any printed documents are transmitted as enclosures, six copies of each should be sent, if they are easily to be procured. In case of newspapers or other printed documents, of which only a portion may require attention, the portion referred to should be cut out, and pasted on foolscap paper, with a note at the head of the date and title of the paper from which it is extracted, the five extra copies required being annexed in an appendix.

177. Despatches forwarded to the Secretary of State should be accompanied by a schedule, and likewise with a statement of the numbers and dates of all despatches which the Governor may have received from the Secretary of State since the preceding occasion, in lieu of a separate acknowledgment of each despatch.[2] Duplicates of all important despatches, and of their principal enclosures, should be transmitted to the Secretary of State from the Cape of Good Hope, and all Colonies to the eastward thereof with which there is no telegraphic communication.

178. All addresses or petitions to the Queen, on parchment, must be accompanied by a transcript on official paper. Protests by Legislative or Executive Councillors should be unfailingly sent home, and if questions respecting legislative proceedings are referred to the Secretary of State, the reference must always be accompanied by extracts from those proceedings.

179. Every Legislative Act must be accompanied by a statement from the Law Officer of the Crown to the effect that, in his opinion, the Royal Assent may properly be given thereto, or ought not to be, and also by a report from the Governor, or from the Law Officer, giving all requisite explanation respecting the object of the Act, the motive in which it originated, and any legal or political question which it may involve. Such a report should be sent separately with any Act of unusual importance. Other Acts may be transmitted in batches as they receive the Governor's assent.

180. For the due preparation of Drafts of Acts, special rules are laid down in the Governor's Instructions.

181. Every Act must be enrolled in the Chief Court of Justice in the colony. For the practice of engrossing and enrolling Acts in this country, see the Appendix (page 309).

182. In the month of January each year, or as soon after as may be practicable, a complete collection should be published, for general information, of all Acts or Ordinances enrolled during the preceding year, and six copies of such collection of Acts, &c., shall be sent home.

183. Whenever it may be found necessary to address the Secretary of State in a more unreserved manner than a Public Despatch would admit with propriety or convenience to the public interest, such communication should be marked "Confidential;" but care must be taken that the regular series Despatches shall contain a full account of all important transactions in the Colony, so that when Parliament may call for information as to any of those transactions a clear and connected view of what has taken place may be afforded by the numbered Despatches, without adding those which are "Confidential."

184. It will, however, rest with the Secretary of State in every case to decide whether such "Confidential" Despatches are or are not to be considered and recorded as public documents.

[2] A footnote at this point in the regulations provides a copy of a circular despatch of 8 March 1870 on the matter.

185. No allowance on account of travelling expenses will be made to any Officer or other person bringing Despatches to this Department, unless the intelligence transmitted be of such a nature as to appear to the Governor to justify the sending it by a special messenger.

186. Every Governor is enjoined to cause the Secretary of State's Despatches, addressed to himself, as well as copies of his own, addressed to the Secretary of State, whether "Confidential" or not, to be deposited in the Government House, if this has been the usual place of deposit for them, or in some other safe Building belonging to the Government.

187. Governors are forbidden to withdraw any public document so deposited, on retiring from their Governments.

188. Governors are also forbidden to give copies of the Secretary of State's Despatches, or Instructions, or to allow them to be taken, unless under a general or special authority from the Secretary of State. But when Responsible Government is established the Governor is generally at liberty to communicate to his Advisers all despatches not "Confidential."[3]

§ II. *Mode in which the Officers administering subordinate Governments are to conduct their Official Correspondence.*

189. The colonies of Barbados, St. Vincent, Grenada, Tobago, and St. Lucia, are consolidated into one General Government, called the Government of the Windward Islands; the Colonies of Antigua, Montserrat, St. Christopher, Nevis, the Virgin Islands, and Dominica, into a second, called the Government of the Leeward Islands; and the Settlements of Sierra Leone, Gambia, the Gold Coast, and Lagos into a third, called the Government of the West Africa[4] Settlements. The Officers administering the subordinate Governments are, in the West Indies, called Lieutenant Governors or Presidents, in the West Africa Settlements, Administrators.

190. The correspondence of the Governors-in-Chief with the Secretary of State must be conducted in the mode which has been established by the preceding Regulations; but they will take care to keep the series of Despatches, relating to each Colony within their respective Commands, detached and separate from the rest.

191. During the absence of the Governor-in-Chief from any Island or Settlement comprised within his Command, the Officer administering the Government of that

[3] The footnote at this point in the original reads: 'By Circular of 10 July, 1871, Despatches are reclassified: - 1. *Numbered*, which a Governor may publish unless directed not to do so. 2. *Secret*, which he may, if he thinks fit, communicate, under the obligation of secrecy, to his Executive Council, and may make public if he thinks it necessary. 3. *Confidential*, which are addressed to a Governor personally, and which he is forbidden to make known without express authority'.

[4] A footnote added by the editor of the *Colonial Office List* notes that the "West African Settlements are now divided into two Governments of the 'West Africa Settlements' and the 'Gold Coast Colony'".

Island or Settlement should correspond with him on all subjects connected with this Office, and should transmit to him all Official Reports and information touching the same, and should apply to him for all such instructions as he may require for his guidance in the discharge of his duties.

192. If, during the absence of the Governor-in-Chief from any subordinate Government within the limits of his Command, exigencies should arise, in which it may be necessary that immediate instructions should be obtained from the Secretary of State, the Officer administering a subordinate Government is authorised to apply to the Secretary of State direct for instructions in relation thereto, if by so doing the Secretary of State can receive his Despatch at an earlier date than would be practicable through the intervention of the Governor-in-Chief.

193. Every such Officer shall be required to transmit by the earliest opportunity to the Governor-in-Chief, or Officer administering the General Government, a copy of every Despatch or communication which he may, under this permission, address direct to the Secretary of State.

194. The Secretary of State will communicate his answer to any such Despatch, as may be most expedient, either to the Governor-in-Chief or direct to the Officer from whom he may have received it, transmitting in the latter case a copy of the answer to the Governor-in-Chief.

195. Officers administering subordinate Governments will be guided, in their correspondence with the Governors-in-Chief, by the general Regulations which have been established by the Secretary of State in the preceding sections of this Chapter.

196. So long as the Governor-in-Chief is not present within the limits of his command, the above instructions must be understood to attach to the Acting Governor-in-Chief.

§ III. *Military Correspondence.*

197. The Governors of Colonies, commanding Her Majesty's Troops therein, must separate their correspondence with the Secretary of State for the Colonies, and the Secretary of State for War, in the following manner:-

198. Whatever related to the discipline of the Troops, or to the employment of them in any ordinary and established Service, or to the relief of the Troops after their time of local Service shall have expired, or to the interior economy of Her Majesty's Land Forces, will properly form the subject of correspondence with the Secretary of State for War exclusively.

199. In the event of actual hostilities with any Foreign Enemy, or of any extraordinary employment of the troops for the maintenance of the public peace, such occurrences must be reported both to the Secretary of State for War and to the Secretary of State for the Colonies.

200. In the event of its being thought necessary to make or to advise any Military Convention with the Officer in command of the Troops of any Foreign Power, a Governor commanding Her Majesty's Troops will at the same time report to the Secretary of State for the Colonies, and to the Secretary of State for War, the measures which he may have so taken, or those which he may wish to recommend for adoption.

201. In case it should be necessary, in order to render the Governor's Military Reports intelligible, to make reference, in his correspondence with the Secretary of State for War, to topics connected with his Civil Authority, he will in every such case at the same time bring under the notice of the Secretary of State for the Colonies the questions of Civil Government to which he may thus have had occasion to advert.

202. As any attempt to define the limits of a Governor's Civil and Military Correspondence may, from the nature of the case, be imperfect, and may omit to provide for some unforeseen exigency, he will best fulfil the joint pleasure of the Secretary of State for War and the Secretary of State for the Colonies by connecting his Civil Correspondence exactly as he would conduct it if he possessed no Military Command, and *vice versa.* The two functions of Governor and of Commander of the Forces, though for the time combined in the same person, should be regarded in this respect as entirely separate, and the reports made by the Governor in each capacity should be made precisely in the same manner as if that combination of powers did not exist.

203. The preceding instructions will apply also to the Governor's Correspondence respecting the Service of the Commissariat.

204. The respective officers employed under the War Office are in all cases without exception to give timely notice to Governors of any communications which they may intend to send home, affecting such Governors or the orders given by them, so that Her Majesty's Government may be simultaneously made acquainted with the opinions of the Governors and with the opinion of those Officers on any matter on which it is requisite that the views of both should be known.

205. When the Civil Governor of a Colony shall have occasion to report upon, or bring under the consideration of the Secretary of State for the Colonies, matters which involve military as well as civil considerations, or which require the decision or concurrence of the Secretary of State for War, the Governor will first communicate with the Officer in Command of the Forces in the Colony respecting the matters in question; and having obtained that officer's opinion or observations thereupon, he will transmit the same with his own report to the Secretary of State for the Colonies.

206. The Officer in command of the Forces is similarly instructed, to obtain the opinion of the Governor before reporting to the Secretary of State for War, or to any other Officer under whose general command he is placed, on any matter which involved civil as well as military considerations, or which cannot be decided without reference to the Secretary of State for the Colonies.

207. The Officer in command of the Forces has been instructed to send to the Governor

duplicates of all Reports on whatever subjects, other than those relating to discipline and the routine of the service, which he may have occasion to send to the Secretary of State for War or to any other Officer under whose general Command he is placed. In case the Governor considers that these Reports require the consideration of the Secretary of State for the Colonies, he is to forward the duplicates with his observations by the same mail which conveys the original Report to the Secretary of State for War.

§ IV. *Naval Correspondence.*

208. Governors of Colonies should communicate with Officers of Her Majesty's Navy, and should convey notices of different kinds to Commanders of Foreign Vessels in Colonial waters, in the following mode.

209. The Governor will write in his own name to any Senior Naval Officer (that is to say, the Senior Officer then within his immediate reach), holding the rank of Flag Officer, Captain, or Commander, but will communicate with any Senior Officer of lower rank through his Private Secretary. In no case will he communicate through the Colonial Secretary, whose functions are of a different character, and whose Office should not be the place of deposit for communications between the Governor and Officers in Command of Her Majesty's Naval forces.

210. Any notice or direction, conveyed by the Governor's authority to the Commander of any Foreign Vessel, should be conveyed through the Officers of the Colonial Government, and not through the Officers of Her Majesty's Navy, whose intervention should not be applied for, unless the directions conveyed through the ordinary channel should fail to produce their effect.

§ V. *Correspondence between the Postmaster-General in this Country, and the Postmasters, Packet Agents, &c. in the Colonies, upon matters affecting the Governor, or Orders given by his Authority.*

211.)[5]

212.)

213.)

214.)

215. Whenever any Postmaster, Packet Agent, or other Public Functionary acting under the *immediate* Orders and Instructions of Her Majesty's Postmaster-General, shall have occasion to transmit to the Postmaster-General any complaint or representation

[5] In the original numbers 211–14 are missing. This is true of the versions printed in the *Colonial Office Lists* of 1868–1907 inclusive. Versions of the regulations concerning correspondence provided in the 1867 and 1908 *Lists* are very different to those for the intervening years, and it is not clear if subsections have been accidentally omitted from the 1868–1907 volumes, or if appropriate renumbering has not been done at the time of amendment.

respecting the conduct of the Local Government or of any of its Officers, he must simultaneously place in the hands of the Governor a copy of so much of any such report as it may be requisite for the Governor to answer, so that the complaint and the explanation may reach this Country at the same time.

216. Should the Governor have occasion to make to the Secretary of State any complaint or representation respecting the conduct of an Officer employed under Her Majesty's Postmaster-General, he will apprise such Officer of the precise nature of the complaint or representation which he proposed to forward, in order that the Officer to whom it related may be enabled at once to transmit to the Postmaster-General any explanation which he may have to offer with respect to his conduct.

§ VI. *Correspondence of Individuals.*

217. Persons in a Colony, whether Public Functionaries or private individuals, who have any representations of a public or private nature to make to Government, should address them to the Governor of the Colony; or, if the Colony be a dependency of a Governor in Chief, then to the Officer in the immediate administration of its Government.

218. The duty of the Governor or Administrator of the Colony is to receive and act upon each such representation as public expediency or justice to the individual may appear to require, with the assistance in certain cases of his Executive Council; and if he doubts what steps to take thereupon, or if public advantage may appear to require it, to consult or report to the Secretary of State. Every individual has, however, the right to address the Secretary of State if he thinks proper. But in this case he must transmit such communication, unsealed, and in triplicate, to the Governor or Administrator, applying to him to forward it in due course to the Secretary of State.

219. Every letter, memorial, or other document which may be received by the Secretary of State from a Colony otherwise than through the Governor, will, unless a very pressing urgency justifies a departure from the rule, be referred back to the Governor for his report.

220. This rule, requiring transmission of correspondence with the Secretary of State through the Governor, is based on the strongest grounds of public convenience, in order that all communications may be duly verified, as well as reported on, before they reach the Secretary of State. It extends, therefore, to communications relating to public affairs as well as the concerns of the writer; to those of all Public Functionaries of whatever rank, and to those from public bodies.

221. Petitions addressed to the Queen, or the Queen in Council, memorials to Public Officers or Boards in Her Majesty's Government, &c., must be in like manner sent to the Governor for transmission home.

222. The Governor is bound to transmit to the Secretary of State every communication

so received by him, accompanied by such report as its contents may appear to him to require.

223. He is to do this with all reasonable despatch, consistently, however, with the delay requisite for the preparation of such report.

224. The Public Officers and other inhabitants of the Windward and of the Leeward Islands and of the West Africa Settlements, will look upon the Governor-in-Chief of each of those Governments as the Referee on all occasions when they are dissatisfied with the judgment formed upon their cases by the Lieutenant-Governor of the particular Island or by the Administrator of the Settlement in which they may reside.

225. If they should wish to appeal from the judgment of the Governor-in-Chief to that of the Secretary of State, they are of course at liberty to do so, adhering strictly to the regulations which are above established.

226. In any reports to be made, either by Lieutenant-Governors or Administrators to the Governors-in-Chief, or by the Governors-in-Chief to the Secretary of State, of questions for decision, they will adopt the following rules:-

227. The Report should comprise three distinct divisions: the first containing a simple narrative of the facts of the case, in the order in which they have occurred, as collected from the documents under consideration, showing merely the substance of the statements made, and of the rights asserted, or the complaints alleged by the respective parties concerned; the second containing the views of the writer as to the merits or demerits of the parties, or the justice of their several claims or complaints, with the reasons upon which those views proceed; and the third, the decision at which the writer has arrived, after a full investigation of the whole case.

228. In any Report or Despatch addressed to the Secretary of State, care should be taken to refer the Secretary of State to former documents in his possession which may bear on the case, with their dates. But this is not to prevent the writer from embodying the substance of such former documents in his Report or Despatch, if he judge that greater clearness or saving of labour is thereby attainable.

§ VII. *Attestation of Documents.*

229. The attestation of Signatures to Documents can only take place upon a full knowledge or intimate belief in the genuineness of those Signatures, and as a general rule, the Secretary of State can only undertake to attest those of Governors or Officers administering Governments.

230. Persons, therefore, who may have occasion to instruct their friends or agents in any Colony to send to them certificates, or powers of attorney, or judicial acts, for legal use in this Country, should take care to have these documents authenticated in the Colony by the Officer administrating the Government.

231. The same rule must particularly be observed by the Governor in sending home

> documents which, after being verified in England, are intended to be used in foreign Countries. The last signature attached by way of attestation to any such document must invariably be one which is known, and can therefore be certified to in this Department. If possible it should always be that of the Officer administering the Government.[6]

[6] *Colonial Office List* (1878), pp. 285–8.

Appendix 6
File registration numbers

With the introduction of a file system in 1927 blocks of subject file numbers were allocated for each series of correspondence as described at p. 106. Blocks of numbers varied between 1927 and 1934 as shown in table 1, but were standardised between 1935 and 1951 as shown in table 2. Between 1935 and 1951 the Economic 'block' 15,001–20,000 was sub-divided for categories such as 'commodities' or 'supplies'; the basic breakdown is shown in table 3.[1]

[1] Further details are provided in Thurston, vol. 1, pp. 407–15.

Table 1. Allocation of Colonial Office file registration numbers, 1927–34

Subject	1927	1928	1929	1930	1931	1932	1933	1934
Nigeria	1–530	1–381	382–703	704–1,022	1,023–310	1,311–	1,001–400	21,001–400
West Africa	1–530	4,001–120	4,121–230	4,231–352	4,353–480	4,481–	1,401–600	21,401–600
Gold Coast	4,001–690	6,001–294	6,295–563	6,564–816	6,817–7133	7,134–	1,601–2,000	21,601–22,000
Sierra Leone	4,001–690	9,001–205	9,206–367	9,368–531	9,532–722	9,723–	2,001–300	22,001–300
Gambia	4,001–690	12,001–78	12,079–180	12,181–267	12,268–382	12,383–	2,301–500	22,301–500
Military (WAFF & KAR)	8,001–208	13,001–226	13,227–417	13,418–579	13,580–757	13,758–	2,701–3,000	22,701–23,000
Kenya	10,001–559	15,001–445	15,501–980	15,961–16,393	17,001–414	18,001–	3,001–500	23,001–500
Uganda	14,001–396	20,001–203	20,251–475	20,476–676	21,001–187	22,001–	3,501–800	23,501–800
Zanzibar	14,001–396	23,001–143	23,151–266	23,267–387	24,001–117	24,501–	3,801–4,000	23,801–24,000
East Africa	17,001–235	25,001–184	25,201–380	25,381–562	26,001–165	27,001–	4,001–200	24,001–200
Africa	–	–	–	–	–	28,001–	4,201–300	24,201–300
Tanganyika	18,001–21,112	29,001–288	29,289–603	29,604–898	30,001–269	31,001–	5,001–300	25,001–300
Nyasaland	18,001–21,112	33,001–178	33,179–354	33,355–522	34,001–156	34,157–	5,301–800	25,301–500
Northern Rhodesia	18,001–21,112	35,001–469	35,218–469	35,470–716	36,001–263	36,264–	5,501–800	25,501–800
Somaliland	22,001–712	38,001–102	38,103–210	38,211–306	38,501–610	38,611–	5,801–6,000	25,801–26,000
Mediterranean	22,001–712	39,001–508	39,509–932	39,993–40,366	41,001–458	–	–	–
General	25,001–28,000	50,001–52,000	60,001–62,000	70,001–72,000	80,001–82,000	90,001–91,650	10,001–13,000	30,001–33,000
Gibraltar	–	–	–	–	–	98,301–400	19,401–500	39,401–500
Malta	–	–	–	–	–	98,401–550	19,501–700	39,501–700
Cyprus	–	–	–	–	–	98,551–800	19,701–20,000	39,701–40,000
Personnel	–	–	–	–	–	91,651–900	9,001–10,000	29,001–30,000
Straits Settlements	28,001–29,000	52,001–300	62,001–300	72,001–300	82,001–300	92,001–250	13,001–300	33,001–300
Malay States	29,001–30,000	52,301–600	62,301–600	72,301–600	82,301–600	92,251–500	13,301–600	33,301–600
Borneo and Sarawak	31,701–50	52,601–700	62,601–700	72,601–700	82,601–700	92,501–93,550	13,601–700	33,601–700
Hong Kong	30,001–800	52,701–53,000	62,701–63,000	72,701–73,000	82,701–83,000	92,551–850	13,701–14,000	33,701–34,000
Eastern	30,801–31,700	53,001–150	63,001–150	73,001–150	83,001–150	92,851–950	14,001–200	34,001–200
Wei-Hai-Wei	31,751–800	53,151–200	63,151–200	–	–	–	–	–
Ceylon	31,801–32,800	53,201–650	63,201–650	73,201–650	83,201–650	92,951–93,250	14,201–500	34,201–500

Table 1 continued

Subject	1927	1928	1929	1930	1931	1932	1933	1934
St Helena	34,801–35,000	53,651–800	63,651–800	73,651–800	83,651–800	93,251–350	19,101–200	39,101–200
Fiji	34,301–800	53,801–54,100	63,801–64,100	73,801–74,100	83,801–84,100	93,351–550	18,401–700	38,401–700
Western Pacific	33,801–34,300	54,101–500	64,101–500	74,101–500	84,101–500	93,551–900	18,701–19,100	38,701–39,100
Mauritius	32,801–33,500	54,501–900	64,501–900	74,501–900	84,501–900	93,901–94,150	14,501–900	34,501–900
Seychelles	33,501–800	54,901–55,000	64,901–65,000	74,901–75,000	84,901–85,000	94,151–250	14,901–15,000	34,901–35,000
British Guiana	38,201–39,000	55,001–240	65,001–420	75,001–240	85,001–240	94,251–500	15,001–300	35,001–300
Barbados	37,501–700	55,241–300	65,241–300	75,241–300	85,241–300	94,501–650	15,301–500	35,301–500
British Honduras	37,901–38,200	55,301–450	65,301–450	75,301–450	85,301–450	94,651–800	15,501–700	35,501–700
Leeward Islands	39,501–900	55,501–700	65,501–700	75,501–700	85,501–700	94,876–95,050	15,801–16,000	35,801–36,000
Grenada	39,001–500	55,701–800	65,701–800	75,701–800	85,701–800	95,051–150	16,001–100	36,001–100
St Lucia	39,001–500	55,801–50	65,801–50	75,801–50	85,801–50	95,151–200	16,101–200	36,101–200
St Vincent	39,001–500	55,851–900	65,851–900	75,851–900	85,851–900	95,201–300	16,201–300	36,201–300
Bermuda	37,701–900	55,901–56,000	65,901–66,000	75,901–76,000	85,901–86,000	95,301–400	16,301–400	36,301–400
Jamaica	35,701–36,500	56,000–250	66,001–250	76,001–250	86,001–250	95,401–650	16,401–700	36,401–700
Bahamas	37,301–500	56,251–400	66,251–400	76,251–400	86,251–400	95,651–750	16,701–800	36,701–800
Trinidad	36,501–37,300	56,401–600	66,401–600	76,401–600	86,401–600	95,751–950	16,801–17,000	36,801–37,000
West Indies	35,201–700	56,601–750	66,601–750	76,601–750	86,601–750	95,951–96,100	17,001–200	37,001–200
Falklands	35,001–200	56,751–57,000	66,751–67,000	76,751–77,000	86,751–87,000	96,101–300	19,201–400	39,201–400
Iraq	40,001–44,000	58,001–59,000	68,001–69,000	78,001–79,000	88,001–89,000	96,301–97,000	–	–
Palestine	44,001–48,000	57,001–58,000	67,001–68,000	77,001–78,000	87,001–88,000	97,001–98,800	17,201–700	37,201–700
Transjordan	44,001–48,000	59,401–550	69,401–550	79,401–550	89,401–550	97,701–850	17,701–900	37,701–900
Aden	48,001–49,000	59,251–400	69,251–400	79,251–79,400	89,251–400	97,851–98,000	17,901–18,100	37,901–38,100
Middle East	49,901–50,000	59,001–250	69,001–250	79,001–250	89,001–250	98,001–300	18,101–400	38,101–400
Establishment	60,001–84	99,001–400	99,001–400	99,001–400	99,001–400	99,001–400	8,501–700	28,501–700
Reparation claims	55,001–138	99,501–90	99,501–90	99,501–90	99,501–90	–	–	–
Chief Clerk (and Honours)	50,001–350	47,000–467	47,000–489	48,000–419	49,000–308	49,500–50,000	8,701–9,000	28,791–29,000

Table 2. Allocation of file registration numbers, 1935–51

Subject	File registration numbers	Subject	File registration numbers
General	1,001–10,000	Seychelles	58,001–500
Defence and general	10,001–11,000	Sarawak	58,501–59,000
Welfare, students	11,001–500	Economic Eastern	59,001–700
Social services	11,501–13,000	Brunei	59,701–60,000
Defence	13,001–15,000	British Guiana	60,001–61,500
Economic [for breakdown see below]	15,001–20,000	Leeward Islands	61,301–63,000
Economic Palestine	16,550–99	Grenada	63,001–750
	19,510–99	St Lucia	63,751–64,250
Personnel	20,001–22,000	St Vincent	64,251–65,500
Communications	22,001–25,000	Dominica	65,151–500
Telecommunications	24,001–100	Barbados	65,501–66,500
International relations	25,001–26,000	British Honduras	66,501–67,500
Honours	26,001–27,000	Bermuda	67,501–68,000
Appointments, recruits, training	27,001–28,000	Bahamas	68,001–500
Research	28,001–29,000	Jamaica	68,501–70,000
Nigeria	30,001–31,000	Trinidad	70,001–71,000
Gold Coast	31,001–32,000	West Indies	71,001–72,000
Sierra Leone	32,001–33,000	United States bases	72,001–75,000
Gambia	33,001–500	Palestine	75,001–77,000
West Africa	33,501–34,000	Transjordan	77,001–78,000
Military Africa	34,001–35,000	Aden	78,001–79,000
Military general	36,001–37,000	Middle East	79,001–80,000
St Helena	35,001–500	Fiji	85,001–86,000
Kenya	38,001–40,000	Western Pacific	86,001–87,500
Uganda	40,001–41,000	St Helena	87,501–88,000
Zanzibar	41,001–42,000	Falkland Islands	88,001–500
Tanganyika	42,001–43,000	Gibraltar	88,501–89,000
Central Africa	43,001–44,000	Malta	89,001–90,000
Nyasaland	44,001–45,000	Cyprus	90,001–91,500
Northern Rhodesia	45,001–46,000	Mediterranean	91,501–92,000
Somaliland	46,001–46,500	Defence general	94,001–96,000
East Africa	46,501–47,000	Information	96,001–97,000
Africa	47,001–200	Economic relations	97,001–250
Malay Straits	50,001–51,500	Economic general	97,251–500
Malay States	51,501–53,000	British Council	97,501–600
North Borneo	53,001–500	Legal (1950)	97,601–850
Hong Kong	53,501–55,000	Prize Court (1951)	97,851–98,000
Eastern	55,001–500	Special care	98,001–600
Ceylon	55,501–57,000	Statistics	98,201–500
Mauritius	57,001–58,000		

Table 3. Economic Division breakdown of file registration numbers by principal subjects, 1935–51

Principal subject	File registration numbers
Commodities	15,000–99
Currency	15,100–200
Miscellaneous: tariffs etc.	15,201–99
Commercial relations	15,300–99
Forestry and miscellaneous subjects	15,400–99
Financial: currency, loans, defence finance regulations, etc.	15,540–69
Agriculture	15,570–699
Financial: taxation, etc.	15,700–999
Commodities [1939]	16,000–70
War trade	16,100–59
Financial: war damage, banking, etc.	16,200–599
Survey, public works, etc.	16,600–99
Land utilisation and tenure	16,700–849
Malta supplies	16,850–99
Supplies: general subjects	16,900–99
Supplies: commodities	17,000–299
Post war and relief requirements and supply arrangements	17,300–99
Supplies: allied colonial territories	17,400–49
Reserves for food supplies	17,450–99
Food supplies	17,500–999
Commodities [1940–2]	18,000–119
Statistics	18,120–99
Trading with the enemy and enemy property	18,200–99
Supplies: miscellaneous [1940–2]	18,300–29
Shipping cargo	18,330–499
Export licences, etc.	18,500–99
Import licences	18,600–9
Trading with the enemy [1940–3]	18,610–19
Supplies: oil and coal [1940–2]	18,620–39
Industrial development	18,650–750
Miscellaneous subjects	18,751–827
Economic action allied territories	18,900–49
Middle East Supplies Centre	18,950–99
Miscellaneous subjects	19,000–199
Reoccupation of Far East	19,200–49
Economic planning	19,250–99
Reparations and economic security	19,261
Co-operation	19,350–99
Programming of colonial requirements	19,400–599
Bulk ordering of supplies	19,500–99
Production of commodities	19,600–999

Appendix 7
Specimen search

The Jameson Raid

At the end of December 1895 Dr Leander Starr Jameson, an administrator in Cecil Rhodes's British South Africa Company, led a military force from Bechuanaland into the Transvaal intending to join the non-Boer European workers (known as Uitlanders) in overthrowing the government of Paul Kruger. The raid was a disaster. The Uitlanders of Johannesburg and the Rand did not revolt and Jameson's force was captured four days after crossing the frontier and handed over to the British authorities. Jameson was tried under the Foreign Enlistment Act and served a short prison sentence in Britain, but then returned to South Africa.[1] Rhodes, implicated in the conspiracy although it is unclear if he actually planned it, was forced to resign from his post as prime minister of the Cape, and Afrikaner opinion throughout South Africa rallied in support of Kruger. The German Kaiser, William II, congratulated Kruger on repulsing the raid – an action which caused resentment in Britain where it was seen as a provocative intervention in a purely British affair and put a strain on Anglo-German relations.[2]

In Britain an inquiry was demanded into the aggressive act against an independent foreign state; a Parliamentary select committee subsequently absolved the secretary of state for the colonies, Joseph Chamberlain, of any involvement in the affair although he admitted that he knew of the potential Uitlander uprising. Judd has noted that 'An unrepentant Rhodes treated the inquiry with breathtaking insolence, even remarking to the Liberal leader of the opposition, Lewis Harcourt, "Nobody is going to name a country after you"'.[3]

A search for records relating to the raid might start with the online catalogue and a simple search on 'Jameson Raid'. The result as at 21 September 2007 was as follows, but readers should be aware that subsequent enhancements to the catalogue will have resulted in a rather different and almost certainly fuller listing.

[1] Where he served as prime minister of the Cape from 1904 to 1908.

[2] The German emperor's message, known as the 'Kruger telegram', is the subject of a specimen search in Foreign Office records set out in Michael Roper's guide *The Records of the Foreign Office, 1782–1968* (Public Record Office, 2002).

[3] D. Judd, *Empire: the British Imperial Experience from 1765 to the Present* (London, 1996), pp. 161–2.

Catalogue Reference	Title/Scope and Content	Covering Dates
CAB 37/42/34	i [Case of officers concerned in the Jameson Raid.]	printed or circulated in 1896 July 31
CAB 41/24/37	i Forces in unhealthy parts of Africa; Reinstatement of officers involved in the Jameson Raid.	1898 May 10
CAB 41/24/38	i Reinstatement of officers taking part in the Jameson Raid; Persian loan; West Africa.	1898 May 17
CO 879/45/1	i South African Republic: disturbances (Jameson Raid) and general affairs: further correspondence. (339 pages)	1896 January 16 - 1896 April 30
CO 879/46/3	i Affairs of the South African Republic, including the Jameson Raid and the Reform Movement; further correspondence. (730 pages)	1896 March 20 - 1897 April 17
CO 879/48/7	i South African Republic: disturbances (Jameson Raid) (39 pages) Copy of the South African Republic Green Book, number 1 of 1896.	1895 December 30 - 1896 April 16
CO 879/51/1	i Affairs of South African Republic, including position of Africans, Cape Coloured persons and British Indians, the Jameson Raid, and the dynamite monopoly; further correspondence (730 pages)	1897 October 18 - 1898 December 15
CO 879/55/2	i Affairs of South African Republic, including Jameson Raid, position of Africans, British Indians and Cape Coloured Persons, the dynamite monopoly, and the Edgar case; further correspondence. (625 pages, 1 map)	1898 December 15 - 1899 June 8
CO 879/58/4	i Settlement of claim of the government of the South African Republic for an indemnity for damages caused by the Jameson Raid, with detailed statement of expenses incurred. (52 pages)	1898 November 9
CO 879/59/13	i Affairs of the South African Republic, including Jameson Raid indemnity, franchise proposals, and preparations for war; further correspondence (980 pages, 1 map)	1899 June 9 - 1899 December 15
DO 35/1196	i RECORDS: Extract from "Cape Times" re Jameson Raid.	1943-1946
PCOM 8/177	i GREY, Colonel Raleigh; JAMESON, Leander Starr; WHITE, Colonel Henry Frederick; WHITE, Major Robert; WILLOUGHBY, Sir John Cristopher: Jameson Raid, South Africa	1896-1897
WO 32/7845	i OVERSEAS: South Africa (Code 0(AU)): Boer War: Jameson Raid: Proceedings relating to trial of Dr Jameson and others. Correspondence concerning position of commissioned officers convicted. Report of Select Committee.	1896-1898
WO 108/413	i The case of the officers implicated in the Raid on the Transvaal (Jameson Raid)	1896 Aug 05

It will be noted that the only Colonial Office records revealed by this search are from the Africa confidential print series, CO 879. This series has been entered into the catalogue fairly recently; browsing the previously available finding aid[4] results in fewer precise references since much material about the raid is concealed in descriptions referring merely to 'affairs of South African Republic'. Paradoxically, however, one reference immediately identifiable in the handbook, 'South African Republic; Disturbances (Dr Jameson's Raid); Correspondence (CO 879/44/4)' does not appear in the results shown above because a search on the 'Jameson Raid' (as it is generally known) will not bring up 'Jameson's Raid'. Searching on 'Jameson's Raid' will not help either because the catalogue does not recognise the apostrophe in 'Jameson's'.[5] Substitute a space for the apostrophe, however, and this and two other additional references will be found:

Catalogue Reference	Title/Scope and Content	Covering Dates
CO 879/44/4	*i* Disturbances in the South African Republic (Dr L S Jameson's Raid): correspondence. (91 pages)	1895 December 30 - 1896 January 18
FO 881/6725X	*i* AFRICA: Desp. South African Republic. Events arising out of Dr. Jameson's Raid. (L.G., Feb. 7, 1896)	Feb. 4, 1896
WO 32/7839	*i* OVERSEAS: South Africa (Code 0(AU)): Dr Jameson's raid into South African Republic: Terms of surrender to Boers. Disposal of prisoners to England and incidents aboard S.S. VICTORIA Trial of military members of force.	1896

One might try a search on 'Jameson' alone. This is a little risky with a common name, and indeed in this case produces 620 results. But the search can be made manageable by restricting the date range to 1895 to 1905 (the range of the results shown above with the exception of the much later Dominions Office file). There are now 42 results. Several of these are irrelevant, relating for example to Board of Trade company records, the service of officers in the army and navy, and Colonial Office correspondence from British Guiana concerning another 'Jameson', but the search also brings up some important references that we have not seen before. There are records of the director of public prosecutions, the Treasury solicitor and the Prison Commission concerning the case against Jameson and his associates; a Home Office file on the treatment of Jameson and other prisoners; a file of the Admiralty Transport Department concerning Jameson's return to the UK; and photographs from the Copyright Office of Jameson and his officers.

As noted above, a search of TNA's new catalogue now produces a different result, and reveals additional material held not only at TNA but also elsewhere.

[4] Public Record Office, *List of Colonial Office Confidential Print to 1916* (HMSO, London, 1965)

[5] See appendix 9 for hints on using the catalogue.

Records of the Colonial Office

Where else might we look for Colonial Office material? Appendix 1 shows us that record series listed under 'South Africa' do not start until 1902, and that for earlier material we need to look under 'South Africa High Commission'. Here the original correspondence series is listed as CO 417, with registers in CO 545. There are no indexes; CO 714 comes to an end in the 1870s.

The register for 1895–6 (CO 545/7) varies slightly from the standard described in chapter 6 in that 'despatches' are divided into three 'cuts' for 1. British Bechuanaland, Bechuanaland Protectorate, and British South Africa Company; 2. Orange Free State, South African Republic [Transvaal]; and 3. Basutoland, German Protectorate [i.e., Namibia]. These are followed by cuts for 'offices' and for 'individuals' as is usual. As the volume covers 1895 and 1896 and the raid took place at the very end of December 1895 the first year's entries can be quickly skipped through, although there may be useful background on subjects such as the grievances of the Uitlanders. There are then numerous references throughout the remainder of the register which are clearly or potentially relevant, including:

First cut: British Bechuanaland, Bechuanaland Protectorate, British South Africa Company.

The first obvious mention of the Jameson Raid appears to be in a despatch from Sir Hercules Robinson, high commissioner in and for South Africa and governor of the Cape, dated 24 January 1896: 'B[ritish] B[echuanaland] Police. Pay due to some of Dr Jameson's force'. The immediately previous entry, however, reads: '1. Remounts purchased by Co[mpany]. 2. Books etc at Pitsani Potlogo'. Your secondary reading[6] will have told you that the abortive raid started from Pitsani Potlogo, 24 miles north of Mafeking. That this register entry is stamped as being printed as the confidential print 'African no. 505' (now held under the reference CO 879/45/1 and already identified above) seems to confirm that it is relevant.

Second cut: Orange Free State; South African Republic

A very early reference, made possible of course only by the use of the telegraph, is dated 30 December 1895 and described as 'Uitlander agitation'. (Printed as African no. 501 (CO 879/44/4, also noted above) and printed for Parliament as C. 7933, February 1896). Thereafter over 50 pages within this cut of the register contain references to the raid or its aftermath.

Third cut: Basutoland; German Protectorate.

Only one relevant reference: 10 March 1896. 'No truth in rumoured intended application of Cape Government to Portuguese Government for arrest of Mr Rhodes'.

Fourth and subsequent cuts: offices.

[6] For example, Elizabeth Longford, *Jameson's Raid: the Prelude to the Boer War* (2nd edn., London, 1982).

Relevant material is noted under: Houses of Parliament; Admiralty; Privy Council Office; Law Officers; Treasury (mainly Treasury solicitor, but including, 25 and 27 February, list of names and addresses of troops transported on the *Harlech Castle*, and a police report of the arrest of Jameson and others and their conveyance to Bow Street Police Court in London); Foreign Office (for example report from Berlin of the emperor's telegram to Kruger, and correspondence regarding US citizens involved in the raid and imprisoned in Johannesburg); 'Miscellaneous Offices' (including communications from the president of the South African Republic, Reuters, the London Chamber of Commerce, Dublin Castle, various newspapers and periodicals including *The Times* and *Country Life*, the London office of the British South Africa Company, and a draft despatch from Chamberlain to Robinson).

The cut for correspondence from 'individuals' includes Cecil Rhodes's letter of resignation as well as letters from individuals in South Africa with knowledge of the events sent to people in the UK and subsequently forwarded to the Colonial Office.

Although all these references are to correspondence in the Colonial Office series CO 417, they also clearly indicate the interests of other government departments, organisations and individuals in the matter, and may suggest other sources.

Using the date of writing given in the register and the category of correspondence, for example despatches: South African Republic; or Treasury; or an individual with a name beginning with 'S', all references can be easily traced to the original correspondence in CO 417.[7] If you are concerned with the fine detail, and have time, you may be tempted simply to work through all the correspondence in CO 417 for the months following the raid – but note that there are 48 volumes for 1896 alone. With less time for research it is probably sensible to start with the confidential print in CO 879, but always be aware that correspondence and other papers are likely to have been edited, and internal minuting is rarely included. A few points about the content of some of these CO 417 volumes follow:

CO 417/177 includes considerable minuting by the secretary of state Joseph Chamberlain. As noted elsewhere this is unusual in this period and shows the importance of the raid. The following volume, CO 417/178, contains a single despatch from Sir Hercules Robinson providing 'a consecutive narrative [of] the various steps taken by me in connection with Dr Jameson's raid', with 480 enclosures. The first minute sheet notes that the correspondence was printed for Parliament as C. 8063 of April 1896 and for the Colonial Office as African no. 505, although an official suggests that not all papers warrant printing.

CO 417/179 is almost entirely concerned with the raid, and includes a letter from Jameson to Sir Jacobus de Wet, the British agent in Pretoria. CO 417/188 includes the list of troopers who took part in the raid; CO 417/189 includes the Foreign Office letter reporting on the 'Kruger telegram' as well as correspondence concerning US citizens involved in the raid. A letter from the British

[7] See chapter 6 for details of the arrangement of correspondence and use of contemporary finding aids.

South Africa Company in CO 417/197 forwards a reproduction of the terms of surrender. CO 417/203 includes a letter from an English clergyman forecasting a South African war.

In 1895–6 there were two British colonies in southern Africa in addition to the territories administered by the British South Africa Company: the Cape and Natal. As noted above, Sir Hercules Robinson was high commissioner in and for South Africa, as well as governor of the Cape, and his voluminous correspondence in CO 417 suggests that relevant material will be concentrated there. But clearly the Cape correspondence in CO 48 (with registers in CO 336) should not be neglected. The Natal correspondence in CO 179 (registered in CO 357) should also be considered.

Other series relating to the Cape and Natal may also be useful. CO 51/303, the volume of Cape sessional papers described as 'Votes and Proceedings of Parliament, 1896', includes questions asking if the Cape government has made any expression of opinion about the Jameson 'inroad', and about the importation of firearms in connection with the raid, and there is a report of a debate on the raid among other relevant material. CO 51/310, Appendix II to the Votes and Proceedings of the Cape Parliament 1897, includes the report of a Select Committee on the Jameson Raid, with a minority report (both reports in English and Afrikaans), minutes of proceedings, minutes of evidence, appendices, and a detailed index. The Cape *Government Gazette* for January to June 1896 (CO 52/74) is likely to include reports and official statements. Equivalent series for Natal are in CO 181 and CO 182. TNA also holds official publications of the South African Republic in the 'green books' series CO 477.

Records of the Foreign Office

Given the implications of the raid for Britain's diplomatic relations with foreign states (primarily but not only Germany) it is worth giving some attention to Foreign Office records.

Before 1906, most FO correspondence is arranged in country-based series. Access to these is through two parallel series of registers. These are the departmental diaries and registers in FO 566, and the so-called library series in FO 605. The FO 566 registers are contemporary, while those in FO 605 were compiled in the Foreign Office library at a later date. The FO 605s, which are produced on microfilm, have internal indexes. The FO 566s, currently produced as original documents, are indexed by FO 738 (1891–1905 only). Note that these are indexes to the registers, not indexes to the correspondence itself. For the period we are concerned with here only FO 566 is relevant; the other series finishes in 1890.

The most relevant index volumes are FO 738/1–2, Africa 1891–6, covering subjects commencing with Ab-Ky and La-End, respectively, and piece 18, Germany, 1891–1905. Not all indexes were checked, but some references were also found in FO 738/8 (United States), FO 738/10 (Austria), FO 738/15 (Denmark) and FO 738/17 (France).

FO 738/2 includes a section 'Transvaal: incursion of Dr Jameson' (with cross-references from 'Jameson' and other terms). It includes references to the opinions of the Portuguese, Dutch, Belgian and German governments, and of Swedish, Swiss and US individuals involved in the raid.

This index relates to the Africa register in FO 566/1645. It gives dates and page numbers which lead you to that register, and enable you to find specific references within it.

The register in FO 566/1645 is a subject register, not one associated with a single series of correspondence. It does not relate directly and solely to the Africa series of correspondence, FO 2, in the way in which each Colonial Office series of registers (after 1849) relates to the correspondence arranged under the same colony (or subject) name. The register is arranged by 'cuts' for each British embassy for which there is correspondence concerning Africa. See especially the Berlin cut for despatches from the British ambassador, Sir Frank Cavendish Lascelles, concerning German opinion and the 'Kruger telegram'.[8]

Registers in FO 566 are arranged with incoming correspondence recorded on left-hand pages, and outgoing on the right; telegrams are entered in red ink. The letter 'O' noted against outgoing correspondence indicates that no draft was kept.[9] In the register referred to here there are references to the printing of correspondence. Foreign Office confidential print of the period is in the series FO 881, and much of Lascelles's correspondence concerning the Transvaal can be found in the print 'Affairs South of the Zambezi, Part 13, January–June 1896' (FO 881/6910) – clearly not a description which will be readily found in a catalogue search for records relating to the Jameson Raid.

To locate the original correspondence is usually quite straightforward, but there is a possible complication in this case. The register cut is marked 'Berlin' (or other city in which the British embassy was based), whereas the correspondence series are listed under the name of the country. There are several series of correspondence for Germany, but for this period (after the unification of Germany) the main series is FO 64, Prussia and Germany, which relates to Prussia up to 1870; after 1870 to the German empire. Within FO 64 and other country series correspondence is catalogued by date and by the names of ambassadors and other diplomatic and consular officials. Lascelles's correspondence is in FO 64/1375–6,[10] and 1378–89; the last five volumes relate specifically to Africa.

FO 64 also contains correspondence between the Foreign Office and the German ambassador and his staff in London. These are listed under the term 'domestic' and the names of German diplomats. Again one of the 1896 volumes relates specifically to Africa (FO 64/1396) and may well be relevant.

[8] Private papers of Lascelles are included in the series FO 800, Foreign Office, Private Offices: Various Ministers' and Officials' Papers at FO 800/6–20, 1895–1908. The last volume is an index to 'subjects of most importance'.

[9] For a more detailed explanation of the use of the registers see L. Atherton, *'Never Complain, Never Explain': Records of the Foreign Office and State Paper Office 1500–c.1960* (PRO Publications, London, 1994).

[10] FO 64/1377 is listed under the name of Lascelles's deputy, Gosselin, but continues the run of despatch numbers used by Lascelles, and, as it covers the period April to June 1896, is likely to be relevant.

As noted above, the index entries in FO 738 include references to the interests of other European governments and of the US in events in the Transvaal. These can be tracked through the registers in FO 566 to Foreign Office correspondence relating to those countries in the same way as the German example given above.

Like the Colonial Office, the Foreign Office printed certain of its correspondence; one print relating to the Jameson Raid has been identified in the searches shown above.

Embassy and consular archives included within Foreign Office series are the records created by British embassies and consulates in foreign countries and subsequently returned to London. They include the correspondence of ambassadors and consuls with the Foreign Office, and correspondence between those individuals and the local ministry for foreign affairs and other contacts. For Germany in our period they are:

FO 244, Prussia and Germany, correspondence, 1784–1913
FO 246, Prussia and Germany, registers of correspondence, 1823–1939

Roper searched these records for papers relating to the 'Kruger telegram' but found nothing additional to that located in FO 64.

Not quite an illustration

The cartoon by Edward Fairfield, a Colonial Office official, shown at figure 56 is considerably earlier than the Jameson Raid, being dated October 1893 when the British South Africa Company was asserting its constitutional right to negotiate with African rulers. It clearly demonstrates, however, the often strained relations between the British government and the company.[11]

[11] Fairfield's drawings were clearly well known to his colleagues. A letter in CO 301/60 from Oscar Arthur, describing himself as a 'spirit medium', claims to include 'spirit drawings'. An official comments, 'The spirit drawings hardly come up to Mr Fairfield's style'.

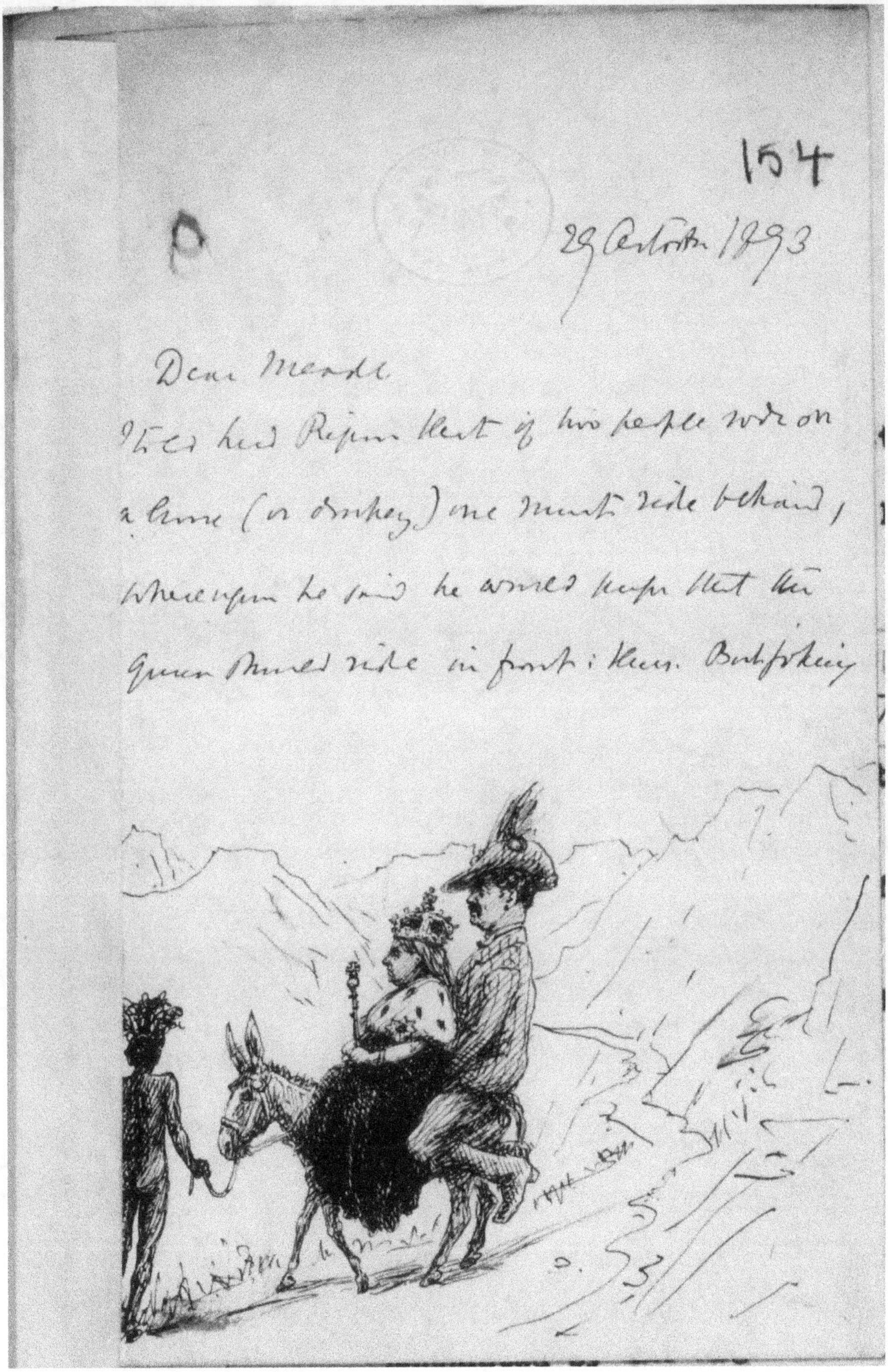

Figure 56. CO 417/110, High Commission for South Africa: Original Correspondence, 1893, fo. 154. Cartoon by Edward Fairfield, a Colonial Office official, appended to his note to a colleague.

Appendix 8
Sources for biography and family history[1]

The records of the Colonial Office and related departments held at TNA include a wealth of material about people living and working in the British dependencies. Information about colonial officials is much easier to find than that relating to private individuals, and details of useful sources are given below, but in all cases locating information may depend more on serendipity than on a structured search. Family historians in particular should be warned that there is little in these records that will demonstrate relationships and thus allow family links to be traced or confirmed. And much useful material, for example records of births, marriages and deaths, census returns, and business records, is more likely to be found in the national archives or register offices of the former colonies than in London.

Anyone searching for individuals living in the Caribbean region, whether ancestors or not, can do no better than to start by consulting Guy Grannum's guide.[2] With its descriptions of the type of material to be found in Colonial Office series such as the gazettes, blue books and naval officers' returns it is likely also to provide some pointers to researchers concerned with other parts of the empire. Its coverage ranges widely over sources in the records of government departments other than the Colonial Office.

Colonial officials

Mention of a colonial official may conjure up a picture of a governor in his white uniform and plumed hat receiving a royal visitor or touring 'up country', or a district officer dealing with the minutiae of tax gathering and petty crime in rural Africa. But a colonial government was much like any other government, whether national or local – it needed a range of specialists to staff its technical departments: lawyers, doctors, educationalists, foresters, engineers, agriculturalists, police and prison officers, and many others.

Throughout the early history of the British empire there were innumerable local arrangements for the appointment of officials, some enshrined in law, others in long practice. Some staff were appointed by the governors, some by the secretaries of state, and the most senior by royal warrant. By at least 1862 this variety of practice was formalised by the simple expedient of allotting a salary

[1] An earlier version of this section appeared in *Ancestors*, 30 (Feb. 2005).

[2] G. Grannum, *Tracing Your Caribbean Ancestors* (London, 2012).

range to the three categories: up to £100 p.a., appointment by the governor; between £100 and £200, appointment by the secretary of state (often on the recommendation of the governor); and above £200, appointment by the secretary of state in the name of the reigning monarch. Of course, it was not always quite as straightforward as this: the governor might not be able to make a recommendation and would ask the Colonial Office to suggest names; in the case of technical appointments another UK government department would frequently be asked to suggest suitable candidates; and there was always a pool of aspiring candidates who had asked for a post, or been recommended by a relation or friend.

The Colonial Service

The reality of a 'Colonial Service' is a comparatively modern one; it began to take shape in the first half of the 19th century, but not until the early 20th century did the various branches of the service begin to be unified. 'Unification' meant that serving officers would be eligible for transfer to vacancies in other colonial territories, and would be considered when such vacancies arose, and it led to changes in recruitment and improvements in training. The separate 'branches' remained. The administrative service, unified in 1932, provided the district officers, district commissioners and the generalist civil servants in the colonial governments. Gradually the specialist services were also unified: the Colonial Legal Service, established in 1933, or the Colonial Medical Service, established the following year, etc. Kirk-Greene has quoted the definition of 'The Colonial Service' used by the Colonial Office in 1948 – 'the term in use for the aggregate of the basic services of all the Colonial Territories for the government of which the Secretary of State for Colonies is responsible'.[3] And those last few words pinpoint another complexity – the Colonial Service was separate from the Indian Civil Service or the Sudan Political Service, and from the Colonial Office itself which was staffed through the 'Home' Civil Service.

Sources at The National Archives

The complexities of the service and the varied methods of appointment are inevitably reflected in the documentary sources. The first, and most important, point to make is that there are no discrete series of service records as there are for the Army or the Royal Navy. On the whole, there is more likely to be career information about an individual, rather than personal or family detail. And there is no guarantee that there will be anything at all.

Systematic sources exist for the 19th and 20th centuries only: the published *Colonial Office List* and the annual 'blue books of statistics'. The *List*, published from 1862 to 1966 with a gap during the Second World War, provides short biographical notes on senior staff showing appointments, honours and often education. Any military service is likely to be noted – and, of course, opens

[3] A. Kirk-Greene, *On Crown Service: a History of HM Colonial and Overseas Civil Services, 1837–1997* (London and New York, 1999).

up other possibilities for research.[4] If school, university or membership of a professional body is noted this may also lead to records maintained by those organisations. Figure 57 is an extract from the 1935 *List* showing the entry for Sir Arnold Hodson. It notes education, service in the South African war, a wide range of official appointments and a number of publications – all of which might be followed up. As an official who rose to be a governor (of the Falkland Islands, Sierra Leone and the Gold Coast) his despatches will be found in the correspondence series for those dependencies. It is less common to find photographs of officials, but in Hodson's case there are pictures of him in full uniform at a durbar in Kumasi (see figure 58). Even more unusually there is evidence of Hodson's leisure pursuits: three files contain details of children's pantomimes organised by him in the Gold Coast between 1936 and 1938.[5] In 1933 Hodson contributed to a radio broadcast to mark centenary commemorations of the abolition of slavery, stating, 'Think for a moment of what those countless Africans sold into slavery must have suffered. They were seized by armed bands of white savages …' (CO 267/642/22).

HODSON, SIR ARNOLD WIENHOLT, K.C.M.G. (1932), C.M.G. (1922).—Ed. Italy, Mulgrave, Castle, and Felsted; in Central Queensland, 1900-1902; joined Australian Commonwealth Horse for service in S. Africa, 1902; in Transvaal, 1902-4; sub.-inspr., Bech. Prot. pol., 1904; specially employed in connection with Damara war (med. and clasp); mem. of Ngamiland mission, 1906; ag. asst. comsnr., Mar. to May, 1910, and Mar. to Dec., 1911; dist. comsnr. and 1st cls. mag., Somaliland, 1912; H.B.M. consul for Southern Abyssinia, 1914; ditto, S.W. Abyssinia, 1923; served part time in European War; present at coronation of Empress Zoditow, 1917; 3rd cls. Star of Ethiopia; African Gen. Ser. Med. and Clasp, Jubaland, 1917-18; attchd., Abyssinian army in expedition against Tigre, 1919 (med. and clasp); late capt., Royal Sussex Regt. (Territorials); has passed Cape Univ. mag. law exam.; Somali language, lower standard; Galla language, higher standard; gov. and commdr.-in-chief, Falkland Is. and their dependencies, Dec., 1926; ditto, Sierra Leone, May, 1931; ditto, Gold Coast, 1934; author "Trekking the Great Thirst," "Seven Years in Southern Abyssinia," "Where Lion Reign," joint author of "A Practical Galla Grammar."

Figure 57. *Colonial Office List*, 1935.
Biographical note on Sir Arnold Hodson.

The alphabetical arrangement of the *Colonial Office List* biographical notes means that an individual can be readily located if you do not know the territory in which he[6] served – but you need a good idea of the time period. The blue books on the other hand are arranged by colony, so unless you are prepared to trawl through numerous volumes you need to know *where* an

[4] Information from the 1939–66 *Lists* has been assembled in Kirk-Greene, *Biographical Dictionary of the British Colonial Service*.

[5] CO 96/731/8, CO 96/740/9 and CO 96/749/8.

[6] Although 'he' is used for convenience throughout this appendix, many women worked in the colonial service.

Figure 58. CN 3/21, Farewell Durbar at Kumasi, Asante (Ashanti), September 1941.
Sir Arnold Hodson, retiring governor of the Gold Coast, returns Crown lands in Kumasi to the Asantehene.

individual served, as well as approximately *when.* They cover the period from about the 1820s (although starting later for some dependencies) to the 1940s, and can be found in the Colonial Office 'miscellanea' series for each colony as listed in appendix 1.

The advantage of the blue books is that they usually list far more junior employees of colonial governments than does the *List*, but the information they provide is brief: post, date and manner of appointment, pay and allowances, and dates of leave.[7] The 'date and manner of appointment' *may* lead to original correspondence. As well as information about individuals, the original correspondence series occasionally include lists of staff, but the collections of staff lists for British Central Africa and Nyasaland, the East Africa Protectorate, Nigeria, Somaliland, and Uganda were returned to the Colonial Office in 1956.

If you are looking for someone who served before about 1820, when the blue books start, a search is unlikely to be feasible unless you know where he served (or at least one territory if he had various appointments). If he was very senior, perhaps a governor, colonial secretary or attorney-general, there may be an entry in a standard reference work such as the *Oxford Dictionary of National Biography*. Otherwise it may be sensible to start with a good history of the colony during the period in question. If that fails, search the Colonial Office 'original correspondence' series for the dependency. If your man served in the British colonies in North America or the Caribbean before 1740 a good source is the indexed *Calendar of State Papers Colonial, America and West Indies*. Use of the CD-ROM edition published by Routledge in 2000, or ProQuest's online version published in 2007, both available through any of the public computers at TNA, allows you to search across all 40 volumes.

The second important point to bear in mind is that a formal recruitment process of the type with which we are now familiar is a comparatively recent development. The old system of 'patronage' was based largely on personal knowledge of candidates or of their family or friends, and appointment frequently followed a letter from someone asking for a colonial appointment for a son, nephew or friend. Such letters generally emphasise the suitability of the individual for a colonial appointment, but may give little personal or career information. Application forms started to be used only in the late 19th century.

'Original correspondence'

Although noted above as being the most useful source for pre-1820 research, this correspondence can provide a treasure trove for any period. Remember always, however, that you may find nothing and a search may be lengthy and complicated. Details of the arrangement of the correspondence and its various finding aids are given in chapter 6.

[7] Twentieth-century blue books may give far less information. The Palestine blue book for 1938 (CO 821/13), for example, lists only the more senior of the thousands of staff then employed.

A series of 'original correspondence' is held in The National Archives for each colony (but *not* for India and some other territories administered by the India Office; see below), and is listed in appendix 1. Original correspondence consists of despatches from the governors, and correspondence with other government departments, organisations and individuals in the UK, on matters concerning the colony in question. From 1927, when the Colonial Office introduced a file system, the correspondence is adequately described in the catalogue, but before that date correspondence is bound up in chronological order and the use of contemporary registers and indexes is usually required to identify relevant material. For the post-1926 period standards of cataloguing vary. Some entries name individuals: for example, a 1930 file in the Jamaica series is described as 'Superintendent, Public Work Department, First and Second Class vacancies; Offer of posts to Mr C Spence (First Class) and Mr E V Williams (Second Class). Contains earlier papers of 1930 including application forms and references'. The application form submitted by Spence is for a promotion. It gives date of birth, name of father, marital status, number of children, education and employment. The form from Williams is for an appointment; it also gives his mother's maiden name, and her place of birth and nationality at birth. On the other hand, two files for the Leeward Islands in the same year are described simply as 'Vacancy: Sub-Inspector of Police', and 'Vacancy: Inspector of Schools' – worth investigating further if you are looking for people who served in such capacities in that part of the world, but probably too vague if your information is less specific.

Some pre-1927 correspondence for British colonies in the Caribbean has recently being catalogued. Within this project we made the decision to name individuals as frequently as possible, and among the catalogue entries which have emerged are, 'Reports death of Samuel Osborne Gibbes, Receiver for the Confiscated Estates of Grenada, who died on 22 January; reports appointment as Acting Receiver of Robert Otway' (Grenada, 1807); 'Reports appointment of Mr Norman Stokes to be inland revenue officer of District E' (Barbados, 1879) and 'Vacant judgeship; application from Mr Dillett "a gentleman of colour". Appointment of William John Anderson, son of the attorney-general of the Bahamas currently practising as a barrister in the Bahamas' (Turks and Caicos, 1874). Requests for appointments, promotions, transfers or increased pay were often presented in the form of petitions or memorials, and these too can be found in the original correspondence. In 1919, for example, an Indian clerk in the Railway Department of Nigeria complained that prices had doubled since the start of the First World War, but that his salary remained the same. The numerous enclosures to his petition, including details of his weekly expenditure and his family responsibilities, give a vivid picture of his particular kind of expatriate life.

As well as information about appointments, promotions, transfers and pensions, the 'original correspondence' series also include material about the misdemeanours of officials: a 'trifling difference' which led to 'the disgraceful scene of two public Officials horsewhipping and assaulting each other in the market place of Kingstown' (St Vincent, 1875); or, the previous year, charges of incompetence and unfitness for office against the colonial engineer of St Vincent following the collapse of two bridges constructed by him in 1872. And inevitably there are incidents of petty pilfering and drunkenness.

Records of patronage and of the personnel departments

'Patronage' was handled in the early 19th century by the General Department within the Colonial Office. Among the records of that department, the documents referenced CO 325/8–23 hold returns of colonial appointments and registers of applications, 1809–59. CO 323/117–40 contain applications for colonial appointments, 1819–35, and it is possible that other documents within the series include similar material. But they are generally letters soliciting colonial appointments for family and friends, rather than applications from candidates themselves, and tend to give little information although they are of some interest. For example, one correspondent wrote on behalf of the son of dissenters who had cast him off without the proverbial penny when he decided to go into the church – he would make an ideal clergyman in a healthy colony the writer claims. The letters are arranged and indexed by the name of the petitioner rather than the job hunter, and do not indicate whether the request was granted.

Later papers are in the 'Patronage' series CO 429, which covers the periods 1867–70 and 1881–1919. The first volume, for 1867–70, contains similar letters to those noted for CO 323. Some correspondents asked for a specific post; others asked more generally for a colonial appointment; and requests from serving officials for promotion or transfer are also to be found. Many give a reason for the request – scarcity of engineering jobs in England, needs a warm climate for his sick daughter, own health has put him on half pay from the Indian Army. Some send references, some give age – but no details of date of birth or parentage have been noted. Unfortunately, the later part of this correspondence, from 1881, contains only a small selection of the original collection. You would therefore be advised to start with the registers in CO 430. These give very limited information, but may aid a search in the original correspondence series. The 'lists of applicants' in CO 430/14–18 provide indexes to the registers. It is clear from the registers that by at least the late 1880s the Colonial Office was asking applicants to complete forms. Very few applications have survived; for example, of 69 entries under the initial 'G' in the register for 1887–90 only five sets of correspondence have been selected for permanent preservation. One of these includes a completed application form – for a Dr Going, appointed to a medical post in the Falklands. A printed form was also sent to referees, and there are some examples of such standardised references.

Following reorganisations within the Colonial Office, similar correspondence continues in CO 877, Appointments (1920–52). Related material is in CO 850, Personnel (1932–52), and CO 1017, Colonial Service Division, later Overseas Service Division (1948–66). CO 850 and CO 1017 are much concerned with policy rather than personal cases, and those files which do concern individuals tend to concentrate on one aspect of a career, for example transfer, extension of appointment, pension, misconduct or application for funding for a course. The files listed under a heading such as 'discipline under colonial regulations' are not usually described by name in the catalogue, but simply in words such as 'Kenya: inefficiency', or 'Trinidad: irregularities'. They can provide considerable information about an individual, but inevitably concentrate on his or her misdeeds. Files concerning applications for grants may give career statements.

Also to be considered ...

Commissions for the most senior colonial officers, such as governor, chief justice, chief auditor, naval officer and councillors, were recorded in the Privy Council registers (PC 2 and PC 5), letters patent (C 66) and colonial entry books (CO 324). The appointment was also announced in the *London Gazette* (ZJ 1) and in the colonial gazettes. A separate 'gazette' series exists for each colony (for example CO 132, Hong Kong; CO 32, Barbados; CO 63, British Columbia). Among government announcements the gazettes will often give notifications of appointment, promotion and transfer, retirement, leave of absence and resumption of duty. Some serve the function of a local newspaper and may include obituaries, or tell you that Mr and Mrs William Williams have returned from leave and will be at home to their friends on Wednesday afternoon.

Sources outside The National Archives

For individuals who served in India and related territories, the most important sources will be found among the Asia, Pacific and Africa collections at the British Library. For Sudan, material can be found at the Sudan archive in Durham University Library: the archive was founded in 1957, the year after Sudanese independence, to collect and preserve the papers of administrators from the Sudan Political Service, missionaries, soldiers, businessmen, doctors, agriculturalists, teachers and others who had served or lived in Sudan during the Anglo-Egyptian condominium. Private papers of former colonial officials may survive in local and academic archives in the UK and overseas: the National Register of Archives can help to locate them. Papers of, and interviews with, former colonial officials, collected from the 1960s under the Oxford Colonial Records Project and formerly at Rhodes House Library, are now in the Commonwealth and African Collections at the Bodleian Library, University of Oxford.

A quite considerable number of memoirs of former colonial officials and specialists have been published.[8]

[8] See T. Barringer, *Administering Empire: an Annotated Checklist of Personal Memoirs and Related Studies* (Institute of Commonwealth Studies, School of Advanced Study, University of London, 2004). An updated edition is available through the Overseas Service Pensioners Association website (http://static1.squarespace.com/static/545a147ce4b042d9849bcd29/t/54c127ebe4b03df342088def/1421944811735/220115+Bibiliography+with+title+1.pdf [accessed 6 March 2015]). Terry Barringer continues to add newly published items to her database, which she is willing to share with researchers. She can be contacted by email at tab1003@cam.ac.uk.

Appendix 9
Access to the records and use of online catalogues

Access to UK public records

Arrangements for access to the records in the 19th century varied from department to department and often required special permission. In 1908 an interdepartmental committee considered if existing restrictions could be relaxed, and recommended that records pre-dating 1838 should be made generally available. Further recommendations gradually advanced this opening date, but it was not until 1958 that there was any real conformity. The Public Records Act of that year then introduced a '50-year rule', which was reduced by further legislation in 1972 to 30 years, meaning that a document dated 1975–6 would become open on the first working day of 2007.[1] Applications from departments seeking to close or retain records for longer periods are scrutinised by the Advisory Council on National Records and Archives, which is chaired by the Master of the Rolls and composed of members of Parliament, academics, researchers and archivists. Those it agrees with are passed to the Lord Chancellor for final approval. Records not meeting current selection criteria may be destroyed or otherwise disposed of.[2] As noted in chapter 6 (p. 104) authority for the destruction of 'valueless' documents was first granted in 1877; it has been estimated that by the 1980s approximately 15 per cent of Colonial Office records were being selected for permanent preservation.

Section 45 of the Constitutional Reform and Governance Act 2010 amended section 3(4) of the Public Records Act by reducing the 'open' date from 30 years to 20 years. A phased transition to a 20-year-rule is taking place over ten years from 2013; two years' worth of government records are to be transferred each year until 2022.

We should not, of course, make the mistake of assuming that such legislative requirements are necessarily complied with. An extreme example of failure to comply was admitted by the FCO in 2013. See chapter 8.

A Freedom of Information Act (FOI) was passed in November 2000 and came fully into effect from 1 January 2005. FOI gives people a right of access to information held by UK 'public bodies', widely defined. FOI applies to information whatever its age, and whether it is at TNA or is still

[1] There were always some exceptions to this rule; most commonly for published material such as government gazettes and records of public inquiries.

[2] For details of TNA's collection policy see http://www.nationalarchives.gov.uk/documents/records-collection-policy-2012.pdf [accessed 6 March 2015].

held by the originating department. The 30-year standard closure period no longer determines access; instead, information is assumed to be 'open' unless one of the exemptions – the grounds on which information may be withheld – applies.

FOI simplifies the process for researchers wishing to access 'closed' or 'retained' material. If a closed document has already been transferred to TNA, and is described in the catalogue, a request for its status to be reviewed can be made online. If it is held by the creating department a request must be made to that department.

The catalogue

Since publication of the first edition of this guide in 2008 there have been major enhancements to the catalogue, which is now known as 'Discovery' and is available at http://discovery.nationalarchives.gov.uk or from the TNA home page. One of the most significant of these is that previously separate databases have been incorporated so that 'Discovery' now covers not only records held by TNA, but also those held by more than 2,500 archives and institutions across the UK, and some abroad. It holds more than 32 million descriptions of records. Over 9 million are available for download. Guidance on use of the catalogue and latest developments is provided through a 'Discovery help' link from the home page. New users of the catalogue are advised to look at these sections, but a little more is said here about the catalogue's coverage of the records of the Colonial Office and related departments. The specific points about using the search option provided in the 2008 edition of this handbook have been omitted here, it being considered more sensible for researchers to seek advice on use of the catalogue and ongoing developments from TNA.

Although almost all of the documents deposited in TNA have been catalogued to some extent, very many of the catalogue entries provide no information about the subject matter covered. This is true of the majority of the records held under the 'CO' departmental code up until 1927 when a registered file system was introduced for correspondence (see pp. 105–9). Before that year the series of 'original correspondence' for individual territories, regions or Colonial Office subject departments have usually been described simply by the type of correspondence and the date range. For example:

CO 267/20 Sierra Leone, Despatches and Miscellaneous, 1781–4
CO 323/183 General, Offices and Individuals, 1815 January–May
CO 583/2 Nigeria, Despatches, 1913 January–April

In these cases the catalogue can provide no further information and, as described in chapter 6, it is necessary to use original registers and indexes to identify relevant subject matter – or alternatively to search the individual bound volumes of correspondence.

Since the initial launch of an online catalogue in March 2001, TNA has focused on a variety of data improvement projects. Two are specific to Colonial Office records of the pre-1927 period.

From 2004 to 2007 external funding allowed the cataloguing of about half of the 'original correspondence' for the British West Indian colonies, and it is hoped that this project can be completed. A second project commenced in May 2005 to list the documents in part of the General Department original correspondence series (CO 323/623–956, 1914–26). In both cases cataloguing is to item level, that is to individual despatches or letters within the bound volumes; itemised descriptions are released as the cataloguing is completed. Examples from these projects are as follows:

> CO 28/107/5, 1831 Jan. 14. Case of John Thomas, enslaved naval pensioner: states that Greenwich Hospital pensions have hitherto been paid by the collector of taxes. Suggests in this case that part should be sent to the collector, and part to the protector of slaves, and states 'I shall take care that the money is expended in the way that may appear to me most advantageous for John Thomas and his children'. No. 4, folios 10–11.
>
> CO 28/107/6, 1831 Jan. 16. Forwards papers in the case of the fatal shooting of James Clarke, 'a free black man',[3] by William Goodridge Mandeville, 'a white man', and reports that Mandeville has escaped justice as the jury ignored the bill to amend legislation relating to testimony. With petition of Hester Clarke, wife of the deceased, complaining that the evidence of free black people has been considered inadmissible. Unnumbered, folios 12–25.
>
> (Two items, of 77, from a volume of despatches from Sir James Lyon, governor of Barbados.)
>
> CO 323/627/1, 1914 Dec. Zanzibar. Detention of two motor vessels from the Norwegian steamer *Troldfos* as conditional contraband of war. Resident Pearce, Unnumbered telegram.
>
> CO 323/627/2, 1914 Dec. Gibraltar. Detention of the Italian steamer *San Giorgio* on charges of carrying contraband cargo. Governor Miles, Unnumbered telegram.
>
> (Two items, of 88, from a volume of General Department correspondence from various sources concerning contraband and prize court proceedings.)

There are two ways of finding out if the catalogue provides detailed itemised descriptions for your record series, for example CO 28, Barbados original correspondence:

a) Using the browse screen to check all individual references within CO 28. Some records series will have more detailed item descriptions below the piece level. The 'browse by reference' box will help you to display the relevant part of the list.

b) Searching for all the references within CO 28 by date. In the 'advanced search' screen, type

[3] Policy throughout this project has been to use terminology given in the documents rather than to risk obscuring original meaning or removing nuances by substituting modern terms. Thus descriptions such as 'coloured', 'coolie', 'mulatto' and 'lunatic' have been retained, but put into inverted commas.

only an asterisk, as a 'wild card', into the 'find words' field. Then type 'CO 28' into 'any of these references' field, and add a specific date (year) or date range as required. Then click on 'search' and the result will show if itemised descriptions are included.

Records of the Dominions Office, Commonwealth Relations Office, Commonwealth Office and Foreign and Commonwealth Office are, in general, well catalogued. Foreign Office correspondence series, however, are not catalogued in any detail until the 1950s, and the use of original registers and indexes held at TNA is required.

Only if a record series has been catalogued in detail is it possible to use the search facility within the online catalogue to identify documents concerning a particular subject or individual. In such cases the catalogue provides a wonderful tool allowing researchers to identify material which might never have been found through the old method of trawling laboriously through the paper listings (or browse screen) of those series identified as most relevant. But there are some pitfalls. The catalogue has been developed over a period of many years; cataloguing standards and the terminology used have varied; place names, or at least their spellings, have changed.

In the case of place names, the contemporary form as given in the document is almost always the only form used in a catalogue description. If you are concerned with Ghana or with Sabah in the periods before independence the names Gold Coast or North Borneo should be used; the Greek island now known as Kefalonia is recorded as Cephalonia; the Malaysia state of Melaka as Malacca. The main exception to this rule is in the case of maps, many of which have been catalogued in some detail in recent years and alternative names recorded.

For other searches try using alternative search terms. For example, 'prison', 'gaol' and 'jail' give different results, as do 'sleeping sickness' and 'Trypanosomiasis'. Be careful also of using a modern term for an historical event. Recent catalogue enhancements have added 'Morant Bay' to references to the Jamaican 'rebellion' of 1865, but some entries may retain the description 'insurrection' – the contemporary term – which might be missed.

An explanation of the means of identifying the modern references of files which have been catalogued and renumbered since their receipt at TNA is given at p. 111.

Other records searchable through TNA's catalogue

As noted above, TNA's new catalogue 'Discovery' now incorporates information about records held elsewhere which was previously made available via the National Register of Archives, Access to Archives (A2A), the ARCHON Directory and the Manorial Documents Register. An introduction to the first three of these, taken from the 2008 edition of this handbook and possibly not up to date, follows.

In 1945 the National Register of Archives (NRA) was set up under the Royal Commission on Historical Manuscripts (also known as the Historical Manuscripts Commission or HMC) to carry out a more comprehensive survey of all privately owned collections and papers. This was done in conjunction with local voluntary county committees and, increasingly, with county archivists. From 1959 the NRA was developed as the central collection, storage and retrieval point for information about historical records. In 1998 it contained more than 42,000 unpublished reports and lists of collections of historical papers in private and public hands in the United Kingdom and overseas. In 2003 the Public Record Office and the Historical Manuscripts Commission came together to form The National Archives, and the NRA reports are now available for consultation by the public at The National Archives. The computerised indexes, together with many of the reports, are available via TNA's website.

The NRA database allows searches for private and business papers, and is perhaps particularly useful for the private papers of individuals. There are, for example, 12 entries for Sir Thomas Stamford Raffles, the founder of Singapore, including not only four separate collections of papers in the British Library, but also papers held by the Royal Asiatic Society, Duke University in North Carolina, the universities of Cambridge and Aberdeen, the National Maritime Museum, the National Library of Scotland and the National Archives of Indonesia. There are links to the entry for Raffles in the *Oxford Dictionary of National Biography*[4] and to a bibliography compiled by the Royal Historical Society.[5] Entries show if TNA holds paper catalogues of holdings in other archives, and if so give their reference numbers. As you will have noticed, although this database is known as the National Register of Archives, and claims to be reasonably comprehensive only for the UK, it does include some references to overseas archives. The NRA database is linked to the ARCHON directory, which includes contact details for record repositories in the United Kingdom and also for institutions elsewhere in the world which have substantial collections of manuscripts noted under its indexes.

TNA also hosts 'Access to Archives' – known as A2A – the English strand of the UK archives network, a database containing catalogues of archives collections held locally in England and Wales and dating from the eighth century to the present day. The A2A database does not yet offer a full description of *all* local archives but it is regularly updated. At the time of writing it contains 10.1 million records relating to 9.25 million items held in 414 record offices and other repositories. Repeating the 'Raffles' search in A2A gives 24 hits from 14 separate catalogues.[6] Unlike the National Register of Archives database which records the existence of relevant material but gives no details of content (although there are sometimes links to catalogues), A2A provides catalogue entries for all selected records.

[4] *Oxford Dictionary of National Biography* (Oxford, 2004) (http://www.oxforddnb.com [accessed 7 Jan. 2008]).

[5] The Royal Historical Society Bibliography of British and Irish History (http://www.rhs.ac.uk/bibl/ [accessed 7 Jan. 2007]).

[6] Twelve of the catalogue entries are from the India Office Records held at the British Library; the other two are from Hampshire Record Office (noting correspondence from Raffles), and the Brynmor Jones Library at the University of Hull (noting a single item: a grant signed by Raffles).

Bibliography

Acts of the Privy Council of England, Colonial Series, 1613–1783 (HMSO, London, 1908–12)

An Alphabetical Guide to Certain War Office and Other Military Records Preserved in the Public Record Office (Public Record Office Lists and Indexes, 53, HMSO, London, 1931)

Calendar of State Papers Colonial, Colonial Series (HMSO, London, 1860–1994)

Calendar of Treasury Books, 1660–[1718], Preserved in the Public Record Office (32 vols. in 64, HMSO, London, 1904–62)

Calendar of Treasury Books and Papers, 1729–[1745], Preserved in Her Majesty's Public Record Office (5 vols., HMSO, London, 1897–1903)

Imperial and Commonwealth Conferences (List and Index Society, 280, 2000)

Journal of the Commissioners for Trade and Plantations, 1704–1782 (HMSO, London, 1920–38)

D. Anderson, 'Mau Mau in the High Court and the 'lost' British Empire archives: colonial conspiracy or bureaucratic bungle?', *Journal of Imperial and Commonwealth History*, 39 (2011), pp. 699–716

C. M. Andrews, *Guide to the Materials for American History, to 1783, in the Public Record Office of Great Britain* (London, 1912; repr. 1965)

S. R. Ashton and S. E. Stockwell, *Imperial Policy and Colonial Practice 1925–1945*: pt. 1, *Metropolitan Reorganisation, Defence and International Relations, Political Change and Constitutional Reform*; pt. 2, *Economic Policy, Social Policies and Colonial Research* (British Documents on the End of Empire, ser. A, vol. 1, HMSO for the Institute of Commonwealth Studies, University of London, 1996)

The West Indies. ed. S. R. Ashton and D. Killingray (British Documents on the End of Empire, ser. B, vol. 6, The Stationery Office for the Institute of Commonwealth Studies, University of London, 1999)

L. Atherton, *'Never Complain, Never Explain': Records of the Foreign Office and State Paper Office 1500–c.1960* (PRO Publications, 1994)

M. K. Banton, 'The Colonial Office, 1820–1955', in *Masters, Servants and Magistrates in Britain and the Empire, 1562–1955*, ed. D. Hay and P. Craven (Chapel Hill, NC, and London, 2004)

M. K. Banton, 'Destroy? 'Migrate'? Conceal? British strategies for the disposal of sensitive records of colonial administrations at independence', *Journal of Imperial and Commonwealth History*, 40 (2012), pp. 321–35

M. K. Banton, 'Record-keeping for good governance and accountability in the Colonial Office: an historical sketch', in *Integrity in Government through Records Management*, ed. J. Lowry and J. Wamukoya (Farnham, 2014)

Maps and Plans in the Public Record Office, 4: *Europe and Turkey*, ed. G. Beech (London, 1998)

The Cambridge History of the British Empire, ed. E. A. Benians and others (9 vols., Cambridge, 1929–59)

Missionary Encounters: Sources and Issues, ed. R. A. Bickers and R. Seaton (Richmond, 1996)

B. L. Blakeley, *The Colonial Office, 1868–1892* (Durham, NC, 1972)

P. J. Cain and A. G. Hopkins, *British Imperialism*: vol. 1, *Innovation and Expansion, 1688–1914*; vol. 2, *Crisis and Deconstruction, 1914–1990* (London, 1993)

J. W. Cell, *British Colonial Administration in the Mid-Nineteenth Century: the Policy-Making Process* (New Haven, CT, 1970)

A Guide to the Naval Records in The National Archives of the UK, ed. R. Cock and N. A. M. Rodger (Institute of Historical Research, London, 2006)

J. Darwin, *The Empire Project: The Rise and Fall of the British World-System, 1830–1970* (Cambridge, 2011)

K. G. Davis, *Documents of the American Revolution, 1770–1783* (Shannon, 1972–81)

K. M. DeSilva, *Sri Lanka*: pt. 1, *The Second World War and the Soulbury Commission 1939–1945*; pt. 2, *Towards Independence 1945–1948* (British Documents on the End of Empire, ser. B, vol. 2, HMSO for the Institute of Commonwealth Studies, University of London, 1997)

Sir R. Furse, *Aucuparius: Recollections of a Recruiting Officer* (Oxford, 1962)

C. Fyfe, *A History of Sierra Leone* (Oxford, 1962)

Joe Garner, *The Commonwealth Office 1925–68* (London, 1978)

G. Grannum, *Tracing your Caribbean Ancestors* (London, 2012)

Lord Hailey, *An African Survey* (Oxford, 1938; revised 1956)

C. Hall, N. Draper, K. McClelland, K. Donington and R. Lang, *Legacies of British Slave-ownership: Colonial Slavery and the Formation of Victorian Britain* (Cambridge, 2014)

H. L. Hall, *The Colonial Office: a History* (London, 1937)

D. P. Henige, *Colonial Governors from the Fifteenth Century to the Present* (Madison, Wis., 1970)

R. Hyam, *Britain's Imperial Century, 1815–1914: a study of Empire and Expansion* (London, 1976; new edn., Basingstoke, 1993)

The Labour Government and the End of Empire, 1945–1951: pt. 1, *High Policy and Administration*; pt. 2, *Economics and International Relations*; pt. 3, *Strategy, Politics and Constitutional Change*; pt. 4, *Race Relations and the Commonwealth*, ed. R. Hyam (British Documents on the End of Empire, ser. A, vol. 2 (HMSO for the Institute of Commonwealth Studies, University of London, 1992)

The Conservative Government and the End of Empire 1957–1964: pt. 1, *High Policy, Political and Constitutional Change*; pt. 2, *Economics, International Relations, and the Commonwealth*, ed. R. Hyam and W. R. Louis (British Documents on the End of Empire, ser. A, vol. 4, The Stationery Office for the Institute of Commonwealth Studies, University of London, 2000)

Sir C. Jeffries, *The Colonial Office* (London, 1956)

Sir C. Jeffries (ed.), *A Review of Colonial Research 1940–1960* (London, 1964)

Sir C. Jeffries, *Whitehall and the Colonial Service: an Administrative Memoir, 1939–1956* (London, 1972)

Sudan: pt. 1, *1942–1950*; pt. 2, *1951–1956*, ed. D. H. Johnson and S. R. Ashton (British Documents on End of Empire, ser. B, vol. 5, The Stationery Office for the Institute of Commonwealth Studies, University of London, 1998)

P. Jones, *Britain and Palestine, 1914–1948: Archival Sources for the History of the British Mandate* (Oxford, 1979)

D. Judd, *Empire: The British Imperial Experience from 1765 to the Present* (London, 1996)

Egypt and the Defence of the Middle East: pt. 1, *1945–1949*; pt. 2, *1949–1953*; pt. 3, *1953–1956*, ed. J. Kent and S. R. Ashton (British Documents on the End of Empire, ser. B, vol. 4, The Stationery Office for the Institute of Commonwealth Studies, University of London, 1998)

A. H. M. Kirk-Greene, *A Biographical Dictionary of the British Colonial Service 1939–1966* (London, 1991)

A. Kirk-Greene, *On Crown Service: a History of HM Colonial and Overseas Civil Services 1837–1997* (London, 1999)

A. Kirk-Greene, *Britain's Imperial Administrators, 1858–1966* (Basingstoke, 2000)

P. Knaplund, *James Stephen and the British Colonial System 1813–1847* (Madison, Wis., 1953)

P. H. Kratoska, *Index to British Colonial Office Files Pertaining to British Malaya* (12 vols., Arkib Negara, Malaysia, 1990)

R. V. Kubicek, *The Administration of Imperialism: Joseph Chamberlain at the Colonial Office* (Durham, NC, 1969)

Calendar of State Papers, Colonial: North America and the West Indies 1574–1739, consultant editors K. Ordahl Kupperman, J. C. Appleby and M. Banton (CD-ROM, London and New York, 2000)

B. V. Lal, *Fiji* (British Documents on the End of Empire, ser. B, vol. 10, The Stationery Office for the Institute of Commonwealth Studies, University of London, 2006)

J. M. Lee and M. Petter, *The Colonial Office, War and Development Policy: Organisation and the Planning of a Metropolitan Initiative, 1939–1945* (Institute of Commonwealth Studies, University of London, 1982)

T. O. Lloyd, *The British Empire 1558–1995* (Oxford, 1996)

E. Longford, *Jameson's Raid: the Prelude to the Boer War* (2nd edn., London, 1982).

W. R. Louis, *Imperialism at Bay: the United States and the Decolonisation of the British Empire, 1941–1945* (Oxford, 1977)

W. R. Louis, *Ends of British Imperialism: the Scramble for Empire, Suez and Decolonisation* (London, 2006)

Sir F. D. Lugard, *The Dual Mandate in British Tropical Africa* (Edinburgh and London, 1926)

M. Lynn, *Nigeria*: pt. 1, *Managing Political Reform 1943–1953*; pt. 2, *Moving to Independence* (British Documents on the End of Empire, ser. B, vol. 7, The Stationery Office for the Institute of Commonwealth Studies, University of London, 2001)

W. David McIntyre, *Winding up the British Empire in the Pacific Islands* (Oxford, 2014)

P. Mansfield, *The British in Egypt* (London, 1971)

The Cambridge Illustrated History of the British Empire, ed. P. J. Marshall (Cambridge, 1996)

N. Mansergh, *The Commonwealth Experience* (London, 1969)

P. Murphy, 'Censorship, declassification and the history of end of empire in Central Africa', *African Research and Documentation*, 92 (2003)

P. Murphy, *Central Africa*: pt. 1, *Closer Association, 1945–1958*; pt. 2, *Crisis and Dissolution, 1959–1965* (British Documents on the End of Empire, ser. B, vol. 9, The Stationery Office for the Institute of Commonwealth Studies, University of London, 2005)

Overseas Service Pensioners' Association (OSPA): for lists of OSPA Research Project Occasional Papers and transcripts of Witness Seminars and Conferences, see http://www.ospa.org.uk

Oxford History of the British Empire, editor-in-chief, W. R. Louis: vol. 1, *The Origins of Empire*, ed. N. Canny; vol. 2, *The Eighteenth Century*, ed. P. J. Marshall; vol. 3, *The Nineteenth Century*, ed. A. Porter; vol. 4, *The Twentieth Century*, ed. J. M. Brown and W. R. Louis; vol. 5, *Historiography*, ed. R. W. Winks (Oxford, 1998–9)

S. H. Northcote, *Papers on the Re-organisation of the Civil Service: Presented to Both Houses of Parliament by Command of Her Majesty* (HMSO, London, 1855)

W. Oldham, *Britain's Convicts to the Colonies* (Library of Australian History, Sydney, 1990)

B. Pappalardo, *Tracing Your Naval Ancestors* (Public Record Office, 2003)

Sir C. Parkinson, *The Colonial Office from Within, 1909–1945* (London, 1947)

Maps and Plans in the Public Record Office, vol. 2: *America and West Indies*, ed. P. A. Penfold (London, 1974)

Maps and Plans in the Public Record Office, vol. 3: *Africa*, ed. P. A. Penfold (London, 1982)

Atlas of British Overseas Expansion, ed. A. N. Porter (London, 1991; 1994)

B. Porter, *The Lion's Share: a Short History of British Imperialism 1850–2004* (4th edn., Harlow, 2004)

Public Record Office, *List of Colonial Office Confidential Print to 1916* (HMSO, London, 1965)

R. B. Pugh, 'The Colonial Office', in *The Cambridge History of the British Empire*, vol. III, ed. E. A. Benians, Sir J. Butler and C. E. Carrington (Cambridge, 1959)

R. B. Pugh, *The Records of the Colonial and Dominions Offices* (PRO Handbooks no. 3, HMSO, London, 1964)

R. Rathbone, *Ghana*: pt. 1, *1941–1952*; pt. 2, *1952–1957* (British Documents on End of Empire, ser. B, vol. 1, HMSO for the Institute of Commonwealth Studies, University of London, 1992)

A.D. Roberts, 'The Imperial Mind', in *Cambridge History of Africa, VII, 1905–40* (Cambridge, 1986)

K. Robinson, *The Dilemmas of Trusteeship: Aspects of British Colonial Policy Between the Wars* (Oxford, 1965)

R.E. Robinson, 'The Journal and the transfer of power, 1947–51', *Journal of Administration Overseas*, 8 (1974), pp. 255–8

M. Roper, *The Records of the War Office and Related Departments 1660–1964* (PRO Publications, 1998)

M. Roper, *The Records of the Foreign Office, 1782–1968* (Public Record Office, 2002)

Royal Commission on Historical Manuscripts, *Private Papers of British Colonial Governors 1782–1900* (HMSO, London, 1986)

J. C. Sainty, *Colonial Office Officials: Officials of the Secretary of State for War, 1794–1801, of the Secretary of State for War and Colonies, 1801–54, and of the Secretary of State for Colonies, 1854–70* (Institute of Historical Research, London, 1976)

Administering Empire: the British Colonial Service in Retrospect, ed. J. Smith (London, 1999)

S. C. Smith, *Malta* (British Documents on the End of Empire, ser. B, vol. 9, The Stationery Office for the Institute of Commonwealth Studies, University of London, 2006)

A. J. Stockwell, *Malaya*: pt. 1, *The Malayan Union Experiment, 1942–1948*; pt. 2, *The Communist Insurrection, 1948–1953*; pt. 3, *The Alliance Route to Independence, 1953–1957* (British Documents on the End of Empire, ser. B, vol. 3, HMSO for the Institute of Commonwealth Studies, University of London, 1995)

A. J. Stockwell, *Malaysia* (British Documents on the End of Empire, The Stationery Office for the Institute of Commonwealth Studies, University of London, 2004)

D. Sunderland, *Managing the British Empire: the Crown Agents, 1833–1914* (Woodbridge, 2004)

D. Sunderland, *Managing British Colonial and Post-Colonial Development: The Crown Agents, 1914–1974* (Woodbridge, 2007)

D. B. Swinfen, *Imperial Control of Colonial Legislation 1813–1865: a Study of British Policy Towards Colonial Legislative Powers* (Oxford, 1970)

A. Thurston, *Guide to Archives and Manuscripts Relating to Kenya and East Africa in the United Kingdom* (London, 1991)

A. Thurston, *Sources for Colonial Studies in the Public Record Office*, vol. 1: *Records of the Colonial Office, Dominions Office, Commonwealth Relations Office and Commonwealth Office* (British Documents on the End of Empire, ser. C, vol. 1, HMSO for the Institute of Commonwealth Studies, University of London and the Public Record Office, 1995)

A. Thurston, *Sources for Colonial Studies in the Public Record Office*, vol. 2: *Records of the Cabinet, Foreign Office, Treasury and Other Records* (British Documents on the End of Empire, ser. C, vol. 2, The Stationery Office for the Institute of Commonwealth Studies, University of London and the Public Record Office, 1998)

C. Whitehead, 'Sir Christopher Cox: an imperial patrician of a different kind', *Journal of Educational Administration and History*, 21 (1989), pp. 28–42

C. Whitehead, *Colonial Educators: the British Indian and Colonial Education Service 1858–1983* (London, 2003)

M. Wight, *The Gold Coast Legislative Council* (London, 1947)

S. S. Wilson, *The Cabinet Office to 1945* (HMSO, London, 1975)

TNA research guides

Research guides are intended to provide an introduction to individual research topics, or details of how to use certain records. A large number have direct or more limited application to colonial affairs and are listed here. Many more relate to subjects touched on in this guide, for example military operations and service records. All are available online through TNA's website at http://www.nationalarchives.gov.uk, perhaps under a different title.

America and West Indies, Transportation to, 1615–1776
America and West Indies: Calendars of State Papers Colonial, 1574–1739
America and West Indies: Colonies before 1782
American Revolution
Australia, Transportation to, 1787–1868
Boundaries, International: Maps and Other Documents
Colonial Office: Advisory Committees
Colonial Office: Registers of Correspondence, 1849–1926
Colonial Office: Registers of Correspondence, 1926–51
Colonies and Dominions, Researching British
Dominions Office
Emigrants

Emigrants to North America after 1776
Government Gazettes of the British Empire and Commonwealth
Immigrants
Imperial and Commonwealth History, Sources for
Indian Indentured Labour, Family History Sources for
Ireland: Roger Casement
Ireland: The Easter Rising 1916
Irish Genealogy
League of Nations
Maps and Plans: Overseas Relations
Palestine: Land Registration before 1948 (Research Note)
Slave Trade, British Transatlantic: Abolition
Slave Trade, British Transatlantic: Acts of Parliament
Slave Trade, British Transatlantic: Britain and the Trade
Slave Trade, British Transatlantic: Emancipation
Slave Trade, British Transatlantic: Introduction
Slave Trade, British Transatlantic: Slavery
Using The National Archives to Search for Maps, Plans and Architectural Drawings

Index

Note: the use of bold text for page numbers indicates the main entry for records relating to an individual dependency or group of dependencies.

www.ingramcontent.com/pod-product-compliance
Lightning Source LLC
LaVergne TN
LVHW060726310826
846742LV00015B/44